MW01201312

The Spy and the State

THE SPY AND THE STATE

The History of American Intelligence

JEFFREY P. ROGG

OXFORD
UNIVERSITY PRESS

OXFORD
UNIVERSITY PRESS

Oxford University Press is a department of the University of Oxford.
It furthers the University's objective of excellence in research, scholarship,
and education by publishing worldwide. Oxford is a registered trade mark of
Oxford University Press in the UK and in certain other countries.

Published in the United States of America by Oxford University Press
198 Madison Avenue, New York, NY 10016, United States of America.

Some ideas in this work have been previously published in Jeffrey P. Rogg, " 'That the Republic Should Suffer No Harm': The Constitutional Conundrum of the Executive, Secret Intelligence, and the Rule of Law," International Journal of Intelligence and Counterintelligence 32 (July 2019), reprinted by permission of the publisher (Taylor & Francis Ltd, http://www.tandfonline.com), and Jeffrey P. Rogg, "The U.S. Intelligence Community's 'MacArthur Moment,' " International Journal of Intelligence and Counterintelligence 33 (August 2020), reprinted by permission of the publisher (Taylor & Francis Ltd, http://www.tandfonline.com).

Library of Congress Cataloging-in-Publication Data
Names: Rogg, Jeffrey P., author.
Title: The spy and the state : the history of American intelligence / Jeffrey P. Rogg.
Description: New York, NY : Oxford University Press, 2025. |
Includes bibliographical references and index. |
Identifiers: LCCN 2024062323 (print) | LCCN 2024062324 (ebook) |
ISBN 9780197678732 (hardback) | ISBN 9780197678749 (epub)
Subjects: LCSH: Intelligence service—United States—History. | Secret service—United States—History. | Security sector—United States—History. |
Espionage, American—History. | National security—United States—History.
Classification: LCC JK468.I6 R634 2025 (print) | LCC JK468.I6 (ebook) |
DDC 327.1273009—dc23/eng/20250213
LC record available at https://lccn.loc.gov/2024062323
LC ebook record available at https://lccn.loc.gov/2024062324

Printed by Sheridan Books, Inc., United States of America

The manufacturer's authorized representative in the EU for product safety is
Oxford University Press España S.A., Parque Empresarial San Fernando de Henares,
Avenida de Castilla, 2 – 28830 Madrid (www.oup.es/en).

For my grandfather, Harold, and my father, William,
who set examples I can never hope to equal

Contents

Acknowledgments

GIVEN THE LENGTH of this book, it is with sincere regret that I cannot devote the same number of pages to all those who supported and enriched this history with their contributions, but I shall endeavor to do them justice in these all-too-brief acknowledgments. First, I am humbled to have Susan Ferber as my editor. Susan has edited several books in the outstanding Oxford History of the United States series. I am grateful Susan gave me the opportunity to share how intelligence history can help fill in some of the missing pieces of American history.

My lasting thanks to my patient advisor, Jennifer Siegel, who during my first year as a PhD student asked only that I promise not to submit a 500-page dissertation. A man of my word, I presented her with a 1,000-page tome instead. She has continued to support my growth as an academic and historian with steady reassurance and sound counsel. Thank you, Jennifer, for taking a chance on one more PhD advisee. I am also indebted to dissertation committee members Peter Mansoor, COL (USA, ret.), who guided me through the history of American civil-military relations, and Paula Baker, who introduced me to the intellectual history of American liberalism. A directed reading with John Brooke convinced me that I had to start my inquiry into US civil-intelligence relations at the beginning with the Revolutionary War.

Never would I have imagined as a green undergrad at Swarthmore College that I would write a book inspired by Samuel Huntington. It was there that I took courses with James Kurth, a former advisee, mentee, and dear friend of Huntington's for over forty years. I likewise consider myself lucky to have Professor Kurth as a teacher, mentor, and friend. I continue to greatly enjoy and benefit from our wide-ranging and always elucidating conversations.

My fellow Swattie and friend Nick Reynolds pointed me toward excellent archival sources and reviewed several of these chapters. As a former intelligence professional and now formidable intelligence historian, Nick has continued to be a terrific sounding board for ideas. Nick also connected me with Jay Venables, who lent a sharp editorial eye to the introduction and first chapter. Hugh Wilford offered outstanding critical review and much-appreciated motivation that saw me through the final revisions of the manuscript. I also want to highlight professors, mentors, colleagues, and friends who have sharpened my work and encouraged me along the way: Gen Lester, Kevin O'Connell, Steve Marrin, Richard Valcourt, Jan Goldman, Aaron Bateman, Diana Bolsinger, John Gentry, Mark Stout, Chris Faulkner, Steve Shinkel, Seamas Mulvihill, Joseph Pierce, David Priess, and Dave Oakley.

The Ohio State University Department of History and Lynde and Harry Bradley Foundation sponsored several of my research trips and conference presentations as well as a writing semester to finish the draft of my dissertation. My colleagues in the Department of History offered helpful peer review. I had the incredible opportunity to revise the first draft of the book while a postdoctoral fellow in the Department of National Security Affairs at the US Naval War College. I was honored to have Steve Knott, whose own *Secret and Sanctioned* was an early inspiration for this book, as my NWC faculty mentor. Derek Reveron, Tom Nichols, and Matt Towner read portions of the draft and tested me on the ideas. Conversations with Andy Stigler helped me keep intelligence situated within the broader context of American national security and statecraft.

Archivists are the unsung heroes and heroines of historians. The archivists at the National Archives helped steer me when I wandered in rudderless to begin my research. Lauren Theodore of NARA II took the time to find and scan the originals of some of the pictures in this book, including my favorite, the superb sketch of the *Bahama* in Chapter 5. Archivists at the Library of Congress, Sanford Historical Society, American Antiquarian Society, University of Virginia Library, Beinecke Rare Book and Manuscript Library, and several presidential libraries also helped me locate documents and pictures for this history. Sim Smiley relocated and scanned some of the pictures appearing in this book that I had first taken on my cellphone in my rush to gather research as a graduate student.

I will always treasure the support of my dad, Bill, and aunt, Fay, who cheered me on and read every single page of this book . . . twice! They constantly asked me when I would send them the next chapter, keeping me on schedule. My mom, Ruth, and brother, Jon, also entertained my historical meanderings as I updated them on my work. My friends Alex and Chris—the better two of our three musketeers' triumvirate—are the "men in the arena," or as we jokingly toast, "the men in the field." This history is in part a tribute to them and others like them—including my friends Jason, Henry, Graeme, Noah, Ben, Howard, Dave, Chris, Mike, and both Matts—who have humbly served the American republic while seeking no recognition for themselves. Fishing trips in my hometown, Tampa, with Bob Mitulinsky gave me some respite from writing along the way. On one such trip, I was staying with Kyle Kalwary, my best friend of over thirty years, when I noticed on his wall a framed newspaper clipping from the front page of the *Tampa Tribune* dated April 11, 1984, that included a headline on the Reagan administration and CIA covert action in Nicaragua. My thanks to Kyle for always keeping me on task (even while on vacation) and being a friend I could always count on. Hannah Yang edited some of the photographs in the book, but more importantly helped take care of my bullmastiff, Teddy, while I worked on the original draft.

Finally, I conclude with my best friend and bullmastiff pup, Teddy, who often slept quietly under my desk as I worked and was with me every step of the way. He ensured that I ventured outside at least a few times a day. I will always cherish our walks together in Goodale Park in Columbus, Ohio, on the trails in Falls Church, Virginia, and along the ocean in Newport, Rhode Island. It was on these walks that I had some of my best brainstorming sessions. Teddy stopped and smelled the flowers for me and greeted everyone he met with a wagging tail. He epitomizes the "gentle giant" and doesn't have a bad bone in his body. He exhibits traits to which humans should aspire. Already wiser than me in many ways, Teddy also must now rank among the most knowledgeable dogs in the world in the field of American intelligence history.

I wrote the original acknowledgment above for Teddy in my dissertation in the fall of 2020. Although I did not know it at the time, he had terminal cancer, and I would have to say goodbye a short time later. Teddy saw me through the research and writing of what became this book. I could not have asked for a better writing companion or friend.

Abbreviations

ACLU	American Civil Liberties Union
AEF	American Expeditionary Forces
AFSA	Armed Forces Security Agency
AI	artificial intelligence
ANCIB	Army-Navy Communications Intelligence Board
APL	American Protective League
AQAP	Al-Qaeda in the Arabian Peninsula
AUMF	Authorization for Use of Military Force
BEW	Board of Economic Warfare
BMI	Bureau of Military Information
BOI	Bureau of Investigation
CFR	Council on Foreign Relations
CIA	Central Intelligence Agency
CIAA	Coordinator of Inter-American Affairs
CIG	Central Intelligence Group
COI	Coordinator of Information
COINTELPRO	Counterintelligence Program
COMINT	communications intelligence
CTC	Counterterrorism Center
DCI	Director of Central Intelligence
DCIA	Director of the Central Intelligence Agency
DCS	Defense Clandestine Service
DDCI	Deputy Director of Central Intelligence
DIA	Defense Intelligence Agency
DIGOS	General Investigations and Special Operations Division (Italy)
DNC	Democratic National Committee
DNI	Director of National Intelligence

DNSA	Director of the National Security Agency
DOD	Department of Defense
DOJ	Department of Justice
EO	executive order
FBI	Federal Bureau of Investigation
FISA	Foreign Intelligence Surveillance Act
FISC	Foreign Intelligence Surveillance Court
FISCR	Foreign Intelligence Surveillance Court of Review
FOIA	Freedom of Information Act
HPSCI	House Permanent Select Committee on Intelligence
HUMINT	human intelligence
IG	Inspector General
IIC	Interdepartmental Intelligence Committee
INR	Bureau of Intelligence and Research
IRTPA	Intelligence Reform and Terrorism Prevention Act of 2004
JCS	Joint Chiefs of Staff
JIC	Joint Intelligence Committee
JIS	Joint Intelligence Staff
JPWC	Joint Psychological Warfare Committee
JSG	Joint Study Group
JSOC	Joint Special Operations Command
JTTF	Joint Terrorism Task Force
MID	Military Information Division (1885–1903)
MID	Military Intelligence Division (1918–1942)
MIS	Military Intelligence Service
NCTC	National Counterterrorism Center
NGA	National Geospatial-Intelligence Agency
NIA	National Intelligence Authority
NIMA	National Imagery and Mapping Agency
NRO	National Reconnaissance Office
NRP	National Reconnaissance Program
NSA	National Security Agency
NSC	National Security Council
NSCID	National Security Council Intelligence Directive
NSDD	National Security Decision Directive
NSL	National Security Letter
ODNI	Office of the Director of National Intelligence
OGC	Office of General Counsel

OLC	Office of Legal Counsel
ONE	Office of National Estimates
ONI	Office of Naval Intelligence
OPC	Office of Policy Coordination
ORE	Office of Reports and Estimates
OSO	Office of Special Operations
OSP	Office of Special Projects
OSP (2002–3)	Office of Special Plans
OSS	Office of Strategic Services
OWI	Office of War Information
PBCFIA	President's Board of Consultants on Foreign Intelligence Activities
PDB	President's Daily Brief
PDDNI	Principal Deputy Director of National Intelligence
PFIAB	President's Foreign Intelligence Advisory Board
PIAB	President's Intelligence Advisory Board
PSP	President's Surveillance Program
R&A	Research and Analysis
SASC	Senate Armed Services Committee
SIGINT	signals intelligence
SIS (Army)	Signal Intelligence Service
SIS (Britain)	Secret Intelligence Service
SIS (FBI)	Special Intelligence Service
SISMI	Military Intelligence and Security Service (Italy)
SSCI	Senate Select Committee on Intelligence
SSU	Strategic Services Unit
STANCIB	State-Army-Navy Communications Intelligence Board
TECHINT	technical intelligence
USCIB	United States Communications Intelligence Board
USIB	United States Intelligence Board
WMD	weapons of mass destruction

Introduction

THE SECRETS BEHIND THE STARS AND STRIPES

RIGHT NOW, AS you read these pages, someone could be watching you or at least collecting information about you. This observation is not intended to cause alarm, only to alert you to the reality that intelligence is all around us. From your internet activities (you may have purchased this book online) to the devices we use and carry with us (the computer, phone, or tablet you might be reading this on), we willingly hand over volumes of personal information every day. Yet, we also often protest invasions of our privacy, especially by the government. Privacy is foundational to freedom, but for intelligence, it is a hurdle to overcome. Intelligence is currently changing state and society as we know it, so the more fully we understand it, the better prepared we are to protect our privacy and, with it, our liberty.

Intelligence is in the news almost every day. But what is intelligence? Most people would probably say secret information. Perhaps they may explain it through comparisons to "spies" like James Bond or organizations like the Central Intelligence Agency (CIA). These are good starting points. Many definitions of intelligence focus on the secret collection and analysis of information. Intelligence also broadly refers to a state's secret activities because it involves not only collecting and analyzing information but also protecting secrets and acting in secret. Together, these activities represent the four core missions of intelligence: collection, analysis, counterintelligence, and covert action. In short, intelligence is a secret sphere of information and action to support national security.[1]

The Spy and the State uses the word "intelligence" in three different ways. First, in the customary sense of secret information. Second, as a distinct profession and institution of national security apart from others—namely, military, diplomacy, and law enforcement. Third, as a system, which includes the functions, activities, and oversight of the organizations collectively known today as the US Intelligence Community, or USIC. But the history of American intelligence requires looking beyond intelligence itself.

Intelligence evolves in response to its interaction with the government and society it serves. This interaction, referred to throughout the book as civil-intelligence relations, should inform intelligence history, but it has been all but absent from the record.[2] In drawing this connection, *The Spy and the State* borrows from the work of Samuel Huntington, who explained how the American military has interacted with and been shaped by the US government and civil society in his groundbreaking 1957 book, *The Soldier and the State: The Theory and Politics of Civil-Military Relations*.[3] These pages will examine the history of American intelligence through the lens of civil-intelligence relations and the major themes of control, competition, coordination, professionalization, and politicization. Essential throughout is the relationship between intelligence and the American people.

The great French leader Georges Clemenceau once declared, "War is too important to be left to the generals." Likewise, intelligence is too important to be left to the spies. The US Constitution begins, "We the People." That spirit imbues the Constitution with meaning and vests in the American people the responsibility for their country. This book therefore consistently references the "American people" and emphasizes their central role in civil-intelligence relations and US intelligence history.[4] Americans, both individually and collectively, have shaped intelligence in the past and will continue to do so in the future. The American people and the intelligence community that serves them deserve a thorough inquiry into the nature of their relationship and the causes of their periodic conflicts. Both sides can learn from the history of the spy and the state.

A Constant Crisis in Civil-Intelligence Relations

The American people harbor many myths and misperceptions about intelligence. They also celebrate the folklore surrounding the Founders, who charted the unsteady course of American intelligence history. Gouverneur Morris, who wrote the Preamble to the Constitution, claimed that he and the other delegates to the Constitutional Convention were "plain, honest men."[5] They were doctors, lawyers, planters, merchants, and businessmen. But there were also a few spymasters among them. These same men who constructed the foundational document of the United States did not mention intelligence in it. To be fair, they could not: The stain of espionage would discredit them and their work. As a result, the country has had to muddle its way through, always struggling to weigh the role of intelligence in national security and statecraft against constitutional principles and precepts. Not surprisingly, contradictions and inconsistencies have abounded.

Some of the most revered figures in US history have used and, in not a few cases abused, intelligence. According to the popular folktale, George Washington famously professed as a youth that he could not tell a lie. Yet, the historical Washington disclosed to Noah Webster that he relied on deception to help win the Revolutionary War. In explaining how he planned the decisive Yorktown campaign of 1781, he recounted "that much trouble was taken and finesse used to misguide & bewilder [the British] . . . by fictitious communications." Not limiting his ruses to the enemy, he even acknowledged, "Nor were less pains taken to deceive our own Army."[6]

As President, Washington sent Gouverneur Morris—hardly one of the "plain, honest men" he professed to be—on an intelligence-gathering mission of sorts to Great Britain. In his instructions to Morris, Washington expressed his desire to learn "the sentiments and Intentions of the Court of London" and explained that it "appear[ed] to [him] most expedient to have these Inquiries made informally by a private Agent." Rather than appoint an official diplomat, which would require the advice and consent of the Senate under the newly ratified Constitution, Washington decided to send Morris in the ambiguous role of a diplomat-spy to "obtain the information in question."[7] Senator William Maclay, apparently bemused by the nature of Morris's work, recorded in his journal that Morris "acted in a strange kind of capacity, half pimp, half envoy, or perhaps more properly a kind of political eavesdropper about the British Court."[8] Washington gave Morris his assignment before there was even a means to compensate him for it. He eventually paid him from the Contingent Fund for Foreign Intercourse, later more appropriately called the Secret Service Fund, which American presidents would draw upon throughout the nineteenth century to finance intelligence missions. He also neglected to report Morris's activities to Congress for a full year, likely a deliberate oversight.

Washington was not the only President who could keep a secret or tell a lie. Amid the strife of the Civil War, "Honest Abe" Lincoln, who praised a government "of the people, by the people, for the people," found no fault with manipulating the public through propaganda and may have used intelligence to intervene in the political process to ensure the electoral defeat of Democrats critical of his war policies.[9] Franklin D. Roosevelt, who comforted the American people during the dark days of the Great Depression and Second World War by hosting "fireside chats" over the radio, accepted political intelligence on his rivals from FBI director J. Edgar Hoover and unleashed the Bureau to root out fascist and communist sympathizers. Echoing John Winthrop, John F. Kennedy told his fellow Americans, "We must always consider that we shall be as a city upon a hill—the eyes of all people are upon us," yet he approved aggressive covert action operations that he hoped to keep from the eyes of the world and the American people.[10] Following Kennedy's example, Ronald Reagan also spoke of America as a "shining city on a hill," and he, too, sanctioned covert operations across the globe while evading or ignoring congressional intelligence oversight in the process.[11] Even a shining city on a hill casts a shadow.

While paying lip service to American ideals, these presidents resorted to intelligence measures that were at odds with the very principles they were intended to defend. Setting political rhetoric aside, the President has a duty to protect the American people. In turn, the American people must ensure their country lives up to its principles. The problem is that intelligence will never live up to American principles, and the American people often fail to live up to them as well. The American people have been consistently inconsistent in setting and adhering to their own expectations for intelligence, so the relationship between intelligence and the American people has been tumultuous. Different versions of the same dilemmas appear repeatedly over time. Try as it might, the United States has been unable to "fix" some key, recurrent problems in American civil-intelligence relations. Instead, intelligence has existed in a state of dynamic tension with US civil society. Undoubtedly aware of this, government officials or officers from agencies like the CIA will often try to reassure the American people that intelligence is not "un-American." To the contrary, it is inherently "un-American."

For a country that values honesty, transparency, and forthrightness, intelligence presents a serious set of challenges because it involves secrecy. Kennedy observed that "the very word 'secrecy' is repugnant in a free and open society; and we are as a people inherently and historically opposed to secret societies, to secret oaths and to secret proceedings."[12] One could add "secret intelligence." Intelligence formally allows, and at times requires, some citizens to lie to and keep secrets from other citizens. Intelligence officers lead lives of secrecy and deception—and not just vis-à-vis adversaries but also in their relationships and interactions with their fellow Americans. They conduct missions on behalf of a public that cannot know about them and yet, as a nation, is collectively accountable for them. Thus, there is fundamental opposition between intelligence, which is a pillar of national security, and an informed citizenry, which is a pillar of the American constitutional system.

Intelligence is antithetical to American principles in other respects. It involves using surreptitious means to shape events. For example, US intelligence has participated in coups and electioneering against foreign states and democratically elected leaders. Furthermore, intelligence inevitably involves invasions of privacy. This is not limited to intrusive measures like electronic surveillance of personal correspondence or spies who act as confidants and friends. Intelligence also attempts to penetrate the human mind, determine intentions, and influence decision-making.

None of this is to say that intelligence officers themselves are un-American, but rather that their profession, by its very nature, is. Perhaps in recognition of this, Allen Dulles, the longest-serving Director of Central Intelligence, once tried to assure the American people, "An intelligence service in a free society... mirrors in its membership the society which it serves."[13] But that has not really been the case for the United States, and intelligence has not been "a mirror held up to the face of American society," as historian Rhodri Jeffreys-Jones countered.[14] American intelligence history is not exactly a representative history because intelligence has not truly represented all of the American people all of the time. Certainly, there have been intelligence agents and officers from virtually every element of civil society throughout American history—from James Armistead Lafayette, the slave who volunteered to spy against the British during the Revolutionary War, to Genevieve Grotjan, the cryptologist who broke Japan's Purple Code before the Second World War. However, intelligence has generally only been as representative as any other part of the government was at any point in time. Furthermore, during periods of danger and public panic, the government has wielded intelligence against political, religious, racial, and ethnic minorities, often with the complicity and sometimes the active cooperation of other citizens. So, apart from the intrinsic divisions between intelligence and the American people, intelligence has divided the American people themselves.

As another alternative remedy to the ills of American civil-intelligence relations, representatives from across civil society and government, including intelligence officials, have at times suggested that US intelligence operations should comport with American principles.[15] However, the reverse usually happens: The American people have proven more willing to temporarily tolerate controversial intelligence activities in order to feel safe than the intelligence community has proven able to ensure its operations live up to the highest American ideals. Too often, the American people throw these ideals to the wind when faced with danger, only to reproach their elected representatives and their intelligence establishment—though rarely themselves—after a war or emergency ends. A problematic pattern has emerged. The country has incorporated, abandoned, and then reincorporated different versions of the same types of intelligence activities, like spying on American citizens, that always generate public outcry throughout US history. Relatedly, the public has generally only paid fleeting attention to intelligence in moments of crisis and controversy. Vacillations like these are hardly a formula for stability, which in turn helps explain the persistent instability in US civil-intelligence relations.

When it comes to intelligence, the United States always seems to come up short in striking the right balance between secrecy and transparency, policies and principles, and security and liberty. Never in perfect equilibrium, the scale tilts one way or the other, producing periodic tensions between the American people, their government, and their intelligence community. As a result, the United States has experienced waves of intelligence controversies that have tested the spirit of the country and its Constitution. Each time, the American people forget and must relearn the same hard lessons, despite the fact that many of the intelligence challenges they face have deep historical roots.

A History of Failure or a Failure of History?

Intelligence lies behind some of the watershed moments in the nation's history, starting with the sequence of events that led to the "shot heard 'round the world" and the birth of the United States. Intelligence not only shaped the course of US history but also determined the actual shape of the country—from the Lewis and Clark expedition to the annexation of Hawaii. Accordingly, understanding American intelligence history is essential to understanding American history.

Therein lies a challenge. Intelligence involves secrecy and requires that certain information not become known outside the classified channels of the US government.[16] However, the United States has a hard time keeping secrets. Many secret intelligence activities became public affairs that dominated the headlines of the time and developed into some of the great crises in the nation's history. These crises have defined American intelligence history, in some cases at the expense of civil-intelligence relations. Further contributing to the challenge of understanding intelligence are the misunderstandings that frequently accompany it. Their sources often lie not only in actual events but also in literature, film, and media because Americans have always had an appetite for intelligence in the form of nonfiction, novels, movies, and TV shows. The mixture of fact and fiction has led to conflicts in how Americans perceive intelligence. Add in propaganda and disinformation, and assembling an accurate picture of intelligence may seem impossible for the average citizen.

The secrecy surrounding intelligence also engenders suspicion. The American people have historically harbored serious doubts about intelligence. This can be a good thing for the health of a democracy since public opinion can act as a check on intelligence. But suspicion can be unhealthy when it leads to conspiracy theories. American intelligence history is full of such theories: that Franklin Roosevelt knew about, but did not prevent, the Japanese attack on Pearl Harbor; that the CIA played a role in JFK's assassination; or that the intelligence community is hiding evidence of extraterrestrial life.[17] Secrecy has also had the untoward effect of concealing American intelligence's track record, which further distorts public perceptions of it.

Kennedy once acknowledged to an audience of CIA officers, "Your successes are unheralded, your failures are trumpeted."[18] Ironically, he offered this conciliatory comment at an award ceremony for Allen Dulles, who was forced to resign as head of the CIA after months of scrutiny over the spectacular intelligence failure of the Bay of Pigs. Not nearly as gracious at the time, Kennedy supposedly fulminated that he wanted to "splinter the C.I.A. in a thousand pieces and scatter it to the winds."[19] Failures, scandals, and abuses mar perceptions of the CIA and the intelligence community more generally.

In this respect, intelligence failure is often as much the product of perception as it is of reality. There is a crucial distinction between actually failing and being perceived to have failed.[20] In perceiving intelligence to have failed, the public has failed to appreciate the purposes and limitations of intelligence. Intelligence exists in a world of uncertainty in which it must take risks both operationally and analytically. One should reasonably expect it would have a mixed record of success and failure. Instead, the country exhibits a zero-tolerance posture toward intelligence failure, particularly when it involves a surprise attack that costs American lives. This attitude is partly born out of the belief that intelligence's main function is to predict impending events, like Pearl Harbor or 9/11. But does intelligence fail when it cannot predict every single event yet to pass, large or small? While warning is certainly a key function of intelligence analysis, prediction is not. Intelligence has often provided warning of events in a general sense of trends and intentions, even if it has not predicted the precise day and time when something catastrophic would occur. The American people should have high standards for their intelligence community, just not impossible ones.

It is a truism of American intelligence history that there are no policy failures, only intelligence failures. This is because policymakers usually find it more convenient to make intelligence the scapegoat than to question or even admit the roles they played. At times, policymakers have either failed to heed intelligence warnings or failed to act on them. Presidential administrations have also pursued policies that set the course for intelligence failure. In some cases, these policy failures developed slowly or snowballed over multiple presidential administrations. In others, events overtook even the best-laid plans, resulting in unexpected, adverse outcomes. Secrecy compounds the problem when presidents rely on covert action to try to save a failed policy or win a quick policy victory on the cheap. If a covert operation fails and becomes public, it often precipitates more policy failure. Thus, policy failure becomes intelligence failure becomes policy failure, but intelligence almost always shoulders the blame and almost never receives a fair hearing in the court of public opinion.

One valuable role of intelligence history is to set the record straight. Two general biases often inform accounts of American intelligence history. On the one hand, there are its skeptics, especially among journalists, academics, and historians, who display a bias against intelligence and tend to focus on its abuses or failures. On the other, there are its defenders, especially among former intelligence officers, who try to explain away failures and dismiss critics for never having faced the hard choices intelligence imposes in practice. Neither side is wholly right or wrong. American intelligence organizations have committed grievous abuses that seem to support negative stereotypes. At the same time, intelligence is an essential element of national security and statecraft that has made the country safer and informed important foreign policy choices. Those who conduct intelligence operations or make intelligence policy can be heroes or villains like anyone else. Importantly, this book will highlight where the American people have failed by allowing or even abetting some of the problems they attribute to intelligence alone. Where intelligence appears to have failed, the entire country has often failed with it.

The Spy and the State aims to address many of the failures and misperceptions marking American intelligence history—and it must begin with the title of the book itself. Intelligence practitioners and scholars distinguish between an intelligence officer, who serves the state as a member of the intelligence community, and a spy, who is the person an intelligence officer recruits as a source of information in another country. The title of this book therefore commits a breach of intelligence etiquette, but *The Intelligence Officer and the State* just did not have the same ring to it. Over time, policymakers, the press, and others have referred to those individuals now called "intelligence officers" as spies, special agents, executive agents, secret agents, and other names as intelligence professionalized in the United States. The book will therefore use these names as they appeared at the time in primary sources. Similarly, this historical narrative rests on primary sources, ranging from personal correspondence to legislative records to news articles. It also references popular culture, such as literature and film, as well as public polling to show how intelligence appears in American civil society throughout US history. Finally, while this book incorporates elements of political, diplomatic, military, and even social, cultural, and administrative history, it is first and foremost a work of intelligence history.

A Road Map for Reading American Intelligence History

The history of American intelligence is roughly divided into four distinct eras marked by changes to the US intelligence system that occurred during transitions between war and peace. Partly due to the precedent set by Washington and Morris, intelligence was a discretionary activity controlled by the President with little outside oversight or interference from the earliest days of the United States through the Civil War. The congressionally authorized Secret Service Fund allowed presidents to hire spies or fund intelligence operations as they saw fit. Partisan politics combined with the separation of powers to stoke competition between the President and Congress over intelligence control and oversight. Moreover, American spies were all amateurs who temporarily performed intelligence missions and then returned to their normal occupations, so intelligence was not a formal profession of national security.

The period from the Civil War to the Second World War witnessed the emergence of the early US intelligence "community" as the large executive departments of government created their own intelligence services. Departmental control of intelligence displaced presidential control. The new intelligence organizations and their parent departments competed over different intelligence functions and missions, and intelligence was subordinated to other professions of national security. One problematic example was the combination of law enforcement and domestic intelligence, which resulted in political intelligence scandals. There was still no independent intelligence organization or profession despite glimmers of both. As the scale of American involvement in the world grew, coordination and professionalization became central challenges for intelligence.

The period from the Second World War to the end of the Cold War began with an attempt to address the coordination problem facing American intelligence by creating the CIA. More intelligence agencies and organizations were also created, often as the result of bureaucratic competition over key functions, leading to the formation of the modern US Intelligence Community. Coordination among the warring tribes within this community continued to frustrate those seeking to reform it. Although it was unable to achieve its mandate to coordinate intelligence, the CIA heralded the long-delayed professionalization of American intelligence as its own distinct profession of national security. The CIA also became a special covert and clandestine arm of US foreign policy, contributing to many myths and misperceptions that the American people still hold about their intelligence community. Relatedly, revelations of abuses carried out by intelligence organizations, especially the CIA, reignited the battle between the President and Congress over the smoldering issue of intelligence control and oversight. While Congress devised a new intelligence oversight system in response, politicization accompanied the change and planted the seeds for more partisan conflict as politicians and parties have often exploited intelligence for political purposes.

The fourth and final era, from the end of the Cold War to the present, led to the rise of the contemporary American intelligence state. Following a brief period of postwar malaise, the 9/11 attacks shook the United States from the illusion of a peace dividend. Unsurprisingly, intelligence took the fall for 9/11, widely regarded as the greatest intelligence failure since Pearl Harbor. The result was another attempt to coordinate intelligence and the belated creation of the position of Director of National Intelligence after decades of proposals and debate. At the same time, policymakers and the public looked to intelligence to keep the country safe from terrorism. The intelligence community harnessed new technology to create a vast surveillance system that has endured. Inauspiciously, intelligence abuses and scandals that struck at the heart of American constitutionalism did not produce major intelligence reform. The American people now face intelligence challenges that threaten both their liberty and their security with even fewer prospects of balancing the two.

The longer history of intelligence, the world's "second-oldest profession," attests to its enduring role in human affairs. The question was never if the United States would incorporate intelligence into national security and statecraft but, rather, what its nature and shape would be. In each period of American intelligence history, old problems persisted, and new ones surfaced. Blowback, a CIA term for the unintended consequences of covert operations, is often only a matter of time.

A common refrain among intelligence analysts is that intelligence requires asking the right questions. As you read this history, ask yourself if you would trade your liberty for security, or rather how much liberty you would exchange for more security. Perhaps a better question is whether you would be willing to trade someone else's liberty for your own security. For intelligence officials or practitioners reading the book, put yourself in the shoes of your fellow citizens, deprived of the secrets upon which you base your own worldviews, as you consider the same questions. Have some of the more intrusive or aggressive intelligence measures the government has implemented really made the country safer, and if so, at what cost? What are the proper uses and realistic limitations of intelligence, especially in a representative government and free society? How much was the current American intelligence system the product of a coherent design and how much was it the result of bureaucratic or personal rivalries, wars and national emergencies, and the churn of democratic politics? These and other questions go to the heart of civil-intelligence relations and even the foundations of the American republic. Archibald MacLeish, the eminent poet, Librarian of Congress, and, notably, recruiter for the Office of Strategic Services, mused, "We have learned the answers, all the answers: It is the question that we do not know."[21] If this book leaves its readers a little less certain and inspires them to ask more questions, it has accomplished its purpose.

PART ONE

The Eagle's Eyes: The Dawn of American Intelligence

1

A Revolution Sub Rosa

THE SHADOW WAR FOR INDEPENDENCE

AT THE CORNER of Vanderbilt Avenue and East 44th Street in New York City, affixed to the present-day building that hosts the Yale Club of New York, a small plaque reads, "At the British artillery park near this site Nathan Hale captain in the U.S. Army, Yale graduate of 1773, apprehended within enemy lines while seeking information, was executed on the morning of September 22, 1776. His last words were 'I only regret that I have but one life to lose for my country.'" He was twenty-one years old.

Although historians debate the site of Hale's execution, the Yale Club is an appropriate place to commemorate one of America's first spies. In addition to Hale, Yale University has produced a number of famous spies over the years, including many from the founding generation of the CIA. Outside Connecticut Hall, Hale's former dormitory on Old Campus, Yale honors Hale with a statue—one that is also reproduced outside the CIA headquarters in Langley, Virginia. As an intelligence mission, Hale's was a total failure. Still, history remembers him as a hero. Hale symbolizes the complicated and contradictory relationship the American people have always had with intelligence.

In the late summer of 1776, George Washington and the Continental Army were hard-pressed as they tried to defend the city of New York from British forces that were massing on Long Island. Washington wanted more information about the British, including their numbers, movements, and plans. He ordered Lieutenant Colonel Thomas Knowlton to form a special unit to conduct reconnaissance missions for the Continental Army. Reconnaissance was one way to try to get information, but what Washington really needed was a spy.

In early September, Washington asked Knowlton to find a volunteer for an intelligence-gathering mission behind enemy lines. As if the assignment was not risky enough, finding a volunteer would be even more challenging.

Americans looked down on espionage as dishonorable, especially for an officer of the Continental Army. The first man Knowlton selected for the mission, Lieutenant James Sprague, refused. Sprague reportedly told Knowlton that he was willing to fight the British "at any time or place" but "could never consent to expose himself to be hung like a dog."[1] Even the punishment reserved for spies—hanging—was considered a disgrace.

Knowlton then approached Hale, who hesitated and consulted his friend Captain William Hull. Hull discouraged him from accepting the mission, arguing that "the propriety of it was doubtful . . . such a service was not claimed of the meanest soldier." Besides, Hull asked, "who respects the character of a spy, assuming the garb of friendship but to betray?" Hull continued, "The very death assigned him is expressive of the estimation in which he is held. As soldiers, let us do our duty in the field; contend for our legitimate rights, and not stain our honour by the sacrifice of integrity." But Hale countered Hull's warning about honor and espionage, reasoning that "every kind of service, necessary to the public good, becomes honourable by being necessary."[2]

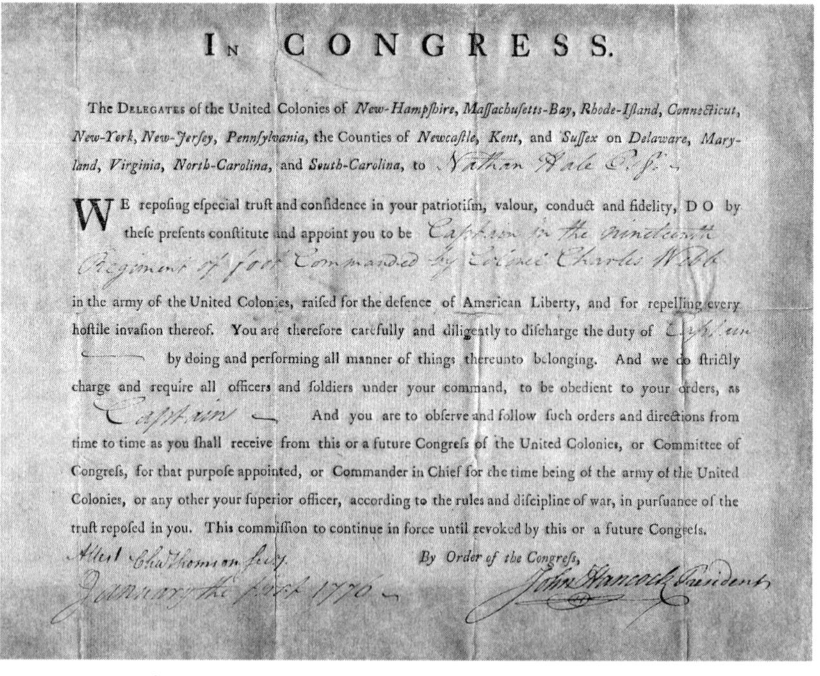

IN CONGRESS.

The DELEGATES of the United Colonies of *New-Hampſhire*, *Maſſachuſetts-Bay*, *Rhode-Iſland*, *Connecticut*, *New-York*, *New-Jerſey*, *Pennſylvania*, the Counties of *Newcaſtle*, *Kent*, and *Suſſex* on *Delaware*, *Maryland*, *Virginia*, *North-Carolina*, and *South-Carolina*, to Nathan Hale Esq.

WE repoſing eſpecial truſt and confidence in your patriotiſm, valour, conduct and fidelity, DO by theſe preſents conſtitute and appoint you to be Captain in the nineteenth Regiment of foot Commanded by Colonel Charles Webb in the army of the United Colonies, raiſed for the defence of American Liberty, and for repelling every hoſtile invaſion thereof. You are therefore carefully and diligently to diſcharge the duty of Captain by doing and performing all manner of things thereunto belonging. And we do ſtrictly charge and require all officers and ſoldiers under your command, to be obedient to your orders, as Captain. And you are to obſerve and follow ſuch orders and directions from time to time as you ſhall receive from this or a future Congreſs of the United Colonies, or Committee of Congreſs, for that purpoſe appointed, or Commander in Chief for the time being of the army of the United Colonies, or any other your ſuperior officer, according to the rules and diſcipline of war, in purſuance of the truſt repoſed in you. This commiſſion to continue in force until revoked by this or a future Congreſs.

Attest Chas Thomson Secy. *By Order of the Congreſs,*

January the first 1776 John Hancock President

FIGURE 1.1 Hale's commission as a captain in the Nineteenth Regiment of Foot. Hale suffered the punishment reserved for spies "according to the rules and discipline of war" alluded to in the commission—death by hanging. Autograph letter and original commission of Nathan Hale, GEN MSS 1146, Beinecke Rare Book and Manuscript Library, Yale University.

Hale's response betrayed his character. He was simply too forthright and trusting to be a good spy.[3] This would be his downfall. Robert Rogers, of "Rogers' Rangers" fame, gained Hale's confidence and convinced him to reveal his mission.[4] Hale also made other amateur mistakes, like using his real name, failing to adequately conceal the documents containing his intelligence reports, and choosing a poor cover as a schoolteacher.[5] The British arrested Hale on September 21 and charged him with espionage. By that point, events had overtaken Hale's mission. The British landing at Kip's Bay on September 15 had forced Washington to retreat to Harlem, leaving the city to the British. Hale was taken to the new British headquarters in modern-day midtown Manhattan and then hanged the next morning. This early foray into espionage cost Hale his life and reinforced the need for effective intelligence in America.

While Hale will always be remembered as a hero of the Revolutionary War, perhaps no American of the period has come to personify villainy and treachery more than Benedict Arnold. Following a period of distinguished service in the Continental Army, Arnold became disenchanted with the cause. Despite his heroic actions in battles at Quebec and Saratoga, where he suffered grievous injuries, he was passed up for promotion and later court-martialed. He also married Peggy Shippen, daughter of a Loyalist family and former paramour of Major John André, the head of British intelligence in North America. Arnold agreed to spy for the British, becoming a foil to Hale. After receiving command of the critical Continental Army position overlooking the Hudson River that later became the home of the United States Military Academy at West Point, he planned to help the British take the fort. Arnold narrowly escaped to British-held New York City after John André was captured by American militiamen following a secret meeting between the two.

The capture of André and exposure of Arnold was a professional and personal accomplishment for Major Benjamin Tallmadge, a military intelligence officer for the Continental Army and close friend of Nathan Hale. In fact, during André's captivity, Tallmadge related to him the story of his "much loved Classmate in Yale College." When André insisted that his and Hale's cases were different, Tallmadge replied that the two cases were "precisely similar, & similar will be your fate."[6] Still, in their brief time together, Tallmadge quickly grew to respect André. The two intelligence officers even shared a handshake under the gallows before André's execution, proving there is honor among spies.[7]

The history of American intelligence reflects the folklore of the Revolutionary War. In Hale and Arnold, the United States had its first

FIGURE 1.2 A self-portrait drawn by André on the eve of his execution. Yale University Art Gallery.

exemplars of intelligence heroes and villains. Mirroring these two contrasting characters, American intelligence has had its tremendous successes as well as its catastrophic failures. Public attitudes toward intelligence have likewise shifted between poles, with the American people eagerly, perhaps too eagerly, supporting intelligence at some points in US history and fearing, even loathing, intelligence at others.

The American Revolution anchored the first great era of US intelligence. The war was formative for American intelligence, not least because its leading figures authored the Constitution and established the United States. Among the most prominent Founders were the nation's first intelligence officers. Many of their documents even reference "intelligence." At the time, "intelligence" could mean any new or important information. In some contexts, the word signified secret information. But more importantly, the sources prove that those engaged in intelligence activities during the war knew they were conducting intelligence as it is understood today. They presided over intelligence missions, gathered information through surreptitious means, and initiated covert action operations to undermine the British war effort. They also attempted to preserve the secrecy of their activities—from the public, from governing bodies, and, at times, from each other.

The First American Intelligence "Conspiracy"

At the Green Dragon Tavern, a public house in Boston's North End, the "Mechanics," a shadowy offshoot of the better-known Sons of Liberty, plotted a revolution. Unfortunately for the patriots, there was a spy in their ranks. Dr. Benjamin Church, a man with impeccable colonial credentials, was passing information to General Thomas Gage, the commander of the British forces then garrisoning Boston. Even before the "shot heard 'round the world," the intelligence game was afoot.

The revolutionaries eventually discovered Church's duplicity when they intercepted and decrypted a coded letter he had addressed to a British officer in Boston. In the letter, an alarmed Church claimed it was "scarcely possible to escape discovery" and provided detailed instructions on how to contact him, including to "write... largely in cypher" and "sign some fictious name." He concluded with a warning: "Make use of every precaution or I perish."[8] Church was lucky. He narrowly avoided the hangman's noose, perhaps on the technicality that the Continental Congress had not mandated the death

FIGURE 1.3 Watercolor sketch of the Green Dragon Tavern: "Where we met to Plan the Consignment of a few Shiploads of Tea, Dec 16 1773," John Johnson. Courtesy of the American Antiquarian Society.

penalty for espionage.[9] Congress corrected this oversight on November 7, 1775, decreeing that "all persons convicted of holding a treacherous correspondence with, or giving intelligence to the enemy, shall suffer death, or such other punishment as a general court-martial shall think proper." The same day, the Continental Congress passed a resolution, "That Dr. Church be close confined in some secure gaol in the colony of Connecticut, without the use of pen, ink, and paper, and that no person be allowed to converse with him, except in the presence and hearing of a Magistrate of the town, or the sheriff of the county where he shall be confined, and in the English language, until farther [*sic*] orders from this or a future Congress."[10] Apparently, Congress feared that Church had more information he could divulge and sought to isolate him. Church was banished from Massachusetts, along with other Loyalists, in 1778. He left on a ship bound for the West Indies that was lost at sea.

Although Benedict Arnold became the most notorious spy of the war for American independence, Church could have been the most dangerous, as he exposed the Boston leadership of the revolution to capture or worse. Fortunately, Gage idled at the instructions of Lord Dartmouth, the British Secretary of State for the Colonies, who had written him that "the first essential step to be taken towards re-establishing Government, would be to arrest and imprison the principal actors & abettors."[11] But instead of nipping the revolution in the bud by decapitating its leadership, Gage chose to act on other intelligence he had by targeting the revolutionaries' munitions depot at Concord. The British set out for Concord, and the Mechanics responded based on their own intelligence network by hanging two lanterns in the Old North Church and sending riders to warn the minutemen who would fight the first battles of the war at Lexington and Concord.[12]

The American Revolution thus began as a conspiracy, a secret plot initiated by a few, like those who met at the Green Dragon Tavern. Ironically, these men believed that they were the ones facing a conspiracy—a conspiracy within the British government to destroy their liberty.[13] But not all colonists wanted independence from the Crown. A considerable number were Loyalists who considered the rebellion and its leaders treasonous. Others were unsure. The revolution's leaders converted a conspiracy by a small group into popular resistance, widespread civil unrest, and, as events unfolded, a full-blown war. But until the revolutionaries had the support of a sufficient number of Americans, they risked arrest and execution for treason. Realizing the precariousness of their position, they resorted to propaganda, an intelligence function, to set the conditions for a revolution.

American history now celebrates the propaganda of the revolution as the intellectual efforts of patriots rather than the plotting of a few conspirators. For example, Thomas Paine would be hailed as the master pamphleteer of the American Revolution. George Washington commended Paine's propaganda in a letter to Richard Henry Lee in 1784, observing that "his 'Common Sense,' and many of his 'Crises' were well timed, and had a happy effect upon the public mind."[14] Propaganda carries negative connotations in an open society like the United States, where citizens believe there must be a free exchange of ideas divorced from hidden agendas or influences. That the revolution was later seen as a reasonable reaction to the excesses of the British government tends to undermine how extreme the demand for independence was for many colonists at the time. The secret meetings of groups like the Mechanics attest to their understanding of the seriousness of their plot or, from the British point of view, their crime. Moreover, the fact that propaganda was transmitted through town halls, newspapers, and pamphlets gives it a more innocent air. All these factors tend to undercut the role of intelligence in igniting the Revolutionary War. However, what was being transmitted by revolutionaries to the American people to shape public opinion was propaganda.[15] For their part, the British might have considered what the revolutionaries were doing to stir up the colonies a disinformation campaign.

Perhaps Americans have reinterpreted the propaganda that emerged during the American Revolution because it featured political principles that became the intellectual cornerstones of the United States. Samuel Adams, a prominent propagandist, stressed that the rights of the American colonists were "principally, *personal security*, *personal liberty* and *private property*," or, as the Declaration of Independence later declared, life, liberty, and the pursuit of happiness.[16] While the Declaration of Independence also frames these rights as "self-evident," in many ways the United States owes its independence and foundational values to this wartime propaganda.

Can Congress Keep a Secret?

As the American Revolution gained momentum and popular support, the secret meetings of groups like the Mechanics transformed into gatherings of formal committees created and authorized by the Continental Congress. Initially, these congressional committees played an active role in overseeing and controlling intelligence. At the outset, it appeared that Congress would be the principal stakeholder in American intelligence. However, a different model triumphed. Intelligence increasingly became the province of a few leading figures as intelligence scandals erupted in the Continental Congress, casting doubt on its ability to responsibly manage the government's secret activities.

The Continental Congress purportedly understood the value of secrecy. As one indication, it instituted oaths of secrecy for its members. The principle of transparent government hardly had a place in an insurgent American government at war. However, both personal and political divisions in the Continental Congress created layers of secrecy that undermined intelligence initiatives.

On November 29, 1775, the Continental Congress issued a series of resolutions that created the Committee of Secret Correspondence, America's first intelligence organization. The Continental Congress also stipulated that the committee's members, who included the famous Founders Benjamin Franklin and John Jay, would "lay their correspondence before Congress when directed."[17] On December 12, 1775, the Committee of Secret Correspondence directed its first agent, Arthur Lee, to report back from Europe regarding "the disposition of foreign powers toward us," including the admonition, "We need not hint that great circumspection and impenetrable secrecy are necessary."[18]

However, Lee resolved to keep secrets from certain members of the Committee of Secret Correspondence. In a letter dated February 13, 1776, he flatly stated that Franklin and Jay "are men whom I can not trust." Lee goes on to say, "If I am to commit myself into an unreserved correspondence, they must be left out.... This letter, therefore, is to you, sir, and not to the committee.... The selection of them instead of inspiring confidence, gives me... apprehension."[19] In a letter the next day, Lee again wrote, "I am not a little surprised that it should so happen that these two men are upon such a committee, while others are omitted with whom I am known to be in habits of communication and confidence. I therefore trust this with you and not with the committee, in whom I can not repose any confidence until those two men are removed."[20] Rather than report to the Committee of Secret Correspondence, the proper organizational channel for his intelligence activities, Lee reserved for himself the right to choose to whom he would communicate and what. American intelligence therefore began as an interpersonal endeavor rather than an organizational one.

But Congress also realized that public oversight could jeopardize the clandestine activities of the Committee of Secret Correspondence. Accordingly, on May 10, 1776, when Congress resolved to have the committee report on its operations thus far, it granted the committee the necessary discretion of "withholding the names of the persons they have employed or with whom they have corresponded."[21] In doing so, it acknowledged the need to protect what today are known as "sources and methods" in the intelligence community.

For its part, the Committee of Secret Correspondence had its own reservations about sharing information with the Continental Congress. In an internal memorandum for the committee dated October 1, 1776, Benjamin Franklin and Robert Morris shared intelligence about a shipment of arms and ammunition France was going to deliver to the American revolutionary forces. They included a caution against spreading the contents of the memorandum:

> The above intelligence was communicated to the subscribers... and on our considering the nature and importance of it, we agree in opinion that it is our indispensable duty to keep it a secret, even from Congress.... We find, by fatal experience, the Congress consists of too many members to keep secrets.[22]

The committee realized that a large, fractious Congress could not keep secrets, so it decided to deliberately violate the section of its charter stipulating that its members would "lay their correspondence before Congress when directed." John Jay reiterated this position in a letter to Robert Morris on October 6, 1776:

> I wish the secret committee would communicate no other intelligence to the Congress at large than what may be necessary to promote the common weal, not gratify the curiosity of individuals. I hint this, because a copy of a letter from A.L. [likely Arthur Lee] to that committee has lately been sent by a member of Congress to a gentleman of his acquaintance who is not a member of Congress. I came by this intelligence in such a way as to speak with certainty, for I have seen the copy, but at the same time in such a way as not to be able with propriety to mention names. You will be pleased, therefore, to make no other use of this information than to induce the greater caution in the committee. For as to binding certain members in the House to secrecy by oaths or otherwise would be just as absurd as to swear Lee (no matter which of them) to look or feel like Ned Rutledge.[23]

Jay captured a persistent challenge to protecting classified information: leaks. During the Revolutionary War, members of the Committee of Secret

Correspondence leaked information to members of the Continental Congress, then members of the Continental Congress leaked information to members of the public.

Secrecy requires discretion, but secrecy also lends itself to discretionary decisions to share or withhold information. Just as Lee was determined to keep information from certain members of the Committee of Secret Correspondence, they, too, resolved not to divulge information to the Continental Congress. As a result, the Continental Congress exercised diminishing control and oversight of intelligence during the war. Intelligence also generated personal and political fractures in both the Continental Congress and the Committee of Secret Correspondence.

Diplomats by Day, Spies by Night

Securing an alliance with France was essential to American grand strategy in the Revolutionary War but the French did not want to risk open hostilities with Britain over what could be a potentially failed effort in North America. American agents in France had to conduct their affairs undercover to avoid any appearance of an outright alliance that would embarrass the French. At the time, European states mixed intelligence with diplomacy in the form of what Francis Wharton, whom Congress later appointed to compile the official correspondence of the Revolutionary War, called the "secret diplomatist," essentially, a diplomat-spy.[24] Despite the American animus against this style of "Old World" statecraft, the Committee of Secret Correspondence endorsed the activities of diplomat-spies, leading to a blurring of the two roles that ultimately suited neither.

In March 1776, the Committee of Secret Correspondence sent instructions to Silas Deane, formerly a delegate to the Continental Congress, to prepare him for his role as a diplomat-spy in France. The committee provided Deane with a cover story and warned him that he must conceal his identity as an American agent. The committee also told Deane that he would "for some time be engaged in the business of providing goods," explaining, "This will give good countenance to your appearing in the character of a merchant... it being probable that the court of France may not like it should be known publicly that any agent from the Colonies is in that country." Among other responsibilities, the committee directed Deane to encourage and facilitate the provision of arms and supplies by France; discover the conditions required by the French for a formal treaty or alliance; "keep a daily journal of all... material transactions, and particularly of what passes in your conversation with great personages"; and communicate with Arthur Lee and Edward Bancroft, another American agent in London, thus creating an intelligence network in Europe.[25]

Deane made good on his instructions. He collected intelligence on the disposition of European states toward American independence, negotiated supplies and armaments for the revolutionaries, and recruited French officers to travel to America as liaisons and military trainers for the Continental Army. But, other than two letters in June, Deane did not hear from the committee until November. Failing communication with the committee, he was forced to act on his own initiative. He soon extended his intelligence activities to include the far more aggressive—and self-appointed—mission of covert action.

One of the more mysterious and audacious operations in which Deane was implicated was a plot to sabotage British shipyards. The scope of the plot and evidence of Deane's involvement are murky, but apparently a volunteer named James Aitken, pseudonym "John the Painter," approached Deane in September 1776 and offered to assassinate King George III and raze the shipyard at Portsmouth.[26] In November, Aitken successfully burned parts of the navy yard, planted bombs in three ships, and set fires to homes in Bristol. When the British finally arrested Aitken, he confessed that he had received payment for the sabotage from Silas Deane.[27] It is unclear if the Committee of Secret Correspondence, let alone the Continental Congress, would have endorsed this provocative and impulsive covert action operation because it risked inflaming British public opinion and exposing France's collusion with the Americans. But, without orders from America, Deane saw himself as having no other choice but to devise his own plans.

Sporadic communication from America was a source of some consternation for Deane and the French. In October 1776, he penned a letter expressing both his and the French government's frustration with the Continental Congress, pleading, "For Heaven's sake, if you mean to have any connection with this kingdom, be more assiduous in getting your letters here." He enclosed critical intelligence on the foreign policy of several European countries and closed by expressing his confidence that he could "obtain a loan for the Colonies if empowered."[28] Still awaiting a response, he again begged the committee for guidance in November.[29] The following month, Deane wrote with exasperation, "The want of intelligence has more than once well-nigh ruined my affairs. Pray be more attentive to this important subject, or drop at once all thoughts of a foreign connection."[30] In the same letter, Deane mentioned that "Dr. Bancroft has been of very great service... no man has better intelligence in England; but it costs something."[31] Bancroft's service was costing the Americans much more than money: He was a double agent working for the British and had gained access to the inner workings of the American diplomatic and intelligence effort in Europe.

Deane was unaware when he wrote this letter that Benjamin Franklin had arrived off the coast of France and had already penned a letter to him. Franklin informed Deane that he had brought with him "several letters for you from the committee, which I do not send forward because I know they contain matters of consequence, and I am not certain of their safety in that way."[32] Secrecy therefore trumped correspondence in the Committee of Secret Correspondence. In addition to these letters, Franklin also eventually brought a mole to Paris who undermined his effort to preserve the secrecy of American activities in France—Dr. Edward Bancroft.

Deane and Franklin decided to exploit their position as guests of the French government and harass the British until either the British and French went to war or the British drove the French into a military alliance with the Americans.[33] Their primary means to achieve this goal was privateering operations based out of French ports.[34] The idea backfired when Britain and France nearly did go to war after American privateering operations precipitated a diplomatic crisis between the two European rivals in the summer of 1777.[35] Franklin and Deane's intelligence operations had the opposite of the diplomatic effect they desired, as their activities actually jeopardized French relations with the American commission. The Americans got their first taste of blowback. In this case, blowback almost undermined the critical diplomatic negotiations taking place.

The American contingent in Paris further strained diplomatic relations with France and exposed a more pernicious problem when a personal dispute originating among the diplomat-spies in France turned into a partisan dispute in the Continental Congress. Franklin arrived in France as a member of the American commission that the Continental Congress had elected in September 1776. The original commission included Franklin, Deane, and Thomas Jefferson.[36] Jefferson declined the position and, instead, Arthur Lee, the first American agent in France, joined Franklin and Deane.[37] Lee still harbored an animus against Franklin, so the commission was divided, with Lee on one side and Franklin and Deane on the other. The personal rivalries exploded when Lee exploited his political connections in the Continental Congress to have Deane recalled from France in late 1777. Lee and his allies accused Deane of grift during his covert dealings with the French and of having ties with pro-British Loyalists in America.[38] In response, Franklin and John Jay rallied Deane's own political allies in Congress.

It was in this context that Thomas Paine, the celebrated author of *Common Sense*, became perhaps the first major American figure to leak classified information. In April 1777, a resolution of the Continental Congress renamed the Committee of Secret Correspondence the Committee for Foreign Affairs.[39] Congress elected Paine as the committee's secretary. The position included an oath "to disclose no matter, the knowledge of which shall be acquired in consequence of such his office, that he shall be directed to keep secret."[40] Paine revealed France's covert aid to the American colonies as part of the factional strife between Deane and Lee and their respective allies in Congress.[41] The leak occurred as part of Paine's famous pamphleteering in a piece titled "Common Sense to the Public on Mr. Deane's Affair."[42] Conrad-Alexandre Gérard, the French plenipotentiary to the Continental Congress, lodged a formal complaint against the "indiscreet assertions contained in these passages," emphasizing that "the author is an officer of Congress, and... he takes advantage of his situation to give credit to his opinions and to his affirmations."[43]

The scandal could have potentially cost America its vital alliance with France, a price the American revolutionaries could not afford to pay. The Continental Congress took the extraordinary step of publicly rebuking Paine. The delegates issued a joint statement declaring that they "disavow[ed] the publications referred to" and stressed that "they have not authorized the writer of the said publication to make any such assertions as are contained therein, but, on the contrary, do highly disapprove of the same."[44] As punishment, Paine was dismissed from the Committee for Foreign Affairs.[45]

Deane suffered the brunt of the blowback, however. He returned to Paris in 1780 in disgrace and financial ruin. He eventually moved to Ghent, then London, and died of an illness in 1789 just after boarding a ship bound for America. He was never able to salvage his reputation or fortune. Redemption only came fifty years later in 1842 when a congressional investigation cleared Deane's name and paid his estate $37,000. As Deane's example showed, mixing intelligence and diplomacy was bad, but mixing intelligence and politics was far worse. The diplomat-spies of the Paris delegation managed to turn their intelligence operations and petty personal disputes in the shadow war against Britain into an open, partisan war in the Continental Congress.

The American commission in France was also plagued by counterintelligence problems. The British successfully planted a spy in their ranks. Edward Bancroft was an ideal choice for a spy because he was a former student of Silas Deane and the private secretary of Benjamin Franklin. Only Arthur Lee did not share the other two's cordial relationship with Bancroft.

Proof of Bancroft's duplicity comes from Bancroft himself. He revealed his espionage activities in a 1784 letter to the Marquess of Carmarthen, the British Secretary of State for Foreign Affairs. He claimed that he had originally refused to spy because it was "repugnant to [his] feelings," but he had changed his mind, citing his supposedly high-minded conviction that the American colonies should remain part of the British Empire. The letter exposed his much more cynical—and likely—motive as being financial compensation for his services to the Crown. Bancroft reported that he lived in the same house as Franklin and Deane, was privy to arms shipments and negotiations with France and other European states, and saw the correspondence sent by the Continental Congress and its "Secret Committees" to the commissioners.[46]

Franklin shrugged off any warnings. Juliana Ritchie, wife of a Philadelphia merchant who might have been an acquaintance of Franklin's, wrote to him that he was "Surrounded with Spies."[47] Thanking her, he nonetheless replied, "It is impossible to discover in every case the Falsity of pretended Friends . . . and more so to prevent being watch'd by Spies, when interested People may think proper to place them for that purpose." Furthermore, he claimed "to be concern'd in no Affairs that I should blush to have made publick; and to do nothing but what Spies may see and welcome."[48] Of course, as a member of the Committee of Secret Correspondence and diplomat-spy in Paris, Franklin had plenty to hide from both the public and the British.

In the event, the British had thoroughly infiltrated the American commission to Paris. In addition to Bancroft, Captain Joseph Hynson and Jacobus Van Zandt, two American expats in Paris, befriended the commissioners and spied for the British.[49] For all his concerns about secrecy and security, Arthur Lee managed to have his personal diary taken and copied. Worse yet, his own private secretary, John Thornton, turned out to be a British spy.[50] The British also intercepted American letters. Francis Wharton lamented, "As more than half of our correspondence met this destiny, the enemy was informed of the plans of Congress at least as freely as were the ministers of Congress abroad."[51] Given the degree of suspicion with which American diplomat-spies regarded one another, and the Committee of Secret Correspondence regarded the Continental Congress, it is reasonable to conclude that "the British Foreign Office was far better informed of American activities [in Europe] than was Congress itself."[52]

Although the paramount goal of the American diplomat-spies was to secure an alliance with France, intelligence occasionally undermined this effort. Even when it did not, the British were well aware of the Americans' activities. The American commission in France ultimately succeeded in its overarching mission in spite of itself. If anything, the real task for the American diplomat-spies was simply not to fumble the whole affair. Benjamin Franklin, who was already a celebrity in Europe, was at his best wooing the French at parties and salons as a diplomat, not scheming in the shadows as a spy.[53] American diplomacy—for all its own shortcomings—had a greater effect than American intelligence in Paris, and the issues that arose from blending both functions jeopardized the French alliance.

The American diplomat-spies in Paris provided several cautionary lessons about vesting both diplomatic and intelligence responsibilities in the same people. Likewise, the dual diplomatic and intelligence roles of the Committee of Secret Correspondence revealed greater problems with intelligence control and oversight. American intelligence was fractured, uncoordinated, and unprofessional even before the establishment of the United States. However, one man rose above the fray during the American Revolution and eclipsed the rest in both his understanding and application of intelligence.

George Washington, Commander in Chief and Spymaster in Chief of the Continental Army

Despite an inauspicious start with Hale's capture and execution, Washington was a quick study. Over the course of the war, he became a skilled and prudent administrator who personally managed the Continental Army's intelligence operations.

Washington's private correspondence reveals his keen interest in and aptitude for intelligence. In a letter to Colonel Elias Dayton, he explained that he wanted to know "the Enemy's situation & numbers—What kind of Troops they are, and What Guards they have—their Strength & where posted." He emphasized, "The necessity of procuring good Intelligence is apparent & need not be further urged—All that remains for me to add, is, that you keep the whole matter as secret as possible. For upon Secrecy, Success depends in most Enterprizes of the kind, and for want of it, they are generally defeated, however well planned & promising a favourable issue."[54] Secrecy became a theme in Washington's letters and a salient feature of his intelligence system.[55]

For example, he wrote to Major John Clark to commend him on his intelligence operations: "I…think you have fallen upon an exceeding good method of gaining intelligence," adding that "too much secrecy cannot be used, both on account of the safety of your Friend and the execution and continuance of your design, which may be of Service to us."[56] He likewise encouraged Benjamin Tallmadge to "observe the strictest silence" in handling communication from Abraham Woodhull, alias "Samuel Culper," of the famous Culper spy ring.[57] Washington also controlled the channels through which he communicated with agents in the field and employed a system of codes and ciphers specific to each intelligence network. He even used a recipe for invisible ink created by John Jay's brother James to conceal important messages.[58]

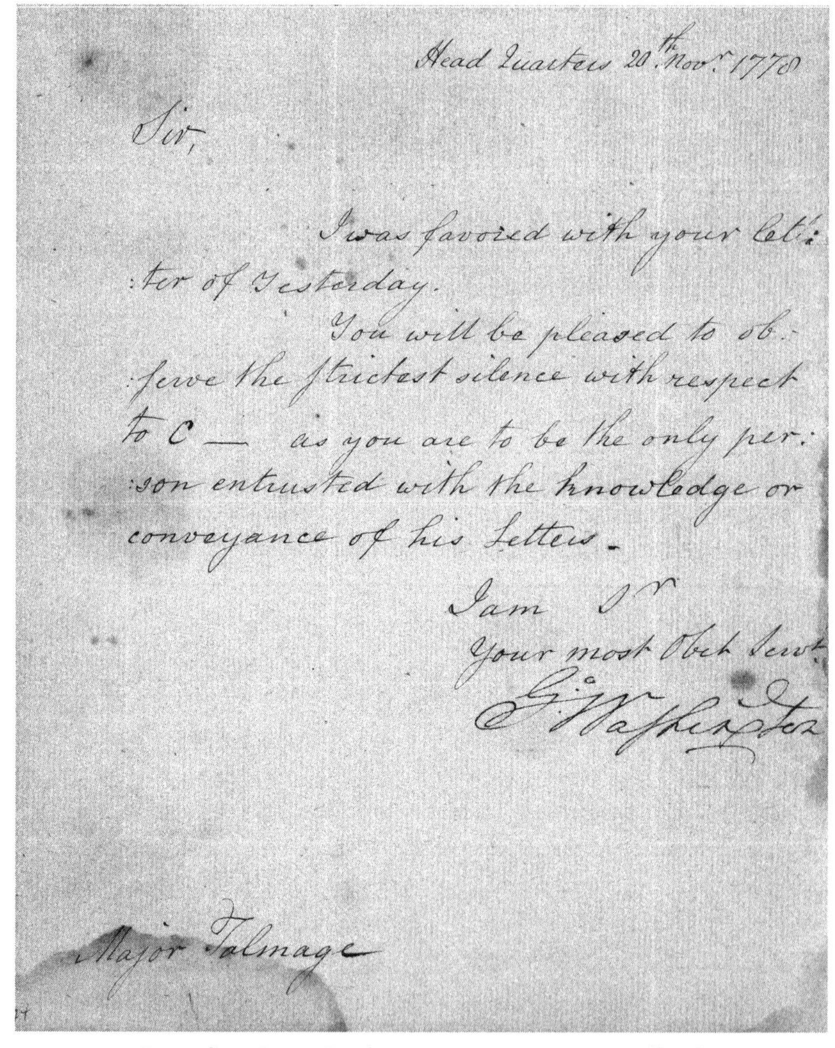
Head Quarters 20th Novr 1778

Sir,

I was favored with your Let:
:ter of Yesterday.
You will be pleased to ob:
:serve the strictest silence with respect
to C— as you are to be the only per:
:son entrusted with the knowledge or
conveyance of his Letters.

I am Sr
Your most Obet Servt
G. Washington

Major Talmage

FIGURE 1.4 Letter from George Washington to Major Benjamin Tallmadge instructing him to "observe the strictest silence with respect to C——," Samuel Culper. Walter L. Pforzheimer Papers, General Collection, Beinecke Rare Book and Manuscript Library, Yale University.

Apparently, Washington became so proficient at keeping secrets that some of his agents almost became victims of his success. In January 1778, three such agents, John and Baker Hendricks and John Meeker, were detained by revolutionaries in New Jersey as British spies and faced trial and the possibility of execution. Washington promptly wrote Governor William Livingston that they were "employed... to procure intelligence of the movements of the Enemy while upon Staten Island" and urged him to halt their prosecution. He explained, "You must be well convinced that it is indispensably necessary to make use of these means to procure intelligence. The persons employed must bear the suspicion of being thought inimical and it is not in their powers to assert their innocence, because that would get abroad and destroy the confidence which the Enemy puts in them."[59] It was a close call for those men, yet a testament to Washington's abilities as the spymaster in chief.

Washington also proved willing to go to extremes in the shadow war with the British. For example, he authorized at least three kidnapping plots, including one to seize King George III's son while the young heir to the throne of England was visiting New York City.[60] He ordered his intelligence officers to recruit Quakers who "would be least liable to suspicion from either party."[61] He even directed Reverend Alexander McWhorter, the chaplain of the artillery brigade, to use the last rites of two condemned spies as an opportunity to extract every last drop of information from them. He determined that "these unfortunate men are acquainted with many facts respecting the enemys affairs," calculating that "while it serves to prepare them for the other world, it will naturally lead to intelligence we want."[62] Furthermore, Washington eagerly supported intelligence operations to intercept and decode British communications, writing General Philip Schuyler, "I think the intelligence obtained thro' that channel may be depended upon, and will eventually be of very great consequence to us."[63] In sum, Washington embraced intelligence in all of its forms and functions, including ones that would have offended the sensibilities of Americans at the time.

There were flaws in the Continental Army's intelligence system under Washington given that he was its primary administrator and consumer.[64] The burdens of personally managing not just the army's intelligence operations but the entire army were apparent. Washington once confessed to Nathaniel Sackett, the leader of one of his spy rings, "It runs in my head that I was to correspond with you by a fictitious name, if so I have forgot the name and must be reminded of it again."[65]

Washington's intelligence operations required a great deal of money. The Continental Congress's persistent issues with raising funds for the war effort meant that Washington occasionally had to rely on his personal wealth and the largesse of others. For example, he privately solicited Robert Morris, the "Financier of the Revolution," to bankroll his efforts.[66] Spymasters drawing on their own means have little incentive to submit to congressional oversight if Congress is not supplying the funds, and Congress's oversight of Washington's intelligence operations became as problematic as its oversight of the Committee of Secret Correspondence.

The Continental Congress ended up financing some of Washington's intelligence efforts, but only a few members of Congress had much of a role in the process, namely, the president of Congress, the superintendent of finance (Robert Morris), and certain members of the Secret Committee.[67] There was little in the way of reporting requirements for Washington. While the Committee of Secret Correspondence was, by congressional resolution, supposed to report on its activities to the Continental Congress—and even then, it did not—Washington was not subjected to any similar oversight or control mechanisms. When other members of the Continental Congress attempted to implement oversight of Washington's intelligence activities, several leading figures blunted their effort.[68]

Washington's secrecy and discretionary control established a precedent for intelligence in the future United States. Over the course of the war, as his intelligence networks and operations expanded, his intelligence model emerged: "Washington believed in an intelligence structure with central direction and focus but decentralized implementation of these activities."[69] No formal intelligence profession or organization developed during the Revolutionary War in part because of Washington's personal control over the Continental Army's intelligence system. This "hub-and-spoke" model of intelligence coordination and control extended into his presidency and continued to define intelligence in the early American republic.

Culture and Counterintelligence

Colonial Americans were ideologically predisposed to distrust the features of a powerful central government—for example, a standing army and intelligence. Espionage was an affront to the sense of forthrightness and decency valued by both the British and the Americans. The treachery of Benjamin Church and Benedict Arnold also certainly colored American public perceptions of espionage. The charge of spying further exacerbated the sting of accusations of treason or disloyalty to either side's cause—independence in the American case, reunification in the British case. As distasteful as intelligence was, the problem of British espionage reinforced the need for a robust counterintelligence campaign.

The very nature and conduct of the war complicated both sides' counterintelligence operations. The Revolutionary War was a civil war on two levels. First, it began as a war between British subjects and the Crown. Second, it expanded to a war between American revolutionaries and pro-British Loyalists in the colonies. In this internecine conflict, both the British and the Americans could exploit a common language and culture alongside divided allegiances in the shadow intelligence war that accompanied open hostilities. The shared kinship and history in the colonies made it difficult and divisive to identify enemy spies in the ranks. For example, Samuel Purviance Jr. denounced as a spy Thomas Webb, a former officer in the British Army during the Seven Years' War who had returned to America as a Methodist preacher. Purviance claimed, "The character under which he travels affords him the very best opportunities of making observations."[70] Based on this accusation, Webb was held as a prisoner of war until his wife secured his release in a prisoner exchange approved by George Washington.

To be fair, the revolutionaries faced a real danger from British sympathizers and Loyalists. They were outnumbered by Loyalists in some parts of the colonies; in others, the revolutionaries' hold on towns and cities was precarious. The Continental Army was at a quality and quantity disadvantage against the superior British Army. Loyalist spies threatened to provide critical intelligence to the British that endangered the Continental Army and the cause of independence. In short, the revolutionaries could not afford the subversion and sabotage of Loyalists, so they acted aggressively to identify and punish Loyalists or suspected Loyalists. People on both sides turned against one another, often on the basis of rumor alone.

Because it was easier for agents to pass among adversaries due to common heritage, language, appearance, and culture, aggressive counterintelligence was a priority for each side. In a letter to Josiah Quincy, George Washington confided, "There is one evil I dread, and that is, [British] spies.... I wish a dozen or more of honest, sensible, and diligent men, were employed... to question, cross-question, &c.... I think it a matter of some importance to prevent them from obtaining intelligence of our situation."[71] Washington offered to compensate Quincy for setting up a counterintelligence network. Like other areas of operations, American counterintelligence efforts were disorganized and discretionary. Networks and committees sprang up throughout the colonies without any formal system or authority to coordinate and control them.

For example, in May 1776, New York's legislature appointed a committee to tackle the issue of "intestine enemies."[72] When Washington and the Continental Army were trying to hold New York City in the summer of 1776, Washington wrote to New York's Secret Committee of "the Necessity of falling upon some Measure to remove, from this City and its Environs, Persons of known disaffection and Enmity to the Cause of America."[73] He hoped New York's counterintelligence committee would help rid them of the scourge of British spies. Although the city fell to the British, New York's counterintelligence committee still managed to conduct its counterintelligence campaign around the colony of New York during the war.

In September 1776, the New York Provisional Convention upgraded its informal counterintelligence committee by resolution, formally creating the Committee and First Commission for Detecting and Defeating Conspiracies. The powers granted to the committee were expansive and discretionary, including the mandate "to apprehend, secure or remove such persons whom they shall judge dangerous to the safety of the State . . . and in general to do every act and thing whatsoever which may be necessary to enable them to execute the trust hereby reposed in them."[74] Accordingly, the committee detained, questioned, and adjudicated suspects as counterintelligence threats.[75]

Perhaps the most striking feature of New York's counterintelligence committee was the ideological, almost crusading, conviction that defined its operations. One resolution of the committee stated that "it is the duty of every virtuous citizen when a mortal blow is aimed at the liberties of his country to stand forth in an open & spirited manner & to assist by his example by his council or by his arms in vindicating and defending her cause."[76] American civilians answered the call and became eager abettors in the counterintelligence campaign against Loyalists or suspected Loyalists. The same people who proclaimed their devotion to the rule of law and resentment toward the Crown and Parliament for flouting it resorted to mob rule and accused their fellow citizens of treachery, often without evidence.[77]

New York's counterintelligence committee blurred the lines between domestic intelligence and law enforcement, an enduring problem in the United States. It also combined intelligence and police powers with the roles of judge and jury, affording the accused little in the way of legal due process. John Jay was on this extrajudicial committee long before he became the first Chief Justice of the United States Supreme Court. As a further irony, leading

American figures, like Jay, who fought for independence from what they viewed as a tyrannical British government, embraced counterintelligence, which is one of the most invasive ways a government can target its own citizens. Worst of all, the American people showed their tolerance and support for extreme intelligence practices when they felt threatened. Out of a volatile combination of patriotism, fear, and sometimes even individual greed, ordinary Americans proved far too willing to spy on and report their fellow Americans.

The United States would continue to face the challenge of balancing counterintelligence and domestic surveillance with American ideological values and civil liberties. The result has always been the same: tremendous vacillations between the poles of liberty and security in civil-intelligence relations. Trust is perhaps the most important element in the relationship between the spy and the state because it takes a great deal of trust to tolerate secret intelligence organizations and activities in a constitutional state and open society. All too often during the Revolutionary War, trust broke down amid personal, political, and public conflicts precipitated by intelligence.

The Revolution Sub Rosa in Retrospect

The Revolutionary War established several patterns and parameters for American intelligence that would shape its structure and evolution in the young United States. Over the course of the war, the Founders made a determined shift away from congressional oversight and control of intelligence to discretionary oversight and control by certain individuals charged with diplomatic, military, and law enforcement functions. These figures later drew upon their experiences to create precedents that proved to be a durable, if deleterious, foundation for American intelligence. George Washington, the Commander in Chief and spymaster in chief of the Continental Army, blurred intelligence with the military. In the American delegation in Paris, Benjamin Franklin blurred intelligence with diplomacy. As a member of the Committee and First Commission for Detecting and Defeating Conspiracies, John Jay blurred intelligence with law enforcement. Furthermore, the improvised and discretionary nature of intelligence during the war characterized American intelligence well into the twentieth century. The Revolutionary War therefore set American intelligence off on a perilous course insofar as it impeded the development of intelligence as a recognized, independent profession or organized, coordinated institution.

The most damaging legacy of the American Revolution lay in the interaction between intelligence and the American people. Intelligence was everywhere during the war. However, the American people either did not recognize it or disregarded it due to the secrecy surrounding it and their unfamiliarity with its missions or their outright bias against espionage. The Founders, widely respected at the time, never familiarized the American people with intelligence. To an extent, they could not. They hid their activities from others "not only so as to protect the cover of the agents concerned," a commendable sign of their awareness of the need to protect sources and methods, "but also to avoid tarnishing the public image of their cause."[78] And so, America's Founders allowed the public to continue to harbor ideological animosities against espionage and intelligence while they secretly conducted those very same operations due to the harsh demands of war. All this secrecy impeded understanding and became a basis for more controversies.

Discreetly reflecting on the role of intelligence during the Revolutionary War, George Washington wrote Noah Webster, "The knowledge of innumerable things, of a more delicate and secret nature, is confined to the perishable remembrance of some few of the present generation."[79] How much of the record is lost with that hallowed generation, the American people may never fully know. But they can be sure that even if intelligence was not always readily apparent, it was unquestionably pervasive in their war for independence.

2

The Founders, the First Citizen, and the First American Intelligence System

IN 1976, AMID the bicentennial of the Declaration of Independence and at the height of congressional scrutiny into a deluge of American intelligence scandals, Senator Charles Mathias lamented that "the intelligence operations of the Government have been the exclusive prerogative of the executive branch." He declared, "For nearly 40 years, Congress has abdicated its constitutional responsibilities to oversee and check the conduct of intelligence operations by the executive."[1] Not only was there a much longer history behind this problem, but the Constitution also does not explicitly mention intelligence, let alone spell out a role for Congress in it. This omission is all the more noteworthy considering several of its drafters were deeply involved in intelligence operations in the Revolutionary War. Still, intelligence was nowhere to be found in the laws and political system of the United States at its creation. But the country quickly redressed this omission.

At the instigation of Washington, the First US Congress enacted the first piece of American intelligence legislation, authorizing the Contingent Fund for Foreign Intercourse, which allowed him to pay for espionage and intelligence activities without interference from Congress. Congress quickly came to regret its decision to give the President such broad powers without any oversight. In addition, the Contingent Fund impeded the professionalization of American intelligence because the President relied on amateur spies who would conduct intelligence operations before returning to their normal occupations. While other national security professions developed during the nineteenth century, a distinct intelligence profession never emerged.

Intelligence controversies likewise accompanied the birth of the United States. The country soon descended into bitter partisan strife with the rise of the two-party system. The warring sides realized that intelligence could serve partisan political purposes, creating a precedent for mixing intelligence and politics.

A Constitutional Crisis in the Making

The architects of the Constitution faced a monumental challenge. They set out to create a stable government that would serve the principles for which they had fought. They were greatly concerned with the relationship between the citizen and the state, and especially the fragile balance between liberty and security. The Founders knew there could be no liberty without security. Creating a central government that could protect national security loomed large in the minds of the delegates to the Constitutional Convention. At the same time, they worried about the threat that a strong central government and national security institutions posed to American principles, including liberty, popular sovereignty, and civic participation in government.

The young United States faced not only the reality of its military weakness vis-à-vis the established powers of Europe but also the threat of subversion through their intelligence activities. Britain, Spain, and France all conducted intelligence operations in North America in the years after the Revolutionary War.[2] The Framers were aware that the new American government was the target of foreign intelligence. In his record of the Constitutional Convention, James Madison worried, "The Ministers of foreign powers would have and make use of, the opportunity to mix their intrigues & influence with the Election... it will be an object of great moment with the great rival powers of Europe... to have at the head of our Government a man attached to their respective politics & interests."[3]

Given their previous concerns about conspiracy and secrecy in the British government, it is ironic that many of the same individuals conducted the meetings and proceedings of the Constitutional Convention in secret. On May 29, 1787, the day that Edmund Randolph opened the debate, the Convention established rules to guide its proceedings. Among them was one specifying "that nothing spoken in the House be printed, or otherwise published or communicated without leave."[4] If transparency is one of the principles of American constitutionalism, secrecy helped create that very system of government.

What emerged from the secret proceedings of the Convention was the Constitution, which contained clauses dealing with national security. Most of these provisions in the Constitution concern the military, while others discuss matters such as domestic order, treason, and foreign policy. There is no plan or design for an American intelligence system or organization. To be fair, the Framers had their share of conflicts over the prospect of a professional military without raising the trickier issue of spying.[5]

In the absence of any explicit discussion of intelligence, the only option is to read it into the Constitution. Historians, legal scholars, and national security professionals often do so by borrowing from the Commander in Chief Clause in Article II, Section 2 of the Constitution.[6] Already the commander in chief of the armed forces under the Constitution, the President is likewise the spymaster in chief of the intelligence community. Meanwhile, the President's constitutional control over intelligence activities occupies a gray area between the President's authorities with respect to war powers and foreign affairs.[7] Nevertheless, only by analogizing intelligence to other areas of the Constitution can people interpret the intelligence authorities of the President and the US government.

The issue then becomes one of determining the boundaries between Congress and the President in overseeing and controlling intelligence—the problem Senator Mathias highlighted in 1976. The separation of powers was a major area of debate during the creation and ratification of the Constitution. The *Federalist Papers* and ratification debates in state legislatures therefore are essential sources to examine the Framers' intent with respect to intelligence.

The term "intelligence" appears in a few places in the *Federalist Papers*. During this period, intelligence generally meant new information: Newspapers and periodicals were sources of intelligence, just as they provide open-source intelligence (OSINT) today. The Founders preferred other terms, like "secret service," to describe espionage and clandestine activities.

However, in Federalist 64, John Jay, former counterintelligence official and member of the Committee of Secret Correspondence during the American Revolution, used "intelligence" in a modern-day sense. Jay took the position that Congress should defer to presidential control and secrecy in intelligence matters:

> It seldom happens in the negotiation of treaties, of whatever nature, but that perfect SECRECY and immediate DESPATCH are sometimes requisite. These are cases where the most useful intelligence may be obtained, if the persons possessing it can be relieved from apprehensions of discovery. Those apprehensions will operate on those persons whether they are actuated by mercenary or friendly motives; and there doubtless are many of both descriptions, who would rely on the secrecy of the President, but who would not confide in that of the Senate, and still less in that of a large popular Assembly. The convention have done well, therefore, in so disposing of the power of making treaties, that although the President must, in forming them, act by the advice and

> consent of the Senate, yet he will be able to manage the business of intelligence in such a manner as prudence may suggest.[8]

Jay defended the President's prerogative to recruit and employ spies. His argument perhaps reflected his wartime experience. Having witnessed the fallout of Paine's leak and the factionalism of Congress that undermined secrecy and diplomacy, Jay believed that a single, capable individual could manage secret intelligence operations better than a committee of Congress. In these passages, Jay stressed that the President must guard intelligence sources and methods even if it meant keeping secrets from Congress and the American people. Finally, he understood that there was a difference between overt diplomacy and covert intelligence in achieving foreign policy goals.

Alexander Hamilton indirectly made the case for presidential control over intelligence in Federalist 70. Like Jay, he believed that a single president could protect secrecy better than a large legislative body: "Decision, activity, secrecy, and despatch will generally characterize the proceedings of one man in much more eminent degree than the proceedings of any greater number; and in proportion as the number increased, these qualities will be diminished."[9] In Federalist 75, he insisted that "accurate and comprehensive knowledge of foreign politics; a steady and systematic adherence to the same views; a nice and uniform sensibility to national character; decision, secrecy, and despatch, are incompatible with the genius of a body so variable and so numerous" as Congress.[10] Jay and Hamilton therefore recognized that the needs of intelligence were best suited to the executive office of the President.[11]

The Statement and Account Clause in Article I, Section 9 was another place where intelligence implicitly made its way into the Constitution.[12] At issue for the Founders in the language of the clause itself was the problem of government secrecy. George Mason originally recommended that public expenditures be "annually published," but James Madison proposed an alternative (ultimately adopted) that they only need be published "from time to time."[13] These two delegates took their disagreement back to their home state of Virginia for the ratification debate. There Madison had to defend his position against the firebrand patriot Patrick Henry.

Henry dissected the proposed Constitution with rhetoric grounded in American principles. Denouncing a standing army and Congress's "unlimited and unbounded power of taxation," while professing that "the first thing I have at heart is American liberty," he turned his attention to the Statement and Account Clause and its provision of "from time to time."[14] Henry argued that the wording "from time to time" was "very indefinite and indeterminate: it may extend to a century."[15] He warned that politicians "may carry on the most wicked and pernicious schemes under the dark veil of secrecy. The liberties of a people were nor ever will be secure, when the transactions of their rulers may be concealed from them." However, Henry confessed, "I am not an advocate for divulging indiscriminately all the operations of government. . . . Such transactions as relate to military operations, or affairs of great consequence, the immediate promulgation of which might defeat the interests of the community, I would not wish to be published, till the end which required their secrecy should have been effected."[16]

George Mason, who wanted annual reporting requirements, adopted the same view as Henry during this debate, submitting to the logic that "in matters relative to military operations, and foreign negotiations, secrecy was necessary sometimes."[17] But the Statement and Account Clause still bothered Henry, who brooded, "By that paper the national wealth is to be disposed of under the veil of secrecy: For the publication from time to time will amount to nothing; and they may cancel what they may think requires secrecy."[18]

The Founders' acknowledgment that some functions of government, like military operations, diplomatic affairs, and presumably intelligence, may be kept secret gave the President a pathway to keep secrets from Congress. In turn, Congress and the US government kept secrets from the American people. In terms of intelligence and the Framers' intent, the Constitution supported presidential control, narrowly, and government secrecy, more broadly.

Despite his own arguments in favor of presidential secrecy in the *Federalist Papers*, Hamilton identified the larger problem facing the Founders as they created the constitutional system. In Federalist 8, he observed,

> Safety from external danger is the most powerful director of national conduct. Even the ardent love of liberty will, after a time, give way to its dictates. The violent destruction of life and property incident to war, the continual effort and alarm attendant on a state of continual danger, will compel nations the most attached to liberty to resort for repose and security to institutions which have a tendency to destroy their civil and political rights. To be more safe, they at length become willing to run the risk of being less free.[19]

Blurring the Bill of Rights

It is not the Constitution proper but the amendments known as the Bill of Rights that place restraints on intelligence. Like the Constitution, none of the amendments explicitly cover intelligence; however, their provisions contain pieces that would seemingly restrict certain functions of intelligence. For example, the First Amendment imposes limits on government censorship of the press or surveillance of dissident groups. The Fourth Amendment offers some protection to the American people from intrusive government intelligence activities like wiretapping or other forms of surveillance. Additionally, US citizens have challenged some of the federal government's intelligence policies on Fifth Amendment due process grounds.[20] However, like the Constitution, these provisions are open to interpretation and therefore generate potential conflicts between the US government and intelligence establishment, on one side, and the American people, on the other.

When in peril, the United States tends to use intelligence in ways that curtail liberty and circumvent the Constitution and Bill of Rights based on arguments appealing to national security. By not writing intelligence clearly and unambiguously into the Constitution or the Bill of Rights, the Framers—either intentionally or unintentionally—gave the government the opportunity to sidestep the protections offered by those documents. When the executive or legislative branch exceeds its authorities, it is left to the judicial branch, as the ultimate arbiter of the Constitution, to set the boundaries between the liberty of the citizen and the power of the government. The same logic that claims the Constitution gives the President and Congress powers over intelligence also ensures that the judiciary has a role to play, though it has generally deferred to the President and broad executive powers in times of war.

The American constitutional and intelligence systems create additional gray areas for intelligence. The Bill of Rights purportedly restricts both domestic intelligence and law enforcement activities that violate its provisions. But the surveillance capabilities and methods available to intelligence, the secrecy with which intelligence operations are conducted, and the ways in which intelligence can evade judicial oversight all result in unique challenges to American civil liberties protected by the Constitution. Instead of clarifying this constitutional problem, the United States has compounded it by mixing domestic intelligence and law enforcement in terms of professions, powers, and legal authorities.

The lack of any explicit provisions covering intelligence in the Constitution meant that the United States would have to rely on trial and error in designing laws to guide American intelligence. The Founders apparently trusted the President to exercise considerable discretion and control over intelligence activities with limited interference or oversight by the other branches of government. Perhaps they did so out of their collective intuition that George Washington would be the first President.

America's First "Black Budget"

It was ultimately the actions—not just the words—of the first crop of elected officials that created and cemented the first American intelligence system. They developed the ideas, laws, and precedents that would shape American intelligence, including the critical issue of funding it. The Constitution gave Congress a measure of oversight—and therefore control—over presidential activities through the power of the purse. Even if the Founders intended to grant the President broad powers to control intelligence and keep it secret, Congress could still try to make the President account for how those funds were spent. The question was whether Congress would give itself a role in intelligence oversight.

The first and most important piece of intelligence-related legislation to be passed by Congress authorized the Contingent Fund for Foreign Intercourse, known later as the Secret Service Fund. The idea was not originally American. The British had a "secret service fund" under the Secretary of State for Foreign Affairs, and in 1782, Parliament passed an act regulating secret service funding. The United States soon followed suit.[21]

As President, Washington knew he had to compete with the European powers still intent on undermining the young American republic. Just as he looked to intelligence when he found himself at a disadvantage as a general in the Revolutionary War, Washington would again need intelligence as President. However, it was clear from the Constitution and the small American military establishment that there would be no formal, powerful American intelligence establishment, so it was left to the new President to outline what form it would take.

On January 8, 1790, in his First Annual Message to Congress, which became the State of the Union Address, Washington declared,

> The interests of the United States require, that our intercourse with other nations should be facilitated by such provisions as will enable me to fulfill my duty in that respect, in the manner, which circumstances may render most conducive to the public good: And to this end, that the compensations to be made to the persons, who may be employed, should, according to the nature of their appointments, be defined by law; and a competent fund designated for defraying the expenses incident to the conduct of our foreign affairs.[22]

Although Washington did not directly address intelligence, his speech set in motion what became the basis for the President's personal intelligence system.

Rather than immediately granting Washington's request for a special fund for foreign affairs, Congress debated giving the President discretionary control over public money. One possible use of the money emerged during this debate. Representative Thomas Scott declared, "I know occasions, at times when the Legislature is not sitting, will present themselves, when money for secret services may be required; yet, in these cases, proof must be made of the expenses before they will be allowed in account, and any which are conceived to be improper will be rejected."[23] Importantly, Scott's speech acknowledged that the American government would employ "secret services" as an instrument of statecraft and implied that Congress should exercise oversight of these activities through its power of appropriation.

However, Congress eventually deferred to presidential discretion. In July 1790, it approved an act granting the President a fund of $40,000 "for the support of such persons as he shall commission to serve the United States in foreign parts, and for the expense incident to the business in which they may be employed," adding that "the President shall account specifically for all such expenditures of the said money as in his judgment may be made public, and also for the amount of such expenditures as he may think it advisable not to specify."[24] Congress included a sunset clause of two years, which meant it intended for the fund to be a temporary allocation.

Washington immediately drew from the Contingent Fund to support the activities of two agents. First, there was Gouverneur Morris on his mission to Britain to collect intelligence on the Crown for Washington. Morris's mission began before the creation of the Contingent Fund, so Washington was already determined to use informal agents to obtain intelligence even before Congress implicitly sanctioned the practice.[25] Furthermore, the payments to Morris did not arrive until after congressional approval of the Contingent Fund and came via the fund itself, so Washington's use of the fund demonstrated that he understood it was for intelligence activities. Second, there was David Humphreys, whose prior experience included being an aide de camp to Washington and intelligence agent with Franklin in Paris. His instructions included an order to "avoid... all suspicion of being on public business."[26] Humphreys's mission also began about a month after Congress allocated the Contingent Fund—additional evidence that Washington had conceived of a role for intelligence agents in American statecraft and that the Contingent Fund would be used to pay them.[27]

The Second United States Congress reallocated the Contingent Fund in 1792 and 1793. The 1793 act provided that any certificates for expenditures "shall be deemed a sufficient voucher for the sum or sums therein expressed to have been expended," even if they did not specify how the money was used.[28] In other words, the new act reestablished the principle that the President could conceal the individuals and operations supported by the Contingent Fund.

The Contingent Fund became a yearly allocation that the President could use as he saw fit. As he had done during the Revolutionary War, Washington personally directed intelligence operations on behalf of the United States. By its own doing, Congress surrendered any serious intelligence oversight function it could have reserved for itself through its appropriations authority. One reason Congress perhaps acquiesced to Washington's singular control of intelligence was his ability to overcome political divisions, though by the time he left office, he faced bitter recriminations from partisan corners.

A Farewell and a Warning

In the first two presidential elections, Washington ran essentially unopposed, suggesting what a unifying figure he was. However, the polarizing effects of the emerging two-party system were already apparent in his first term. By the second term, Washington's political adversaries and their allies in the press attacked the great statesman himself. The *Aurora General Advertiser*, founded by Benjamin Franklin's grandson Benjamin Franklin Bache, smeared Washington. An author going by the name "Calm Observer" accused Washington of overdrawing his presidential salary and compared him with Julius Caesar and Oliver Cromwell.[29] Thomas Paine also published a scathing pamphlet in the *Aurora* condemning Washington as "treacherous in private friendship . . . and a hypocrite in public life."[30]

Much of the rancor in domestic politics was the product of US foreign policy. While the recently independent Americans were building their new state, Europe was in the throes of the French Revolution. Although the French had aided the Americans in their hour of need, Washington declared US neutrality during the French Revolution and subsequent French Revolutionary Wars. The Washington administration then sought to avoid conflict with Britain and establish favorable trade terms, resulting in the Jay Treaty. The treaty reinforced the emerging American political system by further dividing the two existing political parties. The Federalists, led by Alexander Hamilton, supported friendly relations with Britain, while the Democratic-Republicans, led by Thomas Jefferson and James Madison, were passionately pro-France. The Jay Treaty cemented the partisan divide.

James Monroe, a Democratic-Republican whom Washington appointed Minister to France in 1794, was a political casualty of the schism. The Jay

Treaty doomed Monroe's efforts to manage Franco-American relations. Washington recalled Monroe in 1796. Following his return, Monroe exchanged increasingly heated correspondence with Secretary of State Timothy Pickering. In one letter, Monroe charged Pickering with "opening a door in [his] office for the reception of *spies* and *informers*, to whose communications ... implicit faith is given, although their names, their characters, and even the purport of their denunciations be withheld." Appealing to American attitudes toward the Old World and its history of political surveillance, Monroe declared, "This practice is of great antiquity, and is now in use in the despotic Governments of Europe, but I hoped never to see it transplanted to this side of the Atlantic, especially in the degree to which you extend it."[31]

In all these events, Washington, shrewd spymaster and equally perceptive politician that he was, foresaw a problem that would perpetually plague American politics. In his Farewell Address, he warned the American people of the "dangers of [political] parties" and the "baneful effect of the spirit of party generally." Washington also alerted the country to the "mischief of foreign intrigue," signaling that foreign states would try to subvert the United States by exploiting its political divisions. He therefore famously instructed his fellow Americans to avoid foreign entanglements.[32] Washington perceived that mixing intelligence and politics threatened the unity of the country. But political affairs in Europe were already affecting US domestic politics. No sooner had Washington left office than the country erupted with rancorous partisan accusations and recriminations between the parties. Intelligence would feature prominently in the political turmoil.

3

Bitter Bedfellows

IDEOLOGY, INTELLIGENCE, AND OPPOSITION POLITICS

IT WAS ONLY natural that Americans would be hostile to intelligence because the federal government could use it to threaten liberty, the foundational principle that set the course for American independence and a new system of government. But decisions about everything from the economy to national security generated political divisions in the young United States. The emerging political parties dragged intelligence into their partisan struggle by accusing each other of intelligence-related conspiracies in an effort to turn the American people against their rivals.

British intelligence historian Christopher Andrew observed, "Ever since John Winthrop set out to build a 'city on a hill' in Puritan Massachusetts, Americans had believed that their country was guided by uniquely high ethical principles. They regarded peacetime espionage, if they thought of it at all, as a corrupt outgrowth of Old World diplomacy, alien to the open and upright American way."[1] Imagine the shock that many Americans must have felt when they discovered that their revered Founders had been engaged in the sordid business of intelligence and espionage during the Revolutionary War.

The Fall of the Federalists

In 1796, John Gardner, who went by the pen name Aurelius, revealed in the pro-Federalist *Columbian Centinel*, "There is in this country a nefarious conspiracy, not only against the distinguished characters at the head of the federal government, but against the constitution itself. How far it has been instigated by the secret service money of any of the powers at war, is not for me to say.... Foreign influence is an excellent assistant to *ambition*."[2] Sensational stories of secret plots and conspiracies soon saturated the press as a diplomatic scandal involving France fed fears of foreign intrigue and fanned the flames of partisan strife.

John Adams, a Federalist, defeated Thomas Jefferson, a Democratic-Republican, to become the second President of the United States. The new Adams administration sent a delegation to France consisting of Charles Cotesworth Pinckney, John Marshall, and Elbridge Gerry in 1797 to avoid a war between the erstwhile allies. The French conducted their diplomacy informally through intermediaries, who sought bribes in return for negotiating with the Americans. The American delegation realized the talks were going nowhere and returned home.

Meanwhile, the divisions between the Federalists and the Democratic-Republicans widened as the Federalists sought appropriations in Congress for war with France. The pro-French Democratic-Republicans opposed war, and instead sought the disclosure of the diplomatic dispatches between the Adams administration and the American delegation to Paris. When Adams released the papers to Congress, he redacted the names of the French pseudo-diplomats to the initials X (Baron Jean-Conrad Hottinguer), Y (Pierre Bellamy), and Z (Lucien Hauteval), giving the scandal its name, the XYZ Affair.[3] The papers proved that the French did not conduct negotiations in good faith, providing fodder for the Federalists. However, rather than seek a declaration of war from Congress, Adams resisted his own party. Instead, the United States and France engaged in the Quasi-War at sea featuring a nascent US Navy.

The worst consequences of the XYZ Affair and Quasi-War in the United States were a product of internal events rather than external threats. A pervasive fear of spies and foreign intrigue helped the Federalists rush the Alien and Sedition Acts through Congress in June and July 1798. The Alien Acts granted broad powers to the President to designate foreign-born individuals residing in the United States as national security threats and have them deported.[4] The legislation prompted vigorous debates in Congress concerning the President's power over domestic intelligence and the problem of giving him the authority to label individuals as spies or subversives.

Supporting the act, Representative Harrison Gray Otis argued that "it would not be proper to wait until predatory incursions were made—until the enemy was landed in [the] country...before any steps were taken," and expressed his "opinion that when an enemy authorized hostilities, that was the time to take up that crowd of spies and inflammatory agents which overspread the country like the locusts of Egypt, and who were continually attacking [American] liberties."[5] Representative Joseph McDowell retorted that "it was said the country swarmed with spies and seditious persons. If this was the case, he should be glad if gentlemen would point them out." Otherwise, he opposed the measures as "too large a power" to grant the President.[6]

Representative Edward Livingston fiercely opposed the Alien Acts as not only unconstitutional but also "a direct violation of its fundamental principles." He believed the acts gave the President far too much power to wield against "the guilty or innocent victim, whom his own suspicions, or the secret whisper of a spy, have designated" as an enemy. Rather than such legislation being a measure for eliminating spies, Livingston argued, "spies, informers, and all that infamous herd ... fatten under laws like this." He insisted, "The system of *espionage* being thus established, the country will swarm with informers, spies, delators, and all that odious reptile tribe that breed in the sunshine of despotic power." He also warned that "the people of America ... watchful against foreign aggression, are not careless of domestic encroachment; they are as jealous ... of their liberties at home as of the power and prosperity of their country abroad."[7]

Livingston's speech raises three challenges to American civil-intelligence relations. First, he highlighted the danger of executive overreach in terms of leveraging intelligence to designate, surveil, detain, and even deport people as spies and subversives. Second, he captured the ideological tension between American principles and intelligence, including the bias Americans held against espionage. Finally, he identified a crucial difference between what Americans would support being done in their defense overseas and what they would tolerate at home. Despite the protests of Livingston and others, the laws passed.

The following year, Livingston presented a petition from "alien" residents who had emigrated from Ireland, requesting the repeal of the Alien Acts. Representative James Bayard objected to Livingston's petition. Claiming that "he had reason to believe there were many intriguers among us, employed not only to debauch the minds of the people, but acting as spies upon the country," he exploited both spy fever and party politics to defend the acts.[8] Representative Albert Gallatin stridently condemned the acts, warning that "when the present fervor is past ... all those measures which are calculated to eradicate from our minds the principles of our Revolution, and to concentrate power in the Executive, will prove obnoxious to the people of America."[9] He argued that the acts' defenders relied "on the same ground which is to be a pretence and a justification for every act of domestic oppression." He scoffed at their fearmongering, remarking that they "cannot be serious when they tell us of the employment of the active talents of a numerous body of French citizens here as emissaries and spies" quite simply because "notwithstanding all the clamor of last Summer, and notwithstanding the two laws passed on that subject, not a single French citizen has been removed."[10] Majoritarianism narrowly carried the day for the Federalists, and the Alien Acts remained in force.

The Sedition Act restricted the ability of American citizens to speak out against the US government. The act criminalized a broad set of activities customary in a representative government and protected under the Bill of Rights, such as newspaper editorials that ridiculed the US government or President.[11] The Federalists used the Sedition Act to prosecute Democratic-Republican journalists, writers, and even a congressman.

As part of the propaganda war that accompanied the Quasi-War, the Federalists claimed to have discovered a series of alleged plots against the United States.[12] For example, the Taylor Plot was a contrived story that the discovery of French military clothing in Philadelphia was evidence of an impending French invasion. The Ocean Plot was a rumor that French privateers attacked an American merchant vessel called the *Ocean* and killed everyone onboard. The Tub Plot was the most sensational of the alleged conspiracies.[13] The Federalists "discovered" a plot by the French government to incite a slave revolt in the United States following an intelligence tip by the US consul to Hamburg regarding the passage of a French agent to Charleston. The agent allegedly hid his instructions in a shipping tub. It is unclear if the original tip by the consul in Hamburg was genuine or part of the larger Federalist propaganda campaign. Regardless, the Federalists used intelligence to appeal to the public's deeply rooted fears of foreign intrigue to justify expanding the government's powers at the expense of American principles like freedom of the press.

The Democratic-Republican press dismissed every alleged plot as a Federalist invention—"fake news" in today's parlance. Yet, they also engaged in propaganda and tapped into civil society's fear of foreign intrigue. William Duane, editor of the *Aurora*, claimed in a July 1799 article that the British secret service had spent $800,000 in the United States to influence American policy.[14] This article became the subject of an urgent letter from Secretary of State Timothy Pickering to Adams.[15] One solution was to prosecute Duane, like his predecessor Benjamin Franklin Bache, under the Sedition Act.

Amid the political intrigue and partisan strife, Vice President Thomas Jefferson even claimed he was under surveillance. He once arrived late to tea with Mrs. Deborah Logan, wife of the prominent Pennsylvania Democratic-Republican Dr. George Logan, claiming "he was himself dogged and watched in the most extraordinary manner," and "that in order to elude the curiosity of his spies he had not taken the direct road."[16] Perhaps one of the worst abuses of intelligence in a representative government is using it to spy on political rivals, and the United States was already experimenting with political surveillance this early in its existence.

If their intent was to use intelligence to remain in political control, the Federalists' plan failed. The Alien and Sedition Acts became central campaign issues in the election of 1800, which saw the Federalists lose the presidency to the Democratic-Republicans and Thomas Jefferson. After his election, Jefferson pardoned those imprisoned under the acts, and Congress reimbursed those who were fined.

The Federalist party suffered blowback beyond the ballot box. It declined as a political party, eventually collapsing and dissolving two decades later. What did not wane were the precedents set during this formative period. The legislative acts and executive actions of the US government during the Quasi-War foreshadowed two trends during future wars and periods of emergency. First, the Alien and Sedition Acts played upon public suspicions of foreign intrigue and domestic subversion to justify granting the executive branch broad powers to target a vulnerable class of people, not just foreign-born residents and American citizens but any minority group suspected of harboring grievances against the country or of being especially susceptible to foreign influence. Second, accusations of disloyalty or collusion provided a basis for using intelligence to target political opposition. In fact, just as the Federalists used intelligence to target the Democratic-Republicans during the Quasi-War, the Democratic-Republicans would do the same against the Federalists ahead of the War of 1812.

Political Intelligence or Opposition Research?

Like his Federalist predecessors, Jefferson availed himself of intelligence as President. An April 1802 article in the *Columbian Centinel*, titled "Secret Service Money," highlighted the political hypocrisy. The author claimed that during the Washington and Adams administrations, the Democratic-Republicans "raised the most furious yelping whenever occasions, few and special as they were, occurred of such a nature as to require a momentary privacy" and insisted that "a government of a free country should not keep any secret . . . from the view of the people."[17] Jefferson secretly requested funding from Congress for the Lewis and Clark expedition, innocently publicized at the time as an exploratory mission but, by design, a strategic reconnaissance of North America to secure the United States from Spain, France, and Britain. He also sent secret agents both near and far—from the Native American territories to the Barbary Coast—to advance American interests.[18]

Jefferson's successor, James Madison, continued the same policy and relied on intelligence to expand America's territory and reduce Europe's footprint and influence in the New World.[19] These twin policy goals conflicted with European, and particularly British, interests. Madison therefore faced the problem of growing hostilities with Britain.

In a political reversal of the Quasi-War, the Democratic-Republicans supported a war against Britain, while the Federalists opposed one. The New England states became the hotbed of Federalist discontent. The United States once again faced the prospect of foreign interstate war and domestic political conflict. Seeking ways to discredit the Federalists, the Madison administration took advantage of intelligence provided by a disgruntled, opportunistic spy for the British.

The story began during Jefferson's presidency, when tensions with the British were mounting. The Governor-General of Canada, Sir James Craig, wanted to gauge American public opinion about a potential war with Britain and determine whether the Federalist-leaning New England states might support the British or perhaps even rejoin the Crown as colonies.[20] He needed a spy and eventually found one in John Henry.

Henry had served as an officer in the US Army during and after the Quasi-War. Following his service, Henry studied law in Vermont, managed a farm, and authored pro-Federalist pieces in local newspapers. He then moved to Montreal with the intention of practicing law. Henry professed his support for the British government. When Britain and the United States nearly went to war in July 1807, he offered his services to the Canadian militia. In short, he was an ideal recruit for British intelligence.

But Henry had other ideas. He had hoped to become a judge, but his appointment was blocked by the Lieutenant-Governor of Canada, Francis Gore. Disappointed, Henry found himself in Boston on business, where he wrote letters on the state of American politics and public opinion to Herman Witsius Ryland, personal secretary to Governor-General James Craig. Ryland passed these letters off to Craig, who forwarded them to London. In one missive, Henry alleged that he attended a meeting in Boston in which prominent individuals expressed "a firm determination . . . that they will not co-operate in a war against England," adding that "I can with confidence infer that in case of a war, the States on our borders may be detached from the Union."[21] Continued communication between Henry and Ryland encouraged Henry to seek some sort of employment from Craig.

When Madison became President in 1809, Craig took his quest for information a step further. In January 1809, he instructed Ryland to formally solicit Henry's help.[22] Ryland informed Henry of Craig's "idea of employing you on a secret & confidential Mission to Boston," during which Henry would carry a cipher that Craig would supply.[23] Another letter provided Henry with "careful instructions, marked 'most secret and confidential'" that directed him to gather intelligence on "the state of public opinion," "the probability of war," and "the comparative strength of the two great parties into which the country is divided and the views and designs of that which may ultimately prevail."[24]

Henry took to his intelligence work as both a collector and an analyst. His letters suggested the treasonous intentions of the Federalist party. One written from Vermont in February 1809 claimed that "the federal party declares, that in the event of a war, the state of Vermont will treat seriously for itself with Great Britain... without any regard to the policy of the general government."[25] A month later, Henry reported that the state of Massachusetts had similar intentions.[26] Yet another letter offered Henry's analysis of Madison as President.[27]

In May 1809, Henry received instructions from Ryland to return to Montreal. At first, he only requested compensation for his expenses to the extent that they exceeded his personal resources.[28] However, given his earlier professional aspirations, he likely expected some sort of political appointment in return for his services. Henry hoped to become the sheriff of Montreal, but he did not obtain the position.[29] So he wrote to Lord Liverpool, the Colonial Secretary, to request an appointment as Judge Advocate General of Lower Canada or as a consul in the United States. He followed up to say that he never received compensation for his intelligence services to the Crown, save traveling expenses.[30] The British government apparently never sufficiently compensated Henry for his intelligence work, embittering him.

Trouble began while Henry was traveling from England to Boston in the late fall of 1811 and along the way met a Frenchman who introduced himself as Count Édouard de Crillon. The two shared confidences, and Crillon evidently won Henry's trust. Henry confided his disappointment in how he was treated in return for his important services to the British; he even carried the papers that recorded his intelligence dealings, which he probably showed to Crillon.[31] Either Henry or Crillon or both agreed that the documents were valuable and that the US government would probably pay a high price for them. Once in Boston, Henry met with Elbridge Gerry, the Democratic-Republican governor of Massachusetts, who wrote Henry a letter of introduction to President Madison.[32] Crillon also wrote a letter to the French Minister to the United States explaining that "he had the good fortune to form an acquaintance with a person employed by the English government in a secret mission to New England."[33]

Eventually, both Henry and Crillon found themselves in Washington, peddling the intelligence they had in Henry's papers. In a meeting with

Secretary of State James Monroe, Henry offered to sell his documents to the US government for £25,000.[34] Monroe and Madison countered that they had a maximum budget of $50,000. Henry turned down the offer, but Crillon intervened with a solution.

Henry and Crillon struck a deal. Henry understandably wanted to retire someplace out of the reach of the British government, and Crillon could provide the title to his family's estate on the border of France and Spain. He would hand over the deed to Henry in return for a portion of the $50,000 payment by the US government. The combination of the $50,000 (minus Crillon's share) and the estate satisfied Henry.[35] The parties reached an agreement, and the Madison administration gained documents of potentially enormous intelligence value.

Madison and Monroe must have believed that the information was worth the price. On March 9, 1812, Madison sent the papers to Congress, along with a cover letter explaining that they contained the workings of a "secret agent" of Britain engaged in "intrigues" for the purpose of "destroying the Union."[36] The next day, a letter from Representative Ebenezer Seaver claimed that the Committee of Foreign Relations had examined the papers and confirmed their authenticity.[37] The Madison administration and Democratic-Republicans probably thought they were on the verge of achieving a major political victory.

The papers immediately ignited a partisan debate in Congress. Representatives Timothy Pitkin and Josiah Quincy contended that the papers did not name any Federalist conspirators or provide any evidence of Federalist collusion with Britain.[38] In a reversal of the plots alleged by the Federalists during the XYZ Affair, the Democratic-Republicans found themselves losing the propaganda battle.

The Democratic-Republicans sputtered a number of excuses. Representatives John Rhea and George Troup argued that the papers were evidence of British intrigue in the United States. Robert Wright blamed Henry and announced that he would not, "without inquiry, take the words of a spy, traitor, and villain as truth." James Fisk tried to capitalize on perceptions of Old World unscrupulousness by suggesting that, while the British government had no problem engaging in the sneaky business of espionage, it was beneath the US government to do the same.[39]

Congress opened an investigation into the Henry Affair and deposed Crillon. Crillon related the sequence of events, how he had come to know Henry, and what Henry told him, but conveniently left out the details of the deal Henry and he had made with the Madison administration. Crillon also claimed that he had received "threatening letters, and was advised by his friends that he was surrounded by spies." While he protected the Madison administration from involvement in Henry's dishonorable double-dealing, he provided no actual evidence of Federalist collusion with the British.[40]

Similarly, Henry's letters did not name any names or offer any concrete evidence of Federalist collusion with the British. Instead, they contained a combination of information Henry read in Federalist newspapers and plots that Henry claimed he had heard as he snooped around New England—what intelligence officers jokingly refer to as RUMINT, rumor intelligence. Worse still, the letters were not even originals, but were copies that Henry had rewritten or perhaps concocted.

The Madison administration came under fire when the enterprising Federalist congressman Josiah Quincy traced Treasury warrants and managed to discover just how much money the administration had paid Henry.[41] According to Quincy, Madison and Henry conspired "to conceal the nature of the transaction."[42] To accomplish this, Quincy claimed that Madison "avail[ed] himself of the power entrusted to him as President over the secret service fund" by taking $49,000 from the Contingent Fund for Foreign Intercourse, by then known as the Secret Service Fund, while the remaining $1,000 came from the contingent fund of the Department of State via John Graham, its chief clerk.[43] Quincy further explained that Henry wrote a letter from Philadelphia on February 20, 1812, "ten or twenty days after the terms of purchase had been settled and the money paid," in which he falsely professed to have handed over the documents "voluntarily," that is, for free.[44] A review of the warrants in the Treasury ledger of the United States for the year 1812 shows two payments on February 10, 1812, to John Graham, one for $1,000 and the other for $49,000.[45]

The $50,000 payment constituted the entire sum of the Secret Service Fund for the year 1812 and is roughly equivalent to $1 million today.[46] More importantly, $50,000 was more than the cost of a brig, about equal to that of a sloop-of-war, and a good measure toward the price of a frigate—all ships that the United States desperately needed as war with the British loomed. Now it is clear why Madison and Monroe told Henry they could not afford to pay more than $50,000. The purpose of using the Secret Service Fund in this episode is equally clear: Madison could conceal from Congress that he had spent public money for private political purposes.

The Federalist members of the House of Representatives published an open letter to their constituents exposing the Henry Affair. They declared, "It was cause of regret that a communication should have been purchased by an unprecedented expenditure of secret service money, and used by the Chief

Magistrate to disseminate suspicion and jealousy; and to excite resentment among the citizens, by suggesting imputations against a portion of them, as unmerited by their patriotism, as unwarranted by evidence."[47] The secrecy surrounding the Madison administration's intelligence coup was blown once newspapers published the details of the political and intelligence scandal.[48]

The Madison administration begged Joel Barlow, the American minister in Paris, to find Henry and ask him to specifically name each Federalist he accused of colluding with Britain.[49] At this point, the whole episode unraveled. As it turns out, Crillon was an impostor named Paul Émile Soubiran, who was wanted around Europe for his many grifts.[50] The estate that Crillon had deeded Henry did not exist. When Henry arrived in Paris, he learned about Crillon's fraud. Henry wrote to Barlow and Monroe, requesting money to make up for the imaginary estate.[51] But by this point the considerably embarrassed Madison administration was finished with both Henry and Crillon.

One lesson from the Henry Affair is to beware the wrath of a spy once scorned. While Henry initially performed his services for the British out of a sense of loyalty to the Crown, he also demonstrated his excessive ambition and tendency toward self-aggrandizement. When he decided that he had not been adequately rewarded for his services, he sold his work to the United States. When he lost credibility and favor with the Americans, he returned to work for the British, although in the much-diminished capacity of collecting information about any alleged misconduct by Queen Caroline, whom George IV sought to divorce.[52] Henry therefore exhibited an elastic understanding of the word "allegiance," and he, too, learned a lesson common to many other intelligence turncoats. Ambiguous allegiances and secret missions can undermine their credibility and prospects, as they have already proven themselves to be disloyal.

The fear Henry stirred in a country already so suspicious of espionage and intrigue lingered. A few months after the scandal, the United States and Britain did, in fact, go to war. In January 1813, amid the war, Henry's name resurfaced in Congress, with one representative warning the entire body, "Secret service money—England and France both have the character of knowing how to use it to advantage... they, France and England, are both willing to have such men as Henry amongst us."[53] Allusions to the Henry Affair also reappeared in an editorial in March 1814 in which the author, H. Niles, expressed his hope that "our glorious institutions may prevail and flourish, in defiance of the secret service money of princes, and the intrigues of ambitions."[54] Alarmist in the context of war and never entirely secure in peace, Americans tend to see spies and subterfuge everywhere.

The Founders Unmasked

All this conspiracy and intrigue created the perfect atmosphere for a good spy thriller. Published in 1821, *The Spy: A Tale of the Neutral Ground*, was James Fenimore Cooper's second novel.[55] In addition to catapulting its author to fame, it was arguably the world's first spy novel. But the book was not without controversy in its day. Both *The Spy* and the public's reaction to it reveal valuable information about American attitudes toward intelligence at the time.

In *The Spy*, George Washington employs Harvey Birch, a peddler, to spy on the British in Westchester County, New York, the "neutral ground" between British and American lines in the Revolutionary War where both sides engaged in spy games. As Cooper explains in the book's opening scene, "Great numbers . . . wore masks, which even to this day have not been thrown aside; and many an individual has gone down to the tomb, stigmatized as a foe to the rights of his countrymen, while, in secret, he has been the useful agent of the leaders of the Revolution."[56]

So, too, with Harvey Birch. Locals, unaware of Washington's arrangement, suspect that the shadowy Birch is a British spy, so he is considered a traitor by his own countrymen. Birch keeps his real allegiance and his relationship with Washington secret at the risk of his own life and reputation. Even after the war, when Birch nobly declines a reward for his services and explains that he spied out of a sense of patriotism, Washington instructs him, "You must descend into the grave with the reputation of a foe to your native land."[57]

In *The Spy*, Cooper reminds Americans of their ambiguous relationship with intelligence, also citing the example of Nathan Hale, whose actions and death proved that espionage and honor are not necessarily incompatible.[58] In fact, he revisits the opposing attitudes Americans exhibited toward soldiers and spies. In one scene, when one American claims Birch is "one of the most notorious spies in the enemy's service," another observes, "He may be a spy—he must be one . . . but he has a heart above enmity, and a soul that would honour a soldier."[59] Birch himself comments on how differently spies and soldiers were treated. While spies die "on the gallows of a murderer . . . the man who fights, and kills, and plunders, is honoured; but he who serves his country as a spy, no matter how faithfully, no matter how honestly, lives to be reviled, or dies like the vilest criminal!"[60]

Despite the book's popularity, Cooper received reprimands from those who could never consider espionage a noble trade, even if in the service of American liberty. For example, in an 1823 letter, Maria Edgeworth protested, "No sympathy can be excited with meanness, and there must be a degree of

FIGURE 3.1 George Washington, seated on the left holding a book, and Harvey Birch, standing on the right with cloth over his arms, in a mid-nineteenth-century scene designed by T. H. Matteson and engraved by Charles Burt. Library of Congress.

meanness ever associated with the idea of Spy. Neither poetry nor prose can ever make a spy an heroic [c]haracter. From Dolon in the Iliad to Major Andre, and from Major Andre to this instrument of Washington, it has been found impracticable to raise a spy into a hero."[61] An editorial in the *North American Review* in 1831 remarked, "The character of the Spy is bold and striking... though the voluntary descent to a degrading occupation would hardly seem perfectly consistent with the lofty tone of moral feeling, which disinterested patriotism supposes or inspires."[62] Others equivocated. William Gilmore Simms judged Cooper's "conception of the Spy, as a character... a very noble one. A patriot in the humblest condition of life... enduring the persecutions of friends, the hate of enemies... enduring all in secret, without a murmur,—without a word, when a word might have saved him,—all for his country; and all, under the palsying conviction, not only that his country never could reward him, but that, in all probability, the secret of his patriotism must perish with him, and nothing survive but that obloquy under which he was still content to live and labour." However, Simms believed that Cooper was writing in terms of an ideal, adding "that such a character is not often to be found."[63]

In contrast to the American animus, a French writer who reviewed the book for the Paris *Globe* in 1827 declared, "The grand figure of the spy, who dominates the entire tableau, is an original conception, strong and profoundly moral." This reviewer also departed from other critics who "have judged Washington's role in the action to be unworthy of the historical man," instead appraising "his role to be constantly dignified."[64] Aside from the topic of espionage, it was Cooper's portrayal of Washington in *The Spy* that courted controversy.

Cooper begins the book with Washington traveling in disguise and under an assumed name, gathering information like a spy himself. Cooper's portrayal of such an illustrious American figure shook some readers at the time. In a review in the *Port Folio* in February 1822, Sarah Hale seethed, "The manner in which Gen. Washington is introduced is a serious defect. He should have worn the disguise of Mr. Harper to the last; for it is offering too great violence to our veneration for this immortal man to exhibit him, unattended and almost in sight of the enemy . . . skulking in a hut to obtain an interview with a pedlar-spy. Moreover there is nothing done by him, which could not have been effected by an inferior agency."[65] Although Washington might have overseen spies, he was not supposed to sneak around like one himself.

W. H. Gardiner agreed in a piece in the *North American Review* in July 1822. He drew a remarkable distinction between Washington's role as a spymaster in the American Revolution and Cooper's portrayal of Washington in *The Spy*. Gardiner noted approvingly "that no military commander ever availed himself of a judicious system of *espionage* with more consummate address, or greater advantage to his cause, than General Washington."[66] However, Gardiner scolded Cooper for his decision to cast Washington as a spy himself:

> Until we see undoubted evidence of the fact, we shall not hesitate to deny it. The whole character of Washington is against it. His station, his trust, than which none could be higher, are against it. The opinion of those most intimate with him, by their official relations, is entirely against it. Nay, it was almost physically impossible. His remarkable stature and physiognomy, his lofty carriage, the unbending dignity of his whole demeanor, and, above all, the notoriety of his person making detection almost certain, rendered him the most unfit of all men to practise such a deception. We are compelled to believe, therefore, that our author has deviated from historical accuracy, in a point where he

> should most scrupulously have adhered to it. When such a personage as Washington is made to move in the scenes of fiction ... he should appear, if he would appear safely, only as his countrymen have known and must ever remember him, at the head of armies, or in the dignity of state.[67]

In Gardiner's estimation, Washington must maintain a distinguished distance from the disreputable deeds and dirty tricks of spies even if he availed himself of their services.

In publishing *The Spy*, Cooper exposed the still largely unknown relationship that the Founders had with intelligence during the Revolutionary War. He claimed that the idea for the book originated in conversations with a gentleman whose identity he protected but who "had been employed in various situations of high trust during the darkest days of the American revolution." This anonymous individual was "chairman" of "an especial and secret committee." The unnamed storyteller also "did not mention the name of his agent."[68] Cooper therefore protected his source, who protected his own source. But there is enough in Cooper's biography and the introduction to *The Spy* to tie the pieces together. Historians have identified Cooper's source as John Jay, and Cooper's fictional spy, Harvey Birch, as Enoch Crosby, who spied for Jay.[69] Crosby's own memoir, *The Spy Unmasked or, Memoirs of Enoch Crosby, Alias Harvey Birch, the Hero of Mr. Cooper's Tale of the Neutral Ground*, appeared only a few years later and made the same claim.[70]

Public perceptions of espionage help explain Jay and Cooper's concern with protecting sources. In the same scene where Birch refuses a reward for his service after the war, Washington cautions him, "Remember that the veil which conceals your true character cannot be raised in years—perhaps never.... I have told you that the characters of men who are much esteemed in life depend on your secrecy."[71] As they part ways, Washington again reminds Birch, "Remember ... that in me you will always have a secret friend; but openly I cannot know you."[72] Cooper's Washington seemingly understood that he had to protect his reputation and the reputation of those "much esteemed in life," like Jay and the other Founders from an American public that scorned both espionage and those who practiced it.

Of course, the real Washington was an ardent admirer of the dark arts of intelligence and espionage. He had set a course for American intelligence as a product of his example and experience in the field as a general and in office as the President. At his instigation, Congress granted the President the

Contingent Fund, which gave America's chief executive control over intelligence with virtually no oversight or transparency. The combination of the American people's suspicion of executive power and the American political system's division between two political parties led Congress to reconsider this decision. For nearly half a century, Congress debated its role in American intelligence, creating confusion not only over constitutional boundaries between the President and Congress, but also over the question of a distinct intelligence profession.

4

The President's Private Fund for Part-Time Spies

CONGRESS HAD ONLY briefly considered the scope of the Contingent Fund before passing the act. As a result, the Contingent Fund exposed the problems that accompanied the undefined role of intelligence in American constitutionalism and foreign policy. The Constitution gave the President the power to appoint ambassadors and other foreign service officials with the advice and consent of the Senate. In 1798, the House revisited its responsibility to appropriate funds to compensate American officials abroad, raising questions about the ambiguous position of diplomat-spies.

Leaving aside the constitutional issue, Representative James Bayard argued that it was imprudent for the House to infringe upon the President's responsibility for foreign relations at such a precarious moment for the young United States. Bayard explained, "Ambassadors had been called 'honorable spies' to watch the operations of foreign Governments, in order to inform their own Government of every proceeding likely to affect it.... [S]urely, if ever there were an occasion which called for such spies, it was the present."[1] Representative William C. Claiborne ridiculed Bayard and other congressmen for wanting to keep apprised of affairs overseas. Echoing Washington's Farewell Address, Claiborne urged Congress to stay out of "the politics of Europe... with that continual confusion and warfare" and counseled his countrymen "to keep aloof from the intrigues and designs of European Princes, as well as Republics." If the situation in Europe was as bad as Bayard suggested, then "what possible good," he wondered, "could honest American Ministers render to their country from a residence in those countries?" Claiborne concluded with a parochial defense of American isolationism, noting that "an immense ocean separates the United States from those countries," so he saw no need for those officers whom Bayard "called our honorable spies abroad."[2]

Just as Bayard and Claiborne muddled intelligence and diplomacy, Representative Chauncey Goodrich also stumbled with the distinction between the two. If the House would not provide for the compensation of "diplomatic agents abroad," then the President would have to "descend to the same low means with other nations, and depend upon spies for information." Moreover, Goodrich perceived the problem Congress would face with intelligence oversight, for "when [the President] got this information it would not be from authority, and therefore such as he could not communicate to the Legislature."[3] Nathaniel Macon likewise observed that "if our foreign Ministers were done away, we should have secret spies," although he "believed we had now not only public, but secret spies." The United States apparently had not learned from the missteps of the American mission to France during the Revolutionary War because Macon also mentioned a recent report "which showed that we had had a secret spy in a public Minister who had engaged in a plan which might have involved this country in a war, had it not been timely discovered."[4]

Congress was conflating and confusing diplomacy and intelligence both in constitutional terms and in terms of their status and legitimacy as professions of national security. Some congressmen believed diplomats could act as "honorable spies," but to use "secret spies" was below the stature of the President and the United States. Others saw the need for both overt public officials and covert agents—though few would countenance secret agents as "officers" of the US government. The result was the belated development of an American intelligence profession and clashes between the President and Congress over US foreign policy. Congress wrestled with the constitutional question of official presidential appointments like ministers and plenipotentiaries, which required the Senate's advice and consent, and the Contingent Fund, which allowed the President to employ unofficial agents at his own discretion and without notifying Congress. In turn, the President was able to steer foreign policy without congressional interference, generating opposition in Congress that resulted in decades of debates over the nature of American intelligence.

From Contingent Fund to Secret Service Fund

In April 1802, a House committee alarmingly noted executive attempts to expand the scope of the Contingent Fund. The Secretary of War had decided that "expenditures for secret services, rendered in relation to the duties of the

War Department, are to be admitted" under the same discretionary authority guiding the Contingent Fund. Subsequently, the Secretary of the Treasury chose to extend the Contingent Fund's discretionary reporting authority to the Departments of State, War, and Navy, which President Thomas Jefferson recognized by signing two vouchers on behalf of the War Department. The House committee insisted that "the policy of this law, the committee do not intend to question, but it is clear that it extends only to cases of compensation, for what are usually termed '*secret services,*' " citing the Contingent Fund acts for the years 1793, 1798, and 1800 as evidence of congressional intent that these types of services are "expressly confined to foreign intercourse." The House committee "entertain[ed] no doubt as to the illegality of this measure, as it is authorized by no law whatsoever." With respect to War and Navy, it concluded "there is no necessity nor propriety for applying the principle of secret service money to either of those Departments."[5]

Although Congress conceded to presidential discretion over "secret services," it sought to limit this realm of executive power. It did not intend for the executive branch to hide military activities under the same principle. Congress would also attempt to distinguish diplomatic and intelligence activities and officers under the terms of the Contingent Fund, but with little success. Although it had intended to draw boundaries between military, diplomatic, and intelligence activities through the Contingent Fund, it ended up creating more confusion. In the absence of clear laws or even understandings, ideology and experience shaped intelligence in the early American republic.

Congress did, however, acknowledge the President's responsibility to withhold the names of secret agents paid out of the Contingent Fund. When the House took up a resolution calling on the President to provide a list of names of persons holding "offices under the Government of the United States" during the War of 1812, Representative Robert Wright objected to the "disclosure of the names of persons employed in secret service," considering the threat posed by British agents in the United States. Wright then proposed an amendment, subsequently adopted, that the President would only need to list the names of those "holding office or employment of a public nature," thereby exempting those agents engaged in "secret service."[6]

The list of America's "special agents" during this period reveals the spectrum of activities in which they engaged, from observing events and obtaining information to making treaties and negotiating with foreign states.[7] For example, Joel Poinsett, who served multiple presidential administrations in diplomatic and intelligence capacities, incited revolutions, supported juntas, and engaged in a covert proxy war for influence against British intelligence agents in Latin America.[8] Poinsett was also recognized by the junta in Buenos Aires as an official representative of the US government even though he admitted that his credentials "were not directed to them, nor signed by the President," an achievement that Charles Lyon Chandler, an American consul and historian of US foreign relations, deemed a "decisive diplomatic triumph, for Poinsett had caused himself to be recognized as his country's representative before any European power had even accredited anyone to the Junta."[9] Poinsett personified and defined US foreign policy in Latin America ever since by combining overt public relations with covert political activity.

When Congress returned to the Contingent Fund in March 1818, it did so without the benefit, or perhaps burden, of the experience of the founding generation, which had retired from public service.[10] Thus, Congress continued to fumble its way forward. Speaker of the House Henry Clay questioned the Monroe administration's nomination of three men for a public mission to South America.[11] Clay claimed that the administration had compromised the mission by publicizing it and argued that it should have been kept secret, along with the identities of its agents. He insisted that the "proper course" for the President "to have adopted... was to dispatch an individual unknown to all parties; some intelligent, keen, silent, and observing man, of pleasing address and insinuating manners, who, concealing the object of his visit, would see and hear everything, and report it faithfully." He was concerned that the appointed commissioners would not have enough time to fulfill their intelligence-gathering purpose even "if they were acquainted with the language, manners, and habits, of the country," raising the problem of using amateur spies who had no background in the language or culture of the countries in which they were spying. Regarding the Contingent Fund and presidential power, Clay explained that "if the compensation of the Commissioners [to South America] had been made from that fund... it would not have been a proper subject for inquiry." He therefore took issue with the public dimensions of the commission, claiming instead that it should have been a secret intelligence operation.[12]

Representative John Forsyth's response was revealing. He referred to the men whom Monroe had appointed as "intelligent agents" and acknowledged that the purpose of the "secret service fund" was "the employment of spies throughout the world."[13] Forsyth's admission made it clear that the Contingent Fund was the "black budget" for intelligence in the early American republic. But the debate over the public or secret nature of the mission involved a deeper constitutional question. Clay challenged the authority of the President to appoint the three men as public officials.[14] Likewise, Representative Joseph

Hopkinson questioned the President's power to appoint ministers, plenipotentiaries, or—as Forsyth argued—spies.[15] Lingering issues about the role of intelligence in the United States surfaced in this debate.

First, there was no professional corps of intelligence officers with the background, education, or experience in regions of interest, straining the government's ability to effectively gather information. Additionally, because the United States did not clearly distinguish between diplomatic and intelligence officers and activities, the President could appoint individuals who blurred the lines between the two. Fundamentally, Congress was struggling to define its own oversight role for intelligence, as the Contingent Fund was the closest thing to statutory law guiding American intelligence. However, the fund created constitutional questions without clear answers.

President Washington's Precedent

As often happens in political disputes in the United States, the tables turned, and Clay found himself the object of attack in Congress as Secretary of State in the administration of John Quincy Adams. At issue was the Adams administration's decision to send a US delegation to the Congress of Panama, a meeting of Latin American states organized by Simón Bolívar in 1826.[16]

Senator Martin van Buren, who opposed the delegation, explained that the President had a few options: He could send a "private Agent, at the public expense, with proper credentials," he could send the current US Ministers in Colombia and Mexico, or he could appoint ambassadors to the Congress of Panama with the advice and consent of the Senate and a corresponding congressional appropriation for their mission. But, Van Buren added, even "if the Senate do not approve, or Congress refuse the appropriation, either of the other measures may still be adopted. Their execution is within the constitutional competency of the Executive, and the contingent fund will supply the means." The Contingent Fund therefore seemed to provide the President with a mechanism to avoid constitutional or congressional constraints over foreign policy.[17]

In what Henry Wriston ranks as "the longest reported passage in any congressional discussion" on the Contingent Fund, Senator Thomas Hart Benton turned Clay's logic of 1818 against the Adams administration.[18] As Clay had done in 1818, Benton argued that the mission to Panama should have been unofficial and of a more intelligence-like character, citing Washington's appointment of Gouverneur Morris in 1790 as an example. Benton contrasted the "questionable and clumsy shape of a formal Embassy" against "the active, subtle, penetrating, and pervading form of unofficial Agents, speaking the language of the country, and establishing themselves on the basis of social intercourse in every Minister's family," deciding "this is precisely what we should have done."[19]

In an equally long-winded response, Senator Littleton Waller Tazewell challenged the President's control over intelligence activities by appealing to American principles. Tazewell warned the Senate that "the power granted by the People to the Executive, although made by the Constitution but a schoolboy's snow-ball, in a few turns would become a monstrous avalanche, that must one day crush themselves." Tazewell worried that Presidents had expanded their control over US foreign policy by employing unofficial agents using the Contingent Fund rather than going through the constitutional process of appointing public officials with the advice and consent of the Senate. They had done so partially due to the absence of explicit provisions directly addressing the distinctions between the two.[20]

To distinguish the two roles, Tazewell relied on his own interpretation of a precedent set by George Washington. In 1792, Washington asked Revolutionary War–era naval hero John Paul Jones to negotiate an end to the conflict between the United States and Barbary pirates in Algiers. Tazewell contended that the President's constitutional power of appointment in this case derived from his position as the Commander in Chief of the military while the United States was at war. After Washington selected Jones for the mission, Secretary of State Thomas Jefferson informed Jones that the nature of the mission had to be kept secret to avoid interference by European states, thus making Jones a secret agent and the whole mission a secret. Tazewell decided that Jones acted as a "secret agent" of the President rather than a "Public Minister," explaining that "the idea of a *secret Minister* was one much too absurd to have entered such a head as that of either Washington or Jefferson."[21] In the event, Jones died before he could begin his mission, as did his replacement, so the mission was left to Colonel David Humphreys, one of the earliest recipients of compensation from the Contingent Fund.[22] Remarkably, Tazewell cited a precedent that Congress had already discussed and resolved through a change to the Contingent Fund in 1810.

The amended Contingent Fund legislation of May 1, 1810, specifically addressed the continued hostilities between the United States and Barbary pirates.[23] In the act, Congress stipulated that American consuls to the Barbary states were public officers and not secret agents as they previously had been. Congress had therefore seemingly distinguished between intelligence agents and diplomats at least with respect to the Barbary question.

FIGURE 4.1 Littleton Waller Tazewell, representative, senator, twenty-sixth governor of Virginia, and prolific speaker. National Portrait Gallery, Smithsonian Institution; gift of Mr. and Mrs. Paul Mellon.

But Tazewell's sermon demonstrates how Congress continued to confuse diplomacy and intelligence, and diplomatic officers and intelligence agents. Wriston concludes that Tazewell's "doctrine of precedents... did not fit the facts with which he was dealing," because "his shocked assertion that Washington and Jefferson would never dream of a secret minister is belied by their Revolutionary experience."[24] Ironically, Tazewell claimed for himself a special authority to preach about the virtues of George Washington, "understanding the character of President Washington, as I think I do."[25] Like the reviewers who rejected Washington's dealings with intelligence in *The Spy*, Tazewell revealed how American attitudes regarding intelligence were informed more by ideology and mythology than history and reality.

"Privileged Spies" and "Secret Ministers"

In 1831, Congress revisited the Contingent Fund and presidential power in the matter of the "Turkish Commission," the first American foray into diplomatic relations with the Ottoman Empire. Once again, it debated the issue of public versus secret ministers as part of the larger debate over the blurring of American intelligence and diplomatic activities.

Tazewell delivered another protracted speech to oppose an appropriation for the mission because President Andrew Jackson had appointed commissioners without the advice and consent of the Senate. Senator Elias Kane interrupted him to draw a distinction between public ministers and "secret ministers or private agents," whom the President could appoint without advising the Senate "because such appointments were not specially provided for in the constitution." Tazewell dismissed Kane's argument, claiming "under that provision of the constitution which authorizes the appointment of public ministers, the President, by and with the advice and consent of the Senate, may appoint such ministers secretly. They may be instructed to depart secretly. They may be accredited secretly. They may negotiate . . . secretly. Nay, they may conclude a secret treaty. . . . In this sense, such ministers may properly be termed secret ministers; but they are nevertheless public ministers." Despite having deemed the idea of a "secret minister" absurd in his speech in 1826, Tazewell accepted the existence of secret ministers, but only insofar as they were public ministers appointed secretly.[26]

Tazewell then lectured the Senate on why the distinction between diplomats and intelligence officers mattered. He began by contrasting public ministers as diplomats with secret agents as intelligence officers. He advised, "As a simple individual, I would humbly suggest to [the President] . . . that whenever he stands in need of secret agents who are really designed to be such, he had better abstain from putting his own name to the warrant given to them, and never permit it to be authenticated by the great seal. Such a proceeding may sometimes prove hazardous, and I think it would not be very creditable to the nation whose seal it is." He added, "It is only because secret agents are not officers of the United States, but the mere agents of the President, or of his Secretaries, or of his military or naval commanders, that I disclaim all participation in their appointment." Tazewell therefore recognized the appointment of secret agents at the secretary and departmental levels of the military despite the House committee in 1802 having opposed this extension of Contingent Fund authority. However, he did not entertain the idea of secret agents, meaning spies, as a professional class of government officers. In case his sentiments remained in doubt, he announced, "Sir, it mortifies me to hear the high functionaries of the nation degraded by a comparison with such gentry as these; and their secret commissions assimilated to the warrants of messengers, or the secret letters to spies." Thus, while Tazewell argued for American intelligence, he was against an American intelligence profession.[27]

Senator Edward Livingston's response to Tazewell further confused the boundaries between intelligence and diplomacy. He unhelpfully offered that "there are grades in diplomacy which give different ranks and privileges—from an ambassador to a secret agent." Livingston attempted to distinguish between the two by explaining that ambassadors require appointment by the President with the advice and consent of the Senate "because public missions required no secrecy." However, the "framers of the constitution knew the necessity of missions, of which not only the object but the existence should be kept secret," and they "wisely... left [their] appointment solely to the President."[28]

Senator John Forsyth, having already debated the scope of American intelligence activities with Clay in 1818, reappeared to defend presidential secrecy and discretion with respect to the Contingent Fund. He again presented the fund as essentially a congressional budget for American intelligence activities. He criticized Congress for attempting to exert any oversight over these intelligence activities. Forsyth sarcastically commented, "If a desire was felt that any subject should be bru[i]ted about in every corner of the United States, should become the topic of universal discussion, nothing more was necessary than to close the doors of the Senate chamber, and make it the object of secret, confidential deliberation," concluding that "the art of keeping State secrets is no better understood now than it formerly was."[29] Just as the Committee of Secret Correspondence felt that the Continental Congress's failure to protect secrets entitled the committee to conceal its operations from Congress, Forsyth claimed that Congress's continued tendency to leak information disqualified it from overseeing presidential intelligence activities.

Forsyth also challenged Tazewell's distinction between informal spies and official diplomats. He began with a brief explanation of the history of the Contingent Fund: "The experience of the confederation having shown the necessity of secret confidential agencies in foreign countries, very early in the progress of the Federal Government, a fund was set apart, to be expended at the discretion of the President of the United States on his responsibility only, called the contingent fund of foreign intercourse." However, whereas Tazewell "supposed that this fund was for the payment of spies in foreign countries, who might be imprisoned or hung, if detected... as the United States were not bound to protect them," Forsyth differentiated between "American citizens [who] would be entitled to protection" and "this term spy." He continued:

> Foreign ministers are defined to be privileged spies, sent abroad to lie for the benefit of their country.... If the President can, on the strength of this contingent fund, appoint spies, he can appoint the privileged

> spies. But on what ground does the gentleman narrow down the use of this contingent fund? It was given for all purposes to which a secret service fund should or could be applied for the public benefit. For spies, if the gentlem[a]n pleases; for persons sent publicly and secretly to search for important information, political or commercial; for agents to carry confidential instructions, written or verbal, to our foreign ministers, in negotiations where secrecy was the element of success; for agents to feel the pulse of foreign Governments, to ascertain if treaties, commercial or political, could be formed with them, and with power to form them, if practicable. Such uses have been frequently made of this fund.[30]

Forsyth's speech was remarkable in underscoring the state of American intelligence. He seemed content to continue to blur diplomacy and intelligence through the covert diplomacy of diplomat-spies. In this respect, he did not display the same ideological animosity toward espionage as Tazewell did. Instead, he defended American spies who acted for the benefit of the country, foreshadowing the eventual recognition of intelligence agents as officers of the US government. Finally, Forsyth made clear that the Contingent Fund was indeed a secret service fund, "entrusted to the absolute discretion of the President."[31] Based on Tazewell's and Forsyth's speeches, there was no consensus about the contours of American intelligence at the time.

Congress Still Confounded

The following year, in 1832, when Tazewell, Clay, and Forsyth again debated the Contingent Fund, Forsyth reiterated his position that the Contingent Fund was "under the immediate control of the President; he decides on its application for himself, and is responsible to no one."[32] Given the regularity of these debates over the Contingent Fund, one might surmise that the early American republic engaged in a flurry of covert diplomatic activity. However, Clay made the curious observation, "The fund for contingencies for foreign intercourse had increased very much, and it was seldom that any of it was expended. . . . During the last administration, by a proper economy, nearly the whole of this contingent fund had been saved."[33]

It would not remain so, and in 1842, Congress felt compelled to address the uptick in the President's use of executive agents. Senator Levi Woodbury wanted to amend the congressional appropriation bill to prevent the payment of "special agents abroad, appointed without the consent of the Senate or any act of Congress authorizing it," although he admitted that "occasional temporary contingent employments were at times necessary, and were not affected by this proposition." Senator William Preston agreed that "it was necessary to put some restraint on the practice which had grown up under the late Administration, of sending special agents abroad, under various pretences," but also "contended that occasional agents were necessary, and might be employed by the Executive, according to his constitutional function, though not permanently authorized by law; being but temporary in their object, as occasion required."[34]

But there was still the issue of what kind of "special agents" Congress meant. Former Vice President, now Senator, John C. Calhoun "was opposed to this system of employing, and paying salaries, to officers not authorized by law, as there could be no limit to appropriations under such a system," calling them "abuses of the contingent fund." Preston, who had wanted to restrain the practice, nonetheless "contended it was necessary to send special agents to such places as Central America...for the purpose of deriving information as to the existing state of things, with a view of ascertaining how the interests of the United States may be affected or promoted thereby."[35]

In this same vein, Senator James Buchanan did not object to Woodbury's amendment except to the extent it might "deprive the Government of the power of appointing special diplomatic agents, whenever it may become necessary to do so." He made clear just who these "special diplomatic agents" were: "There was no Government on the face of the earth that had not secret agents abroad...[and] to have a nomination made and confirmed by the Senate, according to the ordinary method of appointing diplomatic agents, would defeat the very purpose of the appointment, because the necessary secrecy would not be preserved." He argued that "this amendment...would deprive the Executive of this power; a power so essential to the interests of any country, that no Government on the face of the earth was destitute of it." He even recalled from his time abroad, "There never was a dispatch sent to me...that had not been opened and read by every Government through which it passed," remarking that the "American eagle, placed upon it in the city of Washington, became a most miserable turkey buzzard before it reached its destination." While Buchanan conceded that US Presidents had abused their power, he decided to vote against the amendment, because he "would not, for the sake of saving a few dollars, or for the sake of condemning the abuses of discretion on the part of the Executive...afford the Government an excuse for not sending agents abroad—secretly, if you please, whenever the interests of the country require it." In fact, he "believed there had not been money enough spent by this Government for secret services in regard to foreign relations," noting that "one legation at St. Petersburgh ... had obtained copies of every State document desired." Although "he did not say that he approved of the practice," he deemed it "occasionally a necessary one, and the Executive should not be tied up in regard to it."[36]

Buchanan captured the host of issues confronting Congress with respect to the Contingent Fund. He voiced his ideological disapproval of espionage while at the same time recognizing the necessity of it. Moreover, he yielded to presidential discretion, even if it meant accepting occasional presidential abuse. He, like Preston, seemed to believe that intelligence should be a temporary function, rather than a permanent profession. Finally, his language reflected Congress's ongoing confusion over the boundaries between diplomacy and intelligence.

Notably, some of the congressional debates over the Contingent Fund had their origins in political partisanship, while others exposed personal rivalries in Congress. Intelligence was therefore ammunition for personal and partisan attacks. Disagreements over the Contingent Fund ultimately fractured congressional unity, leaving presidential discretion and control of intelligence untouched.

Executive Outcomes

While Congress debated the Contingent Fund, American Presidents continued to use it to employ agents for intelligence purposes and hide their intelligence operations from Congress and the American people. The case of Duff Green drew an official response from President John Tyler in 1844 when Congress attempted to assert oversight. An amateur general during the War of 1812, Green later became a journalist, an insider in several presidential administrations, a relative by marriage of John C. Calhoun, and a railroad entrepreneur. He added amateur spy to his resume when Tyler charged Green with the mission of influencing Anglo-American relations in London, including advocating in favor of the American annexation of Texas. When Tyler used Green's reports to try to justify annexation to the American people and Congress, the Senate questioned the relationship between Green and the President.

A resolution of June 12, 1844, requested that Tyler inform the Senate "whether Mr. Duff Green has been paid any money out of the Treasury of the United States, or out of the contingent fund for foreign intercourse."[37] On June 17, Tyler defended the presidential prerogative to protect intelligence activities paid for through the Contingent Fund from Congress, though he admitted that "in this particular instance I feel no desire to withhold the fact that Mr. Duff Green was employed by the Executive to collect such information, from private or other sources, as was deemed important [for] undertaking a negotiation then contemplated, but afterwards abandoned."[38] Tyler chose to "declassify" Green's identity, though not exactly his mission, in accordance with presidential discretionary control over intelligence.

Further sparring continued in the Polk administration. Congress heard rumors about the abuse of the Contingent Fund by Secretary of State Daniel Webster during his service under the Harrison and Tyler administrations, and on April 9, 1846, the House issued a resolution requesting Polk to "cause to be furnished . . . an account of all payments made on President's certificates from the fund appropriated by law, through the agency of the State Department, for the contingent expenses of foreign intercourse," including "copies of all entries, receipts, letters, vouchers, memorandums, or other evidence of such payments, to whom paid, for what."[39] Essentially, Congress wanted oversight of all activities conducted through the Contingent Fund.

Polk refused. He drafted a long response that cited the original act of 1790 and ensuing acts of 1793 and 1810, which he explained were still in force. While sensitive to "the strong and correct public feeling which exists throughout the country against secrecy of any kind in the administration of the Government, and especially in reference to public expenditures," Polk still perceived the need for secrecy in the case of activities conducted under the Contingent Fund.[40] In defense of this specific area of presidential secrecy, he wrote:

> The experience of every nation on earth has demonstrated that emergencies may arise in which it becomes absolutely necessary for the public safety or the public good to make expenditures the very object of which would be defeated by publicity. . . . In no nation is the application of such sums ever made public. In time of war or impending danger the situation of the country may make it necessary to employ individuals for the purpose of obtaining information or rendering other important services who could never be prevailed upon to act if they entertained the least apprehension that their names or their agency would in any contingency be divulged. So it may often become necessary to incur an expenditure for an object highly useful to the country. . . . But this object might be altogether defeated by the intrigues of other powers if our purposes were to be made known by the exhibition of the original papers and vouchers to the accounting officers of the Treasury.[41]

Citing the act of 1810, Polk concluded that he was "bound by a high sense of public policy and duty to observe its provisions and the uniform practice of my predecessors under [the Contingent Fund.]"[42] In one fell swoop, he settled both the language and legislative intent of the Contingent Fund.

Historian Matthew Karp claims that "no president had explicitly defended, on principle, the idea of absolute executive secrecy in foreign policy" until Polk.[43] Polk's response to Congress also illustrated how Presidents tend to defend their predecessors' intelligence powers against congressional interference despite political differences.

Polk had another good reason to defend discretionary presidential control over American intelligence activities. The United States was on the brink of war with Mexico in April 1846. Polk sent executive agents to Mexico, first to avoid war, then to end it as quickly as possible once it began. He instructed William Parrott to contact leaders in the Mexican government but also told him that he was not "at liberty to communicate to them [his] official character" until he was able to "clearly ascertain that they are willing to renew our diplomatic intercourse." So, Parrott was to be a spy before he revealed himself as a diplomat. Likewise, Moses Beach was instructed "never to give the slightest intimation, directly or indirectly, that [he] was an agent of this government" except if it would "smooth the way to peace." Covert diplomacy supplanted overt diplomacy. However, covert diplomacy did not prevent war, and covert intelligence operations undermined overt US diplomacy with Mexico.[44]

The Mexican-American War generated a surge of opposition from Congress and the American people. In response, Polk attempted to use intelligence—namely, covert action—to avoid a large-scale, unpopular war. He approved a covert operation to help Antonio López de Santa Anna, the former President of Mexico then living in exile in Havana, Cuba, take back power in return for peace negotiations favorable to American interests.

Thomas Hart Benton recorded that the details of the coup plan "leaked out." Of course, the US government denied the plot. However, any hope for plausible deniability evaporated when Santa Anna returned to Mexico with the help of the US Navy and a US passport. Benton wrote, "It is probably the first time in the history of nations that a secret intrigue for peace was part and parcel of an open declaration of war!" However, once Santa Anna returned to power, he denounced the United States, "the most so, perhaps, to cover up the secret of his return." Santa Anna became a tyrant who "crushed the liberal party" and committed other acts of violence against his own people—"all the natural consequence of trusting such a man: the natural consequence of beginning war upon an intrigue with him." Benton concluded by wondering "But what must history say of the policy and morality of such doings?"[45] In intelligence terms, he worried about blowback, which would continue to be a feature of US intelligence activities in Latin America.

Intelligence on the Eve of the Civil War

In the early American republic, amateur spies performed their services temporarily, as needed, and then returned to whatever trade or occupation they had as civilians. Spies did not remain spies, nor did they develop an expertise in intelligence that was then passed along in formal or informal training and education to a new crop of spies. The Contingent Fund did not produce, nor did the country attempt to create, an American intelligence profession or institution.

The American ideological bias against spies was another factor that impeded the professionalization of intelligence. While members of Congress like Tazewell and Buchanan expressed their distaste for espionage, they still recognized its necessity. Similarly, when Daniel Webster, whose first tenure as Secretary of State saw Congress request full disclosure of Contingent Fund activities, again became Secretary of State in 1850, he revealed his attitude toward espionage in his correspondence with the Austrian chargé d'affaires, Chevalier J. G. Hülsemann.

The Taylor administration dispatched Ambrose Dudley Mann as a special agent to Hungary during its war for independence from Austria.[46] As Taylor later informed the Senate, Mann's mission was to recognize the independence of Hungary should it win the war with Austria. Correspondence from Mann revealed that he was acting as both a spy and a diplomat. Mann explained in his letters that he "deemed it prudent to avoid any mention whatever of the nature of [his] mission." He distinguished himself from a diplomat, writing that he "rejoice[d]...that the President bestowed upon [him] the appointment of confidential agent...A more delicate or complicated mission...was never confided even to the most experienced and accomplished diplomatist." Furthermore, Mann decided that his "duties would be better discharged by standing still and watching minutely the effect of the events that were transpiring—than by an imprudent risk or premature diplomatic intercourse with the Hungarian minister of foreign affairs."[47]

Hülsemann opposed Mann's mission as inconsistent with "the principle of non-intervention, so formally announced by the United States as the basis of American policy, and which had just been sanctioned with so much solemnity by the President in his inaugural address of March 5, 1849." He suggested that the American officials who dispatched Mann "were exposing their emissary to be treated as a spy."[48] Webster rejected Hülsemann's attempt to "give this odious name and character to a confidential agent of a neutral Power, bearing the commission of his country, and sent for a purpose fully warranted by the law of nations."[49]

In precariously balancing the role of the diplomat-spy, Mann preferred the spy, while Webster preferred the diplomat. Moreover, this episode echoed the Turkish Commission debate between Tazewell and Forsyth. The United States had failed to distinguish between diplomats and spies, and had not determined whether these executive agents were entitled to the protection of the US government if they were captured, thereby threatening not just the status but the very lives of diplomat-spies like Mann. Thus, the combination of American principles and constitutional ambiguity undermined the ability of policymakers to concretely distinguish between intelligence and other elements of statecraft.

Mann offered a final warning in this debate. After witnessing the defeat of the Hungarians and the brutal response by the Austrians, he addressed the outcry from the American people and their demand that the US government should "suspend all diplomatic intercourse with Austria." He argued, "If we desire to be instrumental in redeeming our species from political bondage and misrule, we must rely upon the force of our example made apparent by the peaceful dissemination of the benign practical workings of our doctrines."[50] Mann, who had acted as a diplomat-spy, advocated for overt diplomacy based on American principles, suggesting that the United States could best steer world events by transparently displaying its foundational values and ideas.

The Contingent Fund created lingering uncertainties over how to incorporate intelligence into the US government. Amid this confusion, it proved a flexible instrument for Presidents to control intelligence and to use it as an alternative or complement to overt military and diplomatic action. However, these precedents would be challenged as intelligence activities and agents were absorbed into military, diplomatic, and law enforcement missions during the Civil War, ushering in a new era in American intelligence history.

5

Uncivil-Intelligence Relations in the Civil War

FIVE MONTHS AFTER the outbreak of the Civil War, Henry Shelton Sanford, who was officially the US Minister to Belgium but unofficially the Union's spymaster in Europe, penned a letter marked "Confidential" to his boss, Secretary of State William Seward. In it, he outlined serious weaknesses in the Union's intelligence operations in Europe. Detailing the Confederacy's intelligence network, he warned Seward that "the work of the rebel agents has spread beyond the limited means I have or can command even to carrying on imperfectly this work." He implored Seward to "urge that the Government immediately adopt a policy which will enable me to carry on a comprehensive and liberal system of operations or instruct me to relinquish entirely all further effort in this channel."[1]

However, the Union did not take up Sanford's suggestions in Europe or North America. Its intelligence activities during the Civil War remained discretionary, disorganized, unprofessional, and utterly unsuited to the scale of the conflict. The dysfunctions in Civil War–era intelligence reflected the limitations of the first American intelligence system and tensions in civil-intelligence relations.

Aside from the strain President Abraham Lincoln experienced as he personally tried to manage the Union's war effort, the Civil War also required a commensurately large intelligence effort.[2] Lincoln alone could not manage the intelligence needs of the war. Instead, control of intelligence began to shift to the executive departments as the War, Navy, and State Departments drew from the Secret Service Fund to support their own intelligence agents and missions. This signaled a break in the intelligence system established by the Contingent Fund.

Diplomats and Detectives or Amateur Spies and Aspiring Professionals?

The United States entered the Civil War with an intelligence system dependent on amateur spies and without the benefit of professional intelligence organizations. Still, both the North and the South needed intelligence on the other. So, they relied on diplomats, like Henry Shelton Sanford, and detectives, like Allan Pinkerton—amateurs involved in intelligence work. The rough contours of an intelligence profession, defined as often by what it is not as by what it is, surfaced in the writings and biographies of the amateurs who took part in the shadow struggle during the Civil War. Sanford and Pinkerton especially provided instructive accounts of American intelligence in this era.

Allan Pinkerton had made a name for himself as a private detective before the Civil War. He investigated train robberies for the Illinois Central Railroad in the 1850s among many other celebrated cases. Pinkerton even claimed to have stopped an assassination attempt on Abraham Lincoln on the way to his presidential inauguration.[3] At the outset of the war, Pinkerton wrote that Lincoln summoned him to Washington for the purpose of "organizing a secret-service department of the government." Pinkerton, like Sanford, realized how uncoordinated American intelligence was and believed "that anything approaching to a systematized organization or operation would be for a time impossible." He instead returned to his detective business, but General George McClellan, a personal friend of Pinkerton's who had also worked for the Illinois Central Railroad, convinced him to join the war effort.[4] Pinkerton's professional experience informed his wartime intelligence work. Among the abilities and sensibilities that he brought to this work was an earnest attention to secrecy that rivaled Washington's own during the Revolutionary War. In fact, Pinkerton himself worked under the nom de guerre of Major E. J. Allen.[5]

Pinkerton assiduously attempted to protect his sources and spy networks. The spymasters of the Civil War kept logs of their expenses in order to receive reimbursement from the Secret Service Fund. Pinkerton hid the identities of his agents on the statements of account that he provided to the War Department by using three letters for each agent, presumably the initials of his operatives' names—a rudimentary code, but better than none.[6] In October 1862, Pinkerton recorded that John Potts, the disbursing clerk of the War Department, would not compensate him for his expenses unless he provided the names of his agents. He rejected any attempt to force him to reveal their identities and defended the role of secrecy in what he styled as "detective" work. He explained to Peter Watson, the Assistant Secretary of War, that "if they (the operatives) once became known their efficiency to a very great extent was destroyed and inasmuch as in all Detective Service more or less personal risk had to be encountered, I so far insured against this by holding the knowledge of who my operatives were in my own hands." If this secrecy was weakened or broken, he bristled, "in my opinion, the efficiency of the Detective system is destroyed. Secrecy is its strength and publicity its weakness."[7]

Only six months earlier, in April 1862, Pinkerton had lost one of his favorite agents, Timothy Webster, the first person executed for spying during the Civil War. At this point, Pinkerton reported that several other agents of his "were under sentence of death in Rebeldom" while many more were working at considerable risk behind enemy lines.[8] As he later explained in his memoir, he was willing to divulge his sources and methods, but only to "as few persons as possible," an early nod to the need-to-know basis for classified intelligence.[9] Pinkerton also offered further information about these "operatives," as he called them, in his memoir. For example, he would use individuals of "both sexes" who were "ostensible representatives of every grade of society, from the highest to the most menial."[10] They wore disguises and assumed identities as necessary. Moreover, as there was no formal classification system to safeguard secrets during the Civil War, Pinkerton and others endeavored to protect their work through other means. Some of the envelopes containing their official correspondence were marked "secret service," which may have limited their circulation.[11] Those charged with intelligence work sometimes wrote "Confidential" or "Very Confidential" on their letters—a classification marking of sorts. Pinkerton was essentially describing the pre-professional intelligence "tradecraft" that American spies and spymasters were adopting in response to the operational challenges they were facing.

Like Pinkerton, Henry Shelton Sanford was supremely suited for intelligence work, but for different reasons. Sanford was a scion of old New England families, a well-traveled polyglot, and a confidant of William Seward. He had always nurtured diplomatic ambitions. As a stepping-stone to what he hoped would be an appointment as Minister to France, he proposed himself as Minister to Belgium in his letters to Seward's political advisor, Thurlow Weed. Weed pressed Seward, who in turn pressed Lincoln, and Sanford found himself in Paris en route to his posting in Belgium just as war broke out in April 1861.[12]

In his instructions to Sanford, Seward wrote that "the most important duty of the diplomatic representatives of the United States in Europe will be to counteract by all proper means the efforts of the agents of that... confederacy at their respective courts," continuing the Contingent Fund's tradition of blurring

FIGURE 5.1 Allan Pinkerton as Major E. J. Allen (left) flanks Abraham Lincoln (center) with Maj. Gen. John A. McClernand (right) from the Battle of Antietam. Library of Congress Prints and Photographs Division, LC-B817–7949.

intelligence and diplomacy.[13] Sanford took to his spy work immediately and kept Seward apprised of his activities.[14] Like Pinkerton, he was concerned with secrecy, not only marking his letters "Confidential" but also deploying an array of codes using numbers, letters, and names.[15] By July, Sanford informed Seward that he knew "of the movements of . . . every citizen engaged in the aid of revolution" and was able to "give information to our agents in the countries where they were going."[16] So, in addition to his role as a diplomat-spy, Sanford added counterintelligence official to his responsibilities.

These exchanges provide context for Sanford's urgent letter to Seward of September 1861. He was impressed by the Confederacy's approach to intelligence, writing that spies for the South were "men of tact, bold but discreet, familiar with the languages of the people with whom they are to act and supplied with ample means to carry out successfully whatever course of proceedings they judge adviseable." By comparison, he found the Union's intelligence operatives in Europe unsuitable "to meet the present emergencies. Our consuls, the few who have arrived at their posts are mostly inexperienced, ignorant of the languages, unacquainted with the people among who they are, their habits and customs and consequently about as efficient as deaf mutes."[17] Just as the Committee of Secret Correspondence wanted Silas Deane to become proficient in Parisian French and Thomas Hart Benton thought "unofficial agents" should speak the language of the countries in which they

FIGURE 5.2 Henry Shelton Sanford was a diplomat-spy and ardent advocate for a more coordinated, comprehensive Union intelligence effort. Library of Congress Prints and Photographs Division, LC-USZ62-130858.

traveled, Sanford wanted operatives to be fluent in the languages of the places where they were undertaking intelligence work.

Aside from Pinkerton and Sanford, other spymasters and spies of the Civil War adapted and innovated in ways that signaled their appreciation for the subtleties of intelligence.[18] Lafayette Baker, Pinkerton's rival, later described his view of the model "detective," really spy, in his memoir written after the Civil War; the necessary traits included "shrewdness, great self-reliance and self-control, discretion, courage, and integrity."[19] But intelligence itself continued to blur professional boundaries: diplomacy in the case of Seward and Sanford, and law enforcement, in the case of Pinkerton and Baker.

A Purse Divided Against Itself

Sanford knew his work in Europe would require no small investment by the Union. While still in Paris in May 1861, he wrote to Seward, "I hope you will provide for sufficient secret service fund[s] when congress meets," adding, "I have no objection to spend my money freely for the cause," an act of generosity his accountant probably regretted.[20] Apparently Sanford did not obtain enough funds because in August he informed Seward that although he believed he had identified "every agent of the Rebellion who has come over here as well as some of their most important local intermediaries," he was unable, "from want of pecuniary means," to exploit this surveillance opportunity.[21] In September, Sanford again asked Seward for sufficient funds to conduct his intelligence operations.[22] A month later, Sanford told Seward bluntly, "The Contingent Fund allowed this Legation . . . does not cover its postages alone."[23] Because the Secret Service Fund failed to meet Sanford's expenses, he was forced to resort to self-funding. By 1863, he had spent more than $10,000 of his own money on his intelligence activities.[24]

Seward later reported to Congress that he spent roughly $41,000 on payments to secret agents during the war.[25] Meanwhile, the War Department spent far more Secret Service Fund money on intelligence activities in North America than the State Department did in Europe.[26] There was no formal arrangement guiding the Secret Service Fund for the Union during the war, as departments, organizations, and individuals vied over the same pot of money.

Competition for money from the Secret Service Fund, as well as the secrecy that continued to define its use, encouraged interpersonal—rather than interorganizational or interdepartmental—intelligence relationships. Even with the shift away from the president and toward departmental control, individual autonomy and discretionary decision-making continued to mark the American intelligence system. There were no formal structures, provisions, or procedures guiding the coordination, oversight, and management of intelligence outside of the subjective judgment of spymasters, generals, and policymakers. As a result, intelligence "stovepipes," or situations in which individuals or groups restrict the flow of information, developed. Paradoxically, this situation both impeded and advanced elements of intelligence professionalism.

Seward's Stovepipes

In addition to the lack of coordination affecting the Secret Service Fund, the executive departments failed to coordinate their intelligence activities as a joint enterprise. This was apparent in the naval blockade of the Confederacy, a central pillar of the Union's grand strategy. While the Navy was responsible for intercepting ships with supplies and armaments bound for the Confederacy, Union diplomat-spies in Europe needed to provide crucial information about the names and cargoes of these ships before they left port. The uncoordinated effort to identify and interdict blockade runners revealed the shortcomings in the Union's intelligence system.

Among his many recommendations, Sanford urged Seward to arrange for a Union steamer to patrol the English coast to intercept ships identified as blockade runners. He also explained that the steamer must be prepared to "act on information received."[27] This would require some process for sharing intelligence between the State and Navy Departments. At times, the intelligence was quite good. For example, in March 1862, Sanford informed Seward that a ship, the *Bahama*, was due to leave Hamburg with cannons and small arms destined for the Confederacy.[28] In the letter, Sanford described the *Bahama* and even included a sketch of the vessel.[29] However, the case of another blockade runner, the *Fingal*, not only revealed the inadequacies of interdepartmental coordination between the State and Navy Departments but also highlighted deficiencies in intradepartmental coordination within the State Department.

Sanford was not the only US minister in Europe involved in intelligence operations. Charles Francis Adams Sr., son of John Quincy Adams and grandson of John Adams, was the US Minister to Britain during the Civil War. Like Sanford, Adams also had intelligence responsibilities. Aiding Adams in his endeavors was Freeman H. Morse, the US consul in London. Throughout the summer of 1861, many of Adams's letters to Seward concerned ships containing contraband bound for the Confederacy.[30] Both Adams and Sanford were

FIGURE 5.3 Sketch of the *Bahama* (1862). National Archives and Records Administration.

engaged in redundant intelligence collection operations without the other knowing it. They discovered the overlap in a dispute over reimbursement through the Secret Service Fund, making this an instance in which the fund inadvertently led to better intelligence coordination. Sanford and Adams alerted Seward to the situation at nearly the same time.

The Navy had sent Commander W. M. Walker to Europe to gather intelligence on Confederate privateers and arms shipments. Like Pinkerton and Sanford, Walker used money from the Secret Service Fund to support his operations. When the Navy recalled Walker, he left $500 in an account. Sanford informed Seward that he had asked Walker to leave this money to help cover expenses for his intelligence operations targeting the *Fingal*. Meanwhile, Adams had instructed Freeman Morse to use the leftover funds for his own surveillance of the *Fingal*. Sanford explained to Seward that his agents could have obtained this information, noting, "It is likely to be a needless waste of money to employ various parties unbeknown to each other to accomplish the same business."[31]

Eight days later, Adams wrote a letter to Seward criticizing Sanford for believing himself "entitled to this money to conduct certain operations of his own in this country of which I know little or nothing." Echoing Sanford, Adams pointed out "that the Department is incurring unnecessary expense in a double system of investigation." Adams also confessed to Seward, "It is no part of my wish to prosecute this line of duty," hinting, "I cannot help thinking that the supervising of it would be more likely to be economically as well as effectively carried on under Mr. Morse alone on this side than as it is now managed."[32] Unlike Sanford, who relished intelligence work, Adams intimated that he preferred his diplomatic duties. So, he suggested a division of labor: He would fulfill his obligations as the ambassador to Britain, while Morse would assume a role approximating the present-day chief of station, or the chief US intelligence officer in a foreign state. Sanford, who acted like the head of Union intelligence in Europe, was complicating the intelligence effort by running his own operations in Britain without Adams' or Morse's knowledge. Adams concluded his letter by requesting that Seward provide instructions to better organize Union intelligence activities in Europe.[33]

Seward needed to figure out how to coordinate the intelligence work of his department. His resolution was to instruct Sanford to hand over his intelligence assets and sources in Britain to Morse, who would oversee all Union intelligence activities there.[34] By establishing distinct areas of operation for the two men, Seward expected cooperation, rather than competition, between them in the future.

A few months later, when Sanford produced intelligence on an arms shipment from England, Seward reminded Sanford to work with Adams. Seward also informed Sanford that he "communicated to the War Department and to the Navy Department, respectively, proper portions of the information."[35] Seward and the State Department lurched toward a more organized intelligence system by addressing the problems associated with the hub-and-spoke model of intelligence coordination that had defined American intelligence since the Revolutionary War. As for the *Fingal*, it was later captured by the Union and served in the Union Navy for the duration of the war. Perhaps its greatest contribution to the war effort was helping to streamline at least some of the Union's intelligence work.

Pinkerton's Private Eyes

Like other spymasters, Allan Pinkerton also relied on the Secret Service Fund to support his intelligence operations.[36] But the Secret Service Fund did not buy his loyalty. Pinkerton's highest allegiance was to General George McClellan—not money, the Union Army, the US government, or even the cause of the war. In fact, one major reason Pinkerton wrote his memoir was to defend both himself and McClellan from their critics. Pinkerton especially wanted to address accusations that they had grossly overestimated the numbers of Confederate soldiers at critical points in the war, most notably before the Battle of Antietam in September 1862.

Days before the battle, McClellan received perhaps the greatest intelligence coup of the war. An enlisted soldier discovered an envelope containing three cigars wrapped in a piece of paper that turned out to be Special Orders No. 191, General Lee's order of movement for his Army of Northern Virginia in Maryland. McClellan confidently telegraphed Lincoln, "I have all the plans of the rebels," and allegedly told General John Gibbon, "Here is a paper with which if I cannot whip 'Bobbie Lee,' I will be willing to go home."[37]

Antietam was the bloodiest day of battle in American history. Although a Union victory, it came at a fearsome price—higher than one might have expected considering McClellan had foreknowledge of the enemy's movements. Already a notoriously dilatory commander, McClellan proved equal to his reputation. He missed several opportunities ahead of the battle to attack Lee's army while it was divided, the key piece of intelligence that Special Orders No. 191 had revealed.[38] During the battle itself, McClellan did not fully commit his army; a third of McClellan's forces did not even fire a shot.[39] Even with fresh reinforcements, McClellan failed to attack the outnumbered, exhausted Confederate army the following day because "he was still hypnotized by a vision of Lee's limitless legions."[40]

Both McClellan's contemporaries and later observers attributed his battlefield decision-making to his glaringly mistaken belief that Lee's army outnumbered his own. If so, it was a devastating intelligence failure given the Union's use of scouting, reconnaissance, prisoner interrogations, spies, and informants to estimate Confederate strength. As McClellan's spymaster, Pinkerton shared the blame for Antietam.

Edwin Fishel, the authoritative historian of intelligence in the Civil War, exonerates Pinkerton, but also emphasizes that a "neurotic general and a sycophantic intelligence officer . . . is surely a dangerous combination."[41] Pinkerton could never remain objective in his dealings with McClellan and apparently adjusted his assessments to appease the general. Pinkerton's personal loyalty to McClellan and McClellan's own political ambitions also damaged civil-intelligence relations.

In his memoir, Pinkerton claimed to have spied on Lincoln, the Cabinet, and other Union officers as part of his effort to serve the political interests of McClellan. He personally traveled to Washington to observe Lincoln and reported back to the general in letters. Pinkerton also acted as a messenger between McClellan and Lincoln, trying to manipulate the president's opinions in favor of McClellan.[42] In doing so, he acted more in the capacity of an intelligence contractor than an intelligence officer. No formal or institutional ties bound Pinkerton to the Union, so he "regarded his service as a personal one to his friend and former business associate [McClellan] rather than as a professional one to the United States government."[43] When Lincoln removed McClellan from command a few months after Antietam, Pinkerton left as well, taking his intelligence network and all the information it had acquired with him. These departures cleared the way for the creation of the Bureau of Military Information, the closest approximation to an organized intelligence service to this point in American history.

The Brief Bureau of Military Information

General Joseph Hooker took command of the Army of the Potomac in January 1863, following the short tenure of General Ambrose Burnside, McClellan's replacement. Hooker had exhibited an aptitude for intelligence while he was still serving under McClellan. He employed his own spies, consulted Lafayette Baker's secret agents, and used intelligence gleaned from the new surveillance platform of air balloons, even making ascents in the balloons himself.[44] If anyone was going to establish a more organized military intelligence system, it would be Hooker.

Pinkerton's departure left the Army of the Potomac without a spymaster, and since he took all his intelligence work with him, he also left it virtually blind. Hooker's chief of staff, Major General Daniel Butterfield, later exclaimed, "We were almost as ignorant of the enemy in our immediate front as if they had been in China."[45] Hooker was determined to create an intelligence organization, but he needed the right man to lead the new outfit. Hooker found him in the person of Colonel George H. Sharpe.

Sharpe, like Sanford, struck the figure of the gentlemanly, amateur intelligence officer. Hailing from Kingston, New York, Sharpe was "well-connected, well-educated, and well-moneyed."[46] Educated at Rutgers and Yale Law School and proficient in French and Latin with a touch of Italian as well, he served as an attaché in Vienna and Rome in the early 1850s. Sharpe joined the 20th New York Militia before the war, and following a few breaks in service, he recommissioned as a colonel in command of the 120th New York Infantry. He likely came to the attention of Hooker while serving under him at Fredericksburg.[47] Within the first two weeks of taking command of the Army of the Potomac, Hooker offered Sharpe a position on his staff to head a new intelligence service.

The organization began as the Secret Service Department and underwent a few name changes before it became the Bureau of Military Information

(BMI).[48] Sharpe and his staff apparently abandoned the words "Secret Service" because Pinkerton and McClellan had already discredited the term. They also wanted to avoid alerting the Confederates to the new intelligence organization. The BMI further concealed its hand by couching its correspondence under the heading of the "Office of the Provost Marshal General," a good cover because Sharpe's official position was deputy provost marshal.[49] The "Bureau of Military Information" was a fitting name given the expansive intelligence role it assumed.

The BMI was the first "all-source" intelligence service in American history.[50] "All-source" refers to intelligence collected using a variety of methods—for example, human intelligence, signals intelligence, and open-source intelligence. In the case of the BMI and Civil War, it included spies, scouts, balloons, mail intercepts, and newspapers. The BMI also overcame a limitation in Seward's State Department, where intelligence sharing was based on interpersonal communication. Instead, the BMI became a clearinghouse for intelligence. Hooker did his part by incorporating the information gathered by the BMI into military decision-making as a staff function.[51] More importantly, Sharpe and the BMI outlasted Hooker's command of the Army of the Potomac. In the BMI, the Union Army finally had some stability and structure in its intelligence effort.

The success of the BMI model quickly became apparent. It was able to provide Union generals with a crucial picture of the Confederate order of battle before and during the Battle of Gettysburg.[52] From that point on, there was better intelligence sharing throughout the Union Army. General William Rosecrans requested intelligence reports from the BMI on Confederate movements in Tennessee, and General Ulysses S. Grant eventually drew Sharpe and the BMI into his General Headquarters in the spring of 1864.[53] However, when the war ended, the Army determined that the BMI had served its purpose, so it was disbanded.

Despite its contributions, the BMI was part of a larger transformation that took place during the Civil War and had consequences for the evolution of American intelligence. With the transition from presidential to departmental control, intelligence was firmly subordinated to other institutions of national security—namely, the military under the War and Navy Departments and diplomacy under the State Department. At the same time, Baker and Pinkerton personified how domestic intelligence was subordinated to law enforcement. As the Contingent Fund had already illustrated with diplomacy, mixing intelligence and other institutions of national security created inconsistencies and conflicts.

Death to Spies!

On April 24, 1863, Lincoln signed General Orders No. 100, Instructions for the Government of Armies of the United States in the Field, more commonly known as the Lieber Code, after its author, Francis Lieber. This groundbreaking attempt to write down the laws of war preserved traditional biases against espionage.

While a uniformed soldier earned the protections of a prisoner of war, no such protections existed for the ignoble spy. Article 88 of the Lieber Code provided a formal definition of a spy as "a person who secretly, in disguise or under false pretense, seeks information with the intention of communicating it to the enemy," prescribing the punishment of death by hanging "whether or not he succeed in obtaining the information or in conveying it to the enemy."[54] Nathan Hale, hero that he was, would have found no reprieve under American law almost a century later.

But the Lieber Code fumbled with how it treated other intelligence functions in war. In Article 101, the code reached the confusing conclusion, "While deception in war is admitted as a just and necessary means of hostility, and is consistent with honorable warfare, the common law of war allows even capital punishment for clandestine or treacherous attempts to injure an enemy, because they are so dangerous, and it is difficult to guard against them."[55] Intelligence operations have always been a feature of war, but defining exactly what they were, deciding which organizations or institutions would be responsible for them, and trying to construct boundaries around them in law would continue to be a point of friction in American civil-intelligence relations.

The Lieber Code also attempted to address the uneasy relationship between diplomacy and intelligence. The code accorded ambassadors, diplomats, and other plenipotentiaries a form of diplomatic immunity.[56] But it insisted that "unauthorized secret communication with the enemy is considered treasonable by the law of war. Foreign residents in an invaded or occupied territory, or foreign visitors in the same, can claim no immunity from this law."[57] The State Department had already faced the foreign policy fallout from a similar situation involving a British diplomat.

Collusion, the Confederacy, and the Crown

Aside from stopping blockade runners, another vital element of the Union's grand strategy was to prevent an alliance between the Confederacy and European states, particularly Britain. Britain declared neutrality in the war, but that did not mean it was not involved. Intelligence provided the basis for the Union's formal diplomatic protests to the British government that exposed either its tacit cooperation with blockade-running or its inability to prevent its own citizens and crown colonies from profiting from it.[58] In turn, diplomat-spies like Sanford and Morse used diplomatic cover for their intelligence activities. Intelligence informed diplomacy and vice versa in the Civil War, but the two functions also blurred and created a diplomatic crisis between the Union and Britain.

In August 1861, the Union detained the Confederate citizen Robert Muir, who was en route to England with letters for Lord John Russell, the British Foreign Secretary, and also in possession of a passport issued by the British consul in Charleston, Robert Bunch.[59] Seward instructed Adams to warn the British against allowing its diplomatic officers to help Confederate agents.[60] Exhibiting the same principled hypocrisy that is a feature of American civil-intelligence relations, Seward expressed his indignation at the prospect of British intrigue in the United States even as his own diplomats conducted intelligence operations across Europe.

Seward wrote Adams that "suppression of the correspondence between parties in that insurrection with each other in this country and in foreign countries is [a] measure which is essential to the suppression of the insurrection itself." However, the Union had to be careful not to violate norms of diplomacy by intercepting letters bound for a neutral government. Seward expressed his hope that the British government would not complain about "the breach of our international postal treaty under such circumstances" and other measures the Union was taking against Confederate agents.[61] As valuable as intelligence was to diplomacy, it also could complicate diplomatic relations.

Not all the letters intercepted along with Muir were under British diplomatic seal and were therefore fair game to open and investigate. In one of these unsealed documents, Seward believed he found evidence of collusion by both Bunch and Pierre Joseph Belligny de Sainte-Croix, the French consul in Charleston, who were arranging treaties of commerce between the Confederacy and the British and French governments, respectively.[62] Seward was determined to extinguish Anglo-Confederate shadow diplomacy by targeting Bunch. He informed Adams that the State Department "must revoke the exequatur [official recognition] of the Consul [Bunch] who has not only been the bearer of communications between the insurgents and a foreign Government" but also engaged in treaty negotiations with the Confederates.[63]

As it turns out, Bunch was both a consul and an intelligence officer like Freeman Morse, the Union's consul in London. Bunch had arrived in the

United States well before the war, acting as vice consul in New York City from 1848 to 1853 before taking up his post in Charleston in 1853. Bunch grew to despise slavery, the American South, and southerners.[64] He wrote dispatches to London warning the British government not to support the Confederacy.[65] But he played his role with such skill that he "not only convinced the people around him in Charleston that he accepted their ways and their world, he... also convinced Seward's spies."[66] If Bunch overplayed his hand, so did Seward.

Seward came to believe he had evidence of an emerging conspiracy between the British government and the Confederacy, and he likely leaked the contents of the letters he had taken from Muir to the press.[67] The Union already faced the problem of Confederate spies in the North, and the American people continued to suspect that European intrigue was occurring in the United States. Press reports fed the public's spy mania. The *New York Herald* initially reported the details of Muir's arrest and Bunch's connection in August 1861.[68] A few weeks later, in an article titled "Important Developments from the Carpet Bag of a Spy," the *Herald* reproduced portions of a few of the letters that were supposedly found on Muir, including one that Seward may have leaked.[69] The *Herald* also called for Seward to pursue the matter with the British and French governments and revoke diplomatic protections for European diplomats if necessary.[70] The *New York Times*, the *Chicago Daily Tribune*, the *Cincinnati Daily Press*, and even the *Richmond Dispatch* also reported on the controversy.[71] In many cases, the papers advocated that Seward adopt a tougher stance toward diplomacy with Britain.

In the case of Seward and Bunch, intelligence created diplomatic friction between the Union and Britain against the interests of both states and to the benefit of the Confederacy. To make matters worse, what Seward might have intended as a tactical leak to the press became a strategic deluge that restricted his ability to maneuver by drawing the American people into the ongoing scandal. Ironically, he took a stand against other attempts to use intelligence to target the press and public opinion during the war.

Propaganda, Public Opinion, and the Press

Propaganda became the subject of an ideologically charged debate between Seward and Sanford. Sanford proposed that the Union "speedily organize an efficient movement of the press in our favor in London, Paris, and Germany" to influence the people of Europe and the policies of European states toward the Union.[72] Sanford was not alone in his propaganda efforts. Seward appointed John Bigelow, an editor and owner of the *New York Evening Post*, as consul in Paris to foster French public sympathy for the Union.[73] But Seward displayed the same principled hypocrisy toward propaganda as he did toward diplomacy.

Sanford reported unfavorable European press coverage of the 1864 presidential election and proposed establishing a Union-subsidized paper on the Continent to "give authoritative information touching the war, our finances, and the general progress of the country."[74] In December 1864, Seward rejected the idea on ideological grounds, saying that "there is no need that the United States should compromise their just dignity by employing other than the customary diplomatic defenders in any part of the world." In Seward's opinion, "We stand or fall not by means of foreign love or hate but exclusively by reason of our own physical and moral strength."[75]

Sanford tried again in February 1865, offering to set up a French-language pro-Union journal in Europe. Seward acknowledged "the injury we suffer from uninterested misrepresentations in Europe" and understood "the great benefit we should derive from a paper that should be able to convey to the European mind truthful information concerning our country, the administration of its Government, and the workings of our political and social systems." Nonetheless, Seward ruled out what might have been a Civil War–era equivalent to the Voice of America.[76]

The Union's relationship with its own press was more ambiguous than what Seward represented. The American principle of a free press, enshrined in the First Amendment, stood in the way of wartime censorship. As a result, newspapers were sources of good intelligence for the enemy. Hooker began his command of the Army of the Potomac by ordering his frontline troops to stop exchanging Northern newspapers with Confederate soldiers, a common practice in this war between brothers and cousins.[77] General William Tecumseh Sherman had particular distaste for journalists, often referring to them as "spies."[78] He even went so far as to court-martial a reporter as a spy.[79]

The Union government often tried to impose censorship, though it usually failed in its attempts. Journalists adopted the techniques of spies to gather information and then skirt censorship, including disguising themselves to sneak into military camps and using coded language so their stories would make it past the censors.[80] The Lincoln administration enlisted the support of the Northern press through "the application of incentives bordering on bribery," leading prominent publisher and Republican politician Thurlow Weed to quip that "Mr. Lincoln deemed it more important to secure the 'Herald's' support than to obtain a victory in the field."[81]

Despite the military priorities of Hooker and Sherman, newspapers revealed military secrets that endangered soldiers.[82] Some Americans therefore paid for the principle of a free press with their lives. The Civil War also revealed the tendency of the American people to forsake their principles, constitutional rights, and civil liberties in other ways.

Intelligence Against All Enemies, Foreign and Domestic

Domestic intelligence in the Civil War reflected many of the same insidious trends as it had in the Revolutionary War. Both wars were fought on American soil and turned Americans against each other. The Union waged a domestic intelligence campaign of staggering size and scope. Individuals were appointed as "detectives" and given a combination of intelligence and police powers so they could spy on and arrest those they accused of disloyalty.[83] Lincoln's suspension of habeas corpus also meant that citizens of the Union did not have the same constitutional protections as they had during peacetime. In this context, the problem of mixing intelligence and politics was combined with the Union's domestic intelligence campaign to produce a landmark case in American constitutional law.

Many citizens of the Union were sympathetic to the Southern cause, so the Lincoln administration targeted its political opposition in the North, particularly the "Copperheads," or Northern Democrats who opposed the war and the Union cause. In the summer of 1864, the Republican governor of Indiana, Oliver P. Morton, was running against Democrat Joseph E. McDonald. Reflecting the earlier precedents of the XYZ and Henry Affairs, Morton settled on a campaign strategy that "Democrats would be tainted with treason, and patriots must repudiate them."[84] Union military authorities in Indiana arrested several prominent Democrats who were critics of Lincoln, including local politicians, journalists, and a lawyer named Lambdin P. Milligan. The men were members of the Order of the Sons of Liberty, an offshoot of the Knights of the Golden Circle, an organization dedicated to undermining the Union war effort. Union spies surveilled the men in order to uncover the conspiracy and obtain incriminating evidence. When Union military authorities learned of weapons and ammunition being stored by the state leader of the organization, they arrested the men, charged them with treason and conspiracy, and condemned them to death in a military tribunal. In 1866, the Supreme Court finally reviewed the case in *Ex parte Milligan* and ruled that

American citizens cannot be tried in military tribunals as long as civilian courts are available and operating.[85]

Ex parte Milligan set a judicial precedent with respect to the US government's powers over American citizens in wartime. But the role of domestic intelligence in the trial and events surrounding it has been overlooked. One opportunistic journeyman turned detective-spy named Felix G. Stidger only agreed to testify at the trial in exchange for a large amount of money.[86] Stidger had previously misrepresented a political meeting of Democrats as a secret meeting of the Order of the Sons of Liberty, further calling into question the intelligence behind the defendants' arrest and Stidger's testimony.[87] Many of the other "witnesses" at the trial "were government detectives, a few were out-and-out scoundrels, and others were personal or political enemies of the accused."[88] Guilt or innocence aside, Milligan was among the many American citizens targeted for government surveillance based as much on political allegiance as actual treason.

Echoing the American Revolution, domestic intelligence proved just as likely to be abused for personal gain as employed for national defense during the Civil War. Paid detectives arrested and extorted innocent people. For example, in September 1863, two "detectives," Edward Shanley and Joseph Scott, detained a war refugee from the South and demanded a bribe to release him. They were subsequently court-martialed and dismissed from their duties as detectives.[89] Incidents like these did not inspire much faith in intelligence work.

The Civil War witnessed the blending of intelligence, military, and law enforcement functions, and their assignment to amateur detectives, military officers, or even civilian opportunists. This system failed to protect citizens against arbitrary abuses of power. It also complicated efforts to professionalize intelligence, as different executive departments all continued to conduct domestic intelligence operations. In what emerged as a longer trend in American intelligence history, the country's failure to resolve crucial distinctions between law enforcement and intelligence would come at the expense of civil liberties and produce periodic political scandals.

Public Accounts and Professional Responsibilities

Perhaps Pinkerton and Baker felt that the end of the war signaled an end to their need to preserve secrets. Both men published memoirs exposing sources and methods from their experiences during the war that ultimately served their own purposes. Pinkerton used his memoir to defend General McClellan and himself and to address an ongoing dispute over the death of Timothy Webster,

Pinkerton's favorite agent.[90] Furthermore, he still had a detective agency to run, and this popular memoir would boost his business.[91] Baker, Pinkerton's chief rival, also used his memoirs for self-defense and self-aggrandizement.

In their books, both Pinkerton and Baker inflated their roles during the war.[92] Notably, each man claimed to have headed the "United States Secret Service" during the war. But no organization by that name existed. Instead, they ran self-styled "secret service" organizations during overlapping periods of the Civil War.[93] Additionally, neither served with the BMI, originally named the "Secret Service Department." Memoirs like Pinkerton's and Baker's were "written more for profit and fame than to render an accurate depiction of intelligence work during the war."[94]

The one man who did not publish a memoir and who had a far stronger claim to running the "Secret Service" was George Sharpe. After the war, Sharpe served in a variety of political, diplomatic, and public roles, but, "when it came to the activities of the BMI and its operatives, Sharpe maintained a sphynx-like silence... understanding that discretion was not only the better part of valor but also essential for maintaining the anonymity of former scouts and spies still living in the South to protect them from vengeful ex-Confederates."[95] A eulogy to Sharpe in his hometown paper, the *Kingston Daily Freeman*, described Sharpe's recruits and illustrated his appreciation for key characteristics of the intelligence profession:

> To get information it was necessary to get all kinds of men: smart men, men who could act their parts, men of constant resource and fidelity. The first requirement of the work was to be a good judge of men, a man who knew human nature, and knowing it, had the capacity to sympathize with all its faults, ambitions, desires, and excellences. He had to have a man of the most approved fidelity—proof against the allurements of power and money.[96]

More than any of his contemporaries, Sharpe approached the model of an intelligence professional.

Lessons Still Not Learned

Historians debate whether the Civil War represented the dawn of professional intelligence in the United States.[97] Even if there were flickers of an intelligence profession, the fire never caught. What extinguished the flame that had been kindled during the Civil War?

In his memoir, Lafayette Baker emphasized America's ambiguous relationship with intelligence. Baker connected the American people, their principles, and their political system to the pendulum effect that war and peace had on intelligence. He explained, "In a republic the people govern... [and] an official espionage [system] in the time of peace over their conduct, by some of their own number, is contrary to the genius of the institutions they create and control. But when war, especially its most fearful form, a civil conflict, exists, the unnatural condition of things calls for the detective service, to watch and bring to justice the enemies of the State, who are plotting its ruin."[98] Baker also blamed Congress for failing to address the shortcomings of the Contingent Fund by not establishing a more formal intelligence system through legislation. He claimed, "Had Congress passed a law at the outset of the Rebellion, authorizing the organization of a detective police, with a head responsible only to the War or some other Department, no complaints would ever have been heard against a detective police system."[99]

Then again, Baker's own actions after the war justified the American people's suspicions of intelligence and resistance to it in peacetime. He recounted in his memoir how he and his agents spied on President Andrew Johnson after the war. When Johnson angrily confronted him, demanding, "How dare you place detectives at my door?" Baker responded that it was "high time that somebody interfered" in Johnson's business. In response, Johnson "most unceremoniously charged" him with "villainous espionage." Like Pinkerton, Baker exploited his position to spy on the President of the United States, representing a grave breach of civil-intelligence relations.[100] Still, Baker—a better commentator on civil-intelligence relations than model for them—helped explain why the United States entered the Civil War without a distinct intelligence profession or institution and why it abandoned the progress it had made once the war ended.

The trend that Baker identified in American civil-intelligence relations continued after the Civil War. An article in *Beadle's Monthly* in 1866 titled "The Spy System in Europe" compared intelligence in the United States and Europe. The author opened by musing, "Few persons, even among those who have made the complete tour of Europe, are aware of the extraordinary surveillance under which they passed," as opposed to the United States where he explained that "no spy dogs his steps." The author concluded, "Here, where Government *is* the people, a spy would be an anomaly—tolerable only in a time of war, and then only so far as the public safety required;—when the danger ceased, even the most vengeful enemy would be free from surveillance, save by officers of the civil law whose province it was to take cognizance of actual offenses against the Statutes."[101]

Embedded in this account were unresolved tensions concerning foreign and domestic intelligence, the role of intelligence in war and peace, and the limits of the American people's understanding of their own government's intelligence activities. Moreover, the United States approached intelligence in fits and starts depending on the level of the threat environment. There was no continuity in American intelligence, except perhaps its discontinuity. Each successive war saw the country engage in intelligence activities on an even greater scale, and each postwar period revealed the challenges that retrenchment posed. After the Civil War, the United States failed to pursue any permanent, meaningful reforms to the coordination, control, and oversight of intelligence. Despite the earnest warnings of individuals like Henry Shelton Sanford and the examples provided by figures like George Sharpe, American intelligence remained discretionary, disorganized, uncoordinated, and unprofessional.

PART TWO

The Birth of the US Intelligence Community: The Competition to Control Intelligence

6

Intelligence in the Service of a New Empire and Old Institutions

THE UNITED STATES emerged from the Civil War an even stronger nation. Farsighted domestic and international observers recognized that it would play a major role in global affairs. However, the country also remained mired in the illusion of itself as a small republic that was above Old World intrigue and imperial ambition, despite its annexations following the Mexican-American War. Intelligence would help extend the United States beyond the boundaries of North America as an instrument of an expansionist, even imperialist, foreign policy.

American intrigue that ultimately resulted in the annexation of Hawaii rekindled the debate over the Contingent Fund and the questions surrounding diplomat-spies. While Congress continued to struggle with the distinction between diplomacy and intelligence at the expense of professional intelligence, the military departments adopted a different approach to resolving tensions between the intelligence and military professions. They established military intelligence organizations in response to transformations in warfare and departmental priorities. The creation of the country's first permanent military intelligence services therefore heralded not the long-awaited professionalization of American intelligence but instead the subordination of intelligence to a professionalizing American military.

The new military intelligence services had the opportunity to prove their worth when the United States went to war with Spain in 1898. What began as a conflict over the remnants of the Spanish Empire in the Western Hemisphere became a war to extend the American empire into the Eastern Hemisphere when the United States took the Philippines from Spain. In the brutal war turned counterinsurgency campaign that followed, a crop of green US military officers honed intelligence techniques and methods that they eventually brought back to the United States for domestic use. Rather than serve American principles of freedom and self-determination as an independent profession, intelligence served American imperialism under the old guard of the State, War, and Navy Departments.

Trouble in the Tropics

Over the course of the nineteenth century, the United States extended its grasp over the North American territories that now form the continental United States. By the end of the century, the United States also had increasing ties to the distant Kingdom of Hawaii. During the same period, Hawaii experienced a change in its system of government from a dynastic monarchy to a constitutional monarchy. In 1875, Hawaii's newly elected king, David Kalākaua, signed a trade agreement between the Kingdom of Hawaii and the United States. But the United States had more than economic interests in mind.

Hawaii was a valuable piece of geostrategic real estate. In 1887, the US Navy acquired coaling and stationing rights to a natural anchorage on Oahu known to the Hawaiians as Wai-Momi, or "Pearl Water," and to Americans as Pearl Harbor. That same year, a rebellion by mostly American and European settlers forced Kalākaua to sign a new constitution, known as the "Bayonet Constitution," that largely disenfranchised Asians and Native Hawaiians, diminished the power of the monarchy, and empowered wealthy Hawaiians, Americans, and Europeans. The United States was setting the conditions for the annexation of the Hawaiian Islands.

The American quest to annex Hawaii began in the administration of President Benjamin Harrison as a covert action operation under the control of the American Minister to Hawaii, John Stevens. American intelligence activities included working with pro-annexationists on the islands and employing propaganda in US newspapers that emphasized the military importance of the islands and accused the British of secretly subverting American interests in Hawaii.[1] Stevens weighed in, claiming that "annexation alone will put an end to these ultra British intrigues."[2] The pro-annexationists in the US government did not want it to appear that the United States was annexing Hawaii outright, so intelligence provided the middle road between conventional military conquest and overt diplomatic negotiations in order to accomplish foreign policy goals. In one of the troubling hypocrisies that has continued to burden US civil-intelligence relations, although Americans feared foreign intrigue in their country, the US government was guilty of its own intrigue in the affairs of a foreign state.

In January 1891, Kalākaua died in San Francisco while on a tour of the United States. His sister Lili'uokalani assumed the throne and immediately set about to restore the power of the monarchy and the rights of native Hawaiians by drafting a new constitution to replace the Bayonet Constitution. This attempt provided the pretext that pro-annexationists in Hawaii and their supporters in the US government needed.

The coup took place in January 1893, predominantly led by American residents of Hawaii. Stevens requested US Marines, who were part of the American naval contingent in Hawaii, to land in Honolulu under the guise of protecting US citizens and their property. Queen Lili'uokalani abdicated her throne, and the pro-annexationists declared a provisional government led by Sanford Dole, a cousin of Hawaiian Pineapple Company founder James Dole. Stevens immediately recognized Hawaii as a US protectorate. Both President Harrison and Secretary of State John W. Foster denied any official US involvement in the coup.[3] But Harrison had "discreetly encouraged white settlers in Hawaii to rebel against Queen Liliuokalani and when they did, Secretary of State Foster endorsed the landing of American troops at Honolulu to support them."[4] Foster also later publicly advocated for annexation of Hawaii.[5] The Harrison administration therefore relied on the plausible deniability that covert action offers to shield itself from culpability and criticism.

After Harrison lost the 1892 presidential election, he was succeeded by Grover Cleveland, who had supported free trade with Hawaii and the naval station at Pearl Harbor in his first administration but had opposed annexation. Within days of his second inauguration, he rescinded the treaty that would have annexed Hawaii and dispatched James Henderson Blount, an anti-annexationist who had recently retired from Congress, to Hawaii to investigate the coup.

The Blount Report alleged that "without the previous assurance of support from the American minister [Stevens] and the actual presence of United States troops no movement [i.e., coup] would have been attempted, and if attempted would have been a dismal failure resulting in the capture or death of the participants in a very short time."[6] In her abdication of power, Queen Lili'uokalani had also intimated that she would not have relinquished her crown without US involvement. She had to "yield to the superior force of the United States of America, whose minister plenipotentiary, his excellency John L. Stevens, has caused United States troops to be landed at Honolulu and declared that he would support the said Provisional Government."[7] Other palace insiders and pro-monarchists concurred that she would not have ceded power without the intervention of US troops.[8] Blount reached the damning conclusion that "but for" American intervention, the coup never would have taken place.[9]

The Blount Report convinced Cleveland that the proper course of action was to restore Queen Lili'uokalani to the throne. But the Queen rejected Cleveland's demand of amnesty for the members of the coup, and even then, Sanford Dole, the new president of the Republic of Hawaii, refused to relinquish power.[10] Cleveland decided to forward the Blount Report to Congress and let it deal with the whole mess.[11]

Senator George Frisbie Hoar, a vocal anti-imperialist who opposed the annexation of Hawaii, delivered a speech in which he called into question not Stevens's activities in support of the coup but Blount's mission to Hawaii. Hoar argued that the President had the power to appoint ambassadors, public ministers, consuls, and other official plenipotentiaries with the consent of the Senate; inferior officers created by Congress; and "a mere agent as a messenger, or spy, or a person to gather or convey information."[12] He charged Cleveland with blurring the first and third categories by secretly appointing Blount, who went to Hawaii on an information-gathering mission as an executive agent but then assumed the powers and responsibilities of an official diplomat once there by negotiating with both the former Queen of Hawaii and the provisional government.

Hoar, like other members of Congress before him, wrestled with the relationship between intelligence and diplomacy in the American constitutional system and US foreign relations. He claimed that an American spy "so appointed, could be in no sense an officer of the United States, would take no oath of office, could exercise no official function, and could do no act whatever which could have any binding force on the United States... merely because he has done it."[13] As a corollary, Hoar suggested that spies were also not entitled to the same protections as diplomatic officers. The CIA later established its own pattern of blending diplomacy and intelligence with its distinction between "official cover" officers, who work under the cover of an American diplomatic position and therefore have diplomatic immunity, and "non-official cover" operatives, who do not have any official ties to the American government and likewise do not have the same diplomatic protections.

Hoar found Blount's attempts to exercise power over the US military particularly galling. Blount, who was nicknamed "Paramount Blount" for the expansive authority he exercised in Hawaii, had ordered American troops back onto their ships.[14] Hoar recognized the right of the president to send "a private agent of his... on board a ship, or fleet, of another country, as a spy in

FIGURE 6.1 Senator George Frisbie Hoar: for US intelligence but against US intelligence officers. Library of Congress.

time of war, or to gather information in time of peace," but he did "not think the sending such spy to observe and report upon the conduct of high military and naval officers of this country should be encouraged."[15] Thus, he also carved out a distinctive sphere for foreign intelligence as opposed to intelligence operations that involved spying on Americans.

Hoar captured many of the contradictions afflicting American intelligence across the nineteenth century. While acknowledging the distinctiveness of and need for intelligence as an instrument of statecraft, he still exhibited a distaste for and distrust of the business of espionage. Consistent with the tradition of the Contingent Fund, he believed the President could appoint American citizens as amateur spies to work on behalf of the United States, but they were not a class of professional officers within the US government, which further undermined the professionalization of American intelligence.

Hoar's speech was part of his motion to refer the entire affair to the Senate Committee on Foreign Relations. The committee began an investigation chaired by Senator John Tyler Morgan, a former Confederate general, leader of the Ku Klux Klan, and ardent imperialist, and later published its findings. Against Blount's conclusions, the Morgan Report exculpated Stevens of any conspiracy to aid the coup. As a result of the impasse, Cleveland recognized the provisional government. The United States formally annexed Hawaii in 1898 under the expansionist presidency of William McKinley and in the middle of the Spanish-American War. During that war, and just as it had in Hawaii, intelligence served American expansionism as the United States launched an imperial adventure to seize the Philippines from Spain. The Spanish-American and Philippine-American Wars would also test the young military intelligence services of the War and Navy Departments.

The First Permanent US Intelligence Services

Following the Civil War, the US military professionalized at the expense of an independent American intelligence profession.[16] Military professionalization and industrialization were part of a global transformation in warfare beginning with the French Revolutionary and Napoleonic Wars. Industry assembled the tools of war for massive levies of troops, while new railroads could transport them quickly to the battlefield. Advancements in technology like the telegraph transformed the speed at which information and orders could be conveyed, allowing for centralized command of the battlefield. Military staffs composed of professionally educated and trained officers planned the movement and operations of massive armies equipped with the latest weaponry. War planning became a persistent, organized, systematic feature of national security.

Military intelligence assumed more urgency due to these changes, as it was needed for states to discover their adversaries' plans and to support their own military planning. Fundamentally, states incorporated intelligence organizations and functions into their military establishments not in recognition of a distinct intelligence profession and certainly not out of admiration for espionage, but simply on account of military necessity. In 1850, Austria led the way in establishing the first military intelligence service, the Evidenzbureau, followed by the Deuxième Bureau in France in 1871 and an intelligence branch called Sektion (or Abteilung) IIIb in Germany in 1889.[17] When the American military created its first permanent military intelligence organizations, the Navy's Office of Naval Intelligence (ONI) in 1882 and the Army's Military Information Division (MID) in 1885, it was acting on the same impulse driving European states to do so.[18]

ONI and MID suffered from neglect as small, new organizations. Both were chronically understaffed and underfunded. Without any hint of irony or concern for secrecy, on April 20, 1889, the *Army and Navy Journal* announced, "With four officers abroad collecting information, and a small corps of clerks at work under Mr. Peck, the Army Intelligence Bureau may be considered as practically established."[19] Not only was the private Pinkerton Detective Agency bigger than ONI and MID, but General James Weaver, who ran for President on the ticket of the newly formed Populist Party in 1892, warned that "the army of Pinkertons ... is greater by several thousand than the standing army of the United States."[20]

As a further blow to intelligence, ONI and MID became buried in the military bureaucracies of the Navy and War Departments. For example, the Navy Department immediately undermined the independence of the ONI by attaching it to the Bureau of Navigation, where it became an advocacy instrument for navalists.[21] Two of its early commanders departed in frustration after failing in their efforts to build up the fledgling service.[22] ONI also developed a rivalry with the equally young Naval War College in Newport, Rhode Island.[23] However, with the support of Secretary of the Navy Hilary Herbert and later Assistant Secretary of the Navy Theodore Roosevelt, ONI became a key contributor to the Navy's war planning. At least American officials acknowledged the value of intelligence, even if it was to be subordinated to military purposes.[24]

However, military officers viewed ONI and MID as something of a professional backwater and perhaps temporary punishment. Furthermore, they were not permanently assigned to ONI or MID, depriving each service of continuity in leadership and staffing. Without career military intelligence officers, the two organizations did not benefit from loyal, dedicated, and ranking officers to defend them within the larger military establishment. Intelligence was only one among many competing sub-bureaucracies of the Navy and War Departments during a period of tremendous change for the American military.

Indeed, bureaucratic competition quickly plagued MID. In October 1890, Congress enacted a law giving the Army Signal Corps control over the communication of military information via the telegraph and telephone. Notably, Congress emphasized that "the operations of said corps shall be confined to strictly military matters," perhaps anticipating the potential harm that wiretapping could inflict on civil liberties and constitutional rights.[25] But the act unwittingly exposed MID to a power grab within the Army.

In January 1892, Adolphus Washington Greely, the Chief Signal Officer, sent a letter to Secretary of War Stephen Benton Elkins in which he argued that the Signal Corps should control Army intelligence. He began by claiming that Congress's act of 1890 gave the Signal Corps exclusive responsibilities in the field of Army intelligence and declared that "the work of collecting military information is acknowledged in other Armies to be of the greatest importance, and it demands the attention of a permanent head, who should be held fully responsible for its efficient condition." Furthermore, he insisted that "the work . . . of summarizing military information from original sources shall be done by the officers of the Signal Corps."[26] In response, Elkins issued a memorandum in January in which he adopted Greely's position.[27]

This decision naturally riled the Adjutant General's Office, which oversaw MID. Adjutant General John C. Kelton countered that the "functions of the Signal Corps are clearly limited by section 2 of the act mentioned . . . to the collecting and transmitting of information by means of 'telegraphy or otherwise.'" Kelton pointedly noted that the "only legislation which expressly recognizes the existence of an 'Information Division' is found in the Army appropriation acts of 1888, 1889, 1890 and 1891, and the last named act . . . went into effect subsequent to the law reorganizing the Signal Corps." He also explained that MID was "not yet either in the scope of its work or in the rank and number of its personnel, abreast of the sections of the general staff of foreign countries known as 'Intelligence Departments.'"[28] Congress was assigning intelligence functions and responsibilities to different organizations while MID was still on unsteady ground both in terms of legislation and resources, demonstrating how disorganized and fractured the American government was with respect to developing a coherent intelligence system.

Fortunately, General John Schofield, the Commanding General of the Army, offered his own rebuttal to the Signal Corps. He explained that the "Adjutant General's Department [was] the only staff department whose duties relate[d] to *all* branches of the military service" and stated that it helped him "in digesting information." He decided the Adjutant General was "of necessity the custodian of all the military information which is important in the operations of an army" and ordered that all information gathered across the Army should be preserved in that office and presented to him from there. At the same time, he added that it was "superfluous to organize another intelligence department." Finally, with respect to staffing, he advised that "the officers detailed for temporary service abroad for the purpose of collecting information should be chosen from among the most enterprising and intelligent of all departments of the Army." Schofield understood the need for a competent military intelligence service, apart from the more distinct functional role of the Signal Corps. However, he also implied that military intelligence was a temporary duty for professional military officers, thereby undermining the concept of professional military intelligence officers.[29]

MID managed to survive the Signal Corps's offensive. In March 1892, General Orders No. 23 reaffirmed the place of MID in the Adjutant General's Office with its responsibility for the "collection and classification of military information of our own and foreign countries."[30] Even if ONI and MID existed precariously within large government departments rife with bureaucratic competition, their work would illustrate how some intelligence was better than no intelligence when the country went to war with Spain in 1898.

Intelligence and the American Empire

Unlike in previous conflicts, the United States did not need to create intelligence organizations from scratch when it went to war with Spain. As standing services in peacetime, MID and ONI were able to compile information even before the onset of hostilities. By 1892, MID "had turned its full attention on Cuba" and was assembling reports and information of military value, including maps of railway systems, the locations of defensive positions, and notes on the sentiments of the Cuban people.[31] Under the stewardship of Richard Wainwright from 1896 to 1897, ONI's "principal planning effort was directed at possible conflict with Spain."[32] A year later, Wainwright would find himself on the *Maine* when it exploded in Havana harbor, precipitating the Spanish-American War.

By this point, both ONI and MID were making extensive use of the military attaché system for intelligence collection. Naval attachés in London, Paris, Berlin, and Italy established extensive spy networks that provided intelligence on Spanish diplomatic and military activities in Europe.[33] MID provided maps of Cuba and Puerto Rico to the Army and intelligence liaisons to Cuban revolutionaries fighting the Spanish while also exploiting information from the military attaché in Madrid on the movements of the Spanish army.[34] The Signal Corps did its part by intercepting communications through telegraph lines both in the United States and abroad.[35]

But the United States still faced some of the same problems that it had encountered during the Civil War in the coordination, dissemination, and exploitation of intelligence. There were problems with professionalism as well. Many ONI agents provided nothing better than what they "gleaned from newspaper clippings, rumors, and casual conversations." Still others failed to provide any intelligence but nonetheless charged the Navy "for imaginary spy trips."[36] Importantly, ONI and MID were military intelligence services, so their limitations in intelligence often reflected the shortcomings of the American military.

Ironically, anti-imperialism helped rally the American people around the flag during the Spanish-American War. In fact, the United States adopted the cause of Cuban independence when it went to war with Spain. But the geographical and political ground shifted when the United States sent an expeditionary force to the Spanish colony of the Philippines. At the end of the war, Spain granted Cuba its independence and ceded Guam and Puerto Rico to the United States. The McKinley administration demanded the Philippines as well. Spain relented for the price of $20 million and signed the Treaty of Paris, ending the Spanish-American War.

The idea of American imperialism was fiercely contested in the United States. The American Anti-Imperialist League, whose membership included Andrew Carnegie, Mark Twain, and Grover Cleveland, opposed the annexation of the Philippines. Senator Hoar inveighed against the proposal in Congress. But an increasing number of influential politicians and prominent citizens viewed imperialism as a measure of American power and key arena of competition with Europe. In the end, the Senate ratified the Treaty of Paris, and the United States officially became an empire. For its part, the Philippines declared its independence while the United States and Spain were still fighting. Neither power recognized Philippine independence, while the Philippine government, led by Emilio Aguinaldo, did not recognize the Treaty of Paris. In the end, the United States and the new Philippine Republic went to war.

The United States had transformed from a republic fighting an empire to an empire fighting a republic. From the start, its efforts in the Philippines were hampered by insufficient intelligence. Although the American expeditionary force quickly overwhelmed the conventional Philippine military, US forces lacked maps, knowledge of the local language and culture, and other basic information to assist their military operations. The campaign bogged down as the Filipinos turned to guerrilla tactics that exposed American weaknesses in intelligence. Over the course of a bloody counterinsurgency, the "Filipino flair for counterintelligence and the American appetite for information combined to create an advanced form of military espionage that fused combat intelligence and political surveillance," historian Alfred McCoy observed.[37]

A small but influential corps of US military officers cut their teeth during the conflict. Among them was Ralph Van Deman. A graduate of Harvard and then medical school, Van Deman became an infantry officer before landing at MID, where he spent a few uneventful years until transferring to the

Philippines. His formative experience there led him to become the "father of U.S. military intelligence," the epithet by which Van Deman is commonly known today.[38]

Van Deman recorded that the military governor, General Arthur MacArthur, tasked him with organizing a Military Information Division of the Philippines.[39] He required each of the 450 information posts on the Philippine Islands to supply his division with a sketch of the territory surrounding the post and a description of any important Filipinos in the vicinity.[40] Beyond compiling information, the Military Information Division of the Philippines ran spies and conducted human intelligence operations. Van Deman claimed that "undercover agents" of MID-Philippines discovered a plot to attack Manila and assassinate key military officers in the city.[41] Under Van Deman, American colonial intelligence operations did not constrain themselves to the battlefield but also infiltrated deep into Philippine domestic politics and civil society to root out insurgents and subversives. He expanded the practice of keeping index cards with information on as many influential Filipinos as he could. Van Deman became so obsessed with keeping files on people that, as a retired major general in 1952, he had records on a quarter million suspected communists in the United States. Aside from MID-Philippines, the Philippines Constabulary combined police, military, and paramilitary functions, employing both Americans and Filipinos in a massive surveillance apparatus that relied as much on political intelligence and coercion as overt force to pacify the Philippines.[42]

American forces also revived a particularly ugly method of interrogation that the Spanish had first brought to the Philippines. The "water cure" involved repeatedly forcing water into a prisoner's mouth until the interrogators received the information they sought or a confession. Eyewitness reports of this technique shocked American audiences and led to investigations in Congress by the Committee on the Philippines.[43] In response to the outrage, several US officers were court-martialed. In reviewing one case, US Army Judge Advocate General George B. Davis asserted, "No modern state, which is a party to international law, can sanction, either expressly or by a silence which imports consent, a resort to torture with a view to obtain confessions."[44] Even so, the Philippine-American War was not the last time American intelligence officers would use the "water cure."

If the United States was going to apply what it learned about intelligence in the Philippines—for better or worse—it would have to wait for an even larger war. In the meantime, the writings of one of the Army's leading thinkers and the Navy and War Department's treatment of their military intelligence services suggested the country had failed to absorb some of the key lessons of the recent wars.

The First Manual on Military Intelligence

Arthur Lockwood Wagner's experience at West Point made him an unlikely candidate for a serious military reformer and thinker. Wagner finished near the bottom of his class while managing to rack up 731 demerits.[45] Yet, he went on to become a military educator, prolific writer, and chief of MID. In 1893, Wagner wrote *The Service of Security and Information* as an instructor at the Infantry and Cavalry School in Fort Leavenworth, Kansas. Wagner republished his manual on military intelligence in 1903 following his service in both the Spanish-American and Philippine-American Wars.

By way of introduction to the topic, Wagner instructed his audience, "Information in regard to the enemy is the indispensable basis of all military plans," adding that it was by then common practice for states to have a "bureau of military intelligence at the headquarters of the army" responsible for this information.[46] If intelligence was indispensable in war, then so were spies.

Wagner distinguished between two classes of spies, military and civilian, claiming that the first category "consists of officers or soldiers, who from patriotism or a sense of military duty, assume a disguise, and penetrate the enemy's lines to gain information." In fact, he declared that military spies "are often men of the most exalted character and distinguished courage, and deserve a better fame, and a better fate if captured, than that usually accorded to spies," citing both Nathan Hale and John André as examples.[47] Perhaps because the military had embraced intelligence in the form of ONI and MID, the practice of using military spies was no longer quite as dishonorable as it had been in earlier eras.

Civilian spies were a different matter. These spies "often deserve all the obloquy so freely cast upon spies in general," although Wagner excused those "actuated solely by motives of disinterested patriotism." Still, he determined that "whatever may be their motives or individual characteristics, spies are indispensably necessary to a general; and, other things equal, that commander will be victorious who has the best secret service."[48] He, like others, viewed espionage as a necessary evil, but he felt compelled to distinguish the "good" spies from the "bad" ones.

Wagner also identified a few characteristics of intelligence professionals that he found difficult to balance against the ignoble nature of the occupation: "A spy should be intelligent, conscientious, and faithful—qualities hard to find in a man whose very occupation bespeaks habitual deceit and a want of principle." In the same vein, he believed that the "services of a spy permanently attached to a command are likely to be much more valuable than those of one who is employed only for the single occasion."[49] The United States had ample evidence—from Benjamin Tallmadge and the Culper spy ring in the Revolutionary War to George Sharpe and the BMI in the Civil War—that established spymasters and spy networks were far better than fly-by-night operatives and operations. Nevertheless, the United States still lacked professional intelligence officers and organizations.

In discussing how a leader must manage the "secret service of an army," Wagner described the ideal figure as "a peculiar combination of detective and general." He stressed that "it is not sufficient that he should be a detective alone," mentioning that the "chief of McClellan's secret service," Allan Pinkerton, had failed to provide McClellan with accurate intelligence.[50] Notably, Wagner was only able to describe an intelligence professional by referencing two other professions since an independent intelligence profession was difficult to imagine, even for a reformer like Wagner.

If Wagner's manual advanced the field of military intelligence, it nevertheless impeded the professionalization of intelligence. Wagner covered a remarkable range of issues pertaining to intelligence, from double agents ("double spies") and counterintelligence ("Guarding against hostile spies") to signals intelligence ("Use of the telegraph") and open-source intelligence ("Newspaper correspondents 'the plague of modern armies'"). However, much of his book focused on tactical intelligence missions, like scouting and reconnaissance, which were already well established in conventional military doctrine. Even his republished manual made few references to advances made in intelligence in the Spanish-American and Philippine-American Wars. Wagner instead insisted in his preface that these experiences "evolved nothing radically new on the subject herein treated, [although] they have afforded some valuable illustrations of the application of old principles to new conditions."[51]

Intelligence Between War and Peace

In 1893, the same year Wagner first published his manual on military intelligence, MID chief John B. Babcock wrote a memorandum stating that his organization did not have adequate resources or staff. He also claimed that it was "impossible to conceive of any contingency arising which would necessitate the transportation of an army from our shores to wage war in the interior of Europe."[52] His assessment proved fatally flawed when the United States entered the First World War a little over two decades later. In the interim, the transition from the nineteenth century to the twentieth also proved to be a perilous time for American intelligence.

In 1899, Congress finally formally recognized the Office of Naval Intelligence, assigning to it a permanent civil service staff.[53] However, in a letter to the Chief of the Bureau of Navigation, which oversaw ONI, Chief Intelligence Officer Richardson Clover protested this change in ONI's workforce.[54] Clover acknowledged that before congressional recognition, "the existence of [ONI] has heretofore been precarious," but he preferred and even insisted on the use of military "Staff Intelligence Officers" over civilians.[55] The mix of professional naval officers and civilian clerks continued to produce conflicts within the organization that ultimately led to a reduction in its staff.[56]

The Navy did not provide ONI with the necessary room to grow, figuratively or literally. In March 1900, Clover's successor, Captain Charles D. Sigsbee, wrote to the Chief of the Bureau of Navigation grumbling that ONI did not have sufficient space in the building it shared with other components of the Navy and War Departments in Washington, DC.[57] The Navy Department also wrestled with where intelligence fit within the larger naval bureaucracy. In 1909, it suddenly moved ONI from the Bureau of Navigation to the Office of the Aid for Operations and changed the title of ONI's leader from the "chief intelligence officer" to the "director of naval intelligence."[58] Constant changes and stressors deprived ONI of stability and strength, sapping the morale of its staff.[59]

Around the same time, the War Department and the Army underwent organizational reform under the stewardship of Secretary of War Elihu Root. Like ONI's role in the Navy, MID would purportedly help the Army with war planning. The War Department created a General Staff and moved intelligence out of the Adjutant General's Office to the Office of the Chief of Staff.[60] The reorganization created new intraorganizational conflicts that impacted intelligence. MID continued to receive its own funds through congressional appropriations, which complicated its incorporation into the General Staff.[61] MID was also caught in the bureaucratic struggle between the Chief of Staff and the Adjutant General. A War Department General Order in 1907 mandated that all official Army correspondence pass through the Adjutant General's Office, which had the effect of impeding the transfer of military information from officers in the field to MID and risked the secrecy of MID operations.[62]

Having survived the Signal Corps's attempt to swallow it in 1892, MID again fought for its independence beginning in 1907 when the Third (War College) Division of the General Staff tried to incorporate MID into its ranks, initially under the simple pretext of sharing the same building in Washington, DC.[63] MID lost the battle in 1908 when the War Department reshuffled.[64] Another reorganization in 1910 placed the collection and distribution of military information in the War College Division, effectively burying Army intelligence deep within the War Department bureaucracy. Like ONI, MID found itself suffering from low morale.[65]

One salutary development in military intelligence during this period was an effort to coordinate the work of ONI and MID. In 1890, the Ordnance Department of the War Department wrote to the Chief Intelligence Officer of ONI requesting that ONI share any relevant information on foreign countries it collected.[66] In 1902, the Adjutant General reported that, by mutual agreement between MID and ONI, there would be a "system of exchange of information whereby professional data received in one office, which is of interest or value to the other, is promptly furnished for notation and carding," adding that the "Chief Intelligence Officer of the Navy has always been ready to cooperate heartily with this division."[67] The cooperative spirit seemed to spread. A memorandum for the Chief of Staff of the War Department in 1913 remarked that "relations with the State Department and the Navy Department... are extremely cordial and quite intimate. The State Department sends to this division all information that seems to be of value.... In the same way monographs prepared by the Navy and other information received by it is sent here, and the same are reciprocated."[68]

The role of the State Department in this intelligence-sharing arrangement might have disappointed John W. Foster, who had denied complicity in the coup in Hawaii even though he likely encouraged it as Secretary of State in the Harrison administration. In 1906, Foster reflected on the history of American diplomacy and expressed hope for its future—a future without the stain of intelligence. He noted that ever since its independence, "the standard of diplomacy was very low" for the United States, and "even in time of peace it did not hesitate to make use of bribery, espionage, and deliberate deceit." These problems reflected a longer pattern of mixing intelligence and diplomacy as a product of the Contingent Fund. But as the country entered a new century Foster perceived a shift and declared, "No self-respecting government to-day would countenance such practices in its foreign intercourse.... It is a matter of just pride to every citizen of the United States that his government and its representatives abroad have done their full share in purifying diplomacy and making it stand for the best ideals of mankind."[69] Like Babcock's sorely misplaced assumption that US troops would not fight a war in Europe, events would soon prove Foster wrong.

American intelligence at the end of the nineteenth century foreshadowed some of the controversies and scandals that would cast a shadow over the twentieth century. In Hawaii, the executive branch used covert action to bring about the fall of a foreign, popular government and its replacement with a pro-US puppet government. Intelligence can serve the cause of liberty or oppression, and it would continue to tilt the scales one way or the other throughout the twentieth century. But intelligence itself remained overshadowed in the US national security establishment. The State Department continued the tradition of the diplomat-spy, exploiting the constitutional penumbra it created to evade congressional oversight, though not congressional debate. The Navy and War Departments created small military intelligence services embedded in larger offices and bureaus that all experienced retrenchment and reshuffling during a period marked by military reform. Despite promising signs of cooperation, there were also portentous signs of competition as the US government began to grapple with the challenges of coordinating and controlling the activities of an expanding intelligence establishment.

7

The Blurry Blue Line

DOMESTIC INTELLIGENCE AND THE ORIGINS OF THE FBI

THE STATE, WAR, and Navy Departments, representing the diplomatic and military institutions, had successfully subordinated intelligence. One major institution of national security was still missing: law enforcement. Although the Navy and War Departments created the first permanent American intelligence services with ONI and MID, the Treasury Department also had its own "secret service." At the end of the Civil War, it established a law enforcement organization to investigate counterfeiting and financial crimes. However, the Secret Service soon began to mix its law enforcement responsibilities with domestic intelligence functions.

When the United States went to war against Spain, the American people responded with their typical bellicosity. Spy mania created a fertile environment for domestic intelligence to operate without much regard for constitutional protections. Worse yet, President Theodore Roosevelt subsequently used the Secret Service to spy on Congress. Once again, intelligence was wrapped up in politics and ideology, leading to congressional investigations and debate. As an outgrowth of the scandal, the Department of Justice (DOJ) created a Bureau of Investigation, known today as the Federal Bureau of Investigation (FBI). Even though Congress and the American people opposed a domestic "spy system," the Bureau of Investigation followed the Secret Service's path of blurring law enforcement and intelligence, setting the conditions for more controversies and competition to come.

Lincoln's Last Order

According to popular folklore, Abraham Lincoln approved the establishment of the United States Secret Service on April 14, 1865.[1] It was an inauspicious start for an agency that would eventually assume responsibility for protecting

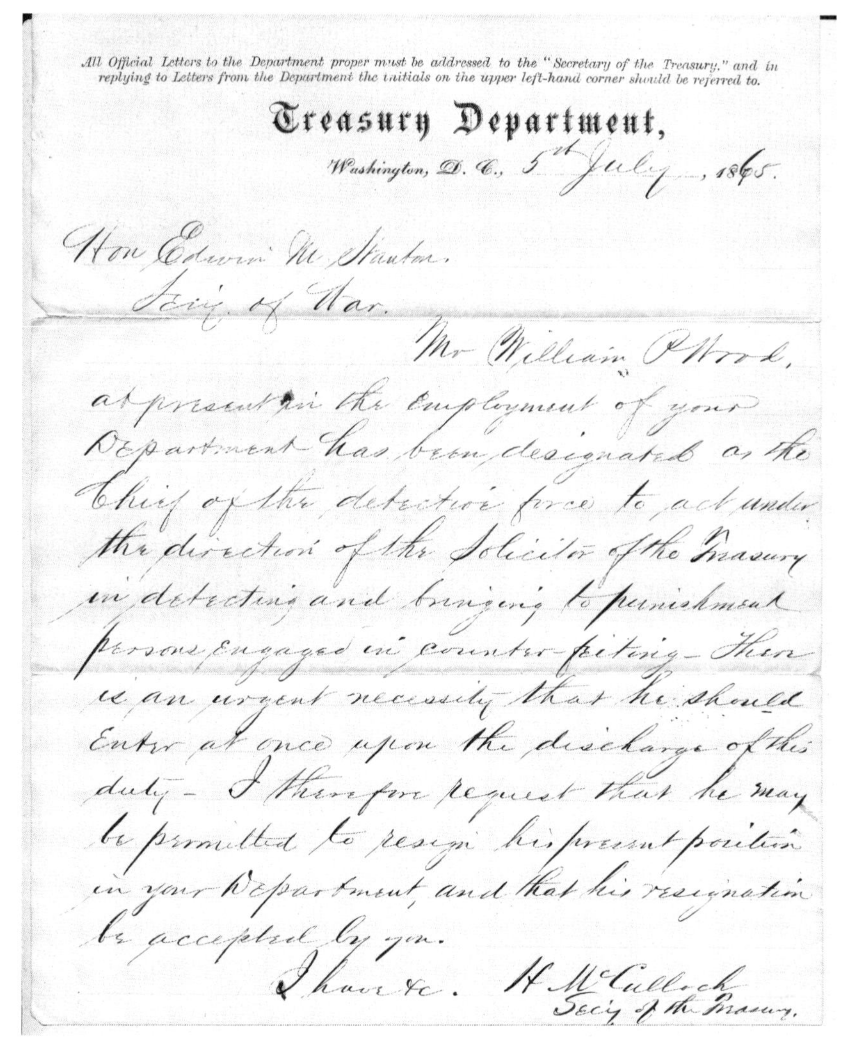

All Official Letters to the Department proper must be addressed to the "Secretary of the Treasury," and in replying to Letters from the Department the initials on the upper left-hand corner should be referred to.

Treasury Department,

Washington, D. C., 5th July, 1865.

Hon Edwin M Stanton.
Secy of War.

Mr William P Wood,
at present in the employment of your Department has been designated as the Chief of the detective force to act under the direction of the Solicitor of the Treasury in detecting and bringing to punishment persons engaged in counter-feiting— There is an urgent necessity that he should enter at once upon the discharge of this duty— I therefore request that he may be permitted to resign his present position in your Department, and that his resignation be accepted by you.

I have &c. H McCulloch
Secy of the Treasury.

FIGURE 7.1 This July 5, 1865, letter from Hugh McCulloch to Edwin Stanton created the US Secret Service. The letter mentions nothing about domestic intelligence. National Archives and Records Administration.

the President because John Wilkes Booth shot Lincoln at Ford's Theatre that same evening. The formal creation of the Secret Service would have to wait until July 5, when Edward Jordan, the solicitor of the Treasury, appointed William P. Wood the Chief of the United States Secret Service Division.[2] A letter by Secretary of the Treasury Hugh McCulloch to Secretary of War Edwin Stanton explicitly stated that the purpose of the service was to find and punish "persons engaged in counterfeiting," a significant challenge the United States faced during and after the Civil War.[3] However, the Secret Service adopted other functions in subsequent years, going well beyond investigating financial crimes.

Like ONI and MID at their inception, the Secret Service lacked a legislative charter that would guide its activities and set its boundaries. Since it had no statutory authority giving it police powers, its agents were unable to act as normal police officers in obtaining search warrants or making arrests, "thereby relegating the new government detectives to the role of informants." Furthermore, the first crop of Secret Service agents was a mixed bag: About a third of the force was made up of former police officers or detectives with unremarkable or even disreputable records, while up to half of the early recruits had criminal backgrounds. These "operatives," as Wood called his agents, circumvented the organization's restrictions on police powers by employing the "citizen's arrest" and using shady methods that created an unfavorable public impression of the young Secret Service.[4]

In 1869, Hiram C. Whitley, a spy and detective during the Civil War, replaced Wood as Chief of the Secret Service. Whitley initiated a series of sweeping reforms and amended Wood's earlier handbook of instructions to guide the conduct of the Secret Service and its agents.[5] This *Circular of Instructions to Operatives* blurred intelligence and law enforcement functions. Whitley emphasized that the job required secrecy and at times deception, including the need to "assume a variety of characters." He also expanded the role of the Secret Service beyond counterfeiting and Treasury crimes to include all crimes falling under the purview of the Department of Justice.[6] For example, under his leadership, the Secret Service waged a campaign to arrest members of the Ku Klux Klan.[7]

Just as the Secret Service was finding its footing, Whitley, Assistant Chief Ichabod Crane Nettleship, and a few Secret Service agents were implicated in a corruption scandal.[8] President Ulysses S. Grant changed the leadership of the Treasury Department in response, and the new Secretary of the Treasury, Benjamin Bristow, ordered his solicitor, Bluford Wilson, to investigate the Secret Service. Wilson issued a long report, which delved into the organization of the Secret Service, its funding, and its mission. Wilson acknowledged that the "employment of such a detective force is not now, and never has been expressly authorized by any act of Congress." He identified several congressional appropriations related to anti-counterfeiting, implying that if there was any congressional mandate for the Secret Service's activities, it was limited to the anti-counterfeiting mission. Wilson also took the opportunity to comment, "Upon principle I am radically opposed to any organized system of espionage in connection with our . . . government," implying the Secret Service was acting more like a domestic intelligence service than an anti-counterfeiting law enforcement organization.[9]

In a follow-up report, Wilson recommended that the Secret Service focus on "detecting and preventing counterfeiting and other frauds on the government."[10] But the Secret Service succumbed to "mission creep." In 1879, Assistant Secretary of the Treasury H. F. French authorized disbursements to Secret Service agents "for any services which have been performed or may be hereafter performed under the direction of the chief of the Secret Service Division," specifically stating that these could be "cases other than the ordinary purpose of suppressing counterfeiting and illegal coinage."[11]

In 1894, the Secret Service uncovered a threat against President Grover Cleveland from Colorado gamblers. At that point, the Secret Service unilaterally extended its responsibilities to include protecting the President.[12] That same year, it expanded its role in presidential security in response to the arrival in Washington of members of Coxey's Army, a group of disgruntled, unemployed workers who also had made threats against Cleveland. The Secret Service refined its ability to conduct surveillance of individuals and groups that threatened the President and deployed these skills during the Spanish-American War.[13]

Taking the Lead During the Spanish-American War

When John E. Wilkie, the Chief of the Secret Service, summarized his organization's work during the Spanish-American War, he began by reassuring his fellow Americans that there "was nothing spectacular about the work... for there were wholly lacking the military features which the public so generally associated with that branch of the Government's service."[14] Instead, Wilkie described counterintelligence operations conducted by an "auxiliary secret service force" of Americans who spoke Spanish and had lived in South America, Spain, or Cuba.[15]

One of the Secret Service's notable successes during the war was uncovering the "Montreal Spy Ring." The Spanish government used Canada as a staging ground for espionage operations in the United States. The Secret Service identified Ramon de Carranza, a former naval attaché to the United States, as Spain's spymaster in Canada. In one operation, Secret Service agents shadowed a man who met with Carranza in Toronto, entered the United States, visited the Navy Department in Washington, and then attempted to mail a letter back to Canada. Wilkie's men intercepted and decoded the letter. The Secret Service agents, supposedly led by Wilkie himself, arrested George Downing, who later hanged himself in jail.[16]

The real bombshell exploded when a Secret Service agent gained entry to Carranza's residence in Montreal under the pretense of looking to rent it after Carranza's lease ended. The agent stole a letter addressed from Carranza to Don José Gomez Ymay, a Spanish admiral, that became known as the Carranza Letter. The US government sent a photograph of the letter to the British, and the *New York Herald* published a translation of it on June 5, 1898, in an article titled "Carranza Letter Gives Proof of His Spy System." Aside from confirming that Carranza had organized a spy network in North America, the letter revealed crucial military and economic information about Spain's war effort. Carranza maintained his innocence, but the British government forced him to leave Canada.[17]

The Secret Service "owed its success in part to a calculated willingness to overlook Constitutional and legal niceties."[18] Among other offenses to American laws and values, the Secret Service intercepted US mail and arrested and detained individuals without charge.[19] By Wilkie's own admission, the Secret Service watched more than six hundred "suspects" in the United States during the war. They "were professors, diplomats, doctors, merchants, cigarmakers, marines, electrical experts, government employés of foreign birth and uncertain antecedents, capitalists, milliners, dress-makers, society women and servants." Often individuals across this broad spectrum of society were surveilled on the basis of letters reporting rumors and suspicions.[20]

As in the Revolutionary War and Civil War, members of the public turned their fellow Americans over to the government for surveillance. People in places as far away as Denver, Colorado, wrote to their congressmen, the Secret Service, Chief Wilkie, and President McKinley himself to convey their suspicions. Some letters included pictures of the accused. An anonymous tipster claiming to be a Spaniard from Grand Rapids, Michigan, warned, "Place no weight in statements emanating from the Catholic church; trust no Spanish priest or sister of mercy." A letter sent from Montreal and signed by "A HATER OF SPANISH TYRANNY IN CUBA" claimed that a W. F. B. Henry was the "head of the Spanish Spy System at present operating in the States [and] he needs very careful watching." Another letter warned that Allan Pinkerton's son Robert had been employed by Spain and was a counterintelligence threat to the United States because he could acquire information through his brother William, who was working for the Secret Service during the war. The New York *World* even printed a picture purporting to illustrate a Spanish spy, including the tools of the espionage trade, so that readers could identify operatives like him in their midst.[21]

Around the same time, the *Indianapolis News* ran an exposé of Wilkie and the role of the Secret Service in the war. It alerted the public to the shift in the

THE WORLD: SUNDAY, MAY 8, 1898.

Z, TYPE OF SPANISH SP

THIS WORLD PICTURE WAS IMMEDIATELY RECOGNIZED BY THE CUBAN JUNTA AS A FAITHFUL REPRODUCTION OF THE SINISTER COUNTENANCE OF MATIAS FERNANDEZ.

SEVERAL members of the Cuban Junta in a critical examination of this portrait declared it to be a perfect likeness of Matias Fernandez, who is registered in the books at the Cuban headquarters as one of the most dangerous and expert spies in the employ of the Spanish Government. For years here and in Havana Fernandez has successfully pursued his occupation. But at length he became too well known to be useful to the Spanish Government and finally received a delicately suggestive request from the Junta to try a change of air. Until the outbreak of the war he was indistinctly reported from Mexico and later from Nashville.

Within the last two weeks he has been seen in this city again, and the Junta wonders what he has in view.

FIGURE 7.2 A newspaper depiction of "the sinister countenance of Matias Fernandez," who was "one of the most dangerous and expert spies in the employ of the Spanish Government." Included in the illustration are the tools of the trade. National Archives and Records Administration.

Secret Service's mission occasioned by the war, explaining, "During times of peace the secret service is engaged in looking after criminals who take to counterfeiting for a living.... But the demands of war lend additional bite to the spicy quality of the service." As for the Secret Service agents themselves, the article prosaically acknowledged that "they are spies" and "many people are prone to look down on them." However, the article insisted, "It must be considered that spies in time of war are absolutely necessary." Thus, an entrenched pattern of American civil-intelligence relations reflecting shifting attitudes toward intelligence in war and peace continued, and while the Spanish-American War temporarily saved the Secret Service from scandal, the end of the war once again exposed it to public scrutiny.[22]

The Not-So-Secret Service

The Secret Service had exploited its lack of a congressional mandate to undertake activities well outside its original mission. The assassination of President

William McKinley by anarchist Leon Czolgosz in 1901 revealed not only its failure to protect the President but also its violation of congressional appropriations that had limited the organization to anti-counterfeiting investigations.[23] However, McKinley's assassination raised public awareness of the issue of presidential security and had the paradoxical effect of giving the Secret Service an even greater stake in that task. The Secret Service also expanded its investigations, instituting a practice of maintaining lists of possible threats.[24] Particularly contentious was the Secret Service's practice of loaning its agents to other executive departments for their own investigations. These many self-appointed roles and responsibilities finally drew congressional scrutiny.

Senator George Frisbie Hoar proposed a bill that would give the Secretary of War and the military the responsibility for protecting the President. Senator Edmund Pettus, a former Confederate and leader of the Ku Klux Klan, supported Hoar's position, arguing that a "secret service is not composed of the kind of men to whom ought to be intrusted such an important duty."[25] Like Hoar, Pettus believed the military, not spies, should guard the President. But other senators quickly denounced Hoar's proposal for a modern Praetorian Guard as incompatible with American principles.[26] The Hoar legislation and subsequent versions of the bill failed to make it through Congress. The appropriations bill for 1907 amended the Secret Service's responsibilities to include protecting the President of the United States. In the interim, the Secret Service continued to protect McKinley's successor while also performing some questionable activities for him.

The Secret Service became caught up in an interbranch dispute between President Theodore Roosevelt and Congress that would shape the future of federal law enforcement and domestic intelligence in the United States. Roosevelt was President in the middle of the Progressive Era. He professionalized, expanded, and empowered the civil service as part of a broader movement toward creating an American administrative state.[27] He increasingly came into conflict with his own Republican Congress over his reformist policies, which effectively increased the power of the President vis-à-vis Congress.[28] The Secret Service entered the fray when it loaned agents to the Departments of the Interior and Justice to investigate public land fraud, resulting in the arrests of many Republicans, including members of Congress.[29] A rumor began circulating that Roosevelt had deliberately turned the Secret Service and its surveillance powers on members of Congress, which Roosevelt himself seemed to confirm.[30]

On January 3, 1904, a story in the *Chicago Inter Ocean* raised questions about the recent politicized activities of the Secret Service. Comparing Wilkie to Joseph Fouché, the notorious head of the French police during the Revolutionary and Napoleonic eras, the paper commented that Wilkie and the Secret Service were "desirous of doing the secret detective work for the whole government and [were] not particular about drawing the line between lawmakers and lawbreakers." According to the article, Congress expressed "an utter abhorrence [to] such a scheme," deeming it "absolutely contradictory to the democratic principles of government." Moreover, the Secret Service was not the product of congressional action and was being used as a weapon against members of Congress "with a view to involving them in scandals that would enable the bureau to dictate to them as the price of silence." In response to the scandal, Congress set out to determine if public funds had "been used to build up a general secret-service system and create a Fouche in the Federal government."[31]

Roosevelt later claimed that the author of the article in the *Inter Ocean* was L. W. Busbey, the private secretary to the Speaker of the House. He denounced the piece as an "utterly unwarranted attack on the Secret Service... and its chief."[32] It appears that Roosevelt used the Secret Service to determine the origins of the *Inter Ocean* article, illustrating that it investigated not only politicians but also the press on the President's behalf.[33]

The *Evening Star* echoed the *Inter Ocean*'s report with a series of articles on the Secret Service in the spring of 1908. On April 21, the *Star* covered the Secret Service's custom of loaning its agents to other executive departments for investigative work. The article claimed that aside from flouting the congressional appropriations that limited the Secret Service to anti-counterfeiting and presidential protection duties, the organization was also collecting an extraordinary amount of information on public and private citizens, "whether of an official, personal, social, or scandalous nature." In one instance it loaned an agent to the Navy Department to gather evidence later used in a "sensational divorce case."[34]

The next day, the *Star* printed a story bearing the headline "Espionage Exists" and warning in its subtitle, "Spy System Invades Privacy of Citizens." This article drew a contrast between domestic intelligence and law enforcement. The paper quoted Representative Walter Smith, who highlighted "the hostility on the part of Congress to the spy system" and American opposition to the idea "that a general system of espionage is being conducted by the general government." Smith also endeavored to distinguish between the authorities Congress granted to the Secret Service versus the functions it adopted on its own and "the abuse of this spy system."[35]

Representative Joseph Swagar Sherley took a principled stand on the issue that also emphasized distinctions between law enforcement and domestic intelligence: "It does not strike some of us as being in accord with American ideas of government to undertake, by a system of spying on men and prying into what ordinarily would be designated as their private affairs, to determine whether or not a crime has been committed and to make the efficiency of a department dependent, not so much upon the presentation in an orderly and legal way of a case properly brought as upon the 'nosing' of the secret service men." Sherley worried that there was "a growing tendency to look upon the employment of special agents whose chief attribute is their ability to spy."[36] It was very clear Congress did not want the Secret Service performing a domestic intelligence role on either legislative or ideological grounds.

Congress debated the future of the Secret Service on the floor of the House on May 1, 1908. Sherley framed the discussion around the "pronounced abuses growing out of the use of the Secret Service for purposes other than those intended."[37] Representative Michael Driscoll worried about similar organizations sprouting up across the executive branch, arguing that "there should not be a secret-service bureau in each Department, any more than there should be a Government printing office in each Department," and supporting the existing arrangement of detailing agents from the Secret Service to other departments as needed.[38] Representative James Tawney countered by questioning whether it was "necessary for [the United States] to maintain a permanent secret-service organization in the various Executive Departments of the Government."[39]

The scandal marked Congress's first attempt to assert intelligence oversight in the twentieth century. Wilkie tried to head off additional congressional intervention by sending a letter to the chairman of the Committee on Appropriations on May 5, 1908.[40] But Congress acted on its intentions and stipulated in a sundry civil appropriations bill it passed on May 27 that the Secret Service could no longer loan its agents to other executive departments.[41] As an unintended consequence, Congress inadvertently encouraged the proliferation of domestic intelligence organizations and activities throughout the executive branch, which would generate bureaucratic competition and further impede intelligence coordination and professionalization.

For his part, Roosevelt did not allay the concerns of Congress or the press regarding Secret Service overreach. In his annual message to Congress on December 8, 1908, he remarked that the motivation behind congressional action was "that the Congressmen did not themselves wish to be investigated by Secret Service men."[42] In interviews with the press, Roosevelt also intimated that "reports of secret service men on Congressmen would prove interesting reading."[43]

Days later, a headline in the *New York Times* announced, "Roosevelt to Tell Congress's Secrets." The article promised that the resulting "political slaughter" would be "appalling." Continuing the combative language, the article declared that the President was "supplied with ample ammunition for the assault... He has gathered a vast amount of interesting information concerning Congressmen from the Secret Service, whose work... has given it opportunity to unearth a considerable number of nuggets in the rich political field of exploitation."[44] But in his official correspondence with Congress, Roosevelt high-mindedly proclaimed, "To use the Secret Service in the investigation of purely private or political matters would be a gross abuse."[45] From the President's perspective, no public servant was above the law; from Congress's perspective, the President was turning an executive domestic security service against the US legislature for political purposes.

Representative Sherley remarked that in his "reading of history," he could "recall no instance where a government perished because of the absence of a secret-service force, but many there [were] that perished as a result of the spy system." Appealing to American principles, he declared, "If Anglo-Saxon civilization stands for anything, it is for a government where the humblest citizen is safeguarded against the secret activities of the executive of the government."[46] Representative John Fitzgerald added, "It has never been the policy to establish a central police or spy system in the Federal Government."[47] The Senate Committee on Appropriations concurred in February, asserting, "It has never been the intention of any Congress to build up a spy system of that character."[48] Representative Smith attempted to capture the common spirit of Congress when he submitted, "We ought all to be able to agree that some detective force is necessary in the enforcement of the criminal laws; and that... in a free country, no general system of spying upon and espionage of the people... should be allowed."[49] Of course, the Secret Service had been doing both.

On January 27, 1909, Wilkie testified before Congress. He and Sherley debated at length the power of the Secret Service to investigate crime as a law enforcement function versus conduct surveillance consistent with domestic intelligence. In one key exchange, Sherley questioned Wilkie on his previous assertion that the Secret Service "had never engaged in the collection of information except in the solution of some particular case of alleged crime." Wilkie responded affirmatively and further offered, "In my opinion no service of that kind should be used for personal or political purposes." Sherley was not content with this answer and pressed him on whether he thought it was a good idea for "such a force [to] gather information that in their judgment might be of value to the Government without regard to an investigation." Wilkie responded, “No, sir; not at all.”[50] He also insisted that “no member of the Secret Service or anyone acting for the Secret Service has ever shadowed a Congressman or Senator.”[51]

Sherley and Wilkie’s exchange reflected yet another congressional attempt to distinguish between law enforcement, which Congress accepted as a necessary function of government, and domestic intelligence, which it scorned as a “spy system.” Wilkie cunningly defended the Secret Service as performing the former function, not the latter. But the Secret Service was about to have competition for both roles.

The (Federal) Bureau of Investigation

While the Secret Service was busy fending off accusations that it was spying on members of Congress, Attorney General Charles J. Bonaparte took advantage of the controversy to create a new organization within the Department of Justice. The problem with the Treasury Department loaning out Secret Service agents to other executive departments was that those other department heads did not control the Secret Service agents. Bonaparte wanted a detective service under his control—perhaps a fitting ambition for the great-nephew of Napoleon Bonaparte, who established the Sûreté, France’s first national detective force. So, he petitioned Congress for a “detective force” or “special agent force.”[52] The *Evening Star* quoted him as saying that Congress’s opposition to “the spy system applies rather to the method of doing the work than to the work itself.”[53] Bonaparte did not distinguish between domestic intelligence and law enforcement and appeared ready to have the Department of Justice adopt both roles, just like the Secret Service. Also, like the Secret Service, Bonaparte set up his own organization without congressional legislation.

Officially, the Bureau of Investigation (BOI) was established in 1909 by Attorney General George W. Wickersham. But, as Wickersham explained in a report to Congress, Bonaparte assembled a small corps of agents for the previously unnamed bureau in July 1908.[54] The first Chief of the BOI, Stanley Finch, recorded that nine former Secret Service men were assigned to him on July 1, 1908, to “form the nucleus of a force to perform the work for which operatives have heretofore been borrowed from the Treasury Department.”[55] The Secret Service was therefore very much responsible for the establishment of the BOI not only in terms of the controversy precipitating its creation but also through staffing and training its first crop of special agents.

Congress soon received word of yet another instance of an executive department unilaterally forming an intelligence service. When Wilkie testified before Congress in January 1909, he was asked whether "the Department of Justice organized a secret service division during this fiscal year." Curiously, Wilkie at first answered evasively, but intimated that it had.[56] Wilkie bristled at the new competition. Taking the opportunity to air his grievances with both Congress and the new rival organization, he told a Boston newspaper, "Since the law taking our men away from the Department of Justice went into effect that department has organized a secret service or detective force of its own.... The only thing the fathers of the prohibitive law [i.e., Congress] accomplished was an additional expense to the Treasury," implying that the BOI was an unnecessary redundancy.[57] Wilkie attempted to keep the two organizations' investigations separate in response. He instructed one of his agents to "be careful in the future not to call upon agents of the Department of Justice to make any investigation of counterfeiting matters for you. Use other sources to get your information."[58] The bad blood between the Secret Service and BOI would continue to impede information sharing and intelligence coordination.

For its part, Congress continued to hold a grudge against the Secret Service. Budget cuts, likely a byproduct of congressional limitations on the scope of the Secret Service's activities, forced Wilkie to lay off a number of his operatives beginning in April 1909.[59] Congress even undermined the Secret Service's responsibility for presidential security by extending the same role to the BOI. In fact, the Secret Service and BOI (later FBI) would compete over this prestigious mission until Congress recognized the primacy of the Secret Service by statute in 1951.[60]

Attorney General Bonaparte did not escape congressional inquiry either. Representative Tawney asked Bonaparte whether he had created his own organization to perform detective and secret service work, to which Bonaparte flatly responded that he "was obliged to."[61] When pressed further, Bonaparte contended that he would not have created the organization "without the express authority of Congress if it had not become a matter of necessity."[62] Representative Sherley lectured Bonaparte as he had Wilkie. He inveighed against the potential for the BOI to "breed the abuses that have always been inherent in such a service," sermonizing, "It is a known fact of history that many governments have gone to their fall by virtue of the magnifying and enlargement of the spy system."[63]

The committee asked Bonaparte if he thought "that there should be a secret political service in this country," to which he responded, "There is no reason in the world for such a service, and the law would not authorize it." The committee then questioned whether the new organization would be tempted to undertake investigations for political purposes. Bonaparte conceded that it would.[64] Congress therefore highlighted the very problem that had emerged with the Secret Service and wondered whether the Department of Justice's new organization would do any better. As an additional challenge to Bonaparte, a few members of the committee expressed their doubts that Congress could ever hope to investigate intelligence scandals if the President or executive departments refused to provide secret information.[65] Furthermore, they asked Bonaparte whether Congress should make it a felony for a government official to use a secret service organization for political purposes.[66] In both cases, Bonaparte demurred and left it to Congress to try to prevent such abuses of power.

In the short period of time between congressional investigations into the Secret Service and the creation of the BOI, Congress attempted to exercise a remarkable degree of oversight and control with respect to domestic intelligence. The growth of the American administrative state, with more formal bureaucracies and civil service positions, required more than just the executive branch to design it; it required funding and statutory support. Congress briefly found its voice in national intelligence policy by using appropriations and legislation to shape the Secret Service.

But Congress failed to correct the root problems it apparently set out to address with respect to the Secret Service when it came to the BOI. It did not create a legislative charter for the BOI, ignoring the irony that the BOI was the result of a unilateral order of an executive department, just like the Secret Service. It also overlooked the fact that the BOI relied on appropriations to fund a growing range of operations, illustrating how it took advantage of mission creep just as the Secret Service had.[67] Above all, Congress still did not formally distinguish between law enforcement and domestic intelligence, allowing the BOI to adopt both missions. To the extent that Congress exercised any oversight and control over intelligence during the opening decade of the twentieth century, it was fleeting and, ultimately, futile.

Intelligence in the Shadow of the American Century

The challenges afflicting domestic intelligence at this hinge point in American intelligence history reflected unresolved questions of civil-intelligence relations. In ideological terms, Congress adamantly opposed domestic intelligence based on American principles, although it recognized the need for federal law enforcement. In structural terms, there was no constitutional provision, act of Congress, or executive order that both created a federal law enforcement agency and explicitly prohibited it from conducting domestic intelligence. The difficulty is that law enforcement and domestic intelligence can overlap in terms of their activities, methods, and investigations. Almost inevitably, the United States blurred the two—not surprising given the precedents set during the Civil War and the country's continued resistance to the concept of a distinct intelligence profession.

Indeed, law enforcement and intelligence fundamentally differ as professions. Law enforcement is focused on investigating crimes that have already occurred and is motivated by finding, arresting, and prosecuting criminals. Intelligence is focused on identifying and preempting threats and is oriented toward using sources to gather more information. Not only are they distinct professions, but they also require separate organizations for constitutional, legal, ethical, policy, and political reasons.[68] Problematically, American law enforcement organizations successfully co-opted domestic intelligence beginning with the Secret Service in the late nineteenth century and the Bureau of Investigation in the early twentieth century.

Other dynamics of civil-intelligence relations were also steering developments in the American intelligence system. The proximate effect of a political-intelligence scandal and the ensuing interbranch competition between Congress and the President was the creation of yet another intelligence service, the BOI, that would compete with the Secret Service. Congress attempted to limit domestic intelligence by placing restraints on the Secret Service's functions but failed to do the same with the BOI. More generally, it failed to adequately oversee and regulate the executive branch's growing number of intelligence services. Against congressional intent, the Secret Service soon resumed domestic intelligence, as did ONI, MID, and the BOI. But this emerging US "intelligence community" would prove to be hardly a community at all.

From the start of what Henry Luce later dubbed the "American Century," intelligence was the area of national security in which the country was least equipped for the demands placed on it. Lingering biases across civil society and government against espionage undercut any effort to create an independent intelligence organization or profession. The very institution charged with helping policymakers understand and shape events before they were caught unprepared was just a few small organizations buried within much larger departments of the federal government. These organizations and departments would vie over intelligence roles and responsibilities even while purportedly cooperating to root out spies, saboteurs, and subversives in the shadow of the First World War. It was not the war abroad that ignited the competition to control intelligence, but rather the war at home and the question of which of the young US intelligence services would lead the fight.

8

Intelligence in No-Man's-Land

AS AMERICAN DOUGHBOYS marched off to the tune of George M. Cohan's 1917 hit "Over There," the secret agents of America's fledgling intelligence organizations could have answered with their own jingle, "Over Here," because they were already engaged in a shadow war with Germany on American soil. On the eve of the Great War, America's intelligence organizations were small, understaffed, and underfunded. Facing the threat of German sabotage and subversion at home, each service expanded dramatically. The question was whether their combined efforts would prove greater than the sum of their parts or whether the individual organizations would undermine the entire enterprise.

During the First World War, all the services in the intelligence community conducted domestic intelligence operations. Their operations overlapped, causing clashes in the undefined, disorganized, and unstructured arena of American intelligence. A troubling trend emerged, as bureaucratic competition over domestic intelligence fueled more aggressive intelligence operations, which then stoked even more bureaucratic competition. The result was less coordination than the country needed under wartime conditions.

Spy fever again gripped the country. Despite the bitter competition within the intelligence community, US intelligence organizations unleashed their combined efforts on the American public in a campaign to root out German secret agents and saboteurs. And, once more, the American people rallied to the cause. Private citizens and interest groups eagerly identified accused spies and subversives. One group, the American Protective League, became a major auxiliary to the intelligence services, blurring a critical line between public and private intelligence. Domestic intelligence appeared to be a truly national effort in the First World War, but rather than unifying the country and the intelligence community, it ended up dividing both.

Intelligence Entrenches at Home

When Europe went to war in 1914, the United States declared neutrality, although it continued to trade with the Allies and extend them loans. Germany responded by launching a campaign of espionage, propaganda, and sabotage in the United States. The US government had to respond to this intelligence threat. In May 1915, President Woodrow Wilson approved a request from Secretary of State William Jennings Bryan to use the Secret Service to surveil German diplomats.[1]

In late July, two Secret Service agents trailed George Sylvester Viereck, a prominent German American literary figure, and Heinrich Albert, nominally a commercial attaché but actually a German spy, as they rode in an elevated train car in New York City. The surveillance team split up when Viereck exited at a stop, leaving agent Frank Burke to watch Albert. When Albert accidentally left his briefcase on his seat as he deboarded, Burke grabbed it and jumped off the train. Albert chased after him, but Burke escaped. After translating the contents of the briefcase, the Secret Service realized it had discovered a treasure trove of information about Germany's ongoing intelligence operations in the United States.

The Wilson administration leaked the documents to the press. The *World* ran a cover story on August 15, announcing, "How Germany Has Worked in U.S. to Shape Opinion, Block the Allies and Get Munitions for Herself, Told in Secret Agents' Letters." The article accused Count Johann von Bernstorff, the German ambassador to the United States, Franz von Papen, a military attaché, and Hugo Schmidt, a representative of Deutsche Bank, of propaganda and other acts of subversion.[2] Germany's commitment to the shadow war in the United States was massive. The German ambassador had more than $150 million (over $4 billion today) with which to "pursue a propaganda campaign, purchase munitions for Germany, and conduct an espionage campaign aimed at denying war material to the Allies."[3]

German intelligence operations escalated as the war went on. In July 1916, Lothar Witzke, a German naval officer turned spy, and Kurt Jahnke, a German American turncoat, sabotaged a munitions depot in Jersey City, New Jersey, housing weapons bound for the Allies. Known as the "Black Tom explosion," the blast left fragments embedded in the Statue of Liberty and allegedly was felt as far away as Philadelphia and Baltimore. A few months later, an explosion rocked the Kingsland munitions factory in Lyndhurst, New Jersey, and was later determined to be an act of sabotage carried out by Theodore Wozniak.[4] These attacks and other allegations of German sabotage sparked a massive wave of spy mania that allowed the US government to deploy domestic intelligence on an unprecedented scale.

The State Department Seizes the Initiative

Unlike the Navy, War, Treasury, and Justice Departments, the State Department still lacked its own intelligence organization. Robert Lansing, the new Secretary of State, was determined to change that. He also perceived a problem with the American intelligence system at large. In a private letter to Wilson in November 1915, Lansing noted that there was "an unfortunate and probably unavoidable lack of coordination between the different Departments of the Government charged with" intelligence functions. He explained that bits of information constantly flowed into the Departments of State, War, Navy, Justice, and Treasury, which individually were useless but when combined could present a clearer picture. Lansing decided that there should be a "single office where all this information must be instantly transmitted without red tape." He proposed the establishment of "a central office" to act as "the clearing house for the secret reports of the various Departments."[5]

Lansing argued that the State Department should be the home of the new office because "none of [the other] Departments is legally or by organization fitted to handle these matters alone." For example, the Justice Department was "charged with the gathering of evidence by which the Attorney General may proceed to prosecute for a definite crime." Meanwhile, "the Secret Service [was] charged with the protection of the President and the protection against counterfeiting and customs frauds." Lansing therefore requested that "an Executive Order be issued placing all these matters under the authority of the Department of State, directing all Government officials and Departments to transmit immediately to the Department of State any information received along these lines and to collect at the request of that Department any information asked for."[6]

Lansing's letter addressed several defects in American intelligence. First, the US government desperately needed to resolve the issue of intelligence coordination. Lansing's proposed office would be an all-source intelligence outfit that would "keep the President accurately informed day to day," thereby returning a measure of direct supervision and control to the President.[7] In addition, the office would coordinate intelligence activities. Finally, an executive order would help institutionalize intelligence and address the historical lack of provisions structuring the country's intelligence system. But Lansing's proposal exacerbated the very problem it aimed to address. Although Lansing correctly pointed out that both the BOI and the Secret Service were fundamentally law enforcement agencies, each organization had assumed responsibility for domestic intelligence. The new State Department intelligence office would be caught between the two bureaucratic rivals without presidential intervention.

In the end, Wilson never issued an executive order. So, Lansing went ahead and simply established his own Bureau of Secret Intelligence in April 1916. He later acknowledged that it was "organized without sanction of law and had no legal standing," referring to it as an "extra-legal bureau."[8] He appointed Leland Harrison, a Harvard College and Harvard Law graduate and career diplomat, head of the office. Lansing rather prosaically recorded the occasion by writing in his desk diary, "Harrison summoned + informed of purpose."[9] The State Department's first "Special Agent" was Joseph M. Nye, a former Secret Service agent. Aside from his intelligence activities, Nye's duties included providing protection details for foreign diplomats in the United States.

According to Lansing's account, the Bureau of Secret Intelligence conducted an extraordinarily wide range of activities: It organized domestic intelligence operations, which it then assigned to the Secret Service or passed on to the BOI; became a hub for information collected by ONI and MID; ran intelligence agents overseas in Europe; and liaised with the intelligence services of the Allies.[10] In attempting to coordinate intelligence, the Bureau of Secret Intelligence prioritized foreign policy. Lansing's approach therefore "allowed the sinister hand of the spy to be regulated by the dexterous hand of the diplomat."[11] In this respect, Lansing departed from his father-in-law, John W. Foster, who had expressed his hope that American diplomacy would be done with the sordid business of espionage. Under Lansing's model, the United States continued to blur intelligence and diplomacy.

To his credit, Lansing at least aspired to coordinate the competing organizations of the intelligence establishment. But he also disrupted perhaps the next, logical step for the government: to create an independent, professional organization to coordinate intelligence. Moreover, his Bureau of Secret Intelligence was a small office within the larger office of Frank L. Polk, counselor of the State Department.[12] Polk in turn appointed an assistant counselor, Gordon Auchincloss, to help him oversee the Bureau of Secret Intelligence. Without the size or bureaucratic power to accomplish Lansing's purpose, the Bureau of Secret Intelligence depended on the goodwill and cooperation of the other executive departments and their intelligence services.

Crossing Wires and Cutting Cooperation

Wilson had put the Secret Service back in the intelligence business despite the express order of Congress a little under a decade earlier. The Secret Service quickly readjusted to its old role. But Attorney General Thomas Watt Gregory opposed what he perceived to be the Secret Service's intrusion on the BOI's bureaucratic turf. In 1916, he obtained from Congress an amendment to the Justice Department's appropriations statute that allowed it to conduct investigations on behalf of the State Department, fully intending that BOI agents would replace Secret Service agents.[13] With this directive in hand, the BOI began conducting its own domestic intelligence operations.

Perhaps to preempt open bureaucratic conflict, Lansing again wrote to Wilson in April 1917 about the "coordination of the secret service work of this Government," which he deemed a "matter of very great importance." He claimed that the State Department had been the "Clearing house" for intelligence, both foreign and domestic, and listed the various organizations involved in the undertaking. He asserted that all the services must "work in complete harmony otherwise there will be duplication of work and frequent 'crossing of wires.'" Lansing had spoken with Secretary of the Treasury William McAdoo, who suggested that Chief William Flynn of the Secret Service should coordinate the American intelligence effort. But Lansing noted that Flynn lacked experience in international affairs. Additionally, he suspected that the Justice Department would reject Flynn due to the "extreme jealousy between the secret agents of Justice and those of the Treasury," adding that they "both seem[ed] willing to report to the State Department but not to each other." Lansing also opposed McAdoo's proposal because the arrangement "would make the Treasury the head office of this work, which ought to be under the Department of State." Lansing similarly resisted putting Alexander Bruce Bielaski, the director of the BOI, in charge because he, too, lacked the appropriate knowledge of international affairs, plus the arrangement "would be entirely unacceptable to Flynn and his men." While professing that he did not want any more responsibilities, Lansing nevertheless argued that the State Department should have the "central office of secret information of all sorts" and be responsible for "harmonizing the domestic work" given the "friction and jealousy" between the Treasury and Justice Departments. As things stood, the ongoing bureaucratic competition between the Secret Service and the BOI was undermining the American intelligence effort.[14]

In a letter to Wilson a week after Lansing's, McAdoo complained that the Secret Service and BOI were "crossing wires with one another." Moreover, he observed that in order to "overcome this difficulty, we established... a sort of 'clearing house agency' in the State Department." But McAdoo did not believe the State Department was up to the task due to the small size of its intelligence office and its other responsibilities. Instead, he argued that the "work of an Intelligence Bureau, properly organized, ought to have the undivided attention of a suitable head and a competent staff of assistants." So, McAdoo recommended—as Lansing had in 1915—that Wilson "create by Executive Order a Bureau of Intelligence" within either the State or Treasury Departments and mandate that all other intelligence organizations report to it to solve the problem of intelligence coordination.[15]

McAdoo's proposal sparked a bureaucratic war. Even the Postmaster General, Albert S. Burleson, wrote Wilson to protest. The US Postal Service played a critical role in domestic intelligence through the surveillance and censorship of mail. McAdoo proposed channeling the Postal Service's operations through the new bureau. Burleson countered that "it would not make for the efficiency of the post office inspectors force to place them even indirectly under such a bureau as the Secretary of the Treasury recommend[ed]." He claimed that his investigators already reported to the Department of Justice and that it would impede their work to have to report to "two different Departments and receive instructions from each."[16]

But the real opposition came from the Attorney General. Gregory called Wilson's attention to the congressional debate a decade earlier and the bill that limited Secret Service activities to anti-counterfeiting and presidential protective security. He informed Wilson that "not long after the outbreak of the present European War the Secret Service of the Treasury began to interfere in many of the problems which the Bureau of Investigation of this Department was working on and in some instances seriously embarrassed it in the development of important and carefully-laid plans."[17] He added that the Secret Service refused to share information with the BOI in some cases. Referring to McAdoo's letter, Gregory insisted that he knew of "no cases where any wires have been crossed except in instances where the Secret Service invaded the jurisdiction of the Department of Justice." Gregory asked Wilson to restrict the activities of "each of these secret service branches of the Government" to the roles assigned to them by Congress, although Congress had not explicitly assigned a domestic intelligence role to any organization. Gregory also considered the existing system of intelligence coordination through the State Department satisfactory. Perhaps as "conditions develop new machinery may become necessary," he admitted, but for the moment the US government was "in danger of creating too much machinery."[18]

McAdoo rejected Gregory's accusations. In a response to Wilson, he bitterly claimed he did not "care three straws about the organization of the Bureau of Intelligence; it was merely a suggestion which [he] thought would find ready acceptance on the part of the other Departments."[19] He also wrote to Gregory to address his claim that the Secret Service was intruding on the BOI's turf, countering that the BOI was just as guilty of doing the same.[20] McAdoo turned his back on his own proposal for a new office to coordinate intelligence and made a power grab on behalf of the Secret Service instead.

In another letter to Wilson, McAdoo explained that the State Department, Army, and Navy had all requested intelligence help from the Secret Service. He saw an opportunity to plant Secret Service agents in the War, Navy, and State Departments—a direct challenge to the decision Congress had made a decade earlier to forbid the Secret Service from loaning agents to other departments. Urging swift action, he warned that the "public interest [was] being hurt by the failure to organize quickly the necessary [intelligence work] of the various departments."[21] To cement his point, McAdoo wrote yet another letter to Wilson after the Secret Service arrested a German agent in New York. Polk and the State Department's Bureau of Secret Intelligence had been aware of the agent due to Secret Service reports but allowed the man to remain free. Assessing the "German spy system [as] highly organized and operating efficiently," he pressed Wilson to "soon take action to make more effective the secret service agencies of the government."[22]

Competition over Coordination

Wilson had an opportunity to implement revolutionary intelligence reform. Instead, he let the competition in his administration fester until he finally wrote to Gregory to ask him to "cooperate with the Secretary of the Treasury and Mr. Polk [in the State Department] in working out . . . a plan for the cooperation" of their intelligence organizations.[23] But even a presidential dictate was not enough to force the departments to resolve their dispute. Alluding to an acrimonious Cabinet meeting in November 1917, Wilson admitted that he felt "derelict in not having sought a remedy" to the intelligence coordination problem "at the time [McAdoo] suggested it." However, Wilson confessed that he was still unsure "as to what the best remedy" was, despite Lansing and McAdoo having presented him with their proposals.[24]

For its part, Congress eroded both intelligence coordination and civil liberties by passing the Espionage Act just as the first doughboys were en route to France in June 1917.[25] The act criminalized a wide range of activities, from exposing US national security secrets to promoting disloyalty in the armed forces. In May 1918, Congress amended the Espionage Act with the addition of the Sedition Act. The Sedition Act of 1918 reflected the spirit of the Sedition Act of 1798, even mirroring its language: It proscribed uttering, printing, writing, or publishing any "disloyal, profane, scurrilous, or abusive language about the form of government of the United States, or the Constitution of the United States."[26]

The Espionage and Sedition Acts worked in concert with domestic intelligence during the war by giving American intelligence organizations the statutory tools with which to arrest and charge individuals suspected of espionage, sabotage, propaganda, or subversion. These organizations often ran roughshod over citizens' constitutional rights. As another unintended consequence, they spurred on bureaucratic competition, as every intelligence service embraced the domestic intelligence mission, enabled by congressional legislation.

Congress further added to the chaos and confusion by granting a temporary reprieve to the Secret Service to conduct domestic intelligence operations. In a sundry appropriations act of June 1917, it authorized the President "to direct, without reference to existing limitations the use of the persons [Secret Service agents] employed hereunder if, in his judgment an emergency exists which requires such action" for one year.[27] Of course, Wilson had already taken that liberty in May 1915, apparently without notifying Congress. In July 1918, Congress reenacted the statute for another year.[28]

When Congress tried to tackle the problem of intelligence coordination, the executive branch intervened. In early 1918, a series of events alerted Congress to weaknesses in the country's intelligence system, including the resignation of Secret Service Chief William Flynn over the problem of cooperation with the Justice Department and a letter from Theodore Roosevelt to Senator George Chamberlain, chairman of the Committee on Military Affairs, raising the question of a central intelligence organization.[29] In congressional hearings, Senator Chamberlain asked Ralph Van Deman, who had risen through the ranks since the Philippine-American War to become the head of Army intelligence, whether it was not "a duplication of work to have so many intelligence departments in the different branches of the Government." Van Deman parried by saying it might have been possible to coordinate intelligence "if we had started out with one secret service organization and that organization had been in existence for years and was working smoothly... but to try to form such an organization now would mean slowing up the whole work for months, or perhaps a year, before you could get into operation." Determined that there would be "duplication even with a single organization," Van Deman minimized the issue and claimed that "we are getting along now with practically no useless duplication."[30] His opinion aside, interdepartmental rivalry was eclipsing interdepartmental cooperation.

On March 6, 1918, the major American intelligence services assembled in New York at the direction of Special Assistant Attorney General John Lord O'Brian.[31] As O'Brian later revealed, these "so-called Intelligence conferences" had started earlier in January between Army intelligence and the BOI "as a matter of convenience and without official authority or sanction."[32] On March 1, he alerted Gregory to the upcoming meeting, explaining that Secret Service Chief William Moran wanted his organization incorporated into the war effort "either by establishing some central control or by agreeing on some system for establishing a clearinghouse." O'Brian perceived the impending power struggle, warning Gregory that it was "obvious that when the representatives meet in conference... the chief question will be whether the other services are willing to adopt some plan by which the Treasury Secret Service will have its powers broadened and be put on a[n] even footing with the War, Navy and Justice Departments."[33] These three departments would ensure that did not happen.

On March 7, O'Brian informed Gregory of what had transpired at the previous day's meeting. The attendees were the heads of the various intelligence organizations, including Van Deman of Army intelligence, Harrison of the Bureau of Secret Intelligence, Moran of the Secret Service, and Bielaski of BOI. O'Brian proposed two possible plans. The first option was to create a "central bureau of Intelligence, with a director appointed by the President and responsible to him." O'Brian noted that "all present agencies [would be] sub-ordinate to the director," who would control all operations conducted by the others. The second proposal was to "create, without a central bureau, some clearing house through which all war information could be cleared and assigned, in order that each service interested might have the benefit of information gathered by other services." Predictably, the "Treasury alone spoke favorably" of the first plan, while the "Army opposed this plan very strongly." The second plan made Army intelligence the clearinghouse for information—a role the State Department had already reserved for itself—which the Treasury opposed "unless the Treasury Secret Service could be set free and engage in war work generally." O'Brian decided there must be some sort of compromise between the Treasury and Justice Departments, but that would require "some central authority... to stand between the Treasury Department and the Department of Justice, in order to prevent duplication, determining what work should be done from day to day by each Department."[34]

While the meeting was intended to arrange for better coordination, the Justice, War, and Navy Departments used it to successfully block the Treasury's quest for a new intelligence system. Ultimately, the three departments conspired to deal the Secret Service out of domestic intelligence and end any effort to create a separate organization empowered to coordinate intelligence.[35] They accomplished both goals. They also undermined the role of the State Department and the Bureau of Secret Intelligence by establishing their own system for sharing information and assigning key responsibilities to Army intelligence.[36] But the military intelligence services assumed an outsized role in domestic intelligence at their own expense.

Military Intelligence on the Home Front

The First World War found the military intelligence services at their lowest point since they were founded. Preparation for and entry into the war rejuvenated them, while ongoing technological innovations revolutionized their organization, culture, and operations. Balloons gave way to planes for aerial reconnaissance, and the radio complemented the telegraph. The operations and equipment associated with trench warfare, submarine attacks, and airpower required trained specialists to collect and process information. Furthermore, the expanding means of collection meant that there was much more information to be collated and analyzed. The military implemented much-needed intelligence reforms, including creating "offices and staffs, complete with intricate divisions of labor, precise support and logistical services, [and] hierarchical management structures."[37]

Paradoxically, the military continued to advance intelligence professionalization while impeding it at the same time. Those involved in intelligence during the First World War sensed the distinctiveness of their role, but their organizations were subordinated under executive departments representing other institutions of national security. The United States was not ready to embrace a formal intelligence profession or institution due to a combination of factors in civil society and government. With the rise of the American administrative state and Progressive Era reforms, however, there was greater faith in the ability of new technology and skilled professionals to address the challenges of governance and statecraft. Technocracy, a term first proposed by William Henry Smyth in 1919, would combine scientific knowledge and industrial management to organize and coordinate the workings of the US government.[38] A strong technocratic strand was embedded in American intelligence culture during this period, generating a partiality toward—and even dependence on—technological means of intelligence collection.[39]

Before the First World War, the Army consigned its intelligence component to the War College Division, which in turn converted it into a small office that dealt more with maps and reports than intelligence operations. Ralph Van Deman proposed that the War College Division establish a Military Intelligence Section (MIS), which it belatedly did in May 1917. As its chief, Van Deman continuously pressed to expand MIS both in terms of its size and the scope of its activities. An office that employed five military officers and two civilian clerks in May 1917 grew to over a thousand civilians and nearly three hundred military officers by the armistice in November 1918. Its budget likewise jumped from an original congressional appropriation of $11,000 for FY 1918 to $1 million that year and over $2 million for FY 1919. Borrowing from the British system of "positive intelligence" and "negative intelligence," Van Deman divided MIS into two major branches. Positive Branch focused on collecting military, political, economic, and social intelligence overseas, while Negative Branch performed counterintelligence and domestic intelligence in the United States. In distinguishing between the two realms but operating in both, MIS was straddling a fault line in American civil-intelligence relations.[40]

MIS's operations pivoted decidedly toward domestic intelligence as a product of its leadership and bureaucratic politics. Following in the tradition of Army intelligence during the Civil War and his own experience in the Philippines, Van Deman turned to law enforcement officers and civilian detectives for his first crop of counterintelligence agents.[41] He also incorporated the index card system for gathering information on potential subversives that he had used in the Philippines.[42] At the same time, MIS shifted toward domestic intelligence for geographical and organizational reasons. The American Expeditionary Forces (AEF) were thousands of miles away in France, and General John J. "Black Jack" Pershing, the commander of the AEF, created his own intelligence staff, G-2, to focus on Europe.[43] MIS steadily expanded its operational reach and organizational power to the point that it was involved in virtually every area of domestic intelligence, from postal censorship to passport control to fraud investigations relating to arms procurement. Van Deman clearly had grand ambitions for Army intelligence, but MIS was trespassing in other departments' bureaucratic territory, stoking more competition.

For a time, Van Deman managed to keep both himself and MIS out of trouble. He successfully steered between the feuding BOI and Secret Service. MIS became the de facto middle-ground organization when the BOI and Secret Service vied over missions or responsibilities.[44] But he eventually provoked a confrontation with the Justice Department when he proposed trying enemy aliens and Americans accused of sedition in military tribunals rather than civilian courts.[45] John Lord O'Brian, who had formerly conspired with Van Deman to cut the Secret Service out of domestic intelligence, voiced his concern to Gregory that MIS was encroaching on the Department of Justice's jurisdiction.[46] At the same time, Van Deman's constant political maneuvering on behalf of MIS rankled his military superiors.[47]

Van Deman ended up a casualty of bureaucratic competition. In June 1918, Secretary of War Newton D. Baker transferred him to G-2 AEF in France. The Army finally formally established the Military Intelligence Division (MID) of the General Staff in August 1918, only a few months before the end of the war, and put Colonel Marlborough Churchill, formerly of the AEF General Staff, in charge.[48] Ironically, this personnel swap—in part born of the bureaucratic competition between Van Deman and his rivals at G-2 AEF—improved the previously adversarial relationship between MIS and G-2 AEF.[49] This was likely little consolation to Van Deman, who had coveted leadership of the Army intelligence service he had done so much to build. Even so, MID would experience drastic cuts to its workforce after the war, losing over half its military officers and most of its civilian staff.[50]

ONI was a relatively overlooked office in the large naval bureaucracy before the outbreak of the First World War. While the course of the war and events like the sinking of the *Lusitania* alerted the Navy to the need for intelligence on German naval operations, it was the domestic sabotage campaign by Germany that put ONI back in business. ONI was responsible for securing American ports, shipping, cargo, and naval factories. Direct US intervention in the war further refined its mission. The breadth of ONI's domestic responsibilities led its director, Rear Admiral Roger Welles, to recruit hundreds of civilian detectives and naval officers to conduct surveillance. Like Pershing in France, Admiral William Sims, the head of American naval operations in the European theater, formed his own intelligence section in London, effectively undercutting ONI operations overseas. In response, ONI pivoted its main effort to domestic intelligence, devoting only a quarter of its personnel to foreign intelligence. The combination of spy hysteria and a large surveillance network led ONI to abuse its power. ONI reports identified suspicious individuals on the rather thin basis that they "looked, spoke, or allegedly acted like Germans." ONI also displayed a rather cavalier attitude toward constitutional protections. In one case, ONI held a suspect whom it described as a "tall, blond German" for months without charge simply for having worked in a chemical dye factory and for spending time around the waterfront.[51]

ONI never grew to the same size as the other services during the war and sometimes had to rely on them for help when its own resources fell short. Still, ONI punched above its weight. Welles claimed that by November 1918, ONI was investigating fifteen thousand potential cases of domestic espionage and subversion a week.[52] After the armistice, it faced the same pattern of retrenchment as MIS/MID. Although ONI headquarters had over three hundred reserve officers in late 1918, only twenty-four remained by July 1920. It also closed its branch offices in 1918 and sent personnel home.[53] Its budget shrank from over $1 million for FY 1918–19 to a paltry $65,000 for FY 1919–20.[54] Once again, the fortunes of the military intelligence services rose and fell with the war—and with the sentiments of a fickle American public.

Mobilizing the Home Front

Echoing previous conflicts, the American people threw themselves into the war effort, including the domestic intelligence campaign. Aside from sensational headlines, even mere rumors stoked their fear and anger. The public did not limit its suspicions or hostility to the substantial population of German and East European citizens and immigrants residing in the country. The US government, intelligence services, and large segments of civil society questioned the loyalty of minorities, especially African Americans and Mexican Americans, whom they suspected were targets of German subversive efforts.[55] Van Deman personally harbored the same prejudice, leading to Army domestic intelligence operations targeting those groups.[56] Meanwhile, ONI "became obsessed with pursuing American Jews."[57] Ordinary Americans aided these efforts by keeping a lookout and reporting their suspicions to the government, in effect becoming a proxy intelligence force. Given that the small intelligence community lacked the capacity to perform all the domestic intelligence investigations required by the spy hysteria, it leveraged their voluntary participation as agents for domestic intelligence operations.

One group in particular was at the center of the domestic intelligence campaign. The American Protective League (APL) was the brainchild of Albert Briggs, a wealthy Chicago businessman.[58] In February 1917, Briggs approached the BOI with a proposal to create an all-volunteer private organization that would assist with its mounting responsibilities. Bielaski, BOI's chief, personally approved of the plan on the condition that the arrangement remain secret. Anyone could join the APL, including citizens without any background in intelligence or law enforcement. Nevertheless, the APL claimed to operate under the direction of the BOI. In fact, the application for

Vol. I WASHINGTON, D. C., JUNE 4, 1918 No. 1

President Signs Espionage Act

SIGNED by President Wilson on May 16, the amended espionage law opens a new chapter in the work of the American Protective League. For the first time we have an inclusive law under which to operate—a law broad enough in its scope and classifications to cover and define as serious crimes a multitude of offenses which were classed as minor by our peace-time code but actually offered serious hindrances to this country's military operations and preparations.

For the first time, too, heavy penalties have been provided for acts and speeches which before could hardly be punished at all under the law. Maximum sentences of twenty years imprisonment and $10,000 fine are not to be taken lightly either by disloyal and pacifist citizens or by unfriendly or enemy aliens who have made it their business, since war was declared, to invent and circulate discreditable stories about almost every phase of America's war activities.

Watch—and Help

THE SPY GLASS hopes, in coming issues, to sweep an editorial horizon as wide as the League itself. This number is a beginning only; our effort will be to grow into a magazine and news bulletin in which the more important developments affecting the League and its work can be brought quickly to the attention of members everywhere. New laws—new rulings by the Department of Justice—new court decisions—new evidences of enemy propaganda and espionage—better methods of handling cases—improved systems for dispatching correspondence, filing and office routine—any and every bit of useful information will be passed along to Chiefs and Members. Some of the humor and pathos of the day's work will be included—but in that you must aid. So send in your suggestions and contributions. Help us to focus THE SPY GLASS on your job.

Disloyalty Now a Crime

No distinction is made between the disloyal talk or act of a citizen and the hostile speech or deed of an alien, enemy or otherwise. The act or speech is the offense and whoever commits it must pay the penalty—though the law allows a good deal of latitude to the court in determining the latter.

All this means a tremendous simplification of every member's labors. So far-reaching and important are the provisions of the amended law—so clearly does it indicate the chief kinds of spying and of propaganda which the League must combat, that the whole catalogue of crimes may well be set down here for study and ready reference in months to come. Omitting the preliminary enacting clauses and breaking up the main section into handy paragraphs, the amended law now reads as follows:

OFFENSES:

I—False and Interfering Reports

SECTION 3. Whoever, when the United States is at war, shall willfully make or convey false reports or false statements with intent to interfere with the operation or success of the military or naval forces of the United States, or to promote the success of its enemies,—

II—Obstructing Bond Sales, etc.

—whoever shall willfully make or convey false reports or false statements, or say or do anything except by way of bona fide and not disloyal advice to an investor or investors, with intent to obstruct the sale by the United States of bonds or other securities of the United States or the making of loans by or to the United States,—

III—Inciting or Causing Mutiny

—whoever, when the United States is at war, shall willfully cause or attempt to cause or incite or attempt to incite, insubordination, disloyalty, mutiny, or refusal of duty, in the military or naval forces of the United States,—

IV—Obstructing Enlistments

—whoever shall willfully obstruct or attempt to obstruct the recruiting or enlistment service of the United States,—

V—Attacks on Government, Flag, etc.

—whoever, when the United States is at war, shall willfully utter, print, write, or publish any disloyal, profane, scurrilous, or abusive language about the form of government of the United States, or the Constitution of the United States, or the military or naval forces of the United States, or the flag of the United States, or the uniform of the Army or Navy of the United States, or any language intended to bring the form of government of the United States, or the Constitution of the United States, or the military or naval forces of the United States, or the flag of the United States, or the uniform of the Army or Navy of the United States into contempt, scorn, contumely, or disrepute,—

VI—Encouraging Resistance

—whoever shall willfully utter, print, write, or publish any langauge intended to incite, provoke, or encourage resistance to the United States, or to promote the cause of its enemies, or shall willfully display the flag of any enemy,—

VII—Curtailing Production

—whoever shall willfully by utterance, writing, printing, publication, or language spoken, urge, incite, or advocate any curtailment of production in this country of anything or things, product or products, necessary or essen-

FIGURE 8.1 The first issue of *The Spy Glass*, the APL's periodical to educate and inform its civilian membership, announced the amendment to the Espionage Act known as the Sedition Act of 1918. National Archives and Records Administration.

enrollment as an APL volunteer explicitly stated that it was "Organized with the Approval and Operating under the Direction of the United States Department of Justice, Bureau of Investigation."[59] The arrangement was ripe for abuse and scandal.

The APL essentially acted as a para-intelligence force during the war. It had as many as 350,000 members spread across hundreds of cities conducting millions of investigations on their fellow Americans.[60] It also produced a periodical for its members called *The Spy Glass*, which was marked "*Confidential*." Issues contained letters to the APL from officials, including Attorney General Gregory and MID chief Marlborough Churchill, thanking the APL for the work it was doing.[61]

APL members carried badges labeled "Secret Service," which naturally infuriated the real Secret Service. McAdoo made his displeasure clear in a series of letters to the Attorney General and the President. He feared the effects of setting a "miscellaneous horde of so-called Secret Service operatives... loose upon the country to pry into the business of peaceful citizens," warning Wilson that "suspicion will be engendered among our people, smoldering race antagonisms will burst into flame, and the melting pot of America will be a melting pot no longer, but a crucible out of which will flash the molten lead of suspicion and dissension."[62] McAdoo vehemently opposed the APL's use of the term "Secret Service Division" and the practice of giving its volunteers badges and identification cards bearing the words "Secret Service" as "detrimental to the public interest." He claimed that the Secret Service had already received complaints about the APL's activities due to public confusion between the two organizations. He also argued that the Department of Justice could not grant intelligence and law enforcement powers to the APL and that no department or official of the US government was actually in control of the APL. McAdoo concluded by warning Wilson that the "Government cannot escape responsibility for their activities whatever they may be."[63]

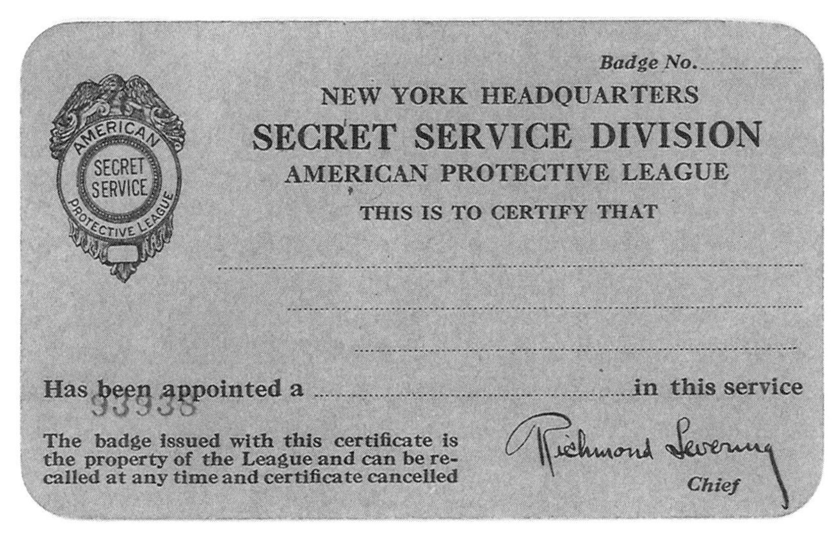

AMERICAN SECRET SERVICE PROTECTIVE LEAGUE

Badge No. ....

NEW YORK HEADQUARTERS

SECRET SERVICE DIVISION

AMERICAN PROTECTIVE LEAGUE

THIS IS TO CERTIFY THAT

....

....

....

Has been appointed a .... in this service

The badge issued with this certificate is the property of the League and can be recalled at any time and certificate cancelled

Richmond Levering

Chief

FIGURE 8.2 This "Secret Service Division" badge was handed out by the American Protective League. Woodrow Wilson Papers, Library of Congress.

Alarmed by McAdoo's letters, Wilson wrote to Gregory that "it would be very dangerous to have such an organization operating in the United States" and wondered "if there is any way in which we could stop it."[64] Gregory tried to reassure him that the APL was "a patriotic organization" and was "tremendously helpful in the work of the Bureau of Investigation." He insisted that the APL had "no official status" and its "members serve[d] without the slightest expense to the Government, and not a single officer or member receive[d] compensation from any source."[65] He also included in the letter the offending badge McAdoo had mentioned and an "Application for Enrollment as a Volunteer in the Secret Service Division American Protective League."

McAdoo made the mistake of using his letters warning about the APL to simultaneously lobby for a central intelligence organization and the Secret Service's continued role in domestic intelligence. His complaints therefore appeared to be as much a product of bureaucratic and personal rivalry with Gregory as genuine concern about the APL and its potential for abuse. Moreover, timing was on the APL's side. The debate over the APL coincided with the first conscription registration on June 5, 1917. The US government needed the APL's manpower to help register the millions of men eligible for the draft. The APL would also provide the muscle for "slacker raids" to round up alleged draft dodgers. Moreover, in June 1917, Congress was on the cusp of passing the Espionage Act. The APL and its national network could help investigate and enforce the sweeping provisions of the law. Amid the spy mania and war fever, Americans proved that they were "more concerned about spies than about civil liberties."[66]

Bureaucratic competition festered as the APL expanded its support from the BOI to the military. While the APL provided the ONI with both operatives and intelligence, it was the APL's relationship with Army intelligence that led to a rupture in the alliance between the BOI and the military intelligence services.[67] Echoing McAdoo's concerns, Van Deman wrote in his memoir that the creation of vigilante groups "devoted to the running down of spies ... was an extremely dangerous development and it was evident that these organizations must be stopped in their activities at once." However, he considered "that if one of these organizations could be developed into a national group that could be trusted to obey orders and do nothing except what they were told to do that they might be of great value to the government."[68]

Rather than stop APL vigilantism, Van Deman decided to co-opt it. An APL liaison office soon became its own subsection of Army intelligence.[69] The Army also commissioned several leading APL activists as officers, in part to extend military control over the league's operations.[70] In exchange, APL members allowed the Army's role in domestic intelligence to remain largely hidden from the view of the American people during the war.[71] But the decision to embrace the APL backfired on Van Deman, as his rivals in the Treasury and Justice Departments exploited public outcry over the APL's many excesses to challenge his influence and persuade Army leadership to transfer him to Europe.[72]

The APL proved a poisoned chalice for American intelligence. The ensuing struggle between rival organizations to control the APL spurred the wider, ongoing bureaucratic competition over domestic intelligence. The credibility of intelligence was damaged when the American people turned against the APL and the intelligence services for allowing a private organization of US citizens to violate the rights of their fellow citizens as well as constitutional boundaries and principles.

The staggering scale of the APL's activities in the war can be matched in astonishment only by the scarcity of its successes and the abundance of its abuses. Despite conducting roughly six million investigations during the war, the APL ultimately failed to find a single German spy.[73] Although the military used APL members to "make loyalty checks, investigate the background of passport applicants, probe the qualifications of prospective citizens, and enforce liquor and vice control around military bases," as it turned out, "for the most part… the volunteer patriots spied on their neighbors, looking for any sign of disloyalty."[74] Like the domestic intelligence organizations that it aided, the APL went beyond searching for German spies or saboteurs and spread its net to include spying on alleged draft dodgers, socialists, and labor unions. In September 1918, twenty-five hundred APL members joined BOI agents, military personnel, and police in massive "slacker" raids in New York and New Jersey that resulted in fifty thousand arrests without warrants or probable cause.[75] A scathing article in the *New York Times* criticized the Attorney General for authorizing the raids, underscoring how he did "not cite any rule or regulation providing for the assistance of soldiers, sailors and members of any private organization when slacker raids were to be conducted."[76] American civil society's patience for domestic intelligence was running low, and the APL helped drain it further. The APL's influence waned beginning with the Armistice, and it was finally disbanded in February of 1919, although APL veterans found roles in future domestic intelligence operations.[77]

Problems Postponed

Just as intelligence seemed poised to occupy a permanent, powerful—though not yet professional—place in the American national security establishment, it found itself caught between warring executive departments and fleeting public support. The intelligence war that accompanied American involvement in the First World War was not only against Germany but also between intelligence organizations and their parent departments. Bureaucratic competition fostered an even more aggressive domestic intelligence campaign as each organization fought to outdo the other. The President of the United States, nominally the chief national intelligence officer and consumer, missed a critical opportunity to establish a coordinated intelligence system. Instead, intelligence remained under the control of a few key executive departments representing different institutions of national security, further divided by competing Cabinet secretaries and intelligence services. With the end of the war, America's intelligence organizations found their size and power greatly diminished due to military retrenchment, despite having reached their strongest position yet in the national security establishment.

The American people bore some responsibility for the outcome. When spy fever gripped the country, Americans enthusiastically aided the intelligence effort. Gregory reported that the Department of Justice was "hampered by the circulation of unfounded reports, running into the hundreds," along with the "hundreds" of tips based on newspapers, pamphlets, books, speeches, or even private conversations reported by Americans "every day."[78] Lansing commented on behalf of the State Department that "some of these [tips] were investigated but the great majority were considered too fantastic and improbable to be worthy of a second thought."[79]

The aggressive domestic intelligence campaign that everyday Americans voluntarily joined during the war helped generate a popular backlash against intelligence after the war ended. In his memoirs published in 1935, Lansing decried the "extraordinary mania" of this period, which he likened to "the witch-hunting mania of the seventeenth century." He lamented how "many an innocent German-American ... was suspected and spied upon by his neighbors and on their insistent demands became the subject of investigation by agents of the government." On the problem of intelligence coordination, he observed that "the rivalries of the several services and the mutual jealousies of their chiefs prevented anything being done." Lansing presciently understood that the "desirable consolidation could only have been effected by creating a new and independent executive agency in charge of all secret investigations, but this was impossible under the existing laws."[80] Such an agency was another world war away. In the meantime, even as the need for a coordinated, professionalized US intelligence system grew, so too did American opposition to intelligence in peacetime.

9

A Return to Normalcy

OVER THE SHORT period of American intervention in the First World War, domestic intelligence operations pivoted from countering German espionage to targeting socialist subversion. Socialism had been a revolutionary movement since the mid-nineteenth century, but the Russian Revolution and its goal of spreading communism globally threatened the United States and the American way of life. American intelligence was in the early stages of fighting the shadow war that would define it for the next century.[1] Just who qualified as a "socialist" or "subversive" became a matter of government judgment and public suspicion, but the primary targets were anarchists, labor unions—particularly members of the Industrial Workers of the World (IWW), also known as "Wobblies"—and, of course, supporters of the Socialist Party of America, like Eugene Debs. This new domestic intelligence campaign would conflict with American civil society's own campaign to "return to normalcy."

Those advocating for isolationism ignored the glaring lesson of the First World War that the United States was a global power with global interests. Moreover, the American people continued to harbor myths about their country and considered it above sneaky intelligence activities in peacetime, whether at home or abroad. Many policymakers and prominent Americans agreed. Yet, the need for robust peacetime intelligence had never been greater, as states negotiated a dizzying array of military, economic, and political agreements to try to avert another cataclysmic war. Unlike in generations past when ministers, ambassadors, and other plenipotentiaries had wide latitude to represent their countries due to delays in communication with their governments back home, the telegraph allowed states to exert closer oversight over their diplomatic officers. Intercepting and decrypting diplomatic traffic offered an information advantage in these negotiations. The United States exploited this advantage—for a time. But bureaucratic competition among executive departments and the country's ideological opposition to intelligence in peacetime resulted in the country once again being unprepared for the next war.

Seeing Red

Beginning in April 1919, a series of mail bombs were sent to a number of notable Americans, including Supreme Court Justice Oliver Wendell Holmes, Jr., business magnate John D. Rockefeller, and Attorney General A. Mitchell Palmer. The bombs failed to kill their targets, but they did injure a few innocent parties. The press picked up the story and was quick to identify the culprit. On May 1, 1919, the *New York Times* announced that the "nation-wide bomb conspiracy... has every earmark of I.W.W.-Bolshevik origin."[2] On May 4, the *Times* again singled out socialists, reporting that the "Lenin-Trotzky Government has managed to transmit to this country a fund that totals between $400,000 and $500,000, which is being used to finance the Bolshevist 'diplomatic' activities in the United States," adding that the IWW advocated "the overthrow of the Government, sabotage, and confiscation of private property." But the article assured readers that the government had an "indexed file of alien and domestic agitators" and that "these troublemakers... have been under almost continuous surveillance ever since the outbreak of war in Europe."[3]

On June 2, 1919, the conspirators sent out more bombs, with nine detonating in eight cities. The bomb destined for Palmer blew up prematurely, killing its deliverer and narrowly missing the Attorney General's neighbors, Assistant Secretary of the Navy Franklin Delano Roosevelt and his wife, Eleanor, who had just walked by his house. The *Times* continued to assail the socialist menace, warning that "Russian Reds Are Busy Here" and reporting on the propaganda and subversion efforts of labor unions in the United States.[4] While suspicion fell on socialists, the historical consensus is that the bombings were the work of the Galleanists, followers of Italian anarchist Luigi Galleani. The collective frenzy surrounding the bombings whipped up anti-socialist sentiment across the country, again creating a permissive environment for American intelligence organizations to launch a campaign that operated outside of constitutional boundaries.

The perpetrators of the May 1919 bombings made a mistake in targeting Palmer. Despite his Quaker roots, Palmer quickly and vigorously vowed to dismantle the vast, subversive socialist network he claimed was operating in the country. Ironically, Palmer had been a critic of the APL in the First World War and, as Attorney General, released thousands of those detained in BOI and APL raids during the war. He also rejected any further intelligence cooperation between the Department of Justice and APL. However, Palmer's mercy toward the victims of BOI excesses apparently did not extend to socialists, whom he targeted with a vengeance. The *New York Times* quoted Palmer's promise that the US government would "protect itself against attacks from within as carefully and as forcefully as it has shown itself able to protect itself against attacks from without."[5]

Palmer named William Flynn as the new chief of the BOI. Flynn, who had been Chief of the Secret Service and resigned in 1918 in part due to competition with the BOI, now led his former organization's foremost rival. Palmer also established a Radical Division, subsequently renamed the General Intelligence Division, in the BOI to root out socialists and other subversives, and put the twenty-four-year-old J. Edgar Hoover in charge.

Hoover feverishly set to work, "launching an unprecedented experiment in peacetime political surveillance."[6] Unlike his boss, he had no problem employing former APL operatives. In just three months, he assembled files on over sixty thousand people suspected of being radicals and political dissidents.[7] Hoover was not just collecting information for its own sake. His intelligence-gathering operations culminated in massive raids beginning on November 7, 1919, which coincided with the second anniversary of the Bolsheviks' seizure of power in Russia. The so-called Palmer Raids were carried out nationwide from November 1919 through February 1920. Thousands were arrested in a grossly disproportionate and heavy-handed manner, often without warrants and based on hearsay alone. American public support for invasive domestic intelligence practices, already eroding at the end of the First World War, collapsed following the Palmer Raids.

Hoover's investigation of socialist conspiracies during his formative years perhaps predisposed him to a lifelong tendency to see socialism everywhere, which would mark his approach to intelligence. His suspicions—and the resulting investigations—were all-encompassing. Not only would he identify the radicals in civil society who posed a threat to the US government, but he was also determined to uncover the threat of subversives within the US government itself. In the process, Hoover stoked even more bureaucratic competition and made political enemies at the expense of American intelligence. Hoover first clashed with Assistant Secretary of Labor Louis F. Post, who objected to the Bureau's methods and the Palmer Raids. Post began dismissing cases against those detained, infuriating Hoover. Author Tim Weiner claims that this personal rivalry was the origin of Hoover's political surveillance of anyone who could stand in his way, including Presidents, members of Congress, and other public figures.[8]

The Hoover-Post rift led to a debate over the government's reaction to the subversive threat in a Cabinet meeting on April 14, 1920. Palmer argued that

Post was endangering the country by releasing subversives. Josephus Daniels, the Secretary of the Navy, recorded that Wilson instructed Palmer to not let "this country see red," that is, not to fear-monger.[9] Daniels agreed, adding in his memoir that Palmer "was seeing red behind every bush."[10] However, Weiner believes that Palmer deliberately misconstrued Wilson's message as "a go-ahead for his campaign to cleanse the country of the Communists."[11]

Hoover and Palmer were convinced that socialists would attempt a nationwide uprising on May 1, 1920, the international socialist holiday May Day. Newspapers around the country sounded the alarm, and cities deployed forces in the streets to prepare for the assault.[12] But the feared socialist uprising never took place. A wave of condemnation followed. One congressman fulminated that no person had "done more to unsettle the nerves of the American people than the Attorney General."[13] Many respected legal scholars opposed the government's domestic intelligence operations, including Harvard law professor Felix Frankfurter, Harvard Law School dean Roscoe Pound, and Columbia Law School dean Harlan Fiske Stone. The *New York Times* cited a report by twelve eminent lawyers stating that the Department of Justice "under guise of a campaign for suppression of radical activities acting by its local agents throughout the country...has committed continual illegal acts."[14] Crying wolf one too many times exhausted the public's patience for intrusive domestic intelligence activities. Whereas spy hysteria had previously led the American people to throw their support behind intelligence, the intelligence community's overzealous response now led them to fear it.

Goodbye to the "Gum-Shoe" Days?

The dramatic expansion of US intelligence organizations during the First World War was rivaled by their equally dramatic contraction following the end of the war and the First Red Scare. The reasons ranged from the personal to the principled to the bureaucratic, but the changes of the interwar period left a lasting mark on American intelligence.

The State Department, which had hastily organized its first intelligence service, abandoned it almost as quickly in the interwar period. Robert Lansing, who had created the Bureau of Secret Intelligence, turned against intelligence in the fashion of the times, writing in 1921,

> Muttered confidences, secret intrigues, and the tactics of the "gumshoer" are discredited. The world wants none of them these days. It

> despises and loathes them.... The statesman who seeks to gain his end by tortuous and underground ways is foolish or badly advised.[15]

Lansing was referring to secret negotiations at the Paris Peace Conference that produced the Treaty of Versailles. Army MID officers had accompanied the American commission and collected intelligence for Wilson to use in the negotiations.[16] The United States therefore continued to combine intelligence and diplomacy, despite the sentiments of diplomats like John W. Foster and Lansing. But these activities would not continue through the State Department's Bureau of Secret Intelligence, known after the war as U-1. In 1927, Secretary of State Frank B. Kellogg shut down U-1, leaving the State Department to again find itself scrambling to stake its claim in intelligence when the Second World War broke out.[17]

A change in leadership shifted the Office of Naval Intelligence's mission and methods. In May 1919, Albert P. Niblack became the director of ONI and made his vision for the organization clear. In his history of ONI, Niblack stated, "It has been the aim of the office to use only reputable business methods and avoid anything savoring of 'gum-shoe' methods," a shift away from ONI's questionable activities during the war.[18] Furthermore, he insisted that the "Military Intelligence Division of the War Department naturally has much more to do with internal affairs of the United States than the Office of Naval Intelligence," although he did end by arguing for closer cooperation between ONI and MID.[19] Niblack's timely pivot away from domestic intelligence saved ONI from the public outcry that accompanied the more egregious abuses of the First Red Scare.[20]

In contrast, MID stayed in the domestic intelligence game following the First World War and joined the BOI in the Palmer Raids. But retrenchment quickly caught up with MID. A review of MID in 1921 suggested cuts to Negative Branch, which was responsible for counterintelligence and domestic intelligence. Army intelligence head Stuart Heintzelman warned, "The suspicion of gum-shoe work is doing the Army much harm."[21] But the greatest harm to MID was self-inflicted.

In the fall of 1922, First Lieutenant W. D. Long, the post intelligence officer for Vancouver Barracks, Washington, sent a letter addressed to law enforcement officials in Oregon stating, "The intelligence service of the Army has for its primary purpose the surveillance of all organizations or elements hostile or potentially hostile to the Government of this country, or who seek to overthrow the government by violence."[22] The letter named a few of these groups, including the Wobblies, socialists, the Communist Party, and the

American Federation of Labor, and requested the cooperation of local law enforcement in gathering information on them. The letter ignited a firestorm that reached the halls of Congress.

In response to the outrage, Secretary of War John Weeks made a statement to the press in which he set out to correct "the possibility of a public misunderstanding of the proper function of military intelligence in time of peace." He stressed, "The surveillance of domestic organizations or groups is not at all the purpose of the military intelligence division." While the First World War had "necessitated special measures," he explained that those had ended with the war. Weeks also wrote personal letters of apology and clarification to the leaders of some of the organizations Long had named, including the Brotherhood of Railroad Trainmen and the American Federation of Labor. Weeks attempted to assuage the public and possibly correct public perceptions of military intelligence, but his response still left open the possibility of further domestic intelligence operations by MID in a time of war.[23]

By the mid-1920s, Army intelligence reflected the mood of the day and distanced itself from domestic intelligence and the business of espionage more generally. A 1924 book, *Military Intelligence: A New Weapon in War*, by Lieutenant Colonel Walter C. Sweeney, emphasized the recent transformations in military intelligence and underscored the technophilic culture of the US intelligence establishment.[24] The book balanced the increasing amount of information, the new methods and means of collecting it, and the need for specially trained intelligence personnel against what Sweeney perceived to be the diminished value of spies. Aside from noting the "insidious nature of espionage," he determined that "modern warfare and the conditions surrounding it have caused the profitable use of spies and agents in enemy countries to be very greatly limited in comparison with what it was in former days." Convinced that "spying in enemy front line zones by military personnel is an impracticable, difficult and unprofitable task under present conditions of warfare," Sweeney pronounced, "A good airplane photograph of the front and rear areas of a division sector will convey more information of value in a few moments of study than could be produced by the long-continued efforts of many officer or soldier spies."[25]

Sweeney also examined another area of espionage that he called "War Propaganda" which resembled what today is known as covert action. According to Sweeney, this was a "new weapon of war" that included the types of subversion and sabotage the United States experienced at the hands of German intelligence agents during the First World War. Sweeney declared that this area of intelligence was "of such a detestable nature that it will never be employed by the United States," although the country's history of covert action went back to the Revolutionary War. He also argued that War Propaganda was "not operated by military personnel but by civilians" and "chiefly is directed against the civilian population in the homeland." Citing the Army's recent wartime experience, he explained, "To use military personnel for the purpose of combating civilian activities is not only a waste of military forces, but, particularly in the United States, is poor policy because it puts the military service in a bad light among its own people since it makes the military too active in purely civil affairs." Sweeney recommended that, rather than having the military carry out this work, the United States "create a new agency and method of defense" to counter War Propaganda. Sweeney's proposal for a new agency to conduct domestic intelligence would never suit the BOI and its new director.[26]

In an episode that reflected the scandal that had led to its creation, the BOI spied on members of Congress during the tenures of BOI Director William J. Burns and Attorney General Harry M. Daugherty from 1921 to 1924.[27] Daugherty and Burns used the BOI to intimidate Daugherty's political rivals in Congress, a brazen act of political intelligence exposed by congressional hearings into the so-called Teapot Dome scandal in the Harding administration. Following the resignations of both Daugherty and Burns in 1924, leadership of the BOI passed to Burns's deputy, J. Edgar Hoover. The Teapot Dome scandal and other BOI controversies taught Hoover to stay out of Congress's crosshairs and avoid scandals.[28] He learned to deftly wield intelligence to intimidate political rivals without becoming a victim of civil-intelligence relations like his predecessors. Hoover had no time to waste.

The American Civil Liberties Union (ACLU) was formed in January 1920 in response to the BOI's excesses during the Palmer Raids. The ACLU turned domestic intelligence on its head and began monitoring the BOI's activities. Its May 1924 report titled "The Nation-Wide Spy System Centering in the Department of Justice" stated that the BOI was a "secret police system actively infringing upon the civil rights of citizens."[29] In turn, Hoover had BOI agents spy on the ACLU; he even somehow managed to plant a spy on the ACLU's executive board.[30] Hoover also met with Roger Baldwin, an ACLU founder, and persuaded him that the BOI was no longer spying on American citizens and had discontinued the application of "the illegal methods so long used by the Bureau of Investigation."[31]

If external opposition to BOI operations was not going to stop Hoover, perhaps an internal order would. It was Daugherty's replacement as Attorney General, the famous jurist Harlan Fiske Stone, who appointed Hoover as

FIGURE 9.1 The new Director of the Bureau of Investigation, J. Edgar Hoover, seated at his desk in December 1924. Library of Congress.

head of the BOI. Stone had opposed the Palmer Raids and lectured Hoover on the dangers of mixing intelligence and law enforcement:

> There is always the possibility that a secret police may become a menace to free government and free institutions, because it carries with it the possibility of abuses of power which are not always quickly apprehended or understood. It is important that its activities be strictly limited to the performance of those functions for which it was created and that its agents themselves not be above the law or beyond its reach. The Bureau of Investigation is not concerned with political or other opinions of individuals. It is concerned only with their conduct and then only with such conduct as is forbidden by the laws of the United States. When a police system passes beyond these limits, it is dangerous to the proper administration of justice and to human liberty, which it should be our first concern to cherish.[32]

Stone clearly drew a line he expected the BOI to follow, and Hoover ostensibly acknowledged the new limitation on his authority. He wrote to Stone that although the BOI continued to receive information on communist activities, "the Bureau is making no investigations of such activities, inasmuch as it does not appear that there is any violation of a Federal Penal Statute involved."[33]

But Hoover was never going to abandon his mission to root out the radicals. Tim Weiner observes, "The risks of being caught spying on Americans were great," but to Hoover, "the risks of not spying seemed greater."[34] He realized that he had to keep the BOI's "political intelligence operations absolutely secret," so he assigned fewer agents to the domestic surveillance of socialists and subversives.[35] Hoover also picked up where John Lord O'Brian had left off in the First World War, and the BOI emerged as the principal US domestic intelligence organization by the mid-1920s, even if barely. John Fox, the FBI's official historian, concludes, "By the time the formal structure of the US Intelligence Community was created in 1947, responsibility for domestic counterintelligence had already been assigned and acted on by the Bureau for more than 25 years."[36] Under Hoover, the BOI, later FBI, won one of the major institutional and bureaucratic wars in American intelligence history by achieving supremacy over domestic intelligence, a function it still controls to this day.

To achieve his goals, Hoover exploited the BOI's blurry background as both a law enforcement agency and a domestic intelligence service. The BOI's intelligence operations managed to fly under the radar for the next decade as Hoover embraced the BOI's law enforcement role. The BOI began taking down brutal gangsters and mobsters like "Baby Face" Nelson, "Pretty Boy" Floyd, Al Capone, John Dillinger, and "Machine Gun" Kelly. Swashbuckling portrayals of BOI agents and operations in news and film won them the admiration and respect of the American people. This popularity would serve the Bureau well when it returned to performing visible domestic intelligence operations.[37]

Although domestic intelligence activities received the most attention, the First Red Scare occasioned other calls for intelligence reform. William Pinkerton, son of Allan Pinkerton, observed that America's intelligence organizations "were working practically independently of each other, under separate managements and inexperienced investigators, with different plans of operation, often on the same cases, and because of the lack of centralization and cooperation more often spoiled than accomplished, results." Worried that the country only just " 'got by' with its secret service work during the last four years," Pinkerton advocated the establishment of a "Federal secret service of ample size... [with] trained detectives that will centralize, connect up and weave together data." In short, Pinkerton envisioned a "centralized clearinghouse of secret service data for the protection of the people." Thus, the First

Red Scare produced yet another proposal for a new organization to coordinate intelligence, but once again, the United States failed to act.[38]

An American Intelligence Experiment

In September 1919, Woodrow Wilson, who had neglected sorely needed intelligence reform during the First World War, publicly called for peacetime intelligence. He urged his fellow Americans to abandon their historical bias and embrace intelligence:

> Plans must be kept secret. Knowledge must be accumulated by a system which we have condemned, because we have called it a spying system. The more polite call it a system of intelligence. You can not watch other nations with your unassisted eye. You have got to watch them by secret agencies planted everywhere.[39]

Wilson also invoked the memory of the recent war as all the more reason why America needed intelligence. He noted many countries had intelligence services but that "the German secret service found out more than the others did, and therefore Germany sprang upon the other nations unawares, and they were not ready for it."[40]

The United States had to know what the rest of the world was thinking and planning. Spies were not the only option. Advances in technology had propelled communications intelligence, or COMINT, as an essential function for states to understand the intentions and actions of allies and adversaries alike. During the First World War, Army intelligence included a COMINT subsection, MI 8, under the command of Major Herbert Yardley. Yardley was very much the father of MI 8, if not the father of American COMINT. He began his career in the State Department as a code clerk and became interested in cryptology, the practice of coding and decoding correspondence. The Army recognized the dismal state of military cryptology—the Germans had quickly compromised the Army's Code Book of 1915—and commissioned Yardley in 1917. When he took command of MI 8, Yardley set about recruiting staff. He quickly grew MI 8 from a staff of 2 to 165.[41]

In the course of the First World War, MI 8 intercepted and deciphered the telegrams of Germany, Argentina, Brazil, Chile, Costa Rica, Cuba, Mexico, Spain, and Panama.[42] It also decrypted a challenging, enciphered letter from Lothar Witzke, one of the German saboteurs in the United States.[43] During its first eighteen months, the section read 10,735 foreign messages and solved about fifty different codes and ciphers.[44] In comparison, Yardley alleged, the Navy's cryptologic bureau had failed to decipher a single cipher or code message.[45] The Code and Cipher Solution Section of MI 8 went on to perform cryptologic work for the War, Navy, State, and Justice Departments, proving the value of its interagency work.[46]

The only capable rival to MI 8 was the US Army Signal Corps. It was here that William Friedman began his career. Friedman was introduced to cryptology by his wife, Elizabeth Smith Friedman, an accomplished cryptanalyst in her right and one of the first group of female codebreakers who would shape the field.[47] William Friedman ended up in the Code Solution section of the AEF's Radio Intelligence Section during the war and subsequently moved to the Signal Corps. With retrenchment following the war, Friedman and Yardley found themselves engaged in the same intelligence function in different organizations competing for diminishing funds, which began a lifelong bureaucratic, professional, and personal rivalry between the two cryptologists.

After supporting the American Peace Commission to France, Yardley returned to the United States in March 1919 only to discover MI 8 was in a dismal state due to personnel and budget reductions. Yardley brought the issue to the attention of General Marlborough Churchill, the head of Army intelligence, who in turn discussed it with General Peyton March, the Army Chief of Staff. March explained that the Army simply did not have sufficient funds to maintain a full cryptologic bureau.[48] Out of financial necessity, the War Department would have to share ownership of the organization if it wanted to preserve the cryptologic function. According to Churchill, it would be necessary "to secure the assistance of the State Department if the work of the [code and] cipher section [was] to continue."[49] Fortunately, the State Department agreed. However, like domestic intelligence, COMINT in the interwar period would face what had emerged to be two of the foremost challenges of American civil-intelligence relations: bureaucratic competition and ideological aversion.

The First World War had already demonstrated to Lansing and others that forcing intelligence coordination between departments through a single organization was a futile goal. Perhaps fostering intelligence cooperation between departments through a single organization was possible. The War and State Departments decided to jointly fund Yardley's new COMINT organization, the Cipher Bureau, which began its operations in October 1919. Yardley proposed a $100,000 budget for his new outfit.[50] Bureaucratic competition was immediately apparent because the State Department said it would only pay its $40,000 stake in the Cipher Bureau if the Navy Department was excluded from the arrangement.[51] The War Department agreed and provided the remaining $60,000. Importantly, the Cipher Bureau was not an independent intelligence service, but instead was a subordinate organization of the State and War Departments. A combination of interpersonal (Yardley and Friedman), intradepartmental (the Army Signal Corps and the Cipher Bureau), and interdepartmental (the State and War Departments) rivalries guaranteed the Cipher Bureau would not survive.

Additional factors further complicated the Cipher Bureau's assimilation as a new intelligence organization. Due to a legal proscription against spending State Department funds in Washington, DC, Yardley was forced to set up shop in New York City. This meant that both the State and War Departments had less oversight of Yardley, who had a strong individualist streak. Even more confusion surrounded the status of the Cipher Bureau's employees. Yardley and Friedman noted that the staff was on a secret payroll with no record of civil service.[52] Although the State Department provided a substantial portion of the Cipher Bureau's budget, Yardley told one of its officials point blank, "I am not a State Department employee."[53] Yardley underscored that the Cipher Bureau was under military leadership and paid tribute to Marlborough Churchill, calling him a "fine general officer under whom we served."[54] He also recorded with pride that he received the Distinguished Service Medal.[55] Meanwhile, a War Department document in 1931 decoupled Yardley's position in the Cipher Bureau from his military commission as a reservist, explicitly stating that "his service... after the termination of his war commission in 1919 was as a civilian."[56] The same tension with departmental loyalties applied to other members of the Cipher Bureau, as Yardley recounted how a bureaucratic issue arose with one of his employees who had remained on the Justice Department's payroll.[57] Revealingly, the US government did not know where or how to assimilate intelligence officers as a professional body in the national security civil service.

The State and War Departments never seemed to settle on which department would administratively own the Cipher Bureau.[58] During its brief existence, it apparently operated for various periods under the oversight of both the State and War Departments, under the control of one but not the other, and independently. Perhaps on account of the bureaucratic confusion, Yardley exerted a large degree of personal control over the Cipher Bureau. Friedman claimed that it was so "far away from *direct* supervision of anybody connected with the War Department or of G-2... that nobody knew what was going on, how the office was administered, etc."[59] As an intelligence organization, the Cipher Bureau operated in a truly ambiguous environment of control and oversight.

Still, the Cipher Bureau was not self-funded. It was financially dependent on the War and State Departments, which made it vulnerable to postwar military retrenchment. After only one year in operation, the Cipher Bureau suffered a cut of half of its initial $100,000 budget. While the State Department paid its $40,000 in 1921, the War Department dropped its funding to $10,000, arguing that the Cipher Bureau's operations were primarily helping the State Department. Further budget cuts in 1924 forced Yardley to reduce the Cipher Bureau's staff by half. In its last year of existence, 1929, the Cipher Bureau's budget was a paltry $25,000, with the State Department fronting $15,000. The staff consisted of Yardley, one code and cipher expert, one translator, one secretary, and two clerk-typists.[60]

Military intelligence, generally, and COMINT, specifically, had to compete for dwindling resources amid growing bureaucratic competition. The existence of multiple COMINT organizations in the War Department taxed its budget allocations, and Friedman's Office of the Chief Signal Officer, the Cipher Bureau's main competitor, faced its own cuts. Rivalry with the Navy further intensified the competition over COMINT. The Navy had been excluded from the Cipher Bureau but still depended on it for COMINT.[61] The Cipher Bureau was simply spread too thin to satisfy all its possible intelligence consumers across several executive departments. In 1922, the Navy officially established its own COMINT organization, OP-20-G, which began to compete with the Cipher Bureau and Signal Corps.[62]

The Cipher Bureau was also impacted by the ideological retrenchment of the period. The national backlash against domestic intelligence hurt the Cipher Bureau's COMINT capabilities. For example, the Army did not have a robust system of radio intercept stations with which to provide COMINT organizations like the Cipher Bureau with raw intelligence.[63] The Cipher Bureau had to rely on the generosity and complicity of private telegraph companies to collect communications between foreign governments and their representatives in the United States. Telegraph companies became less willing to deliver copies of messages over the course of the 1920s.[64] Then, in February 1927, Congress passed a law prohibiting the interception of radio communications.[65] In response, Yardley claimed that his office was "forced to adopt rather subtle methods" to access foreign communications, possibly including thefts, bribes, or break-ins.[66]

Whether budgetary constraints, staff cuts, leadership, or lack of access to information correlated to declining productivity or not, the Cipher Bureau's performance deteriorated over the course of its existence. If the funding and work of the Cipher Bureau ebbed, the War Department's desire to maintain its COMINT function did not. In 1929, Major O. S. Albright of the Signal Corps, who supervised the cryptologic activities of the War Department, ascertained that the Cipher Bureau's operations almost exclusively benefited the State Department. Furthermore, the Cipher Bureau no longer trained new cryptologists, the primary purpose for which the War Department had originally funded it. Finally, Albright reasoned that the Signal Corps should house all the cryptologic work of the War Department, instead of the existing arrangement, which distributed responsibilities among three different components: the Adjutant General, the Signal Corps, and the Cipher Bureau. Albright therefore recommended that the Signal Corps should absorb the Cipher Bureau's functions. The Army Chief of Staff and Secretary of War approved Albright's recommendations, so the Cipher Bureau's continued existence depended on the State Department.[67]

When Henry Stimson, the new Secretary of State, learned of the Cipher Bureau's existence in the spring of 1929, he famously declared, "Gentlemen do not read each other's mail!" and ordered the State Department to stop funding the organization.[68] Stimson emphasized that this period of US foreign relations was one of "peace and trust," so in that spirit he closed the Cipher Bureau, unapologetically adding that "he never regretted" it.[69] McGeorge Bundy, Stimson's co-biographer, even recorded that Stimson was "always... proud" of his decision.[70] Cutting COMINT from the State Department would have far-reaching effects on the American intelligence system.

At stake in the survival of the Cipher Bureau was the bureaucratic future of communications and signals intelligence in the United States. While the State and War Departments were deciding the fate of the Cipher Bureau, Friedman created the Signal Intelligence Service (SIS) to consolidate Army COMINT. To add insult to injury, the cryptologists in Friedman's newly formed SIS used files obtained from the Cipher Bureau to jump-start their own work.[71] Thus, a key intelligence discipline, requiring a specially trained corps of intelligence professionals, continued to be subordinated to another institution of national security. Friedman even expressed his hope that the SIS would achieve a "proper organization and development in peacetime in preparation for operations at maximum efficiency in war."[72] Moreover, a 1939 memorandum determined that the "primary mission" of the SIS was to ensure Army cryptology was prepared for war.[73] The Cipher Bureau therefore not only represented another failure of interdepartmental cooperation and coordination but also foreshadowed the ultimate victory of the military in its efforts to control US signals intelligence, just as the BOI, later FBI, won the bureaucratic competition over domestic intelligence.

The Cipher Bureau was a remarkable organization for its time. In many ways, it illustrated the natural evolution of American intelligence. This brief experiment evolved as a quasi-independent, quasi-professional intelligence agency funded by a coalition of executive departments to preserve an essential intelligence discipline in peacetime. The Cipher Bureau lost the battle to survive due to double envelopment by its patrons as a product of larger bureaucratic and ideological battles over the structure and shape of the US intelligence system.

The Wrath of a Spy Once Scorned

Besides discarding the Cipher Bureau, the US government abandoned Yardley as well. It still needed to learn the lesson that it had to take care of its intelligence officers or risk having highly trained professionals expose the country's secrets to foreign states and public audiences. Indeed, Yardley went on to ply his trade by working for Canada and China. He also got his revenge in a tell-all book.

In 1931, Yardley released *The American Black Chamber* to considerable fanfare. The day after the book's publication, officials from the State and War Departments emphatically denied either the existence of the Cipher Bureau or their knowledge of it.[74] American civil society debated Yardley, his book, and the Cipher Bureau.[75] Some believed Yardley was a patriot who exposed nefarious intelligence activities that offended American principles. Others viewed him as a traitor who jeopardized national security. This early episode marked another controversial area of American civil-intelligence relations as the country struggled to distinguish between whistleblowers and traitors.

Yardley claimed that the rough treatment he received at the closing of the Cipher Bureau left him indigent, so the book sales represented a sort of severance pay.[76] He also defended his book based on his own sense of patriotism. He insisted that he "had hoped to bring home to [his] government and to the public the dangerous position that America holds by abolishing the Black Chamber."[77] Regardless of his intentions and personal beliefs, Yardley drew national and even international attention to the Cipher Bureau, its activities, and its sudden demise.

After taking so much care to stress secrecy to his staff in the Cipher Bureau, Yardley abandoned this sacrosanct pillar of intelligence professionalism in his book.[78] The Cipher Bureau's greatest coup undoubtedly involved codebreaking during the Washington Naval Conference. In 1921, nine nations assembled for the first arms control conference in history. There, these countries would set limitations on the size of their navies, a pivotal measure of power in the international system. The Cipher Bureau worked feverishly to decode Japanese diplomatic communications between Tokyo and Washington, even deciphering a new code that the Japanese developed immediately before the conference.[79] In his book, Yardley shared the correspondence between the Japanese government and its diplomats, including the message instructing the negotiators to accept a final ratio of 5 American and 5 British to 3 Japanese in terms of naval tonnage. The diplomatic advantage provided by COMINT was of inestimable value. As Yardley quipped, poker is an easy game when you know your adversary's hand.[80] Aside from Japan, Yardley named other states the Cipher Bureau had successfully targeted, including England, France, the Vatican, Mexico, Spain, and the Soviet Union. Finally, he provided examples of the codes the Cipher Bureau intercepted and how it went about decrypting them. Thus, Yardley committed the grave sin of exposing intelligence "sources and methods" in *The American Black Chamber*.

Yardley attempted to capitalize on the success of his first book by publishing a second, but the Justice Department invoked the Espionage Act of 1917 to seize the manuscript.[81] At the behest of the State and War Departments, Congress hurriedly passed an act that explicitly prohibited intelligence officers who had access to diplomatic codes from publishing them.[82] The law achieved its narrow purpose, blocking the publication of Yardley's second book. Still, the damage had been done. Yardley had revealed more objectionable intelligence activities to the American people during a period in which their suspicion of intelligence already ran high.

From the Roaring Twenties to the Threatening Thirties

The collective failure to develop a robust peacetime intelligence system left the country woefully unprepared for the threats it faced both at home and abroad as the horizon darkened throughout the 1930s. Given the pressures of the period, it should be no surprise that yet another proposal for a central intelligence organization failed in 1929.

That year, John A. Gade, a diplomat, naval officer, and architect drafted his plan for "some sort of central Intelligence Agency... reporting directly to" the President. Gade identified many of the issues that others had highlighted before him: a lack of coordination, the redundancy in intelligence functions and activities, and the need to return intelligence to presidential supervision and control. Although Gade preferred to place his proposed organization in the State Department, he believed that it should initially be independent, staffed by representatives from each of the existing intelligence organizations. He also insisted that this new organization would not be a "national secret service [which] the sentiment of every American of common sense bitterly opposed." Gade's proposal made its way to ONI and MID, where each organization promptly and perfunctorily rejected it.[83]

With the government closing or retrenching its existing intelligence organizations, some enterprising amateurs saw the virtues of intelligence and attempted to preserve it, even if informally. In 1927, a few American elites formed a secret society cryptically called The Room. It was the brainchild of Vincent Astor, scion of one of America's richest families. The Room's membership included prominent businessmen, academics, attorneys, and diplomats. Among the more notable members were two of President Theodore Roosevelt's sons, Theodore Jr. and Kermit; John W. Foster's grandson Allen Dulles; and Andrew Mellon's son-in-law, David K. E. Bruce. These men used their travels and connections to gather information, which they then shared in an apartment located in a brownstone on the Upper East Side of New York City.[84] The Room hearkened back to the tradition of the Mechanics, who met at the Green Dragon Tavern. Like the Mechanics, this amateur intelligence society was not a professional intelligence organization, and its members were not professional intelligence officers. Education and upbringing were not necessarily replacements for training and professionalization, and in this respect, The Room raised another issue that burdened much of American intelligence history.

From the earliest days of the country, it was often America's elites who spearheaded the growth of the intelligence establishment. That was particularly the case in the First World War and interwar periods. For example, Ralph Van Deman and his replacement, the already aristocratically named Marlborough Churchill, were both Harvard graduates, while Frank Polk and Gordon Auchincloss in the State Department were alumni of Yale.[85] To fill MID's ranks, Van Deman "consciously recruited almost exclusively from the class which ... may be called the 'best citizens of the community,'" while "ONI brought a similar class of people ... some of them golf or tennis buddies of Assistant Secretary of the Navy Franklin Roosevelt."[86] Former CIA officer and intelligence historian G. J. A. O'Toole suggested that the presence of these "clubbable young aristocrats" in an occupation that "their Victorian fathers and grandfathers would have deemed dishonorable" helped dispel "any lingering doubts of the propriety and respectability of the cloak-and-dagger trade."[87] Even if they perhaps resolved the place of intelligence in their own ranks, they created other problems for American civil-intelligence relations.

The tinge of elitism affected how intelligence officers used intelligence against their fellow citizens and, in turn, how their fellow citizens perceived intelligence. Raised with privilege, and in some cases prejudice, MID and ONI's "upper class officers... were unlikely to be particularly sympathetic to the marginalized portions of American society" that they targeted for surveillance.[88] Furthermore, this American intelligence caste system—the more conspiratorially minded might say cabal—influenced US foreign policy in sympathy with imperialism, which would embitter some parts of the world toward the United States.[89] Relatedly, the elitist background of intelligence officers would feed conspiracy theories in an American public that already nurtured suspicions of the shadowy world of intelligence.

For all their education and experience, the elites at the head of the American intelligence establishment continued to fail it in some of the most fundamental respects, especially the coordination of its organizations and activities. Looking back on American intelligence during the First World War, a BOI agent recollected in 1938, "There were probably seven or eight such active organizations operating at full force during war days and it was not an uncommon experience for an Agent of this Bureau to call upon an individual in the course of his investigation, to find out that six or seven other Government agents representing as many other investigative agencies had been around to interview the party about the same matter." With one eye toward the past and another toward the future, he predicted, "The experience had in those days was so convincing in the lesson it taught, as to make it certain that in the event of another World War, some central control should exist to correct the old evils."[90] Alas, the United States did not correct the very problems that individuals like Henry Shelton Sanford, Robert Lansing, or John Gade aimed to address, leaving the same issues of intelligence professionalization and coordination unresolved as ominous signs of another world war loomed.

10

Navigating into the Gathering Storm with Hoover at the Helm

J. EDGAR HOOVER emerged from the Oval Office on August 25, 1936, with a mandate and a mission. President Franklin Delano Roosevelt had just endorsed a new domestic intelligence campaign to be led by Hoover and his FBI. Roosevelt often relied on a broad reading of presidential authority as he dramatically overhauled the American administrative state with the New Deal and led the country through the Second World War. Intelligence was another area in which Roosevelt expanded executive power through presidential orders and directives.[1] For his part, Hoover had carefully played the bureaucratic game since 1924, establishing a name for himself and his Bureau as America's premier crimefighters. That patience appeared to pay off, as Hoover seemed poised to become America's first intelligence czar.

Both Hoover and Roosevelt were attempting to exercise individual control over intelligence at different levels. As President, Roosevelt directly inserted himself into intelligence affairs—albeit in his own unwieldy, meddlesome way—after decades in which Presidents largely left intelligence to the warring executive departments. Hoover made his bid for control by maneuvering the FBI and himself into the center of the intelligence community. But winning control required coordinating intelligence, a goal that would again be thwarted by bureaucratic competition.

Charting a Cautious Course

Hoover's experience during the First Red Scare and its aftermath had taught him to avoid intelligence scandals and the associated bad publicity. In 1931, when the House introduced a bill that would have authorized the BOI to investigate communists, Hoover turned down the opportunity. He framed his decision in terms of the ambiguous boundary between law enforcement and domestic intelligence. He suggested to Congressman Hamilton Fish, who chaired the House committee investigating communists, that "it would be better to make it a crime to participate in such activities," explaining that even if the Bureau was authorized to conduct surveillance of communists, "it would be in the position of having a mass of material with which nothing could be done, because there [was] no legislation to take care of it." In a nod to another lingering problem, Hoover added that "the Bureau has never been established by legislation, but operates solely on an appropriation bill."[2]

The following year, Hoover expounded his reasons for turning down Congress in a letter to Attorney General William D. Mitchell. He portrayed the issue as one of transparency, claiming that "the work of the Bureau of Investigation at this time is . . . of an open character not in any manner subject to criticism, and the operations of the Bureau of Investigation may be given the closest scrutiny at all times." He believed this would change "were the Bureau to embark upon a policy of investigative activity into conditions which, from a federal standpoint, have not been declared illegal and in connection with which no prosecution might be instituted." Hoover also worried that "the Bureau would undoubtedly be subject to charges in the matter of alleged secret and undesirable methods . . . as well as to allegations involving charges of the use of 'Agents Provocateur.' "[3] Hoover feared the public outcry if the BOI visibly jumped back into the domestic intelligence business—at least before the country was ready for it.

Opportunities continued to come Hoover's way. In October 1933, he turned down another invitation for the BOI to conduct domestic intelligence operations, this time on behalf of the Immigration Service.[4] The next appeal came from Roosevelt himself. In a White House meeting of May 1934 attended by Hoover, the Attorney General, the Secretary of the Treasury, and the Chief of the Secret Service, Hoover recorded that Roosevelt desired a "very careful and searching investigation of" the Nazi movement in America with particular attention to whether the German embassy and consulates were involved. Hoover emphasized that the attendees agreed that there should be "one clearing house for information upon this activity" and revealingly proposed that the "investigation should be considered a so-called intelligence investigation," with reports moving directly from Hoover to the Attorney General to the President. Hoover could not turn down the President, so he accepted Roosevelt's request and instructed BOI field offices to investigate Nazis. In doing so, he was also carefully setting the conditions to place himself and the Bureau at the center of the intelligence system he was shaping.[5]

But Hoover declined other chances to broaden his intelligence mandate. For example, he reported to the Acting Attorney General in 1935 that the

State Department approached him about the possibility of sharing information on communists with foreign intelligence or law enforcement services. He dutifully insisted that the Bureau only investigated violations of federal law. Besides, he explained, the "little information... obtained by this Bureau relating to the activities of these radical organizations" was "of no value when existing laws do not permit a prosecution," repeating the argument he had made in 1931.[6] However, some claim Hoover had continued to spy on communists for the State Department in accordance with Congress's 1916 statute allowing the BOI to conduct targeted investigations on its behalf.[7] If so, the wary Hoover may have preferred this narrow arrangement to what the State Department now proposed, reasoning that intelligence sharing with foreign services exceeded his mandate to perform investigations strictly for the State Department. Certainly, he would have wanted to avoid the possible exposure of an international network of spy services that would have almost certainly produced public backlash.

Hoover's stated reluctance to conduct domestic intelligence operations does not explain why he was willing to accept Roosevelt's request to surveil the Nazi movement in the United States in 1934. Hoover likely wanted to build his credibility with the President to ensure his own political survival.[8] Moreover, there was a difference between decisions reached in a secret meeting of senior officials, including the President, and overt or formal requests from Congress and other executive departments. Additionally, if Hoover could connect Nazi activities to German consulates and diplomats, then he perhaps could find legislative cover under the 1917 Espionage Act or another statute. Intentions and obfuscations aside, Hoover and the Bureau's domestic intelligence activities were bound to grow alongside the dual threats of communism and fascism in the mid- to late 1930s.

On August 24, 1936, Hoover met one-on-one with Roosevelt. According to Hoover, the President was "desirous of discussing the question of the subversive activities in the United States, particularly Fascism and Communism." In response, Hoover described a range of communist activities, suggesting that he had persisted with domestic intelligence despite his earlier declarations to the contrary. Even if his prior investigations into communists or Nazis were confined to specific individuals or groups, the meeting with Roosevelt inevitably required expanding the Bureau's operations. For that to happen, Hoover wanted legal cover. He explained to Roosevelt that the Bureau could conduct investigations on behalf of the State Department under the existing law from 1916. Hoover coaxingly informed Roosevelt that there was not "at the present time" a "governmental organization which [was] getting any so-called 'general intelligence information'" on the topics of interest to the President. Hoover hinted that if Roosevelt were to arrange for the State Department to make the appropriate request, he and the Bureau were ready to provide their assistance.[9]

At that point, the meeting turned to two familiar themes of American intelligence history: secrecy and bureaucratic competition. Roosevelt expressed his reluctance to make "a formal request... through the State Department because of the many leaks therein." This comment reveals why Hoover perhaps rejected the State Department's invitation to work with foreign intelligence services in 1935: he feared leaks that would invite public scrutiny. As a solution, Roosevelt told Hoover that he would put a handwritten memorandum of his request to the Secretary of State in his personal safe at the White House. He instructed Hoover to return to the White House the following day for a meeting with Secretary of State Cordell Hull to make the necessary arrangements. As a final matter, Roosevelt "suggested" that Hoover "coordinate any investigation along similar lines" with the "Military or Naval Intelligence Services," but not the Secret Service, which Roosevelt felt "should confine themselves strictly to the matter of protecting his life." This meeting echoed the March 1918 meeting led by John Lord O'Brian where the BOI and military intelligence services effectively cut the Secret Service out of domestic intelligence. In 1936, the President himself endorsed the arrangement and placed Hoover right at the center of the US intelligence establishment.[10]

The next day, Roosevelt, Hoover, and Hull walked through the pro forma process of having Hull request that the Department of Justice investigate communism and fascism on behalf of the State Department.[11] Roosevelt stressed that "both of these movements were international in scope" and therefore "fell within the scope of foreign affairs over which the State Department would have a right to request an inquiry be made." Unlike any previous, specific investigations the Bureau might have made on behalf of the State Department, this request was for a general, national intelligence operation. Perhaps due to the gravity of the discussion, Hull wondered aloud about memorializing the meeting's decisions in writing, but Roosevelt claimed that "it would be sufficient that the President, the Secretary of State, and [Hoover] should be the ones aware of this request," although he added that Hoover should inform the Attorney General.[12] Other stakeholders in American intelligence were excluded from the decision-making as well.

Congress was noticeably absent from the arrangements between Roosevelt and Hoover. It is possible Roosevelt realized that he would never obtain the legislation he sought if he went to Congress, which had a strong isolationist bloc among his Republican opposition and was focused on the economy.[13] Instead of troubling himself with Congress, Roosevelt invoked the historical precedent of personally supervising intelligence with no congressional oversight or interference. He simply excluded Congress from having any role in intelligence, rather than risk Congress curtailing intelligence operations. Just as Wilson had given permission for the Secret Service to conduct domestic intelligence operations in May 1915, in direct violation of the limitations set by Congress, Roosevelt did the same in 1934, in a departure from existing statutory policy.[14] In 1936, Roosevelt adopted the broadest possible reading of the 1916 law to authorize a wide-ranging intelligence campaign. He subsequently continued to issue both official and unofficial presidential directives into the late 1930s, but in doing so, he made "no attempt to clarify what domestic intelligence functions were authorized by statute and what functions were based on an implicit claim of inherent presidential power."[15] The problem was as old as the country itself. The Founders had failed to provide for the basic contours of intelligence in the Constitution, so they left the boundaries open to interpretation and competition between the two branches.

Hoover found himself in a precarious position. He was not going to allow secret Oval Office meetings to position him or the Bureau to take the fall if domestic intelligence operations became public and prompted congressional investigations. He wanted a record of events, but the record is part of the problem because only Hoover's memoranda of his verbal communications with Roosevelt and other senior officials survive. In this respect, it is difficult to know exactly what Roosevelt authorized and any limitations he might have imposed.[16] Having already made a memorandum of the meeting with Roosevelt and Hull—despite Roosevelt's response to Hull that the decisions made at the meeting would not be recorded in writing—Hoover followed up with another memorandum to his special assistant, Edward A. Tamm, on September 10, 1936. In it, he carefully reiterated the hierarchy of policymakers—from the President to the Secretary of State to the Attorney General—and legal procedures defining the new domestic intelligence program, including Roosevelt's instruction to coordinate the investigation with ONI, MID, and the State Department. Tellingly, Hoover concluded the memorandum, "This, therefore, is the authority upon which to proceed in the conduct of this investigation, which should, of course, be handled in a most discreet and confidential manner."[17]

Hoover took advantage of the President's instructions to slowly and secretly enlarge the Bureau's range of intelligence operations and his personal control over the larger intelligence effort. He recorded that in his August 24 meeting with Roosevelt, the President was "interested in ... obtaining a broad picture of the general [communist] movement and its activities as may affect the economic and political life of the country as a whole."[18] Of the August 25 meeting, Hoover again made it a point to say that the President wanted a "survey" made of communist and fascist activities, suggesting an open-ended investigation.[19] The problem was that Roosevelt's intent was open to interpretation. Just as A. Mitchell Palmer had taken Wilson's admonition to "not let the country see red" as authorization for massive domestic intelligence operations, Hoover adopted an expansive interpretation of Roosevelt's instructions, which inevitably meant giving him and his organization more power.[20]

In the event, Roosevelt was unlikely to restrain Hoover's intelligence activities. As early as 1933, Hoover was fielding White House requests for political intelligence, which eventually extended across the political spectrum to include right-wing opposition to the New Deal, the left-wing Communist Party presidential candidate, Earl Browder, and obstructionist members of Congress.[21] Roosevelt used the information provided by Hoover as part of his response to the formidable isolationist movement.[22] One of the targets was Charles Lindbergh, the acclaimed aviator who was a Nazi sympathizer and vocal anti-interventionist.[23] So, in addition to using intelligence for personal political purposes, Roosevelt also used it to advance his foreign policy goals.

Not only did Roosevelt welcome intelligence on his political rivals, but he was also willing to circumvent constitutional protections as he thought necessary. For example, he issued a confidential memorandum to the Attorney General authorizing the Bureau to conduct wiretaps for intelligence purposes despite both congressional legislation and Supreme Court precedents limiting the practice. Roosevelt's directive acknowledged that "under ordinary and normal circumstances wiretapping by Government agents should not be carried on for the excellent reason that it is almost bound to lead to abuse of civil rights." But he believed that wiretapping was essential to intelligence, which he distinguished from law enforcement. Although judicial precedent applied to wiretapping for law enforcement purposes, he claimed that the Supreme Court's decision in *Nardone v. United States* did not intend this "to apply to grave matters involving defense of the nation."[24]

Once again, Hoover interpreted Roosevelt's instructions broadly. The Bureau's wiretapping operations exploded, netting intelligence ranging from the political to the personal and fostering in the Bureau a dangerously misplaced sense of organizational independence apart from both the President and the Attorney General.[25] In the case of Lindbergh, it "collected derogatory information that clearly had no useful purpose other than to discredit" him, especially with regard to his "moral character."[26] Hoover conducted political intelligence operations not only for the President's benefit but also for his own by monitoring the inner workings of the Roosevelt administration. In one case, Tamm, his trusted deputy, reported to him about the influence Supreme Court Justice Felix Frankfurter had on Roosevelt's presidential appointments.[27] Hoover would work every angle to shore up his position with the President. He also accommodated Roosevelt's preference for in-person communication and often avoided notifying the Attorney General of their meetings.[28] Hoover therefore established a relationship with Roosevelt that led the President to vest him with increasing intelligence powers.

Hoover's machinations during the 1930s were as careful as they were at times confusing. To be fair, he had to navigate several challenges, including blurry boundaries between law enforcement and domestic intelligence, vague statutory authorities, interbranch competition between the President and Congress, and the growing threat of communism and fascism in the United

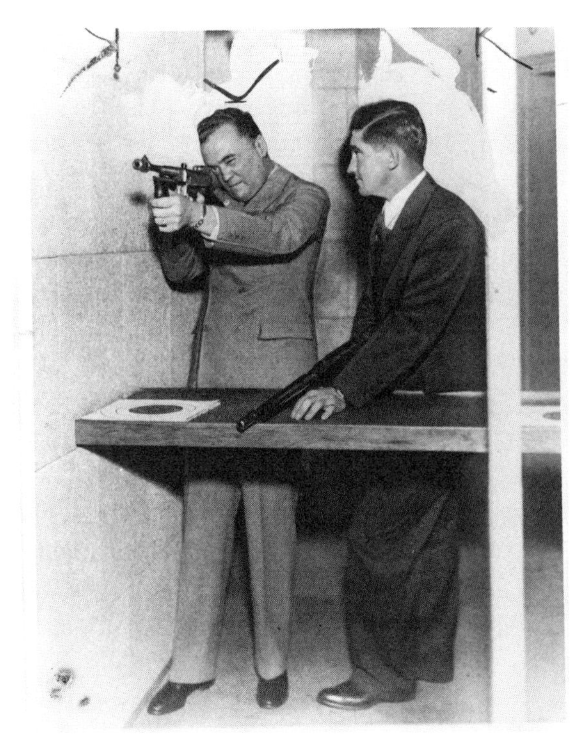

FIGURE 10.1 Hoover, head of the newly minted FBI, shows Mickey Cochrane, the manager of the Detroit Tigers, how to shoot a tommy gun in September 1935. Library of Congress.

States—the entire enterprise made all the more complicated by a fickle American public. Hoover received a bureaucratic status boost for his efforts. First, in 1933, Roosevelt consolidated the Bureau of Prohibition and the Bureau of Investigation into a larger Division of Investigation, headed by Hoover.[29] Then, in 1935, Congress finally formally established the Federal Bureau of Investigation. Notably, the enabling statute made the FBI's first and foremost function the "detection and prosecution of crimes," but did not mention anything related to intelligence.[30] It was just as well with Hoover, who was enhancing his and the Bureau's position without any pushback from the President, Congress, or the American people.

Hoover "Has the Problem Well in Hand"

Immediately after concluding the two August 1936 meetings with Roosevelt, Hoover set to work organizing a new American domestic intelligence campaign. In September, he sent out orders to the FBI's field offices stating, "The Bureau desires to obtain from all possible sources information concerning subversive activities being conducted in the United States by Communists, Fascisti, and representatives or advocates" of any radical groups. Furthermore, he demanded, "No investigation should be initiated into cases of this kind in the absence of specific authorization from the Bureau, but you should forward to the Bureau information obtained from all sources."[31] Hoover wanted to be the hub for American intelligence. By closely monitoring and directing investigations himself, he aimed to avoid the scandals that afflicted the Bureau during the First Red Scare.

A public relations disaster nearly derailed Hoover's grand design before he could implement it. In February 1938, Guenther Rumrich, a naturalized US citizen, was arrested by the New York City police as he tried to impersonate Secretary of State Cordell Hull in order to obtain blank passports at the New York Passport Office. At first, the State Department was unsure if it wanted to hold Rumrich on the relatively minor charge of impersonating Hull. But then a tip came in from the British. MI5, the British domestic intelligence service, was surveilling a German intelligence asset who had been routing Nazi communications through Britain for over a year. One series of correspondence was with a German spy in the United States code-named "Crown." When MI5 discovered a plot against the commander of Fort Totten in New York City, it passed the information to the War Department. A search of Rumrich's home and subsequent confession by Rumrich himself revealed that he was "Crown." The United States had caught its first German spy.[32]

Hoover initially opposed the FBI's involvement in the case due to the "messy jurisdictional issues" and a "complete absence of coordination among the State Department, War Department, FBI, New York City Police Department, and British Security Service."[33] However, the case was too important, and the FBI took over the investigation. Hoover assigned Leon Turrou, an FBI agent, to handle Rumrich's interrogation. The interrogation was an intelligence gold mine, as Rumrich revealed his sources and methods. Turrou began to uncover an extensive German spy network operating in the United States.

At this point, the conflict between law enforcement and intelligence in the FBI's organizational culture almost cost Turrou, the FBI, and Hoover dearly. A proven and capable law enforcement officer, Turrou fell short as an intelligence officer. He told the suspects he was investigating that they were subject to subpoenas to testify before a grand jury. Predictably, most of them fled the country. Rather than celebrate the discovery of this German spy ring, the press blamed Hoover and the FBI for the spies' escape. Still worse, Turrou had been leaking details of the investigation to the press and was summarily dismissed from the FBI for violating its nondisclosure agreement. Turrou challenged his dismissal. He also attempted to capitalize on the case—and the American people's mixed reaction of fascination and fear—by selling his story to the *New York Post*. In response, the US government obtained a court order barring its publication. Turrou's attorney underscored the irony that "one of the most prolific sources of news . . . was J. Edgar Hoover, who was Mr. Turrou's Chief." The press also protested the government's attempts to silence Turrou. The publisher of the *New York Post* even wrote to Roosevelt, who took the Department of Justice's side due to the sensitivity of prosecuting the first German espionage case since World War I.[34]

Turrou persisted. In 1939, he published a book, *Nazi Spies in America*. His story was also sensationalized in the film *Confessions of a Nazi Spy* that same year. He later defended himself in his 1949 autobiography, *Where My Shadow Falls*, claiming that "in 1938" the FBI "had no counterespionage service," which meant that "the ferreting out of spies by the FBI had had no precedent."[35] He was not entirely correct, given the scale of the BOI's domestic intelligence operations during the First World War and First Red Scare. In the interim, Hoover had worked hard to rehabilitate the organization's image in the eyes of the American people. With Turrou's bungling of the Rumrich case, the Bureau's first major public foray back into domestic intelligence had collapsed spectacularly.

Hoover was undaunted. In October 1938, he penned an internal memorandum for the FBI in which he insisted that "investigative activities and protective measures [must be] handled by one central agency, the Bureau."[36] To do so required endorsement from the very top, and Hoover fortunately had the President's ear. The Rumrich affair had forced Roosevelt to respond to a media frenzy that again kindled the public's fear of German espionage and sabotage. In press statements, Roosevelt acknowledged the country's intelligence shortcomings and promised reforms to strengthen its intelligence establishment. He instructed Attorney General Homer Stillé Cummings to convene a meeting of senior officials to discuss the current state of American intelligence.[37]

On October 20, 1938, Cummings replied to Roosevelt with a letter that included a memorandum from Hoover. Hoover opened by stating that the "purpose of this memorandum will be to present the present purposes and scope of the three phases of domestic intelligence handled by the three intelligence services of the United States Government, namely, the Military Intelligence Division; the Office of Naval Intelligence; and the Federal Bureau of Investigation, together with suggestions for expansion and such further coordination as may be effected along this general line." Suddenly, the Bureau was no longer a law enforcement agency, but one of three American intelligence services—Hoover excluded the Secret Service or any other organization from their ranks. Additionally, he informed Roosevelt that the FBI, ONI, and MID had "developed a close and coordinated plan of cooperation," including a division of responsibilities in which ONI and MID would "restrict their activities to those matters which pertain to the two armed services" and the FBI would investigate "strictly civilian matters of a domestic character." However, Hoover's real purpose in drafting the memorandum was not to outline the state of American intelligence but to propose changes that would secure his and the Bureau's control over it.[38]

Hoover explained to Roosevelt that "the structure which is already in existence is much broader than espionage or counter-espionage, but covers in a true sense real intelligence values to the three services interested." He mentioned that the FBI had a special school for new agents that also trained a few ONI officers. He wanted to enlarge the school to train FBI, ONI, and MID agents "in general intelligence work," emphasizing that it was a "special class of work."[39] On the one hand, Hoover seemed to recognize that intelligence was a distinct profession and that intelligence as an institution extended beyond the traditional fields of espionage and counter-espionage. On the other, intelligence would remain subordinated to the military and law enforcement professions under Hoover's proposal.

Standing in Hoover's way was a familiar obstacle. In order to execute his master plan, Hoover appealed to Roosevelt for the "utmost degree of secrecy in order to avoid criticism or objections which might be raised to such an expansion" of the US intelligence system. He explained that the "word 'espionage' has long been a word that has been repugnant to the American people," and therefore suggested that "it would seem undesirable to seek any special legislation which would draw attention to the fact that it was proposed to develop a special counter-espionage drive of any great magnitude."[40] Of course, it was Hoover who proposed the expansion and Roosevelt who would have to publicly support Hoover if the two sought congressional legislation. Roosevelt, who had already demonstrated his predilection for secrecy and unilateral executive action, did not need much convincing. Hoover recorded that Roosevelt approved the proposal in a private meeting on the Presidential Special Train on November 2, 1938. During that meeting, Roosevelt also informed Hoover that he had instructed the Director of Budget to include appropriations of $50,000 for MID, $50,000 for ONI, and $150,000 for the FBI.[41] Thanks to Hoover's efforts, the FBI was overtaking its competition as the most powerful organization in the US intelligence community.

Hoover and the FBI also received a boost from the press. In December 1938, an article in the *New York Times* bearing the rather plain title "Spies" announced that "Army and navy intelligence officers and agents of the Federal Bureau of Investigation are busier today in watching the activities of suspicious persons than at any time since the [First] World War." It naively claimed that "the peacetime spy in America has scant 'pickings'... There are few real secrets, military or otherwise, here or elsewhere," and so "the spy's role is limited," adding that "much of his time... is spent in a desperate search for the obvious." The *Times* opined that "the creation of any super-espionage military agency is both unnecessary and undesirable," insisting that it would be "alien to American tradition, and no glorified 'OGPU' [Soviet security service] or secret police is needed or wanted here." Instead, "a civilian agency of the Government already has the problem well in hand," meaning the FBI. Despite its missteps in the Rumrich affair, the FBI still had more public support for domestic intelligence work because it was a civilian agency and therefore seemed less threatening than a military service. Hoover's attempts to woo the public through the FBI's law enforcement activities and persuade the President through personal overtures were paying off.[42]

Overcoming Old Obstacles

Although Secretary of State Cordell Hull had given Hoover the legal cover to expand the FBI's domestic intelligence operations, it was the State Department that first resisted Hoover's power grab in early spring 1939. Assistant Secretary of State George Messersmith initially tried to go behind Hoover's back by calling a meeting of representatives from the intelligence community, specifically excluding the FBI. Messersmith claimed at the meeting that Roosevelt had tapped him to coordinate domestic intelligence investigations—the same role Hoover thought Roosevelt had assigned to him.[43] One explanation for the redundancy was that Roosevelt once bragged that he "never let [his] right hand know what [his] left hand does," so it is possible that he assigned the same function to both men.[44]

In another version of this story. Roosevelt wanted Messersmith to gather all the heads of the intelligence agencies together, which he did. However, Hoover declined the invitation and did not attend. When Messersmith reported the FBI director's conspicuous absence to Hull, and Hull reported it to Roosevelt, Roosevelt told Hoover to attend the next meeting or be prepared to submit his resignation.[45] Regardless of which account is correct, Messersmith was positioning the State Department to be at the center of the US intelligence system. Hoover fought back.

Hoover complained to the new Attorney General, Frank Murphy, about the State Department's intrusion on the intelligence arrangement he had so carefully cultivated. Claiming that Messersmith intended to divvy up domestic intelligence investigations among different organizations, Hoover argued that he "consider[ed] centralization of all information in cases of this type in one agency absolutely essential to the proper conducting of proper investigations." The Justice, War, and Navy Departments had formed a coalition against the Treasury and State Departments in 1918. The old alliances stood fast in 1939, and ONI and MID became auxiliaries in Hoover's effort to control intelligence.[46] To this end, Hoover warned Murphy that "the Treasury Department and the State Department were reluctant to concede jurisdiction" and asked him to "take appropriate action with reference to other governmental agencies, including the State Department, which are attempting to literally chisel into this type of work." At Hoover's instigation, Murphy wrote to the President to argue against an interdepartmental intelligence committee led by the State Department in favor of an interdepartmental committee made up of the heads of the FBI, MID, and ONI.[47]

Roosevelt accepted Murphy's reasoning and issued a directive temporarily resolving the ongoing bureaucratic competition in June 1939. The directive stated that it was the President's "desire that the investigation of all espionage, counterespionage, and sabotage matters be controlled and handled by the Federal Bureau of Investigation of the Department of Justice, the Military Intelligence Division of the War Department, and the Office of Naval Intelligence in the Navy Department," adding that the "directors of these three agencies are to function as a committee to coordinate their activities." Crucially, Roosevelt mandated, "No investigations should be conducted by any investigative agency of the Government into matters involving actually or *potentially* any espionage, counterespionage, or sabotage, except by the three agencies mentioned above." He then ordered any other agencies currently conducting investigations of these kinds to "refer immediately" to the FBI "any data, information, or material that may come to their notice bearing directly or *indirectly*" on these areas. Through this directive, Roosevelt essentially adopted Hoover's proposal of October 1938.[48]

However, Hoover faced a legal problem. He no longer wanted to work under the 1916 statute that required the State Department to make requests before the FBI could open investigations because it provided the State Department with some grounds to claim it should be responsible for intelligence coordination. Hoover had to abandon his long-held deference to Congress's 1916 statute. When he provided Murphy with his proposal to boost the FBI's intelligence resources and operations in 1938, he had acknowledged that it was "not within the specific provisions of prevailing statutes."[49] In lieu of congressional statutes, Hoover accepted presidential approval as sufficient authority. Roosevelt issued a directive on September 6, 1939, that the FBI "should take charge of investigative work in matters relating to espionage, sabotage and violations of the neutrality regulations."[50] Two days later, Roosevelt declared a limited national emergency and approved an expansion of the FBI to meet the threat. Echoing Wilson's warning twenty years earlier, Roosevelt told the press that he had to empower the FBI to prevent the country from being caught off guard by German sabotage, propaganda, and subversion as it had been before its official involvement in the First World War.[51]

The American public responded to the emergency by again supporting intrusive domestic intelligence measures. Letters and telegrams poured in, often addressed directly to the President. Some purported to identify individual spies and subversives. A telegram by Marietta Warren of Tyler, Texas, implored the President, "Please demonstrate your sincerity in eliminating fifth column activities by getting rid of Harry Bridges... without delay."[52] Others offered their ideas for countering the fifth column. Herbert Adams, possibly a Harvard acquaintance of Roosevelt, wrote the President a personal letter addressed "Dear Franklin," in which he recalled the work of the American Protective League. While confessing that he had "never learned how large the success of this body was," he suggested the President create "an organization based upon similar principles, but set up along different lines," that would "function in utmost secrecy without violating cherished individual liberty."[53]

Support for Hoover and the FBI as well as domestic intelligence in general persisted throughout the war. For example, the Sheriffs' Association of Texas "unanimously endors[ed] the work and policies of the Federal Bureau of Investigation as administered by the Honorable John Edgar Hoover, its Director, as well as the manner in which the FBI under his able direction has discharged its war-time responsibilities as the national coordinating investigative agency in matters pertaining to espionage, sabotage, and subversive activities."[54] The spy fever and hysteria of the Second World War culminated with one of the worst, targeted violations of constitutional rights in US history, the mass internment of Japanese Americans, which was supported by the President and upheld by the Supreme Court. As Herbert Adams's letter revealed, the American people had not learned the lessons of history.

The greatest risks to Hoover's designs during the interwar period were public exposure and congressional scrutiny. A new world war and a new wave of spy mania allowed him to justify the FBI's activities to both audiences. In their comments to the press, Hoover and Murphy reassured the country that, unlike the First World War, this time the "detection and punishment of spies would be characterized by no irresponsible witch hunts." Murphy announced that "we will not act on the basis of hysteria," conceding that "twenty years ago inhuman and cruel things were done in the name of justice." Hoover added for good measure, "Let there be no hysteria, no unbridled trampling upon the rights of innocent persons."[55] Hoover also began to brief Congress on FBI intelligence activities after Roosevelt's proclamation of a limited national emergency, protected by the cover of presidential authority. He informed Congress that the FBI had created a General Intelligence Division and was authorized to perform intelligence investigations pursuant to the President's orders of September 1939. Congress did not protest.[56]

In fact, Congress began its own investigations. In 1938, the Dies Committee, better known as the House Committee on Un-American Activities, convened to investigate fascist and communist subversion in the United States. Its chair, Martin Dies Jr., pushed Roosevelt to root out subversive elements embedded in the US government itself. The FBI had files on government employees, some of which were built through information gained by illegally breaking into the offices of left-wing movements.[57] In a letter to Attorney General Robert Jackson, who replaced Murphy, Representative Jerry Voorhis explained that the "Department of Justice and the Dies Committee are by their very nature complementary agencies." Although the Dies Committee had "neither the power, the facilities nor the personnel to enter" into the domestic intelligence arena, Voorhis suggested that it could carry out "the work of exposing to the light of public knowledge matters concerning such organizations and groups which may not be violations of our laws but which are nevertheless clearly inimical to the cause of the preservation of our Constitutional Democracy."[58] Rather than act as a restraining element on domestic intelligence, Congress embraced the new campaign.

Mixing politics and intelligence eventually entangled Roosevelt, Hoover, and Dies. Hoover and Dies thought Roosevelt was too restrained and wanted him to let them conduct their investigations without any interference. This was a problem for Roosevelt because Dies, though a Democrat, had turned against the New Deal and was wielding his committee against the administration and its domestic agenda.[59] In a reprise of earlier politicized intelligence investigations, the President ordered the FBI to investigate Dies in 1942 for a possible campaign payment from a German national, likely as a check on the congressman.[60] Perhaps remembering his experience with the May Day scare and Palmer Raids, Hoover expressed his frustration with Dies's public fear-mongering about conspiracies that never came to pass and charges that the FBI was "negligent" in investigating some of the alleged offenses.[61] Unlike his fellow Americans, Hoover had learned the lessons of history and used them to his advantage at the expense of civil-intelligence relations.

Hoover Heads an Intelligence Steering Committee

With neither the public nor Congress standing in the way of his efforts to construct the intelligence system he wanted, Hoover turned to the arrangement that Roosevelt had instituted in June 1939. The new troika, comprising the heads of the FBI, ONI, and MID, became known as the Interdepartmental Intelligence Committee (IIC). Hoover initially opposed the interdepartmental committee model when the State Department tried to take the helm, but he accepted the new arrangement because he had whittled down the competition to what he must have regarded as the more manageable military intelligence organizations. As a consolation prize, the IIC allowed a State Department representative to attend meetings except when it held "closed" discussions.[62] First Messersmith and then Assistant Secretary of State Adolf Berle attended as a "friendly link with FDR" but "never functioned as the *coordinator*" of the IIC.[63] Representatives from other excluded organizations and departments were able to attend as well, but the responsibility for coordinating and steering intelligence lay with the IIC.

The IIC attempted to overcome the bureaucratic competition that had plagued American intelligence in the last war. The three organizations successfully navigated past their conflicts over counterintelligence and domestic intelligence. With the help of Ralph Van Deman, who came out of retirement to assist, they agreed to a series of "Delimitation Agreements" that created spheres of responsibility for each organization.[64] The FBI assumed sole responsibility for investigations involving civilians in the United States except for US territories in the Canal Zone, Guam, Samoa, and the Philippines.[65] Ultimately, the Delimitation Agreements between the FBI, on one side, and ONI and MID, on the other, cemented the FBI's control over domestic intelligence by 1942, concluding a major bureaucratic struggle that had been ongoing since the First World War.[66]

But the IIC ran into trouble when it took up the issue of American espionage operations overseas. At the time, there was no US organization dedicated to gathering human intelligence (HUMINT) from overseas. Moreover, there were no professional intelligence officers specially trained in HUMINT; instead, the country relied on amateur enthusiasts like Vincent Astor or on military attachés. HUMINT became a new bureaucratic battleground and fault line for the IIC.

Adolf Berle, the State Department representative to the IIC, spoke to Roosevelt about forming a unit dedicated to HUMINT. Curiously, Roosevelt told Berle that he wanted the FBI to be responsible for foreign intelligence collection in the Western Hemisphere and for ONI and MID to share responsibility for the rest of the world.[67] The three organizations memorialized this arrangement in a memorandum of agreement. The memorandum also recorded that Hoover created a Special Intelligence Service (SIS) to conduct operations in the Western Hemisphere. The SIS would obtain information "primarily through undercover operations," so the FBI was expanding its intelligence mandate into the foreign intelligence collection realm.[68]

This new division of labor, especially the blending of the FBI's domestic and foreign intelligence activities, became an area of contention in the IIC. The G-2, or head of Army intelligence, Brigadier General Sherman Miles, wanted the SIS to restrict itself to counterintelligence investigations overseas. One MID memorandum referred to any arrangement giving the FBI supremacy in the Western Hemisphere as "wholly unacceptable to M.I.D." It firmly stated, "The F.B.I is *not* solely 'responsible for foreign intelligence work in the Western Hemisphere,'" asserting that if "any department of the Government has primacy in the foreign intelligence field, it is the Department of State."[69] ONI also joined the fray. In fact, the Director of ONI, Rear Admiral Walter Stratton Anderson, had already preempted the FBI's SIS in name and mission by creating a Special Intelligence Section to conduct foreign intelligence operations—a week before Roosevelt's decision.[70]

Hoover held some key advantages over MID and ONI that allowed him to temporarily blunt his competition. As military organizations, MID and ONI changed leadership with some regularity. Miles was new to the G-2 job in 1940 and "was no match for Hoover."[71] In the case of ONI, Anderson "fell under the spell of the FBI director, who was only too eager to tutor the novice intelligence director in the business of security."[72] Additionally, Hoover played the ONI and MID heads against each other, using his sway over Anderson to tip the balance whenever Hoover and Miles disagreed.[73] Furthermore, Hoover had led the Bureau since 1924 and had no challengers from within or without the organization. He had built his brand and had gained public recognition. Having also skillfully gained the confidence of Roosevelt, he had a degree of credibility with the President and the American people that the ONI and MID heads would never have. In terms of leadership of the IIC, Hoover emerged as the first among equals.

Hoover's High-Water Mark

Journalist Don Whitehead recounts a perhaps apocryphal story that Roosevelt proposed putting Hoover in charge of all government intelligence agencies in October 1940, but Hoover rejected the offer, claiming "that plan would be very good for today, but over the years it would be a mistake."[74] Perhaps Hoover preferred the position he had made for himself at the center of the IIC. That way any congressional or executive scrutiny would fall on the entire committee rather than on the FBI and Hoover alone. Perhaps Hoover's experience with bureaucratic competition taught him that attempting to coordinate American intelligence was a fool's errand and that it was better to be the head of the FBI at the center of the IIC. By maximizing the FBI's intelligence powers compared to ONI and MID, and his own against the directors of the two military intelligence organizations, Hoover would be the de facto leader of the American intelligence establishment.

At nearly the same time that Roosevelt allegedly made his offer, an anonymous author wrote a document, titled "Information," arguing that the United States was "a 'no snooping' nation" and that the FBI should coordinate intelligence as a "single central information source for all government activities."[75]

Aside from the fact that the United States had always been a snooping nation, Hoover had managed to convince policymakers and the public that the FBI had stayed away from snooping until called upon to lead the government's intelligence activities. Hoover, by force of experience, influence, and manipulation, had steered himself and the FBI into the center of the American intelligence system. This brief period in the fall of 1940 proved to be the height of Hoover's control over American intelligence.

11

Donovan's Finest Hour

AS YET ANOTHER war raged in Europe and another shadow war developed in the United States, J. Edgar Hoover and the FBI stood poised to dominate American intelligence. The intelligence requirements of the Second World War eclipsed anything the United States had experienced in its history. Even Hoover and his newly empowered FBI would never be able to meet the scale of the intelligence effort the war required. Furthermore, they had focused on domestic intelligence at just the time when the United States needed foreign intelligence more than ever. Another individual and organization emerged to challenge Hoover and the FBI for the position at the top of the US intelligence establishment.

William J. Donovan was Hoover's foil in many ways and drew upon his own experience, celebrity stature, and political access to position himself as America's intelligence czar. He would have to settle for the title of "Coordinator of Information." In Donovan's Office of the Coordinator of Information (COI), the United States would finally have an independent intelligence organization responsible for the full range of activities associated with intelligence today. The purported goal of the COI was to coordinate intelligence for the President, but the wily Roosevelt had other advisors contending for this role. Donovan also inflamed rivalries by expanding the COI's operations into areas covered by existing intelligence organizations. Although Donovan and the COI faced tremendous bureaucratic competition, they managed to disrupt the American intelligence system and set in motion the long-awaited creation of an independent intelligence profession and organization.

Wild Bill Interrupts Hoover's Rodeo

Donovan could have won his nickname, "Wild Bill," at many points in his life. His standout football career made him a big man on Columbia's campus. He then attended Columbia Law School, where he was a student of Harlan Fiske Stone and a classmate of Franklin Roosevelt. After law school, Donovan moved back home to Buffalo, New York, where he practiced law alongside John Lord O'Brian, who had played a role in the bureaucratic competition over intelligence during the First World War. Donovan's personal associations foreshadowed his own future in intelligence.[1]

Life as an attorney would never satisfy Donovan's thirst for adventure, so he and some associates formed an Army National Guard cavalry unit that found its way to the US-Mexico border as part of General John J. Pershing's force pursuing Pancho Villa. No sooner had Donovan returned to Buffalo than he was commissioned as an officer with New York City's famous "Fighting 69th" regiment.[2] Donovan bravely led his battalion into battle during the First World War and was wounded by gunfire and gas. As a testament to his valor and leadership, he received three Purple Hearts, the Silver Star, the Distinguished Service Medal, the Distinguished Service Cross, the French Croix de Guerre, and the Medal of Honor. When Donovan received the last decoration in 1922, he removed the medal from his neck and presented it to the soldiers of the regiment, insisting, "It doesn't belong to me.... It belongs to the boys who are not here, the boys who are resting under the white crosses in France or in the cemeteries of New York, also to the boys who were lucky enough to come through."[3] This was the mettle of the man who became so influential in American intelligence history.

Not surprisingly, Donovan's return to normalcy in the early 1920s did not suit him. In 1924, he joined his former Columbia Law professor Harlan Fiske Stone, the newly minted Attorney General, in the Department of Justice as Assistant Attorney General for the Criminal Division. This put Donovan in direct supervision over J. Edgar Hoover. Differences in character and mutual distrust quickly characterized their relationship and generated a professional and bureaucratic rivalry that carried over to the FBI and CIA. Through his friendship with O'Brian, Donovan became involved in intelligence when he moved to New York City after leaving the Department of Justice in 1929. O'Brian's influence likely led Donovan to join The Room, the secret intelligence network of elite New Yorkers led by Vincent Astor.[4]

Donovan's efforts to court Roosevelt as part of his ascent in American intelligence challenged the relationship Hoover had carefully cultivated with the President. Donovan and Roosevelt first joined forces when Donovan visited Italy and Ethiopia in 1935–36, likely on an intelligence mission directed by Roosevelt.[5] He followed this initial foray with subsequent fact-finding trips to watch German army maneuvers in the summer of 1938 and to monitor the events of the Spanish Civil War.[6] This underscored the key distinction between Donovan and Hoover's experience: while Hoover spent the 1930s

FIGURE 11.1 Donovan as a doughboy in France, September 1918. He already wears two decorations on his uniform: the ribbons for the Distinguished Service Cross and the French Croix de Guerre. National Archives and Records Administration.

looking inward, Donovan spent the same period looking outward. Donovan steeped himself in foreign policy, traveling extensively and learning about conditions around the world as global tremors reverberated back to the United States. Hoover and Donovan therefore personified fundamental differences in intelligence that had consequences for the division of domestic and foreign intelligence responsibilities between the FBI and CIA.

The real break for Donovan came in 1940, just as Hoover was approaching the peak of his power. Seeking to temper political rivalries in anticipation of American involvement in the Second World War, Roosevelt appointed Republicans to his Cabinet. First, he invited Frank Knox, the publisher of the *Chicago Daily News*, to become the Secretary of the Navy. In turn, Knox proposed that Roosevelt name Donovan the Secretary of War. The President professed his admiration for Donovan but claimed he did not think it would be politically prudent to have two Republicans in such influential roles in his administration, even though he settled on another Republican, Henry Stimson, who became Secretary of War for the second time in his career.[7]

That July, Donovan was summoned to a meeting with the President and the Secretaries of State, War, and Navy. They wanted him to make a trip to Britain to study its response to German subversion. France had just surrendered to Germany, so the more likely and practical purpose of the trip was to assess Britain's ability to defend itself. The British gave Donovan access to virtually the entire government, including Prime Minister Winston Churchill and the royal family. Donovan also received a cordial welcome from Britain's intelligence establishment, including Stewart Menzies, the head of Britain's Secret Intelligence Service (SIS), also known as MI6, and Admiral John Godfrey, the head of the Naval Intelligence Division.[8]

The British, who were under the impression that Donovan was traveling on behalf of Roosevelt and was even a close friend of the President, feted Donovan to secure an advocate who had Roosevelt's ear.[9] In fact, Donovan was still working his way into Roosevelt's confidence. The relationship that emerged between the British and Donovan proved mutually beneficial: As the British courted Donovan, Donovan courted the British, and each courted Roosevelt on behalf of the other. When Donovan took another trip across the Atlantic in the winter of 1940, the British made sure he had company.

William S. Stephenson was a Canadian veteran of the First World War, a jack-of-all-trades, and a source of inspiration for the fictional James Bond. He was also the British spymaster in the United States. Churchill and SIS chief Menzies charged Stephenson, code-named "Intrepid," with running intelligence operations in the Western Hemisphere through the British Security Coordination (BSC), located in New York City.[10] While Stephenson quickly established a working relationship with Hoover and other prominent Americans, it was Donovan whom Stephenson and the British chose to "cultivate" almost "as if [he] were a British agent of some sort." Fiercely independent, Donovan was no one's agent, but he certainly admired British intelligence and would represent British interests and ideas in his efforts to transform American intelligence.[11] So influential was Stephenson in this eventual pillar of the Anglo-American "special relationship" that Donovan later told an interviewer, "Bill Stephenson taught us everything we ever knew about foreign intelligence operations."[12]

Stephenson, who likely contributed to the initial misrepresentation that explains Donovan's grand welcome on his first trip to London, "kept on overselling Donovan" ahead of his second trip.[13] During the long journey, which included a weeklong stop in Bermuda, Stephenson sparked Donovan's fascination with British intelligence operations. After parting ways with Stephenson in London, Donovan went on to witness commando training in

FIGURE 11.2 "Big Bill" Donovan presents "Little Bill" Stephenson with the Medal for Merit for his (secret) services to the United States during the war in a ceremony in November 1946. Library of Congress.

Britain and long-range desert patrols in Libya.[14] The interests of the two decorated Great War veterans overlapped. In December 1941, Stephenson set up the school known as Camp X in Ontario that trained British and American personnel in intelligence and special operations during the war. Aside from their professional association and common concerns, a personal friendship blossomed between the two men, with observers distinguishing Donovan as "Big Bill" and Stephenson as "Little Bill" due to the differences in their height. But whereas Stephenson was already a formidable figure in British intelligence, Donovan was still searching for his place in American intelligence. He would have Stephenson's help. Shortly after their trip, Stephenson cabled Churchill, "I have been attempting to maneuver Donovan into job of coordinating all United States intelligence."[15]

Churchill and the upper echelons of the British intelligence establishment recognized the disorganized state of their American cousin's intelligence system and understood both the challenges and the opportunities that accompanied it. The British themselves were in the process of coordinating their own intelligence system through the recently created Joint Intelligence Committee (JIC).[16] The Chairman of the JIC, Victor Cavendish-Bentinck, had a rather jaundiced view of American intelligence, writing in May 1941 that he "believe[d] that their intelligence departments are primitive and rather inexperienced," also noting that "there is little contact or collaboration between American Government Departments."[17] As a result, the British had to forge separate liaison relationships with each of the competing American intelligence services. Intelligence sharing between the two unofficial allies was difficult and quite risky, especially as the British could not afford any leaks of their highly secretive and successful ULTRA signals intelligence program that intercepted Nazi communications. The British nudged Roosevelt to revisit the coordination problems facing US intelligence, stressing that it would be better to have one person lead it—and they had just the man in mind.[18]

Donovan was undoubtedly brimming with ideas when he landed back in the United States in March 1941. He immediately met with Roosevelt and members of the Cabinet on his return. The timing was auspicious, as Roosevelt had just directed Stimson, Knox, and Attorney General Robert Jackson to make a study of the American intelligence system.[19] According to Stimson, Roosevelt and his Cabinet were hampered by a "twilight zone" in intelligence produced by the "conflict of the three intelligence agencies," the FBI, ONI, and MID. Roosevelt offered two possible solutions, based on the French and British models. France had a joint board, much like the IIC that Hoover then dominated. In Britain, "a gentleman known as 'Mr. X'" coordinated intelligence and resolved disputes between separate offices. Roosevelt ordered his Cabinet to "confer as to the institution of a similar solution for our country in case we got into war."[20] Donovan emerged not as a "Mr. X"–style anonymous adjudicator but as a new individual and bureaucratic force in the ongoing competition over American intelligence.

Revisiting Roosevelt

Personal, political, statutory, and international factors converged and contributed to the events that made 1941 a turning point in US intelligence history. While Donovan was certainly a central catalyst, it was Roosevelt who ultimately chose to reform American intelligence. It was noteworthy that Roosevelt would seemingly give so much authority to Donovan because he was not a President who liked to delegate too much power to any of his subordinates. British historian John Ranelagh argues that when Roosevelt "agreed to the establishment of COI . . . he was agreeing to the creation of another channel of influence rather than to the replacement of existing ones," concluding that "Donovan was simply another competitor in the ring."[21]

Roosevelt's actions and decisions during this crucial period raise several questions. Why did Roosevelt personally oversee so many changes to intelligence during the late 1930s and early 1940s, including instances where he assigned lines of responsibility to intelligence organizations as they fought with each other? Also, why did he suggest a coordinating authority modeled after the French or British systems if chaos and competition were what he preferred? The American system in 1941 was competitive enough to satisfy Roosevelt's devious leadership style.

Roosevelt was perhaps the most engaged President in matters of intelligence since Washington. He had his first dalliance with intelligence as Assistant Secretary of the Navy during the First World War, praising British naval intelligence in his journal and promising to deliver a more effective American naval intelligence effort.[22] After his election as President, he tapped naval officers for special intelligence missions.[23] Roosevelt displayed a continuing appetite for intelligence in the 1930s through the unofficial network of Vincent Astor and The Room and his presidential directives to Hoover. Despite his personal preference for competition among his subordinates, after the outbreak of the Second World War, Roosevelt perhaps realized he needed more coordination when it came to intelligence. While the three intelligence chieftains presided over their fiefdoms and competed within the IIC model, the arrangement excluded or devalued other organizations and departments that contributed to the national intelligence enterprise. But the system was too uncoordinated to satisfy the President's intelligence requirements.

Roosevelt's personal way of doing business and managing the presidency involved working through individuals rather than bureaucracies. So, his first step in reasserting control over intelligence recalled the hub-and-spoke model during the era of the Secret Service Fund. He created an informal intelligence channel through the journalist and writer John Franklin Carter. Carter had his own secret sources and sent Roosevelt reports on a range of topics from March 1941 to April 1945, paid for using "special unvouchered funds made possible by the military appropriations act of 1940."[24] Whatever his merits, Carter did not have a mandate to coordinate the work of official intelligence organizations. Furthermore, the scale of US involvement in the world required more than small, secret arrangements between the President and a trusted agent.

The world of 1941 was enveloping the United States with threats. However, the US intelligence system left Roosevelt "groping in the dark" because each intelligence organization and executive department formed "a separate empire of knowledge," and "no means existed for gathering and evaluating information from different sources at the national level."[25] Global events were overwhelming not only this intelligence system, composed of squabbling departmental organizations, but also the entire American government—and that included a micromanaging and mischievous President. In the summer of 1941, Roosevelt broke with the past and signed an order creating a new, independent office to coordinate American intelligence, an idea dating back to Lansing and McAdoo in the First World War.

Intelligence Coordinator or Controller?

Before Donovan's official entrance on the intelligence scene, Hoover was the central figure in American intelligence, if not its effective coordinator. But he overplayed his hand in the IIC and the cracks in the committee system of intelligence coordination were beginning to show. The debate over a Delimitation Agreement between the FBI, ONI, and MID, along with Roosevelt's decision to vest the FBI with foreign intelligence responsibilities in the Western Hemisphere, created confusion and competition in a body that supposedly existed to prevent precisely these types of problems.[26] Despite Roosevelt's order, MID sent officers to conduct intelligence operations in Latin America.[27] The relationship between Hoover and Army G-2 Sherman Miles broke down, as did Hoover's relationship with ONI chief Alan Kirk. Although Kirk expressed his hope for continued FBI-ONI cooperation and a "cordial" relationship with Hoover, a schism opened in the first month of Kirk's tenure when he found out the FBI was performing investigations in Guam and Samoa in violation of the Delimitation Agreement.[28] Not only was Hoover's influence over the IIC slipping, but his role as the President's chief intelligence counselor was also in jeopardy.

Hoover was a natural favorite while the President was worried about fascism and communism in the United States, but his focus on the home front left Roosevelt with an incomplete view of the world. Even then, Hoover continued to focus on the wrong enemy at the wrong time. Attorney General Francis Biddle admonished Hoover because Roosevelt believed the FBI "was spending too much time investigating suspected Communists…and ignoring the Fascist minded groups."[29] Beyond the type of intelligence that Hoover had to offer, his position in the American intelligence system would also limit him. Hoover's station was beneath the Attorney General and, try as he might, he could never truly be, first and foremost, the intelligence counselor to the President of the United States. Furthermore, the FBI was subordinated to the Justice Department and had a law enforcement role, which meant it could never be the independent organization that the country needed in an exclusive intelligence role. An intelligence coordinator and chief intelligence advisor to the President would have to be an independent individual in an independent organization.

ONI indirectly produced its own possible claimant to the title of intelligence coordinator. Vincent Astor, former naval reservist and founder of The Room, continued to conduct unofficial, volunteer intelligence missions for Roosevelt during the 1930s. He even made a survey of Japanese activities in the Pacific along with Kermit Roosevelt on his personal yacht, the *Nourmahal*. With the onset of the Second World War, The Room became The Club, and Astor established a relationship with the BSC in New York City. He also started to leapfrog ONI to communicate directly with Roosevelt. Roosevelt sent a letter to the Chief of Naval Operations, Harold Stark, stating that he had "requested [Astor] to coordinate the Intelligence work in the New York area." Although the letter from Roosevelt sanctioned Astor's activities, Astor still had no official intelligence title.[30]

In the spring of 1941, Astor told Adolf Berle, the State Department representative to the IIC and a Roosevelt confidant, that he "desired to become a coordinator of intelligence."[31] Soon after, Roosevelt appointed Astor as "Area Controller for the New York Area." The President's memorandum explained that in "order to coordinate the interested activities and to eliminate duplication of effort . . . all intelligence and investigational activities undertaken in the New York Area by the representatives of the Departments of State, War, Navy, and Justice shall be coordinated through a single agency—to be known as the Area Controller."[32] Astor's transition from unofficial amateur to official intelligence officer came at a cost: He traded his independence and direct access to the President for a role in a bureaucracy characterized by infighting.[33] It was John Franklin Carter who remained an independent operator with special access to the President. Carter, who was running his own intelligence operations in New York through T. R. Coward, the president of the Yale Club, spoke with Astor about the disorganized state of intelligence efforts in the city.[34] He reported to the White House that "Astor is still very confused and suspicious about the whole problem of investigation in the New York district. . . . The F.B.I. says there is a great deal of duplication of effort and Astor says there is not."[35]

Astor succumbed to the stress of the job. First he was hospitalized for a stomach procedure. Then his position became public as the result of a leak, further undermining his work.[36] While he retained his title, his responsibilities continued to diminish, and he finally requested that Roosevelt discharge him as Area Controller in August 1944 so he could return to private life.[37] The regional issues that Astor faced as Area Controller of New York foreshadowed the national issues Donovan would face as the Coordinator of Information.

As for the Army, Sherman Miles warned Army Chief of Staff General George C. Marshall in April 1941 that there was "a movement [a]foot, fostered by Col. Donovan, to establish a super agency controlling *all* intelligence," emphasizing that "such a move would appear to be very disadvantageous, if not calamitous."[38] Ironically, it was Miles who was most alarmed by Donovan's rising star, and it was Miles who unintentionally helped set the conditions for Donovan's ascent. The first mistake Miles made was opposing an internal Army proposal to establish an American analogue to the British JIC.[39] Instead, he proposed a new office of representatives from the major intelligence-producing agencies that would meet and share information, but withdrew this idea, claiming that "a single 'clearing house' for the entire government was not feasible."[40] Perhaps in an attempt to narrow any role Donovan might have in intelligence, Miles conceded that he could act "as the coordinator between the three intelligence agencies in any conflict which may arise *within the field of countersubversion*."[41] But Donovan would not be so easily contained.

By this point, the only thing the leaders of the IIC fundamentally agreed upon was stopping Donovan. To this end, they drafted a series of reports to reassure Roosevelt that the present system was functioning well and there was no need for any overhaul or reform.[42] One report undermined the IIC's own argument by admitting that "each of the three Services have responsibilities to their own Department which lies outside the scope of their coordinated activities."[43] As the IIC tried to preempt the creation of a superseding office for intelligence coordination, it made a last-ditch effort to reduce bureaucratic competition by deconflicting FBI, ONI, and MID activities at the national and regional levels.[44] These efforts proved to be too little, too late.

Amid all the propositions, wrangling, agreements, and appointments in the spring of 1941, Donovan outlined his own proposal for a new intelligence organization, which he sent to his friend, Secretary of the Navy Frank Knox. Donovan opened by stressing that "intelligence operations . . . should be headed by someone appointed by the President directly responsible to him and to no one else." Hearkening back to the tradition of the Secret Service Fund, Donovan proposed that the new organization "should have a fund solely for the purpose of foreign investigation and the expenditures under this fund should be secret and made solely at the discretion of the President." He also envisioned that it would "have sole charge of intelligence work abroad" and not take over domestic responsibilities handled by the FBI, thereby supporting the functional division that was emerging between foreign and domestic intelligence. Donovan's letter included a description of Britain's SIS as a rough model for his new organization.[45]

But Hoover can fairly claim that he and the FBI made their own study of British intelligence before Donovan.[46] Early on, Hoover had extended FBI cooperation to Stephenson and the BSC, and the Bureau was instrumental in helping British intelligence establish a foothold in the United States. Hoover also sent FBI agents to Britain in November 1940, a month before Donovan took his second trip, and wrote a series of memoranda to Roosevelt in March 1941 based on their findings. When Donovan claimed he was responsible for the warm reception the FBI agents received from British intelligence, Hoover bristled, scribbling on the bottom of an FBI agent's memorandum, "If I recall correctly I think we were there before the Colonel [Donovan] arrived."[47] Even then, this acknowledgment would have been little consolation to Hoover, who wanted to remain the key figure in American intelligence.

In his study of British intelligence, Hoover noted that "British officials believed that if the Security Service [MI5] and SIS [MI6] were combined, a more effective organization would result."[48] He was perhaps making a self-serving argument to join foreign and domestic intelligence in one organization—his. However, he still offered a discerning insight about intelligence: the division between foreign and domestic work compromised the effectiveness of intelligence, as well as the ability to coordinate it. In trying to capture control of both, Hoover was overreaching, especially given the country's historical separation of the two based on American principles as much as bureaucratic competition. In contrast, Donovan's proposal would be more concordant with the constraints facing intelligence in the United States.

Besides, Donovan had more political capital than Hoover on both sides of the Atlantic.[49] Major players in the British and American governments actively supported Donovan in May 1941. Knox appealed to Felix Frankfurter, Roosevelt's "one-man employment agency," to find a leading role for Donovan in American intelligence. Stephenson had already laid the groundwork for his friend through his high-level liaison between the British and American governments. Admiral Godfrey made a trip to the United States where he and his aide, Commander Ian Fleming, who later created James Bond, advocated for reforming the American intelligence system with Donovan somewhere in the machinery. Finally, Roosevelt's ambassador to Great Britain, John Winant, endorsed Donovan's ideas and suggested Donovan take the lead in implementing them.

Roosevelt had to find a position for this popular and politically connected individual one way or another.[50]

To top it all off, Donovan was still actively making his case for the job. He drafted a memorandum that expanded on his previous letter to Knox. It began more like a treatise, declaring, "Strategy, without information upon which it can rely, is helpless." Donovan worried that the United States was "lacking [an] effective service for analyzing, comprehending, and appraising" intelligence and therefore claimed it was "essential that we set up a central... intelligence organization which would itself collect either directly or through existing departments of government, at home and abroad, pertinent information concerning potential enemies." The heart of Donovan's proposal was for a "Coordinator of Strategic Information who would be responsible directly to the President," although this figurehead would have the assistance of an "advisory panel" comprising representatives from the FBI, ONI, MID, and other intelligence-oriented agencies. Donovan's organization would draw personnel from these other services and promised that it would "neither displace nor encroach [upon]" any of them. His self-styled Service of Strategic Information would provide the President with "accurate and complete enemy intelligence reports upon which military operational decisions could be based."[51]

Donovan was proposing something novel: an independent intelligence organization that would report only to the President rather than a Cabinet-level intermediary like all the other US intelligence services. This organization would focus on foreign intelligence collection, an area in which the United States lacked continuity and expertise. Donovan explained that this work would require specially trained officers across a range of technical and subject-matter expertise rather than fly-by-night staffing by military officers, as in ONI and MID. But bureaucratic competition ensured that neither the new organization nor its leader would truly be able to coordinate American intelligence.

Clashes Behind the Curtain

Bureaucratic competition and behind-the-scenes scrambling continued in the period between Roosevelt's decision to appoint Donovan the Coordinator of Information and his formal presidential order to that effect. A particular point of contention was Roosevelt's initial idea that the COI be a military position. The Army especially opposed Donovan holding a military rank, fearing that he and the COI would usurp military responsibilities and authorities.[52] Even without the rank, the Army did not want Donovan to have any purview over information that could be used to shape strategy. Various drafts of the order eventually signed by Roosevelt used the terms "strategic," "defense," and "national security" with respect to the COI's structure and functions, and even referred to the office of the COI as the "Strategic Intelligence Service."[53] It was unclear just what type of information Donovan would coordinate, and the Army was doing its best to influence the parameters of Donovan's role. In the end, Donovan and his new organization would be civilian.

Word leaked to the press before Roosevelt signed the document creating the COI. The *New York Times* reported on July 6, 1941, that Donovan was "Slated for Big Post."[54] On July 10, it announced that Donovan "will soon be named to a post as Coordinator of Intelligence Information," a position and concept "without precedent." Describing how the State Department, Army, and Navy all produced intelligence, the article noted that the longer reports gathered by these departments only reached the President as "short digests," but that they "suffer[ed] in the digesting, since each digest [was] prepared by an official necessarily preoccupied with the special interests of his own department." Donovan and his new independent office would be expected "to take original reports and analyze them in relation to each other, in a manner impossible at present, simply because there is no agency of the government with the freedom from other routine necessary to this task."[55]

This news article gave the American people a revealing look into their intelligence system. It publicly identified the absence of an independent intelligence organization in the American national security establishment and raised awareness about the lack of coordination among the existing intelligence services. The *Times* also highlighted that the President was not receiving a coordinated, finished intelligence product based on all-source analysis. The insider information in the article and its astute evaluation of the state of American intelligence suggest leaks by pro-Donovan sources.

Roosevelt formally established the Office of the Coordinator of Information and appointed Donovan by presidential order on July 11, 1941.[56] A statement from the White House explained that the COI would "collect and assemble information . . . from the various departments and agencies of the Government" but noted that Donovan's "work is not intended to supersede or to duplicate, or to involve any direction of or interference with, the activities of the General Staff, the regular intelligence services, the Federal Bureau of Investigation, or of other existing departments and agencies."[57] Perhaps in support of the new initiative, an article in the *New York Times* the following day alleged that Roosevelt "told associates that the scattered reports which came to his desk often were hopelessly confusing."[58]

Other elements of the COI suggested its role would go beyond coordinating and analyzing information. The legacy of the Secret Service Fund was resurrected in spirit in the COI's funding. The COI's budget derived in part from unvouchered presidential funds, which would enable the President to conceal the COI's operations from congressional and public scrutiny. In the original letter sanctioning the arrangement, the Bureau of Budget revealed that the unvouchered funds would be used for spies. Just as Congress had once debated whether the Contingent Fund was for spies or executive agents, someone crossed out the word "spies" in the letter and penciled the word "agents" above. The letter explained that "most of these agents will have to operate on an undercover basis, and it will be desirable to employ them from unvouchered funds."[59] Another reason the COI needed unvouchered funds was that Donovan wanted to personally recruit his staff and skirt cumbersome government procedures.[60]

The Bureau of Budget also made clear that the COI might undertake roles beyond espionage. In the event of war, the COI would use unvouchered funds to engage in "subversive activities," including sabotage and propaganda. The COI might even have to "subsidize more heavily... political leaders in the various neutral countries who can be bribed." In a nod to protecting sources and methods, as well as concealing the US government's role in these covert operations, the Bureau of Budget stressed that "the funds used for these purposes cannot be traced back to their source, as the lives of the agents and the success of their missions will depend upon the secrecy with which the transactions are handled."[61]

The document creating the COI even alluded to these activities. An ambiguous provision authorized it to "carry out, when requested by the President, such supplementary activities as may facilitate the securing of information important for national security."[62] James R. Murphy, Donovan's executive assistant in the COI, claimed that there was an "unwritten part of COI" based on "the President's direction to Donovan to organize an undercover service" and that "right from the beginning it was understood by those of us who were there that the important part of Donovan's job was to organize an intelligence service."[63] Likely based on Stephenson's interpretation, the BSC recorded in 1944 that although Roosevelt's directive establishing the COI "was not very specific, it was interpreted by Colonel Donovan as the green light for him to take steps to establish for the first time in U.S. history a real secret world-wide intelligence organization." Upon reading this statement, Donovan wrote in the margin, "No. This was requested by the services."[64] Regardless of any original intention or design, Donovan seemed bent on incorporating every possible type of intelligence mission into the COI, which intensified bureaucratic competition.

Donovan's One-Stop Shop for Intelligence

Writing to the Foreign Office in October 1941, Lord Halifax, the British ambassador to the United States, wondered if Donovan was "proceeding slowly in the exercise of his power for the reason that too abrupt a call upon the state and service departments might result in raising an opposition within those departments and hampering his activities."[65] His impression was mistaken. By the winter of 1941, Donovan was well on his way to raising opposition from nearly all corners of the US government.

Donovan quickly created a Research and Analysis (R&A) branch in the COI and, with the help of Archibald MacLeish, the Librarian of Congress, identified America's leading academics for its staff.[66] R&A was one area in which the COI had a clear mandate, yet it still produced bureaucratic friction since it depended on other intelligence organizations for information. Aside from struggling to gain cooperation from a range of agencies and executive departments, R&A had to compete within the COI for Donovan's attention, which always wandered in different directions in an "ever-changing Donovanesque free-for-all."[67] Analysis also suffered due to the COI's incorporation of more action-oriented intelligence functions.

As the COI expanded, so, too, did its list of enemies. Donovan organized a propaganda arm and tapped Robert Sherwood, a playwright and the President's speechwriter, to lead the effort. This set the stage for a clash with Nelson Rockefeller, the Coordinator of Inter-American Affairs (CIAA), whose office overlapped geographically with the COI's propaganda service. In response to the strife, observers at the time joked that "the Coordinators would have to be coordinated."[68] Roosevelt was forced to mediate the dispute and took Rockefeller's side, giving the CIAA authority over propaganda in the Western Hemisphere.

The COI faced fiercer resistance over operations in the Western Hemisphere when Donovan created a Secret Intelligence (SI) branch to conduct espionage. At the time, there was no formal intelligence profession or continuity in professional intelligence officers trained in the art of espionage, or HUMINT. A COI memorandum explained that in peace, "information from abroad comes from our diplomatic representatives, government missions, newspapers and radio reporters, and a myriad of everyday sources," while in war, "many of these sources dry up, and we become dependent upon sources other than the normal peacetime ones."[69] The United States needed a dedicated HUMINT organization, and the COI was ready to take on the role. The IIC had already grappled with foreign HUMINT, producing a conflict between the FBI, on one side, and ONI and MID, on the other, that Roosevelt had resolved.

Surprisingly, the Army and Navy seemingly handed off their HUMINT authority to the COI. Adolf Berle remarked that Donovan and the COI "would never have gotten into espionage if General Sherman Miles had not been afraid to organize a spy system."[70] Miles defended his decision by arguing that "the undercover intelligence of the two services [MID and ONI] should be consolidated under the Coordinator of Information" because "an undercover intelligence service is much more effective if under one head rather than three, and... a civilian agency, such as Coordinator of Information, has distinct advantages over any military or naval agency" in conducting clandestine intelligence work.[71] A public profile of Miles in *Life* magazine in December 1940 offered another explanation, which explains why the COI would use unvouchered funds: "More important today than ever before, G-2 has no appropriations to pay for spies, because spies are considered un-American."[72]

The COI replaced ONI and MID in the bureaucratic fight with the FBI over HUMINT. Hoover reminded Roosevelt of the IIC arrangement, and the President reissued his directive giving the FBI "all responsibility" for intelligence in the Western Hemisphere.[73] An FBI memorandum recorded that "Col. William Donovan called and seemed considerably 'put out' that the President had signed the above directive," claiming that "the Agents of the FBI could not gather material necessary for his purposes, but that his agent[s] should work together with the FBI." Donovan argued that the COI should have control over all intelligence in Central and South America—on top of picking up ONI and MID's overseas espionage operations—and that the FBI should only be responsible for the United States and its territories.[74] Donovan therefore wanted US intelligence to be separated into foreign and domestic spheres, a conceptual and functional division he would continue to advocate.

Espionage was one thing, but Donovan wanted the COI to go even further and conduct commando missions, sabotage, and other special operations. His fascination with special operations proved to be a liability for himself and his organization. Upon American entrance into the Second World War, Donovan volunteered to leave the COI and assume command of a fighting unit, his first of a few failed attempts. Frustrated each time, he would take wildly risky trips into combat zones, perhaps to sate his thirst for battle. He would have to settle for bureaucratic fighting in Washington instead.

Intelligence Ad Lib

As a result of Donovan's expansive vision, the COI was creating redundancies in American intelligence. These redundancies cost money, drawing the Bureau of Budget into the dispute. As early as July 1941, Bernard L. Gladieux, who led the Bureau of Budget's effort to prepare the country for the impending war, sent a memorandum to Roosevelt requesting "clarification as to the scope and functions of this new office" because "some of the proposed plans for Colonel Donovan's agency impinge so directly upon a variety of activities of existing agencies."[75] By September 1941, Gladieux lamented that the "situation [was] becoming increasingly acute as Donovan tend[ed] to move into areas of activity already occupied by established agencies."[76]

In a November 1941 meeting with the Bureau of Budget, Donovan grumbled that "he had been unable to obtain a sympathetic hearing on his programs." Perhaps looking for areas of less overlap, budget officials encouraged Donovan to pursue espionage and special operations as "his first order of business." While Donovan certainly did not need any prodding when it came to the more active areas of intelligence, he remarkably responded that "the Coordinator's principal interest was in information and was not in strategy or in action to be taken."[77] Nonetheless, that very same week, Donovan sent his proposed budget for the COI for FY 1942 to Roosevelt. It included funding for propaganda, counterespionage, and "secret activities." The president went line by line, writing "OK" next to items or "OK for [an amended amount]," indicating that, as busy as he was, Roosevelt was still personally invested in Donovan's designs for the COI.[78]

All these schemes were only in their developmental stages in 1941. In the process of constructing an intelligence empire, Donovan was encircling himself with bureaucratic rivals who saw the COI, and especially its leader, as a threat to their intelligence domains. Donovan was bound to clash with Hoover, who nurtured his own imperial ambitions for American intelligence. In November 1941, Hoover's right-hand man, Edward Tamm, informed him that the *New York World-Telegram* was preparing "an 'exposé' of Colonel Donovan's organization . . . predicated upon the principle that the majority of the personnel in Donovan's organization are incompetent to perform the duties assigned to them and further that many of them have 'politically shady' backgrounds."[79] Assistant Secretary of State Samuel Breckinridge Long agreed, recording in his diary, "One most important thing to be controlled is Donovan" because "his organization is composed largely of inexperienced people" who had access to sensitive information and "use[d] it ad lib."[80] Even America's entrance into the war did not dampen the personal and organizational hostility.

12

An Intelligence Failure and an Intelligence Insurgency

AS OF DECEMBER 1941, the COI had created a lot of commotion with little action, except rousing other departments and organizations against it. In his dual roles as the country's intelligence coordinator and the head of a new, independent intelligence organization, Donovan faced many challenges, not the least of which was his tendency to distract himself from his principal role of coordinating intelligence. Then again, even if he had invested more effort in the job, bureaucratic competition was so ingrained in the American intelligence system that he likely would have found little success in the struggle.

The country's first real experiment in intelligence coordination failed at an inopportune time. The surprise attack at Pearl Harbor was a formative moment in US intelligence history. Pearl Harbor would become the subject of a searching congressional investigation, countless subsequent examinations, and even conspiracy theories.[1] Blame tends to fall on the intelligence community, but it was also a collective, cumulative failure rooted in the country's historical approach to intelligence.

Although at first glance the moment seemed conducive to the growth of the COI, the reverse proved true. As a new organization without a departmental patron, the COI faced existential threats from the old guard of executive departments that dominated intelligence.[2] Realizing that the COI would not survive as an independent intelligence organization, Donovan rebranded it as the Office of Strategic Services and subordinated it to the military. The purpose and place of the two organizations in the American intelligence system fundamentally differed, but what did not change was the precarious position of Donovan's outfit.

An Infamous Intelligence Failure

On November 17, 1941, just a few weeks prior to the attack on Pearl Harbor, Joseph Clark Grew, the American ambassador to Japan, cabled Washington to warn officials that although "our present most important duty perhaps is to detect any premonitory signs of naval or military operations" he doubted that he would be able to provide "substantial warning" of an impending attack.[3] Grew had already reported in January 1941 that he had heard the Japanese were planning "a surprise mass attack on Pearl Harbor" and that this information had come "from many sources."[4] From this initial tip, the United States had nearly a year to detect and prevent the attack, yet it failed to do so.

Even if the pieces were there, no one put the puzzle together due to failures in intelligence collection, analysis, and coordination.[5] On account of a bureaucratic division of labor and separate organizational focus, ONI and MID missed an opportunity to work together and discover that Japan had planned massive, near-simultaneous surprise attacks stretching from Hawaii to the Philippines. MID busied itself with the Japanese Army, which would strike the Philippines on December 8, 1941, while ONI tracked the Japanese Navy, which would carry out the attack on Pearl Harbor on December 7.[6] MID received a cryptic report in June 1941 about the construction of a Japanese submarine fleet destined for Hawaii, but it doubted the credibility of the report, and it is unclear what it did with the information.[7] Meanwhile, ONI dismissed Grew's warning. In late 1941, ONI was more concerned about the threat of Nazi U-boats, spies, and saboteurs on the Atlantic coast than a conventional Japanese military attack in the Pacific.[8] Nevertheless, ONI reported on November 26 that Japan was organizing a task force composed of its largest carriers, although the report misjudged the geographic targets of this fleet.[9] As late as December 4, an ONI report also noted heavy Japanese radio traffic, "large scale shifts in key diplomatic personnel," a "mass exodus of Japanese residents" across North and South America, and specific Japanese interest in and attention to Hawaii.[10]

The FBI provided its own critical piece of intelligence ahead of the attack. Robert L. Shivers, the FBI Special Agent in Charge in Honolulu, reported that the FBI intercepted a telephone call from the cook at the Japanese consulate claiming that the consul general was "burning and destroying all his important papers."[11] Shivers had been acting on a request from the local ONI office to confirm intelligence that the Japanese government had ordered several of its diplomatic outposts in the United States and around the world to destroy their telegraph codes and other secret documents. The destruction of the codes meant war was imminent. Japanese consuls and ambassadors were to relay the code word "HARUNA" back to Japan once the codes were destroyed. On the evening of December 2, the Japanese consul general in Hawaii, Nagao Kita, sent the confirmation code back to Tokyo.[12] Given that the United States was intercepting Japanese communications, why was it unable to provide warning of the attack on Pearl Harbor?

Herbert Yardley and his book, *The American Black Chamber*, had alerted Japan to US codebreaking capabilities.[13] In response, Japan distributed copies of Yardley's book to its embassies and built its first cipher machine to encode official communications.[14] Japan continued to develop increasingly robust codes and cipher machines throughout the 1930s. William Friedman claimed that codebreaking became more difficult due to Yardley and blamed him for the "losses of thousands of lives," though he likely sought to deflect any blame from his own Signal Intelligence Service for failing to intercept Japanese communications that might have revealed Japan's plans.[15] A 1948 Senate report also connected Yardley to the attack, concluding that the "inability to decode the important Japanese military communications in the days immediately leading up to Pearl Harbor was directly ascribable to the state of code-security consciousness which the revelations of a decade earlier had forced on Japanese officialdom."[16] This focus on Yardley can distract from the larger ills of American civil-intelligence relations that made the United States vulnerable in the years ahead of Pearl Harbor.

Congress had already complicated the work of communications intelligence by prohibiting radio intercepts in 1927. It doubled down with the Communications Act of 1934, which legislated that "no person," presumably including intelligence officers and organizations, "shall intercept any communication and divulge . . . such intercepted communication" or "receive or assist in receiving any interstate or foreign communication by wire or radio."[17] It is possible Congress prohibited intercepting domestic and international communications for ideological reasons like the ones that led to the shuttering of the Cipher Bureau. It is also likely the executive branch failed to explain to Congress the necessity of communications intelligence in the modern world of the telegraph and telephone, although the public's response to Yardley and *The American Black Chamber* likely would have forced Congress's hand anyway. Nonetheless, Congress put American COMINT officers in the difficult position of having to flout or figure out a way around US law. For example, in weighing the law and its criminal consequences, Signal Corps officer Joseph O. Mauborgne rationalized that "these penalties apply, of course, to the work done by the entire Signal Intelligence Service, but they may be ignored, as this service operates in compliance with existing directions of the Secretary of War."[18] Revealingly, Mauborgne also subordinated this type of intelligence work to the military, which created even more problems. The United States was struggling to incorporate signals intelligence (SIGINT), of which COMINT is a subcategory, as an emerging intelligence discipline in the years before Pearl Harbor.

Army and Navy SIGINT continued apace during the 1930s, with particular emphasis on Japan through a secretive project known as MAGIC. When Japan developed a new code or cipher machine, MAGIC worked its magic and cracked the code. In September 1940, Genevieve Grotjan, a civilian cryptanalyst with SIS, broke Japan's most difficult code to date, code-named PURPLE. Friedman declared, "Without a doubt we are experiencing one of the greatest moments of the Signal Intelligence Service," and allowed his staff to enjoy a round of Coca-Colas to celebrate Grotjan's achievement before they all returned to work.[19]

So successful and sensitive was the Army's SIGINT work that Mauborgne, who became the Army's Chief Signal Officer, decided in 1940 that he had to keep the SIS's activities secret from the new Secretary of War—the same man who had claimed that "gentlemen do not read each other's mail" when he was the Secretary of State. However, as Secretary of War, Henry Stimson was no longer opposed to reading other people's mail. With his change in executive departments came a change of heart, which was not out of character for Americans who harbored very different views of intelligence in wartime versus peacetime. Stimson also grounded his principled hypocrisy on the distinction between diplomatic tact and military necessity, divisions that were apparent in how the country was tackling SIGINT.[20]

Continuing a trend that began when the SIS took over from the Cipher Bureau, military control over SIGINT expanded before the Second World War. Aside from regional and organizational differences dividing Army and Navy intelligence collection, SIGINT drove another wedge between the two. Logically, the SIS targeted the Japanese Army, and OP-20-G, the Navy's signal intelligence organization, targeted the Japanese Navy. The missing link was diplomatic communications, a glaring deficiency left by the closure of the Cipher Bureau. The Army and Navy had to divert resources to cover Japanese diplomatic communications and coordinate their efforts in the process. The solution they arrived at in the fall of 1940 was an "odd-even day" agreement that had the Army and Navy switch off the days they covered diplomatic traffic. It was an astoundingly ineffective solution that made it difficult to track Japanese communications and created redundancy in the Army and Navy's work.[21]

Even if Stimson had come around to codebreaking as war loomed, the larger military bureaucracies still had not. Both the SIS and OP-20-G suffered from insufficient personnel and resources, "generated at least in part by a lack of respect for the intelligence profession."[22] In the case of OP-20-G, covering diplomatic communications strained precious time and resources, while the Navy Department's focus on the Atlantic over the Pacific compounded the problem.[23] OP-20-G spent more time and attention on Japanese diplomatic traffic than on intercepting Japanese naval messages and deciphering the especially difficult Japanese naval code JN-25.[24] These messages offered one principal avenue for uncovering Japan's plan to attack Pearl Harbor. Intercepting and decoding communications was one thing, but compiling and analyzing all the different pieces was another. In this respect, naval intelligence also failed.

Despite the challenges facing it, ONI still had more military information on Japan than any other American intelligence organization did before Pearl Harbor. Having studied the Japanese attack on Port Arthur, which began the Russo-Japanese War in 1904, ONI concluded that "Japan considered the surprise attack on the enemy's main military facility before declaring war a primary aspect of war planning." Had ONI analyzed all available information together in the context of its historical understanding of Japanese military doctrine, it could have at least offered an estimate that Japan would attack Pearl Harbor. Perhaps for this reason, Berle recorded in his diary on December 7 that although "it was a bad day all around... if there is anyone I would not like to be, it is Chief of Naval Intelligence."[25] Indeed, Rear Admiral Theodore Wilkinson, who was the Director of Naval Intelligence at the time, would subsequently offer his own account of ONI's lapses. He later testified during Congress's investigation of the attack that Japan had taken an interest in the disposition of American naval forces at Pearl Harbor, and he commented that it "was an evidence of their nicety of intelligence." Even so, he admitted in further testimony that he could not recall ONI holding any discussion on the Japanese threat to Pearl Harbor preceding the attack.[26]

There were plenty of targets to pick from to blame for Pearl Harbor: individuals like Yardley or Wilkinson, organizations like SIS or ONI, collection disciplines like HUMINT or SIGINT, and intelligence missions like collections or analysis. But there was no single scapegoat. Rather, Pearl Harbor was the culmination of failures of American intelligence.

The intelligence establishment was composed of relatively weak intelligence services subordinated to larger executive departments that were bureaucratically more prepared to fight each other than a foreign adversary. The existing services had been primarily inward-looking, so limitations in foreign intelligence collection, particularly in the form of HUMINT, produced blind spots. Although SIGINT was the most productive form of foreign intelligence that the United States was collecting, it was also the most secretive, so there were restrictions on sharing its vital clues. The United States still struggled with coordinating intelligence, and in the case of Pearl Harbor this meant pulling together all possible strands of information.

The surprise attack on Pearl Harbor shook the country's long-standing perceptions and prejudices regarding the role of intelligence in peacetime. It was virtually guaranteed that the intelligence system the United States had before the war would not look the same after. There was already one person who was radically disrupting American intelligence, and on December 7, 1941, the former Columbia gridiron star was attending a football game in New York City when the loudspeaker announced to the entire stadium that "Colonel William J. Donovan . . . was being paged by Washington."[27]

From Coordinating Information to Offering Strategic Services

That very day, Donovan flew to Washington and went straight to the COI to consult his staff en route to see the President. Even if Donovan had focused on coordinating intelligence, it was unlikely the COI would have been able to piece together enough information to prevent Pearl Harbor. The organization was only five months old and lacked access to crucial intelligence sources, including MAGIC. Like the Navy, it focused more on Europe than Japan—so much so that it was Donovan who ended up filling in his staff on what had happened at Pearl Harbor. By midnight, Donovan was meeting with Roosevelt in the Oval Office. While the short conversation veered from Pearl Harbor to the impending war, it is unclear just how much the President and his intelligence coordinator actually discussed intelligence.[28]

If either Roosevelt or Donovan intended the Coordinator of Information to coordinate information, neither made it the focal point of the organization. Roosevelt, who "thrived on genteel intrigue," perhaps overindulged Donovan, whose mind abounded with ideas. The President occasionally joined in, and the two continued to bat around ideas through the winter of 1941–42, in one case quite literally. In what was likely the most far-fetched scheme of the entire war, Roosevelt forwarded Donovan a letter he received proposing that the United States find a way to deploy bats against Japan. Donovan worked on an operation to drop these "bat bombs" into Japan that was eventually scrapped after the bats kept dying during testing.[29]

For a secret intelligence organization, the COI certainly did not have a secretive boss. In December 1941, *Look* magazine wrote an article ironically titled "Wild Bill Donovan—Washington's Mystery Man." Jet-setting, millionaire, Wall Street war heroes who receive presidential appointments do not exactly fly under the radar. Just as ironically, the article portrayed Donovan's job and organization as secret while also publicizing its responsibility for intelligence missions like espionage and propaganda.[30]

While Donovan's star may have been rising, the COI was floundering. A summary of its activities in January 1942 read like an attempt to justify its continued existence. The report somewhat tautologically argued that one of the COI's primary accomplishments was the "creation of an articulated organization, staffed by a highly talented force, to perform functions new in concept in the Government of the United States," but for that very same reason, the COI faced the "difficulties inherent in a governmental agency new in its field and unique in its concept."[31] There was some sense to this observation. From the Bureau of Military Information in the Civil War to the Cipher Bureau in the interwar period, similar experiments had failed.

The COI was also making enemies faster than it was winning friends. William Whitney, formerly the COI's London representative, worried that the State, War, and Navy Departments would start poaching the COI's functions as they mobilized for war. He counseled Donovan, "Pick one horse"—coordination, analysis, espionage, propaganda, or special operations—"and ride it as well as your very great talents will enable you to ride it," even though that would never do for Donovan. Based on his observation that the Foreign Office was exercising increasing influence over elements of the British intelligence establishment, Whitney further suggested that Donovan ally the COI with the State Department.[32] But Donovan, ever the soldier, pivoted toward the military. Whether due to bureaucratic awareness or natural inclinations, Donovan "realized that in war the armed forces would predominate and that it would be wise to link COI to military activity."[33] He chose correctly, at least for the duration of the war.

The United States was still not ready for an independent intelligence organization. Roosevelt's patronage was not enough to guarantee the COI's survival. It needed Cabinet-level cover. Donovan also needed outside support to make the move and fortunately found three powerful allies in the British, the US Joint Chiefs of Staff, and the President.[34]

Churchill and the senior British military leadership stressed the role of propaganda, espionage, and sabotage in the war when they met with Roosevelt and the senior American leadership at the Arcadia conference, which ran from late December 1941 to mid-January 1942. Based on their experience, they suggested the United States train and deploy a paramilitary force while the country mobilized for war. Following the rout of British conventional forces on the Continent, the British organized the Special Operations Executive (SOE) as a paramilitary outfit to take the fight to the Germans with Churchill's famous instruction to "set Europe ablaze." But the SOE had only just clung to life against the designs of the UK's War and Foreign Offices.[35] The COI was undergoing a similar bureaucratic struggle and had already planned to adopt the same sneaky espionage and sabotage missions that many senior US military leaders still found unappealing.[36]

Thanks in part to earlier British mentoring, Donovan had a plan in hand. Donovan had sent Robert A. Solborg to attend training with the SOE as a prelude to the COI setting up its own special operations wing.[37] In January 1942, Solborg sent Donovan a memorandum proposing an American "Special Operations Service." He explained that it would "undertake subversive action of every sort and description against the enemy" because the "Axis [was] waging total war and must be answered in the same way," wryly concluding, "Its fifth column must be out-columned."[38] At the same time, Donovan urged Roosevelt to allow him to create a larger force modeled on the British commandos that would conduct raids in Japanese-held territory across Asia with the help of local forces.[39] Perhaps revealing how he really felt about his role as Coordinator of Information, Donovan sent a maudlin "appeal from a soldier to his Commander-in-Chief," in which he proposed the formation of a commando force to rescue American troops in the Philippines and requested the President's permission to serve with it.[40] Donovan would confess to his deputy coordinator and head of the R&A branch, James Baxter, that "while he would prefer direct military duty to his present job he had no intention of leaving the organization."[41] Donovan's desire for action was a distraction from the organization that desperately needed his full attention.

Meanwhile, internal and external opposition to the COI was mounting. Two of Donovan's own appointees turned against their boss. Solborg, who later admitted his displeasure with the "haphazard way and stuntlike propensities of Donovan's procedures," had returned from his special operations training in Britain overly ambitious about his chances of running the COI's secret intelligence and special operations activities. Likely perceiving Solborg as a potential rival, Donovan sent him to Portugal and replaced him with Preston Goodfellow.[42] In an even more brazen act of subversion, Robert Sherwood, whom Donovan selected to run the COI's propaganda arm, the Foreign Information Service, sent a letter to Roosevelt arguing that the COI "should be dissolved" and that its functions should be absorbed by the military intelligence services, the State Department, and, in the case of propaganda, a new agency.[43]

Meanwhile, Adolf Berle, the State Department's point man on intelligence, raised his concerns over Donovan and the COI to the President with the support of Nelson Rockefeller and J. Edgar Hoover.[44] Berle recorded in his diary that Roosevelt "thought Bill was doing a pretty good job on propaganda and something of a job in terms of intelligence."[45] Of Donovan, Berle mused that "you can never quite pin him down to saying what he really does want to do," adding his sense that Donovan "feels that he is quite able to run foreign affairs all by himself."[46] Breckinridge Long, who had already voiced his irritation with Donovan and the COI in 1941, fumed in his own diary:

> Bill Donovan—"Wild Bill"... has been a thorn in the side of a number of the regular agencies of the Government for some time—including the side of the Department of State.... He is into everybody's business—knows no bounds of jurisdiction—tries to fill the shoes of each agency charged with responsibility for a war activity.... He does many things under the *nom de guerre* of "Information" but among others he broadcasts news and "propaganda." Often his broadcasts follow a policy widely divergent from the official foreign policy and from time to time make trouble for us abroad.[47]

The budgetary axe was hanging over the COI as well. Bernard Gladieux wrote in his notes that the "Bureau of Budget would prefer to scatter COI's activities," with the exception of secret intelligence and special operations, as there was "good reason for leaving this within a secret agency such as COI because it deals with such activities as sabotage, placing of agents in foreign countries, etc."[48] A Bureau of Budget outline sent to Gladieux describing the function and budget of every organizational unit of the COI included a "Suggested Disposition" for each one. Tellingly, it suggested abolishing or transferring all of them.[49] Fortunately for Donovan, the military saw an opportunity to absorb the COI and its leader.

One of the Arcadia Conference's lasting contributions to the American national security establishment was the belated creation of the Joint Chiefs of Staff (JCS). US military brass had sat across the table from the British Chiefs of Staff Committee but did not have a comparable body. So, at the suggestion of Admiral William Leahy, the military branches agreed to form the JCS. With British encouragement, the JCS created a subsidiary Joint Intelligence Committee (JIC) that included the ranking intelligence leaders from ONI, MID, State, COI, and other wartime intelligence organizations. The JCS appointed a naval officer, Captain Francis Denebrink, to examine the COI and its value to the military. Denebrink's report of early March 1942 recommended partitioning the COI's existing branches into the JCS, JIC, military intelligence services, and military services more generally.[50] The JCS tapped its secretary, Brigadier General Walter Bedell "Beetle" Smith, to assemble a proposal to present to Roosevelt.

Perhaps having caught wind of the JCS plan, Donovan sent his own memorandum to Roosevelt, explaining that the COI contained four critical intelligence missions that he stressed would be best preserved in a single organization.[51] Rather than remain independent, Donovan offered to subordinate the COI, which he would rebrand as the Office of Strategic Information, to the JCS.[52] In addition to the existing COI missions, he proposed that the Office of Strategic Information formally adopt the missions of foreign propaganda, political and psychological warfare, and the operation of "such special service units as may be directed by the United States Joint Chiefs of Staff." Toward the end of March, Smith forwarded Donovan's plan to Harry Hopkins, Roosevelt's confidant and factotum, adding that the JCS approved it. Rather than compete with Donovan, the JCS seized the opportunity to absorb Donovan and the COI, in effect growing its own bureaucratic power. For his part, Donovan wanted to ensure the survival of his organization and his immediate control over it.[53]

Roosevelt held Donovan and the COI's future in his hands, so Donovan made his own personal overtures to the President through meetings and memoranda.[54] In a letter to Roosevelt in April 1942, Donovan reminded him that "at the very outset of our relationship, it was agreed that I would deal directly with you." He explained that "we have been able to set up for you an instrument of modern warfare" and argued that it should "not be disturbed at home before it shall ever be put to its really crucial work abroad."[55] Whether crediting Roosevelt for the creation of the COI or reminding him that the organization was designed to be his personal intelligence service, Donovan certainly knew how to appeal to his vanity.

Roosevelt equivocated. According to Berle, the President was trying to get Donovan a promotion from colonel to brigadier general, "after which he was thinking of putting [Donovan] on some nice, quiet, isolated island, where he could have a scrap with some Japs every morning before breakfast. Then he thought the Colonel would be out of trouble and be entirely happy."[56] Whether he was joking or not, Roosevelt decided to keep Donovan around. He also seemed to approve of Donovan's ideas—except one. When Roosevelt saw Donovan's plan, he told Harold Smith, the Director of the Bureau of Budget, that he did "not think foreign information [i.e., propaganda] should go to [the] military services."[57]

On June 13, 1942, in two different orders, one an executive order, the other a military order, Roosevelt created the Office of War Information (OWI) and the Office of Strategic Services (OSS), respectively. The OWI assumed the propaganda function that Sherwood suggested belonged in a new agency. The OSS preserved its other core intelligence functions, albeit to a different end under the JCS. Intelligence would serve the military and the war effort, perhaps fitting in the context of the Second World War, but regressive in terms of the COI's original purpose.

The COI was novel as an independent organization tasked with coordinating intelligence for the President. In accordance with Donovan's vision, it quickly evolved into a nearly complete intelligence service that could have professionalized intelligence. What was not novel was intelligence being subordinated to the military in war and the rejection of intelligence coordination in the face of bureaucratic competition. Enduring features of American civil-intelligence relations successfully undermined the creation of the country's first quasi-professional, independent intelligence organization.

An Insurgency in Washington, DC

With both Donovan and his organization further attenuated from the President, and the President perhaps unintentionally signaling a willingness to sever some of the COI's functions with the creation of OWI, the OSS was vulnerable. Nonetheless, Donovan's ambitions were not dampened. He still attempted to fashion the OSS into a single, all-encompassing intelligence service. As a result, the same complaints lobbed against the COI were directed against the OSS.

The Bureau of Budget continued its feud with the OSS. A memorandum reported that the US Army Air Forces' intelligence office was claiming that "only about 15% to 25% of OSS's output appeared... to be original creative work.... The remainder is 'rehash' of the material obtained from other sources," inevitably resulting in "an undue amount of duplication."[58] In a memorandum of a conversation with the Navy in October 1942, Bureau of Budget official William Hall wrote that the "OSS has duplicated Army and Navy facilities" and that "such duplication would tend to increase" over time.[59] However, an evaluation of OSS secret intelligence provided to ONI in November 1942 indicated that ONI found most of the materials provided generally reliable and valuable.[60] Nonetheless, the OSS continued to face accusations that its work was redundant.

The State Department and Bureau of Budget formed an alliance against Donovan and the OSS. Berle told Hall that "Donovan's intelligence efforts have been feeble and what has been accomplished has been done through State, War, and Navy channels." In the same conversation, Hall reported that "Donovan [was] somewhat estranged from the White House now." Perhaps sensing Donovan's diminished personal and bureaucratic power, Hall suggested that "considerable savings in funds and use of personnel could be achieved by dispersal of OSS staff to other agencies," leaving Donovan to lead guerrilla operations for the Army.[61]

That would be a problem because Donovan had powerful enemies in the Army as well. Major General George Strong, the new head of Army intelligence, emerged as one of the bitterest rivals of Donovan and the OSS aside from Hoover and the FBI. Perhaps taking a page from Donovan's playbook, he attempted to duplicate some key COI and OSS functions.

Although his predecessor, Sherman Miles, had essentially handed espionage over to Donovan and the COI, Strong tried to take it back. In the spring of 1942, he approved the creation of a secret espionage unit known as the Pond, led by John "Frenchy" Grombach, a West Point graduate, accomplished fencer and boxer, and radio program producer. Although Grombach had previously been on loan to the COI, he loathed the OSS and believed its publicity made overseas espionage operations more difficult for the United States. By contrast, the Pond was so secret that other intelligence organizations like ONI did not know it existed, although it did form a close working relationship with the State Department and passed counterintelligence reports to the FBI. Grombach dismissed OSS officers as amateurs and even had the Pond keep files on some of them. But the Pond, which existed from 1942 until 1955, may have been too secretive for its own good. It could never compete bureaucratically with formally established intelligence organizations that had official status and allocated resources. The Pond all but disappeared from the historical record until the discovery of some documents in a Virginia barn in 2001. Despite Grombach's gripes about all the OSS hype, apparently too much secrecy can, in fact, be a bad thing for an intelligence outfit.[62]

Besides espionage, Strong also tried to displace the OSS's analytical role. Wall Street attorney Alfred T. McCormack had been appointed by Stimson to set up a small analytic wing for the War Department, which Strong incorporated into Army intelligence. McCormack's group took raw information gathered from the Army's MAGIC signals intelligence program and created finished products that were distributed to the War, State, and Navy Departments, as well as to the President. Notably, the OSS was never among the recipients.[63]

In another blow, Strong prevented the OSS from having access to MAGIC. Instead, it received snippets from the Army and Navy at their discretion. As the Army Chief of Staff, General George C. Marshall, shared Strong's concerns about the OSS's ability to keep a secret. Roosevelt himself deferred to Marshall's decision, further distancing the OSS from the COI model that would coordinate intelligence for the President.[64] The OSS eventually received access to ULTRA, the equally sensitive British signals intelligence program, through its X-2 counterintelligence branch in the spring of 1943. Strong protested, prompting Donovan to write to him and explain that X-2 was a compartmentalized branch that adhered to British security protocols and shielded the ULTRA secret from the rest of the OSS.[65] As a final SIGINT slight, the War Department used MAGIC and ULTRA to test the reliability of OSS intelligence, finding some of its reports to be mere rumor.[66]

In addition to old, established organizational rivals, the OSS faced new competitors as well. The Board of Economic Warfare (BEW), another wartime expediency created by Roosevelt, campaigned against the OSS's R&A branch due to their overlapping work in economic analysis. Looking for allies in its campaign against the OSS, the Bureau of Budget took up the BEW's cause. Gladieux determined that the BEW and OSS "duplicated each other on numerous specific studies" and that "the problem will be solved only if the two agencies are merged."[67] In response, Marshall requested that OSS's R&A and the BEW establish boundaries between their work.[68]

Despite the schism between Sherwood and Donovan resulting in the creation of the OWI, the OSS still took on a propaganda role. In response to the infighting, Roosevelt nearly signed off on an order transferring the OSS from the JCS to the War Department in February 1943, which would have all but ensured its extinction. Fortunately, the OSS had a defender in the JCS. Roosevelt issued Executive Order 9312 in March 1943, which settled the disputed boundaries between the OSS and OWI. Still, the two organizations continued to feud until a "peace treaty" finally settled their differences a full two years after their creation.[69]

Donovan also faced an insurgency within the OSS just as he had in the COI. Several of his senior deputies grew concerned with the OSS's competing missions and peripatetic leadership. Donovan was not content to simply manage the OSS. He wanted to take an active part in overseeing its operations as well. However, he would disappear for months on end to travel to far-flung battle zones and OSS outposts, bravely but needlessly putting himself in danger. Meanwhile, the OSS gained little from Donovan's risk-taking and derring-do. Deciding that Donovan was a better figurehead than manager, OSS deputy director John Magruder proposed that the OSS needed a chief of operations. He also wanted to cut the OSS's paramilitary and propaganda functions so that the organization could focus on collection and analysis. Donovan rejected Magruder's plan and set off on yet another global tour that included an unnecessarily dangerous trip to an OSS base behind Japanese lines in Burma.[70]

Finally, besides Frenchy Grombach's Pond, the OSS faced competition across the pond, or the Atlantic Ocean. Having saved the OSS's paramilitary role from Magruder's designs, Donovan plotted to expand its paramilitary activities in Europe. This worried Britain's MI6 and SOE, which considered the OSS to be amateurs and auxiliaries. OSS and SOE competition over operations in Yugoslavia especially became a point of contention. Tensions boiled over, requiring Roosevelt and Churchill to intervene. It seemed everywhere Donovan and the OSS went, personal and organizational rivalries followed.[71]

An Oh So Special Study in Contrasts

Legends about the OSS remain popular. These myths have colored the public's understanding of the history that gave rise to the CIA and contemporary American intelligence system.[72] Stories of the Jedburgh special operations teams that parachuted into Europe and worked with resistance fighters to sabotage the German military still dominate the collective memory of the OSS.[73] Even before the COI transformed into the OSS, Donovan created Detachment 101, which conducted special operations in the China-Burma-India Theater. OSS teams also worked with Ho Chi Minh and the Viet Minh in Indochina and even played a complicated role in the US attempt to organize Chinese resistance against Japan by simultaneously courting both Chiang Kai-shek and the Kuomintang, on the one hand, and Mao Zedong and the Chinese Communists, on the other. The latter effort ended tragically with the murder of OSS officer John Birch, who is often considered the "first casualty" of the Cold War.[74]

Not to be conflated with the special operations of the OSS were its intelligence and counterintelligence activities. Allen Dulles led OSS espionage operations in Switzerland, recruiting Fritz Kolbe, one of the best human intelligence sources in Berlin during the war.[75] The secretive X-2 counterintelligence branch played a less obvious yet formidable role because it had veto power over both OSS special operations and secret intelligence activities.[76] The OSS even had a maritime unit to help infiltrate intelligence and special operations teams and run reconnaissance missions.

FIGURE 12.1 A cartoon from OSS files parodies what was apparently the popular misconception of intelligence operations in Southeast Asia. Note the reference to "wires crossed," which Robert Lansing and William McAdoo had used to refer to the confusion plaguing American intelligence in the First World War. National Archives and Records Administration.

Far less glamorous, but also influential, was the work of the OSS's R&A branch. Sherman Kent, widely regarded as the foundational figure in American analytic tradecraft, cut his teeth in R&A after a career as an academic historian at Yale. R&A conducted a range of studies across academic disciplines, geographic regions, and policy areas all the way down to the tactical level to sharpen the war effort. Its work later proved useful to the prosecution during the trials of Nazi war criminals at Nuremberg, where Donovan served as a special assistant to the chief prosecutor, Robert Jackson.

But the popular folklore surrounding the OSS tends to obscure its complicated history. The combination of operational and analytical units in the OSS generated tensions between those carrying out the two different mission sets. A letter from R&A officer John A. Wilson to branch boss William Langer captured the differences: "The 'cloak and dagger boys' felt that the 'long-haired' researchists were owlishly impractical... and were insufficiently schooled on security. On the other hand, the researchists felt that the operations people were rashly eager to 'get something done right away,' disregarded the necessity for basic knowledge as controlling action, and therefore made disastrous mistakes."[77] This clash of cultures spurred intra-organizational competition as the different elements of the OSS fought for influence and funding.

As the leader of the OSS, Donovan did not help resolve the tension. He often paid lip service to intelligence coordination and analysis while personally and organizationally steering the OSS toward operations. Jedburgh William Colby recalled that at the OSS's final ceremony, Donovan "referred first to his scholars and research experts in describing the OSS 'team' and only secondly mentioned the 'active units in operations and intelligence who engaged the enemy in direct encounter.' " If Donovan sincerely believed, as he stated, "that scholarship was [the OSS's] primary discipline, that the acquisition of information was to serve it, and that its paramilitary adventures were an adjunct to its authority and expertise in secret machinery," his actions during the war often belied his words.[78]

Neither did the OSS resolve a longer-running problem for American intelligence. Despite its best efforts, it was an amateur organization aspiring to professionalism, not a professional intelligence service. With the help of the British, it rapidly created training programs to learn how to conduct intelligence and special operations. Nonetheless, amateur OSS intelligence officers formed much of the cadre who trained the first class of truly professional intelligence officers in the young CIA. These same OSS amateurs brought their own experiences and stories to the CIA, fundamentally shaping its organizational culture and introducing the same tension that afflicted the OSS in terms of balancing analysis, espionage, and paramilitary operations.

The OSS also continued the tradition of recruiting heavily from the Ivy League and other social elites. Observers at the time joked the organization's acronym variously stood for "Oh So Secret," "Oh So Special," or "Oh So Social." Although its composition was not quite as exclusive as its critics charged, the appearance of elitism in the OSS fed similar charges against the CIA. Some of this criticism is unwarranted. After all, as a new organization without preexisting procedures, recruiting trusted friends and using social networks were among the few viable alternatives. Furthermore, when creating an organization designed to protect secrets and conduct secret activities that require a high degree of trust and confidence, it was perhaps natural to recruit based on common backgrounds and personal bonds.

The presence of high academia in the OSS meant that it included people politically left of center. In fact, the OSS knowingly recruited communist sympathizers, which exacerbated Hoover's suspicion of and animosity toward Donovan and the OSS. When the FBI demanded that Donovan dismiss three communist OSS personnel, he retorted, "I know they're Communists; that's why I hired them." He even reportedly once declared, "I'd put Stalin on the OSS payroll if I thought it would help us defeat Hitler."[79] Curiously, Donovan later lied to Congress, testifying that the OSS vetted its personnel and that no fascists or communists ever made it into the organization.[80]

Donovan probably had to disavow his own recruitment decisions because he had turned the OSS into a counterintelligence nightmare, which the Soviets successfully exploited by planting spies in the organization. Duncan Lee, a Yale graduate who worked for Donovan's law firm and then became Donovan's personal assistant in the OSS, was the highest-placed Soviet spy in the OSS.[81] But Donovan judged the OSS's ideological diversity worth the bureaucratic and security risks. Without diminishing the scale of the counterintelligence dangers that Donovan invited into the OSS, he still set a valuable precedent of sorts by opening its ideological ranks on the condition that personal political beliefs should not affect operational intelligence outcomes. Given that the American intelligence establishment had periodically waded into domestic politics, the OSS at least aspired to separate intelligence from politics in its own organization.

Fighting for the Future of American Intelligence

As difficult as Donovan could be as a boss or bureaucratic rival, he was undeniably a trailblazer. He stood fast against the resistance and setbacks he faced in leading the COI and OSS, and he endeavored to create something new in the American national security establishment. He accomplished that, albeit imperfectly and at great personal and professional risk. Even if he sometimes seemed to take his own life for granted, Donovan passionately defended the existence of the OSS.

The OSS faced near-constant bureaucratic warfare alongside actual warfare during the Second World War. It was not just the organization itself that was at stake when it came to the survival of the OSS but Donovan's vision for American intelligence as well. As officials debated Donovan's proposal for a postwar, peacetime intelligence system, Donovan—and opposition to him—drove the debate.

13

Coordination at Last?

THE AMERICAN INTELLIGENCE establishment traditionally expanded in war and atrophied in peace, but the Second World War proved transformative because the country finally recognized that it needed a robust, permanent peacetime intelligence system. At issue was Donovan's proposal for an independent intelligence organization to coordinate national intelligence efforts and conduct "other" intelligence activities. Once again, the traditional institutions of national security, represented by their executive departments and intelligence organizations, sought to subordinate intelligence. In this case, they resisted the creation of yet another Donovan-devised competitor, much as they had the COI and OSS. In addition to debating plans for a central intelligence organization in the corridors and backrooms of government buildings, officials took the proposition public. Donovan's plan was leaked to the press. His rivals appealed to America's enduring ideological suspicion of a "spy system" by comparing his proposed organization to the Nazi Gestapo. The bureaucratic war therefore played out in the papers and in the court of public opinion.

During this pivotal moment, President Franklin Roosevelt, Donovan's equivocal but essential patron, died while in office. His successor, Harry Truman, who disliked Donovan, disbanded the OSS and dismissed its director. Even if Donovan was unable to save his organization or his own job, he permanently transformed the American intelligence system. He set the conditions for an independent intelligence organization and, at long last, profession.

Donovan's Grand Design

Donovan believed that the fate of the OSS and the future of American intelligence were intertwined, but he had to protect the OSS before he could devote more attention to the question of postwar intelligence.[1] Two memoranda in October 1942 required Donovan to address these interrelated issues.

First, Donovan received a letter from Charles Eliot, the Director of the National Resources Planning Board, inquiring about the OSS's wartime activities as well as any postwar plans for the organization.[2] Second, General George C. Marshall requested clarification regarding the functions of the OSS in a memorandum to the Joint Psychological Warfare Committee (JPWC).[3] Continuing their previous assault on the COI, Donovan's various rivals tried to dismember the OSS by claiming that each of its functional branches was conducting operations already being performed by other organizations or departments of the government.

In a long memorandum that read more as an organizational study, Donovan responded to the JPWC by describing each OSS branch, as well as what distinguished its work from efforts elsewhere in the American intelligence establishment. For example, he tied OSS R&A to the COI's responsibility for "collecting all information and data bearing on a particular subject or problem, and analyzing a great variety of intelligence in order to secure an over-all picture"—in other words, all-source intelligence analysis. Donovan especially took pains to outline why the OSS was better suited to espionage than ONI and MID. He explained that its use of unvouchered funds allowed it to protect sources and methods. He emphasized that espionage required officers "with years of experience in the various geographic fields of operations" and "intimate knowledge of locale," unlike military officers who constantly rotated in and out of positions. Donovan also argued that ONI and MID officers lacked "adequate training in . . . good secret service work." Finally, he stressed that espionage requires collecting intelligence beyond purely military matters, to include economic and political information, implicitly connecting the OSS's Secret Intelligence and R&A branches. Donovan defended the OSS as a whole through the unique contribution of each of its functional parts. But there was more to this memorandum than a mere explanation of why these intelligence functions belonged in a single organization. Donovan had effectively outlined a distinct intelligence profession.[4]

He went further toward rationalizing his concept in September 1943, when he drafted a report bearing the ponderous heading "The Need in the United States on a Permanent Basis as an Integral Part of Our Military Establishment of a Long-Range Strategic Intelligence Organization, with Attendant 'Subversion' and 'Deception of the Enemy' Functions." In this treatise, Donovan made the case for a permanent peacetime intelligence organization in general and for the OSS to be that organization specifically. However, he painted a confused picture of postwar intelligence by recommending the creation of a quasi-independent, largely civilian intelligence service, housed within the military institution, that would conduct national intelligence operations and analysis. Notably, unlike the COI, this proposed organization would not report directly to the President. The OSS was a subordinate component of the JCS at this time, so perhaps Donovan wanted to appease his bureaucratic patrons.[5]

Donovan refined his ideas over the subsequent year. By the fall of 1944, there was a widespread sense in the US government that the end of the war in Europe was in sight, which made the future of postwar intelligence an urgent question for the existing stakeholders.[6] To support Donovan, the OSS committed part of its brain trust to the problem of postwar intelligence. In August 1944, it produced a memorandum proposing a Central Directorate of Intelligence to coordinate intelligence, with a Central Intelligence Service responsible for several functions then being performed by the OSS.[7]

On September 1, 1944, another OSS memorandum took up the need for a "single, professional agency" after the war. It opened by citing the country's historical failure to preserve intelligence in peacetime: "'Between wars' we have allowed our expensive, improvised galaxies of intelligence systems, with their overlapping operations and duplicated functions to lapse into skeleton organizations leading for the most part a kind of *pro forma* existence, or to perish outright," until "at the next emergency we have again been forced to expand and recreate intelligence systems, with untrained personnel and often without clear directives or any very definite ideas of how to do it or what it is all about anyhow." The authors acknowledged that "it has been commonly felt that intelligence work, particularly undercover intelligence work, was not quite nice or polite, that it was somehow un-American," but they speculated that "public opinion has been changing in this connection since Pearl Harbor shattered our complacency." Furthermore, the memorandum firmly stated, "Intelligence cannot be departmentalized," so it proposed an independent "Department of Information which would include all the Intelligence services of the various Departments in one coordinated organization." This was surely an outcome the other executive departments would never allow.[8]

Donovan needed a pretext to begin his lobbying campaign for his new agency. The moment arrived when Roosevelt instructed the Bureau of Budget to begin preparing for postwar retrenchment at the end of September 1944. Harold Smith sent a memorandum to Donovan requesting OSS plans for a drawdown after the war.[9] Donovan received similar requests in September and October from Senator Harry Byrd, chairman of the Joint Committee on Reduction of Nonessential Federal Expenditures. Donovan and the OSS prepared a spirited defense for a postwar OSS, if not in name, then in design, functions, personnel, and, of course, leadership.

In dictated notes outlining "The Basis for a Permanent World-Wide Intelligence Service," Donovan envisioned a "single over-all general strategic intelligence service" that "should be authorized to operate only abroad and not within the U.S." and should not be affiliated with "any law enforcement organization." Existing intelligence services like ONI and MID would continue to "meet the respective needs of their services in combat or operational intelligence," but they should "look to the Central Agency for over-all intelligence," ranging from cryptology to collection to subversion. The agency would also use unvouchered funds so that it could hide its activities. But Donovan invited bureaucratic competition by proposing that representatives of State, Navy, Army, and Air Corps form an advisory board and that the new organization furnish these departments with any information they might require. Realizing his error, Donovan revised this plan in October and decided that while the board would still provide "advice and assistance," the organization would "be administered under Presidential direction." He pointedly emphasized that it was "not necessary to create a new agency" because the "nucleus of such an organization already exist[ed] in the Office of Strategic Services."[10]

OSS officials contributed their ideas as well. For example, John C. Hughes, the head of OSS's New York branch, wrote a lengthy memorandum on postwar intelligence based on feedback from his office that Donovan edited with in-line comments. Hughes claimed that his staff agreed the OSS had become too well known to "be safely continued after the war as the permanent over-all secret intelligence organization of the United States government." He therefore proposed keeping the OSS but establishing another new secret intelligence agency, Service Z, that would work independently of the rest of the American intelligence establishment. Donovan even entertained the idea, agreeing that "the best cover for 'secret' work is in an 'open intelligence system.'"[11]

OSS officer Stacy B. Lloyd recommended that the OSS change its name after the war, become a civilian organization with a civilian director, and operate on "independent and unvouchered funds from the President." Lloyd argued that all the other intelligence organizations in the US government did "not have intelligence as their primary function," and as a result, "either due to pressure of other affairs, to lack of funds or adequate personnel or facilities, the intelligence gathering suffers in time of peace and in time of war is totally inadequate to carry out such activities." Lloyd continued, "An intelligence service cannot be developed rapidly... [i]t cannot be developed by inexperienced personnel... [and it] must work secretly and without dependence on any other bureau or government department." To make his point, he stressed that it took over a year for agents to "become skillful enough to live within their cover and to gather information." Throughout US history, and from diplomat-spies like Henry Shelton Sanford to detective-spies like Allan Pinkerton, there were brief expressions of an American intelligence profession. Lloyd continued this tradition, except this time the country would see the process through.[12]

Nothing was going to change without a fight, however. Donovan and the OSS's ideas leaked to their rivals in government. Roosevelt sent Donovan a note on October 31 with the warning "for your eyes only." Enclosed was a memorandum addressed to the President attempting to preempt Donovan's plan.[13] Its author was likely John Franklin Carter, who had been directing an unofficial intelligence office for Roosevelt.[14] Against Donovan's proposal, the memorandum argued that "reliance should be placed on the alternative method" of "a small and informal office, adequately camouflaged, utilizing chiefly foreign contacts" and "occasional 'look-see' agents in special circumstances." The memo's author also believed that "post-war trends will discourage expenditure of Federal funds for foreign espionage"—not an entirely unreasonable conclusion given the long history of ideological and organizational intelligence retrenchment that took place following wars.[15]

In response, Donovan claimed that his challenger was "in the 'horse and buggy stage' of intelligence thinking" and that it was "the failure for all these years to appreciate the complexity of building and directing intelligence as well as subversive operations over a world-wide network that has made the problem so difficult for us in this war." Donovan reminded Roosevelt that under "your authority and with your support there has been established for the first time in our history an independent American intelligence Service."[16] This response was far shorter and more restrained than Donovan's earlier drafts. In one, he had fulminated that his challenger, presumably Carter, "fail[ed] to grasp the magnitude of the problem" and had "not experienced personally" the challenge of building and leading an intelligence organization. In another draft he had vented, "This proposal is absurd."[17]

Never one to waste a promotional opportunity, Donovan also took Roosevelt's mischievous provocation as an invitation to present the President with his own plan for postwar intelligence, which he did in a historic memorandum of November 18, 1944. Donovan began with two requirements: first, "that intelligence control be returned to the supervision of the President," and second, "the establishment of a central authority reporting directly to [the President] with the responsibility to frame intelligence objectives and to collect and coordinate the intelligence material required by the Executive Branch in planning and carrying out national policy and strategy." Donovan stressed that coordination remained a stumbling block among the different departments and organizations conducting intelligence operations. Furthermore, he intimated that the OSS was best positioned to provide "the trained and specialized personnel needed for the task."[18]

Donovan attached a "Tab A" to this letter to act as a blueprint for an executive order. The unnamed "central intelligence service" would have a director appointed by the President, who performed his duties "under the direction and supervision" of the President with the assistance of an advisory board composed of the Secretaries of State, War, and Navy, along with any other officials the President might choose. The functional responsibilities of the service would be intelligence coordination, collection, analysis, subversion, and a cryptic reference to "such other functions and duties relating to intelligence as the President from time to time may direct." In an acknowledgment, or perhaps preemption, of the ideological opposition of the American people to a spy service and the bureaucratic opposition of the FBI to a potential rival, Tab A stipulated that the new organization would "have no police or law-enforcement functions." The service would also "operate under an independent budget," ensuring its bureaucratic independence and secrecy.[19]

On November 23, 1944, OSS General Counsel James Donovan sent Deputy Director John Magruder a draft executive order that would transfer the OSS to the Executive Office of the President. It specified that the OSS "shall perform such functions and duties with respect to the collection and analysis of information, and shall perform such special services, as the President from time to time may direct." The clause that the OSS would take charge of "coordination of the functions of all intelligence agencies of the Government" was sure to ignite the looming bureaucratic war over Donovan's gambit to shape postwar intelligence. Whether Donovan and the OSS underestimated the competition or overestimated Roosevelt's support, they must have felt the draft order stood a chance. The only thing missing from it was Roosevelt's signature, as the OSS had already taken the liberty of typing the President's name for him at the end of the document.[20]

Ripostes and Rebuttals

Donovan and the OSS were not the only ones planning for postwar intelligence. Hoover, one of the key prewar gatekeepers, offered up his own proposal. The JCS, divided internally between its civilian and military elements, arrived at a plan through hard-fought consensus and compromise. The eventual shape of the postwar intelligence system therefore resulted from the cumulative actions, ideas, and battles among departments, organizations, and individuals.

Hoover wanted American intelligence after the war to resemble what it had been before the war—namely, without Donovan and the OSS. Not surprisingly, Hoover's structure for the postwar system reflected the prewar system. The FBI, ONI, and MID would be responsible for operations, and the State Department would coordinate and analyze the resulting intelligence. Hierarchically, an IIC-type committee of an Assistant Secretary of State and the directors of MID, ONI, and the FBI would manage operations, while a policy board of the corresponding Cabinet-level Secretaries plus the Attorney General would oversee the committee. At the top sat the President, but noticeably absent was a direct conduit for intelligence to the President. Of course, the OSS and its director were nowhere to be found on Hoover's chart.[21]

There were rational as well as bureaucratic reasons for Hoover to cut Donovan and the OSS out of postwar intelligence. Aside from targeting Nazi espionage, the FBI continued to monitor communism during the war, so Hoover and the FBI clearly recognized what the country's major postwar adversary would be.[22] Furthermore, the FBI was beginning to piece together the Soviet espionage plot to steal the secret of the atomic bomb by the fall of 1944.[23] In Hoover's view, Donovan and the OSS could not have a role in the postwar intelligence establishment for the simple reason that they worked with and were compromised by the Soviets.

It was true that Donovan and the OSS liaised with the NKVD, the fearsome Soviet intelligence service, during the war. But the OSS also attempted to collect intelligence on the Soviets. For example, in December 1944, it obtained Soviet military and diplomatic codes from the Finns over the objections of Edward Stettinius, the new Secretary of State. Stettinius raised the issue with Roosevelt. The President did not want to risk the alliance with the Soviets and decided that the OSS should give the codes back, despite the likelihood that the Soviets would change their codes and jeopardize the work of American SIGINT operations. Still, the episode revealed that Donovan and the OSS understood that they had to shift from tactical operations against the Nazis to strategic intelligence against the Soviet Union to prove their value to postwar national security policymaking.[24]

Both Hoover and Donovan apparently understood that communism would replace fascism as the predominant intelligence threat after the war.

But, where Donovan's attention to the Soviet Union was based on his rational calculations of realpolitik, Hoover's motivation was rooted in his obsessive hatred of communism, which quite literally knew no bounds. Additionally, Donovan was willing to concede the domestic intelligence function in all his proposals for a postwar intelligence agency. Hoover would unite foreign and domestic intelligence in the FBI.

Indeed, the FBI expanded its reach outside the Western Hemisphere during the war despite Roosevelt's directive to the contrary. For example, OSS sources in Europe reported the comings and goings of FBI agents to Donovan.[25] The FBI itself documented liaisons, operations, and activities in England, Italy, Germany, France, and even the Philippines and Japan.[26] At the same time, Major Joseph H. Rosenbaum, Donovan's personal eyes and ears in the White House, was campaigning against the FBI's plan to turn its SIS into a worldwide intelligence service.[27] Having already won control of domestic intelligence, Hoover now wanted the FBI to take over foreign espionage in the postwar system. This would be his plan's undoing because it violated a conceptual boundary between foreign and domestic intelligence that was increasingly acknowledged across the US government and American civil society.

The most powerful actor shaping postwar intelligence was the military. The JCS had taken up the topic as early as November 1942 when the chiefs of the Army and Navy declared "the need for coordination and eventual integration of Army and Navy intelligence activity." At the prompting of the JCS, the directors of MID and ONI produced a report that recommended establishing a "Joint Intelligence Agency" that incorporated "all intelligence activities of the Army, Navy, and Office of Strategic Services, except the secret intelligence activities necessary to the special operations of O.S.S."[28] The anticipated consolidation of military intelligence foreshadowed the eventual consolidation of the services themselves into a single department, the Department of Defense, which was another major transformation in US national security following the end of the Second World War.

The JCS endorsed the idea of a central intelligence organization, though not exactly the Central Intelligence Agency that it became. The first reference to a "Central Intelligence Agency" appeared in a 1942 Marine Corps proposal for an information clearinghouse in the Pacific Theater, while the same expression without capitalization was used "in passing" by the OSS later in 1942.[29] In October 1944, while Donovan was drafting his own proposal for postwar intelligence, a JIC paper concluded, "Protection of the national security and advancement of the national interest require the creation of a Central

Intelligence Agency," with a director appointed by the President and responsible to a board composed of the Secretaries of State, War, and Navy. The proposed central intelligence agency would be responsible for national intelligence, coordination of departmental intelligence, and clandestine intelligence operations. Furthermore, it would assemble and analyze information "relating to the over-all security and vital national interests of the United States" and disseminate "national policy intelligence to the President." This JIC proposal captured some elements of the later CIA.[30]

A subsequent report by the Joint Intelligence Staff (JIS), a component of the JIC, also called for a central intelligence agency. However, the real insight in this document was its simultaneously backward- and forward-looking examination of the problems facing American intelligence. The paper cited key analytical failures before the war, such as "German capabilities and intentions in the spring of 1940," and uncertainties after the war, especially "U.S.S.R. capabilities and intentions in the period beginning with the collapse of Germany," stressing that these issues "cut across lines of departmental responsibility." It criticized the United States for moving ahead with "*ad hoc* agreements, proposals, and directives" for intelligence, rather than a coherent plan.[31] Like Hoover and Donovan, the JIC was keenly aware of the challenges of the postwar world, especially the Soviet Union.

However, this proposal dismissed any effort to centralize "all intelligence activities under the United States Government" in a single agency as "unworkable." Instead, it envisioned a body that would coordinate the work of the existing departmental organizations and conduct "those intelligence operations which cannot appropriately be performed by any existing department of agency," likely meaning espionage and perhaps covert action. The report emphasized the need for intelligence staff to remain objective and receive specialized training in analysis and tradecraft. This central intelligence agency would take charge of ensuring standards of training and objectivity for the entire US intelligence establishment, thus putting it at the vanguard of an American intelligence profession.[32]

The JCS did not know the details of Donovan's plan while drafting its proposals until Roosevelt forwarded them in late November 1944.[33] A schism developed between the civilian and military members of the JIS. The military members of the JIS opposed Donovan's proposal, which they deemed "unsound and dangerous." They distinguished between national intelligence and the intelligence requirements of the various departments, while stressing the need to preserve a chain of command. They suggested that a board of the Secretaries of War, Navy, and State should coordinate national intelligence activities. They further recommended that three organizations—the already existing JIC, a new Joint Intelligence Service, and a new Federal Intelligence Directorate—would help coordinate intelligence and conduct coordinated intelligence activities. Like Donovan and the OSS, they enclosed a directive for the President to sign.[34]

The civilians on the JIS drafted their own plan. They credited Donovan with pointing out the "inadequacies" of the existing US intelligence system and advocating for "a greater degree of coordination and centralization." Their plan preserved a central intelligence service with a director appointed by the President but made it responsible to a board of the Secretaries of State, War, and Navy. The civilian JIS staff also suggested that the existing departments and agencies remain responsible for intelligence collection except by clandestine methods, which would come under the purview of the new organization. Crucially, the plan explicitly stated, "Subversive operations abroad [did] not appear to be an appropriate function of a central intelligence service," undoubtedly a blow to Donovan and his penchant for covert action.[35]

A dizzying number of papers, including different versions of each paper, passed back and forth between the military and civilian representatives in the JIS through December 22, 1944, when the JIC met to debate the proposals. The meeting began with the attendees confirming that OSS Deputy Director Magruder, the OSS representative to the JIC, still supported Donovan's plan. He stressed the need for a national intelligence organization that would perform clandestine missions and report directly to the President. Magruder explained that national intelligence involved more than intelligence "of a military nature," which he believed the JIC overemphasized. Moreover, Magruder argued that secret intelligence must remain the exclusive work of a central intelligence agency because "it would be a target at all times for the public, for legislation, and for the enemy.... Whereas, if secret intelligence were incorporated in the body of the larger central agency, we feel it would have excellent cover in being obscured by the over-all operation."[36]

While the JIC examined each plan in detail, Max Ways, who drafted the civilian version of the JIS proposals, identified the fundamental problem plaguing the JIC as "a conflict between two administrative principles... both of which are valid." On the one hand, there was "the need for coordination of government activities" and, on the other hand, was the principle "of the responsibility of the chain of command." Compromise required infringing on both principles. Ways also addressed questions about giving the new central intelligence organization operational control over clandestine activities. His critics thought that mixing intelligence coordination with operations would create biased judgments. Ways stumbled in his response, rationalizing that all organizations display bias, and besides, the new central intelligence organization would only have "a little clandestine operation." The debate would prove prescient, as the later CIA would indeed suffer an identity crisis because it embraced more than "a little clandestine operation."[37]

Major General Clayton Bissell focused on the chain-of-command issue, pointing out that Ways's plan gave the director of the proposed central intelligence organization the ability to "run-around" the Cabinet Secretaries to the President. Furthermore, Bissell believed the director had too much power and discretion in making final intelligence judgments. Using language certain to rile the committee, Bissell sermonized, "Such power in one man is not in the best interest of a democratic government... it is in the best interest of a dictatorship," even going so far as to say it would be a fitting system for Nazi Germany. Comparisons to Nazi Germany would certainly strike a nerve with any audience at this time, and comparing Donovan's proposal for postwar intelligence to Nazi Germany's intelligence system became a source of public outcry when word of it leaked to the press a few months later.[38]

Just as Donovan's plan went to the JCS, the JCS's plans went to Donovan. In a move that was typical of Donovan and perfect proof of the JCS's concerns, the maverick chose to leapfrog his chain of command and write directly to Roosevelt to argue his side. He stressed that the JCS proposal was "strictly military in its concept" and therefore too "narrow" for the demands of national security. He wanted to ensure that the director of the proposed central intelligence agency had the freedom to run the organization without interference from an advisory board—although he had earlier made the same suggestion himself, which he now contrasted with the JCS plan calling for the board to control the director. Naturally, Donovan pictured himself as director of this new organization and Roosevelt as the President in this arrangement, so he probably hoped Roosevelt would intervene on his behalf.[39]

The JIC finally reached a compromise in a move that was likely designed to head off Donovan. The military members accepted the proposal for a central intelligence agency provided that the director be under the control of a National Intelligence Authority (NIA) composed of the Secretaries of State, War, and Navy. The NIA would be responsible for coordinating all government intelligence activities. Furthermore, the director would have to report to an advisory board of the heads of the different existing departmental intelligence organizations. Finally, the new organization would be dependent on the NIA for its budget, ensuring it would be subordinate to the NIA and its committee-style leadership.[40]

Notably absent from the JCS plan were the Justice Department and FBI, although it stipulated that the new central intelligence agency would have no law enforcement powers. A subsequent report explained why. When mentioning that there "have been suggestions that the Attorney General be included in the National Intelligence Authority because of the F.B.I.'s interest," the report stressed that these were law enforcement entities, a "connection from which the Intelligence Authority, in so far as possible, should keep clear."[41] In a continuing bureaucratic war, the military conspired to cut the Justice Department out of the postwar intelligence structure. Hoover would have a place on the proposed directors' advisory board, but he would hardly exercise any control over postwar American intelligence. The JCS plan did not address the crucial division between domestic and foreign intelligence but simply presumed it. The failure to include domestic intelligence as part of a comprehensive plan for postwar intelligence ensured further divisions and competition, especially with Hoover.

While these debates were raging, Stanley P. Lovell, who invented spy gear as the head of the OSS's Research and Development branch, drafted an eloquent defense of a new postwar intelligence system to OSS Assistant Director Edward "Ned" Buxton. Scribbled at the top of the document was a quote from Irish politician John Philpot Curran: "The condition upon which God hath given liberty to man is eternal vigilance." The memorandum opened by stating, "The United States has never had a Secret Intelligence Service [and] . . . [f]ew Americans even know what is meant by the term," so he offered his own global history of intelligence. Lovell identified the key limitation that had stopped the United States from having a permanent, professional intelligence organization in the past, which was the American people. As he explained, "Secrets, themselves" were "held by many to be basically 'un-American,' " and as "a nation of extroverts we have always belittled the covert and clandestine." But, he warned, "the American Way simply would not work" anymore because "success in war—and no less in Peace—is the reward for knowing the facts." He adjudged this historic trade-off as worth it, reasoning that "one day's war expense will pay a year's bill for knowledge." In anticipation of a powerful argument that would resonate with the public and likely prevent a professional American intelligence agency from surviving in peacetime, he acknowledged that it "should have absolutely no police function," adding, "We want no world-wide F.B.I."—which is precisely what Hoover wanted. Lovell also perceived a flaw in the OSS when he observed that "the mixing of intelligence-gathering and subversive activity is usually fatal to both," editorializing that "a secret agent who risks his carefully established 'cover' by acts of sabotage or violence is both a zealot and a fool." To Lovell, the choice for the United States was clear: either create a postwar secret intelligence service or "live as a nation after this war is over in the same black ignorance that preceded it." In short, Lovell presented an incisive analysis of American civil-intelligence relations and captured several of the ideological and structural questions at issue in the debate over a central intelligence organization.[42]

Postwar Planning Disrupted

Two major events intervened in the deliberation process in early 1945. In February 1945, the Donovan plan leaked to the press. Then, in April 1945, Roosevelt died suddenly. It is impossible to know what would have happened without either of these incidents, but they had consequential effects on the postwar intelligence system.

On February 9, 1945, headlines across the country alerted the American people to the ongoing, secret planning for a "Super-spy System" and republished details of Donovan's memorandum of November 18, 1944, indicating a well-placed source. These articles informed readers that the Roosevelt administration planned to create a single spy agency with enormous powers both domestically and internationally. Referring to the proposed agency as an American "Gestapo" certainly inflamed a nation at war with Nazi Germany and became a line that others would parrot. On February 10, an article reported the opposition of several members of Congress to the plan. Senator Edwin Johnson exclaimed, "I don't want any Democratic Gestapo. I can't go along with a proposal for a domestic spy system," while Senator Homer Capehart opposed "any new super-duper Gestapo." The very next day, another article revealed the existence of the JCS plan and republished portions of it as well, signaling that the source was someone who opposed both the Donovan and JCS proposals.[43]

The source of these leaks has been the subject of a lively debate.[44] Donovan's suspicion fell on J. Edgar Hoover. The author of the stories in the papers was Walter Trohan, an enemy of the Roosevelt administration and a media conduit for Hoover. FBI official William C. Sullivan later told an unknown interlocutor in a telephone interview that "Trohan was in our pocket, one of our best prostitutes."[45] He explained that the FBI had hired Trohan's son and discovered he was homosexual, implying that Hoover used this information as leverage over Trohan. Sullivan flatly stated, "Thereafter Trohan printed anything we wanted printed." He added that Hoover had ordered any evidence of his or the FBI's involvement in the leaks destroyed and that Trohan would never acknowledge working on behalf of the Bureau.[46]

AN AMERICAN PAPER FOR AMERICANS

Chicago Daily Tribune

THE WORLD'S GREATEST NEWSPAPER

"BACK TO BATAAN!"

★★ FINAL

VOLUME CIV—NO. 35 C — FRIDAY, FEBRUARY 9, 1945.—34 PAGES — THREE CENTS PAY NO MORE

NEW SIEGFRIED OFFENSIVE!

New Deal Plans Super Spy System

SLEUTHS WOULD SNOOP ON U.S. AND THE WORLD

Order Creating It Already Drafted.

BY WALTER TROHAN

U.S. Building Big Peace Base on Kwajalein

BY HAROLD SMITH

A POOR WAY TO ATTRACT A DOVE

MANILA'S PASIG RIVER CROSSED BY U.S. TROOPS

Yanks Join Fight in South of City.

NAZIS HOLD OUT IN FIVE POCKETS ON FRENCH COAST

BY DAVID DARRAH

CANADIANS HIT FLANK OF LINE; YANKS PUSH ON

Nazi Fortress Falls to U.S. 1st Army.

Yanks Spurn U.S.O. Shows; Hail Belgians

BY JOHN THOMPSON

Tribune Features

Phone as You Ride! It's New Chicago Step

1,479 JAP PLANES MONTH'S BAG BY ARMY AND NAVY

War Summaries

FIGURE 13.1 The *Chicago Daily Tribune* was one of the papers that broke the story about Donovan's plan for postwar intelligence. The story subtitled "Sleuths Would Snoop on U.S. and the World" included a photo of Donovan.

There are other theories as well. Trohan himself later claimed that Steve Early, Roosevelt's secretary, provided the documents because "FDR wanted the story out" to contain Donovan's political ambitions.[47] Trohan's articles were strikingly similar to a scathing anti-OSS memorandum by Colonel Richard Park Jr., a military aide to Roosevelt.[48] In turn, one of Park's sources for the report was "Frenchy" Grombach, the head of the Pond and another Donovan rival.[49] Donovan had made plenty of enemies who all had a motive to see his proposal for postwar intelligence fail.

In response to the outcry, Roosevelt told Donovan to "shove the entire thing under the rug for as long as the shock waves reverberate."[50] Donovan wrote back, fuming that "the disclosure was no mere leak but a deliberate plan to sabotage any attempt at reorganization of this government's intelligence services." He especially opposed the "characterization of the plan as 'Gestapo' " and emphasized that his proposed central intelligence organization would have no police powers.[51] It was undeniably a smear of Donovan and his plan. If anything, it was Hoover who deliberately mixed intelligence and law enforcement in the FBI. As these exchanges illustrate, a combination of petty personal rivalries and bigger bureaucratic rivalries shaped the creation of the postwar intelligence system. And although the American people and Congress had not played a role in the debate thus far, the news stories would ensure that they would have a vote, if not veto power.

In the end, the JCS tabled its plan for postwar intelligence but Donovan did not. Isador Lubin, who was head of the Bureau of Labor Statistics, a Roosevelt confidant, and an advocate for Donovan and the OSS, wrote the President a letter in support of Donovan.[52] Roosevelt sent a memorandum to Donovan on April 5, in which he referenced the proposal of November 18, 1944, and invited him to convene all the intelligence chiefs for a meeting designed to reach a consensus on a central intelligence organization.[53] The next day, Donovan sent several department heads his plan and solicited their feedback. Their responses exhibited varying degrees of skepticism, interest, and enthusiasm. Expressing his doubts in a letter dated April 12, 1945, Secretary of the Treasury Henry Morgenthau Jr. admonished Donovan, "The burdens on the President are now monumental. We shouldn't add to them if we can avoid it."[54] Indeed, the burdens had taken their toll. Roosevelt died that very day.

Chief Justice of the Supreme Court Harlan Fiske Stone swore in the new President, Harry S. Truman. The transition in administrations guaranteed a rupture in postwar intelligence planning. Compared to Roosevelt, Truman "was inexperienced in foreign affairs, mistrustful of secret government activities, and opposed to the unorthodox operating procedures that characterized the Roosevelt-Donovan relationship during the war."[55] It did not help that Truman's introduction to the ongoing bureaucratic battle over postwar intelligence came through OSS nemesis Harold Smith, the Director of the Bureau of Budget.[56] When Attorney General Francis Biddle met with the President in May to discuss intelligence matters, Truman "stated he did not like Donovan's plan." Biddle responded that Donovan should not be responsible for constructing postwar intelligence, and "the President agreed thoroughly."[57] The muckraking reporter Drew Pearson took note in his widely read "Washington Merry-Go-Round" column:

> *General "Wild Bill" Donovan*—of the Office of Strategic Services, sometimes called the "Cloak and Dagger Club" or "Oh So Social," will miss Roosevelt terribly. Donovan ran the giant espionage outfit which tried to find out what was going on behind enemy lines, and he had accumulated the most bizarre assortment of female spies, social register bluebloods and anti-Roosevelt haters ever seen in Washington. As an old personal friend, Roosevelt gave him free rein, including grandiose plans for a postwar espionage service. Truman does not like peacetime espionage and will not be so lenient.[58]

Meanwhile, the OSS was on shaky ground as a military organization subject to inevitable postwar retrenchment and without deep roots in an executive department like its rivals. Another round of damaging newspaper articles, as well as budgetary cuts, hit the OSS in May 1945, just as the war in Europe ended.[59]

The war against Japan continued over the summer, as did the war over intelligence. Donovan took his case to the Senate's Committee on Military Affairs, receiving "hearty agreement" from Senator Harley Kilgore. He wrote to Donovan, "It is my hope that in the future we may be forearmed. In the past we certainly have not been."[60] More important than his expression of support for Donovan's plan was Kilgore's example that at least some members of Congress understood the need for—and approved of—a robust peacetime intelligence system. But then another OSS hit piece by Trohan announced, "OSS Survival Plan Attacked as Plot for US Super-Gestapo."[61] Donovan fought back through his own sources. The *Chicago Daily News* ran a headline countering, "Capital Ax Falling on Our Priceless Spy System."[62] The OSS also undertook an information campaign inside the military. Magruder wrote Donovan in late August 1945 on the necessity of "indoctrinating the Armed Forces as to the value of the work of [the OSS]." For example, he attached a lecture titled "The Philosophy of Intelligence," which argued that the postwar world required a coordinated, peacetime intelligence system steered by a professional intelligence service. The speaker concluded with the soaring observation, "The ostrich is not our national bird, with its head in the sand. Rather the eagle is our emblem who surveys the world seeing far and wide what is taking place round about."[63]

Nevertheless, an impassioned letter from Donovan to Harold Smith on August 25 reflected Donovan's sense that the end was nigh. Donovan tried to barter for time. He contended that the allotted "liquidation budget" would allow the OSS to continue operating through January or February, after which Donovan professed his "wish to return to private life." As a patriot and "private citizen concerned with the future of his country," Donovan warned Smith that there was "no permanent agency to take over the functions which OSS will have then ceased to perform." He then alluded to his plan of November 1944 and attached a "statement of principles" to guide a postwar intelligence system.[64]

The end came far sooner than Donovan expected. Truman signed Executive Order 9621, abolishing the OSS, on September 20, 1945. It transferred the OSS's branches to the State and War Departments and would go into effect on October 1, 1945.[65] Truman also signed a letter to Donovan, thanking him and the OSS for their contributions to the war effort. The letter contained the strikingly counterintuitive suggestion that the reallocation of the OSS components "represents the beginning of the development of a coordinated system of foreign intelligence within the permanent framework of the Government." If the history of the preceding half century had shown anything, it was that interdepartmental coordination of intelligence was a fantasy. Whether sincere or not, Truman offered Donovan consolation "in the knowledge that the peacetime intelligence services of the Government are being erected on the foundation of the facilities and resources mobilized through the Office of Strategic Services during the war."[66]

Postwar Intelligence in Limbo

Truman faced the problem of the new bureaucratic competition he created by extinguishing the OSS. Pursuant to his order, the R&A branch of the OSS went to the State Department, forming the basis for the present-day Bureau of Intelligence and Research. The clandestine and special operations components of the OSS went to the War Department as the newly formed Strategic Services Unit (SSU) led by former OSS Deputy Director John Magruder. Meanwhile, the Bureau of Budget proposed that the State Department should coordinate peacetime intelligence through its leadership of two interdepartmental intelligence committees.[67] With Donovan and the OSS out of the picture, the State and War Departments predictably competed over the direction of postwar intelligence, with J. Edgar Hoover and the FBI also trying to stake their claim.

The President fended off Hoover's push nearly as quickly as Hoover leaped at the opportunity to take advantage of Donovan's professional demise. Hoover had written Attorney General Tom Clark in late August to argue that the FBI's SIS should not only continue its operations abroad but also "extend Western Hemisphere coverage to a world-wide organization." Hoover went on to observe astutely that a new intelligence system would require a legislative charter, which meant congressional debate. Congressional debate, in turn, meant public scrutiny, with all the unexpected or unintended consequences that implied. The FBI was prepared to secretly continue its work and expand its preexisting operations without any untoward publicity.[68]

When Clark presented Truman with Hoover's outline for postwar intelligence, Hoover stuck to his original plan for a committee structure. There would be a superseding "committee to control basic policy" composed of the Secretaries of State, War, and Navy plus the Attorney General and an IIC-styled "operational committee" composed of the directors of the FBI, ONI, and MID, plus an Assistant Secretary of State. Just as Hoover positioned the FBI to be the lead organization in the IIC when he first proposed the prewar coordination system to Roosevelt, he again attempted to do the same in the postwar system he presented to Truman. It was a pivotal moment for American intelligence because Truman was essentially deciding if the United States was going to combine foreign and domestic intelligence.[69]

As the postwar national security threats presented by the Soviet Union and communism were coming into focus, Hoover insisted that "foreign and domestic civil intelligence are inseparable and constitute one field of operation." He claimed that the "theory that police work and intelligence coverage cannot be combined has been entirely dispelled." Still, he recognized that his proposal could face public accusations of creating a "Gestapo" or "political police," which would be "obnoxious to American citizens." But he countered that the FBI's system "operating in the Western Hemisphere throughout the war has engaged in both police and intelligence activities and its record of protecting civil liberties has been highly praised even by the American Civil Liberties Union," which, if true, marked a departure from the mutual suspicions and recriminations that characterized the BOI-ACLU relationship in the mid-1920s. Hoover highlighted the "simplicity of structure and flexibility of operations" of the FBI's SIS. Expanding the SIS would "require no elaborate superstructure," so the "plan, consequently, can be placed in operation immediately by the President," avoiding congressional debate, legislation, or oversight. Hoover therefore aspired to make the FBI the very same type of expansive, "Super-spy" system that Walter Trohan had mischaracterized in the press as Donovan's plan.[70]

Hoover probably did not know that the Bureau of Budget, which was guiding Truman's postwar intelligence planning, had already taken up the question of expanding the FBI's SIS into a global intelligence service and had decided against it.[71] Still, the SIS left its mark on American intelligence. Many SIS officers later joined the new CIA, and SIS "legal attachés" even provided a model for the CIA's station chiefs. None of this would be much consolation to Hoover.[72]

Truman had no intention of empowering Hoover. Apparently, Hoover tried to woo Truman as he once did Roosevelt, with political intelligence about the President's rivals—for example, using wiretaps that captured the conversations of Supreme Court Justice Felix Frankfurter. Truman voiced his objections to Hoover and the FBI in his diary, writing, "We want no Gestapo or Secret Police... [and the] FBI is tending in that direction. They are dabbling in sex-life scandals and plain blackmail.... This must stop." He was equally determined to rein in the FBI's foreign intelligence operations and "confine the FBI to the United States."[73] Truman would ensure that Hoover would not use Donovan's fall to opportunistically wrest control of the American intelligence system back for himself.

However, Truman's order—via Bureau of Budget scheming—for the State Department to "take the lead in developing a comprehensive and coordinated foreign intelligence program" caught the State Department flatfooted.[74] The State Department had not operated an intelligence organization since U-1 was abolished in 1927, and there was already internal opposition to a new one based on its incorporation of the OSS's R&A. An institutional rift between diplomacy and intelligence was apparent, as the foreign service corps viewed intelligence officers with suspicion, particularly given the known communist sympathies among OSS R&A staff. Finally, the State Department's planning for postwar intelligence had sputtered in December 1944. It appears the Bureau of Budget just expected the State Department to follow its formula.[75]

Instead, the State Department put its own spin on the Bureau of Budget plan.[76] At first it planned for two committees, each composed of the Secretaries of State, Navy, and War, with one adding the Secretary of the Treasury and Attorney General, to jointly oversee an Executive Secretary, who was also advised by two interdepartmental groups. The Executive Secretary had two deputies who would oversee a total of twenty committees. The plan avoided a central intelligence organization or any other type of coordinating agency.[77] The State Department then revised this plan to create one overarching National Intelligence Authority composed of the Secretaries of

War, State, and Navy, and chaired by State, but the new proposal still maintained the overburdened and bloated subcommittee structure.[78] The State Department had elevated decades of failed intelligence coordination through the committee system to a high art form.

By comparison, the military establishment had been forward-thinking and innovative. Secretary of the Navy James Forrestal directed fellow Wall Street veteran Ferdinand Eberstadt to make a sweeping study of the American national security establishment over the summer of 1945. The Eberstadt Report offered a proposal for postwar intelligence, including the creation of a central intelligence organization designed to coordinate intelligence. The military also finally "recognized the fact of 'intelligence' as an autonomous field of study and action," or perhaps profession. After all the internal deliberations and disagreements of the previous year, by the fall of 1945, both the Army and Navy were "solidly united behind their conception of a central, independent agency performing the functions of coordination, production, and centralized operations."[79] But they would still have to convince the President, Congress, and the rest of the country.

Magruder's Missive

As if the issue had not received enough attention, a War Department committee headed by Robert Lovett examined the question of centralizing and coordinating intelligence in late October and early November 1945. Magruder wrote a long, lucid memorandum to Lovett that outlined his vision for a new central intelligence agency. Revisiting the OSS, Magruder explained that it "established, for the first time in American history," three critical intelligence missions: "an organized network of secret agents" who collected foreign intelligence, "an organized system of counter-espionage" in foreign countries, and "organized . . . resources" to perform intelligence analysis. Magruder attributed the OSS's shortcomings to "the fact that the United States had no centrally controlled and comprehensive espionage system in being when the war broke out, and no experience in the development and direction of any such system," echoing the sentiments of figures like Henry Shelton Sanford, Lafayette Baker, Robert Lansing, and "Wild Bill" Donovan, among others.[80]

Magruder believed that intelligence suffered from lack of coordination, duplication of effort, impediments to information sharing, and "inadequate team-work." Accordingly, he recommended the establishment of a "central foreign intelligence service" that would be responsible for clandestine foreign intelligence collection and all-source intelligence analysis. Based on his experience, he was concerned with "prevent[ing] the agency from becoming an instrument of policy of a single government department." He also wanted the agency to stick to intelligence and not have any "policy-making function." To ensure that the new organization would not be subjected to charges of using secret intelligence for its own internal political ends, he determined that it would put its "complete concentration upon foreign intelligence." Moreover, he observed that it was "not generally recognized in the United States that the operation of clandestine intelligence is a highly professional pursuit which should be undertaken only by experts," intimating that the new organization would have to professionalize espionage. Finally, he argued that the organization must have an independent budget to protect it from other departments and guard the secrecy of its operations and the identities of its agents. Magruder was not far off the mark in terms of what eventually became the CIA.[81]

Unfortunately, Magruder was an OSS veteran in a decidedly anti-OSS milieu. Furthermore, the SSU and MID were competing in the War Department, as it had two different intelligence organizations to manage. But the real battle over postwar intelligence was interdepartmental and inter-institutional, between the State Department and Bureau of Budget, on one side, and the War and Navy departments, on the other. By January 1946, they reached a compromise of sorts that formed the basis for the postwar peacetime American intelligence system. But the immediate outcome was not the truly independent, professional intelligence organization that Magruder advocated for or that Donovan had long wanted.

PART THREE

The Covert Cold War: The Construction of the Secret National Security State

14

Central Intelligence and Central Problems

With the Soviet threat looming, the United States could not repeat its traditional practice of intelligence retrenchment at the end of the Second World War. The Cold War also required a new national security architecture for the challenges the country faced. The 1947 National Security Act was an ambitious effort to coordinate the entire American national security system: the military with the National Military Establishment, known today as the Department of Defense (DOD); national security policymaking with the National Security Council; and intelligence with the CIA.[1] Congress had to address a broader range of coordination problems than just intelligence. If not disinterested, then certainly distracted, it instituted transformational change for American intelligence in the few short paragraphs legislating the CIA.[2] As a result, the exact form and functions of the CIA became subject to broad interpretation.

The statutory language of the 1947 National Security Act did not capture the spirit of the agency or the full spectrum of intelligence roles it later adopted. Its development was shaped by the OSS veterans who heavily staffed the CIA, contemporary crises like communist subversion across Europe, and a broader identity crisis generated by the CIA's attempt to balance the competing missions of coordination and analysis, on the one hand, and clandestine and covert activities, on the other.[3] While old tensions in civil-intelligence relations would endure and new ones would arise, the creation of the CIA was unquestionably a watershed moment in American intelligence history.

"A Headless Body and a Bodyless Head"

Whereas the concept of a peacetime "spy system" had long been opposed by Congress and the American people in the past, intelligence was finally widely accepted as a necessary element of US national security and statecraft in the aftermath of the Second World War. Despite the recent public relations campaign waged against Donovan, initial press reports and public polling on the subject of a postwar intelligence system seemed favorable.[4] Pop culture expressed through comics, magazines, and movies celebrated American intelligence exploits during the war, like the 1946 films *O.S.S.* and *Cloak and Dagger*.[5] Several factors probably contributed to American civil society's change of heart. Congress was conducting its comprehensive investigation of the Pearl Harbor attack, in which intelligence featured prominently. The dawn of the Nuclear Age also raised the stakes of a surprise attack, requiring persistent vigilance. Furthermore, on March 5, 1946, Winston Churchill gave his famous Iron Curtain speech in Fulton, Missouri, warning Americans of the threat posed by communism, including its "fifth columns." Given the widespread sense of foreboding in 1946, the US government had a window to construct a new peacetime intelligence system.

Truman chose to be transparent with the American people about this decision. In his State of the Union Address on January 21, 1946, he explained that the country would preserve some of its wartime activities, including foreign intelligence.[6] The very next day, he signed a presidential directive largely resembling the JCS plan. It created a National Intelligence Authority (NIA) composed of the Cabinet Secretaries, but instead of a central intelligence agency there would be a Central Intelligence Group (CIG) led by a Director of Central Intelligence (DCI). The difference between "agency" and "group" is noteworthy. Instead of a truly independent agency, the CIG merely combined whatever resources and personnel the executive departments and their intelligence services were willing to contribute to the new organization. Due to budget cuts, the departments, which had always been parsimonious when it came to intelligence, became even more sparing with the CIG, so it did not meet its budgetary or staff requirements. Moreover, the director's control over the CIG was unclear. The DCI had to contend with the covetous intelligence chiefs who sat on an Intelligence Advisory Board and monitored the allocation of resources and personnel to the CIG from their respective offices. As a result, this arrangement "created a headless body and a bodyless head."[7]

The CIG was designed to be a cooperative venture among executive departments and intelligence organizations. If history had proven anything, it was that they were unable to cooperate for long. Since the DCI and CIG had such little control, they could hardly be expected to accomplish the task of intelligence coordination, the primary purpose for which they were established. Still, the CIG was a step toward intelligence coordination, and it introduced changes that would outlast it. One noteworthy innovation was the production of a Daily Summary for the President, a precursor of the President's Daily Brief.[8] The CIG also introduced a Weekly Summary of current intelligence issues, which continued under the CIA. Such all-source intelligence analysis was a welcome innovation for American intelligence.

But Rear Admiral Sidney Souers, the first DCI, was frustrated from the outset. He lasted less than five months on the job. Souers's brief stewardship led him to recommend that the CIG obtain a legislative charter, independent budget, and true organizational independence if it ever hoped to centralize and coordinate intelligence.[9] His successor, General Hoyt Vandenberg, obtained an internal NIA directive that revised Truman's presidential order. It gave the DCI more authority to coordinate intelligence, authorized the DCI to take control of all foreign intelligence activities outside the United States, and ensured that the CIG was adequately funded and staffed.[10]

With his expanded authority, Vandenberg set to work building up the CIG. The CIG acquired the SSU as the new Office of Special Operations, thus absorbing many OSS veterans. For his part, Hoover relinquished foreign intelligence in Latin America with such haste, born of his hostility to the CIG and Truman's postwar intelligence plan, that it was clear he hoped to undermine the new organization and system.[11] In response to these two developments, the CIG assumed responsibility for foreign HUMINT, which contributed to the evolution of the US intelligence community along functional lines. In another test of the new organization and system, Truman requested the first National Intelligence Estimate on the timely topic of the Soviet Union's global intentions and capabilities.[12] The CIG was carving out its spheres of responsibility for espionage and analysis. It was also struggling to break free from historical constraints on independent intelligence. As one CIG official admitted, it was "but one stage, in a long-range growth, far from complete."[13] Given the many weaknesses in the CIG's design, it would not take long to move on to the next stage.

A Public Debate over Secret Intelligence

To shore up their hard-fought yet modest gains, CIG officials pressed for a legislative charter. CIG General Counsel Lawrence Houston drafted a proposed bill to establish a Central Intelligence Agency. The bill would shift the CIG from a dependent, relatively passive agency to an independent, operational agency. However, the Truman administration—namely, Truman's chief counsel, Clark Clifford—balked at the proposal. Houston, with the assistance of his deputies John Warner and Walter Pforzheimer, edited the initial proposal and resubmitted it. The White House attached it to a larger bill that included the far more contentious issue of military unification, but still worried that the CIG's proposal could prevent the entire bill from being approved. Accordingly, the White House drafted its own proposal for a Central Intelligence Agency. The CIG staff was able to offer comments, though it could not make any significant revisions, to what ultimately became the CIA provisions of the proposed National Security Act of 1947 that Truman sent to Congress.[14] And so, intelligence was not the dominant issue preoccupying the President, department heads, Congress, or even the press and public as the country embarked on historic intelligence reform.[15]

For the first time in US history, Congress had the opportunity to debate the establishment of an independent, professional peacetime intelligence organization. Senator Elbert Thomas explained that with "our present world-wide sphere of international responsibility and our position among the world powers, we need the most efficient intelligence system that can be devised," declaring that "there is no returning to the prewar system." Alluding to the CIG, Thomas noted, "We have now a central intelligence agency established by executive action," but contended that "provision for such an agency should be made in permanent legislation."[16]

Not all were as optimistic about the new organization. Congressman Clarence Brown grilled Secretary of the Navy James Forrestal over the authority and scope of the proposed central intelligence agency and its director. For example, he wondered whether the CIA could look at his income tax reports. Concerned about executive power, Brown did not want to establish "any particular central police agency under any President... and just allow him to have a gestapo of his own if he wants to have it." When Forrestal responded that the CIA would be "limited definitely to purposes outside of this country" and that the FBI was responsible for domestic operations, Brown noted that the legislation on the table did not explicitly outline this division. He also observed that the roles and responsibilities of the proposed CIA were vague, while the law, at least purportedly, restricted both FBI and Secret Service activities.[17]

The issue of legislating an American "gestapo"—already a proven rhetorical weapon against intelligence—continued to surface in the House hearings. Brown reprised his questions for Vice Admiral Forrest Sherman, the Deputy Chief of Naval Operations, professing that it was "the duty and the responsibility of the Congress to make certain that we do not set up any gestapo in this country, or any agency which might possibly develop into one."[18] Brown took the position that there were "enough people now running around butting into everybody else's business in this country without establishing another agency to do so," musing, "What we ought to do is eliminate 90 percent of the present snoopers instead of adding to them."[19] Echoing others, Marine Brigadier General Merritt Edson worried that the bill "opens the door toward a potential gestapo or NKVD in the Central Intelligence Agency."[20] In an exchange with Congressman John McCormack, Edson argued that strict legislation was necessary to curtail the CIA's activities, especially with respect to "police powers" and "snooping on civilians." McCormack agreed that the CIA should not adopt the domestic functions of the FBI.[21]

In Senate hearings, Vandenberg tried to assuage common fears and misunderstandings about intelligence and the proposed CIA. While acknowledging the common sentiment "that there was something un-American about espionage and even about intelligence generally," he insisted that "all intelligence is not sinister, nor is it an invidious type of work." Instead, he presented a more sterile view of the CIA's role as an organization primarily focused on the coordination and analysis of information. He cleverly avoided discussing clandestine or covert activities and only indirectly tackled the CIA's contribution to collecting intelligence, steering clear of the spy business. Vandenberg emphasized that the President's directive creating the CIG had denied it a domestic role, which would ensure that "the Central Intelligence Group can never become a Gestapo or security police." Notably, the proposed bill creating the CIA did not have a similar provision at that point in its drafting.[22]

Frederick J. Libby, the executive secretary of the National Council for Prevention of War, picked up on the problem that the bill did not include a stipulation that the CIA would not possess police powers, predicting that it would "become a Gestapo at home and a universal spy system abroad." Libby's testimony went further, characterizing the entire 1947 National Security Act as the militarization of the American republic.[23] In fact, the United States was constructing the national security state, a combination of the administrative state that emerged at the beginning of the century and the military powerhouse the country had become by midcentury.

As a result, the distinction between intelligence in war and peace and whether the CIA would be a civilian or military intelligence agency took on increasing importance during the debate. Under the provisions of the proposed bill, the CIA director could be either a civilian or a military officer. Brown felt that "a uniform sometimes gives a man a little more feeling of power and authority," so he sensed there would be "a feeling of greater security if a civilian is entrusted with such power."[24] General Edson warned that the act had been drafted by military men, gave too much power to the military, and would lead to military domination of the CIA.[25] Vandenberg, as both a military officer and director of the CIG, stressed that national intelligence transcended the narrower category of military affairs, implying the need to ensure the military did not subordinate the CIA.[26]

Among the contributors to this debate was Allen Dulles, an OSS veteran, who sent a long memorandum to Senator John Chandler "Chan" Gurney, the chairman of the Senate Armed Services Committee. Dulles began by describing intelligence as a profession, distinguished by its focus on secrecy, and "not a mere casual occupation." He, too, emphasized that intelligence went beyond military information, necessitating scientific, political, and social expertise. Additionally, he pointed out that intelligence requirements were different in times of peace and war. Therefore, the CIA "should be predominantly civilian rather than military, and under civilian leadership." It would need its own personnel and appropriations and, critically, "have exclusive jurisdiction to carry out secret intelligence operations" and "have its operations and personnel protected by 'official secrets' legislation." In short, he requested an independent, secret, professional intelligence organization, "with proper legislative backing, a correct technical set-up, and adequate leadership."[27]

"Wild Bill" Donovan also penned letters to Chan Gurney, doubtlessly frustrated to be doing so from the discomfort of civilian life. He claimed that the proposal "not only perpetuates the existing evil of bad organization of placing Central Intelligence under a Committee of Three (3) (Secretaries of State, War and Navy) but intensified that evil by putting it under a Committee of Six (6) in the National Security Council." Instead, he suggested the CIA report to the proposed Secretary of National Defense, later the Secretary of Defense, which would have the deleterious effect of subordinating the CIA to the military. However, he also agreed with Dulles that the head of the CIA should be a civilian. He understood that intelligence was "no longer confined to time of war," so it should not come under any individual military service. Donovan continued to confuse his military loyalties with his intelligence sensibilities, but he quickly realized his error.[28] In a follow-up letter to Gurney, Donovan reiterated some of his previous positions, but instead would have the CIA report to the President, just as he had suggested in November 1944. Furthermore, he opposed lumping together postwar intelligence reform and military unification in the same bill because military issues would undoubtedly overshadow intelligence issues.[29]

Gurney consulted Walter Pforzheimer, the CIG's legislative liaison, about Donovan's recommendation. Pforzheimer disagreed with the CIA reporting to the Secretary of National Defense, since it "would contain us within the military establishment, which was not the design at all." Pforzheimer was right in that a central intelligence organization needed to be independent. But he disagreed with Donovan that Congress should delay intelligence legislation. He advised that "if General Donovan and his associates wished to make a fight on our detailed functions, that would be appropriate at the time our enabling legislation comes up."[30] In this case, Donovan was right. Donovan, who seldom concerned himself with day-to-day organizational details or formalities, had always taken pains to outline the proper roles and functions of the COI, OSS, and proposed postwar intelligence organization. Congress failed to pay sufficient attention to the details, and the provisions of the 1947 act as written were too vague for the roles that were immediately demanded of the CIA.

The hearings in both the House and Senate and the statements of congressmen and executive officials tackled the dual, persisting problems of bureaucratic competition and ideological opposition. The legislative history suggested that the CIA would be, first and foremost, another attempt to coordinate the American intelligence system. Bureaucratic competition had undone previous attempts to achieve this aim and, predictably, competition accompanied the CIA from its creation. The CIA, like its predecessors, would join the existing pantheon of US intelligence services as they warred with each other while warring together against America's enemies. Ideological suspicions would also remain despite congressional legislation. The *New York Times* reported that members of the House still had reservations about a "military dictatorship," a "Gestapo," or "an OGPU [Soviet security service preceding the NKVD]," and noted that Congress was taking steps to restrict the agency's police powers.[31]

Congress could have legislated more. However, once the President and Congress reached a consensus on the more pressing matter of military consolidation, any further agonizing over intelligence became irrelevant, unnecessary, and unproductive. Congress passed the final bill, and Truman signed it into law on July 26, 1947.[32] Roscoe Hillenkoetter, who had replaced Vandenberg to become the third Director of Central Intelligence, was the first director of the Central Intelligence Agency. The CIA had a legislative charter that left room for interpretation—and manipulation.

Landmark Intelligence Legislation

The 1947 National Security Act established the CIA as an organization under the new National Security Council (NSC). Although independent in the sense of not belonging to an executive department, the CIA still faced the possibility of subordination to executive departments by making it accountable to the National Security Council rather than the President. The act included tepid language explaining that the CIA's job was to "advise" and "make recommendations to" the NSC "for the purpose of coordinating the intelligence activities of the several Government departments and agencies." It gave the CIA the analytical responsibility to "correlate and evaluate intelligence relating to national security." Moreover, it mandated that the other departments and agencies of the government "shall make available" to the DCI any information essential to national security "to the extent recommended" by the NSC, which in effect made the new agency dependent on the cooperation of the NSC, executive departments, and other members of the intelligence community. If the CIA wanted information from the Director of the FBI, the DCI had to make the request in writing, indicating that Congress knew that cooperation between the two organizations would be problematic. Additionally, the DCI could be either a civilian or a military officer, despite concerns about military domination.[33]

To settle one of the most contentious areas surrounding the CIA, the final version of the act contained the provision that the CIA "shall have no police, subpoena, law-enforcement powers, or internal-security functions" as a buffer against accusations that it would be an American Gestapo.[34] Thus, ideas influenced laws, and Congress gave expression to old American attitudes toward intelligence in legislating the CIA. However, as the country would later discover, congressional bills were not enough to restrain an organization whose raison d'être was secrecy and security.

Furthermore, the legislation might have provided for more expansive powers than Congress intended. The act contained the vague provision that the CIA would "perform such other functions and duties related to intelligence affecting the national security as the National Security Council may from time to time direct."[35] The language in the provision mirrored Tab A in Donovan's November 18, 1944, proposal to Roosevelt in which he suggested that a central intelligence organization would conduct these unnamed activities on behalf of the President. The CIA subsequently used this clause to argue it was given a legislative mandate to perform covert action, a mission that would come to haunt the CIA, the intelligence community, and American civil-intelligence relations.[36]

Ironically, the *New York Times*, which soon became a venue for publicizing CIA failures and scandals, heralded the creation of the CIA. In an article titled "Intelligence Net to be World-Wide," the *Times* marked the occasion as

Congress endorsed "for the first time in American history...an effective world-wide American intelligence service." In one of the greatest understatements in US history, the article stated, "In a democracy change comes slowly"—in the case of an independent, professional intelligence organization, far more slowly than the article's reference to the year and a half between Truman's order creating the CIG and the legislation establishing the CIA. The CIA was the product of decades of thought and debate regarding the nature of intelligence, the distinctiveness of the intelligence profession, and, above all, the need for intelligence coordination—all weighed against a longstanding American bias against espionage. Addressing one of the public's foremost fears, the article promised that "the Central Intelligence Agency will not act within the United States." Grandiloquently and without the slightest historical accuracy, the article concluded that the United States had finally "embarked on the hidden game of international and national security."[37]

Clarity or Confusion in American Covert Action?

Despite the vast differences between the United States and the Soviet Union that set the conditions for their epochal clash, they shared one common interest that would shape global intelligence history. In the aftermath of the Second World War, both countries fundamentally hoped to avoid another catastrophic conventional war and soon faced the cataclysmic threat of nuclear war. Intelligence offered the two rivals a covert way to avoid an overt war. This crucial element of what became the Cold War demanded the clandestine and covert operations that so enamored the OSS veterans who largely formed the first generation of the CIA. The establishment of the CIA also proved timely for an executive branch that was scrambling to fill the gaps that were quickly becoming apparent in US national security and statecraft. In 1947, American policymakers were alarmed by a secret Soviet campaign that targeted the weak, recovering states of postwar Europe. They decided to fight fire with fire.

On March 12, 1947, Truman delivered a speech in support of US assistance to Turkey and Greece in which he famously declared that "it must be the policy of the United States to support free peoples who are resisting attempted subjugation by armed minorities or by outside pressures."[38] This "Truman Doctrine" required countering Soviet covert activities with American covert activities. But it was unclear which department or organization would lead the effort.

In only its second meeting, the NSC took up the issue of "psychological warfare," continuing a discussion from the Second World War over what the term meant and what organization should lead it. Secretary of State George C. Marshall, who had earlier raised those very questions with Donovan, wanted to "eliminate the word 'warfare.'" According to DCI Hillenkoetter, Marshall did "not seem to favor the idea of psychological warfare," even though Under Secretary of State Robert Lovett and Hillenkoetter both reminded him that the Secretary of State was responsible for coordinating psychological warfare activities. The military bowed out as Secretary of the Army Kenneth Claiborne Royall announced that "the Military Establishment did not believe that it should have a part in those activities."[39] The FBI was also out of the foreign intelligence business after Hoover closed the SIS. The new CIA had a cadre of OSS veterans experienced in subversion, overseas logistics already in place, and unvouchered funds for intelligence missions that helped keep them secret.[40] The NSC directed the CIA to take charge of psychological operations to counter Soviet propaganda in December 1947.[41] In the absence of any other takers, and by virtue of experience and opportunity, the CIA was poised to become the covert action arm of the US government, but not without another bureaucratic fight.

In a memorandum of May 1948, George Kennan, the State Department's Director of Policy Planning, announced the "inauguration of organized political warfare," including all overt and covert means "short of war." He astutely observed that the United States struggled to distinguish between war and peace and believed that the country "cannot afford in the future... to scramble into impromptu covert operations." He advocated a sustained covert campaign to counter the Soviet Union. He also proposed creating a "directorate of political warfare operations" in the NSC that would report to the Secretary of State and take charge of any covert activities currently under the CIA or military. Kennan was positioning himself and the State Department to run the country's covert action programs.[42]

The directive NSC 10/2 was an attempt to establish organizational responsibility and lines of authority for covert action. It opened by explaining that "the overt foreign activities of the US Government must be supplemented by covert operations" to counter "the vicious covert activities of the USSR." Since the CIA was already conducting foreign espionage, the NSC determined that there was no need to create a new organization for covert action. Instead, it created an Office of Special Projects, subsequently known as the Office of Policy Coordination, that would be housed in the CIA for this purpose. But the language of the directive made it unclear how the CIA would control its own covert action office. The Secretary of State would nominate the head of the Office of Special Projects with the approval of the DCI and

NSC, clouding the office's leadership and control. Moreover, officials from the State and Defense Departments would ensure covert operations were "planned and conducted in a manner consistent with US foreign and military policies and with overt activities." The directive also specified that the office would "operate independently of other components" of the CIA for "purposes of security and flexibility of operations," creating a bureaucratic fault line in the CIA itself.[43]

The implementation of NSC 10/2 was equally problematic. The new office would exist as an operational arm of the CIA but take its policy guidance from a 10/2 Panel.[44] Kennan, Souers, and Hillenkoetter agreed that NSC 10/2's execution "should reflect the recognition of the principle that the Departments of State and the National Military Establishment [later the Department of Defense] are responsible for the conduct of the [covert] activities" of the CIA, further stipulating that the State Department would take "pre-eminence in time of peace and the National Military Establishment succeeding the pre-eminent position in war time."[45] The State and Defense Departments could subordinate the CIA by controlling its covert operations and yet not be held responsible for them, thus positioning the CIA to be a scapegoat for covert action failures.

NSC 10/2 also included a definition of "covert operations" as "all activities... which are conducted or sponsored by this Government against hostile foreign states or groups or in support of friendly foreign states or groups but which are so planned and executed that any US Government responsibility for them is not evident... and that if uncovered the US Government can plausibly disclaim any responsibility for them." Thus, the directive articulated the principle of plausible deniability. In specifying that covert action operations were foreign intelligence operations, it created a boundary between what was acceptable at home versus abroad. The definition also included different types of covert operations, such as propaganda, economic warfare, sabotage, and subversion, although it distinguished covert action operations from "traditional" military or intelligence activities like armed conflict or espionage. Ultimately, NSC 10/2 operationally put the CIA in the business of covert action.[46]

The CIA's First Report Cards

Policymakers began to scrutinize the CIA from the moment of its creation. Former President Herbert Hoover oversaw a congressionally created commission, known as the Hoover Commission, to examine how the US government was functioning. Ferdinand Eberstadt, who had conducted a study on intelligence in 1945, revisited the intelligence establishment with particular attention to the young CIA. Concurrent with this report, the NSC organized its own investigation of the CIA with the approval of Truman, carried out by a triumvirate of former World War Two intelligence officers and New York lawyers—Allen Dulles, William Jackson, and Mathias Correa. The Dulles-Jackson-Correa Report ("Dulles Report") and the Eberstadt Report, both submitted in 1949, mirrored each other in many ways.

The Eberstadt Report underscored the CIA's early struggles.[47] The report claimed the CIA had "fallen short" as "the major source of coordinated and evaluated intelligence."[48] It briefly entertained the idea of having the CIA report directly to the President, as Donovan had suggested, but determined it was "doubtful whether... he has the time to pay much attention to it."[49] Likewise, the report dismissed proposals to place the CIA under the State Department or military, firmly stating that the "CIA's functions and interests transcend both."[50] In further support of the CIA's independence, the report stressed the need for professional intelligence officers, recruited and trained for that specific purpose. It also discussed the strained relationship between the CIA and FBI, noting that J. Edgar Hoover declined to cooperate with the Eberstadt Committee.[51] Finally, despite acknowledging that "intelligence can best flourish in the shade of silence," the report recommended independent oversight either by a congressional "watchdog" committee or by a presidentially appointed committee, reintroducing the issue of presidential and congressional competition over intelligence.[52] Overall, the report identified many problems, old and new, facing the CIA.

Like the Eberstadt Report, the Dulles Report took stock of the CIA's performance in the areas of coordination, professionalism, and, portentously, covert and clandestine activities. Instead of solving the coordination problem, the CIA became "just one more intelligence agency producing intelligence in competition with older established agencies of the Government departments."[53] The report blamed the 1947 National Security Act for failing to "give the Central Intelligence Agency independent authority to coordinate intelligence" and pointed out that the arrangement protected the bureaucratic fiefdoms of the departmental members of the NSC.[54] In concurrence with the Eberstadt Report, the Dulles Report rejected ongoing departmental attempts to subordinate the CIA. With respect to the organizational rivalry between the CIA and FBI, it challenged the conceptual distinction between separate spheres of foreign and domestic intelligence, commenting that "our intelligence... cannot be sharply divided on any such geographical basis."[55]

Hoover himself had said as much, but his solution would have subordinated the intelligence profession to law enforcement, which the Dulles Report implicitly rejected on the basis of professionalism.

Like the Eberstadt Report, the Dulles Report called for professional intelligence officers trained in operations and analysis. It recommended placing the (misnamed) Office of Special Operations, charged with foreign espionage, and the (deceptively named) Office of Policy Coordination, charged with covert action, into one Operations Division. This new division could conduct its own personnel recruitment and training since clandestine and covert activities required a different skill set than analysis. The report concluded that this arrangement "would, to a large extent, meet the criticism frequently voiced, and with a good deal of merit, that it is essentially unsound to combine in a single intelligence agency both secret operations and over-all coordinating and estimating functions."[56] In doing so, it recognized the practical, cultural, and organizational differences between those who analyze information and those who undertake espionage and covert action.

Aside from not resolving these internal conflicts in the CIA, the Dulles Report proposed to leverage them for external purposes. In a candid, though manipulative, response to the publicity surrounding the CIA's creation, the report took issue with the "unfortunate trend wherein the Central Intelligence Agency finds itself advertised almost exclusively as a secret service organization." It deviously recommended that the CIA "should be presented instead to the public as the centralized coordinator of intelligence...[which] would help to cover rather than uncover its secret operations."[57] Essentially, the Dulles Report recommended a public relations campaign designed to highlight the CIA's congressionally mandated role and conceal the operational activities it had adopted without clear statutory intent.

The CIA's Secret Service Fund

Cold War threats, policymaker preferences, and organizational interests were driving the CIA toward covert and clandestine activities. To be fair, the CIA's legislative charter was vague and incomplete. Underpinning the legislative charter was a similarly vague and incomplete expression of congressional intent. But for CIA General Counsel Lawrence Houston, congressional intent was still clear enough.

Barely a week into the CIA's existence in September 1947, Houston examined the cryptic language of the 1947 National Security Act that subsequently was used to endorse CIA covert action and concluded that, "taken out of context and without knowledge of its history, these Sections could bear almost unlimited interpretation." With respect to propaganda and special operations, Houston warned that "either activity would be an unwarranted extension of the functions authorized" to the CIA "based on our understanding of the intent of Congress at the time these provisions were enacted." Instead, he believed that "Congress was primarily interested in an agency for coordinating intelligence and originally did not propose any overseas collection activities for CIA," let alone covert action. Houston therefore recommended that the CIA should not undertake covert action operations "without previously informing Congress and obtaining its approval of the functions and expenditure of funds for those purposes."[58]

By involving Congress in CIA control and oversight through the power of the purse, Houston was perhaps insinuating that Congress should not leave the same loophole it did when it first authorized the Contingent Fund. He also acknowledged that coordination was the key question Congress purportedly sought to redress by creating the CIA. Ironically, the CIA's pivot to covert action undermined both congressional oversight and intelligence coordination. Still, the CIA needed funding, which meant congressional appropriations.

The CIA proposed legislation specifically addressing its organizational needs. Unlike the 1947 National Security Act, the Central Intelligence Agency Act of 1949 received little serious debate as it made its way through Congress.[59] To the extent that Congress discussed the secrecy surrounding the proposed legislation—or the CIA itself—the *New York Times* cited House minority leader Joseph W. Martin Jr., who argued, "In Washington, if three people know anything, everybody does," alluding to the challenge that leaks would pose. House Armed Services Committee chairman Carl Vinson insisted, "When you're in the spy business you can't go shouting about it from the house tops." The article revealed little about the legislation itself, only offering that it "would give legal authority to the undercover work of the Central Intelligence Agency, the top United States espionage clearing house," and enable the CIA "to hire secretly and spend money freely, and without strings, in carrying on its activities."[60]

The act gave the agency everything it wanted and enshrouded it in congressionally approved secrecy.[61] For example, it exempted the CIA from laws that required "the publication or disclosure of the organization, functions, names, official titles, salaries, or numbers of personnel employed by the agency."[62] Clark Clifford, who had originally opposed transforming the CIG into the CIA, later recorded that the CIA "could evade oversight of its activities by drawing the cloak of secrecy around itself."[63] In this, the agency had the help of executive policymakers desperate for a covert instrument to confront the Soviet Union and a Congress equally preoccupied when it took up the challenge of legislating a secret intelligence organization in peacetime.

For the second time in US history, Congress had legislated itself out of intelligence oversight. The 1949 CIA Act created a "black budget" that demonstrated congressional deference to discretionary executive control of intelligence. The 1949 CIA Act even mirrored the language of the Contingent Fund's reauthorization of 1793, specifying that CIA expenditures could be "accounted for solely on the certificate of the Director and every such certificate shall be deemed a sufficient voucher for the amount therein certified."[64] In an observation reflecting the spirit of the Secret Service Fund, Houston concluded, "Provisions of unvouchered funds and the inviolability of such funds from outside inspection is the heart and soul of covert operation."[65]

Oversight by Other Means

When presented with the opportunity to reexamine the CIA and give itself explicit oversight authority in the 1949 CIA Act, Congress again failed. However, in the place of formal congressional oversight, an informal system evolved. The unofficial congressional "oversight" bodies for the CIA were the appropriations and armed services committees in both the Senate and the House. But oversight was not equally distributed in them. Instead, a few prominent members of these committees, who were also among the most influential members of Congress, took on the responsibility of CIA oversight. In turn, they created unofficial CIA subcommittees within their own committees. These subcommittees rarely met, and when they did, they did so in secret, often on short notice. They also never made transcripts of their meetings or kept copies of classified documents provided by the CIA. They rarely discussed actual CIA operations or scrutinized how the CIA spent its budget.[66] The CIA budget itself was hidden within the Department of Defense budget, although Congress allocated a Contingency Reserve Fund in 1952 that was separate from the CIA's regular budget and designed to be used for "unanticipated large projects" like the development of the U-2 spy plane and other covert and clandestine programs.[67]

Congressional oversight of the early CIA mirrored intelligence oversight during the Revolutionary War in that it was based on interpersonal arrangements. Committee chairmen and the DCI discussed sensitive issues and secret operations in unofficial meetings at their offices and homes, or even over meals. Congress had finally legislated an independent professional intelligence organization, but there was still no legislation or legislative process to adequately oversee it.[68]

Just as political rivalries steered the committee system during the Revolutionary War, political competition shaped early congressional oversight of the CIA. The few congressmen and senators who were privy to CIA secrets wanted to maintain their privileged status and jealously guarded CIA oversight from interference by other committees or members of Congress.[69] But they also managed this system as a matter of national security to shield the agency's work from leaks just as members of the Committee of Secret Correspondence had done.[70] The consensus Congress reached on the CIA reflected a broader "Cold War consensus" between the US government and the American people that gave considerable deference to the President and executive branch to protect the country.[71]

The early system of CIA oversight fundamentally depended on trust between the CIA and Congress. Congress trusted the CIA to protect the country against communism and respected the DCIs, who were either high-ranking members of the military or well-known and well-connected public figures. In turn, the DCIs knew they had to keep a few important members of Congress informed on intelligence matters and sensitive operations.[72] For these congressmen, CIA oversight was a delicate balancing act. They "did not want to be surprised" and "wanted to know enough, if an operation came to light, that they could say they had known about it."[73] At the same time, they wanted to "be able to plead ignorance of specific information so that they would not find themselves compromised politically."[74] The system was "all very cozy, clubby, informal, and unsystematic," kept far from the public eye.[75]

The elite status of the members of Congress conducting CIA oversight was a double-edged sword. Because they were such influential figures in Congress, they were too busy to develop any deep expertise in intelligence oversight or thorough understanding of the CIA, its budget, and its operations. When other committees and members of Congress later challenged the existing oversight system, they were ill-equipped to respond. Another problem was that the CIA's early oversight bodies were the congressional armed services committees, which naturally fixed their attention on military matters. Moreover, the exclusivity surrounding CIA oversight, based on power and personal influence, bred resentment and political competition in Congress.[76] Generational, cultural, and political divisions in Congress would eventually transform congressional intelligence oversight, but the initial approach had sufficient shortcomings to almost guarantee its demise.[77]

One prominent feature of this early era of congressional intelligence oversight is worthy of recognition. Remarkably, the "record is virtually silent with respect to any [congressional] leaks" of CIA activities.[78] The Cold War consensus mitigated the problem of politicization—for a time.

An Agency Apart

For decades, the United States hid intelligence by subordinating it to other executive departments. When MID, ONI, the Secret Service, or the FBI conducted intelligence operations that led to national scandals, their parent departments or Congress reined them in, often arguing that they had exceeded their real mandate, which was not first and foremost intelligence. The CIA was the product of democratic debate and design in Congress, created right before the eyes of the American people.[79] The United States finally had an independent intelligence organization that could not deflect blame. To many Americans, the CIA is what they think of when asked about intelligence. The CIA has therefore often been the scapegoat for all the ills of American intelligence.

Just as Congress eventually reconsidered oversight of the Secret Service Fund, it would reconsider oversight of the CIA and broader intelligence community. Aside from political partisanship in Congress, interbranch rivalry with the President stirred congressional oversight, as it had in the nineteenth century. Furthermore, public revelations of controversial intelligence activities that reignited the American people's resistance to intelligence would compel Congress to act. The CIA bore some responsibility for the turn of events, as it made some mistakes in its initial operations and analysis that invited external scrutiny.

15

The CIA and a Clash of Cultures

BY ADOPTING THE competing missions of intelligence coordination and analysis, on the one hand, and covert and clandestine activities, on the other, the CIA guaranteed that it could not perform all functions equally well. During its early years, the CIA had to make choices that affected its organizational culture. As a product of its OSS roots, bureaucratic bargaining, and the decisions of its leadership, the CIA embraced the covert and clandestine side. This guaranteed the Agency would suffer blowback because these activities represented exactly the sort of sneaky intelligence tricks and deceits that offended American principles.

Measured against the unforgiving yardstick of intelligence failure—whether real or imagined—the CIA exhibited numerous serious "failures" in the early years of the Cold War. Some held unrealistically high expectations for the new organization. Others certainly wanted to see it fail. Regardless, these outcomes caused observers to question the CIA's purpose and effectiveness.

Problems with Prediction

The CIA's first perceived failure occurred in Bogotá, Colombia in April 1948 during the Ninth International Conference of American States. The assassination of liberal presidential candidate Jorge Eliécer Gaitán sparked massive civil unrest, known as the *bogotazo*, and inaugurated the period of internal Colombian civil war known as *la violencia*. The riots endangered the US delegation to the conference, which included Secretary of State George C. Marshall and other eminent Americans like General Matthew B. Ridgway. Senior American policymakers, including Marshall, suspected that communists were behind the unrest.[1] But the press, Congress, and others blamed the CIA for not issuing a warning ahead of the events in Colombia.

New York Governor Thomas Dewey, who was running for the Republican ticket to challenge Truman in the 1948 presidential election, declared that "we apparently had no idea what was going on in a country just two hours bomber time from the Panama Canal." Dewey insisted that the Truman administration "not only has no adequate information about what is going on, but it can't even keep its own secrets." By way of example, he mentioned that the CIA was supposed to be "the most secret thing in our Government" and yet "left-wing newspapers in Paris actually printed the name of the new head of the service before he knew it himself and six weeks before it was announced to the American press." In a final jab against both Truman and the CIA, he claimed that "the United States had the finest intelligence service ever developed operating all over South America under J. Edgar Hoover," but Truman "ordered that entire service discontinued" and "cut off our ears and put out our eyes in our information services around the world."[2]

Congress briefly examined the CIA's "failure" in Colombia, summoning DCI Hillenkoetter to testify before a special committee. Hillenkoetter apparently welcomed the opportunity to defend the Agency. He revealed intelligence showing that the CIA had warned the State Department of potential unrest in Colombia.[3] The *Washington Post* editorial board agreed. After wondering only a few days earlier, "Was the American intelligence system caught napping?" the board exculpated the CIA and determined that "the State Department was at fault in cold-shouldering the warnings." But the *Post* also decided that the episode revealed how "unification of intelligence is still a will-o'-the-wisp."[4] In response to the controversy, Representative Edward J. Devitt proposed—and Hillenkoetter supported—a joint congressional committee modeled on the Joint Committee on Atomic Energy to oversee the CIA, but the proposal foundered due to lack of interest in Congress.[5]

Just as events in Colombia were unfolding, the CIA appeared to miss other key moments in 1948–49. An article in the *Herald Tribune* accused the CIA of failing to warn policymakers ahead of the fall of Czechoslovakia to Soviet-enabled Communists, Yugoslavia's break from the Soviet Union under the leadership of Josip Broz Tito, the victory of the communists in the Chinese Civil War, and the victory of the Israelis in the First Arab-Israeli War. Just as Hillenkoetter rebutted allegations of the CIA's failure in Bogotá, he also addressed these failures, citing evidence that the CIA provided intelligence ahead of each of these events.[6] The issue was not that the CIA lacked information or failed to make analytic judgments with some degree of accuracy. Rather, the CIA's assessments and information did not satisfy or persuade policymakers, which was perhaps an intelligence failure of sorts, but not the CIA's alone.

That said, the CIA made two monumental errors in situations of such significance that anything short of absolute predictive accuracy was absolute intelligence failure. The first involved the Soviet Union's successful detonation of a nuclear weapon on August 29, 1949. While American intelligence focused on defeating Germany and Japan during the Second World War, the Soviet Union devoted some of its intelligence capabilities to targeting the United States, including its top-secret nuclear weapons program. In fact, Soviet intelligence learned about the program a year before it began.[7] Spies like Klaus Fuchs, who worked on the Manhattan Project and in the Los Alamos lab, passed secrets to the Soviet Union.[8] Soviet intelligence stole the secrets behind the atomic bomb, while US intelligence failed to prevent—and then predict—the successful test of a Soviet nuclear weapon.

In July 1948, the CIA estimated that the Soviets would have the bomb as early as 1950, though it settled on 1953 as the most likely date. Notably, the State Department, Army, Air Force, and Atomic Energy Commission all agreed with the CIA assessment.[9] Subsequent CIA analyses parroted these estimates and, to add insult to injury, repeated the same timeline three weeks after the Soviet Union detonated its first atomic bomb.[10] When Hillenkoetter and the CIA reported evidence of a detonation in September 1949, they still hedged, speculating that the presence of radioactive gases over the North Pacific was possibly due to volcanic activity in the region.[11]

The CIA's failure in the case of the Soviet atomic bomb reflected a few of the problems that the CIA was designed to solve. A revealing memorandum by Willard Machle, the Assistant Director for Scientific Intelligence, to Hillenkoetter argued that the CIA still did not have the necessary authority under its legislative mandate to be the "central coordinating agency in the national intelligence structure" and cited "non-cooperation" by the other departmental intelligence agencies as a problem. For its part, the CIA struggled to harmonize its analytical and operational roles. Machle accused the CIA's "collecting offices" of failing to "recognize that they exist only to provide services for the producing offices and agencies," with the result that they "have become ends unto themselves." A fixation on secrecy also affected information sharing within the CIA, creating obstacles to effective coordination within an organization that was established to coordinate US intelligence. In short, the CIA's Soviet bomb failure was partially the result of continued failures of intelligence coordination and analysis within both the American intelligence system and the CIA.[12]

To be fair, the CIA faced other pressing analytical questions. For example, to its credit, it reached the correct and at the time extraordinarily controversial conclusion that the Soviet Union would not attack Western Europe regardless of its perceived aggressive posture.[13] But there is also an inherent tension between assessing general issues, like whether the Soviet Union was planning a conventional military invasion of Western Europe, and answering extremely specific intelligence questions, such as the very time and place a surprise attack would take place. The CIA discovered how this distinction affected its credibility when North Korea launched its invasion of South Korea on June 25, 1950.[14]

The reasons for the CIA's Korea failure were both external and internal. Externally, Korea was not high on the list of the Truman administration's State and Defense Department priorities. These departments dominated the NSC, which had authority over the CIA. There was pressure on the CIA to reflect their institutional priorities, as well as the national priorities of the presidential administration. Essentially, the CIA still lacked the institutional independence to address intelligence issues and raise them with policymakers based on its own professional expertise and analysis. Internally, the CIA had only a few officers in South Korea before the invasion and tended to reuse information from State Department and military reports in its analysis. Finally, CIA analytical products at the time failed to include what are called indications and warnings, which would provide actionable intelligence for policymakers. However, even if they had, the global situation was so precarious in 1950 it is doubtful reports on Korea would have alarmed policymakers any more than reports on other regions under pressure from communism.[15]

Upon reexamination, the CIA did not entirely fail with respect to Korea. Just one week before North Korea invaded South Korea, the CIA Office of Reports and Estimates (ORE) produced a report on the "Current Capabilities of the North Korean Regime," which it distributed to the President, NSC, and State and Defense Departments, among others. The ORE report determined that the "ultimate local objective of the Soviet Union and of the northern Korean regime" was "the elimination of the southern Republic of Korea and the unification of the Korean peninsula under Communist domination."[16] The CIA's analysis of Korea therefore reflected its other alleged failures. The agency was accurate in presenting broad trends but failed to predict the day and hour of an event—perhaps the only actual question that ultimately matters to policymakers and the public. Like the Soviet atomic bomb, the invasion of South Korea provided the CIA with no margin for analytical error.

This last CIA failure resulted in an overhaul of its leadership.[17] Hillenkoetter took the fall for both the CIA and the Truman administration.

General Walter "Beetle" Smith assumed leadership of an organization tarred by the perception of failure. As the former chief of staff to General Dwight D. Eisenhower during the Second World War and later the ambassador to the Soviet Union, Smith brought name recognition to the position of DCI. The highest-ranking military officer to serve as DCI, Smith charmed his way through his confirmation hearing in the Senate Armed Services Committee by telling war stories, and he compelled cooperation, if not outright obedience, from the formerly recalcitrant military intelligence services.[18] He chose William Harding Jackson, former OSS veteran, Wall Street attorney, and coauthor of the Dulles Report, to be his Deputy Director. An intelligence insider, Jackson had been on the short list to head the CIA. The combination of Smith and Jackson ensured the CIA had both external and internal credibility in its top ranks. The pair quickly instituted a reorganization of the CIA.

The Statutory Missions: Coordination and Analysis

Smith and Jackson first had to address the CIA's embarrassing analytic failures. They began by dissolving and dividing the CIA's Office of Reports and Estimates into three offices: the Office of National Estimates (ONE), the Office of Research and Reports, and the Office of Current Intelligence. In 1952, Smith placed these three offices in a Directorate of Intelligence, known today as the Directorate of Analysis.[19] He understood coordination and analysis to be the principal responsibilities of the CIA under the 1947 National Security Act. At a meeting of the Intelligence Advisory Committee, composed of representatives from the US intelligence establishment, Smith declared that the ONE "would become the heart of the Central Intelligence Agency and of the national intelligence machinery."[20] He tapped William Langer, the former chief of the OSS R&A branch, to head it.

Reviewing ONE estimates would be a Board of National Estimates. This board consisted of a brain trust of exceptional individuals personally approved by Smith. The idea for it came from none other than "Wild Bill" Donovan, whom Smith had solicited for advice.[21] Following a familiar pattern of recruitment for American intelligence organizations, the board was heavily made up of liberal, East Coast intellectuals, who clashed with the more conservative defense and foreign policy communities in DC.[22] When Langer steered the composition of the board toward academics, Smith and Jackson became disenchanted with their own design, leading them to establish yet another—albeit unofficial—analytical oversight body of eminent Americans known as the Princeton Consultants.[23]

This hybrid analytical system based on internal CIA analysis and external review by a few picked elites reflected growing pains as intelligence shifted from the work of amateur elites to that of trained professionals. The principal purpose of the system was for CIA analysis to inform national policymaking. However, the use of external oversight and review of CIA analysis had the untoward effect of signaling that analysis by professional intelligence officers was not necessarily any better than that of gifted lay individuals. Moreover, intelligence analysis was still only effective to the extent that policymakers actually paid attention to it.

The relationship between the analyst and policymaker became a point of contention in the famous "Kent-Kendall debate" that took place early in the CIA's history. Sherman Kent, who had served in OSS R&A, helped Langer set up ONE. In 1949, he published *Strategic Intelligence for American World Policy*, a seminal book on intelligence analysis in which he advanced a foundational principle of the American intelligence profession: Intelligence should inform, but never advocate, policy. Kent reasoned that "intelligence must be close enough to policy, plans, and operations to have the greatest amount of guidance, and must not be so close that it loses its objectivity and integrity of judgment." He therefore argued that the only way to guarantee intelligence objectivity and integrity was to keep it separate from consumers and policymakers. As an additional buffer against politicization, Kent also sketched out what he admitted was an artificial boundary between foreign and domestic intelligence.[24]

Willmoore Kendall, who had brief stints as an analyst in the State Department and the CIG, reviewed Kent's book shortly after its publication. He preferred a closer relationship between the analyst and policymaker because the "most crucial aspect" of intelligence "concern[ed] the communication to the *politically* responsible laymen of the knowledge." To do so effectively, he claimed, analysts would have to consider "'domestic' matters," implying political considerations. Kendall also perceived in Kent's work "a compulsive preoccupation with *prediction*, with the elimination of 'surprise' from foreign affairs." In Kendall's view, "The shadow of Pearl Harbor is projected into the mists of Bogotá, and intelligence looks shamefaced over its failure to tell Secretary Marshall the day and hour at which a revolution will break out in Colombia."[25]

Many elements of the Kent-Kendall debate still stand. Reforms to the CIA's analytical mission cannot resolve tensions inherent in intelligence, including the policymaker-analyst relationship, politicization, and the impact of analysis on policymaking. Policymakers and the public continue to nurture the belief that any instance in which intelligence fails to predict an event represents an intelligence (namely, CIA) failure. As a result, the CIA's credibility can suffer at any moment.

The Spoiler Missions: Covert and Clandestine Activities

If analysis had failed in the eyes of policymakers, then perhaps covert action was a way for the CIA to prove itself.[26] When Smith was appointed, the CIA was facing bureaucratic competition with the State Department over covert action. NSC 10/2 had ordered the creation of the Office of Special Projects (OSP) nominally as an office within the CIA, but Marshall appointed Kennan as the State Department representative to the OSP, giving the latter an opportunity to try to exercise personal control over covert action.

In a meeting with DCI Hillenkoetter and others in August 1948, Kennan described political warfare as "essentially an instrument of foreign policy," and, as such, it "must take its policy direction and guidance from the Departments of State and the National Military Establishment." Kennan reserved for himself "specific knowledge of the objectives of every operation and also of the procedures and methods employed in all cases." Consequently, it was unclear just how much control the DCI and CIA would have over the OSP, even though it was a CIA office. The other officials at this meeting largely deferred to Kennan. Hillenkoetter barely fought for the DCI to control the OSP. However, he added that if the State Department was going to provide policy guidance, it must "accept the political responsibility," likely foreseeing inevitable scapegoating of the CIA by policymakers.[27]

Frank Wisner, the man selected by Kennan to lead the OSP, was also in attendance. He decided that "it would be necessary that the head of [the OSP] have continuing and direct access to the State Department and the various elements of the military establishment without having to proceed through the CIA administrative hierarchy in each case." Hillenkoetter approved and in exchange only requested to "be kept informed in regard to all important projects and decisions." Wisner agreed, requiring "broad latitude in selecting his methods of operations" and insisting on "considerable assistance from other Government Departments and agencies, including State and the National Military Establishment."[28] But before Wisner took charge, the Office of Special Projects was given the more anodyne name of the Office of Policy Coordination (OPC).

Wisner, like many others in the early years of the CIA, was a Wall Street lawyer and OSS veteran. He embraced his role as the head of the OPC. William Colby, also an OSS veteran who joined the OPC, recorded that "Wisner landed like a dynamo, read all the intelligence and set out to form a clandestine force worldwide."[29] Due to the vague lines of authority controlling and overseeing the OPC, "Wisner was accountable to virtually no one" and staffed the OPC with like-minded friends from his OSS days.[30] Colby compared the OPC to "an order of Knights Templars, to save Western freedom from Communist darkness—and from war."[31] Aside from Wisner's personality and staff choices, there were other factors that embedded certain features of the OPC's design and organizational culture in the CIA.

In April 1950, the NSC approved NSC 68, the foundational document that largely steered US policy for the duration of the Cold War. The paper, a product of the State and Defense Departments, adopted a confrontational tone and recommended the "intensification of affirmative and timely measures and operations by covert means in the fields of economic warfare and political and psychological warfare with a view to fomenting and supporting unrest and revolt in selected strategic satellite countries."[32] With the onset of the Korean War, OPC budgeting, staff, and operations ballooned between 1949 and 1952: from a staff of around 300 to almost 3,000 (not including nearly 3,500 overseas contractors); from a budget of $4.7 million to $82 million; and from seven overseas stations to forty-seven.[33] The Cold War drove American policymakers to endorse and expand covert action, and the OPC was happy to oblige.

In accordance with its own institutional missions and organizational cultures, the State Department wanted the OPC to conduct political and propaganda operations, and the Defense Department looked to it to perform paramilitary operations and support anticommunist movements across the world. In order to conduct the full spectrum of covert action required by these two very different departments, the OPC employed an organizational system based on distinct projects. In effect, each project was given its own leadership, funding, and staff to support it, rather than a coherent system based on policy objectives, general programs, or regional or national operations. The OPC's approach to operations also undercut control and oversight. OPC headquarters in Washington struggled to maintain control over its own divisions and staff, while they both struggled to control operations by OPC field stations and operations officers abroad. Externally, State and Defense, including their representatives to the OPC, were largely aligned on a policy of aggressive covert operations against the Soviet Union, but they adopted a laissez-faire approach to OPC oversight. All the while, the OPC was still an office within the CIA.[34]

During his tenure, Hillenkoetter "resented the fact that he had no management authority over OPC," and he sparred with State, Defense, and even Wisner.[35] There was also a growing conflict between the Office of Special Operations (OSO), the CIA's foreign intelligence division, and the OPC. They maintained different staffs and conducted separate operations out of the same CIA stations overseas. They also offered different salaries and promotion incentives to their personnel, with OPC employees paid more than OSO employees. OSO officers tended to be quiet, knowledgeable specialists focused on "silent, long-term objectives in espionage and counterespionage," while OPC officers engaged in high-risk operations that produced visible results and garnered the favor of the State and Defense Departments.[36] The resulting intraorganizational rivalry and competition threatened the unity of the CIA, which it could ill afford as a young and vulnerable independent organization.

Beetle Smith began his first week as DCI by announcing that he was taking administrative control over the OPC. Going forward, Wisner and the OPC would take orders from him, not the State or Defense Departments.[37] The Dulles Report had recommended that the OSO and the OPC be placed in a single division under the control of a deputy director reporting to the DCI.[38] In January 1951, Smith appointed the report's namesake, Allen Dulles, to precisely this role. That fall, NSC 10/5 amended NSC 10/2 and "reaffirm[ed] the responsibility and authority of the Director of Central Intelligence for the conduct of covert operations," recognizing Smith's moves to assert control over the OPC.[39]

In 1952, Smith formally consolidated the OSO and the OPC under a Directorate of Plans, the forerunner of today's Directorate of Operations. Wisner became the Deputy Director for Plans and Dulles was elevated to the Deputy Director of Central Intelligence. In order to balance the new directorate's leadership between the OPC and the OSO, Richard Helms, an OSS veteran and OSO officer, became Wisner's second-in-command. But instead of harmonizing the two offices in the new directorate, the "merger resulted in the maximum development of covert action over clandestine collection."[40] The Directorate of Plans also dominated the CIA writ large, accounting for 80 percent of the budget and 60 percent of the personnel. Furthermore, Dulles championed covert action, leading Smith to grow increasingly concerned that these activities were going to undercut analysis, which he considered the heart of the CIA.[41]

Smith cautioned the NSC about the untoward influence of "the field of cold war covert activities, including guerrilla warfare," on the CIA, particularly because he believed they were "probably not envisaged at the time the National Security Act of 1947 . . . was framed." While describing how the CIA "accepted these responsibilities as agents for the major Departments concerned"—that is, State and Defense—he cautioned that they were "not functions essential to the performance by Central Intelligence Agency of its intelligence responsibilities." Instead, he explained, they "were placed in this Agency because there was no other Department or Agency of the Government which could undertake them at the time." Smith warned the NSC that covert and clandestine activities detracted from the CIA's ability to supply valuable strategic intelligence on the Soviet Union and noted that the CIA was still struggling to coordinate intelligence produced by other organizations of government.[42]

Smith was not alone among intelligence officials and officers who questioned the CIA's operational activities and their effect on its other roles. Souers later lamented in a personal letter to Truman that the CIA was "certainly a different animal than I tried to set up for you," voicing his concern that "with so much emphasis on operations, it would not surprise me to find that the matter of collecting and processing intelligence has suffered some."[43] Sherman Kent insisted that intelligence should not be "the carrier out of operations" as a matter of analytic objectivity since executing policy can steer analysis toward policy advocacy.[44] However, he did make a forceful defense for clandestine collection, so he acknowledged a role for CIA clandestine activities, though not necessarily covert action.[45] His rival Kendall worried that covert and clandestine activities were becoming ends in themselves without the oversight or control of policymakers. In another broadside against Kent, Kendall criticized the trend of intelligence to "enormously exaggerate the importance of covert collection, and yet permit it to yield shockingly small dividends." Kendall opined that "the whole question of covert collection . . . requires urgent investigation by a Congressional committee prepared to speak the language of legislative supremacy, and to insist that no democracy can afford to make a simple and . . . irrevocable act of faith in the men called upon to perform this highly explosive function."[46] Like Smith's caution to the NSC about the CIA diving too deep into covert action, Kendall's call for robust congressional oversight went unheeded. Both legislative and executive branch policymakers were intent on fighting the Cold War, and covert action allowed them to confront the Soviet Union on its own sneaky, subversive terms.

These early years witnessed several unsuccessful covert action operations designed to turn the tide of communism. For example, in 1949, a joint CIA program with the British SIS in Albania to support anticommunist partisans failed to gain a foothold in the country. Likewise, attempts to build an anticommunist paramilitary network in Poland crumbled the following year. Meanwhile, divisions between the OPC and the OSO undermined the CIA's effort to establish an espionage network in Ukraine in 1949 and 1950. Finally, during the Korean War, the CIA supported anticommunist Chinese forces. As with the European operations, counterintelligence problems plagued these efforts and almost every mission ended in failure. Moreover, covert action produced blowback. The CIA launched failed forays into China from neutral Burma, which strained Burma's diplomatic relations with the United States—not a good outcome for a US foreign policy that sought containment of communism through relations with third-party states.[47]

Unquestionably, policymakers outside the CIA steered the agency further toward covert action. Furthermore, many of these early covert action operations were initiated by the OPC before Smith asserted CIA control. Still, the CIA assumed responsibility for covert action and would plan and execute some deeply flawed operations. The CIA willingly, even eagerly, acted based on the dubious idea that "*doing something* is better than *doing nothing*," an unsound and underscrutinized approach to national security that would cost the United States dearly.[48]

Even if he had wanted to, Smith would not have a chance to rein in the CIA's covert and clandestine activities. When Dwight D. Eisenhower became President in 1953, he appointed John Foster Dulles as Secretary of State and Allen Dulles became the DCI, "in spite of Smith's objections that he was overenamored with covert operations."[49] The Dulles brothers were heirs of the highest ranks of American diplomacy and intelligence: Their grandfather John W. Foster had overseen the events that led to the fall of the Kingdom of Hawaii during the Harrison administration, and their uncle by marriage, Robert Lansing, had tried to solve the problem of intelligence coordination during the Wilson administration. During the Eisenhower administration, the Dulles brothers coordinated American intelligence and diplomatic activities through a period that witnessed coups, espionage, and the very tricks and devices that their grandfather had purportedly hoped would not color US foreign relations.

Smith enjoyed the President's full trust, having been his former chief of staff during the Second World War, and was tapped for Under Secretary of

State in a move designed to help Eisenhower manage the Dulles brothers. During his year and a half on the job, Smith tried to contain the CIA's covert activities and the growing influence of the Directorate of Plans.[50] In his waning days as DCI, Smith opposed CIA participation in a British plan to overthrow Mohammad Mosaddegh, who as prime minister of Iran had nationalized the Anglo-Iranian Oil Company, later known as British Petroleum, or BP today.[51] But Eisenhower and the Dulles brothers believed that Mosaddegh—despite not showing any inclination toward communism—might fall sway to the communist Tudeh Party and turn Iran into a Soviet proxy. Led by Kermit Roosevelt Jr., a grandson of Theodore Roosevelt and OSS veteran, the CIA joined the British and helped topple Mosaddegh, leading the Shah of Iran to assume power. The coup in Iran produced double blowback: It whetted both American policymakers' and the CIA's taste for covert action and became a source of enduring Iranian hostility toward the United States.

Shortly after the foray in Iran, the CIA supported a coup in Guatemala. The democratically elected Jacobo Árbenz threatened the interests of the United Fruit Company, better known today as Chiquita, an American corporation that had long held extensive land and economic stakes in many states of Latin America. It had also interfered in the internal affairs of those states with the support of the US government.[52] Árbenz's reforms looked suspiciously socialist to the United States. Originally planned but then aborted in 1952, the CIA-orchestrated coup was launched in 1954. In what were clearly conflicts of interest, Allen Dulles had served on the board of the United Fruit Company in the years before the coup and Smith became a member of the board following the coup.

On its face the Guatemala coup represented an intelligence "success" in the sense that the CIA accomplished its mission by replacing Árbenz with a pro-American regime. But many states in Europe and Latin America condemned US intervention in Guatemala, as did the United Nations. In a Cold War competition between the United States and the Soviet Union over global influence, the United States jeopardized its image as being the "good side." US intervention in Guatemala also steeled the resolve of Ernesto "Che" Guevara, who was living in Guatemala at the time. Guevara subsequently became an avowed enemy of the United States and supported communist movements across Latin America, especially in Cuba. For Guatemala, the outcome was worse. Carlos Castillo Armas, the CIA-backed leader of the coup, assumed the presidency, arrested and executed anyone opposed to his rule, and committed grievous human rights violations.

The result was a nearly four-decade civil war in Guatemala between US-sponsored military governments and leftist rebels that killed over a hundred thousand Guatemalans.

The United States and the CIA became victims of these intelligence successes. The CIA and American policymakers were seduced by the promises of covert action. Kennan later expressed remorse for his role in constructing the OPC. After he helped establish it, he admitted that he "scarcely paid any attention to it" and considered it "probably the worst mistake I ever made in government." He wished to disavow "all part that I or the staff took in any of this," declaring, "I should never have accepted... the duty of giving political advice to Wisner's outfit."[53]

The bureaucratic competition between the CIA and State over the OPC occurred at the same moment when intelligence established itself as an independent profession in the United States. By seizing covert action as part of its own declaration of independence, the CIA absorbed an organization and culture that undermined its original statutory missions of intelligence coordination and analysis. But combining these disparate elements was also the goal of the CIA's founding father. As Colby acknowledged, "The creation of the OPC completed the formation of the CIA... [as] an agency almost precisely like the one Donovan had proposed that his OSS become."[54] Brimming with OSS veterans and Donovan disciples, the CIA was the near realization of Donovan's vision for a central intelligence organization. Rather than plot the middle course, Smith's reforms had the untoward effect of further guiding the CIA toward covert and clandestine activities.

Harry Rositzke, an OSS veteran who became one of the first generation of CIA officers, predicted that the "usefulness of covert action operations will be determined by an enlightened or unenlightened American foreign policy." He elaborated that "secret operations, however well executed, like diplomacy and military action, are no better or worse than the foreign policy they are designed to support." American policymakers have often turned to covert action as a panacea without understanding that even a successful covert operation cannot rescue a flawed policy. Worse yet, when covert action failed in the past, the CIA was a convenient scapegoat for policymakers, which in turn, undermined American civil-intelligence relations.[55] However, Rositzke noted one "positive by-product" of early US covert action operations: that "the first generation of CIA operations officers was learning its trade by doing, by developing know-how, both in what to do and what not to do."[56] They became the first true crop of American intelligence professionals.

An American Intelligence Profession

Among the salient problems of American intelligence history that the CIA finally addressed was the professionalization of intelligence. It faced an uphill battle as both the Defense and State Departments attempted to shape, if not outright control, the young CIA. In addition, many of the original cadre of

FIGURE 15.1 A 1950 cartoon celebrates the exploits of "Donovan of Central Intelligence." The CIA had the comic censored even though it is doubtful the real Donovan would have taken issue with the swashbuckling portrayal and bit of publicity. Reprint of original by Golden Age Reprints.

CIA officers were OSS, and therefore military, veterans. A few observant CIA officers perceived the distinction between the military and intelligence professions, arguing for a division between the two. For example, Stephen Penrose, formerly of the OSS, vented his frustration with the military influence, naming that as one of his reasons for leaving the CIA. He "felt there were too many Captains and Colonels placed in charge of divisions who did not have background for the Intelligence type of work." He found the situation all "the more alarming because it occurs at a time when, as almost never before, the government needs an effective, expanding professional intelligence service." In his view, the CIA was "losing its professionals" because it was "dependent in most working branches for imaginative and energetic direction upon career military men of a type which is not apt to be either imaginative or energetic as regards non-military intelligence or procedures." In a nod to its statutory missions, he concluded that the current state of affairs "cannot but nullify the principles of coordination and centralization which were implicit in the establishment of the CIA."[57]

Willmoore Kendall also concluded that the heavy presence of OSS veterans in the CIA marred its analytical edge. He asserted that Kent and others viewed intelligence through a "state of mind... dangerously... *dominated by an essentially wartime conception of the intelligence function*," for the simple reason that they "learned the intelligence business during the war." In fact, Kendall doubted "the very use of the term 'strategic' as opposed to, say, 'foreign policy,' to denote the entire task of intelligence." In short, Kendall implied that the wartime, military experience of intelligence analysts stunted the professionalization of intelligence analysis.[58]

The CIA overcame this and other historical obstacles to professionalization. In a departure from the earlier period of amateur spies, it would recruit and train professional intelligence officers. This transition forced a break in the traditional method of recruitment from Ivy League schools or social clubs. As part of his reforms, Smith instituted a Junior Officer Training Program in 1950 to create a "systematic method to identify, select, and develop career intelligence officers of the highest calibre."[59]

One of this new breed of intelligence officers was Burton Gerber. Unlike the Ivy League insiders and East Coast elites, Gerber and "Middle American graduates of state universities and the military... brought a more democratic face and sense of professionalism to a service that for years had lived off the amateur enthusiasm of its elitist founding fathers, whose notions of secret keeping or secret stealing had been shaped by Yale and Skull and Bones," one of Yale's elite secret societies.[60] Ironically, Matthew Baird, a Princeton and

Oxford graduate who had also been the headmaster of a boarding school, directed the CIA's Junior Officer Training Program, so some of the old ways still persisted. However, the professionalization of intelligence did not solve the problem of elitism, which simply changed forms.

A "Cult of Intelligence" or a New Intelligence Bureaucracy?

The elite tradition of amateur spies from the Northeast and Ivy League at times carried a buoyant sense of noblesse oblige and adventurism. Other times, it lent itself to prejudicial surveillance or advancing US foreign policy in accordance with a particular worldview. Professionalization created an intelligence elite that nurtured its own brand of elitism.

William Colby, who hailed from an educated family and attended Princeton, described the emergent organizational culture at the CIA based on the "missionary zeal, sense of elitism and marvelous camaraderie among [his] colleagues there." He described "how easy it would have been" to "immerse [himself] exclusively in the cloak-and-dagger life."

> Some of my colleagues at the Agency did just that. Socially as well as professionally they cliqued together, forming a sealed fraternity. They ate together at their own special favorite restaurants; they partied almost only among themselves; their families drifted to each other, so their defenses did not always have to be up. In this way they increasingly separated themselves from the ordinary world and developed a rather skewed view of that world... and they looked down on the life of the rest of the citizenry. And out of this grew what was later named—and condemned—as the "cult" of intelligence, an inbred, distorted, elitist view of intelligence that held it to be above the normal processes of society, with its own rationale and justification, beyond the restraints of the Constitution, which applied to everything and everyone else.

Colby explained that he did not fully succumb to the "cloak-and-dagger life," thanks to his wife and her determination to maintain "a normal life for us and the children, no matter how peculiar the profession might be."[61]

Victor Marchetti, who joined the ranks of the CIA in 1955, savaged this "cult of intelligence" in a 1974 book widely ridiculed by his former colleagues. In contrast to the principles of American constitutionalism, Marchetti warned that the CIA fostered a "clandestine mentality" that encouraged "professional amorality—the belief that righteous goals can be achieved through the use of unprincipled and normally unacceptable means." He claimed that "with the cooperation of an acquiescent, ill-informed Congress, and the encouragement and assistance of a series of Presidents, the cult has built a wall of laws and executive orders around the CIA and itself... that has blocked effective public scrutiny" and created a group that "when caught in their own webs of deceit, even assert that the government has an inherent right to lie to its people."[62]

Marchetti stressed that "the public does not even realize how frequently the CIA has failed" and attacked the CIA's analytical and operational records. Instead, Marchetti implied that the CIA's real success was in manipulating the American public based "upon its careful mythologizing and glorification of the exploits of the clandestine profession," even though it acted "almost completely at variance with the apparent intent of the law that established the agency." In his view, the CIA could take up its original purpose of coordinating foreign intelligence for policymakers or continue down its current path of "interference in the domestic affairs of other nations (and perhaps our own) by means of penetration agents, propaganda, covert paramilitary interventions, and an array of other dirty tricks."[63] Unlike amateur spies who performed their services and then returned to regular, civilian life, the CIA had created a standing group of intelligence elites. Over time, this became a source of conspiracy theories that a secret cabal of intelligence officers was manipulating events from the shadows.

The intelligence profession faced more mundane problems in the organizational form of the CIA. Intelligence officers bristled against increasing bureaucratization as the CIA was incorporated into the national security apparatus at the cost of the flexibility and initiative they experienced in the COI or OSS. Colby saw this change as inevitable and even necessary because the CIA "demand[ed] the management techniques of major technical enterprises and government structures, require[d] mammoth financing, and [had to] be closely coordinated with the other elements of America's foreign policy." In his view, the CIA had "quite simply outgrown the old concept of a small, secret intelligence service located at the elbow of the President and to be used by him at his discretion," as Donovan had once conceived of it.[64]

Other old intelligence hands like Harry Rositzke viewed bureaucratization as an unwelcome change and a threat to the CIA's core missions. Rositzke was "firmly convinced that [it was] too big, too bureaucratized, and too tactical in its intelligence targets to give American policy makers what they need." He lamented that it "went the way of the entire intelligence community: a large bureaucracy with large staffs, interminable coordination, and countless echelons of decision making." Contrary to the dynamism, derring-do, and individualism that he believed marked the intelligence profession, he saw the "lethargy and timidity normal to a civil service bureaucracy" as detrimental to a service "whose main business is taking chances based on personal judgment." He wanted to return to the earlier model that Colby implied was no longer relevant or practical. He argued that the United States still needed something along the lines of Vincent Astor's The Room/The Club, John Franklin Carter's intelligence office, or John Hughes's proposed Service Z from the Second World War. Rositzke envisioned a "separate, truly secret intelligence service" composed of "a small professional elite" who would "live under private, mainly commercial, cover reporting by unofficial communications to a small head office in, say, New York," under the leadership of an anonymous chief who reported directly to the DCI. Unable to resolve all the trade-offs between amateurism and professionalism, the CIA could not necessarily give intelligence a democratic face, but it certainly gave it a bureaucratic one.[65]

Governing the Shadows

Professionalization and bureaucratization cut against each other, but they also combined to inform public perceptions of the CIA. One of the most entrenched conspiracy theories about the CIA is that it secretly steers US foreign policy, if not the entire US government, from the shadows. It was already a common charge even in the CIA's early years. Kendall believed that CIA analysis was no longer connected to "the elected officials who, as we hope, are still making the decisions about our foreign policy," but to so-called policy planners. As cogs in a bureaucratic policymaking machine dominated by unelected officials, intelligence analysts were becoming "mere research assistants to the George Kennans."[66] Kendall therefore raised the problem of the undemocratic role of CIA analysis in US national security policymaking.

The same accusation was lobbed at CIA operations. Marchetti accused the CIA of being "intent upon conducting the foreign affairs of the U.S. government without the awareness or participation of the people" while also "recogniz[ing] no role for a questioning legislature or an investigative press." Clark Clifford, who as an advisor to Truman was instrumental in the creation of the CIA and who continued to advise Presidents on intelligence issues, quipped that the "CIA became a government within a government."[67] But, as Rositzke reminded his readers, the CIA was part of the American constitutional system.[68] Among the challenges it posed to US civil-intelligence relations, the CIA reexposed divisions between the President and Congress with respect to intelligence control and oversight.

16

New Oversight and New Organizations

ALL THE ACTIVITY swirling around the CIA attracted the attention of Congress, which had neglected to give itself a clear oversight role in both the 1947 National Security Act and the 1949 CIA Act. In the face of congressional pressure accompanying CIA failures and Beetle Smith's reforms, the President attempted to head off any further congressional intervention through executive intelligence oversight. What emerged was a parallel system characterized by congressional or presidential commissions, like the earlier, concurrent studies of the Eberstadt and Dulles Reports. Meanwhile, initial proposals for a formal system of congressional intelligence oversight failed due to internal divisions in Congress. As a result, Congress continued to neglect its responsibility to oversee the intelligence community.

A succession of presidential oversight reports identified shortcomings in the American intelligence system, which the executive branch aimed to correct by unilaterally creating even more intelligence organizations. These new organizations were the products of bureaucratic competition over key intelligence functions. Furthermore, they were subordinated to the Department of Defense, creating divisions between the DCI and the Secretary of Defense, national intelligence and military intelligence, and the intelligence profession and military profession.

Oversight by Commission

Both the President and the CIA were fortunate that the first major congressional effort to target the CIA was spearheaded by the increasingly unpopular Senator Joseph McCarthy in July 1953. Repeating his well-worn refrain about communism in the ranks, McCarthy summoned William P. Bundy, the chief of staff of the CIA's ONE and liaison to the NSC, to appear before his committee. Instead, Bundy suddenly went on a family vacation that Dulles claimed had been planned for nearly a year.[1] Walter Pforzheimer, the CIA's legislative counsel, recorded that Dulles told him "it was an Agency rule that its employees would not appear before Congressional committees and that only the Director answered to Congressional committees where appropriate."[2] The press picked up the story, including the CIA's apparent opposition to congressional oversight.[3] Dulles also warned Eisenhower that he would resign if the congressional investigation continued.[4] Ultimately, the dogged McCarthy relented. As one of the few government organizations to openly resist McCarthy's witch hunt, the CIA experienced a boost in public popularity.[5] More significantly, the affair pushed the President and the CIA closer together in a united front against congressional oversight.

As the McCarthy-Dulles controversy was unfolding, Congress authorized a second Hoover Commission to investigate the executive branch. The commission's report noted that the DCI was failing to satisfy the dual roles of coordinating the intelligence community and leading the CIA. It recommended that the DCI appoint an "executive officer" or "chief of staff" to oversee and manage operations so that the DCI could focus on intelligence coordination.[6] The intelligence investigation on which the recommendations were based was conducted by a respected general, Mark Clark. Clark submitted two reports in 1955: a classified one for the President and an unclassified one for Congress. The introduction referenced the "intelligence community," and defined it as the "machinery for accomplishing [US] intelligence objectives... when referred to as a whole." This designation cemented the term adopted by policymakers and intelligence officers, and it is still in use today.* The report singled out the CIA for "special attention" because it was "charged with the overall responsibility for coordinating the output of all intelligence forces." The Clark Report unflatteringly characterized the CIA as "a new agency unique and in many ways strange to our democratic form of government" because it "operates without the customary legislative restraints and reins under which other departments must function," concluding that "its work is veiled in secrecy, and it is virtually a law unto itself."[7]

The Clark Report repeated some of the recommendations made by the Eberstadt Report, signaling that some fundamental problems had not been resolved. While it heaped praise on Dulles as "industrious, objective, selfless, enthusiastic, and imaginative," it also observed that as DCI, "he has taken upon himself too many burdensome duties and responsibilities on the

---

* From this point on, the book will refer to the US Intelligence Community by its contemporary shorthand, USIC.

operational side of CIA's activities," resulting in "certain administrative flaws." The report warned that the "glamor and excitement of some angles of our intelligence effort must not be permitted to overshadow other vital phases of the work or cause neglect of primary functions," implying that clandestine and covert activities were eclipsing coordination and analysis. The Clark Report therefore recommended "an internal reorganization of the CIA."[8] Dulles would later address this suggestion, but not in the manner envisioned in the Clark Report. He appointed Lucian Truscott, a decorated Second World War general, as Deputy Director for Coordination, "preferring instead to delegate his coordinating (as opposed to his operating) responsibilities."[9] Yet again, the allure of operations proved far more tempting than the burdens of coordination.

Another missing element that worried the Clark task force was the "absence of satisfactory machinery for surveillance of the stewardship" of the CIA. Accordingly, it recommended a " 'watch-dog' commission as a means of reestablishing the relationship between the CIA and Congress so essential to and characteristic of our democratic form of government," noting that this principle of oversight "was abrogated by the enactment of [the 1949 CIA Act] and other statutes relating to the Agency." To remedy the problem, the task force recommended a commission appointed by the President and Congress that would periodically review not only the CIA but also all other intelligence agencies to "keep the public assured of the essential and trustworthy accomplishments of our intelligence forces, and to enlist public support and participation in the intelligence effort."[10]

The unclassified version of the Clark Report that was sent to Congress reiterated many of the conclusions of the classified report to the President and acknowledged the challenges of intelligence oversight. On the one hand, the report recognized that the CIA "must of necessity operate in an atmosphere of secrecy and with an unusual amount of freedom and independence" that would be impossible if it was "subjected to open scrutiny and the extensive checks and balances which apply to the average governmental agency." On the other hand, it cautioned that "there is always a danger that such freedom from restraints could inspire laxity and abuses which might prove costly to the American people."[11]

However, the Hoover Commission departed from the Clark task force's recommendation of a combined congressional-presidential commission. Instead, it proposed the creation of two different committees, a presidential committee of "experienced private citizens" and a joint congressional committee, further suggesting that they "could collaborate on matters of special importance to the national security."[12] Even if the President and Congress could cooperate on intelligence oversight, a doubtful proposition given the history, the idea that two committees representing each branch could cooperate was even more unlikely. In fact, Eisenhower's reaction to the Hoover Commission marked the onset of a new competition between the President and Congress over intelligence.

Eisenhower perceived the threat that the Hoover Commission posed to exclusive executive control of intelligence, so he attempted to preempt Congress. He tapped another famous general, James Doolittle, to study the covert activities of the CIA and produce a classified report personally addressed to him. In his instructions to Doolittle, Eisenhower cagily "suggest[ed] that [Doolittle] and General Clark confer in order to avoid any unnecessary duplication of work" between their two reports.[13] What Eisenhower really meant was for Doolittle to keep the CIA's covert and clandestine activities "outside the Clark task force's purview."[14]

The Doolittle Commission concluded that the CIA was "doing a creditable job" despite "its relatively short life and rapid expansion." It examined areas like intelligence professionalism and coordination, but it was its cavalier conclusions about covert action that were striking. Reflecting a shortsighted reading of American intelligence history, the Doolittle Report inaccurately professed that "the United States [was] relatively new at the game" of covert action. It championed "an aggressive covert psychological, political and paramilitary organization more effective, more unique, and if necessary, more ruthless than that employed by the enemy," and almost threateningly demanded that "no one should be permitted to stand in the way of the prompt, efficient and secure accomplishment of this mission." Tying the climate of the Cold War to its recommendations, the report argued:

> It is now clear that we are facing an implacable enemy whose avowed objective is world domination by whatever means and at whatever cost. There are no rules in such a game. Hitherto acceptable norms of human conduct do not apply. If the United States is to survive, long-standing American concepts of "fair play" must be reconsidered. We must develop effective espionage and counterespionage services and must learn to subvert, sabotage, and destroy our enemies by more clever, more sophisticated and more effective methods than those used against us. It may become necessary that the American people be made acquainted with, understand and support this fundamentally repugnant philosophy.[15]

But the American people were never made acquainted with "this fundamentally repugnant philosophy." Instead, policymakers and government officials continued to count on a combination of secrecy and a permissive threat environment to conduct covert action without public outcry or scrutiny. Moreover, the Doolittle Commission adopted exactly the opposite position as Kennan, who concluded his famous Long Telegram with a warning: "The greatest danger that can befall us in coping with this problem of Soviet communism, is that we shall allow ourselves to become like those with whom we are coping."[16] The Doolittle Commission fundamentally misunderstood American civil-intelligence relations.

It was never the case that the American people shirked a fight when provoked.[17] They embraced war with an enthusiasm matched only by their eagerness to return to normalcy as soon as the war was over. But the same national security institutions that Americans trusted to protect them in war they feared as a threat to their liberty in peace. The First World War and the First Red Scare should have alerted policymakers and the intelligence community to the mercurial temperament of American civil society. The Cold War consensus and a complacent public were on borrowed time.

The Clark and Doolittle Reports represented more examples of intelligence oversight by commission. In both instances, there was also an interbranch rivalry at play as a presidential commission sought to offset the weight of a congressional commission. The Hoover Commission understood that intelligence oversight had to be more consistent than ad hoc investigations and reports, and consequently recommended separate oversight bodies within both the executive and legislative branches.

Congresses Misses Another Opportunity

Amid intelligence coups abroad and controversies at home, Senator Mike Mansfield proposed a resolution to create a joint congressional intelligence committee first in 1953 and then again in 1954. Mansfield persevered with another attempt in 1955. In introducing his legislation, Mansfield claimed, "As it is now, C.I.A. is freed from practically every ordinary form of Congressional check.... There is no regular, methodical review of this agency, other than a briefing which is supplied to a few members of selected sub-committees." He distinguished between "an essential degree of secrecy to achieve a specific purpose and secrecy for the mere sake of secrecy," observing that "once secrecy becomes sacrosanct, it invites abuse." Perhaps in response, the CIA put up a sign that said "Central Intelligence Agency" outside its headquarters and instructed its telephone operators to answer with "Central Intelligence Agency" when someone called.[18] But the CIA faced stiffer congressional resistance this time. The 1955 resolution gathered more bipartisan support because of the Hoover Commission's recommendations.

"Who are the supermen of the CIA?" Senator Wayne Morse wondered aloud when the resolution came to the floor. They were "not elected officials of the Government," he decided, and therefore "the responsibility as the elected representatives of a free people happens to be ours . . . to protect the people, by serving as a check against the administration."[19] Countering the refrain that secrecy was essential to intelligence operations even in a democracy, Morse argued that "no topic of Government belonging to all the people of the country is too sensitive for the selected representatives of a free people to handle."[20] He further reasoned:

> We are dealing with America's spy system when we are dealing with the CIA; and when we are dealing with America's spy system, we had better take care that we do not deal with a police state system. We do not have to fight communism with a police state system. We did not have to fight Nazism with a police state system. We had better keep on free ground.[21]

Insisting that the "American people have a right to know what kind of spying we are doing and what kind of policy we have," Morse proclaimed that this issue could wreck the "whole ship of freedom which has been built up under our great Constitution."[22]

To prove that these senators were not alone in their concerns, Senator William Langer entered into the record excerpts from numerous press articles supporting Mansfield's resolution for more rigorous congressional intelligence oversight, suggesting that American civil society was invested in the outcome.[23] There were also other constitutional matters at stake, as a few senators worried out loud that the President could conduct a shadow foreign policy through the CIA. But, besides overlooking the first-order problem that the Constitution lacked any explicit provisions dealing with intelligence, Congress was trying to create a constitutional precedent where practically none existed, an exercise made all the more difficult given its historically halfhearted efforts to carve out its own space in intelligence oversight.

The Mansfield resolution ultimately succumbed to rivalry within Congress as the armed services and appropriations committees, which formed the old guard of congressional intelligence oversight, protected their prerogatives.

Senator Leverett Saltonstall, former chairman of the Senate Armed Services Committee, sparred with Mansfield and Morse during the debate. He adopted a deferential approach to discretionary presidential control of intelligence and even blamed Congress for the shortcomings in its oversight of the CIA. Contrary to Morse's alarm at agency secrecy, Saltonstall offered, "It is not a question of reluctance on the part of CIA officials to speak to us. It is a question of our reluctance, if you will, to see information and knowledge on subjects which I personally, as a member of Congress and as a citizen, would rather not have."[24] He also alluded to Congress's need to safeguard sources and methods based on the simple principle of protecting the "the lives of men who are endeavoring to get the information for us."[25]

Senator Richard Russell, the chairman of the Senate Armed Services Committee, took up this defense and argued, "If there is anything in the United States which should be held sacred behind the curtain of classified matter, it is the information of the [CIA]." He further declared that it would

FIGURE 16.1 Congress, dressed as Sherlock Holmes, comes knocking at the CIA's door. It failed to solve the mystery of missing congressional intelligence oversight. Library of Congress Prints and Photographs Division, LC-USZ62-102946. Courtesy of the Gib Crockett estate.

"be better to abolish [the CIA] out of hand than it would be to adopt a theory that such information should be available to every member of Congress and to the members of the staff of any committee."[26] Besides the resistance voiced by these congressional heavyweights, the congressional armed services and appropriations committees had also addressed the need for any new congressional intelligence committee by establishing intelligence oversight subcommittees. In the end, the Senate voted down the Mansfield resolution. Congress may have missed another opportunity to assert its role in oversight, but the President did not.

The President's Private Oversight Board

Eisenhower fumed that Mansfield's resolution "would be passed over his dead body."[27] After the Hoover Commission recommended both presidential and congressional intelligence oversight bodies, Dulles recommended that Eisenhower form a presidential panel before Congress reconvened to discuss a proposed intelligence committee.[28] The President decided to establish his own intelligence board as a ballast against a congressional intelligence committee.

In January 1956, as Mansfield was reintroducing his resolution in Congress, Eisenhower created the President's Board of Consultants on Foreign Intelligence Activities (PBCFIA), known today as the President's Intelligence Advisory Board (PIAB). Per the Hoover Commission's recommendation, the PBCFIA was a body of select citizens first chaired by James R. Killian Jr., the president of the Massachusetts Institute of Technology. Its initial members included distinguished former military officers, like James Doolittle, Richard Connolly, and John Hull, and powerful citizens, such as Benjamin Fairless, Robert Lovett, and Joseph Kennedy. In February 1956, Eisenhower issued Executive Order 10656, officially establishing the board.

The board's task was to review the foreign intelligence activities of the USIC, particularly the CIA. The DCI and other elements of the USIC were authorized to make their activities available to the board for scrutiny.[29] The CIA and USIC had more reasons to share their operations and activities with the President's board than they did with Congress, especially since the board's reviews and recommendations were only advisory. The President could accept or reject its findings and choose what to implement or not, so the President still exercised ultimate authority over intelligence. Above all, the board kept intelligence oversight within the executive branch and among a close circle of presidential confidants. Critically, the President's board "was never intended to operate as an intelligence 'watchdog'" or "as an intelligence policeman," in the manner that Mansfield or later proponents of congressional intelligence oversight envisioned. Instead, it was aimed at "improving both the quantity and quality of U.S. intelligence." For example, on the board's advice, Eisenhower established the US Intelligence Board (USIB), consisting of all the heads of the intelligence community, which would convene and purportedly coordinate intelligence under the chairmanship of the DCI.[30]

With the executive branch overseeing intelligence, it would naturally follow that the President would assume responsibility for intelligence scandals. But the Eisenhower administration created another group that played a critical role in American covert action policy, including who would shoulder the blame for covert action run amok. The NSC established the Planning Coordination Group, made up of representatives from the State and Defense Departments, and later a special representative of the President, which would be notified in advance of covert action programs initiated by the CIA and would be responsible for giving policy approval for such programs.[31] This covert action oversight panel, initially known as the 5412 Group after the series of NSC 5412 directives that created it, or blandly as the Special Group, was intended to provide the President with plausible deniability for covert action.[32]

Notionally, the Special Group disconnected the President from direct responsibility for authorizing CIA covert action operations.[33] A tradition emerged that the CIA became the scapegoat for covert action failures even though the actions were reviewed and approved by presidential administrations pursuant to their foreign policy goals. In some respects, this was inevitable. After all, the CIA was organizationally responsible for conducting covert action operations and therefore became "a fall guy within the Washington bureaucracy." As a result, the State Department, the FBI, and other members of the intelligence community made "sniping at the CIA... a common luncheon sport in Washington."[34] And while the CIA garnered most of the attention, the same period witnessed the expansion of the USIC.

Sending the Wrong Signal

Though the NSA is prominent enough today, observers once joked that the National Security Agency's initials stood for "No Such Agency." Fittingly a descendant of the Cipher Bureau and the Signal Intelligence Service, the NSA was a product of bureaucratic competition. It was not just the creation of the NSA but its position in the broader architecture of the American intelligence system that portended more bureaucratic competition to come.

The parochialism and shortcomings of Army and Navy SIGINT during the Second World War led other departments and organizations, including the State Department and the FBI, to create their own SIGINT programs. Fearing the loss of their monopoly over this increasingly valuable intelligence function, the Army and Navy established a SIGINT coordinating committee in 1944, then the Army-Navy Communication Intelligence Board (ANCIB) in 1945. But this interservice cooperation was not what it seemed. The purpose of the ANCIB was not so much to address competition between the Army and Navy SIGINT components, which still wanted to preserve their individual independence, but rather to protect them from outside competition.[35]

The end of the war raised further challenges. The military had to contend with competition from the outside. First, the ANCIB became the State-Army-Navy Communication Intelligence Board (STANCIB). The board then expanded again to become the United States Communications Intelligence Board (USCIB) when it added the FBI, Air Force, CIG, and later CIA to its membership. Furthermore, in 1948, National Security Council Intelligence Directive No. 9 made the USCIB a component under the direction of the NSC to effect "the authoritative coordination of Communications Intelligence activities of the Government."[36] The very drafting of NSCID No. 9 witnessed the same kind of competition as the bitter debate over the drafting of the directives forming the CIG and then the CIA.[37]

The unification of the armed services in the 1947 National Security Act presaged the unification of the military's SIGINT effort in May 1949 with the creation of the Armed Forces Security Agency (AFSA), "the first government agency to be formed in total secrecy," according to former intelligence analyst and journalist James Bamford.[38] The AFSA faced both external and internal problems. Externally, the State Department and CIA balked at the move, which occurred without any prior notification from the Secretary of Defense.[39] Internally, the SIGINT offices of the Army, Navy, and Air Force opposed AFSA control over their operations. The JCS further whittled away AFSA authorities in directives that essentially undercut its ability to coordinate or control the work of the Army, Navy, and Air Force SIGINT offices.[40] The individual military services did not want the AFSA to control SIGINT, while civilian departments and intelligence organizations did not want the military—either the services or the AFSA—to control it either. The situation was untenable.

The shortcomings in SIGINT, especially during the Korean War, riled Beetle Smith, who wrote a memorandum to the NSC. He cited the uncoordinated nature of the current system "of divided authorities and multiple responsibilities" and concluded by calling for a formal review of all American

SIGINT.[41] The complaints made their way to President Truman, who ordered the review. Composed of representatives from the CIA and the State and Defense Departments, the Brownell Committee determined that SIGINT failed to represent the interests and priorities of all departmental and organizational stakeholders. The report resolved the tension in favor of the military by recommending three levels of structural changes. First, the committee suggested that the AFSA have "the responsibility and authority for providing a unified organization and control of the [SIGINT] activities of most of the federal government." Second, it recommended that the director be a career military professional at the flag or general officer level. Finally, the report proposed that AFSA be "directly subordinated to the Department of Defense as the executive agent of the government for [SIGINT] activities."[42]

On October 24, 1952, Truman issued a presidential memorandum establishing the National Security Agency "to provide an effective, unified organization and control of the communications intelligence activities of the United States." The NSA director would be a military officer designated by the Secretary of Defense in consultation with the JCS. The directive provided for far more NSA control over SIGINT than the AFSA had before it. The presidential directive stipulated that "all [SIGINT] collection and production resources of the United States are placed under [the NSA director's] operational and technical control," which was not the case with any preexisting SIGINT organization. Crucially, the memorandum also positioned SIGINT as a special intelligence activity outside the framework of other intelligence activities, which meant more secrecy and less oversight for the NSA than other intelligence organizations.[43]

However, Truman had to address the same tension the Brownell Report noted in terms of the military and national nature of SIGINT. The memorandum stated that SIGINT is a "national responsibility [that]... must be so organized and managed... to satisfy the legitimate intelligence requirements of all such departments and agencies."[44] Accordingly, the memorandum made the DCI the chairman of the USCIB. However, the composition of the USCIB still remained decidedly in favor of the military. The directive attempted to balance out the difference by awarding the representatives of the State Department and CIA two votes on the board, thus giving the civilian representatives the same number of votes as the military representatives. Recommendations decided by majority vote on the board would be binding on the Secretary of Defense. The USCIB's purported responsibility was to coordinate the SIGINT activities of all departments and agencies—yet another long-awaited benchmark for American intelligence. But the USCIB's coordinating role must be measured against the NSA's functional role in terms of the effects of the creation of the NSA on the American intelligence system.

Implicit in the tinkering that went on with the USCIB and the discussion of the national and military applications of SIGINT was the wider question of subordinating national intelligence capabilities and organizations to the military institution. SIGINT had already proven its tremendous applications in the Second World War. In the context of the Cold War, SIGINT was again an essential function in support of strategic planning and military operations in the event of war with the Soviet Union. This would be the arc of the expansion of the USIC during the Cold War. Organizations that straddled national and military intelligence responsibilities were incorporated as components of the Department of Defense rather than as civilian agencies. The result was that the USIC would face a division in its leadership between the Director of Central Intelligence and the Secretary of Defense, which subsequent intelligence oversight reports and executive decisions only further intensified.[45]

The Competition Up Above

The history of the Cipher Bureau and American SIGINT had already proven that executive departments and agencies do not like to share ownership of key intelligence functions. Satellites that provided both imagery and signals intelligence became the next arena of cooperation that inevitably led to competition. Like SIGINT, overhead reconnaissance promised to be an essential source of intelligence on the Soviet Union. Thus, the intelligence requirements of the early Cold War were a key catalyst for innovations in space technologies. The value of overheard reconnaissance plus the technological innovation required to develop and employ satellites reinforced the need to protect those treasured secrets but also generated the competition over them.

The successful Soviet launch of the Sputnik satellite in 1957 alarmed policymakers and the public alike. They feared that the United States was falling behind the Soviet Union in the "space race," which exacerbated greater fears of a Soviet advantage in science and technology. Contrary to press reports, the Sputnik launch did not take the Eisenhower administration by surprise or represent another case of CIA failure. As early as 1946, Project RAND, the antecedent of the RAND Corporation, was studying the possibility of launching satellites into space and the advantages they offered for intelligence and reconnaissance.[46] In 1950, the RAND Corporation published studies that drew the attention of the CIA to the political and psychological effects that the first successful launch of a satellite would have on the world. A 1954 CIA staff study "emphasized the enormous psychologic advantage to the nation first in space" and suggested that the President issue a directive establishing the US satellite development program.[47] In 1955, the CIA determined that the Soviet Union would be able to field a satellite by 1958, but in 1957, it revised this estimate to the end of that year.[48]

The United States did not stand by idly as the Soviet Union developed its space capabilities. Around 1956, the US Air Force began working on a strategic reconnaissance satellite program that would allow for different collection configurations.[49] But it encountered several obstacles. Eisenhower, who famously warned about the dangers of "an immense military establishment and a large arms industry"—the infamous "military-industrial complex"—in his Farewell Address, was determined to chip away at defense spending, including the satellite program.[50] Moreover, satellites were unproven technology, leading to skepticism across the senior ranks of government, with some officials even joking, "That's for Buck Rogers."[51] Finally, the Eisenhower administration had broadcast its vision for the peaceful exploration and utilization of outer space, so it was determined to have a civil space program serve as the public face of US space activities.[52]

A secret "second story" offered an alternative to the overt Air Force satellite program. The Air Force would announce that it was canceling its current program and starting a new scientific satellite project, but it would continue its strategic reconnaissance satellite development in secret under the CIA. The CIA would keep Project CORONA, as it later was known, secret through its special contracting and funding authorities.[53] The CIA and Air Force had already successfully cooperated in researching, developing, and operating the U-2 reconnaissance plane, so perhaps they could do so in the emerging area of satellite reconnaissance.

Fissures slowly developed over who would lead the US satellite reconnaissance program. In 1955, Eisenhower approved an NSC policy paper that called for a satellite launch by 1958, notably tasking the Secretary of Defense with coordinating the program in consultation with the Secretary of State and the DCI.[54] Following the launch of Sputnik, he established the Advanced Research Projects Agency (ARPA), known today as the Defense Advanced Research Projects Agency (DARPA), to conduct research and development in science and technology, especially with respect to satellite reconnaissance. But Eisenhower also granted the CIA "complete and exclusive control of all of the intelligence phases" of the secret satellite reconnaissance program.

Following some confusion among administration officials over which organization would actually be in charge of the program, the President reiterated his position that the project would be housed in ARPA, under the direction of the CIA. Project CORONA therefore involved a division of responsibilities among ARPA, the Air Force, and the CIA.[55]

In May 1960, the Soviet Union shot down a U-2 reconnaissance plane piloted by Francis Gary Powers in what became an embarrassing public spectacle for the Eisenhower administration. With the vulnerability of the U-2 now apparent and the CIA facing continued obstacles to HUMINT collection in the Soviet Union, satellite reconnaissance became an even more urgent priority.[56] In June, the United States launched a satellite capable of providing electronic intelligence on Soviet radars, and in August, the first CORONA mission successfully provided more imagery intelligence about the Soviet Union than all prior U-2 flights combined.[57] That month Eisenhower also approved the creation of a National Reconnaissance Office (NRO) in order to develop and operate US reconnaissance satellites.

FIGURE 16.2 Francis Gary Powers (seated) reads about his ordeal in the office of Walter Pforzheimer (standing). On the table sits a model of the U-2, the type of spy plane in which Powers was shot down over the Soviet Union. Walter L. Pforzheimer Papers, Beinecke Rare Book and Manuscript Library, Yale University.

The formal establishment of the NRO was a joint act of Deputy Secretary of Defense Roswell Gilpatric, a former Under Secretary of the Air Force, and Deputy Director of Central Intelligence, USAF General Charles P. Cabell, in September 1961. The office would be responsible for overall management of the National Reconnaissance Program (NRP), which involves the collection of all imagery and signals intelligence through overhead reconnaissance. The NRO would fall under the dual leadership of the Under Secretary of the Air Force, Dr. Joseph V. Charyk, and the Deputy Director for Plans at the CIA, Richard Bissell, with a staff drawn from both the DOD and the CIA. The agreement perhaps underestimated the potential for bureaucratic competition when it speculated that Charyk and Bissell would be "acting jointly."[58] To this point, the Air Force and CIA "had cooperated on a cordial loosely structured basis." The directors also held monthly meetings, with Bissell assuming the predominant position. But CORONA's success as an intelligence program drew more attention and resources from the Air Force, and Bissell became distracted by other CIA programs.[59] Following Bissell's resignation from the CIA in February 1962, the "loose arrangement" became unsustainable.[60]

A follow-up agreement between DCI John McCone and Gilpatric in May 1962 determined that there would be a single Director of the NRO (DNRO), jointly appointed by the Secretary of Defense and the DCI. Charyk became the DNRO, giving the Air Force and DOD a bureaucratic advantage in the NRO. But some voices in the CIA felt that CORONA was really a CIA program, and they began to blame the Air Force for any of its shortcomings. James Cunningham, the CIA's Deputy Assistant Director, admitted that "the USAF/CIA relationship has deteriorated to the point where mutual trust is now hesitant and there is speculation on either side of 'power grabs' by the other."[61]

The CIA and Air Force came to blows over funding. Charyk crossed out an entire section on the NRO budget drafted by the CIA, positioning the DNRO against the DCI. When Secretary of Defense Robert McNamara explained to McCone why he believed that the NRO and NSA should fall under the newly established Defense Intelligence Agency (DIA), McCone balked, explaining that "both NSA and NRO transcend strictly military intelligence and... it would be undesirable to have this subordination."[62] The fate of the NRO therefore involved institutional competition between intelligence and the military.

The military continued to incrementally extend its control over overhead reconnaissance and the NRO. In 1963, an agreement between the Secretary of Defense and the DCI stipulated that the Secretary of Defense would appoint the DNRO "from among the officers and employees of the Department of Defense," although with the concurrence of the DCI. In return, the DCI would select the Deputy Director of the NRO from the CIA with the concurrence of the Secretary of Defense.[63] Cunningham also saw another power grab in the designs of the Joint Chiefs of Staff, commenting on one of its proposals that the JCS was trying to "absorb those responsibilities and prerogatives relating to operational control of reconnaissance programs now exercised by the CIA."[64]

A final agreement in August 1965 consummated the DOD's control over the NRO. It made the NRO a "separate agency of the DOD" and gave the Secretary of Defense "the ultimate responsibility for the management and operation of the NRO and the NRP," including selection and supervision of the NRO director.[65] Within the DOD, the NRO faced the same conflicting pressures as the NSA in terms of serving as a national intelligence organization or military intelligence organization, especially as satellite capabilities evolved.[66] The United States therefore built the tension between national and military intelligence into the structure of the Cold War–era intelligence community.

The prospect of a nuclear exchange or conventional war in Europe with the Soviet Union made overhead reconnaissance an invaluable intelligence source for defense planning, so it is understandable why policymakers would vest the NRO in the DOD. Like the NSA, the decision had implications for the balance of power between the military and civilian components of the intelligence community and between the Secretary of Defense and the DCI. But the military faced its own internal divisions over whether military intelligence should support the defense leadership or service members in the field. It also found itself wrestling with the problem of coordinating the ballooning defense intelligence system.

Coordinating Military Intelligence

The competition among the rival military branches over SIGINT had revealed how fractured military intelligence remained despite the consolidation of the services in the DOD. Yet another presidential commission report resulted in an attempt to unify military intelligence in a new military intelligence organization, the Defense Intelligence Agency.[67] The result was one of the most confounding combinations of personnel, responsibilities, and functions in the USIC.

In July 1960, Eisenhower approved a proposal for a Joint Study Group (JSG), composed of representatives from the CIA, DOD, State Department,

Bureau of Budget, NSC, and PBCFIA, to study the foreign intelligence work of the United States. The JSG Report was comprehensive, examining US foreign intelligence across different organizations (e.g., the CIA and the NSA); departments (e.g., State and DOD); and functions (e.g., collection and analysis). Like virtually every other study preceding it, the JSG report highlighted coordination as the salient challenge facing the American intelligence system.

The JSG insisted that there was "no doubt anywhere that the coordinator is and must be the Director of Central Intelligence." But the DCI faced the problem of conflicting responsibilities in managing both the CIA and American foreign intelligence activities. As a result, "other agencies found themselves being coordinated by an organization which from time to time appeared as a vigorous competitor of theirs." One possible solution was to separate the DCI and the CIA. This solution would leave the DCI with a small staff and less bureaucratic power, perhaps meaning less authority to coordinate the USIC. The JSG demurred, suggesting further consideration only if coordination did not improve "after a reasonable time."[68]

Most of the JSG Report focused on the DOD. Besides noting that the majority of USIC personnel were involved in DOD activities, it observed that the military dominated the membership of the US Intelligence Board. This frustrated the board's central purpose: to help the DCI coordinate the entire USIC. The report also determined that silos in the three military intelligence services made it "difficult to achieve an over-all military intelligence view" and impeded defense intelligence and strategic planning at the highest levels of the DOD and JCS. Therefore, it somewhat confusingly recommended coordinating all DOD intelligence activities in the Office of the Secretary of Defense (OSD) while at the same time strengthening JCS authority over intelligence coordination and operations.[69]

When Eisenhower discussed the JSG Report with the NSC in the waning days of his presidency in January 1961, he leaned on George Washington's example and his own experience as a general when he "pointed out that in military history a single man usually dominates the intelligence service of a country at any given time." He even offered his own anecdotes about using military intelligence during the Second World War. He questioned why the "antiquated system of separate intelligence organizations for each Military Service was retained." Surprisingly, DCI Allen Dulles opposed any changes to the existing system. Although the military retained the greater number of votes on the USIB, Dulles probably preferred to keep the board's military composition fractured among the competing services. Perhaps he feared the creation of a unified military intelligence organization that could rival or even eclipse the CIA when equipped with the DOD's resources and budget. However, any subsequent action had to wait for the next presidential administration under John F. Kennedy.[70]

Robert S. McNamara, Kennedy's Secretary of Defense, cited the JSG Report when he directed the establishment of the Defense Intelligence Agency in February 1961. In another example of executive discretion, he stipulated that the DIA must not require new legislation.[71] When McNamara informed Kennedy of his decision, he framed the DIA as an intelligence organization reporting to the Secretary of Defense through the JCS. The DIA would "review and coordinate the intelligence functions retained by the military departments" and would be responsible for supplying military intelligence to the DOD, USIC, and USIB. However, like the NSA, some operational activities and resources would be retained by the separate military services, meaning that the DIA did not completely resolve the problem of military intelligence coordination.[72]

The DOD directive that created the DIA reiterated its authorities and roles—for example, its notional responsibility for coordinating DOD intelligence and acting as the voice of the DOD in national intelligence policy.[73] In a remarkable display of transparency for an organization created by the executive branch and without congressional legislation, the DOD publicly announced the existence of the new agency on August 2, 1961, stating that the DIA's "principal objective" was "unity of effort among all components of the Department of Defense in developing military intelligence."[74]

The DIA mixed civilians and military officers in an organization that blended the military and intelligence professions. It also found itself caught between providing strategic intelligence to the senior defense leadership in Washington and providing tactical intelligence to commanders at the ground level. To add to its responsibilities and rivalries, the DIA eventually entered the world of clandestine operations, in both cooperation and competition with the CIA. Finally, as another DOD intelligence organization, the DIA further weighted the USIC toward the military, making the DOD and Secretary of Defense even more formidable actors in the American intelligence system.[75]

More Organizations, More Oversight?

Allusions to a certain "three-letter agency" almost always conjure thoughts of the CIA. However, the CIA is just one of many three-letter agencies in the

USIC. It was also not the first; the CIA joined the preexisting ONI, MID, and FBI. The early Cold War saw the creation of even more. As the United States added more organizations, they required more oversight, especially as the size and scope of their intelligence activities expanded.

Congress would finally carve out its role in intelligence oversight, but it did so reactively rather than proactively, following revelations of secret intelligence activities that generated public outcry. Furthermore, it was not the DOD and its burgeoning intelligence organizations that created the crisis. Domestic intelligence operations by the CIA and FBI, civilian components of the USIC, ignited public opposition to the American national security state, while the new NSA emerged largely unscathed despite its own domestic intelligence activities. Congress, which had heretofore shirked its responsibility for vigorous intelligence oversight, could no longer sit idle.

17

Who Will Guard the Shadow Guardians?

IN SPITE OF the measures taken to preserve plausible deniability and protect the President from blowback, some covert action failures were just too big to cover up. For example, Eisenhower took responsibility for the shootdown and capture of U-2 pilot Francis Gary Powers in May 1960. An even greater fiasco was the dramatic April 1961 failure of the Bay of Pigs invasion, where the CIA planned to use anti-Castro Cubans to overthrow Fidel Castro. Even though the operation was planned during the Eisenhower administration, Kennedy followed through with it and duly accepted the blame.[1]

Writing two months after the disaster, eminent American historian and former OSS analyst Arthur M. Schlesinger Jr. drafted a memorandum to Kennedy on the subject of CIA reform. Schlesinger reflected, "On balance, CIA's record has probably been very good." Quite possibly informing Kennedy's own comments at the CIA a few months later, he continued, "The triumphs of an intelligence agency are unknown; all the public hears about (or should hear about) are its errors." However, he cautioned, "an agency dedicated to clandestine activity can afford damned few visible errors. The important thing to recognize today . . . is that the CIA . . . has about used up its quota." At the time he was writing, the American people had not learned about all the CIA's errors and indiscretions. Schlesinger predicted, "One more CIA debacle will shake faith considerably in US policy, at home as well as abroad." The CIA had more than one to hide.[2]

Public revelations of intelligence misdeeds in the 1960s and 1970s demolished the Cold War consensus and public support for intelligence along with it. The USIC not only had failed with respect to events overseas but also had exceeded the scope of its authorities in its surveillance activities at home. Secrecy, the essential ingredient that gave intelligence an air of mystery and power, collapsed. In fact, the USIC failed spectacularly at keeping the very secrets that could do it the most harm.

The CIA Confronts Counterculture

While stories began to emerge in the 1960s, the intelligence programs that eventually incited the ire of the American people began in the 1950s. One of the most notorious projects was known as MKULTRA, often remembered as the CIA's "mind control" experiments. The CIA tested drugs, hypnosis, and other methods to collect information or manipulate people on the witting and unwitting, willing and unwilling. The list of test subjects ranges from prisoners like the famous American gangsters August Del Gracio and Whitey Bulger to volunteers like American icons Ken Kesey, author of *One Flew over the Cuckoo's Nest*, and Grateful Dead songwriter Robert Hunter.[3]

Dr. Sidney Gottlieb, who oversaw MKULTRA, also took the program abroad to secret prisons where people were held and interrogated by the CIA. When these CIA experiments later became public knowledge, they reminded a horrified American audience of the torture, interrogations, and experiments

FIGURE 17.1 The consolation prize for intelligence failure: an award and a resignation. JFK presents DCI Allen Dulles with the National Security Medal, November 28, 1961. Just to the right of Dulles stands CIA rival J. Edgar Hoover. Courtesy of the John F. Kennedy Presidential Library.

that had taken place in Nazi concentration camps. Gottlieb also helped develop poisons and toxins as part of the CIA's inchoate plans to kill Patrice Lumumba of the Congo and Fidel Castro of Cuba; he even traveled to the Congo with the poison destined for Lumumba before the latter's assassination rendered the plot moot.[4] Gottlieb's work would significantly damage the CIA's public image.[5]

For a secret intelligence organization, the CIA had never been very secret. Ever since its inception, information about the CIA reached the public, often at the instigation of the CIA itself. As DCI, Allen Dulles looked to enhance his agency's image through spy fiction, even providing authors with stories for their books.[6] After his resignation, he published *The Craft of Intelligence* (1963) to correct public perceptions of intelligence, claiming it was "probably the least understood and the most misrepresented of the professions" in US national security.[7] Dulles claimed that the CIA was "representative of all classes and places," in an effort to counter the dominant narrative that the CIA was "pale, male, and Yale," as observers have quipped.[8] He likewise tried to dispel myths about the CIA as a shadow policymaker for the US government, explaining that its operations received approval from senior American officials. For emphasis, he argued that the CIA was subject to vigorous civilian control and oversight as an organization established by congressional statute and firmly responsive to the executive branch. He painted a favorable picture of congressional oversight even though (or perhaps because) it was informal and hardly scrutinous during his tenure. Dulles was defending the status quo in a period of impending change. He was also ahead of the times in his effort to inspire faith and credibility in the CIA, writing before the rumors and revelations that would profoundly change American attitudes toward the CIA and intelligence.

That same year, former President Truman must have shocked the entire country—and undoubtedly the CIA—when he published an op-ed titled "Limit CIA Role to Intelligence." Truman revealed that his intent in signing the CIA into existence was to establish an all-source collection and analysis organization. However, it had turned into "an operational and at times a policy-making arm of the Government," despite his original intention that it would never "be injected into peacetime cloak and dagger operations." It had strayed so far from this "role that it is being interpreted as a symbol of sinister and mysterious foreign intrigue—and a subject for cold war enemy propaganda." He called for the CIA to "be restored to its original assignment as the intelligence arm of the President" and recommended that "its operational duties be terminated or properly used elsewhere." Truman captured almost two centuries of tensions in American civil-intelligence relations in concluding,

> We have grown up as a nation, respected for our free institutions and for our ability to maintain a free and open society. There is something about the way the CIA has been functioning that is casting a shadow over our historic position and I feel that we need to correct it.[9]

As suspicions about the CIA mounted, David Wise and Thomas Ross published *The Invisible Government* (1964), which claimed that there were two US governments: a visible one and an invisible one. Hidden from the American people and Congress, the "invisible government" was a "loose, amorphous grouping of individuals and agencies . . . not limited to the Central Intelligence Agency, although the CIA is at its heart."[10] The authors urged the President and Congress to work together to "control the intelligence establishment, to place checks on its power and to make it truly accountable," particularly in the realm of covert action. In this respect, contrary to the Doolittle Report and consistent with Kennan, they warned against a free society "succumbing to the enemy's morality by too eagerly embracing his methods."[11] The book also blamed the President for using advisory boards and other mechanisms to resist "the need for greater Congressional control [of intelligence]."[12] In a conclusion complementary to Truman's, the authors decided that the

> secret machinery of the government can never be totally reconciled with the traditions of a free republic. But in a time of Cold War, the solution lies not in dismantling this machinery but in bringing it under greater control. The resultant danger of exposure is far less than the danger of secret power. If we err as a society, let it be on the side of control.[13]

The media debate over the CIA and intelligence continued. In 1966, the *New York Times* ran the first of five successive articles based on months of investigation examining the premise of a CIA-led shadow government. The report cited congressmen, officials, and other sources, including Dulles, who acknowledged that it might be time for a congressional intelligence oversight committee. Nonetheless, the *Times* determined that "whatever its miscalculations, blunders and misfortunes . . . the agency acts today not on its own but with the approval and under the control of the political leaders of the United

States Government." However, it hedged, "What *is* control? And who guards the guards?" It wondered "whether the nation has allowed itself to go too far in the grim and sometimes deadly business of espionage and secret operations" and how far American leaders should "go in approving [intelligence operations] without tarnishing and retarding those ideas of freedom and self-government they proclaim to the world." Like Dulles, Truman, Wise, and Ross, the *Times* was trying to weigh the CIA's role in civil-intelligence relations, a question the country was actively debating throughout the 1960s.[14]

On Valentine's Day 1967, amid advertisements for airlines, cars, clothes, and other gift ideas, the *New York Times* printed a far different advertisement that took up a full page. A left-leaning magazine known as *Ramparts* promoted its March issue, promising a bombshell report on various CIA scandals. The advertisement revealed that the CIA had "infiltrated and subverted the world of American student leaders" and "wormed its way into American institutions," asserting that the "CIA owes the youth of this country an apology."[15] Perhaps trying to scoop *Ramparts*, the *Times* announced in a headline on the front page that very same day, "A Student Group Concedes It Took Funds from C.I.A." The article preempted the magazine's coverage by explaining that leaders of the National Student Association, the largest college student organization in the country, had accepted funding from the CIA but, by the mid-1960s, had high-mindedly and belatedly decided that "a covert relationship with Government agencies was intolerable to an open democratic organization." As Eugene Groves, the association's president, disclosed, the CIA and the National Student Association had joined forces to combat other heavily funded, Soviet-controlled front organizations for foreign students.[16] Yet again, American civil society was complicit in the very intelligence scandals it later found so objectionable.

Another *Ramparts* article by Sol Stern indicted both the CIA and the National Student Association. Stern alleged that the CIA "treated [the association] as an arm of U.S. foreign policy." Moreover, Stern charged that the National Student Association not only served as a conduit for CIA propaganda, but its student members also collected information for the CIA.[17] Marcus Raskin, who contributed to the investigation, explained how the CIA had enticed the young idealists of the National Student Association, only for them to become mere "instruments of the Cold War . . . used by the CIA as contacts, covers and mail drops." Raskin questioned "how do we now face other nations who took us at our word that our students were 'free' and therefore different from the communist-run youth groups?"[18] It appears that the American people had weighed the two competing approaches to the Cold

War expressed in the Doolittle Report and Long Telegram, and they decided that in trying to defeat their enemies, they must not become like them.

The National Student Association was only one example of a broader campaign by the CIA to enlist the American people in the shadow Cold War. It also targeted organizations for recent immigrants and refugees from communist countries; civic groups including trade unions, like the powerful AFL-CIO, and public intellectuals including artists, writers, and filmmakers; and programs for minority groups such as Catholics, women, and African Americans. The CIA even enlisted the help of journalists and periodicals, so the same press that later castigated the CIA for its scandals played a part in some of them. The hypocrisy was equally applicable to the CIA itself, as educated, Ivy League liberal elites justified their use of illiberal measures as necessary to safeguard American principles.[19] The cost of Cold War cooperation between the CIA and American civil society was considerable in terms of public funds expended and reputational capital. US citizens, including some of its best goodwill ambassadors, like students, were suspected of being CIA assets when traveling, living, and working overseas.[20]

Thomas Braden, a former OSS officer and division head in CIA operations, did the CIA no favors in 1967 when he published an op-ed titled "I'm Glad the CIA Is Immoral" in the *Saturday Evening Post*. Braden claimed he knew the truth about the CIA's role in fighting the Cold War and defended its activities as "essential." He rationalized the CIA's illicit support for front groups based on communist subversion of the same nature. As for congressional oversight of CIA activities, Braden sneered, "The idea that Congress would have approved many of our projects was about as likely as the John Birch Society's approving Medicare." Although his moral reasoning was questionable, Braden was unquestionably correct in his observation that "the cold war was and is a war, fought with ideas instead of bombs." He simply failed to recognize how CIA operations would conflict with American ideas.[21] Braden's op-ed did little to burnish the image of the CIA. In publishing the article, he not only exposed the CIA to even more unwanted attention from the American people but also incurred the wrath of his fellow CIA officers, including his former mentor, Allen Dulles, who never spoke to Braden again.[22]

While American civil society was complicit in CIA operations in some instances, it was not in others. In either case, the result was a rupture between the American people, their elected officials, and the intelligence community. The true cost was in the trust between the public and the US government. Between 1966 and 1968, trust in the government fell from 61 percent to 45 percent, and never again rose above 47 percent.[23] The relationship between

FIGURE 17.2 A February 1967 cartoon by Herblock titled "Down the Rabbit Hole" plays upon a scene from Alice in Wonderland to show the CIA's covert activities undermining US institutions. A 1967 Herblock Cartoon, © The Herb Block Foundation.

the spy and the state permanently transformed the relationship between the American people and their government.

Another sign of the times was Congress's 1967 passage of the Freedom of Information Act (FOIA), which sailed through the House with a vote of 306–0.[24] FOIA provided the American people with a legislative instrument to challenge government secrecy. In ensuing years, requests for government records through FOIA have been responsible for the release of materials and evidence concerning landmark events and key players in American history—for example, documents on the Bay of Pigs and J. Edgar Hoover's files. FOIA records from the FBI and the CIA also helped shed light on the invasive domestic intelligence activities from the 1950s to the 1970s that tipped the scales in the long-running debate over congressional intelligence oversight.

From COINTELRPO to CHAOS

In 1956, the FBI launched a series of covert domestic intelligence programs known under the umbrella name COINTELPRO, or Counterintelligence Program. The original target was the American Communist Party, but the list expanded to other leftist organizations and individuals during the 1960s. Troublingly, several Attorneys General, presidential advisors, and even members of Congress knew of the existence of COINTELPRO.[25] Among the techniques the FBI deployed were so-called black-bag jobs, involving lock-picking, safecracking, and other old "gumshoe" tricks that blurred the lines between law enforcement and intelligence and ran afoul of Congress and American civil society.

William C. Sullivan, who headed the FBI's domestic intelligence operations and was implicated in drafting threatening letters to Martin Luther King Jr. as part of COINTELPRO, admitted that the FBI did "not obtain authorization for 'black bag' jobs from outside the Bureau," as they were "clearly illegal." Nonetheless, he saw them as "an invaluable technique in combating subversive activities of a clandestine nature aimed directly at undermining and destroying our nation."[26] Sullivan defended these operations as "naturally pragmatic," later testifying to Congress, "Never once did I hear anybody including myself, raise the question: 'Is this course of action which we have agreed upon, lawful, is it legal, is it ethical or moral.' "[27]

However, Sullivan's boss knew from experience that he had to protect the FBI from public scrutiny. Hoover supposedly put an end to black-bag jobs in 1966. However, in a meeting with Attorney General John Mitchell, DCI Richard Helms, and DNSA (Director of the NSA) Admiral Noel Gayler in the spring of 1971, Gayler "stated that he was most desirous of the FBI resuming the so-called 'black bag' operations." Hoover was opposed, but the Attorney General intervened and said that DCI Helms and Gayler should figure out what they wanted and then he personally would "make the decision as to what could or could not be done."[28]

COINTELPRO ended in 1971 due to public disclosure and private civic action aimed at holding the FBI accountable. A group known as the Citizens' Commission to Investigate the FBI broke into an FBI field office, took COINTELPRO documents, and turned them over to the press.[29] Carl Stern, an NBC journalist, subsequently used FOIA to force the FBI to turn over more COINTELPRO documents.

The FBI was not the only intelligence organization conducting domestic surveillance operations that conflicted with constitutional principles and precepts. Hoover recounted another meeting with the Attorney General, DCI, and DNSA in the spring of 1971 in which the NSA's operations became a topic of discussion. A memorandum claimed that the "NSA develop[ed] significant domestic intelligence while monitoring foreign communications traffic." Although under "its operational directive NSA [did] not have a jurisdictional mandate to produce intelligence relating to U.S. citizens," this information was still "given to CIA and the Bureau on an extremely confidential basis and has been referred to by the highly classified code name 'Minaret Traffic.' " Hoover felt the FBI "should take advantage of any resources of NSA and CIA which can be tapped." Furthermore, both the DCI and DNSA expressed an interest in exploring opportunities to legalize and expand this practice.[30]

Like the CIA, the NSA relied on the cooperation of civil society to conduct some of its operations. Private companies like Western Union, RCA Global, and ITT World Communications provided the NSA with copies of international communications as part of the secretive Project SHAMROCK.[31] The NSA even produced an internal memorandum with the intention of hiding its domestic surveillance activities despite evidence that they were "clearly outside the foreign intelligence mandate of NSA." It began to intercept the communications of select Americans in the 1960s, culminating with the creation of a "Watch List" from 1967 to 1973, to which the FBI, CIA, Secret Service, and DOD all contributed.[32] The NSA then intercepted communications traffic that included the names of American citizens under its highly classified Project MINARET.[33] The NSA had leveraged its intelligence capabilities for domestic purposes as part of a larger, national campaign involving key players in the USIC.

Even the rivalrous CIA and FBI worked together to spy on Americans. Under a 1966 agreement, the CIA conducted domestic intelligence operations pursuant to FBI requests.[34] However, in 1967, the CIA created its own domestic intelligence program, MHCHAOS, to identify connections between US groups and communist subversion. Just as COINTELPRO blurred law enforcement and intelligence, MHCHAOS broke down "the distinction between 'foreign' and 'domestic' intelligence." From 1967 to 1974, MHCHAOS used methods like mail opening and NSA intercepts to collect intelligence about what were ultimately the "lawful domestic activities of dissident American groups." After Hoover eliminated FBI black-bag jobs in 1966, the FBI relied on the CIA to carry out black-bag jobs and even provided it with names. In the end, MHCHAOS compiled over 7,000 files on American citizens that included the names of over 300,000 more and contained information "wholly irrelevant to the legitimate interests of the CIA or any other government agency," according to Congress. Worse yet, the CIA concluded that there was "negligible foreign influence on domestic protest activity." MHCHAOS proved to be the wrong program, in the wrong place, at the wrong time for the CIA.[35]

The American fiction of separating foreign and domestic intelligence collapsed in a surprising display of bureaucratic cooperation in the USIC. Unfortunately, the target of this cooperation was the American people. Hoover broke off liaison with the CIA in 1970 over leaks, although communication between the two organizations apparently continued without his knowledge. Hoover also tried to distance the Bureau from other organizations in the USIC as they began to question the FBI's counterintelligence work. They claimed that Hoover was "so intent on preventing any embarrassment to the F.B.I. or any sullying of his reputation" that he purposely allowed the FBI's domestic intelligence operations to wither.[36] Still, the damage had been done. Domestic intelligence eroded and ultimately shattered the Cold War consensus that had united the government, the USIC, and the American people.

The CIA's Most Sensitive Secrets

Scrutiny of the USIC, particularly the CIA, escalated in the early 1970s, beginning at the top of the executive branch. President Richard Nixon and his National Security Advisor, Henry Kissinger, viewed the CIA with suspicion. Nixon was particularly aggrieved when the CIA failed to warn him about the 1970 coup in Cambodia, which further complicated the US position in Southeast Asia.[37] Nixon ordered a review of the intelligence community by James Schlesinger, the Assistant Director of the Office of Management and Budget.

The Schlesinger Report of 1971 sought to right an imbalance in the USIC. Although the size and cost of the USIC had exploded, the scope and quality of its analysis lagged. The report determined that distinctions between national, departmental, and tactical intelligence had broken down along with distinctions between military and non-military intelligence. Citing the enduring problem of bureaucratic competition, the report searched for answers in the organization and leadership of the USIC, finding that it was inadequate for the "needs of a modern and technologically complex intelligence community." For example, the DCI, who was ostensibly responsible for coordinating the work of the USIC, "was outranked by other departmental heads who report directly to the President and are his immediate supervisors on the National Security Council." As one possible solution, the report introduced the idea of a Director of National Intelligence (DNI) to oversee the USIC, leaving the DCI to run the CIA.[38] However, Schlesinger's recommendations aimed too high at a time when domestic civil strife over the Vietnam War and unfolding political scandals distracted the administration. Perhaps more problematically, some of his report's proposals would have required new legislation, which meant involving Congress.[39]

The USIC put yet another target on its back when it emerged that the individuals involved in the 1972 Watergate break-in were former officers, agents, or assets of the CIA and FBI. The FBI and CIA proved to be the source of Nixon's political undoing in other ways as well. Mark Felt, the Associate Director of the FBI, was later discovered to be "Deep Throat," the anonymous official who leaked information to Bob Woodward and Carl Bernstein of the *Washington Post*. They uncovered Nixon's role in the Watergate scandal, which eventually led to his resignation. Felt's leaks also named E. Howard Hunt, a former CIA officer, as one of the main conspirators involved in Watergate. In turn, Hunt admitted to a pattern of interference in domestic politics.[40]

The confusion over the CIA, politicization, and the Nixon administration reached its apogee with James Schlesinger's appointment as DCI in 1973. Schlesinger's mission was to institute major reforms, some of which were backward-looking while others were forward-looking. For example, he was to implement Nixon's vision "that the agency had to be changed from being an established bureaucracy and brought back as a presidential instrument," recalling the tradition of the Secret Service Fund and Donovan's plan for an independent intelligence organization. However, in surveying the future, Schlesinger wanted to prioritize technical intelligence over human intelligence. Schlesinger's bias against HUMINT operations, drastic personnel cuts, and position as an outsider made him deeply unpopular at the CIA. After just four months on the job, Schlesinger left the position of DCI to become the Secretary of Defense. But Schlesinger also left behind a poison pill that would subsequently expose the CIA to widespread scrutiny and condemnation.[41]

In May 1973, midway through his short tenure as DCI, Schlesinger issued a memorandum directing all CIA employees to report any activities "inconsistent" with or "outside" the CIA's charter. Citing recent press reports, he emphasized that he would "do everything in [his] power to confine CIA activities to those which fall within a strict interpretation of its legislative charter."[42] Schlesinger later claimed that he believed the request would lead to more information on Watergate. Indeed, it did. For example, Howard Hunt had requested a referral for a retired CIA lockpicker a few months before the Watergate job. However, Schlesinger's memorandum did not specify the scope of the internal investigation.[43]

When William Colby assumed the role of DCI a few months later, he inherited what became a voluminous report known as the "Family Jewels." The nearly seven-hundred-page report covered the objectionable activities the CIA conducted over the years: mind-control experiments, surveillance of journalists and others, assassination plots, and domestic intelligence operations. CIA Inspector General William Broe warned Colby that recent revelations were getting close to revealing the MHCHAOS program and suggested that "a fresh look... might be in order in the light of current events." He added that his office was "particularly concerned about MHCHAOS because of the high degree of resentment we found among many Agency employees at their being expected to participate in it." Colby terminated MHCHAOS in March 1974 and locked the "Family Jewels" report away in his safe, perhaps expecting neither to become public.[44]

Despite earlier instances of public scrutiny, the CIA must have realized that the next investigation would be different when a front-page headline in the *New York Times* on December 22, 1974, blared, "Huge C.I.A. Operation Reported in U.S. Against Antiwar Forces, Other Dissidents in Nixon Years." Unlike the 1966 piece that stated it would investigate the CIA before reaching a conclusion, Seymour Hersh, the author of the 1974 report, rendered his verdict in the opening line. He began the article by concluding that the CIA, "directly violating its charter, conducted a massive, illegal domestic intelligence operation." The article included some of the contents of the "Family Jewels," which triggered "widespread paper shredding at the agency." A few anonymous government sources tried to defend the CIA's activities but conceded that they were "handled in a very spooky way." Some suggested "the laws were fuzzy in connection with the so-called 'gray' area of

C.I.A.-F.B.I. operations," while an official with "first-hand knowledge" stated, "Every one of these acts was blatantly illegal." As Hersh reminded his readers, Colby himself acknowledged in his confirmation hearings that the CIA did not have the authority to conduct the types of "internal security functions" it now stood accused of carrying out.[45]

Hersh's article called into question just how much control anyone was exercising over the CIA. On the one hand, the journalist noted that many junior CIA officers "began waving 'the red flag' inside the agency" out of opposition to domestic intelligence operations. On the other, he alleged that the CIA's counterintelligence division, led by James Jesus Angleton, acted almost independently, highlighting the problem of control within the CIA. The article cited White House transcripts that "could indicate Presidential knowledge about the C.I.A.'s alleged domestic activities."[46] At the very least, Congressman Lucien Nedzi explained during a CIA seminar in November 1973, "an Executive accustomed to approving 'extra-legal' activity abroad became slack in guarding against extra-legal activity at home."[47] One example was the so-called Huston Plan.

In 1970, Tom Charles Huston, an aide to Nixon, proposed a widespread domestic intelligence campaign. The plan originated from a Special Report of the Interagency Committee on Intelligence, "prepared jointly by representatives from the FBI, CIA, NSA, and DIA." The report contained proposals for domestic intelligence operations, including NSA interceptions of US citizens, a mail-opening operation, "surreptitious entry" (i.e., break-ins), and surveillance of groups on college campuses. Many of these operations were already taking place without presidential notice or approval.[48] Hoover "adamantly opposed the plan" and, in a savvy bureaucratic move echoing his meetings with Roosevelt before the Second World War, demanded explicit approval of the Huston Plan from the Attorney General or the President.[49] This must have shaken Attorney General John Mitchell, who advised Nixon to withdraw his approval of the plan, which he did only five days after approving it.

Even without presidential approval, the operations outlined in the Huston Plan continued. The leaders of the FBI, CIA, and NSA continued to meet and discuss domestic intelligence operations.[50] Angleton, the head of the CIA's counterintelligence division, must have shocked Congress in the hearings on the Huston Plan when he claimed, "It is inconceivable that a secret intelligence arm of the government has to comply with all the overt orders of the government." He seemed to be under the impression that the USIC had extraconstitutional powers. Only after relentless pressure from the committee did Angleton withdraw his statement.[51] It also did not help that Hersh's article alleged CIA surveillance of an antiwar member of Congress.[52] All of this was ammunition for a searching congressional investigation into the USIC.

J. Edgar Hoover had learned over the course of his long career to avoid both Congress's and the public's crosshairs. He managed to do so one last time by dying in May 1972, just a few weeks before the Watergate break-in and the subsequent congressional reckoning the FBI faced for COINTELPRO. In his place, Charles Brennan, former Assistant Director of the FBI's Domestic Intelligence Division, described the role of the American people in encouraging the very operations they would come to revile. In congressional hearings on the Huston Plan, Brennan conceded that the White House directed the FBI to conduct certain domestic intelligence operations. However, Brennan added, "I think you have to look at the social, political, and economic complexities that were related... and I think that a vast majority of the American people were subjecting the Representatives of Congress and the members of the White House staff and other people in Government to a great deal of pressure, as to why these things [e.g., domestic terrorist attacks, criminal acts, and other dissident activities] were taking place and why something wasn't being done about these, and I think in a broader context, then, the FBI was getting a tremendous amount of pressure from the White House, in response to the overall problem."[53] Brennan's case for collective accountability would not resonate with Congress or the American people.

The "Year of Intelligence"

The United States had unified, albeit temporarily, around the American national security state. By the 1970s, détente reduced American civil society's fear of the Soviet Union, the Cold War consensus was crumbling, and opposition to the American national security state was growing. The entire state of affairs culminated in 1975, known as the "Year of Intelligence." When in the past the President had sensed a coming wave of congressional or public scrutiny, he ordered a presidential commission to investigate the allegations, which had the effect of stifling the opposition and preempting any further action. Just a few short weeks after Hersh's piece, President Gerald Ford tried the same tactic at the urging of his Deputy Chief of Staff, Dick Cheney.[54] In early January 1975, Ford created the Commission on CIA Activities Within the United States, also called the Rockefeller Commission after its chairman, Vice President Nelson Rockefeller. The commission had a mandate to investigate CIA domestic intelligence activities and, even more contentiously, allegations of CIA plots to assassinate foreign leaders.

Taking stock of the current controversy, the Rockefeller Commission scrutinized the CIA according to the terms of the 1947 National Security Act and proposed reforms to ensure that the CIA would not stray from its mandate in the future. The commission then turned to the problem of intelligence oversight. Like the Hoover Commission before it, the Rockefeller Commission recommended the creation of a congressional Joint Committee on Intelligence to assume the oversight role currently held by the Armed Services committees. It also suggested expanding the role of the President's Foreign Intelligence Advisory Board (PFIAB) to officially include CIA oversight.[55] Ford opted to create an Intelligence Oversight Board that was eventually incorporated as a standing committee of the later PIAB. As for CIA plots to assassinate foreign leaders, the White House intervened and suppressed some of the details, "stripping the report of its independent character" and "drain[ing] credibility from the Commission's investigation."[56] But the buzz around CIA assassination schemes remained in the news, and public curiosity was not satisfied.[57] This time, no amount of presidential preemption would work; the congressional accounting would be thorough and the effects lasting.

It began with the Hughes-Ryan Amendment to the Foreign Assistance Act of 1974, which required the President to issue a presidential finding for any approved CIA covert action operation. If Ford had any reservations about the amendment, Hersh's bombshell destroyed his opportunity to veto it. He signed Hughes-Ryan into law on December 30, 1974—a little over a week after Hersh's article was published. The language of the amendment required the finding to be sent "in a timely fashion ... to the appropriate committees of Congress" and specify "a description and scope of [the] operation."[58] The "appropriate committees" referenced in the law "included the Foreign Relations, Armed Services, and Appropriations committees and five subcommittees—a total of 163 senators and congressmen plus top staffers." Already a leaky ship, the CIA stood little chance of preserving secrecy under these reporting requirements, especially not in the politically charged environment of Congress. Senator Harold Hughes, a cosponsor of the amendment, revealed his real reason behind it when he announced, "I would admit that circumstances might develop in which covert action would be justified in time of war. I find it impossible, however, to envisage any circumstances in time of peace that would justify them."[59]

With this landmark legislation, Congress gave itself "an operational role ... in the execution of intelligence activities."[60] Ford later groused that Hughes-Ryan "effectively shut down covert operations anywhere in the world."[61] Henry

Kissinger, serving as both Secretary of State and National Security Advisor, had a personal predilection toward covert action and warned Ford amid the turmoil, "You will end up with a CIA that does only reporting, and not operations." Ford and Kissinger hyperbolized. CIA covert action operations continued even in 1975. So, too, did public scrutiny. Alluding to the "Family Jewels," Kissinger ominously predicted that political "blood will flow."[62]

A Tale of Two Committees

When Arthur Schlesinger published *The Imperial Presidency* in 1973, he noted with alarm that the President had gained power at the expense of Congress during the early Cold War.[63] But Congress was beginning to fight back. It enacted the War Powers Resolution in 1973, restraining the President's war-making power. In 1974, the Hughes-Ryan Amendment struck at presidential deniability over covert action. Then, in 1975 and 1976, Congress intervened directly in covert action by passing the Tunney and Clark Amendments, which cut off US covert support to rebels in Angola.[64] The now centuries-old issue of formal intelligence oversight became a focal point for Congress.

Only a few months after he left the CIA, Allen Dulles gave an interview on CBS News in which he demurred on the question of a congressional intelligence oversight committee. He explained that subcommittees of the congressional appropriations committees went over the entire CIA budget. He also claimed that they were kept informed of even the most sensitive CIA activities, naming the U-2 spy plane—"the most secret thing we had and the best-kept secret"—as one example. He firmly insisted, "We told them everything they wanted to know."[65] Writing amid the growing controversy in 1974, John Maury, the CIA's legislative counsel, recorded that the DCI or deputy director averaged "30 to 35 committee appearances annually" and that the CIA responded to 175 requests from committee members in 1973 alone.[66] But the old model of congressional intelligence oversight had failed to stop intelligence abuses like COINTELPRO, CHAOS, and the Huston Plan. Those programs, along with the intelligence organizations that participated in them, would be the subjects of the most searching congressional investigation in American intelligence history.

In January and February 1975, the Senate and House each created select committees to investigate American intelligence, eventually known as the Church and Pike Committees after their respective chairmen, Senator Frank Church and Representative Otis Pike. The Pike Committee was frustrated from the start. It was originally chaired by Congressman Lucien Nedzi, but the committee quickly succumbed to political squabbles. As the chairman of the Armed Services subcommittee overseeing the CIA, Nedzi had received briefings about some of the CIA's scandals in 1971 and had chosen not to pursue them any further. A few of Nedzi's fellow Democrats on the committee feared that he would use his position to help cover for the CIA. Nedzi resigned as chairman despite an overwhelming bipartisan vote to keep him in that role, and Pike took over.[67]

The committee proved disastrous for predictable reasons: partisanship, leaks, and political grandstanding. If the problem with the Nedzi Committee was fear of a whitewash, the problem with the Pike Committee was that it "was perceived as having made its mind up to secure the dismantling of the agency before it heard the evidence."[68] One representative directly told the chief of the CIA Review Staff, which worked with both the Church and Pike Committees, "You, the CIA, are the enemy."[69] The CIA liaison to the Pike committee recollected that a committee staffer later admitted to him, "We were trying to embarrass you." The animus was mutual.

Colby called Pike a "jackass" and his staff "a ragtag, immature and publicity-seeking group." CIA officers variously dismissed the committee staffers as "a bunch of juveniles, a miserable bunch," or "flower children . . . running barefoot down the halls, literally barefoot, on occasion," and "really irresponsible and goaded by some sort of drive to make trouble, and terribly inexperienced and naïve."[70] Sharing the CIA's sentiments, the Ford administration refused to cooperate with information requests from the Pike Committee. As a result, the Pike Committee report reactively excoriated the CIA and the President. The entire committee succumbed to partisanship, with the Republicans on the committee voting along party lines to withhold the Pike Report. Even the House itself voted against releasing it.[71]

A leak eventually settled the issue. On February 16, 1976, *The Village Voice* published an article titled "The Report on the CIA That President Ford Doesn't Want You to Read" that exposed the contents of the Pike Report.[72] The problems surrounding the Pike Committee and report undermined whatever virtues the report and committee had, including proposals for USIC budget transparency, stricter oversight of covert action, and the establishment of a strong congressional intelligence oversight committee.[73] It was an inauspicious start to a new era of congressional intelligence oversight.

The Church Committee would at least complete its job and release its report to the public. Nonetheless, political undercurrents rippled through the Church Committee hearings. Chairman Frank Church "made no bones about his personal ambition to run as the Democratic presidential candidate . . . and he saw the congressional investigation as a major plank in his campaign."[74] Ambitions aside, Church attempted to conduct a "responsibly nonpartisan" committee investigation.[75]

Republican and Democrat administrations had overseen and approved of controversial intelligence activities, so each political party could not necessarily target the opposing party's President, as had happened during the many debates on the Secret Service Fund in the nineteenth century. Church needed a different target than the presidency, so he opted to blame the CIA. In this, Church chose the wrong target. Although he did not know it, Church himself was a target of the NSA's MINARET program.[76] Regardless, in one of the most famous lines in American intelligence history, Church suggested that the CIA "may have been behaving like a rogue elephant on a rampage."[77] He voiced his skepticism that any former President approved of the CIA's notorious assassination plots. The Church Committee fixated on the assassination issue to the distraction of its staff; Gregory Treverton joked to fellow staffer Loch Johnson that "the only successful CIA assassination plot has been against the Church committee itself."[78]

Testimony during the Church Committee hearings made it clear that even if the vague language of the 1947 National Security Act was indeed authorization for the CIA to conduct covert action operations, the CIA had strayed from the intent of those policymakers who first empowered it. George Kennan voiced alarm at what CIA covert action had become, explaining, "It did not work out at all the way I had conceived it.…We had thought that this would be a facility which could be used when and if an occasion arose when it might be needed," adding that he and others assumed that "there might be years when we wouldn't have to do anything like this."[79] Clark Clifford claimed that American covert action operations "have gotten out of hand." In a double blow to the principle of plausible deniability and American principles, Clifford explained that "knowledge regarding such operations has become so widespread that our country has been accused of being responsible for practically every internal difficulty that has occurred in every country in the world," and, as a result, "our reputation has been damaged and our capacity for ethical and moral world leadership has been impaired."[80] Kennan and Clifford were not the only seasoned officials to voice their regrets at the Church Committee.

A Dispute Between DCIs

DCI William Colby recognized that the Church Committee meant "a change in the relationship between Congress and the CIA on the one hand, and Congress and the President on the other."[81] He recorded that the

> old power structure of the Congress could no longer control their junior colleagues and hold off their curiosity about the secret world of intelligence. In this new era, CIA was going to have to fend for itself without that long-time special Congressional protection....I cannot pretend that I was happy with this exposure. I was perfectly aware of the troubles it would cause....But I must say that, unlike many in the White House and, for that matter, within the intelligence community, I believed that Congress was within its constitutional rights to undertake a long-overdue and thoroughgoing review of the Agency and the intelligence community. I did not share the view that intelligence was solely a function of the Executive Branch and must be protected from Congressional prying.[82]

Colby had a wider audience than Congress in mind. He "went over the heads of the President and Congress and appealed to the majority in the country, presenting himself as a representative American (which he was not) making the same journey as the majority had made" during the Cold War from supporting US government actions to questioning them.[83] In an extraordinary turn for American intelligence, the DCI opted for transparency over secrecy.

In a public hearing, Colby confessed some of the CIA's sins before Congress and the American people while also trying to defend his agency against the "rogue elephant" allegation. He discussed the CIA's research into biological warfare agents using shellfish toxins and cobra venom, explaining that they were studied as an alternative to cyanide for CIA officers to carry on dangerous missions as an alternative to capture, torture, interrogation, and execution. However, he also admitted the program was "for offensive reasons" and presented a poison dart gun to the committee as proof.[84] He asserted that the CIA and its officers had always "felt very much subject to direct presidential control and responsive to it" and that there were "very few cases in which the agency or its employees have done something that they should not have," but even those activities were "approved by the appropriate authorities at that time."[85] In response to Senator Walter Mondale's question concerning intelligence accountability and presidential control, Colby suggested that not only the CIA but also the American intelligence system was about to experience a historic shift. He observed that the Church Committee had uncovered "a cultural pattern of intelligence activities and the traditions, the old traditions of how they were conducted." He accepted that "those are being changed in America," professing, "And I for one am glad they are."[86]

That Colby was the one to admit all this probably surprised everyone. A dedicated Cold Warrior, he had been an OSS Jedburgh in the Second World War, an OPC operative, and a key player in the CIA's ruthless "Phoenix Program" to capture, interrogate, and kill Viet Cong during the Vietnam War.[87] Colby proved just as courageous in steering his own course for the CIA during the Church Committee hearings.

As a result of his actions, Colby made enemies in the executive branch and even the CIA. Henry Kissinger fumed, "What Colby has done is a disgrace."[88] In a conversation with Ford and other senior administration officials, James Schlesinger exclaimed, "Colby is inclined to be too damned cooperative with Congress."[89] Colby encouraged his staff to cooperate as well. He published a long note in the CIA's employee bulletin outlining cooperation between the CIA and the ongoing congressional investigation, even offering that "employees should... feel free" to speak to the congressional investigatory staff "outside of Agency channels if they so desire," although he reminded them that Congress's "field of interest is CIA activities within this country."[90] For his efforts to protect the CIA, some of Colby's colleagues "called him a traitor," while others "hinted that he was a Soviet agent."[91]

Colby also departed from a precedent set by DCI Richard Helms. During his confirmation hearing to be US ambassador to Iran in 1973, Helms denied

FIGURE 17.3 Colby walks into a hearing of the Rockefeller Commission in January 1975. Could the large binder or briefcase include details of the CIA's "Family Jewels"? Courtesy of the Gerald R. Ford Presidential Library.

that the CIA had supported the recent coup in Chile or provided money to Salvador Allende's opponents.[92] Helms recorded that he felt bound by his oath to the CIA, the President's orders, and the lives of his officers and assets when he was cornered by Congress to make a statement on CIA classified operations in what was a public hearing.[93] CIA covert action in Chile had been a closely guarded secret. When President Nixon first ordered the CIA to instigate a military coup in Chile in 1970, he did so "under the injunction not to inform" the State Department, the US Ambassador to Chile, or even the 40 Committee, his administration's version of the Special Group that was designed to shield the President from association with US covert action operations.[94]

Unfortunately for Helms, the Ford administration released information to the Church Committee that proved the CIA had been involved in Chile. Helms later accepted a misdemeanor charge for misleading Congress. He became the scapegoat for an agency that was already the scapegoat for American intelligence activities during the early Cold War.[95] Helms recollected how after his sentencing, he attended a luncheon of retired Agency officers and "every one of the several hundred guests rose and applauded thunderously."[96]

Although both men were old OSS-CIA hands and committed Cold Warriors, Helms and Colby exhibited starkly different visions for the CIA's future relationship with the President, Congress, and the American people. They even brought their feud before Congress. Helms argued that Colby hurt the CIA by turning over its records to congressional investigators—as well as personally damaged him by helping spearhead the investigation into his perjury charge. He believed that the CIA "wasn't established to keep in touch with the public," whereas Colby countered that the "modern American intelligence community simply cannot be treated as a traditional spy service whose very existence was denied by the monarchs it served." Helms then claimed the CIA's mission was to serve "as staff to the president" and "stay out of the limelight and keep quiet." Colby in turn emphasized "the agency needs to do a better job of educating the public [because] an informed public is an essential element of any national policy." In yet another disagreement over the CIA and politicization, Helms stated that the CIA should not divulge information that could be used to oppose the policies of a presidential administration, whereas Colby contended that the CIA must provide information "even if it doesn't support... policy," optimistically presuming that good information will "hopefully... help change the policy."[97]

FIGURE 17.4 Judge Carl McGowan (left) swears in Richard Helms (center) as DCI on June 30, 1966, while President Lyndon Johnson (right) looks on. Helms should have been a little more careful after swearing in for his congressional testimony in 1973. Courtesy of the LBJ Presidential Library.

The Church Committee hearings illustrated one of the major downsides to congressional intelligence oversight. Congress can exploit its subpoena power and hearings to create conflicts between the President and the USIC. The public testimony of intelligence officers and the secret information that surfaces in these investigations can also be used as partisan weapons. This political weaponization of intelligence under the auspices of oversight is a destabilizing factor in US civil-intelligence relations that threatens to cut intelligence loose into the raging waters between the President and Congress.

Helms and Colby struggled to steer the best course they could for themselves and the CIA. But they could not please all and had to choose to accept either the odium of their fellow intelligence officers or that of policymakers and the public. Both men certainly acted pursuant to what they thought was good for the CIA, which felt the wrath of American civil-intelligence relations more than any other organization investigated by the Church Committee.

And that was the paradox of the Year of Intelligence. The CIA had begun the year with a target on its back. Church called the CIA a rogue elephant, but his own committee's investigation proved that the CIA acted at the behest of the President and NSC, and this included MHCHAOS, the assassination plots, and "every major covert action project from Radio Free Europe to the 1975 intervention in Angola."[98] The same Pike Committee staffer who confessed that it was out to embarrass the agency supposedly admitted, "What we found was so different from what we expected."[99] Although Congress scrutinized the President and Intelligence, it was largely to blame for hundreds of years of weak structural design and oversight.

A Question Without an Answer?

As Schlesinger pondered the problems facing the CIA in his memo to Kennedy, he captured the question at the heart of American civil-intelligence relations, musing, "What sort of secret activity is consistent with the preservation of a free social order?" He concluded that "secret activities are permissible so long as they do not corrupt the principles and practices of our society, and that they cease to be permissible when their effect is to corrupt these principles and practices."[100] But Schlesinger had answered his own question without answering how the United States would resolve it. The convulsions of the 1960s and 1970s had made it clear that intelligence had corrupted or at least transgressed American civil society's principles and practices. Congress's response to Schlesinger's question was that it would arbitrate between intelligence activities and American principles, but even this answer would produce more questions.

18

Americanizing Intelligence?

IT WAS THE last NSC meeting of Gerald Ford's presidency. DCI George H. W. Bush credited Ford's Executive Order 11905 with "putting the Intelligence Community within the proper constitutional framework," although the order "has not received the proper credit on the Hill." Secretary of State Henry Kissinger and Bush went on to discuss the effects of the Church Committee on the state of American intelligence. Kissinger found "no degradation in the quality of intelligence analysis" but decided "the opposite is true... in the covert action area," adding that the United States was "unable to do it anymore." Bush agreed, "Henry, you are right. We are both ineffective and scared in the covert action area."[1]

The NSC meeting then turned its wrath on the courts and Justice Department for how they were handling cases involving espionage and leaks. Bush cited the prosecution of Julius and Ethel Rosenberg, who were convicted of espionage in 1951 and executed in 1953 for passing atomic secrets to the Soviet Union, as an example in which "intelligence information was not regarded as admissible evidence."[2] Now, in 1977, Bush worried that the Justice Department and courts were undermining his responsibility as DCI to protect sources and methods. Kissinger exclaimed in frustration, "The Justice Department does not understand that intelligence problems must be treated in a special category." Ford was more reflective and tried to understand the greater historical shift America was experiencing in terms of civil-intelligence relations: "There is really no experience in the past with this kind of problem. What accounts for the change in the situation at this time? Is it the law, the mood in the country?" He captured the collective confusion of the NSC attendees and undoubtedly many of his fellow Americans when he wondered aloud, "How have things changed so much today?"[3]

Both the law and the mood of the country had indeed changed since Ford took over for Nixon amid all the public outrage and suspicion directed at the US government in 1974. Intelligence had become a prominent feature of national controversies, singled out for failures, scandals, and abuses that had their origins in the policies of elected officials, the national mood, and the actions of the USIC in the precarious context of the Cold War. If the intelligence community was doing things that conflicted with American principles, maybe the answer was to make intelligence "more American."

Intended and Unintended Consequences

Before the Church Committee published its final report in April 1976, the Ford administration attempted to head off further congressional intervention. In October 1975, Ford wrote a letter to each member of the committee, urging them not to publish the report on assassination. He warned that the "public release of these official materials and information will do grievous damage to our country."[4] Church responded to this private plea by publicly embarrassing the President in front of the press, exposing Ford's attempt to "keep [the assassination report] concealed from the American people."[5]

Ford also took other measures to try to mollify Congress and the public. He cleaned house in early November 1975 in a reorganization known as the "Halloween Massacre." He replaced Kissinger with Brent Scowcroft as National Security Advisor (Kissinger remained Secretary of State), Schlesinger with Donald Rumsfeld as Secretary of Defense, and Colby with George H. W. Bush as DCI. Next, he issued Executive Order 11905 in February 1976, which would purportedly guide US foreign intelligence activities, but was just as likely an attempt to preempt the impending recommendations of the Church Committee. This executive order created a new Intelligence Oversight Board, replaced the 40 Committee with an Operations Advisory Group, and proposed an American version of the British Official Secrets Act to prevent leaks from the executive branch.[6] Still engaged in the public debate, Colby dismissed the notion of an American secrets act, claiming there was no need for "muzzling our press or frightening our citizens."[7] EO 11905 also contained a clause forbidding employees of the US government from engaging in "political assassination," an ambiguous prohibition depending on one's understanding of the word "political."[8]

Executive action proved to be too little, too late. This time, Congress would not back down from legislative intelligence reform. The Church Committee and Congress greeted Ford's order "as a positive step" but insisted that "legislative remedies would still be required."[9]

"Restoring" Congressional Intelligence Oversight

The Church Committee report offered three central recommendations for intelligence reform: (1) a vast legislative charter to govern all intelligence organizations, (2) restrictions on covert action, and (3) the creation of permanent congressional intelligence oversight committees.[10] The legislative charter was too broad and the restrictions on covert action too narrow, but the creation of intelligence oversight committees seemed just right for Congress. The Senate acted first by establishing the Senate Select Committee on Intelligence (SSCI) in May 1976. The House followed suit with the House Permanent Select Committee on Intelligence (HPSCI) just over a year later in July 1977.

Several senators heralded the new era of congressional intelligence oversight by claiming they were following the path envisioned by the Founders. Senator Charles Mathias declared that "the Senate has a special opportunity to renew the values of those who founded this country" and that the "creation of a new intelligence oversight structure will reaffirm the principles that are at the center of our democracy."[11] Along those lines, Senator Walter Mondale mourned that the country had strayed from "the principles of American Government established 200 years ago," emphasizing that the "one thing above all that the constitutional framers feared was abuse of governmental power and secret police."[12] Joining them, Senator Frank Church intoned, "The cautions expressed by the Founding Fathers and the constitutional checks designed to assure that policymaking not become the province of a few men have been circumvented through the use of secrecy."[13] Of course, policymaking, especially through the vehicle of secret intelligence, had indeed been "the province of a few men" during the Revolutionary War and early American republic. While each of these senators' protestations aligned nicely with the jaundiced view of intelligence traditionally held by many Americans, they lacked historical grounding. The rhetorical appeal to the Founders belied how they had used intelligence, excluded it from the Constitution, and legislated themselves out of oversight with the Secret Service Fund.

The Senate further debated whether congressional oversight would undermine intelligence. Senator Lowell Weicker acknowledged the need for "having an effective CIA and an effective FBI" but argued "there is no reason why in the achieving of that effectiveness, the Constitution has to be left in the dust."[14] Senator Barry Goldwater countered, "Vital to the performance of our intelligence services is a cloak of secrecy."[15] Senator Dick Clark, who authored the amendment designed to end the CIA's covert action program in Angola, declared that Congress "must chart a new course for our intelligence community" and believed that "the right kind of intelligence committee, with the right kind of powers, at least can help chart that course."[16] Aside from getting the country's early history wrong, some of the senators apparently ignored the lessons of recent history as well. For example, Mondale repeated the yarn that "intelligence agencies in the foreign field started wars without our knowledge and without authority . . . decided to assassinate foreign leaders without our knowledge and without our approval—and indeed, in some instances, without the knowledge of some people high in Government." Although he was "willing to grant that the CIA has to operate in secret, that the FBI has to operate in secret," he called this secrecy a "grievous concession for a democracy to make."[17] Exploiting the rhetoric of representative government, Mondale proposed to transfer intelligence powers from the President to Congress, and so give Congress its own "system in secret" to oversee and control intelligence.

Other members of the Senate concurred. Senator Birch Bayh argued that "a permanent oversight committee with legislative authority is an important first step in gaining control of intelligence activities" and predicted the committee would "serve as a watchdog to keep the intelligence agencies in check."[18] Senator Jacob Javits claimed that there was "one fundamental issue before" the Senate: "whether the business of intelligence shall continue to be the exclusive preserve of the executive branch, or whether Congress shall finally also assume its constitutional responsibilities in this field."[19]

While some senators were confident that their reading of American history made the case for congressional oversight, others greeted the new reforms with cautious optimism. Senator Claiborne Pell, who spoke in favor of a strong congressional intelligence oversight committee, mused:

> It seems odd that in our country's history, every 50 years something of this sort arises. We had the Grant scandals of the 1870's, the Teapot Dome scandal of the 1920's, then we had the Watergate and CIA problems in the 1970's. Let us hope that in the 2020's we do not go through the same cycle again.[20]

Congressional oversight was not the panacea the Church-era generation believed it would be, and the United States did not have to wait fifty years for more intelligence scandals.

Crises and Confusion in the Carter Years

From moralizing and handwringing about the excesses of intelligence and especially the CIA at the beginning of his administration to calling upon them at the end of his term, Jimmy Carter epitomized the ambivalent effects of American principles on intelligence and national security. Carter thought he could usher in a new era of goodwill and transparency, not just at home but across the world. Intelligence was one area for reform within Carter's larger messianic agenda.

Part of Carter's campaign for goodwill and intelligence reform involved trying to work more closely with Congress. Perhaps signaling deference to congressional oversight, he abolished the PFIAB in 1977. He credited SSCI in crafting EO 12036, his own signature intelligence reform signed in January 1978. Asserting that "never before in history has an Executive order by the President had so much congressional input," he stated that it would allow a "joint sharing of responsibility" with Congress to ensure intelligence operations would be conducted "in a legal way."[21]

EO 12036 imposed several restrictions on intelligence activities. For example, it prohibited the CIA from engaging in electronic surveillance in the United States and limited USIC electronic surveillance of communications to or from the United States. The order restricted domestic physical searches to the jurisdiction of the FBI and restricted the interception and opening of mail. Carter amended Ford's prohibition on "political assassination" to just "assassination" and curtailed other "Special Activities." Finally, the order stipulated that the DCI and USIC would keep both the House and Senate intelligence committees "fully and currently informed" of intelligence activities, including a requirement to report "in a timely fashion" any operations "that are illegal or improper." Clearly, EO 12036 targeted the abuses investigated by the Church Committee.[22]

While he appeared to capitulate to congressional intervention, Carter confided in his diary, "I finally signed the executive order for the intelligence community. . . . Now we have to constrain the congressional committees from passing an overly restrictive intelligence charter."[23] Apart from verbal overtures of cooperation with Congress and perhaps more subtle attempts to maintain executive discretion, Carter had his own reforms in mind. Although the Church Committee investigation had refuted the "rogue elephant" comparison, the CIA still faced an intelligence skeptic in Carter. He had campaigned on a platform of rectifying what he called "three national disgraces—'Watergate, Vietnam, and the CIA.'"[24] Moreover, his Vice President, Walter Mondale, had been a forceful critic of the CIA on the Church Committee.

Carter immediately erred in replacing Bush as DCI. The long-standing precedent was that the DCI was an apolitical position not subject to the spoils system in which an incoming administration replaces the previous administration's appointments. Carter, who wanted to break from the past,

FIGURE 18.1 Two CIA skeptics: President Jimmy Carter (left) and Senator Frank Church (right). Courtesy of the Jimmy Carter Presidential Library.

set a new precedent in making the DCI a truly political appointee, which risks politicizing the CIA.[25]

Admiral Stansfield Turner, a career Navy man, aspired to be the Chief of Naval Operations but settled for the job of DCI. Turner voiced uncertainty at Carter's suggestion that he would have the authority to run the entire USIC.[26] Nonetheless, Turner accepted a role for which his military career and personality had ill-equipped him.[27] Carter and Turner proceeded to introduce reforms that clashed with the organizational culture of the CIA and the profession of intelligence.

Like Schlesinger, Turner proved to be an unpopular outsider at the insular CIA. He, too, saw technology and TECHINT as the path forward for the USIC even though the CIA was historically and culturally HUMINT-oriented. Part of this was based on his faith in technology as reliable and unbiased, unlike espionage, which Americans had long seen as "inherently dirty, unethical, unreliable, and potentially explosive."[28] In this respect, there was a sense among CIA officers that Turner "brought the President's moralistic sensibilities to Langley with him."[29] Turner instituted personnel cuts at the CIA, specifically targeting its clandestine division. In a second "Halloween Massacre" in 1977, Turner fired over two hundred operations officers as part of a plan to eventually cut over eight hundred positions.[30] CIA officers bristled. A note appeared on a bulletin board at the CIA with a rhyme written to a tune from Gilbert and Sullivan's *HMS Pinafore*: "He'll be the CNO [Chief of Naval Operations] / So thinks he: Thus why give a fig / For the Agency." Turner responded to the resistance within the CIA by calling its leaders "crybabies."[31]

CIA officers sensed that Turner "thought the CIA was like a battleship, with replaceable crew members on call when needed."[32] Perhaps Admiral Turner "assumed that he could bring the CIA, and American intelligence, to the same standard of operational efficiency he had brought the ships under his command."[33] But the CIA was not a battleship and Turner could not run the CIA like he ran a ship. A rumor in the "Washington Whispers" section of *U.S. News & World Report* in April 1978 claimed that Turner found that his personnel cuts "left the agency with too few qualified officers for important overseas posts." As a result, he "backtracked sharply on retrenchment plans that originally called for the dismissal of 820 agents."[34] Even then, he placed more faith in his own analysis and intuition than CIA analysts. With no appreciation for the professional intelligence imperative to remain apolitical, Turner politicized intelligence as his way of cozying up to Carter. Furthermore, instead of coordination, Turner preferred centralization, with information sharing suffering as a result.[35]

Turner did, however, bring to the position his sense of civil-military relations—namely, his fidelity to the chain of command. At his confirmation hearing before SSCI, Senators Charles Mathias and Birch Bayh, both ardent supporters of congressional intelligence oversight, pressed Turner on his responsibilities as DCI vis-à-vis the President and Congress. Turner affirmed to Bayh "that as long as I am employed in the executive branch of the Government, my loyalty is to the President of the United States" and remarked that "if every member of the executive branch who disagreed with the President went to the press or went to the Congress independently, we would have anarchy in the executive branch."[36] To Mathias's similar question, Turner reiterated, "I believe that deliberations on policy decisions within the executive branch are not necessarily suitable for transmittal to the Congress...and that there are some very delicate details of covert intelligence operations which the committee may not want to hear."[37] Turner therefore exposed himself as possessing a rigid "military sense of loyalty to the chain of command" that informed his actions as the DCI.[38]

This deference to the President made Turner an unusual choice for DCI given Carter's purported goal of closer cooperation between the President and Congress. In a 1982 article entitled "Intelligence: The Right Rules" in *Foreign Policy*, Turner bared his views on some of the tensions inherent in congressional intelligence oversight. Among the dangers he highlighted were the security risks posed by leaks and the "impulse of congressional committees to manage rather than just oversee." He also argued that it was "not the job of Congress to dictate how the president should exercise his executive authorities, which include the use of covert action."[39]

As a further paradox, Turner willingly, even eagerly, shared the shortcomings of his own agency with Congress. He believed that congressional oversight would "ensure against our [CIA] becoming separated from the legal and ethical standards of our society."[40] He dutifully rushed to Congress to expose the recent discovery of a few houses in San Francisco and New York where CIA experiments had taken place in the 1950s. He later "excoriated his own agency" before the House for its handling of the alleged KGB defector Yuri Nosenko, whom some CIA officers suspected of being a double agent.[41] Turner also revealed an equivocal, even hypocritical attitude toward secrecy. On the one hand, he disliked the CIA's secrecy, viewing it not only as "irrational" but also as a tool that "cloaked a wide range of unethical activities."[42] Yet, as DCI, he crowed to the National Press Club that "the threat to our country of excesses in intelligence operations is far less today than any time in our history," but "the real danger is that we will be unable to conduct necessary operations because of the risk that they would be disclosed."[43]

A generation earlier, the Doolittle Report had argued that the American people had to accept intelligence activities of precisely the type that they rejected in the 1970s. Turner reached the opposite conclusion. He expounded, "There is one overall test of the ethics of human intelligence activities. That is whether those approving them feel they could defend their actions before the public if the actions became public," a standard referred to as the "*New York Times* test." However, Turner clarified that "this guideline does not say that the overseers should approve actions only if the public would approve them if they knew of them."[44]

For his part, Carter once declared during his election campaign, "The C.I.A. has spied on our own people. The F.B.I. has committed burglaries. . . . This is a time for change in our country. I don't want the people to change. I want the Government to change."[45] Carter and Turner failed to understand, or refused to accept, the prevailing pattern of US civil-intelligence relations: The American people supported aggressive intelligence activities when they felt threatened, only to withdraw that support when they felt safe. Rather than defend intelligence by acquainting the American people with ethically questionable intelligence operations conducted on their behalf, Turner and Carter wanted intelligence to change to align with American principles.

In this regard, their CIA reforms were riding a wave of American public sentiment that was cresting with détente with the Soviet Union. Turner and Carter viewed some of the intelligence activities of the CIA as "Cold War relics," despite the fact that the Cold War was still ongoing.[46] Turner counted the falling dominoes: Cuban mercenaries in Angola in 1977 and 1978 and in Somalia and Ethiopia in 1979; Soviet-backed South Yemen against North Yemen in 1979; and then the dual shocks of the Soviet invasion of Afghanistan and the Iranian Revolution in 1979. Turner conceded that "despite [the administration's] dedication to human rights and its considerable reservations about the morality of covert actions, [it] turned easily and quickly to covert devices to respond to these despotic acts."[47]

Global events forced Carter to embrace covert action. The threat of a resurgent, expansionist Soviet Union prompted Carter to authorize covert action in the form of nonlethal aid to Afghanistan, which quickly became lethal aid following the Soviet invasion in late December 1979.[48] The invasion itself took the Carter administration by surprise, marking yet another intelligence failure. More intelligence failures stacked up against the Carter administration. In November 1979, revolutionaries stormed the US embassy in Tehran, taking more than fifty American citizens hostage. The following April, Carter ordered a rescue attempt that ended tragically when a helicopter collided with a plane on the secret staging airfield in Iran. Rick Hernandez, one of Carter's aides, called a member of the Democratic National Committee in the middle of the night to say, "We just lost the election."[49]

The American people did not forgive Carter for his failure to secure the release of the hostages in Iran, and he paid at the polls. Iran illustrated yet again how an intelligence failure becomes a policy failure and then a political failure. Ironically, a daring CIA covert operation in January 1980 successfully rescued six Americans who had escaped the embassy the day it was captured. However, the Carter administration kept the CIA's role in the rescue secret due to the ongoing hostage crisis at the embassy. This incredible intelligence success story went unheralded, and the Carter administration suffered from the public's perception of constant intelligence—and therefore presidential—failure.

A Magna Carta for American Intelligence?

While Carter and Turner struggled on a quixotic quest to turn American intelligence into something it never was or could be, Congress pressed ahead with its own idealistic agenda for intelligence reform. The new congressional intelligence oversight committees, HPSCI and SSCI, spearheaded legislation that had the ancillary effect of augmenting their control over intelligence vis-à-vis the rest of Congress. Although Congress passed the Foreign Intelligence Surveillance Act of 1978, the Classified Information Procedures Act of 1980, the Intelligence Oversight Act of 1980, the Intelligence Identities Protection Act of 1982, and the CIA Information Act of 1984, among others, it failed to produce the grand charter for American intelligence recommended by the Church Committee.[50]

The National Intelligence Reorganization and Reform Act of 1978 was supposed to be the signature legislation and Magna Carta for American intelligence. The sweeping bill, S. 2525, adopted the Schlesinger Report's idea of a Director of National Intelligence to coordinate the USIC. Like EO 12036, it also sought to restrict or prohibit specific types of intelligence activities. The bill required the President to establish standards for foreign intelligence collection and to submit them to Congress. Additionally, it stipulated that the President must approve every covert action program and that intelligence officers could not adopt religious, academic, or cultural covers, clearly referring to earlier CIA operations. The bill was even more strict with respect to collecting intelligence on American citizens. Above all, Congress would gain oversight power for all national intelligence activities.[51]

Ambition was the enemy of success in the case of S. 2525. The bill never made it through the hearings. The problems with the bill pivoted around the specificity with which it tried to regulate intelligence activities, the bureaucratic processes it imposed on intelligence operations, and the role of Congress in control versus oversight of intelligence activities. It also came at a time when global events made the Carter administration hesitant to agree to congressionally imposed limitations on intelligence operations.[52]

During the hearings, several prominent former officials testified, including Clark Clifford, William Colby, George Bush, and Richard Helms. Clark Clifford was "unalterably opposed to the enumerations of prohibited activities," including assassinations. He called the regulations "demeaning" and questioned whether anyone in the room was "sufficiently prescient to anticipate with any degree of accuracy what the future may demand in this area."[53] By contrast, Colby wholeheartedly endorsed S. 2525 as "a landmark in the history of intelligence," pointing out that "for many years our political leadership, executive, legislative, and even judicial, viewed intelligence as a special world somewhere outside the law," notably supported by "national consensus." Colby believed the bill would finally incorporate intelligence into the Constitution—the glaring structural problem of American civil-intelligence relations. However, he worried about "legalistic challenges" to intelligence activities and intimated that he wanted to keep covert action operations "within the American arsenal." He therefore would rather not have covert action limited by statute.[54]

Bush, who had expressed his frustration with the state of covert action at the end of the Ford administration, conceded that "Congress should be informed, fully informed" of intelligence activities. But he adamantly opposed the idea that "Congress ought to micromanage the intelligence business." He deemed the reporting requirements to Congress too broad and the language on special activities "too confining." Bush stood "opposed to too much regulation, too much reporting, too much restriction."[55] Richard Helms concurred. He also opposed congressional management of the USIC and explained that "flexibility is essential" in intelligence. Besides, he believed the bill would strain rather than "encourage collaboration between the executive and the legislative" branches due to its burdensome reporting requirements. In his view, it had too many definitions and even these definitions were confusing. Finally, Helms, undoubtedly still resentful of his own treatment for attempting to protect sensitive CIA operations in a public hearing, pushed for the DCI to have greater authority to protect sources and methods.[56] The consensus was that S. 2525 would pose a bureaucratic nightmare for intelligence.

Fundamentally, intelligence involves missions beyond the ability of Congress to legislate with sufficient breadth or narrowness to ensure its effectiveness. S. 2525 erred in this respect because it added caveats to clandestine collection activities, contained ambiguous language, and required an arduous process for implementing covert action.[57] Beyond implementation, Congress would have struggled to legislate all the parameters of covert action.[58] The bill also "impose[d] a truly massive reporting requirement on the intelligence community," taking it to extremes. For example, it compelled the proposed Director of National Intelligence to consult with the Secretary of State and advise the congressional intelligence oversight committees of any proposed liaison relationships between the USIC and foreign intelligence agencies, making it unlikely any foreign government would want to work with the United States, especially given the American propensity to leak secrets. In aspiring to account for every past, present, and future intelligence controversy, S. 2525 made it "unlikely that anything vaguely resembling an effective intelligence community [would] be able to survive under its strictures."[59]

All these problems would fall on the proposed DNI to implement. But this role was equally problematic. The officials who testified at the hearings on

S. 2525 equivocated over how the DNI would usurp, replace, or cooperate with the DCI and the CIA more generally. After all, the DCI was originally created to be the President's chief counselor and coordinator of intelligence, making this new role both a derivative of and affront to the current position of the DCI. While ostensibly giving the President more control over intelligence through the position of the DNI, S. 2525 would constrain presidential control through its many restrictions and reporting requirements to Congress. The DCI already faced enough political pressures in trying to satisfy "the interests of the President, who is head of state but also head of a political party; the bureaucratic needs and demands of his own agency, which may or may not coincide with those of the White House; and the competing interests of other intelligence agencies."[60]

Congress could not resolve these issues. In attempting to legislate everything it legislated nothing because S. 2525 never became law. Amid the noise of the debate, commentary, hearings, and reports in Congress, Bush remarked that the intelligence community needed the support of the American people, and he would "like to see a little more rhetoric . . . emphasizing the need for intelligence."[61]

Progressive or Regressive Intelligence Reform?

The judiciary was a noticeably absent branch of government for most of American intelligence history, appearing only intermittently and generally ineffectively.[62] As part of the reaction against the national security state, the Supreme Court received a slew of appeals and reviewed transgressions into the private lives of American citizens in violation of the First Amendment's guarantees relating to speech, association, and conscience and the Fourth Amendment's prohibition against unreasonable searches and seizures.[63] In a landmark decision in 1972, the Supreme Court applied the Fourth Amendment's protections to electronic surveillance and highlighted the problem of surveillance by the executive branch without congressional legislation or judicial review. In acknowledging the distinctions between intelligence and law enforcement, the Court nonetheless found that judicial approval was required for electronic surveillance. Judicial approval meant that courts would play an integral role in this area of intelligence collection, but the question was how.[64]

In one noteworthy development, the Foreign Intelligence Surveillance Act of 1978 (FISA) incorporated all three branches of government.[65] FISA regulates how the USIC conducts foreign intelligence surveillance activities that could impact American citizens.[66] By the time Congress passed the bill, wiretapping had been a much used and abused intelligence collection method for decades. Due to the proliferation of communications technology, wiretapping by intelligence agencies both intentionally and unintentionally captured the conversations and communications of American citizens.[67] FISA was a structural attempt to balance American civil liberties with innovations in communications technology and the operations of the USIC.

FISA created a special warrant process and even a special court called the Foreign Intelligence Surveillance Court (FISC or FISA Court). Briefly, the Attorney General approves FISA warrants, which are then submitted to the FISC.[68] However, the entire process is cloaked in secrecy: Warrants, court hearings, proceedings, and records are classified and closed to the public. The extraordinarily high percentage of FISA warrants approved has led some observers to question the rigor of FISA and dismiss it as a "rubber stamp." FISA proponents argue that it is precisely because the process is so rigorous and the standards so exacting that FISA warrants are typically approved. As another safeguard against abuse, FISA includes provisions that give oversight authorities to HPSCI, SSCI, and both congressional judiciary committees. Yet, the aggregate oversight of the executive, legislative, and judicial branches still would not prevent FISA abuses. The act also added another layer of complexity to the already problematic wall between foreign and domestic intelligence and the boundary between intelligence and law enforcement.

Following the passage of FISA, Congress changed the appropriations structure for intelligence by instituting an annual Intelligence Authorization Act beginning in fiscal year 1979. Previously, the intelligence budget was hidden within the extremely large defense appropriations budget. With a new separate appropriations budget for intelligence, Congress forced the USIC to be more accountable regarding its programs and operations.[69] Moreover, the act gave Congress a tool to implement further reforms through its power of the purse using future Intelligence Authorization Acts.

Next, Congress revisited S. 2525 as S. 2284, the National Intelligence Act of 1980. This time, Senator Henry "Scoop" Jackson, a Cold War hawk, advised Congress, "I do not think we can account for... all the things that I see that could happen down the road.... My inclination is to avoid writing a charter, a book on this subject, with all of the trouble it can portend for the future."[70] When the hearings for S. 2284 began in February 1980, the United States was still reeling from the events of the Iranian Revolution and the Soviet invasion of Afghanistan. Senator Richard Lugar acknowledged the challenge that national security exigencies imposed on congressional intelligence reform, observing that "the pendulum has been swinging" and recent events meant that "the President of the United States... is [now] desirous of having a very strong intelligence capability and of using it."[71]

Indeed, the pendulum had swung from liberty in the early to mid-1970s to security by the end of the decade. Although Congress's mission to reform American intelligence through a grand charter seemed appropriate and even necessary in the wake of the Church Committee hearings, within just a few years global events reminded both policymakers and the public that the world does not always comport with American ideals. Congress thought it could rationally dictate US intelligence operations line by line. Suddenly, the chaos of the world made Carter and members of Congress question their own wisdom, even values. The tone of the debate shifted from protecting the rights of American citizens to protecting intelligence.

In his 1980 State of the Union Address, Carter called for a new intelligence charter that would "remove unwarranted restraints." Senator Daniel Patrick Moynihan introduced S. 2216 the next day, exclaiming, "It is the K.G.B., not the C.I.A., which threatens democracy." An article in *The Nation* announced "The Agency's Bill" with the subheading "Moynihan Unleashes the C.I.A."[72] S. 2216 proposed repealing the Hughes-Ryan Amendment, revising FOIA to offer the USIC more protection, and imposing criminal penalties on those, including journalists, who outed intelligence officers. In S. 2216, Moynihan offered up "a veritable laundry list of the C.I.A.'s fondest desires."[73] He also opposed S. 2284, the National Intelligence Act of 1980, claiming it was "172 pages of 'don'ts.'" He explained that intelligence was by its nature a "risk-taking enterprise" and worried that S. 2284 would make the USIC "cease to take risks," surely an outcome "that we do not want."[74] In congressional testimony equally representative of the shifting temperament of the times, DCI Turner voiced his preference for Moynihan's bill over S. 2284. Expressing his desire for the "CIA's wish list," he asked the Senate for "relief from the Hughes-Ryan amendment, from the more onerous provisions of the Freedom of Information Act, and for legislation to deal with instances of the revelation of the identities of our personnel."[75] Each of these three prongs of Moynihan's bill became successive pieces of legislation.

As part of this process, S. 2284 metamorphosized from the National Intelligence Act of 1980 to the Intelligence Oversight Act of 1980. Instead of a grand charter to oversee all American intelligence activities, Congress focused on specific aspects of oversight. Like other congressional debates on intelligence, some of the substance was both retrospective and historically underinformed at the same time. For example, Senator Bayh speculated that

FIGURE 18.2 Senator Daniel Patrick Moynihan, who was for the CIA before he was against it. Library of Congress.

had there been an oversight committee since 1947, "some ill-advised programs might have been averted and damage to the United States prevented."[76] But there had been earlier congressional oversight, albeit less fastidious, and the Cold War consensus suggests that the same covert action operations would have been approved. Senator Lugar perceptively alluded to several themes of civil-intelligence relations in weighing congressional intelligence oversight, including the challenge of balancing an effective intelligence establishment with civil liberties, the influence of the prevailing threat environment, and the separation of powers. He explained that there was a "fine line between the desirability of having first-class intelligence capability in this country and the issue of civil rights." Although Americans previously wanted to constrain the intelligence establishment in the early and mid-1970s, he, like his fellow Americans, now wondered how the United States would respond to events involving the Soviet Union, Iran, and Afghanistan, among others. Furthermore, Lugar determined that the proposed oversight bill would put President Carter "between a rock and a hard place," anticipating that "if things really get tough, he's going to have to do some things, and then he's going to have the committee nitpicking back."[77]

Carter had already taken some covert measures, which SSCI knew about from the presidential finding he had signed in December 1979 authorizing the provision of lethal aid and training to the mujahideen fighting the Soviets in Afghanistan.[78] But the creation of HPSCI and SSCI had increased the number of committees to which the President had to report covert action programs to eight under the Hughes-Ryan amendment.[79] The Intelligence Oversight Act of 1980 acknowledged the danger of overreporting such sensitive operations to too many congressional committees. As a result, the bill only required the President to report them to HPSCI and SSCI. The act also gave the President an escape clause in exigent circumstances, allowing for a belated finding or limited notification to the "Gang of Eight," composed of the Speaker and minority leader of the House, the majority and minority leaders of the Senate, and the chairs and ranking members of HPSCI and SSCI.

The Intelligence Oversight Act of 1980 was a milestone in American intelligence history because it established congressional intelligence oversight through formal legislation. DCI Turner noted that this type of oversight system was unprecedented in the world's representative democracies: Not even the UK's Parliament received the type of intelligence briefings that the congressional intelligence committees did.[80] Congress followed this achievement by taking up the other two prongs of Moynihan's bill. But, in choosing between transparency and secrecy while in the grip of renewed global threats, Congress chose secrecy.

The exposure of intelligence abuses in the 1960s and 1970s were not simply sterilized stories about the CIA or USIC. They contained the names and identities of professional intelligence officers. For example, Philip Agee published *Inside the Company: A CIA Diary* (1975) after resigning from his position to protest the CIA's covert operations and support for authoritarian regimes.[81] He included the names of CIA officers, assets, and front organizations in several countries in Latin America in the book, blowing their cover. Not only were Agee and others like him jeopardizing national security by exposing and ruining intelligence operations, they were also risking the lives of intelligence officers and their families. Sadly, Richard Welch, the CIA chief of station in Athens, Greece, was assassinated in December 1975 after a few different periodicals and books, including *Inside the Company*, outed him, although there is some debate over whether they bore responsibility for his death.

To its credit, Congress recognized the danger that intelligence officers faced. In 1982, it passed the Intelligence Identities Protection Act. In promulgating the law, Congress weighed the First Amendment right to criticize government policies, operations, or organizations against exposing individual intelligence officers or agents and their families to danger.

Having protected the "sources" side of intelligence "sources and methods," Congress next turned its attention to the question of "methods." The final leg of Moynihan's bill addressed the threat that FOIA posed to intelligence operations. Congress had to balance transparency and operational effectiveness. The CIA Information Act of 1984 exempted "operational files," so designated by the DCI, from FOIA disclosure requirements. The ACLU submitted an especially strident defense of FOIA, pointing out that only through this act did the public truly learn the extent of the Bay of Pigs, mind-control experiments, and CIA spying on Americans. It described FOIA as a form of public accountability, insisting that "congressional oversight is no substitute for it but should be in addition to it."[82] The ACLU worried that the proposed legislation would exempt the CIA from FOIA.

A CIA memorandum in 1978 reveals that the CIA itself had grappled with FOIA. It was concerned that the act allowed "bits and pieces of information" to reach the public, giving the American people an incomplete picture of events that tarnished its image.[83] The memorandum implied that the options were either total transparency or total secrecy. Through the CIA Information Act, Congress gave the CIA a great deal of latitude in deciding what to keep secret. It later extended this same latitude to other USIC organizations like the NSA and NRO.[84] Although Congress had made transparency its watchword in the mid-1970s, by the mid-1980s secrecy again dominated.

A New Beginning for an Old Problem

Rather than restoring any established historical or constitutional role, Congress finally, formally asserted its claim to intelligence oversight just in time for the country's bicentennial. Following the creation of the permanent intelligence oversight committees, it aimed to cement its role in intelligence through legislation. While it failed to produce a grand charter, Congress still passed successive pieces of legislation that gave it considerably more control. However, congressional intelligence reform in the United States suffers from several grave flaws.

Congressional reform often takes place only in the wake of a perceived intelligence failure, scandal, or abuse, regardless of whether the facts of the case merit broad reform. Thus, reform is contingent on perceptions shaped in response to a crisis rather than as part of a thoughtful and considered process. Congressional legislation is also the product of bargaining among competing political, bureaucratic, and social interests whose power varies. Further reform frequently fails to happen, since busy members of Congress rarely have the time and energy to revisit an issue. This, in turn, means that obsolescent reforms remain in place long past their expiration date. Finally, intelligence reform may only address a particular context and moment in time, leaving the USIC, like the US military, to "fight the last war."

The structural reforms of the late 1970s and early 1980s were the products of a specific time and place. Their actual efficacy and consequences can only be judged by how later events unfolded. Still, they reflected a more assertive Congress than at any other point in American history.

19

The Executive Strikes Back

GLOBAL EVENTS HAD forced Carter to loosen the reins on the CIA despite the rhetoric of his presidential campaign, but his covert campaign failed to achieve any overt outcomes that could secure him a second term. His successor, Ronald Reagan, knew that the Cold War would continue until the Soviet Union—the "Evil Empire"—fell. He made intelligence a pillar in his grand design to win the Cold War. To achieve victory in that war, Reagan was willing to go to war with Congress.

The intelligence activities that took place during the Reagan administration produced the same types of controversies that congressional intelligence oversight was supposed to have resolved. However, the last decade of the Cold War also demonstrated the constraints that the American people can impose on US national security and statecraft. Ongoing covert action operations that were presumably supposed to be secret became the topic of national debate, as the American people supported intelligence activities in some places but not others. While public opinion can be an inconsistent bellwether to guide intelligence policy, it was nonetheless an influential feature of US civil-intelligence relations during the Reagan years.

Unleashing the CIA

Reagan's first dalliance with intelligence was in the early 1950s as part of the "Crusade for Freedom" fundraising campaign for Radio Free Europe, one of the CIA's key propaganda programs in the cultural Cold War. He later gained an inside look at the CIA as a member of the Rockefeller Commission. In comparison to that executive branch commission, Reagan believed that the Church and Pike Committees' investigations were unnecessary and even dangerous as they risked exposing too many national security secrets. He would bring this skepticism of congressional intelligence oversight to the presidency.[1]

Reagan also made intelligence a pillar of his presidential campaign. It was a consistent talking point in his radio commentaries from 1975 to 1979.[2] There was a full section on intelligence in the Republican Party platform of 1980, which vowed to reestablish the PFIAB; introduce legislation to safeguard the secrecy surrounding intelligence officers (the Intelligence Identities Protection Act of 1982) and CIA operations (the CIA Information Act of 1984); and intensify efforts across all of intelligence's core missions, including covert action.[3] Reagan would deliver on each of these campaign promises. On the campaign trail itself, Reagan claimed that "the Ford and Carter executive orders, undue criticism from the public and media, and excessive congressional oversight had hobbled intelligence capabilities."[4] Key members of his team had strong intelligence backgrounds, including his running mate for Vice President, former DCI George H. W. Bush, and his campaign manager, OSS veteran William Casey. Mixing intelligence and politics so closely ran the risk of politicization, which marred Reagan's candidacy from the outset.

For example, an article in the *New York Times* accused the Reagan campaign of using former CIA officers to gather intelligence on the Carter campaign, including its strategy for the televised presidential debates.[5] *Time* magazine reported that Casey "set up a political intelligence-gathering apparatus for the campaign" and "recruited former CIA and FBI agents to gather political information from their colleagues still in active service."[6] Other reports alleged that the Reagan campaign had "moles" in the NSC and CIA who fed Casey information.[7] For his part, Casey "used the term 'intelligence operation' to describe the monitory activity the [Reagan] campaign" was conducting.[8] Rumors also emerged that the Reagan team conducted secret negotiations with the Iranians to prevent the Carter administration from securing the release of the American hostages in Tehran as an "October surprise" ahead of the 1980 presidential election. In exchange, the American intermediaries promised to supply Iran with weapons when Reagan became President. A congressional investigation in 1992 cleared Reagan and his campaign, but former Texas lieutenant governor Ben Barnes revealed in March 2023 that he was a witness to these negotiations as part of the October surprise conspiracy.[9]

Casey aspired to be Reagan's Secretary of State but agreed to be DCI on the condition that "he could have a hand in shaping foreign policy rather than simply reporting the data on which it was based."[10] If Casey wanted to try his hand at policymaking as DCI, then he needed a more aggressive CIA to serve as a policymaking instrument. He did not need to convince Reagan. Just like Carter and Turner, Reagan found a kindred ideological spirit in Casey, who believed "that Communism was the Antichrist," a sentiment with which

FIGURE 19.1 Political or intelligence advice? Casey and Reagan huddle in the Oval Office in January 1983. Courtesy of the Ronald Reagan Presidential Library.

Reagan certainly agreed.[11] The two also remained politically bound, with Casey offering political as well as intelligence advice to the President as DCI.[12]

As an intelligence insider, Casey was a natural choice to reverse Turner's reforms. Turner, the outsider, had demoralized the CIA and himself in the process, according to Casey, who claimed that Turner "radiated defeat" at a meeting in the handover as DCI.[13] Casey radiated confidence when he told SSCI in his confirmation hearing that he would restore morale at the CIA. During the hearing, Casey had to address "one of the buzz phrases" making its way around Washington: "It's time to unleash the CIA."[14] While Casey denied using the phrase himself, he described it as "ways to ease restrictions, to make them perhaps less cumbersome without infringing in any[ ]way on the rights that belong to American citizens." He also stated that he would "want to review the Executive order," meaning Carter's 12036, that had so encumbered the CIA.[15]

In December 1981, Reagan signed EO 12333 to supersede Carter's order. It eliminated many restrictions but preserved a few limitations on intelligence activities, including undisclosed participation in domestic civic groups, human experimentation, and assassination. The order alluded to earlier intelligence scandals by insisting that the USIC had to use the "least intrusive collection techniques feasible within the United States or directed against United States persons abroad," with respect to unconsented physical searches, interference with mail, and other types of electronic and physical surveillance.[16] The changes in EO 12333 affected congressional intelligence oversight, most notably by eliminating the language about the USIC keeping HPSCI and SSCI "fully and currently informed concerning intelligence activities."[17] Turner publicly criticized the Reagan administration for its policy changes based on the "attitude . . . that congressional oversight hobbles intelligence," which was precisely Reagan's perception and motivation for implementing reforms.[18]

EO 12333 also changed the existing reporting requirements for covert action, which became a central battleground between the President and Congress during the Reagan administration. The purpose behind it was "to preclude the need for new legislation" but, being an executive order, it "presented an opportunity for abuse."[19] True to his campaign word, Reagan reestablished the PFIAB to be briefed on intelligence activities, so executive oversight once again competed with congressional oversight. Indeed, the new congressional intelligence oversight system was about to face its first real test. Reagan, who was determined to confront the Soviet Union in every arena, was more than willing to fight the shadow Cold War by unleashing the CIA and the broader USIC—with or without the approval of Congress.

The Origins of the Iran-Contra Scandal

During the Carter administration, a strategic shift took place in Nicaragua from the pro-US Somoza regime to the pro-socialist Sandinista regime. Carter wanted to negotiate a peaceful transition to replace the oppressive Somoza regime, which had been fighting an insurgency by the leftist Sandinistas. When President Anastasio Somoza rebuffed Carter's overtures, the United States withdrew military aid and assistance. However, Carter did sign off on a CIA covert action operation to support pro-democratic forces in Nicaragua against a Sandinista takeover.[20] Meanwhile, Cuban military assistance to the Sandinistas continued. Somoza resigned in 1979 and sought refuge in the United States. The Carter administration refused Somoza's request for permanent asylum, and Somoza settled in Paraguay, where he was assassinated by Sandinistas in 1980. Francisco Urcuyo, Somoza's successor, was in power for only one day before a Sandinista-led junta took control. Cuban and Soviet aid flowed into Nicaragua as the Sandinistas now fended off an insurgency by the right-wing Contras.

With Cuban support, the Sandinista regime began intervening in neighboring El Salvador, which had also been embroiled in a civil war that pitted forces from the right and left against each other. Curiously, Carter provided military support to the pro-US junta in El Salvador despite denying the same support to the Somoza regime. One of the last acts of the Carter administration was to send even more military supplies to El Salvador despite a temporary suspension of aid after the rape and murder of four American Catholic missionaries by members of the Salvadoran National Guard.[21]

Central America teetered on the brink of communist-orchestrated chaos, "boiling like a cauldron," as Soviet Foreign Minister Andrei Gromyko observed. In a national address, Reagan told the American people that he refused to "send an unmistakable signal that the greatest power in the world is unwilling and incapable of stopping Communist aggression in our own backyard."[22] In March 1981, he directed the CIA to "provide all forms of training, equipment and related assistance to cooperating governments throughout Central America in order to counter foreign-sponsored subversion and terrorism."[23] He followed that in December by authorizing the "support and conduct" of "paramilitary operations" in Nicaragua.[24]

Reagan did not limit covert action only to America's backyard. In 1981, he reauthorized Carter's finding to provide weapons to the mujahideen fighting the Soviets in Afghanistan.[25] His administration created or expanded covert action programs in Libya, Angola, Chad, Ethiopia, Liberia, and Cambodia, among others.[26] The combination of escalating covert action operations by the President and more searching scrutiny by Congress led to the resumption of open conflict between the two.

Nicaragua exposed the interbranch sparring over the CIA, covert action, and US foreign policy. The Reagan administration publicly defended US intervention in Nicaragua as an attempt to prevent it from subverting El Salvador and destabilizing the region. But support for the Contras, who aimed to overthrow the Sandinistas, caused some in Congress to wonder if regime change was the real goal. While many members of Congress were sympathetic to Reagan's overall policy of preventing the spread of communism in the Western Hemisphere, congressional opposition to the administration's Nicaragua policy, specifically, resulted in a series of legislative bills known collectively as the Boland Amendments.[27] The first Boland Amendment, attached to the defense appropriations bill for FY 1983, explicitly prohibited the use of funds by the CIA or DOD "for the purpose of overthrowing the Government of Nicaragua."[28] But Congress was inconsistent in trying to balance law and policy because it "had not cut Contra funding; it merely had legislated an impermissible purpose."[29] Policy ambiguity that turned into legislative ambiguity enabled the Reagan administration to circumvent Congress.

The House next introduced a resolution requiring the Reagan administration to disclose information about its activities in Honduras and Nicaragua to Congress.[30] David S. Addington, an attorney in the CIA's Legislation Division, reached back to the Polk administration's refusal to provide Congress with a detailed accounting of the Secret Service Fund and observed that both the President and House "have ample weapons in their legal arsenals" to wage war with each other. Addington bluntly concluded his brief with "*Pragmatic Legal Advice: Compromise*."[31] Neither Reagan nor Congress would compromise.

In September 1983, Reagan signed another finding to support the Contras.[32] Since this one recognized that Congress would not allow US citizens to conduct paramilitary operations in Nicaragua, the Reagan administration decided to work through foreign proxies. Administration officials duly briefed HPSCI and SSCI, and both duly voted to continue covert aid to Nicaragua. But a schism developed in Congress as the House voted to cease all funding for paramilitary groups fighting the Nicaraguan government and the Senate wanted to continue the program. They managed to reach a compromise by passing another Boland Amendment in December 1983 that established a cap of $24 million for Contra funding.[33]

The Reagan administration must have realized that it was operating on a condensed timeline, so it decided to pursue more aggressive operations, including support for attacks by aircraft and speedboats and, even more controversially, an operation to mine Nicaraguan ports.[34] Both HPSCI and SSCI were informed of the mining operation.[35] But, following explosive headlines after several ships hit mines, members of Congress "acted as if they were hearing about it for the first time."[36] Senator Barry Goldwater, chairman of SSCI, claimed that his committee had been deceived by the administration.[37]

The Reagan administration and SSCI ultimately reached an agreement called the Casey Accords in June 1984. Senators Barry Goldwater and Daniel Patrick Moynihan signed a written agreement with Casey requiring the CIA to adhere to more stringent congressional reporting requirements.[38] They must have known that they were taking a risk given that "Casey's frequent appearances [before Congress] often deteriorate[d] into angry exchanges with lawmakers" and he had a well-known "affinity for covert operations," according to an April 1984 biographical sketch of Casey in the *New York Times*.[39] Moreover, Casey was hardly one for formality and procedure. For example, after finding a 130-page book of guidelines for covert operations at the CIA, Casey fumed, "You practically have to take a lawyer with you on a mission. I'm throwing this thing out."[40] The Casey Accords were evidence that existing congressional legislation did not sufficiently address presidential reporting requirements for covert action.

In January 1985, Reagan signed National Security Decision Directive (NSDD) 159, which outlined the process for formulating covert action within the executive branch and included provisions for congressional notification. The directive also required the President to approve covert action findings in writing.[41] Nonetheless, the Reagan administration continued to sidestep congressional intelligence oversight, suggesting that covert action reporting requirements were worth only as much as the paper on which they were printed.

As public and congressional approval of the Reagan administration's support to the Contras collapsed, Congress prepared yet another Boland Amendment to try to end US covert action in Nicaragua once and for all. This time, Congress legislated,

> During fiscal year 1985, no funds available to the Central Intelligence Agency, the Department of Defense, or any other agency or entity of the United States involved in intelligence activities may be obligated or expended for the purpose or which would have the effect of supporting, directly or indirectly, military or paramilitary operations in Nicaragua by any nation, group, organization, movement, or individual.[42]

Although this language seemed airtight, the Reagan administration creatively interpreted it to mean that the legislation did not apply to the NSC. National Security Advisor Vice Admiral John Poindexter and NSC staff member Lieutenant Colonel Oliver North developed a program to continue sustaining the Contras by sending that support through another country. Moreover, while the DOD and CIA could not provide intelligence directly to the Contras, the amendment did not explicitly reference the NSC, which simply passed along DOD and CIA intelligence. The following year, Congress voted to provide humanitarian aid to the Contras but included the Pell Amendment, which attempted to prevent the administration from any continued military support of the Contras through third-party states. Subsequent bills for 1986 and 1987 provided for nonmilitary support and allowed the USIC to share information with the Contras.[43]

It was truly a head-spinning display of strokes and counterstrokes by the executive and legislative branches. The Reagan administration was determined to steer its own course in Nicaragua despite the disapproval of Congress. Congress was not simply withholding appropriations to influence presidential policies but instead attempting to condition the use of funds already appropriated and therefore interfere in presidential policy—perhaps against Supreme Court and other judicial precedents.[44] When Congress legislated the United States out of covert action in Nicaragua, the Reagan administration improvised. The result of this was the Iran-Contra scandal. The NSC created a covert action program that sold US arms to Iran as a way to both fund the Contras and secure the release of American hostages held in Lebanon. Deliberately dodging congressional intelligence oversight, Reagan signed a presidential finding in January 1986 that contained the provision "I determine it is essential to limit prior notice, and direct the Director of Central Intelligence to refrain from reporting this Finding to the Congress... until I otherwise direct."[45] Like so many other covert action programs, the Iran-Contra arrangement was exposed by a leak. When the details emerged in November 1986, the brewing competition between the President and Congress finally boiled over.

More Politics and Politicization

The first and historically logical step was for Reagan to head off a congressional investigation with a presidential commission, which he did in December. The Tower Commission hastily submitted its report at the end of February 1987. By its own admission, the commission was not convened to assign "individual culpability" for Iran-Contra; instead, it had the vague mandate to investigate the NSC as an institution, using Iran-Contra "as a principal case study." The Tower Commission determined that the decision-making process for Iran-Contra had been "flawed," but few officials in the executive branch had any real input due to the secrecy of the program. The report faulted Reagan for signing the January 1986 finding that directed the DCI not to report the program to Congress, also noting that the administration had paid little attention to the "significant questions of law" involved. It concluded that Iran-Contra was "directly at odds with important and well-publicized policies of the Executive Branch," and "the United States never should have been a party to the arms transfers."[46]

The Tower Commission placed some of the blame on Casey for not addressing the problems with the program with Reagan.[47] By this point, Casey, who was called the "father" of the Contras, had already resigned as DCI following his diagnosis of brain cancer. He passed away a short time later, in May 1987. While Casey's death made him a convenient scapegoat for Iran-Contra, his family did nothing to dispel rumors by requesting that "in lieu of flowers, donations...be made to the William J. Casey Fund for the Nicaraguan Freedom Fighters."[48]

Overall, the Tower Commission identified the flaws in the control and oversight of the American intelligence system that had developed out of presidential and congressional competition.[49] Whether intentionally or not, the report contributed to the myth of a rogue intelligence establishment. Reagan did the USIC no favors in a nationally televised address on March 4, 1987. While Reagan admitted that he had approved of the Iran-Contra program, he claimed that he could not remember whether it was before or after the fact. Although he accepted "full responsibility," he claimed to be "angry...about activities undertaken without [his] knowledge" and expressed disappointment "in some who served [him]." Extraordinarily, Reagan voiced his determination "to make the congressional oversight process work," stating that "proper procedures for consultation with the Congress will be followed, not only in letter but in spirit."[50]

Reagan's presidency to date suggested that he intended to follow congressional procedures in neither letter nor spirit. But the Tower Commission also blamed Congress for the scandal, implying that leaks and other security issues explained why the President avoided congressional reporting requirements. The report therefore proposed replacing HPSCI and SSCI with a joint intelligence oversight committee supported by a restricted staff to avoid leaks.[51] The Tower Commission's findings and recommendations did not sit well with Congress, which launched its own investigation into Iran-Contra.

The congressional investigation was politicized from start to finish, and it resulted in majority and minority reports. The majority report identified the "common ingredients of the Iran and Contra policies" as being ones of "secrecy, deception, and disdain for the law." However, the majority report blamed a "small group of senior officials" who "testified that they even withheld key facts from the President."[52] For example, the National Security Advisor "justified his decision not to inform the President...on the ground that he wanted to give the President 'deniability'...and to shield the President from political embarrassment if the [operation] became public." Thus, "deniability replaced accountability." The report then tackled the issue of plausible deniability. As "an accepted concept in intelligence activities," plausible deniability was designed to conceal the role of the United States in a covert action operation, but it did not mean "structuring an operation so that it may be concealed from—or denied to—the highest elected officials of the United States Government itself."[53]

During the congressional investigation, principles of secrecy and plausible deniability ran up against transparency and accountability in the testimony of intelligence and national security officials involved in Iran-Contra. Clair George, the CIA Deputy Director for Operations, professed, "To think that because we deal in lies . . . that therefore that gives you some permission, some right or some particular reason to operate that way with your fellow employees, I would not only disagree with that I would say it would be the destruction of a secret service in a democracy."[54] George's sense of transparency apparently had limits because he was one of several Iran-Contra officials indicted for committing perjury or withholding evidence in Congress. Others included Poindexter, North, Secretary of Defense Caspar Weinberger, former National Security Advisor Robert "Bud" McFarlane, and CIA operations officer Duane "Dewey" Clarridge. President George H. W. Bush later pardoned everyone save North and Poindexter, although those two had their convictions overturned in court.

Casey took part in the investigation before his death and did his best to protect the image of the CIA. He explained in his testimony to SSCI that his agency only played a "support role," adding, "We were not the architects and we did not provide direction." Handwritten on the draft testimony was his observation, "I can't say CIA wouldn't have handled things differently if this had been a CIA operation. Certainly CIA keeps a closer watch on how its agents and programs are run than was done here," although Casey also admitted, "Even we got a little sloppy in providing support." To further clarify the CIA's role in Iran-Contra, another handwritten revision read, "I simply want to repeat, that this was not a CIA operation. We had a limited role, and we were not in a position to demand [any] details or spy on the NSC to find out." Casey concluded his testimony to Congress by emphasizing that he was "deeply concerned about . . . the CIA's credibility," so he had ample reason to disavow the scandal.[55]

On the paramount question of presidential involvement in the scandal, the majority report accepted Reagan's assertions that he did not know of the diversion of funds to the Contras. By their own admission, Poindexter and North claimed that they did not inform the President of their decisions. Still, the report decided that "ultimate responsibility for the events in the Iran-Contra Affair must rest with the President."[56] The report somewhat paradoxically blamed national security officials for acting independently of presidential control while also faulting the President for not exercising sufficient control.

A subsequent seven-year investigation by independent counsel Lawrence Walsh later determined that all the individuals involved in Iran-Contra

CENTRAL INTELLIGENCE AGENCY

CREDO

We are the Central Intelligence Agency.

We produce timely and high quality intelligence for the President and Government of the United States.

We provide objective and unbiased evaluations and are always open to new perceptions and ready to challenge conventional wisdom.

We perform special intelligence tasks at the request of the President.

We conduct our activities and ourselves according to the highest standards of integrity, morality and honor and according to the spirit and letter of the law.

We measure our success by our contribution to the protection and enhancement of American values, security and national interest.

We believe our people are the Agency's most important resource. We *seek* the best and work to *make them* better. We subordinate our desire for public recognition to the need for confidentiality. We strive for continuing professional improvement. We give unfailing loyalty to each other and to our common purpose.

We look to our leaders to stimulate initiative, a commitment to excellence, and a propensity for action; to reward and protect us in a manner which reflects the special nature of our responsibility, our contribution, and our sacrifices; and to promote among us a sense of mutual trust and shared responsibility.

We derive our inspiration and commitment to excellence from the inscription in our foyer: "And Ye shall know the truth and the truth shall make you free."

FIGURE 19.2 The CIA Credo was approved by Casey in 1984 to restore morale at an agency that had been under siege for the past decade. Walter L. Pforzheimer Papers, Beinecke Rare Book and Manuscript Library, Yale University.

"skirted the law, some of them broke the law, and almost all of them tried to cover up the President's willful activities."[57] The Walsh report concluded that Reagan, Bush, Weinberger, Casey, McFarlane, Poindexter, and Secretary of State George Shultz knew about the sale of weapons to Iran and that many administration officials deliberately deceived Congress. But it stipulated that there was no evidence that Reagan violated any criminal statute, nor could it prove that he knew of the diversion of funds from the Iran deal to the

Contras. Regardless, Walsh blamed Reagan for creating the conditions that encouraged others to circumvent the law, including congressional reporting requirements for covert action.[58]

The minority report highlighted the meddlesome role that Congress had played in the events of Iran-Contra. It reached back to historical debates and the constitutional separation of powers between the President and Congress, noting the "ongoing state of political guerrilla warfare over foreign policy between the legislative and executive branches." Furthermore, the report attributed executive branch secrecy to the "history and legitimate fear of leaks" from Congress.[59] During the Carter administration, the new congressional intelligence committees at least attempted to strike a bipartisan tone. During the Reagan administration, they became more adversarial in terms of both the relationship between the President and Congress and the atmosphere of partisan politics in Congress itself.[60]

Lee Hamilton, the chairman of HPSCI, wrote an op-ed in the *Washington Post* criticizing the Reagan administration for its covert action policies. He observed that,

> at present, the Intelligence committees can only sit and listen as the administration outlines a finding and initiates a program. They are unable to block the initiation of a program, and are able to shape policy only to the extent the president accepts their advice.... The policy process is not working well when the Congress can only attempt to block wayward covert actions after the fact, after U.S. prestige and people's lives have already been committed.[61]

Hamilton was making the case for enhancing the powers of the congressional intelligence oversight committees to include veto power over covert action programs. While criticizing covert action operations in Nicaragua and Angola, he notably omitted any mention of CIA operations in Afghanistan, an instance in which Congress stood behind presidential policy. He also ignored implicit congressional approval for covert action operations through appropriating funds for them.

Congress adopted an alternative approach to undermining presidential control over intelligence. Members of the intelligence committees or other members of Congress who gain access to secrets can use leaks to "veto or cripple a policy that a determined minority could not defeat through the formal processes of government."[62] Representative Leo Ryan credited leaks as "an important tool in checking the 'secret government.'"[63] Senator Joe Biden "twice threatened to go public with covert action plans by the Reagan administration that [he thought] were harebrained."[64] Leaks are a potent form of intelligence politicization. They have the effect of holding executive branch intelligence operations hostage to the subjective judgments of individual members of Congress. At the same time, the executive branch will often tactically use leaks to shore up public support for certain policies. Leaks are yet another manifestation of the competition for intelligence control between the President and Congress as well as the politicization of intelligence in American opposition politics.

The congressional intelligence committees were not exactly transparent themselves when they publicly criticized the USIC for lack of transparency. They were briefed on CIA operations during the Reagan administration, but "under the glare of media exposure," they simply denied they had been briefed and accused the CIA of misleading the committees.[65] Already an established practice in the years preceding the formal congressional intelligence committees, Congress continued to exploit its own politicized version of plausible deniability to disavow knowledge of USIC activities that it had indeed known about and even funded.

During the 1950s and 1960s, Congress exhibited a high degree of bipartisanship and cooperated with the President on intelligence policy. As the Cold War consensus crumbled, several of the worst ills of American intelligence history resurfaced, including competition between the President and Congress, politicization and partisanship, and scapegoating intelligence. With the conclusion of the Church Committee, Congress implicitly promised the American people that it would adopt a proactive approach to intelligence oversight and ensure that the abuses of years past could never be repeated. But congressional intervention and oversight did not prevent subsequent intelligence scandals. Moreover, the Reagan administration viewed Congress as partisan, obstructionist, and even unconstitutional in its interference in US intelligence activities. Undoubtedly, some fault for the intelligence controversies of the 1980s lay with the Reagan administration, but Congress was responsible as well. There was even more blame to go around.

The American People at the End of the Cold War

The President and Congress each took their case to the American people. In his op-ed for the *Post*, Congressman Hamilton high-mindedly declared, "The US government should not carry out any covert action that a fully-informed American public would not support."[66] Reagan had invited the American people to influence national intelligence policy during his presidential campaign by making it part of his platform. But, to have any impact, the American people needed to know what the USIC was doing. Through a combination of press reports, leaks, congressional hearings, and executive branch admissions, the American people were more aware of ongoing intelligence operations during the 1980s than at any previous point in US history.

Covert action was a remarkably overt feature of US foreign policy during the Reagan administration, often appearing in news stories that discussed it in detail. For example, an article in *Newsweek* in November 1982 reported that the CIA was "currently running paramilitary operations in about 10 countries, including Afghanistan."[67] In July 1983, a headline in the *San Francisco Examiner & Chronicle* read, "CIA Plan Revealed: Mine 3 Nicaragua Harbors to Halt Flow of Arms."[68] A few months later, *Newsweek*'s front cover announced, "The Secret Warriors: The CIA Is Back in Business."[69] Finally, in 1986, the *Washington Post* published an article of breathtaking scale that mentioned US covert action operations outside well-known ones, including in Chad, Liberia, Ethiopia, Suriname, and Mauritius. The article also noted that the Reagan administration had resurrected the 40 Committee as the 208 Committee to be the "micromanagers of America's new secret diplomacy."[70] Plausible deniability for both the President and the country had been one of the chief concerns of the architects of US covert action policy in the early Cold War. By the end of the Cold War, the press had blown it apart.

The flurry of press revelations exacerbated the confrontation between the President and Congress and contributed to the especially strident debate over Iran-Contra. But Iran-Contra can overshadow the success of US covert action in Afghanistan. Operation Cyclone, the CIA's covert action program to support the Afghan mujahideen, was a key contributor to the Soviet defeat in Afghanistan. The CIA regained its covert action competency—and with it a measure of respect from policymakers and the public—as a byproduct of the Afghanistan campaign. Both Congress and the American people fiercely opposed the Soviet invasion of Afghanistan. Congressman Charlie Wilson, spurred on by the Texas socialite, activist, and philanthropist Joanne Herring, played a pivotal role in funding and championing CIA covert action in Afghanistan, illustrating the assistance Congress and American civil society can offer to executive branch covert action programs.[71]

But Congress and the public can just as easily impede US covert action. Reagan was generally consistent in authorizing covert action in places where he also took overt measures to win the Cold War, but Congress and the American people were not consistent in their responses. This is apparent when comparing the US covert action program to support the mujahideen in Afghanistan with the programs to support the Contras in Nicaragua and UNITA in Angola. Many factors explain why the US public and Congress resisted the latter two, including the alleged human rights violations by pro-American regimes and groups; inherent American sympathy for the right to self-determination being claimed by these postcolonial states; the questionable policy of regime change, especially when it involved democratically elected or publicly supported regimes; and the memory of America's incremental involvement in Vietnam, which began with support for unpopular leaders through intelligence and covert action. Meanwhile, US support for the mujahideen in Afghanistan seemingly represented the foil to each of these conditions by supporting the Afghan people in their resistance to a brutal Soviet invasion and occupation. In this respect, Soviet intervention in Afghanistan was far more overt and bloody than it was in the shadow, proxy wars waged in Central America and Africa with covert Soviet support.[72] Perhaps the bigger problem was that the United States appeared to be doing the same things as the enemy it professed to be better than.

An article in the *Washington Post* commented that the Reagan Doctrine, "coincidentally, mirrors a Soviet doctrine unveiled a quarter-century ago" when Nikita Khrushchev promised that "Moscow's military muscle would be thrown behind 'wars of national liberation' in the Third World, where colonial and leftist groups were struggling against colonial or pro-American regimes."[73] Reagan must have loathed the comparison. But the Reagan Doctrine and its visibility on the global stage forced the American people to once again confront the Doolittle Report's proposition that the United States needed to reconsider its ideals and abandon any rules in its competition with the Soviet Union. The Reagan administration attempted to address this Cold War quandary of civil-intelligence relations in NSDD 159, though it left room for maneuver. The directive stated that "the US will not make use of most of the techniques employed by [its] adversaries." As part of the policymaking process, the directive also claimed that a review of any proposed covert action program would include "legal considerations, Congressional and legislative requirements, [and] public and media issues."[74] Although the Reagan administration seemingly disregarded legal, congressional, and media issues, it did not discount the public dimension.

For instance, in 1983, Casey spoke at Westminster College in Fulton, Missouri, the same venue where Winston Churchill had delivered his famous "Iron Curtain speech" in 1946. Citing Churchill, Casey described the threat the Soviet Union posed to the Free World and the American way of life. He implicitly defended the Reagan Doctrine, alluding to the need for the United States to counter the Soviet Union's global campaign of "subversion and disruption," including in Central America. Casey acknowledged that the Cold War was "a conflict deeply rooted in ideas."[75] Part of the point of his speech was to secure the support of the American people for the Reagan administration, though he knew full well that it was conducting intelligence activities that conflicted with their ideals.

Press revelations prompted more public engagement by the Reagan administration. On May 8, 1984, the *Christian Science Monitor* revealed CIA support for "death squads" in El Salvador.[76] The following night, Reagan gave a speech to the nation defending his policies in Central America.[77] In its analysis of the speech, the *New York Times* observed that Reagan "reached beyond Congress...to try to defend his policy on Central America before the American voter." One administration official explained that the "problem [was] not that the American public [was] opposed to his policy...It's that they just don't understand it," citing questions like who were the "good guys" or what "side" the United States was supporting and why.[78] Like Reagan, members of Congress were also prepared to take their case to the court of public opinion. For example, NSC staffer and former CIA officer Walter Raymond Jr. recognized that the *Christian Science Monitor* piece provided the "backdrop" for a nationally televised "rebuttal" to Reagan's speech by Senators Paul Tsongas and Chris Dodd.[79]

Reagan continued to court the American people throughout his presidency. In national speeches, he tried, to no avail, to explicitly link the covert wars in Afghanistan and Nicaragua to the larger struggle against communism.[80] He also used these addresses to try to convince the American people to pressure Congress to repeal the Boland Amendments and restore US support to the Contras.[81] In a vague mea culpa speech following the exposure of the Iran-Contra scandal, Reagan even suggested that the *New York Times* test would henceforth be the guiding principle for covert action: "I have also directed that any covert activity be in support of clear policy objectives and in compliance with American values. I expect a covert policy that, if Americans saw it on the front page of their newspaper, they'd say, 'That makes sense.' "[82] Reagan therefore invited public debate over one of the most secretive and sensitive areas of intelligence.

Indeed, Congress was not the only branch of government that was indiscreet in terms of leaking covert action operations during the 1980s. Reagan himself revealed his administration's covert action program in Angola in a question-and-answer session with the press. Whether inadvertently or not,

Reagan explained, "We all believe that a covert operation would be more useful to us and have more chance of success right now than the overt proposal that has been made in the Congress"—a startlingly counterintuitive statement. Several administration officials expressed "astonishment" and "surprise," some because of the sensitive nature of covert action and others because they did not even know that the administration had reached a policy decision on Angola.[83] Even then, the American people were already debating the merits of covert versus overt action in Angola by the time Reagan exposed it. A week before Reagan's admission, the Heritage Foundation, a conservative think tank, drafted a report titled "Angola Tests the Reagan Doctrine," which mentioned that administration officials and members of Congress supported covert action in Angola.[84] Then again, there really were not many places for intelligence to hide in the 1980s.

Whereas 1975 was the "Year of Intelligence," 1985 was the "Year of the Spy," so named on account of the arrests of several Americans who were caught spying for foreign countries. When publicized, these arrests led the public to question whether the USIC could keep its own house in order.[85] That same year, a group of journalists and academics joined together to create the National Security Archive, which used FOIA to secure a degree of accountability and transparency from the CIA and the broader USIC.[86] As mainstream media reported on US covert action all over the world, and civic groups actively probed intelligence, the American people were able to express their disagreement with specific, current intelligence operations to a degree they had not been able to before in US history.

A Requiem for Covert Action or the Covert Cold War?

Jeane Kirkpatrick, the Reagan confidant who served as the first female US ambassador to the UN, delivered a eulogy at Casey's funeral in which she related that a journalist had told her, "Bill Casey is a controversial man." She replied, "But, of course...he was a bold committed man in an age rent by controversy."[87] Casey was an agent of controversy during this age, but so too were Congress, the President, the American people, and the intelligence community.

Having just asserted its prerogative to oversee and influence intelligence, Congress struggled with its newfound responsibilities. It abandoned its post–Church Committee goal of a grand charter to categorically establish limits for intelligence but still attempted to legislate the details of covert action. Members of Congress also feigned ignorance of covert action programs they had funded, and they used leaks to undermine US foreign policy and specific ongoing intelligence operations they disliked. Contrary to its promise of a new age of transparency, Congress legislated acts that preserved secrecy, including the CIA's ability to keep secrets from the American people through FOIA exceptions.

Meanwhile, the Reagan administration attempted to evade congressional oversight and interference. Observers at the time noted the regression towards the older American intelligence tradition of executive control and secrecy. Arthur Schlesinger argued that the Reagan administration "gave rise to a body of secret laws, decrees and actions that increased presidential power, reduced presidential accountability, denied Congress and the people essential knowledge about public policy," while Clark Clifford adjudged the Reagan administration's approach as "a secret government operating in a democracy."[88] In taking his case to the American people, Reagan tried to defend his administration's covert action programs by appealing to the very same American principles that covert action affronted. This was a hard sell, as the guerrillas the United States was supporting in Afghanistan and Nicaragua were not models of democracy and human rights.[89] The soaring rhetoric that otherwise served Reagan so well as President could not obtain or maintain the support of Congress and the American people when it came to intelligence.

The November 1982 *Newsweek* exposé on covert action questioned whether such action was even necessary, capturing the enduring suspicion with which Americans regarded intelligence and the impossible standards to which they held it. The article stated that "if the aim of covert action is in line with what Americans generally consider necessary, prudent and moral, most of them will tolerate the means," but undercut this position by warning that "a free society should not sacrifice its principles so lightly." The article proposed that US covert action must "abide by certain rules: don't violate your own principles. Don't make things worse. Don't get caught." It concluded, "It is possible to conduct secret operations in a society like ours, but only with great difficulty. That is the way it should be for missions that so commonly violate basic democratic principles."[90] The authors of the *Newsweek* piece exhibited the same type of equivocation about covert action that afflicted American civil society at large during the Reagan years. Americans supported covert action in some places but opposed it in others. Public support therefore failed to provide coherent guidance for policymakers and left plenty of opportunities for conflict, especially between Congress and the President.

With the President formulating policy, Congress intervening through hearings and appropriations, and the public judging the outcome, the USIC had little chance of averting a scandal. The position was untenable: The USIC would shoulder criticism for a good foreign policy unethically executed or a bad foreign policy ethically executed. Still, intelligence professionals bear responsibility for the operations they conduct. Loch Johnson, an instrumental staffer on the Church Committee, surveyed US covert action from 1947 to 1986 and revealed that nearly all the CIA sources in his study "were clearly biased . . . in favor of covert action." He found that the "weakest link . . . seems to be at the bottom . . . at the level of agents in the field. Here is where rogue elephants are most likely to roam."[91]

At least some intelligence professionals at the CIA perceived the risks of covert action. In 1981, Robert Gates, the CIA's Director of the Executive Staff and head of the Office of Policy and Planning, drafted a memorandum to Casey on the topic of covert action. He reiterated some of the warnings that OSS veteran and CIA officer Frank Lindsay had earlier delineated in 1968. Gates highlighted Lindsay's conclusion that "covert operations should be called upon only when something should be done in a secret manner and only when secrecy is possible." In a statement that would especially hold true in the 1980s, he emphasized, "Large operations cannot be kept secret." Gates outlined how "covert operations are seen as a way to accomplish a policy objective . . . on the cheap, to cope with a problem where no one has any idea how to obtain public support for a solution to the problem, or to use covert action as a short-term tactic to fend off a problem or disaster." He stressed that, instead, "what is important here is a better understanding on the part of policymakers that covert action is rarely a long-term solution to any problem and that they must face up to their responsibilities to develop viable longer-range policies in situations where covert action has bought them some time." The covert action programs of the 1980s exhibited all the issues Gates anticipated.[92]

That the entire country—the government, the USIC, and the American people—stood behind covert action in Afghanistan is the ultimate irony of the period. Like other notable covert action operations during the Cold War, short-term success in Afghanistan later produced long-term blowback and the worst intelligence failure since Pearl Harbor.[93] But, in the late 1980s, Afghanistan was only one theater in a long Cold War that was finally drawing to a close. During this period, the American intelligence system had changed dramatically—from the number of organizations in the USIC and the technology and tradecraft it used to the essential role it played in US national security and the prominent role it held in the government itself. Yet, elemental problems of civil-intelligence relations continued to frustrate the country throughout the Cold War. Perhaps its end would offer the United States an opportunity to restore some balance between the spy and the state.

PART FOUR

An American Intelligence State: US Civil-Intelligence Relations at the Crossroads

20

The Illusory Peace Dividend

THE UNEXPECTED FALL of the Berlin Wall and the sudden disintegration of the Soviet Union caught the United States by surprise. The country had created a vast national security state and a massive, if not always harmonious, intelligence community to help win the Cold War. It had to determine what to do with them now that it was over. The end of the Cold War also ushered in questions about a "peace dividend," so retrenchment again threatened the USIC. During the 1990s, the United States and the USIC had to contend with an even more confounding adversary than the Soviet Union: the apparent lack of any formidable adversary at all.

If the United States faced an existential threat during the Cold War, the CIA faced an existential threat in the peace that followed. Debates about the very survival of the CIA elicited familiar themes of civil-intelligence relations, namely, competition, control, and coordination. In the morass, the President and Congress continued to spar over intelligence. Congress proposed more reforms and held more debates. Meanwhile, the USIC tried to identify missions that would demonstrate its continued relevance to national security. Fundamentally, the United States was grappling with the future of American intelligence amid the uncertainty of the post-Cold War world.

An Epilogue or Prologue to Congressional Reform?

In the epilogue to the 1989 revised edition of *The Imperial Presidency*, Arthur Schlesinger asserted that he was "well aware that covert action has its uses" but was equally "well aware of its limitations, especially in peacetime, and of the problems it presents to a democracy." Upon further consideration, he dismissed covert action as "often easy to detect, always hard to control, and in its nature illegal and immune to normal procedures of accountability," roundly concluding, "Founded as it is on law breaking, deception and lies, it imports bad habits into a democratic polity."

Schlesinger wondered, "What can a democracy do about it?" He arrived at the same answer—and irreconcilable tension of American civil-intelligence relations—that he and others who took up the same question always seemed to when he decided that "clandestine activities should be consistent with official policy and with national traditions and ideals." Recognizing that these are "all pious hopes that an infatuated President may simply ignore," he questioned if "anything [can] be done to compel Presidents to restrain their penchant for dirty tricks." His solution was more congressional oversight and reform, including a CIA Inspector General (IG) answerable to Congress and a forty-eight-hour reporting requirement for covert action findings—proposals already underway in Congress by the time he was writing.[1]

Reagan, like his predecessors, sought to preempt congressional legislation following the Tower Commission and Iran-Contra Reports. He signed a series of three National Security Decision Directives in 1987 that refined the process for drafting, approving, and reporting covert action operations. For example, NSDD 286 mandated prior notification to Congress and included a prohibition on retroactive findings, meaning a presidential finding after an operation has already taken place. It made the CIA the primary organization responsible for covert action absent a specific presidential decision to use another executive department, organization, or entity. However, it also included an exception to the usual notification requirements based on "extraordinary circumstances affecting the vital interests of the United States."[2] But Congress had long since caught on to these executive attempts to escape congressional legislation. Both the Senate and the House introduced bills bolstering their oversight authorities in order "to preclude future administrations from circumventing or changing oversight requirements via executive orders or NSDDs."[3]

The proposed Intelligence Oversight Act of 1988 replaced the ambiguous requirement that allowed the President to report covert action "in a timely fashion" with a strict forty-eight-hour window. Reagan was not going to sign this into law, so although the Senate bill passed, the House bill never went to a vote.[4] Congress suspended its efforts at intelligence oversight reform until the presidential transition to George H. W. Bush, the only former DCI to become President. Not surprisingly, the Bush administration displayed a competitive and begrudging attitude to congressional intelligence reform.

Congress began by creating a statutory CIA Inspector General in 1989 as part of the Intelligence Authorization Act for FY 1990, an idea Reagan had opposed in 1987.[5] Although the CIA had had an Inspector General appointed by the DCI since 1952, the Iran-Contra Report recommended a statutory CIA IG, which would have obligations to both the DCI and Congress.[6] The legislation creating the statutory CIA IG included reporting requirements to the congressional intelligence committees and exceptions under which the DCI could override a CIA IG investigation to protect sensitive operations and information.[7] Establishing the statutory CIA IG therefore involved a careful balancing act. An IG that was too independent threatened both the CIA and Congress: the former by impeding the CIA's activities and the latter by competing with the congressional intelligence committees as its own form of oversight.[8] Notably, the DCI did not block any CIA IG investigations from 1989 until 2004, suggesting the CIA IG has not been too much of an impediment to CIA operations.[9]

Congress launched another salvo against the President with the Intelligence Authorization Act for FY 1991, sponsored by HPSCI chairman Dave McCurdy and SSCI chairman David Boren, who became the principal leaders of congressional intelligence reform efforts in the early 1990s. The proposed reforms included a statutory definition of covert action, a forty-eight-hour reporting deadline for presidential findings, and notification to Congress when the President requested a foreign government or private citizen to conduct covert action on behalf of the United States.[10]

Bush balked. The result was a pocket veto—the first presidential veto of intelligence legislation. Congress and the President fiercely negotiated to reach a compromise. While its fiscal power seemingly gave Congress the upper hand, the Bush administration benefited from public support for the Gulf War, which required the capabilities of the USIC. But the intelligence community needed funding, and it would not have it for FY 1991 without an authorization act. No American politician wants to be accused of not supporting the military or intelligence community in a time of war. Congress blinked.[11]

The final version of the Intelligence Authorization Act for FY 1991 eliminated much of the rigid statutory language that Bush opposed. It repealed the Hughes-Ryan Amendment and required only that covert action findings be made in writing, not be retroactive, and be disclosed "in a timely fashion" if the President did not give prior notice to the intelligence committees or the Gang of Eight. Notably, the act also legislated a statutory definition for covert action.[12] After all the back-and-forth between the President and Congress, the act mostly formalized the standard practices the President and intelligence community had already been following for years.[13]

"New World, New C.I.A."

The CIA always receives the most scrutiny from policymakers and the American people in national debates about intelligence. It often stands to lose the most in these debates. In the early 1990s, the CIA seemingly had the choice of either demonstrating it could conform to American principles or be eliminated altogether.[14] In 1982, Turner predicted, "If the CIA ever again were to overstep its bounds and violate the rights of Americans and if another wave of intense public criticism were to follow, the agency could be mortally wounded."[15] In 1990, amid his reform proposals in Congress, Senator Boren published an op-ed in the *New York Times* titled "New World, New C.I.A.," in which he insisted that the CIA needed to operate "in a manner consistent with the fundamental values of the American people."[16] But the mere existence of the CIA in the absence of the Cold War became problematic. Serious questions were raised about why the United States still needed an independent intelligence organization originally designed to confront the Soviet Union once that threat had passed. The 1990s therefore produced a "cautious, risk-averse climate" at the CIA as it "sought desperately to be 'correct'—to look like the rest of America."[17]

Senator Daniel Patrick Moynihan was ready to celebrate the end of the Cold War with legislation rolling back the American national security state. He introduced the End of the Cold War Act of 1991, a name far more grandiose in its promise than in its substance. A provision titled "Unification of Diplomacy" claimed that "the creation of the Central Intelligence Agency as a separate entity... undermined the role of the Department of State as the primary agency of the United States Government formulating and conducting foreign policy and providing information to the President concerning the state of world affairs." Accordingly, the act proposed transferring all the powers and functions of the CIA to the State Department. The Secretary of State would design this new intelligence system with the input of Congress and the President's Intelligence Advisory Board.[18]

The State Department had been caught off guard when Truman directed it to take the lead in organizing postwar intelligence in the fall of 1945. It was no better prepared this time around. Besides being neither ready nor able, the State Department did not even appear willing to assume the CIA's functions and responsibilities. One former foreign service officer wrote to the *New York Times*, "Through my 22-year Foreign Service career, I found that the Central Intelligence Agency presence was neither necessary, nor in most cases desirable."[19] Moynihan's proposal, which never made it through SSCI, was also regressive because it attempted to subordinate independent intelligence to the diplomatic institution. Furthermore, by closing the CIA, it risked unleashing the same bureaucratic competition and chaos that had accompanied the agency's creation.

Moynihan exhibited little appreciation for intelligence professionalism. He repeated the Church Committee–era libel that the CIA was a shadow foreign policymaker. His conviction that the Secretary of State should "provide information to the President concerning the state of world affairs" conflated "information" and "intelligence." Additionally, he ignored the fact that the DCI presented the President with products derived from both secret and open sources that had been analyzed by professional intelligence analysts. By the 1990s, the CIA had decades of experience selecting, training, and cultivating professional intelligence officers, including operations officers and analysts, who conducted missions and functions far different from those of diplomatic officers. While the State Department still had the small but intellectually powerful Bureau of Intelligence and Research, the vestigial organ of the OSS's R&A branch, its principal customer was the Secretary of State rather than the President.[20] To make his case for the End of the Cold War Act of 1991, Moynihan criticized the CIA's analytical performance, citing the CIA's failure to precisely predict the collapse of the Soviet Union at the end of the Cold War, much as critics had with its failure to predict the detonation of the Soviet atomic bomb at its outset.

Stansfield Turner, who seemed to never miss an opportunity to damage the reputation of the agency he once led, contributed to the widespread view that the CIA had failed spectacularly yet again. In his 1991 *Foreign Affairs* article "Intelligence for a New World Order," he listed a litany of recent intelligence failures, from the Iranian Revolution and Iran-Contra to the Iraqi invasion of Kuwait and ongoing changes in the former Soviet Union. Turner observed that the "quality of intelligence analysis has never met our expectations" in part because it is difficult for "large bureaucracies to go out on a limb... to stake their reputations on forecasting." He stressed "the enormity of this failure to forecast the magnitude of the Soviet crisis." Even if some individual CIA analysts "were more prescient than the corporate view, their ideas were filtered out in the bureaucratic process," and the "corporate view missed by a mile."[21]

Turner cited Moynihan's proposal to fold the CIA into the State Department in his own proposals for intelligence reform, calling the subordination of the intelligence profession to diplomacy the "single greatest advantage of Senator Moynihan's proposal" while ignoring the effects this would have on analytic objectivity and the politicization of intelligence. He argued that while the CIA was "a relatively young organization"—at this point over forty years old—it had "yet to build a well-balanced clandestine service." Reflecting his own biases as DCI, Turner once again challenged the CIA's effectiveness as a HUMINT organization while celebrating the value of technical intelligence. He also believed that the DCI could not be both the coordinator of the USIC and the head of the CIA, so he supported the creation of a DNI. While Turner did not advocate abolishing the CIA, he certainly provided ammunition for its detractors, like Moynihan.[22] In a feedback loop, Moynihan would recycle some of Turner's accusations against the CIA at almost every opportunity: in Robert Gates's confirmation hearings to be DCI in 1991, in his own Moynihan Commission on government secrecy in 1996, in his 1998 book on secrecy, in an interview with Jim Lehrer in 1998, in his farewell to the Senate in 2002, and in a commencement address at Harvard in 2003.[23]

Congressional debate over the fate of the CIA went public in the *New York Times* in May 1991 with dueling op-eds by Moynihan and Congressman Bud Shuster, a member of HPSCI, in a dialogue headlined, "Do We Still Need the C.I.A.?" Moynihan introduced his position by stating that "it is possible, for the first time since the onset of the cold war, to ask whether we need the agency as it is now." He contended, "For a quarter century, the C.I.A. has been repeatedly wrong about the major political and economic questions entrusted to its analysis." Adding insult to injury, he scoffed that "the term [intelligence] has become oxymoronic." In fact, Moynihan claimed that he himself had "forecast . . . the breakup of the Soviet Union with fearsome consequences" in a 1979 *Newsweek* forum. Thinking the CIA had nothing to offer the country, he pilloried its ongoing efforts to find "new work" as "a kind of retirement program for a cadre of cold warriors not really needed any longer." Although Moynihan acknowledged, "Of course we will need continued intelligence capabilities," he did not want the CIA to be part of them.[24]

On the same page of the newspaper, Bud Shuster dismissed Moynihan's proposal as a "recipe for disaster." Shuster derided Moynihan's "thesis that the C.I.A. is synonymous with the cold war and that [since] the cold war is dead . . . the agency should now be buried in the State Department." He rightly worried that vesting the CIA's responsibilities in the Secretary of State would politicize intelligence by making it an instrument for advocating State Department policy. He surmised that the State Department and its diplomats would not want to be responsible for espionage and questioned how a transfer of the CIA's functions to State would affect relations with the DOD and its intelligence components.[25] The CIA still had "plenty of missions other than analyzing the Soviet Union," like countering nuclear proliferation and terrorism. Shuster also offered the historical warning that intelligence retrenchment following the First World War contributed to the failure at Pearl Harbor and felt that the country "should have outgrown the notion that it had little need for intelligence collection and analysis." Instead, the United States needed to "get over the idea that intelligence is dirty, that it represents the abandonment of American innocence and ideals rather than a wise way to preserve those ideals."[26] In their dialogue, Moynihan and Shuster revealed how tensions in American civil-intelligence relations never actually abated, but simply changed forms, especially during transitions between war and peace.

Senator Boren likewise publicly defended the CIA in *Foreign Affairs*. He noted that neither the State Department nor the Defense Department was "equipped to take on the role of lead agency in intelligence." Intelligence also had to remain outside the purview of those two policymaking departments to maintain its objectivity. Besides, the diplomatic and military professions had different priorities than the intelligence profession. As a reformer, Boren called for "change [to] the existing [intelligence] community, including the CIA."[27] The CIA survived Moynihan's first call to abolish it, but there would be another. In the meantime, Congress leveled its sights on the entire USIC as part of the peace dividend.

DCI or DNI?

Since the early days of the Cold War, various commissions and studies of American intelligence had identified the inherent tension in the DCI's leadership of both the CIA and USIC. The need for a Director of National Intelligence—the US intelligence czar proposed in the 1971 Schlesinger Report and the National Intelligence Reorganization and Reform Act of 1978—continued through the 1980s and into the early 1990s. In the wake of Iran-Contra, Senator Arlen Specter, a member of SSCI, "proposed splitting the director of central intelligence job into two posts: a director of national intelligence to be the President's primary advisor on foreign intelligence, supervise all U.S. intelligence-gathering agencies, and serve as a member of the National Security Council, and a director of the Central Intelligence Agency to manage the agency and carry out covert action."[28] Congress had just expended tremendous energy in its fight to coordinate the US military under the Goldwater-Nichols Department of Defense Reorganization Act of 1986, so it is not surprising that a proposal for intelligence coordination stalled.[29] Undeterred, Specter tried again in 1991, but to no avail.

In 1992, intelligence committee chairs McCurdy and Boren each introduced legislation that would establish a Director of National Intelligence.[30] Crucially, the DNI would control national intelligence funds and thus be empowered to coordinate the USIC far beyond any similar authority given to the DCI. A Deputy Director of National Intelligence would be responsible for estimates and analysis, removing this critical function from the CIA. With the CIA no longer the analytical hub for intelligence or the DCI the principal intelligence advisor to the President, the DCI and the CIA would be responsible for espionage and covert action. The legislation therefore addressed an identity crisis that had afflicted the CIA since its inception.

Even the Secretary of Defense would have to ensure the implementation of DNI policies down to the tactical level. Perhaps to mollify the military establishment, both bills offered it a measure of control over the entire USIC by endorsing the appointment of a general or flag officer to the position of DNI or Deputy DNI.[31] Problematically, the DNI would have powers within the DOD that intersected with, and possibly transgressed, those of the Secretary of Defense. So, the legislation continued the troublesome tradition of mixing the intelligence and military professions in the office of the DNI at the expense of an independent American intelligence institution.

The looming question for Congress was how the executive branch would respond. The *New York Times* reported that the bills "seemed to catch officials in the White House, the Pentagon, and the C.I.A. off guard."[32] Meanwhile, the *Washington Post* predicted "stiff opposition," especially from the DOD.[33] McCurdy certainly did not assuage the concerns of competing bureaucracies and officials by announcing that the DNI was "going to be a czar with teeth ... a czar with muscle ... a czar with troops and forces and budget. He will be The Director."[34]

But Boren, who had previously compromised with President Bush on the CIA IG and 1991 Intelligence Authorization Act, again demonstrated the same judiciousness. He explained that he had introduced his bill "to prompt discussion of the issues involved" and that he was "not wedded to any particular proposal at this stage."[35] He added, "It is not our purpose to pass a bill, send it to the White House and have it rejected by the president."[36] In a hearing before HPSCI and SSCI, Boren told the committees that congressional action "may not be needed in all areas to address many of our concerns ... And, indeed, if the Administration could demonstrate that these concerns can be dealt with effectively without legislation, or at least with less legislation, I would certainly be inclined to listen to the Administration and to follow that course of action."[37] Whether intentionally or unintentionally, Boren had presented the executive branch with an opening to preempt Congress.

The major stakeholders in the executive branch, DCI Robert Gates and Secretary of Defense Dick Cheney, intervened. As DCI, Gates faced the greatest loss of power under the proposed legislation, so Boren and McCurdy hinted he would be named the first DNI to secure his support.[38] But Gates had other plans. In his confirmation hearing for the position of DCI the previous year, he had presciently observed that if the executive branch did not take action to transform intelligence, then Congress would. He wisely spent his time preparing for the coming congressional onslaught.[39] When Boren and McCurdy dropped their bills on Congress, Gates was ready. He presented his own proposed reforms to both HPSCI and SSCI that tackled "Community management, Community analysis, integrating the collection disciplines, and strengthening support to the military," virtually all the principal areas of the McCurdy and Boren bills. His intention was to fix the USIC without a DNI. Gates also stressed that he had discussed his ideas with Cheney, demonstrating that the threat of more bureaucratic competition compelled cooperation between the DCI and the Secretary of Defense.[40]

In fact, Cheney had already written to Les Aspin, chairman of the House Armed Services Committee, calling the proposed bills "unnecessary and so severely flawed that selective amendments would not make either of them acceptable." He especially opposed the creation of a DNI that would exercise "inappropriate authority... of internal DoD activities that... must remain under the authority, direction, and control of the Secretary of Defense." Cheney warned Aspin that he would recommend Bush veto either bill—the very outcome Boren wanted to avoid.[41]

The DCI and Secretary of Defense also found an unlikely ally in the ACLU. It pointed out that the proposed DNI would have control over both CIA and FBI intelligence activities, thereby linking foreign and domestic intelligence. This had been a foundational area of ideological and structural division in the American intelligence system that the authors of the 1947 National Security Act and other policymakers had taken pains to address. Moreover, the ACLU encouraged Congress to reconsider the utility of covert action since the Cold War was over, recommending that it prohibit this core mission of intelligence altogether. In general, the ACLU was "concerned with the intelligence community getting involved in non-national security activities," such as international law enforcement. Thus, elements of American civil society joined executive officials to oppose the 1992 congressional reforms, albeit for different reasons.[42]

In the end, neither bill made it past the hearings. Congress likely saw no reason to undertake such radical reforms in the absence of a major failure or scandal. Instead, it deferred to the executive branch to implement Gates's plan. Bud Shuster observed that many of the proposed changes were "needlessly threatening the President's necessary flexibility to structure the intelligence community for the most effective conduct of intelligence activities." He joked that the changes Congress ended up accepting were "from the Tamm[y] Fay[e] Bak[k]er school of legislative cosmetology: rather harmless."[43]

Congress ultimately folded Gates's reforms into the Intelligence Authorization Act for FY 1993.[44] The DCI received a boost in power and authority, just as Gates intended. Congress also settled on a different route for cashing in on the peace dividend. It cut Bush's proposed intelligence budget by 6 percent, which was the largest budget cut to the USIC in over forty years, and mandated that the USIC reduce personnel 17.5 percent by 1997.[45] But reform and retrenchment were part of a broader discussion taking place over a post–Cold War intelligence system.

Debating Intelligence

Boren and McCurdy held news conferences following the introduction of their doomed bills. The *New York Times* reported the legislation was intended to "jolt the Bush administration and Congress into changing the intelligence system to fit the needs of the post-Communist world."[46] The *Washington Post* quoted Boren, "Changes in the world have made the current intelligence structure outdated."[47] The United States faced "new challenges and new uncertainties," according to Boren, which meant that the intelligence system required "considerable recalibration and streamlining."[48] Citing the end of the Cold War, McCurdy argued that "the governmental organizations which have been primarily focused on the Soviet Union must . . . be reevaluated." Furthermore, he told Congress, "Our goal should not be to invent new missions in an effort to justify the maintenance of an immense intelligence apparatus. Rather our goal should be to ensure that our national intelligence agencies are properly focused and structured to respond to those real intelligence needs which can reasonably be expected in the future."[49]

Terms like "recalibration and streamlining" and "properly focused and structured" were synonymous with retrenchment, and Boren and McCurdy admitted as much. Boren stated that Congress could reduce funding for the intelligence community "without damaging our national security interests."[50] McCurdy commented that "the Federal deficit ensures that competition among national security programs for a share of shrinking budgetary resources will be fierce for the foreseeable future."[51] Other members of Congress stridently opposed intelligence retrenchment and what they perceived to be a misreading of history.

Congressman Bob McEwen delivered a vigorous rebuttal, lecturing Congress, "Wise people learn history and do not repeat history." McEwen's history lesson focused on the ebb and flow of intelligence between periods of war and peace. He contrasted intelligence with the military, pointing out that it was "not something that can be built and stockpiled like tanks and missiles." Unlike an assembly line for tanks that can be turned on and off, he explained, "an intelligence system must be nurtured and supported at all times." But he perceived an even more insidious agenda afoot. He claimed that some individuals were trying to capitalize on global changes "to accomplish what they have always desired, to destroy America's intelligence services." McEwen proposed a rather radical departure from the tradition in which military and intelligence retrenchment went together, arguing that "as we reduce our defense spending, we should improve our intelligence capabilities." He concluded with a warning: "If we let our intelligence capabilities slip in order to claim a short-term political peace dividend scalp, we will pay a steep price.... It may come due years down the road, but the price will be paid, and often it is paid in blood."[52]

Bud Shuster agreed, calling intelligence "an early warning system for the very dangerous world in which we live."[53] Similarly, Representative Larry Combest urged Congress not to "close [its] eyes and [its] ears to the very real dangers that remain in this post–cold war world." He reminded Congress that budgetary support for what were originally intelligence programs led to massive innovations and triumphs in "aerospace technology, computer technology, and communications technology."[54] True enough, the American people were the beneficiaries of these Cold War–era technological transformations, but they would also enable state surveillance on a colossal scale.

Like Combest, former DCI Turner was bullish about technological change. Ever the advocate for high technology, he called technical systems "the sword" and HUMINT "the rapier" of future intelligence collection. In the post–Cold War world, economic intelligence would be a key area of competition, but it required spying on allies and adversaries alike. For this work, "impersonal" intelligence collection through satellites and signals intercepts was less offensive to allies than "human, on-site spying." Turner stressed what he perceived to be the expanding geographical and thematic scope of the USIC's responsibilities. He cited the need for political intelligence in countries across the world due to the instability caused by the collapse of the Soviet Union. At the same time, the USIC would have to continue to collect intelligence in the former Soviet Union to ensure continued adherence to arms control agreements and to secure nuclear, biological, and chemical weapons.[55]

Congress was alert to these and other intelligence priorities, including the environment and disease, as it debated intelligence reform in the early 1990s.[56] Gates identified a common feature of the country's post–Cold War challenges: "that they cannot be resolved simply through the application of military force or diplomacy."[57] The end of the Soviet Union and the Cold War were "cataclysmic events in history," Gates cautioned, and "to think that they will pass quietly from the world stage without further troubling us is to be oblivious to history."[58] The end of the Cold War in no way ended the need for a robust American intelligence system.

As expected, much of the focus was on the CIA as the organizational embodiment of the intelligence profession. The *New York Times* reported that the CIA was "casting about for new missions" and called attention to its struggle to find its place in American national security. Along with new missions, it needed new people for operations in new places that required familiarity with different languages and cultures. All the emphasis on "new" was part of an American cultural trend to always look for the new and unprecedented in any postwar period. Still, it was clear that there were plenty of missions for the CIA, even if they were less predictable and perhaps less exciting than during the Cold War.[59]

The nadir for the CIA in the 1990s occurred during the brief and tumultuous tenure of James Woolsey as DCI. Woolsey found himself battling the President, Congress, the press, the USIC, and even the CIA. He had little to no contact with President Bill Clinton, who did not show much inclination or admiration for intelligence.[60] In fact, when a plane crashed on the White House lawn in 1994, some joked that it was Woolsey trying to get an audience with the President. The DCI fared no better with Congress, which accused him of being "overprotective" of the CIA.[61] Meanwhile, McCurdy had predicted that retrenchment would breed greater bureaucratic competition, and sure enough, the DIA and FBI encroached on CIA territory.[62] Rather than protect his agency, Woolsey oversaw personnel and budget cuts to it while also launching new electronic and reconnaissance satellite programs that led Congress to (hypocritically) accuse him of allowing the USIC "to squabble over shares of a shrinking pie."[63] In the tradition of other "outsider" DCIs with technological proclivities, like Schlesinger and Turner, Woolsey saw his reputation suffer with CIA operations officers despite his attempt to defend their work in Congress.[64]

The worst blow to the CIA was the 1994 arrest of Aldrich Ames, a counterintelligence officer, who spied for the Soviet Union beginning in 1985 and continued to spy for Russia after the Cold War ended. In exchange for millions of dollars, Ames passed along classified information, including the identity of several CIA assets, at least ten of whom were arrested and executed.[65] The FBI spearheaded the investigation into Ames as the CIA struggled to accept that it had a spy in its ranks. To make matters worse, Ames compromised FBI sources and methods, enraging the FBI. Ames therefore created further rifts between the CIA and FBI despite public professions of cooperation at the time.[66]

The Ames scandal made the CIA a "laughingstock."[67] It turned Woolsey against the agency he had exhausted personal capital in defending. He vowed to change its "fraternity" culture that "smack[ed] of elitism and arrogance." Promises to change CIA culture had fallen short in previous eras, particularly when made by outsiders like Woolsey. Still, he announced that the "American people [had] the right to ask where the C.I.A. is going after the cold war and after, for that matter, Aldrich Ames."[68] Woolsey would not stay around long enough to find out. He submitted his resignation in December 1994. An article announcing "Woolsey Gives In" appeared alongside another titled "Spy Agency Under Siege" that repeated the lingering question of the day: "What need does a spy agency fill in the post-cold-war era?"[69]

Moynihan offered his own answer and submitted another bill, this one much less discreetly titled: the Abolition of the Central Intelligence Agency Act of 1995.[70] He again proposed vesting the CIA's responsibilities and functions in the Department of State. The act was read twice and referred to SSCI, where no further action was taken. The CIA survived once more, but intelligence still faced immense scrutiny.

Defending Intelligence

If 1975 was the "Year of Intelligence" and 1985 the "Year of the Spy," then 1995 was a year of reflection as six different commissions, panels, and study groups examined the American intelligence system.[71] The Commission on the Roles and Capabilities of the US Intelligence Community, also known as the Aspin-Brown Commission, was perhaps the most consequential of them.

FIGURE 20.1 A 1994 cartoon by Herblock satirizes the CIA's effort to protect its funding during a period of retrenchment and following the arrest of CIA officer Aldrich Ames for selling secrets to Russia. A 1994 Herblock Cartoon, © The Herb Block Foundation.

Loch Johnson and L. Britt Snider, both former Church Committee staffers and scholars of intelligence oversight, believe that an intelligence failure precipitated the Aspin-Brown Commission, but they differ as to which one. Johnson claims that Operation Gothic Serpent in Somalia in 1993, which resulted in the downing of two Black Hawk helicopters, the deaths of eighteen American soldiers, and the capture of a pilot, along with the 1993 bombing of the World Trade Center, forced President Clinton to fire Defense Secretary Les Aspin.[72] Aspin's political severance was his appointment as chairman of the President's Intelligence Advisory Board. Aspin, with the support of Vice President Al Gore and National Security Advisor Anthony Lake, decided to initiate a broad review of the USIC. Meanwhile, Snider posits that the arrest of Ames and recriminations from Congress and the public led Senator John Warner to establish a commission to defend the USIC against the negative publicity created by the Ames case.[73] Regardless of which event might have been primarily responsible, the theme of intelligence failure led the President and Congress to join forces and revisit the role of intelligence in US national security.

If the "Black Hawk Down" incident was the precipitating event for the Aspin-Brown Commission, it was ironic that Les Aspin would lead the commission given that he was the Secretary of Defense at the time. It was even more ironic considering that he was a strident critic of the CIA and a serial leaker who had been removed from HPSCI in 1980 for his propensity to use intelligence for political purposes. After a briefing about US Navy operations in the Persian Gulf in 1987, Aspin called a press conference in which he leaked details of a convoy that resulted in the lead ship striking an Iranian mine. In response, military members of Secretary of Defense Caspar Weinberger's staff quipped, "Les's lips sink ships." Yet, this was the same individual who proposed to study and reform the American intelligence system.[74]

John Warner had entirely different motivations than Aspin for conducting the commission review. He explained in the commission report that he did so because the USIC was "under siege."[75] Warner understood the mercurial nature of the American people. He therefore viewed the commission as an opportunity to rehabilitate the public image of the USIC.[76]

The mixed presidential-congressional commission included nine members (all private citizens) chosen by the President and eight (four private citizens, four members of Congress) selected by Congress.[77] When Aspin died during the inquiry, the chairmanship of the commission passed to Harold Brown, the former Secretary of Defense under Carter. But it was Warner, the intelligence advocate, who really steered the commission. The commission tackled many of the salient questions facing the USIC, focusing on its missions, management practices, existing versus future capabilities, and, as always, coordination. It issued recommendations ranging from a new executive order to govern US intelligence activities to the public disclosure of the intelligence budget. It also noted that the overwhelming majority of the intelligence budget was used by military organizations not under the DCI's control. At the same time, the report explained that many members of the USIC viewed the DCI as biased due to organizational control over the CIA, again reinforcing the need for a DNI-type role.

Congress acknowledged a few recommendations of the Aspin-Brown Report in the Intelligence Authorization Act of FY 1997. It provided new support for the DCI to help manage the CIA and included stronger management authorities to shift money and personnel around intelligence programs. It also required DCI concurrence in the appointment of the directors of the NSA, NRO, and a newly proposed National Imagery and Mapping Agency (NIMA). However, the position of the DCI still suffered in its overall authority and ability to coordinate the USIC, as the creation of NIMA illustrated. Under its enabling legislation, NIMA would be a DOD organization, although the DCI purportedly would be able to influence its operations and mediate conflicts among competing priorities. Once again, the DOD captured a key intelligence function, creating another area of tension between the DCI and the Secretary of Defense in terms of intelligence control and resources.[78]

One of the principal conclusions of the Aspin-Brown Commission was that the "confidence of the public in the intelligence function must be restored," as Warner consistently argued.[79] The commission reemphasized the need for intelligence, and its report "helped educate experts and the public alike on intelligence issues."[80] The Church Committee began with a guilty-until-proven-innocent standard for judging the intelligence community and stressed intelligence failures, scandals, and abuses over intelligence successes. By contrast, the Aspin-Brown Commission balanced its criticism of the USIC with praise. Importantly, the commission observed that "for most Americans, the CIA *is* U.S. intelligence," identifying a common and enduring misperception that made the CIA, and the USIC along with it, the subject of widespread suspicion and scorn.[81] Throughout history, both the President and Congress had done much to undermine public trust in intelligence by making it a scapegoat for their own policymaking failures. As a joint congressional-presidential endeavor, the Aspin-Brown Commission was noteworthy in its attempt to burnish the public's perception of intelligence.

American civil society debated intelligence alongside the US government. The Council on Foreign Relations (CFR) conducted its own review, titled "Making Intelligence Smarter," led by a formidable panel of intelligence and national security experts.[82] The report advocated in favor of espionage and covert action as essential ingredients in US foreign policy. An op-ed in the *Washington Post* parodied the CFR report in its title, "Get Smart: Spies Posing as Reporters is a Stupid Idea." The author had asked Richard Haass, the CFR report's project director, about his position on the CIA's use of "nonofficial covers" for its clandestine service. Haass suggested the CIA should reconsider its policy against allowing case officers to pose as press or clergy. The author of the op-ed recounted the tangled history of the CIA using journalist credentials as cover and the dangers this posed to American journalists overseas.[83]

Haass responded in his own op-ed for the *Post*, calling intelligence "an increasingly valuable foreign policy tool." He made the case for more vigorous covert action operations, including ones that he intimated would require rescinding the prohibition on assassination. He reasoned that the USIC should operate in a manner "little different from the tradition in law enforcement of using criminals to catch criminals," claiming that the policies "should be acceptable so long as the likely benefits outweigh the certain moral and potential political costs." Above all, Haass insisted that "those involved... should know that risk-taking will be supported and that they will be politically protected," because "one problem with the clandestine services has been a lack of initiative brought about by restrictive regulations, a fear of retroactive discipline and a lack of high-level support."[84] In response to Haass, the Director of the Peace Corps wrote his own op-ed playing on intelligence jargon with the title "Don't Spook the Peace Corps."[85] Given the unknowns and challenges of the post–Cold War world, at least some intelligence advocates in civil society wanted to revisit the rules governing how the USIC conducted its business, while other members of the public still had their reservations.

Senator Moynihan was not done with his initiatives and convened a commission to study intelligence's secret ingredient—secrecy. He wanted to impose new restraints on intelligence that would diminish secrecy and compel transparency. The 1997 report of the Commission on Protecting and Reducing Government Secrecy, known as the Moynihan Commission, began with a triumphalist vision of the future based on a myopic reading of the past:

> Major conflict is no longer a prospect; ours is the only nation capable of waging a global war, and we have no such design. The ideological conflicts that arose in 19th century Europe are now largely spent; the totalitarian challenge is no more.... The world, if not at peace, nor likely to be, is even so not in imminent peril.[86]

Adopting the traditional American perception of hard boundaries between war and peace, Moynihan judged the post–Cold War world as one made safe (enough) for democracy. While ostensibly focused on government secrecy,

Moynihan exploited the commission to target the CIA. He believed that the CIA was a "vast bureaucratic system, a source of constant worry," which had ballooned at the expense of both the State and Defense Departments. However, he rightly noted that secrecy had not always served intelligence or the CIA well, as "secrecy begets suspicion, which can metastasize into beliefs in conspiracies of the most awful sort"—for example, that the CIA was involved in the Kennedy assassination. The Moynihan Commission viewed government secrecy as a relic of the Cold War and a principal reason for the Soviet Union's own ultimate collapse. It therefore argued for a new "culture of openness" that apparently did not require the services of the CIA.[87]

Moynihan took his argument even more public by publishing a book titled *Secrecy* the following year.[88] He also celebrated the declassification of records from Project Venona, the heavily classified Cold War–era SIGINT program to intercept Soviet communications. Moynihan's position on Venona was especially ironic. It undermined his stance on secrecy because it was an example of a highly valuable intelligence program successfully kept secret for decades.[89] Despite his best efforts, Moynihan could not resolve the problems and paradoxes of American intelligence history.

American Intelligence on the Eve of the Next Pearl Harbor

Intelligence was on the defensive throughout the 1990s. The USIC survived largely intact because policymakers fundamentally understood that intelligence was an essential and permanent pillar of national security. Still, the USIC was fighting ideological opposition and post–Cold War retrenchment at home while confronting multiplying challenges and threats abroad. It had its choice of missions, but it could seemingly settle on a "jack-of-all-trades, master of none" approach since no major apparent adversary loomed. In congressional hearings, executive meetings, and public debates, "diversification was ever the watchword of those who defended the intelligence bureaucracy or called for its expansion." However, diversification became another source of bureaucratic competition as different intelligence organizations rushed to take on the same missions. Diversification also had the untoward effect of blurring mission focus; after all, some missions had to have priority over others, and it was up to the USIC to identify priorities that policymakers were missing. American intelligence was lost amid the options.[90]

In November 1999, Seymour Hersh published an exposé on the NSA's decline, warning of an "intelligence gap" that "left our spies out in the cold." Hersh listed the NSA's many challenges. There was the organization's loss of prestige among policymakers in Congress and the executive branch. It suffered as a result of bureaucratic competition with the CIA and within the DOD. Above all, it faced ideological opposition from the public as the "traditional American belief in privacy and constitutional protection [was] at odds with a superspy agency capable of monitoring unencrypted telephone conversations and E-mail exchanges anywhere in the world." The NSA's director, General Michael Hayden, reflected, "In its forty-year struggle against Soviet Communism, the N.S.A. was thorough, stable, and focused." Hayden then asked himself, "What's changed?" before answering his own question: "All of that."[91]

The USIC was hardly left toothless by the end of the Cold War. Even if bureaucratically bloated in the eyes of peace dividend advocates, and although perhaps a little lost without an obvious enemy on which to focus its efforts, it was a far more robust intelligence establishment than the United States had ever had during a period of retrenchment following a war. It could still bring incredible resources, personnel, and capabilities to bear against the next threat. The question was whether the United States would pick the adversary or the adversary would pick the United States.

The answer would be both. Terrorism had been a threat to American interests even during the Cold War, but the Soviet Union naturally dominated the day. The Aspin-Brown Commission suggested missions and priorities for the USIC that included counternarcotics, counterproliferation, countering international organized crime, and, of course, counterterrorism.[92] Likewise, in his op-ed for the *Washington Post*, Haass contemplated a role for intelligence in "preemptive attacks on terrorists."[93] The mounting terrorist attacks against the United States in the 1990s—the World Trade Center bombing in 1993, the Khobar Towers bombing in 1996, the embassy bombings in Dar es Salaam, Tanzania, and Nairobi, Kenya, in 1998, and the attack on the USS *Cole* in 2000—foreshadowed the unimaginable to come.

21

A New National Consensus and New National Security State

INSTEAD OF BEING comfortably ensconced in retirement, Gary Schroen found himself back in Afghanistan in September 2001. Schroen was one of the CIA officers who had helped the mujahideen defeat the Soviet Union in Afghanistan during the 1980s. As the Soviets began their withdrawal, the United States decided to close the embassy in Kabul in January 1989, which Schroen argued was a big mistake. He wanted to keep CIA personnel in Kabul to monitor post-Soviet Afghanistan. Events proved Schroen right.[1]

Afghanistan never stabilized. The radical Taliban government that took control of Kabul in 1996 provided a safe haven for Osama bin Laden and his al Qaeda organization. There, they planned attacks against US targets, including the embassy bombings in 1998 and the attack on the *Cole* in 2000. Additionally, bin Laden issued fatwas that declared jihad, or holy war, against the United States in 1996 and 1998. In response, DCI George Tenet declared war on al Qaeda in December 1998.[2] The CIA was almost back in the fight.

In exchange for the Taliban's hospitality, bin Laden and al Qaeda helped it fight a civil war against the Northern Alliance led by Ahmad Shah Massoud, the "Lion of Panjshir."[3] Schroen rekindled the CIA's relationship with Massoud in 1996.[4] Over the next few years, the CIA sent liaison teams, including a team from its Counterterrorism Center (CTC) code-named Jawbreaker, to provide Massoud and the Northern Alliance with money and equipment. The CIA was keen to know when Massoud picked up any intelligence on bin Laden's movements around Afghanistan. But the CIA and the US government equivocated when it came to capturing or killing bin Laden. In 1998, the CIA abandoned a plan to capture bin Laden at Tarnak Farms.[5] In early 2000, it passed along intelligence to Massoud that bin Laden was at Derunta Camp near Jalalabad. Massoud wanted to strike the camp with rockets in the hope of killing bin Laden. CIA attorneys balked at the idea that CIA intelligence would result in a targeted killing operation. Subsequent guidelines were established that allowed the CIA and Massoud only to plan missions to capture bin Laden, which frustrated Massoud and his men.[6]

During one mission to Afghanistan in 2000, CIA officer Gary Berntsen recorded the reaction of Massoud's aide to news that CIA headquarters was ordering the team to pull out of the country: "This is common for America. You make promises and abandon us.... I will never understand your country."[7] Massoud demonstrated his own more subtle understanding of American civil-intelligence relations. He observed that "intelligence people are always aggressive," but they "represented a democracy, they represented an organized society where institutions function with restrictions." Although "the CIA wished to do a lot in Afghanistan... their hands were tied." Massoud decided that it "was not an intelligence failure. It was a political failure."[8] Whether an intelligence or a political failure, the outcome was even more tragic failure.

It began with Massoud. On September 9, 2001, two men posing as journalists who wanted to interview Massoud detonated explosives hidden in a video camera and battery pack, killing the Lion of Panjshir. Two days later, al Qaeda struck the United States. On September 11, as the world watched, hijacked planes hit the World Trade Center in New York City and the Pentagon in Arlington, Virginia, while courageous passengers on United Flight 93 forced another plane to crash in rural Pennsylvania before it could hit its target in Washington, DC. The terrorist attacks on 9/11 shook the United States to its core. The worst attack on US soil since Pearl Harbor destroyed whatever illusion Americans continued to hold of a more peaceful post–Cold War world.

Paradoxically, intelligence appeared to be both the cause of and solution to 9/11. The attacks were the result of an intelligence failure in the most immediate sense of the term because intelligence had not prevented the attacks. Moreover, the President and Congress joined the media and the American people in scapegoating intelligence and heaping criticism on the USIC for its supposed shortcomings in the 1990s that allowed 9/11 to happen. At the very same time, they all also praised the hard work of the patriotic people working in the USIC. The entire country looked to intelligence to confront the threat of terrorism and prevent future attacks.

Intelligence had been on the defensive in the 1990s and now had to rapidly shift to the offensive. Congress had bogged the intelligence community down in hearings and reviews that forced the USIC to defend not just its missions but in some cases its very existence, while also cutting its budget and personnel. The Clinton administration displayed a fleeting interest in intelligence and instilled a risk-averseness in the USIC, especially the CIA, exhibited by its half-hearted attempts to target bin Laden during the 1990s.[9] The Bush administration compounded the Clinton administration's failure to take aggressive measures against bin Laden and al Qaeda before 9/11.

To be fair, the USIC was to blame, too. Upper management in the CIA reflected the political sensitivities and fears of the Clinton administration by aborting missions to capture or kill bin Laden. As always, the organizations in the USIC fought among themselves, particularly over diminished resources. The problem of intelligence coordination, particularly between the CIA and FBI and between foreign and domestic intelligence, became the central debate of 9/11. Like other intelligence failures of the past, the USIC did flash warning signs of an impending attack. For example, the so-called Phoenix Memo, forwarded to FBI headquarters in July 2001, sketched out a plan by bin Laden to send terrorists to US aviation schools, while a CIA President's Daily Brief (PDB) of August 6, 2001, titled, "Bin Ladin Determined to Strike in US," warned of the possibility of an attack, even mentioning the threat of hijacked aircraft.[10] However, like the Soviet atomic bomb or the North Korean invasion of South Korea, it was not enough for intelligence to merely identify trends or to report an enemy's intentions. Policymakers and the public expected the USIC to know the timing of the attacks and stop them. So,

FIGURE 21.1 This cartoon critiques the USIC's failure to prevent the 9/11 attacks. Courtesy Etta Hulme Papers, Special Collections, The University of Texas at Arlington Libraries.

9/11 entered the annals of American intelligence history as the worst intelligence failure since Pearl Harbor.

Following 9/11, Islamist terrorism became the ideological threat and exigency that the United States would have to combat. In the immediate aftermath, the country rallied around a common cause. Reflecting their traditional temperament in times of national danger, the American people were both fearful and bloodthirsty. The President quickly issued executive orders and findings that mobilized intelligence for the Global War on Terror, while Congress relegislated an American national security state. The USIC, which had been somewhat adrift in the 1990s, had a new primary adversary and mission. Reflecting the halcyon days of the Cold War consensus, the pillars of American civil-intelligence relations temporarily aligned to meet the threat.

American Intelligence in a Global War on Terror

Intelligence seemed to provide the best instrument to respond to terrorism. Terrorists do not wear uniforms, and they attempt to blend into civil society. They work as organizations, small networks, or, in some cases, "lone wolf" individuals. Intelligence officers are a foil to terrorists in some respects because they are accustomed to blending in and gaining access to closed-off organizations, groups, and individuals. Moreover, transnational terrorist networks operate across borders in both allied and adversarial states. The US government may not have the diplomatic or law enforcement power to arrest terrorists in some countries, while it may not want to risk the consequences of a military strike in others. Clandestine intelligence collection and covert action allowed the United States to take the fight to the terrorists by uncovering terrorist cells and keeping them off balance through capture-or-kill operations.

But the new security environment following the 9/11 attacks also complicated the Cold War intelligence paradigm that had profoundly influenced the design of the American intelligence system. Although the Cold War had been global, the center of gravity was always the Soviet Union, which steered the USIC's structure, resources, authorities, capabilities, and expertise. The Soviet Union also had a measure of control over its officers, operations, and, to an extent, proxies, allowing the US and Soviet governments to establish some unspoken codes of conduct for their spy games. Furthermore, regardless of the integral role of intelligence, the military still maintained primacy as the key national security institution in the Cold War.

The USIC had to adapt to the Global War on Terror. The geographical shift meant a pivot in terms of language and culture, which in turn required corresponding shifts in the recruitment and training of intelligence officers. The United States faced both state and non-state adversaries with different levels of control and coordination over terrorists, so many of the old rules were out. Although the conventional military was on the front lines in Afghanistan and Iraq, the United States turned to a combination of intelligence and special operations forces to "find, fix, and finish" terrorists on and off the battlefield. But the convergence of intelligence and special operations compounded the old identity crisis plaguing the CIA as primarily analytical or operational in its organizational culture and priorities.

The Global War on Terror tested the USIC and civil-intelligence relations in other ways. Whereas the Cold War largely preserved the arbitrary boundary between domestic and foreign intelligence, terrorists wanted to attack the US homeland by any means possible, meaning the threat was persistent and pervasive. They aimed at "soft," civilian targets, so the USIC had to target those weak points for surveillance and detection to disrupt terrorist plots. As a result, the USIC had to enlist the help of the American people in a war without borders or boundaries. Posters implored the public, "If you see something, say something," which became a pathway for citizens to surveil one another and report back to the government. Terrorism blurred law enforcement and intelligence, as well as foreign and domestic intelligence, two key sources of controversy in American intelligence history. It created an atmosphere of fear, paranoia, and suspicion in an open society and constitutional state that required trust not only between citizens and their government but also between citizens themselves.

By incorporating the American people into the Global War on Terror, the USIC faced challenges to principles of intelligence professionalism. For example, the USIC found itself caught between secrecy and transparency. Intelligence officers instinctively want to protect their coveted sources and methods. Even when it could be in the national interest to know about a terrorist plot, intelligence organizations may want to withhold information about an attack to learn more about a terrorist network or to locate terrorist leadership for capture-kill missions. However, intelligence had to warn policymakers, which in some cases extended to the public, of a possible terrorist threat, which risked undoing all that work. Thus, terrorism placed competing pressures on intelligence.

Indeed, the pressure on the USIC was enormous. As it learned on 9/11, even one terrorist attack was one too many for policymakers and the public. A terrorist attack could come in the form of a knife attack by a lone wolf, a bomb attack by a group, or, in the worst-case scenario, an attack with a weapon of mass destruction (WMD). The expectation was that the USIC would predict and prevent each and every terrorist attack, meaning that it faced the impossible challenge of being both omniscient and omnipotent. Intelligence failure was completely unacceptable. Any miscalculation would hurt the President and Congress politically, so terrorism raised the stakes for both policymakers and the USIC. Even rumors of a possible terrorist attack were enough to send people running, ground flights, disrupt everyday life, and otherwise cause chaos.

Fearful of another imminent attack, the US government, with the consent of the American people, instituted aggressive intelligence measures at home and abroad after 9/11. Intelligence, rather than the military, had to be the main tool against terrorism abroad, while intelligence, rather than law enforcement, had to take the lead against terrorism at home. Given the scale of the threat, the USIC conducted a truly global intelligence campaign that at times tread upon American principles, ensuring there would be conflicts in civil-intelligence relations.

A Phoenix Rises from the Ashes

During the Vietnam War, the CIA spearheaded the Phoenix Program, a joint US–South Vietnamese venture that involved capturing, interrogating, and killing members of the Viet Cong.[11] On September 17, 2001, President George W. Bush signed a secret memorandum authorizing the CIA to capture or kill al Qaeda members around the world. It set the course for targeted killing, extraordinary rendition, and "enhanced interrogation," three essential elements of the USIC's counterterrorism campaign.[12] Bush told reporters that bin Laden faced old-time, Western justice: "Wanted Dead or Alive."[13] Cofer Black, the head of the CIA's CTC, instructed Gary Schroen before he left for Afghanistan,

> I want to give you your marching orders, and I want to make them very clear. I have discussed this with the president, and he is in full agreement.... Your mission is to exert all efforts to find Usama bin Ladin and his senior lieutenants and to kill them. I don't want bin Ladin and his thugs captured, I want them dead. Alive and in prison here in the United States, they'll become a symbol, a rallying point for other terrorists. They have planned and carried out the murder of thousands of our citizens. They must be killed. I want to see photos of their heads on pikes. I want bin Ladin's head shipped back in a box filled with dry ice. I want to be able to show bin Ladin's head to the president. I promised him I would do that. Have I made myself clear?[14]

The message from Bush and Black seemed clear enough: Phoenix was reborn. In fact, in the aftermath of 9/11, Bush announced, "I want the CIA to be the first on the ground."[15] Schroen and his team touched down in Afghanistan on September 26. They were ready, but was the CIA ready?

The CIA immediately began to institute changes, including bringing in new recruits from the military and training them in the ways of intelligence to counterbalance a cautious, bureaucratic culture that some Cold War–era CIA officers perceived to have taken hold.[16] Depending on military veterans to shore up the CIA risked conflating the intelligence and military professions once again. Additionally, counterterrorism appeared to be an especially fitting mission for the operational side of the CIA, which further encouraged a pivot in organizational culture. The CIA, which had spent much of the early Cold War trying to distinguish itself from the military, found itself increasingly enmeshed in paramilitary activities in Afghanistan. Military special operations forces joined the CIA in Afghanistan. They worked closely to hunt for Osama bin Laden and help the Northern Alliance oust the Taliban government. Gary Berntsen promised Cofer Black that "the senior SF [Special Forces] officer attached to me will be my brother. I'll include him in everything."[17]

The Global War on Terror produced growing proximity between the CIA and military special operations, especially the Joint Special Operations Command (JSOC), which blended organizations, professions, and structural authorities as they pertained to intelligence activities conducted by the military or CIA.[18] Intelligence and the military could certainly cooperate well on the ground, as they did in the Phoenix Program during the Vietnam War. However, there has also always been inherent competition between the two in Washington, DC. Since counterterrorism drew budget allocations from Congress, the CIA and military competed for their share of the missions, funding, and prestige that came with it.

Even amid the cooperation between the CIA and military special operations forces in Afghanistan, Secretary of Defense Donald Rumsfeld decided to create an intelligence component in the DOD to eliminate its "near total dependence on the CIA" for HUMINT. The plan signaled the DOD's "bid to conduct surreptitious missions, in friendly and unfriendly states, when conventional war is a distant or unlikely prospect—activities that have traditionally been the province of the CIA's Directorate of Operations."[19] Rumsfeld and the DOD were trying not only to reduce, if not eliminate, the role of the CIA in DOD counterterrorism operations but also to challenge the CIA's primacy in HUMINT, one of its key functional contributions to the USIC.

Ambiguity in applicable US law and congressional oversight over what should be intelligence or military activities and CIA or DOD responsibilities was what gave the DOD an opening and later produced a fight in Congress over it. Rumsfeld had created the new component without congressional authority by using "reprogrammed funds." DOD officials and attorneys reinterpreted statutory distinctions between intelligence and military operations to give the DOD broad authority to conduct what appeared to be intelligence activities outside of military theaters and combat operations.[20] The congressional armed services committees stood behind the DOD. They claimed that the new DOD HUMINT initiative was part of the DOD's budget that they had reviewed and approved. However, the congressional intelligence committees felt that the DOD had deliberately circumvented or manipulated existing statutory authorities to give itself HUMINT capabilities without congressional authority or approval.[21] Members of HPSCI claimed they were unaware of the DOD's program until asked about it by the press, while SSCI members also insisted that they had not been properly informed.[22] The congressional intelligence committees believed the DOD's new intelligence activities more properly belonged under their purview.

The problem was one of statutory language. In a self-inflicted wound, Congress had defined covert action and attempted to distinguish it from "traditional intelligence activities" and "traditional military activities."[23] Senator John D. Rockefeller IV of SSCI exclaimed, "I don't take lightly the distinction between clandestine and covert.... It makes all the difference in the world."[24] Congress was running into problems that implicated different statutory authorities (Title 10 versus Title 50 of the US Code), different intelligence bureaucracies (the CIA versus the DOD's new HUMINT program), and different national security professions (intelligence versus the military).

In the meantime, counterterrorism had given the CIA a renewed sense of purpose. The President and Congress stood behind the CIA, enabling its global intelligence campaign against terrorism. But in endorsing the CIA to take the fight to the terrorists, the United States was reopening debates over executive power, congressional oversight, and intelligence activities. Trouble began with the initial presidential order of September 17, 2001, that sent the CIA to war.

Constructing the New National Security State

Bush's order immediately set off alarm bells at the CIA. Previous Presidents had signed executive orders banning "assassination." But they had also issued findings that broadened the CIA's authority to conduct counterterrorism missions. For example, in 1986, Reagan signed a finding that would allow the CIA to strike terrorists preemptively or capture them overseas for trial in the

United States.[25] Following the embassy bombings in 1998, Clinton authorized covert lethal operations against al Qaeda. Presidents had therefore prohibited assassination but endorsed targeted killing at the same time. Mindful of the past and of when the CIA had been the scapegoat for controversial presidential policies, the CIA "was determined to leave no room this time for 'plausible denial' of responsibility on the part of the president…The paper trail inside government must begin undeniably with 'the political leadership.'"[26] In this, the CIA would find no opposition from the Bush administration.

The President, Vice President, and Cabinet endorsed a vision of executive control over intelligence in line with the Reagan administration and others reaching back to George Washington. The Global War on Terror provided the grounds for Bush "to restore what he rightly saw as the uniquely executive responsibility for authorizing clandestine operations."[27] In the immediate aftermath of 9/11, he met little resistance from Congress, which deferred to the President, just as it had in the early days of the Cold War.

On September 18, Congress legislated the Authorization for Use of Military Force (AUMF), granting the President the power to use "all necessary and appropriate force" against those responsible for the 9/11 attacks "in order to prevent any future acts of international terrorism against the United States."[28] But it rejected language that would have given the President "open-ended authority to act against all terrorism and terrorists or aggressors against the United States anywhere," opting instead to limit the AUMF to "those nations, organizations and persons who aided or harbored the terrorists" responsible for 9/11.[29] Regardless, Bush and succeeding Presidents interpreted their authorities under the AUMF broadly, using it to continue a covert campaign against terrorists across Africa, the Middle East, Southwest Asia, and Southeast Asia.[30] Although members of Congress and the public have expressed concerns about the scope, longevity, and application of the AUMF, Congress has yet to amend or revoke it.[31]

Congress also expanded the powers of the USIC following 9/11 in ways that endangered civil liberties. Like the Alien and Sedition Acts accompanying the spy hysteria of the XYZ Affair and the First World War, Congress hurriedly passed legislation affecting domestic intelligence. The USA PATRIOT Act of October 2001 established the legislative foundation for the American intelligence state. The acronym stood for "Uniting and Strengthening America by Providing Appropriate Tools Required to Intercept and Obstruct Terrorism." The act couched extensive intelligence authorities in language that would appeal to the American people. The act enhanced intelligence powers across a range of missions and functions while blurring or amending earlier statutory or customary limits on intelligence.[32]

For example, the USA PATRIOT Act revisited the arbitrary distinction between foreign and domestic intelligence. It required the Attorney General or any head of a federal law enforcement agency to "expeditiously disclose to the Director of Central Intelligence... foreign intelligence acquired... in the course of a criminal investigation," blurring the boundary between law enforcement and intelligence in the process.[33] The act defined "foreign intelligence information" to mean "information, whether or not concerning a United States person, that relates to the ability of the United States to protect" itself, which could allow the government to bypass the distinctions and protections afforded to American citizens from foreign intelligence collection by agencies, like the CIA and NSA, and from statutory laws, like FISA.[34] In fact, the act amended FISA and expanded government electronic surveillance authorities. It also changed requirements for private information technology and communications companies to hand over customer records to the government and provided a loophole for those companies to "voluntarily" disclose information to the government regarding an immediate threat.[35] The FBI had its investigatory powers increased by amendments to provisions concerning National Security Letters, which allowed it to access the personal records of private citizens.

The USA PATRIOT Act passed both houses of Congress with overwhelming bipartisan support. Congress therefore sanctioned the expansion of both the executive branch's and the USIC's power. However, the Bush administration had already preempted congressional legislation with executive action and had unleashed the vast surveillance capabilities of the NSA.

On October 4, 2001, Bush signed the first authorization in what later became known as the President's Surveillance Program (PSP). The PSP was a collection of presidential authorizations for extraordinary USIC surveillance, primarily conducted by the NSA. Among other prerogatives, this first order allowed the NSA to intercept wire and cable communications into or out of the United States; collect the metadata of telephone and internet providers; and retain, process, analyze, and disseminate intelligence acquired under the order, meaning the NSA could share the results of its surveillance across the government and USIC. The order also ignored FISA requirements "under certain circumstances."[36]

Not only did the Bush administration undermine Congress, but it also cut the judiciary out of intelligence programs that affected the constitutional rights of American citizens. In what became a trend in the Global War on Terror, the executive branch conducted intelligence operations before considering their legality or constitutionality. Bush authorized the PSP before administration attorneys had even offered a legal opinion on it. Although Attorney General John Ashcroft certified the first presidential authorization as to "form and legality" the same day Bush signed the directive, the actual legal analysis occurred later. In November 2001, Deputy Assistant Attorney General John Yoo of the Justice Department's Office of Legal Counsel (OLC) rendered his opinion in a memorandum defending the program.[37] He argued that FISA was an "unconstitutional infringement on the President's Article II authorities" because it "cannot restrict the President's ability to engage in warrantless searches that protect the national security"—the same logic President Franklin Roosevelt applied to wiretapping in 1940 despite congressional legislation and judicial precedent. The Bush administration ultimately argued for the legality and constitutionality of the PSP on the basis of presidential constitutional powers and discretionary presidential control of intelligence.[38]

There was also a practical problem that prompted the Bush administration to launch the PSP. Technology and the way people used it had changed dramatically since Congress first legislated FISA in 1978. The NSA "determined that FISA authorization did not allow sufficient flexibility to counter the new terrorist threat" and that the FISA process was unable to accommodate the number of terrorist targets or the speed with which they changed their communications."[39] DNSA General Michael Hayden claimed that the "NSA could not address the intelligence gap using FISA."[40] Immediately after 9/11, HPSCI asked the NSA for assistance in drafting a congressional proposal to amend FISA, suggesting that HPSCI understood the 1978 act's deficiencies.[41] HPSCI's proposal sputtered, likely because the executive branch feared that a congressional amendment might take too long or might impede NSA activities. The PSP demonstrated how the statutes guiding the USIC obsolesce as intelligence methods and capabilities advance. Congress needs to keep up if it wants to be a stakeholder in intelligence control and oversight.[42] In the event, the executive branch quickly chose to initiate an intelligence program that conflicted with existing legislation but was necessary to meet the new threat. Even so, the PSP probably would not have encountered much resistance in the aftermath of 9/11.

Both the legislative and judicial branches were informed of the PSP and took no action to curb it until it leaked to the press. Hayden briefed members of HPSCI and SSCI in the early days of the program.[43] He also briefed the chief judge of the FISC and the incoming chief judge of the FISC in 2002, and neither "express[ed] any view or comment on the legality or illegality of the PSP."[44] The oversight mechanisms within the USIC itself seemed to sanction the PSP. The NSA Office of General Counsel was briefed on the program the same day it started, while the NSA Inspector General belatedly learned of the PSP a year later. Even then, the NSA IG never opposed the PSP but instead recommended monthly "due diligence."[45] They were not the only ones embracing the PSP.

Ever since the era of the Cipher Bureau, American SIGINT organizations relied on private companies to provide the government with access to their records and systems. Immediately after 9/11, private companies offered their services to the NSA. In fact, the NSA had to turn down their help before the presidential order of October 4 allowed it to exploit private sector resources, although the NSA made it clear that the PSP "was a cooperative program and participation was voluntary."[46] The NSA and American corporations were engaged in a joint surveillance enterprise, but there was one more pillar of civil-intelligence relations still missing.

Careful What You Wish For

Like earlier episodes in US history, the pendulum swung from liberty to security as the American people responded to the 9/11 attacks and terrorist threat by supporting the new national security state. Polling showed that trust in the US government soared to levels unseen since before the intelligence scandals of the 1970s. A majority of Americans agreed that it was necessary to sacrifice civil liberties to fight terrorism, although most people "drew the line against allowing the government to monitor *their own* emails and phone calls."[47] The public would only later find out that bulk data collection by the NSA did not draw that line. Still, the American people were once again willing to trade liberty for security—with some contingencies. However, changes in intelligence brought about by a combination of the Global War on Terror and the Information Age suggest they may never fully recover what was lost in the exchange.

In the menacing days following 9/11, a new national consensus emerged. As in the early days of the Cold War, the US government, intelligence community, and public united against a threat. Once again, the consensus would not last. In fact, it began to crumble soon after its inception, though an American intelligence state would continue to expand and evolve.

22

Reform Without Resolution

ON THE EVENING of 9/11, President Bush wrote in his daily White House log, "The Pearl Harbor of the 21st century took place today."[1] The comparison resonated. Steven Push, who lost his wife in the attacks, summarized the collective mood when he told Congress, "Our loved ones paid the ultimate price for the worst American intelligence failure since Pearl Harbor."[2] All were to blame for the 9/11 failure, but some took more blame than others—intelligence, especially the CIA, as usual. But they had repeatedly warned the President and Congress about terrorism throughout the 1990s, and the President and Congress responded, even if not to the extent that hindsight demanded they should have.

Congress had even created a statutory commission to review the threat of terrorism before 9/11. Released in June 2000, the Report of the National Commission on Terrorism professed, "Good Intelligence Is the Best Weapon Against International Terrorism." It recommended strengthening CIA HUMINT sources, including rescinding a 1995 guideline that restricted recruiting informants from terrorist organizations. Likewise, it found the FBI and DOJ's bureaucratic rules and procedures, including the FISA process, too restrictive. It also suggested increasing funding for the CIA's CTC, the FBI, and the NSA. In the most prescient portions, the report even made pointed recommendations for the government to track possible terrorists passing as students in the United States and to designate Afghanistan as a state sponsor of terrorism. Thus, a year before the 9/11 attacks, a commission highlighted flaws in the country's existing counterterrorism system that commissions after 9/11 blamed on the USIC.[3]

Another pre-9/11 commission made an even blunter assessment of the state of American intelligence. The US Commission on National Security/21st Century concluded in its final report of January 2001, "The basic structure of the U.S. intelligence community does not require change." It proposed strengthening the DCI as one of its narrower reforms yet also stressed the need to maintain an equilibrium between the DCI and the Secretary of

Defense. Nowhere did the report mention a DNI. Mirroring the commission on terrorism, it endorsed a more robust HUMINT capability, including the USIC's need to recruit individuals "not liable to be model citizens of spotless virtue" in order to uncover "terrorist plans and methods." Finally, the report noted the pressing need to "secure the homeland" and to increase funding and resources for the entire USIC. Crucially, both pre-9/11 commissions balanced their criticism of the USIC with tailored recommendations to improve it. There was no need to scapegoat the USIC and no perceived need to fundamentally reshape the entire American intelligence system.[4]

That all changed on 9/11. The next day, Henry Kissinger stated that the US "government should be charged with a systematic response that . . . will end the way that the attack on Pearl Harbor ended—with the destruction of the system that is responsible for it." He feared that until 9/11, the United States had "been trying to do this [counterterrorism] as a police matter, [but] now it has to be done a different way." In addressing whether 9/11 was an intelligence failure, he acknowledged that if he "had been asked whether such a coordinated attack as yesterday's was possible, [he], no more than most people, would have thought so." Kissinger, who had not been nearly as conciliatory toward intelligence when he was National Security Advisor and Secretary of State, probably knew a greater reckoning awaited.[5]

Although the entire country looked to the USIC to prevent subsequent terrorist attacks, it still needed someone to blame for 9/11. Intelligence was the natural scapegoat. An intelligence failure of this magnitude meant a congressional investigation, which would lead to calls for reform and proposals for new legislation. A familiar cycle in American intelligence history began anew.

Congress Makes Its Case

Congressional intervention started with a joint inquiry by HPSCI and SSCI into the 9/11 attacks. The 2002 report's first finding was entirely too predictable: Although the USIC "had amassed a great deal of valuable intelligence regarding Usama Bin Ladin and his terrorist activities, none of it identified the time, place, and specific nature of the attacks that were planned for September 11, 2001." Once again, American intelligence had failed by not providing the tactical intelligence of time, place, and target. The committee also determined that the USIC did not "demonstrate sufficient initiative in coming to grips with the new transnational threats," an observation that just as easily applied to Congress, the President, and the rest of the country during the 1990s.[6] Although prosaically faulting the "U.S. Government as a whole," the Joint Inquiry singled out the USIC for its failure to create a "comprehensive counterterrorist strategy."[7] In this respect, the committee report tied counterterrorism to intelligence coordination. The division between foreign and domestic intelligence was an obstacle to coordinating intelligence and, in the case of 9/11, it had hampered counterterrorism. In the final analysis, the committee concluded that the DCI had failed to coordinate the USIC, while the USIC had failed to coordinate itself.

The Joint Inquiry's recommendations were as predictable as its findings. The report stated that a statutory DNI would "make the entire U.S. Intelligence Community operate as a coherent whole"—the impossible dream of American intelligence for nearly a century and a mainstay of congressional intelligence reform efforts for nearly a half century. It also offered specific recommendations for the different components of the USIC it blamed for 9/11—namely, the CIA, FBI, and NSA. Critically, it focused on the specific threat of terrorism, meaning that its proposals for intelligence reform were directed at terrorism as the exigency of the day more so than any enduring issue with the American intelligence system, although the two overlapped in some respects, like coordination. Finally—and not surprisingly—the joint inquiry emphasized the role congressional oversight should play in structuring and managing American intelligence.[8]

Congress's previous proposals for a DNI and a grand charter to restructure the USIC were unsuccessful because no immediate crisis justified taking drastic measures. Furthermore, key officials in the executive branch had opposed legislative reform, and especially the creation of a DNI. The events of 9/11 gave Congress the cause it needed to drive forward historic intelligence reform. However, the joint inquiry was packaged in typical congressional language and trappings, so it failed to resonate with the American people and did not sate the public's anger or curiosity.

Even while the joint inquiry was ongoing, pressure was building in Congress for an independent commission to study the 9/11 attacks. The relatives of the victims of 9/11 attended the hearings and pushed Congress for more answers.[9] A senior New York City Police Department official expressed his disappointment with the inquiry: "You can hardly point to a cataclysmic event in our history, whether it was the sinking of the *Titanic*, the Pearl Harbor attack, the Kennedy assassination, when a blue-ribbon panel did not set out to establish the facts, and where appropriate, suggest reforms.... That has not happened here."[10] Congress and the American people were aligned, but they had to overcome the opposition of the President.

Fearing political blowback for failing to prevent the attacks, Bush had hoped to keep the 9/11 investigation confined to the joint inquiry rather than a wider, public probe. The Bush administration also worried that a public commission would expose sensitive information about US counterterrorism operations.[11] Furthermore, officials argued that a full commission with hearings, testimonies, and paper requests would consume resources that the USIC desperately needed for the Global War on Terror.[12] Congress tapped into public pressure and prevailed over the Bush administration. The result was the National Commission on Terrorist Attacks upon the United States, or the 9/11 Commission.

The enabling legislation for the 9/11 Commission was incorporated into the Intelligence Authorization Act for FY 2003. The commission was called to "build upon the investigations of other entities, and avoid unnecessary duplication, by reviewing the findings, conclusions, and recommendations of" the Joint Inquiry, among others.[13] Naturally, its report arrived at similar conclusions and recommendations to the Joint Inquiry. However, the 9/11 Commission report read like a narrative and became a national bestseller. In it, the commission expressed its "hope" that the report "will encourage our fellow citizens to study, reflect—and act."[14] It emphasized American principles, proclaiming, "Just as we did in the Cold War, we need to defend our ideals abroad vigorously."[15] The report would shape the contours of the ongoing national debate over American intelligence, framing both the problems and solutions that Congress would later incorporate into the most significant structural intelligence reform since 1947.

Like the Joint Inquiry, the 9/11 Commission tackled the historically entrenched problem of intelligence coordination in the context of counterterrorism. Combining the two, it recommended establishing a National Counterterrorism Center (NCTC) staffed by representatives from across the USIC to produce joint intelligence. Aiming even higher, it took on the problem of coordinating the entire American intelligence system, arriving at the same solution as other congressional and presidential investigations. Echoing decades of proposals, it called for the creation of a "National Intelligence Director"—that is, a DNI—who would have broad powers to oversee the budget and operations of the USIC and who would also supplant the DCI as the principal intelligence advisor to the President. The 9/11 Commission would further curtail the DCI and CIA's influence by shifting responsibility for paramilitary operations to the DOD. Although removing the paramilitary function from the CIA would help resolve its historical identity crisis, it was targeting a pillar of CIA bureaucratic power and prestige, made even more relevant by the ongoing Global War on Terror. Just as it appeared the CIA would gain newfound status and standing, the 9/11 Commission proposed to undercut the CIA's influence and, indeed, independence.[16]

At the same time, the commission was prepared to further empower the FBI, a federal law enforcement agency, in its domestic intelligence role. The report recommended that the FBI develop a "specialized and integrated national security workforce... imbued with a deep expertise in intelligence and national security."[17] In trying to perhaps eliminate the wall between intelligence and law enforcement, the commission risked blurring them even more and contributing to the FBI's own identity crisis. Ironically, despite the care that American policymakers had taken to separate intelligence and law enforcement in creating the CIA, the 9/11 Commission was willing to overlook the inherent conflicts between those two professions in the FBI.

The 9/11 Commission, which included several former members of Congress, joined the joint inquiry in advocating even more vigorous congressional intelligence oversight. It declared this to be "among the most difficult and important" recommendations and dismissed the current oversight system as "now dysfunctional." In its place, it offered two proposals for reform: mirroring the "old model of the Joint Committee on Atomic Energy"—an idea dismissed as early as the 1950s—or maintaining the current model of the two congressional intelligence committees but giving them authorization and appropriation authorities.[18] However, each of these proposals replicated a historical dysfunction associated with congressional intelligence oversight. The former proposal was perhaps too deferential to intelligence, while the latter, post–Church Committee approach was too politically partisan and prone to leaks. Neither was satisfactory.

The Politics of Intelligence Failure

It was not accidental that both the joint inquiry and the 9/11 Commission settled on the premise that intelligence had failed. As tempting as it might have been to blame the other party and exploit national outrage to score a political victory, both Republicans and Democrats stood to suffer blowback because the origins of the 9/11 failure spanned multiple presidential administrations. When SSCI chairman Bob Graham announced the joint inquiry, he claimed that both he and HPSCI chairman Porter Goss were "committed to a fair, non-partisan and thorough process."[19] But "non-partisan" misrepresents the political composition of the joint inquiry and the 9/11 Commission.

The two committees were bipartisan, rather than nonpartisan, bodies.[20] During the joint inquiry, Republicans controlled HPSCI and Democrats controlled SSCI. Meanwhile, the 9/11 Commission was composed of exactly five Democrats and five Republicans. Goss stressed that the joint inquiry was "not a who-shall-we-hang type of investigation."[21] HPSCI member Nancy Pelosi added that HPSCI and SSCI "have a responsibility to ensure that Congress conducts a thorough assessment of the performance of the intelligence agencies leading up to and including September 11th" and that "the best way to do that is to work cooperatively, in a bipartisan manner." She, too, concluded that the "inquiry's purpose is not to assign fault"—at least not politically.[22] Instead, all the 9/11 investigatory bodies would set their crosshairs on the USIC.

First, they would still have to overcome the specter of political partisanship that hung over the proceedings. 9/11 Commission chairman Thomas Kean and vice chairman Lee Hamilton described the political problem facing them: if the "inquiry were to be broadened from examining the performance of the intelligence agencies to include an examination of the wider policy choices of the Bush and Clinton administrations, then it would be far more difficult for Republican and Democratic members of Congress to work in a nonpartisan manner." They recorded that "unanimity did not come easily." Commissioners often "split roughly down partisan lines," and "commissioners themselves [were becoming] targets for politicians and pundits from both sides of the partisan divide." Nonetheless, they credited the commission with producing a "bipartisan report on the most urgent security matter of the day," which would "put the onus on Congress and the president to come together across partisan lines, and to act." The result spared the politicians and scapegoated the USIC.[23]

But the 9/11 Commission investigation revealed that the shortcomings and failures of the USIC reflected the shortcomings and failures of the Clinton and Bush administrations. Each administration had restricted the USIC—namely, the CIA—from targeting al Qaeda to the extent it was willing or able, despite warnings that al Qaeda wanted to launch catastrophic attacks in the United States.[24] In the end, the reports avoided directly blaming one or both presidential administrations for 9/11.

Congress also escaped the commission largely unscathed. When asked in an interview, "Was Congress at fault at all on Sept. 11?" Senator Graham demurred. He claimed that Congress had intended to provide "more resources to the intelligence community" and alluded to other reforms that the congressional intelligence committees had proposed for the USIC.[25] Similarly, the 9/11 Commission acknowledged that previous commissions had "made scores of recommendations to address terrorism and homeland security but drew little attention from Congress."[26] Although Congress conducted hearings about what the USIC was doing in the 1990s, the 9/11 Commission Report noted that "Congress did not reorganize itself after the end of the Cold War to address new threats."[27]

The post-9/11 investigations left the USIC to absorb most of the blame for another intelligence failure, which further undermined the public trust in it after a decade on the defensive. Kean announced that policymakers "were not served properly by the intelligence agencies of this country . . . I can tell you that the two presidents of the United States were not well served by those agencies, and they did not, in my opinion, have the information they needed to make the decisions they had to make."[28] Kean and Hamilton also publicly accused the CIA of not cooperating with the 9/11 Commission investigation in a *New York Times* op-ed provocatively titled "Stonewalled by the C.I.A."[29] As in previous investigations, the USIC was left to fend for itself.

Following the example of William Colby, Cofer Black, the former head of the CIA's CTC, testified before the joint inquiry and turned the tables on both the President and Congress. Although the committee had offered Black a screen to shield his identity, he refused, stoically stating, "I want to look the American people in the eye." He described the CIA's struggles with resources and personnel even as it watched bin Laden and al Qaeda with increasing alarm throughout the 1990s. Countering the joint inquiry's and 9/11 Commission's criticism that a lack of intelligence coordination had led to the attack, Black offered evidence of cooperation between the FBI and CIA to thwart terrorist plots. In fact, Black regretted that he could not share all the USIC's successes in preventing terrorist attacks before 9/11 due to classification restrictions. He concluded by speaking to his own officers from the CTC, telling them that he "was proud of them" and adding that he wanted "the American people to hear this." Black's attempt to set the record straight ultimately fell on deaf ears.[30]

Unfortunately, the pathologies of American civil-intelligence relations were already deeply embedded before 9/11. The 9/11 investigations correctly identified several challenges in the American intelligence system, but the reports failed to adequately identify and explain their historical antecedents. The proceedings themselves also fell victim to some of the same old problems.

FIGURE 22.1 This cartoon depicts the silos in the USIC impeding intelligence coordination. Courtesy Etta Hulme Papers, Special Collections, The University of Texas at Arlington Libraries.

Barriers to Intelligence Coordination and Compromise

Just like on the eve of Pearl Harbor, the United States had the system for which it had bargained on 9/11, including a much-maligned "wall" in intelligence sharing discussed in the 9/11 Commission Report. The "wall" could be interpreted as the professional division between intelligence and law enforcement, the functional division between foreign and domestic intelligence, or the organizational division between the CIA and FBI. These walls represented the evolution of the American intelligence system in response to bureaucratic competition, intelligence professionalization, and ideological opposition, but they were politicized during the 9/11 investigation. Regardless of the bipartisan consensus that emerged in the 9/11 Commission, Republicans and Democrats in government and the press still cherry-picked the hearings and report to blame the other presidential administration for the attacks.

In fact, the 9/11 Commission had to defend one of its own. Attorney General John Ashcroft asserted in his testimony that "the single greatest structural cause for September 11 was the wall that segregated criminal investigators and intelligence agents" in the FBI on account of a 1995 legal memorandum drafted by 9/11 Commission member Jamie Gorelick when she was a Deputy Attorney General in the Clinton administration.[31] Ashcroft declassified the memorandum and pointedly told the commission, "Full disclosure compels me to inform you that the author of this memorandum is a member of the commission."[32] The issue quickly devolved into one of partisanship and blame-shifting. The press joined the fracas. The *New York Times* ran a headline claiming, "Ashcroft Faults Clinton Era at 9/11 Panel," while the *Washington Times* reported that "Gorelick [had] been among the most partisan and aggressive Democratic panel members in questioning the anti-terror efforts of the Bush administration," and called for Gorelick to testify about her role in the 9/11 failure.[33]

In response, Gorelick penned her own public defense in a *Washington Post* op-ed during the 9/11 Commission investigation, claiming that she "did not invent the wall," but that it was a result of the congressionally legislated FISA and subsequent judicial interpretations of it. In her rebuttal, she also blamed the presidential administrations of Ronald Reagan and George H. W. Bush for creating the wall and even argued that her 1995 memorandum had loosened restrictions on information sharing between intelligence officers and criminal investigators to "ensure the flow of information 'over the wall.'" Gorelick therefore jeopardized the precarious bipartisan standing of the panel with her own politicized defense.[34]

Former Senator Thomas Slade Gorton, a Republican on the 9/11 Commission, wrote an op-ed defending Gorelick after the commission concluded. He blamed Congress for legislation that helped build the wall before 9/11, but stressed that it was "not clear that those laws would have prohibited sharing information in this instance."[35] Moreover, the commission report determined that the 1995 memorandum's "procedures were almost immediately misunderstood and misapplied" by the FBI, noting that they "dealt only with sharing between agents and criminal prosecutors, not between two kinds of FBI agents, those working on intelligence matters and those working on criminal matters." As an outgrowth of the internal confusion, the FBI had limited the sharing of intelligence it obtained from the CIA and NSA with FBI criminal investigators.[36] So, the 9/11 Commission avoided a partisan schism by shifting blame back onto the USIC.

The commission's work served to exacerbate divisions within the USIC and American intelligence system. The FBI and CIA sparred over which organization was responsible for 9/11, with former FBI and CIA officials later accusing each other of failing to track the 9/11 hijackers or share intelligence.[37] But there was more at stake than rivalry or culpability. The FBI stood to lose its domestic intelligence function, as some policymakers and observers believed it was time to follow the trend of other countries and establish a domestic intelligence service with no law enforcement powers like Britain's MI5.[38] Throughout its history, the FBI tried to avoid scrutiny of its domestic intelligence operations by hiding behind its cover as a law enforcement organization. It followed the same playbook to divert blame away from itself and protect its bureaucratic fiefdom over domestic intelligence.

Just as John Wilkie had insisted the Secret Service was a law enforcement organization rather than a domestic intelligence service nearly a century before, the FBI made the same claim. During the 9/11 Commission hearings, the FBI contended that it "had not so much failed *on* 9/11 because domestic intelligence was not really part of [its] mission until *after* 9/11."[39] In fact, FBI Director Robert Mueller took steps after 9/11 to make it appear that the FBI was only just becoming aware of its domestic intelligence role by creating an Office of Intelligence and building a cadre of FBI intelligence specialists. Mueller's bureaucratically shrewd changes "supported an argument that the FBI should be given a chance to succeed in a new mission area while the CIA was forced to explain why it had failed at something that had been core to its purpose."[40] As its history shows, the FBI had been a domestic intelligence service since its very creation as the BOI. Hoover consummated the FBI's victory over domestic intelligence, although he tempered those activities at times to avoid congressional or public scrutiny. After Hoover's death and the Church Committee investigation, the FBI conveniently forgot its roots.[41]

The 9/11 Commission accepted the FBI's revisionist history, rejected the idea of creating a new domestic intelligence agency, and suggested that the FBI retain both law enforcement and domestic intelligence functions.[42] The FBI also had its own Joint Terrorism Task Forces (JTTFs) composed of federal, state, and local law enforcement organizations, giving it further bureaucratic power in counterterrorism, so the 9/11 Commission was probably hesitant to intervene at such a perilous time, with the country facing the ongoing threat of terrorism. The FBI's dual authority over national law enforcement and domestic intelligence, combined with its attempts to "snatch turf from the embattled CIA," reinforced the walls between law enforcement and intelligence, foreign and domestic intelligence, and the CIA and FBI.[43]

These walls and their accompanying obstacles were not simply the products of historical singularities like the Church Committee, FISA, or a 1995 memorandum. They rested on a much deeper foundation. Congress itself had played its part in constructing the very walls that it later sought to demolish after 9/11. Just as paradoxically, Congress embarked on what was both the most wide-ranging and yet narrowest reform of American intelligence since 1947.

The Long and Short of IRTPA

What a change an intelligence failure and a few years had made. Whereas the U.S. Commission on National Security/21st Century had determined in January 2001 that the basic structure of the American intelligence system was sound, SSCI chairman Pat Roberts announced in September 2004, "Simply put, the structure of the U.S. intelligence community is defective." He went further, claiming that the "so-called Director of Central Intelligence . . . lacks authority, in statute and in practice, to effectively manage the intelligence activities of the United States." First up was a new statute.[44]

The Intelligence Reform and Terrorism Prevention Act of 2004 (IRTPA) was the long-awaited intelligence overhaul proposed decades prior and frequently revisited without success.[45] However, as the product of an intelligence failure and an exigent threat, IRTPA risked tainting long-term intelligence reform with short-term security priorities. The USIC, already steered toward counterterrorism by policymakers and the public, was given a congressional mandate to make counterterrorism its raison d'être. In doing so, it resumed its focus on a single major adversary, though the multipolar, post–Cold War world should have demonstrated that there were many global challenges besides terrorism. IRTPA would purportedly coordinate the USIC and thwart terrorism in one signature piece of legislation—an impossible goal that, nevertheless, did not stop Congress from trying.

IRTPA finally established the position of the Director of National Intelligence. The Director of Central Intelligence became the Director of the Central Intelligence Agency (DCIA). The act stipulated that the DNI could not simultaneously be the DCIA or the head of any other organization in the USIC. It also specified that the DNI and Principal Deputy Director of National Intelligence (PDDNI) could not both be active-duty military officers. While IRTPA did not mandate that the DNI or PDDNI must be a military officer, the act said it was "desirable" to have one come from the military ranks, likely to mitigate tensions between civilian and military intelligence.[46] It would be the responsibility of the DNI to "ensure maximum availability of and access to intelligence information within the intelligence community," demonstrating congressional intent that the DNI should coordinate intelligence, much as the DCI was supposed to do according to the 1947 National Security Act.[47]

Congressional legislation and intent aside, it would be up to the executive branch to ensure the DNI could coordinate the USIC in practice. President Bush, under considerable pressure from the 9/11 Commission Report and an impending presidential election, had already lent his support to congressionally driven intelligence reform in a White House speech in August 2004. He had asked Congress to establish a "National Intelligence Director" to "oversee and coordinate the foreign and domestic activities of" the USIC. In response to Bush's speech, a reporter mentioned that some of the President's "own advisors oppose creation of a National Intelligence Director" and inquired if the President would "give the new director sweeping budget authority."[48] With the President and Congress aligned behind the DNI, the issue was how much power the DNI would actually have when faced with competition from other executive departments and intelligence organizations.

The Department of Defense Goes to War Against a "Department of Intelligence"

Vice President Dick Cheney and Secretary of Defense Donald Rumsfeld stridently resisted the creation of the DNI. Both men had a history of opposing measures that shifted DOD capabilities and resources to the DCI or a proposed DNI.[49] Just as the Bush administration had initially opposed the 9/11 Commission, claiming it would divert intelligence resources needed for the Global War on Terror, Rumsfeld worried that a massive intelligence reorganization would jeopardize the war effort in Afghanistan and Iraq. He sneered that "we're rearranging the deck chairs of the *Titanic*" and blamed "those amateur brain surgeons... in the Senate."[50]

The bureaucratic battle within the executive branch spilled over into Congress as a rift emerged between the intelligence committees and armed services committees. The Senate Armed Services Committee (SASC) opposed any DNI authorities that would transfer oversight and control over existing DOD intelligence components and resources to SSCI. Furthermore, SASC defended the DOD against being lumped in with the USIC as part of the 9/11 intelligence failure. Congressman Duncan Hunter, chairman of the House Armed Services Committee, echoed Rumsfeld's insistence that IRTPA would affect military and intelligence operations overseas. Genuine concerns over intelligence support to the military during a time of war notwithstanding, money became a central area of contention. The stakes were especially high for the Secretary of Defense and DOD.[51]

The 9/11 Commission noted that the DCI's role in coordinating the USIC's budget never translated into the power to coordinate the USIC and that most of the funding for the USIC remained hidden in the DOD budget.[52] IRTPA ostensibly granted the DNI the power to "develop and determine" the annual national intelligence budget, but this authority amounted to little since the budget was reviewed and approved by the President and four congressional committees.[53] As a result, the DNI was dependent on personal and professional relationships with agency directors.[54] Even in 2007, when relative interpersonal comity existed among the DNI, DCIA, and Secretary of Defense, bureaucratic competition still drove wedges into the USIC.[55] Intelligence was big business for the DOD, and the Secretary of Defense was loath to cede any control to the DNI.

Rumsfeld began to undermine the DNI even before its creation. He asserted "greater independence of action" as Congress was crafting IRTPA until it agreed to "language that he interpret[ed] as preserving much of the [DOD's] autonomy." Under Secretary of Defense for Intelligence General William Boykin explained that the DOD was simply trying to ensure it could meet its obligations because the Secretary of Defense "actually has more responsibility to collect intelligence for the national intelligence program… than does the CIA director." He tied the budget to the DOD's intelligence role: "That's why you hear all this information being published about the secretary [of Defense] having 80 percent of the [intelligence] budget. Well, yea, but he has 80 percent of the responsibility for collection, as well."[56]

One reason such a high percentage of the budget flowed to the DOD was that it went to DOD intelligence organizations like the NSA, NRO, and National Geospatial-Intelligence Agency (NGA). These organizations use extraordinarily complex and expensive intelligence systems and platforms that require funding for research and development, production, and operational deployment. Aside from the simple bureaucratic competition over resources, deeper historical forces were at play. The DOD had won control over several key intelligence functions with the NSA, NRO, and NGA. The division between the DNI and Secretary of Defense over the USIC's membership and resources therefore reflected a longer tradition of subordinating intelligence to the military.

During the debates that produced IRTPA and the DNI, some observers wondered whether it was time to establish a more distinct boundary between intelligence and the military by changing the architecture of the USIC. In an op-ed for the *Washington Post*, John Hamre, the president of the Center for Strategic and International Studies and a former Deputy Secretary of Defense, argued that the "DNI needs to be undergirded with real institutional power" and proposed that the NRO, NSA, and NGA should be transferred to the DNI.[57] Shortly after Hamre's op-ed, Acting DCI John McLaughlin sent a letter to Bush urging him to "give [the DNI] command and control authority over core national intelligence agencies—the CIA, NSA, NGA, and NRO." Worse yet, Rumsfeld faced subversion from within as Generals James Clapper and Michael Hayden, the Directors of NGA and NSA, respectively, entertained the idea of moving their organizations to the DNI.[58]

Congress still needed a way to give the DNI at least some measure of control over the historically warring chieftains of the USIC. To this end, the 9/11 Commission had recommended that the DNI have approval authority over the nominees to lead the various organizations of the USIC.[59] But IRTPA did not give the DNI sufficient appointment authority, leaving the real power with the President and executive department heads.[60] Where congressional legislation proved wanting, the President stepped in to try to strengthen the DNI. In an ultimately unsuccessful effort to bolster the position, Bush amended EO 12333 in 2008 along the dual avenues of appointment and budgetary powers.[61] However, the DNI still does not control the actual means of conducting intelligence collection or operations. Those remain with the different members of the USIC, half of which reside within the DOD. Unlike the Secretary of Defense, who controls the DOD's intelligence organizations, the DNI does not have the same power.[62]

Legislating the DNI was an incredible historical achievement, but IRTPA missed an even more historic opportunity by leaving the USIC's composition fractured among different executive departments and institutions of national security. While there were executive departments representing the military, diplomatic, and law enforcement institutions, there would be no Department of Intelligence representing the intelligence institution. The growing pains associated with the new Department of Homeland Security led the 9/11 Commission to abandon the idea, while SSCI likewise considered it as part of IRTPA before yielding to resistance from SASC.[63] Instead, IRTPA created another independent intelligence organization in addition to the CIA setting the stage for a clash between the old and new orders.

National Versus Central Intelligence

The DCI and CIA had the most to lose under IRTPA. Just as Rumsfeld and Cheney fought IRTPA as current and former Secretaries of Defense, so too did former DCIs. Bush's top pick for the new DNI position, Robert Gates, who had been in line for the proposed DNI position in 1992, still rejected the concept in 2004. He thought Congress was "racing to ruin the CIA." Gates understood that the DCI never had the actual power or authority to coordinate the USIC and that the new DNI would face many of the same challenges. He also predicted that "any provisions transferring Pentagon agencies and their budgets to the [DNI] would be watered down and compromised into meaningless verbiage," which is what happened with the DNI's appointment and budgetary powers. Based on his insights, Gates determined that the DNI "would, in fact, be an intelligence eunuch."[64] He declined the position. Former DCI George Tenet, who resigned in July 2004, also challenged IRTPA and the DNI, claiming that Congress was simply in a "mad rush to rearrange wiring diagrams in an attempt to be seen as doing something."[65]

Congress was considering intelligence coordination in the context of the 9/11 attacks. If it wanted the USIC to focus on counterterrorism, and counterterrorism was the prized mission in bureaucratic competition, then the CIA should notionally have emerged the winner in IRTPA. Instead, the CIA ended up on the losing end.

The CIA pivoted toward the narrower threat of terrorism at the expense of the broader, global responsibilities it had. For example, CIA analysis shifted toward targeting, distracting it from the true purpose of analysis, understanding. At the same time, the DCIA became the "combatant commander in the war on terrorism," leading the "troops," ironically a term Gates used to refer to intelligence officers in almost the same breath that he warned about the military's dominant position in the USIC.[66] The CIA's pivot toward paramilitary operations and counterterrorism did it no favors in terms of intelligence analysis and coordination—the original legislative intent behind its creation.

The CIA also suffered from a structural problem that left it at a disadvantage during the debate over IRTPA. As an independent intelligence organization, the CIA lacked a departmental patron. With the proposed reforms affecting various organizations in the USIC, all but the CIA could take cover under a larger executive department. As the position of the DNI became a legislative certainty, the Secretary of Defense and DOD simply fought for their own interests and left the DCI and CIA to their fate. In IRTPA, the DCI and CIA lost two major levers of bureaucratic power to the DNI: the position of the DCI as the chief intelligence advisor to the President and organizational control over the PDB, the signature intelligence product delivered to the President every day.

In turn, Congress had to resolve questions about the DNI. It had to balance the DNI's proximity to the President with the problem of politicization. During the hearings on IRTPA, several members of Congress raised this issue if the DNI were to be placed in the Executive Office of the President.[67] At the same time, Congress recognized that the DNI must be coequal to the department heads of the executive branch.[68] So, it stipulated that the DNI would be a Cabinet-level position. To fulfill the responsibility for the PDB and other flagship intelligence products, IRTPA legislated a new bureaucratic organization, the Office of the Director of National Intelligence (ODNI), to facilitate the DNI's functions.[69]

With both a national and a central intelligence organization, and a director of national intelligence and a director of (the) central intelligence (agency), how would the two bodies and their leaders interact? Although the CIA would continue to analyze all-source intelligence, the ODNI's analytical staff would coordinate the production of the PDB. In 2009, outgoing DCIA Michael Hayden and outgoing DNI Mike McConnell offered a stark metaphor to explain the CIA-ODNI relationship. In response to Hayden's comment, "Between the two of us there's going to be a trenchline," McConnell remarked, "Anytime you have organizations that have similar interests, you're going to have disputes. And particularly if the two leaders aren't working together and having a partnership and so on, the warfare at the trench level gets to be pretty much a raging battle."[70] The language used by the two directors hardly signaled a coherent arrangement.

Furthermore, with two intelligence advisors to choose from, the President could show favor to one or the other based on personal, policy, or political loyalty as much as any other factor. The fight for the President's ear can therefore create the very politicization that Congress wanted to avoid. And while the ODNI and CIA may be organizationally independent, the relationship between their two directors is not. IRTPA specified that the DCIA "shall report to" the DNI, implying a subordinate status.[71] Yet, in his confirmation hearing for the position of DCIA, Leon Panetta at first insisted that the DNI merely had a coordinating role with respect to the CIA as an "operational arm" of the USIC. Only under some pressure did Panetta later concede, "The DNI is my boss."[72] Nevertheless, Panetta was determined to fight for traditional DCIA authorities.

IRTPA replaced the vague language in the 1947 National Security Act giving the NSC the authority to oversee CIA covert action with a revision that stipulated that the CIA would "perform such other functions and duties... as the President or the Director of National Intelligence may direct."[73] The new language inserted the DNI into covert action in a way that provides divergent authorities and allows the DCIA to simply circumvent the DNI. In fact, during a schism between Panetta and DNI Admiral Dennis Blair over covert action, the White House made it clear that the President still wanted direct control over CIA covert action, reducing the DNI's authority or influence.[74]

Similarly, in another quarrel between the DCIA and DNI during the tenures of Panetta and Blair, the two clashed over which director would choose the top American intelligence officer in each country overseas. Blair insisted that the DNI had the ultimate authority to select this official and that the individual did not need to be the CIA's chief of station, which was the established practice. Panetta refused to cede ground. Members of Congress expressed their displeasure that "the C.I.A. has not accepted its reduced role in the intelligence firmament," with Senator Dianne Feinstein, chairwoman of SSCI, venting, "We need to move intelligence away from the cold war mind-set and the C.I.A. has a problem to some extent accepting that." However, Congress created the conditions for these interagency clashes in legislating IRTPA.[75]

IRTPA singled out the CIA for censure in other ways as well. For example, the act stipulated that the DNI "shall ensure compliance with the Constitution and law of the United States by the Central Intelligence Agency" and the other elements of the USIC.[76] Notably, this provision only mentioned the CIA by name, echoing the long-standing criticism that the CIA was uniquely responsible for unconstitutional intelligence transgressions. IRTPA also adopted the 9/11 Commission's conclusion that the CIA's lack of diversity weakened its ability to operate in the Global War on Terrorism, although it was hardly alone in this regard.[77] Like the 9/11 Commission and the joint inquiry, IRTPA suffered from historical shortsightedness, leading to a multifront assault on the CIA—bureaucratically, operationally, and culturally.

The Federal Bureau of Intelligence

Where the CIA lost ground, an old organizational rival emerged a winner from IRTPA. Rather than punish the FBI by creating a domestic intelligence service just as it had punished the CIA with the creation of the DNI, Congress rewarded the FBI by enlarging its intelligence authorities and capabilities. IRTPA followed the 9/11 Commission's recommendation that the FBI create a national intelligence workforce of "agents, analysts, linguists and surveillance specialists who are recruited, trained, and rewarded in a manner which ensures the existence within the Federal Bureau of Investigation [of] an institutional culture with substantial expertise in, and commitment to, the intelligence mission of the Bureau." Moreover, the act expressly stipulated, "Each agent employed by the Bureau... shall receive basic training in both criminal justice matters and national intelligence matters" and have assignments in each field, legislatively blurring the intelligence and law enforcement professions in a tradition that reached back to the detective-spies of the Civil War. To make its point, IRTPA redesignated the FBI Office of Intelligence the Directorate of Intelligence. In effect, Congress created a Federal Bureau of Investigation and Intelligence.[78]

In another striking example of historical myopia, Congress wanted IRTPA to transform the FBI's organizational culture into something it always was but arguably never should have been. As a DOJ component, the FBI was first and foremost a law enforcement organization, even as it nurtured and performed its domestic intelligence function. Congress intended to combine the competing organizational cultures of intelligence and law enforcement in the FBI to combat terrorism. The FBI was only too happy to oblige with this legislative expansion of its bureaucratic power. Hoover's heirs would have the congressional authority he had always coveted.

Reforming American Intelligence History?

Rather than resolve many of the historical problems plaguing American intelligence, IRTPA simply relegislated or restructured them. Under IRTPA, the relationship between the USIC and DNI mirrored what Thomas Troy described as the relationship between the CIG and DCI: "a headless body and a bodyless head."[79] The DNI inherited many of the same coordination problems faced by the DCI. The DNI oversees the USIC but cannot exactly coordinate it because IRTPA did not give the DNI control over its different organizations or functions.

Truly empowering the DNI would have required even more dramatic reform by institutionalizing intelligence through an executive department. Rather than doing this, IRTPA allowed intelligence to remain broken up among different professions and institutions of national security. Unquestionably, an independent intelligence institution would threaten civil liberties and constitutional rights, which is perhaps why the United States has avoided creating a Department of Intelligence.[80] But different elements of the American intelligence establishment committed abuses throughout US history even without an independent intelligence institution. The country would again be at risk with the invasive type of intelligence and surveillance activities required by counterterrorism. No sooner had the ink on IRTPA dried than a new series of intelligence scandals and controversies rocked the country.

23

Revelation Without Reform

IN THE AFTERMATH of 9/11, the USIC embraced counterterrorism with an almost messianic fervor, both as the mission to save it from the collective malaise of the 1990s and because counterterrorism fundamentally appealed to core features of the intelligence profession. At the urging of a unified country, the USIC aggressively pursued terrorists, killing them in raids and drone strikes or kidnapping and interrogating them under extraordinarily harsh conditions in secret prisons around the world. In a war without borders, counterterrorism also blurred the boundaries between foreign and domestic intelligence, leading the USIC to unleash technologically enabled surveillance on the American people beyond the scope of anything comparable in US history. Inauspiciously, innovations in intelligence and technology combined with the exigency of the Global War on Terror to produce a persistent surveillance state that has proven difficult to dismantle once created.

Every decade since 1975, intelligence somehow made the headlines in a defining way. In 2005, a flurry of controversies involving foreign and domestic intelligence operations splintered the post-9/11 consensus. Reports of intelligence excesses and abuses, conducted with executive approval and congressional oversight, raised questions concerning the scope of the USIC's powers and activities. Congress soon expressed remorse for the legislation it passed in support of the Global War on Terror and subsequent Iraq War. It reacted by investigating the USIC but made no effort to roll back the new American intelligence state. Congress had rushed to pass IRTPA in 2004 and was not going to revisit its landmark legislation so soon. Any subsequent reform enacted in response to the controversies would merely be a temporary, impromptu salve.

"Dead Wrong"

The Bush administration relied on any number of pretexts to launch the war in Iraq in 2003, including an alleged connection between Saddam Hussein and al Qaeda that was disputed by the CIA and other elements of the USIC.[1] However, the main pretext for the war—what DCI Tenet had called a "slam dunk"—was the collective analytical judgment of the CIA, USIC, and many other foreign intelligence services that Iraq possessed weapons of mass destruction (WMDs). Tenet later disputed what he meant by "slam dunk," arguing that he was trying to convey to the Bush administration that they could put together a better "public case," which still risked politicizing intelligence by using it in a narrative to advance a presidential policy. Tenet also claimed that his comment allowed the Bush administration to scapegoat the USIC, CIA, and himself for what was fundamentally a policy decision to go to war in Iraq.[2] Instead of a slam dunk, the country called a foul on the USIC.

Another major intelligence failure meant another investigation. The Bush administration initially resisted yet another commission that could hurt it politically. In June 2003, SSCI began its own inquiry, which scrutinized the USIC rather than the Bush administration.[3] Bush eventually relented and created the Commission on the Intelligence Capabilities of the United States Regarding Weapons of Mass Destruction (WMD Commission) in February 2004. Although its point of origin was different from that of the 9/11 Commission, it followed a similar course and encountered some familiar obstacles along the way.

In contrast to the 9/11 Commission, the WMD Commission was the product of an executive order.[4] The order had two significant effects because it preempted a congressional commission and limited the scope of the commission's investigation. At a White House press conference in which the co-chairmen of the WMD Commission, Laurence Silberman and Charles Robb, "flanked a beaming Bush as if they were bodyguards," Silberman admitted that the commission did not interview Bush or Cheney as part of its investigation because "our executive order did not direct us to deal with the use of intelligence by policymakers."[5] Like the 9/11 Commission, the WMD Commission was bipartisan, ostensibly to preserve the appearance of impartiality, but more likely because the issue of Iraqi WMDs bridged multiple presidential administrations. Furthermore, over one hundred Democratic members of Congress had voted for the resolution that authorized the Bush administration to use military force in Iraq, making the misadventure very much a bipartisan problem.[6] So, the commission's report "direct[ed] its fire at the intelligence professionals—the same ones already beaten up by the Sept. 11 commission and congressional reports—and [gave] the political figures a pass."[7]

Unsurprisingly, the commission concluded that the USIC was "fragmented, loosely managed, and poorly coordinated," and "a 'Community' in name only." Notably, it delivered its report in March 2005, three months after IRTPA was enacted. As a result, the WMD Commission found itself in the problematic position of critiquing the landmark legislation that Congress had just passed to address some of the very same problems the commission highlighted in its investigation. For example, the commission presented four principal recommendations in its cover letter to Bush: (1) give the DNI sufficient power to match the position's responsibilities, (2) bring the FBI "all the way" into the USIC, (3) demand more of the USIC, and (4) rethink the PDB to balance long-term and short-term, or current, intelligence. The commission took aim at the new DNI role, determining that it "could have been a purely coordinating position" or "something closer to a 'Secretary of Intelligence'" but in fact was "neither of these things." Instead, it was "given broad responsibilities but only ambiguous authorities." While the WMD Commission may have correctly deduced IRTPA was incomplete in terms of intelligence reform, it did not help clarify the challenges and limitations of intelligence for an American public that was trying to understand the failures that led to the Iraq war. Ultimately, it offered the stark assessment that the USIC's judgments were "dead wrong."[8]

The USIC had already failed on 9/11, but with the addition of the Iraq WMD failure, the country was laboring under competing conclusions about why the USIC failed in each instance. Former CIA officer Mark Lowenthal juxtaposes the two to highlight the paradoxes:

> In 9/11, intelligence was excoriated for "failing to connect the dots."... But in Iraq, intelligence was blamed for connecting too many dots.
>
> In 9/11, intelligence did not warn intensely enough. But in Iraq, intelligence warned too intensely.
>
> In 9/11, intelligence was faulted for a "failure of imagination." But in Iraq, intelligence had too vivid an imagination.
>
> In 9/11, the failure to share intelligence was seen as a major problem. But in Iraq, too much information... was shared.[9]

The USIC was damned if it did and damned if it didn't.

Politicization also dogged the Iraq WMD failure. In 2002, Secretary of Defense Donald Rumsfeld and his Deputy Secretary of Defense, Paul Wolfowitz, created an Office of Special Plans (OSP) within the DOD to analyze the question of Iraqi WMDs. One former intelligence official at DIA explained, "The Pentagon has banded together to dominate the government's foreign policy and they've pulled it off.... The D.I.A. has been intimidated and beaten to a pulp. And there's no guts at all in the C.I.A." The OSP's defenders countered that the OSP was conducting careful analysis in the place of a derelict USIC. One OSP official claimed, "I did a job when the intelligence community wasn't doing theirs . . . they hadn't done the analysis." Or at least not to Rumsfeld's satisfaction. In other words, if the USIC was not going to politicize intelligence, the OSP would.[10] The OSP had a distinct advantage over the USIC because it was not bound by the same professional intelligence constraint to avoid policy advocacy. A DOD official crowed that OSP "won the policy debate . . . they beat 'em—they cleaned up against State and the C.I.A. There's no mystery why they won—because they were more effective in making their argument. . . . It was a fair fight. They persuaded the President of the need to make a new security policy."[11]

The Iraq War put the USIC in the middle of increasingly ugly partisan attacks. One particularly notorious episode was the unmasking of CIA officer Valerie Plame. Joseph Wilson, Plame's husband and a former US diplomat, ended up on a CIA-funded trip to Niger in February 2002 to investigate a rumor that Iraq was trying to purchase uranium "yellowcake." He reported back that the deal was "highly unlikely," although the CIA "did not regard Wilson's intelligence as definitive."[12] The yellowcake rumor persisted, and Bush repeated it in his 2003 State of the Union Address. Wilson, who had deep connections to the Democratic Party, entered the political minefield by writing an op-ed in the *New York Times* in July 2003 challenging the Bush administration's narrative and questioning its "selective use of intelligence to justify the war in Iraq."[13]

A week after Wilson's op-ed, *Washington Post* columnist Robert Novak exposed Wilson's wife as an undercover CIA officer.[14] In what was almost certainly an act of political retribution, Bush administration officials Richard Armitage, Karl Rove, and I. Lewis "Scooter" Libby had discovered that Plame worked for the CIA and revealed her identity to several journalists. The story outed Plame and essentially destroyed her career.[15]

Justifiably aggrieved, Plame took her case to Congress, where she claimed that her cover was blown for "purely political motives." She disputed accounts claiming she had advised the CIA to send her husband on the fact-finding mission to Niger, flatly stating, "I did not recommend him. I did not suggest him. There was no nepotism involved."[16] However, SSCI's ongoing investigation into Iraqi WMDs uncovered a classified memorandum in which Plame had discussed rumors of an Iraq-Niger nexus only a few weeks before the trip and found evidence of her telling an official that her husband had "good relationships" with officials in Niger and "may be in a position to assist."

Additionally, Plame later told the CIA Inspector General that she had suggested her husband could investigate the Iraq-Niger uranium nexus.[17] The Plame affair continued an earlier American tradition of mixing diplomacy and intelligence, which led to mixing intelligence and politics. It was also one of several sub-scandals of the larger Iraq WMD scandal that battered US civil-intelligence relations. The USIC had more to hide.

Extraordinary Rendition and an Extraordinary CIA Failure

In June 2005, an Italian judge issued warrants for the arrest of thirteen CIA officers on the charge of kidnapping. The scandal became known as the "Imam Rapito" or "Kidnapped Imam" affair.[18] The events had unfolded a few years earlier, in February 2003, when Hassan Mustafa Osama Nasr, aka Abu Omar, disappeared from the streets of Milan. Abu Omar was just one of dozens of accused terrorists the CIA seized as part of its extraordinary rendition program. The program involved capturing accused terrorists and transferring them to a third country for interrogation, which usually involved the use of torture. The CIA sent Abu Omar to Egypt, where he was interrogated and tortured until an Egyptian judge released him in April 2004. He immediately called his wife and reported that he had been kidnapped and taken to Egypt. By speaking about the incident, Abu Omar violated instructions given to him by the Egyptian security services. He disappeared again and did not reappear until his second release from Egyptian prison in February 2007.

In the case of Abu Omar, the CIA operation backfired spectacularly. First, DIGOS, Italy's national law enforcement agency, had already had Abu Omar under surveillance. It had bugged his home phone, cellphone, apartment, and mosque. It also had planted a video camera in his apartment along with a device that recorded keystrokes on his personal computer.[19] The CIA actually tried to mislead DIGOS after the kidnapping by sending it a false tip-off claiming that Abu Omar had fled to the Balkans.[20] Meanwhile, Jeffrey Castelli, the CIA chief of station in Rome, had apparently briefed his counterpart in SISMI, Italy's military intelligence service, about the operation, so Italy seemed to suffer from its own wall between law enforcement and intelligence.[21]

The operation was almost certain to fail due to the sheer recklessness and poor tradecraft of the CIA officers involved. Among the principal purposes of covert action operations is that they remain covert or at least deniable. The CIA mismanaged the Abu Omar operation so badly that any semblance of plausible deniability vanished.

Armando Spataro, an Italian prosecutor in Milan, instructed DIGOS inspector Bruno Megale to figure out who kidnapped Abu Omar. Ironically, Megale untangled the operation through phone tracking software originally provided to DIGOS by the CIA. In one of the many blunders committed by the operatives in Milan, they chose to communicate over traceable cellphones rather than using the walkie-talkies the CIA had provided. DIGOS traced the calls made by these phones to luxury hotels where several Americans had checked in using addresses close to CIA headquarters in Langley, Virginia. The operatives had spent over $100,000 using easily traceable credit cards. When checking into the hotels or renting vehicles, a few of them provided their personal account numbers for frequent flier miles and preferred-guest programs. Some lingered in Milan after the operation and stayed in even more luxurious accommodations. The same unsettling and self-indulgent trend occurred in other operations.[22] Veteran CIA officer Robert Baer later explained that proper tradecraft would have included using satellite phones and paying in cash, while an op-ed in the *New York Times* ridiculed the operatives as "The CIA Gang That Couldn't Snatch Straight."[23] How could so many intelligence professionals have made such amateur mistakes?

The CIA could address the sloppy tradecraft through better training and preparation for future missions, but this should not overshadow the unsteady foundation supporting the entire operation. In the first place, there was dissent between senior CIA officers in Italy, Milan station chief Robert Seldon Lady and Rome station chief Castelli. Italian intelligence officials stated that the idea for Abu Omar's rendition originated with Castelli, who thought the operation would be "a notch in his belt" when the CIA considered him for promotion.[24] Some CIA officials later alleged that Castelli intentionally misled superiors by hyperbolizing the threat Abu Omar posed and questioning DIGOS's surveillance capabilities.[25] For his part, Lady maintained good relations with DIGOS. He had warned Castelli that the abduction would disrupt DIGOS's surveillance of Abu Omar and would damage DIGOS's cooperation with the CIA. An anonymous senior CIA official admitted that he and Stephen Kappes, the CIA's Associate Deputy Director for Operations, approved the operation but did not know about Lady's objections. He also claimed they likely would have stopped it had they known. So, the operation moved ahead despite the apparent objections of the Milan station chief, the man who had to take charge of the operation and subsequently lost his job, his retirement home in Italy, and his wife after its failure.[26]

The Abu Omar operation also revealed confusion in US intelligence policy. In the 1980s, Congress expanded laws aimed at capturing terrorists abroad, while in 1986 the Reagan administration approved more aggressive covert action operations to capture terrorists.[27] The policy continued under the Clinton administration as "rendition," a name invented by National Security Advisor Sandy Berger, who also praised it as a "new art form."[28] In fact, during an Oval Office meeting to discuss an operation in 1993, Vice President Al Gore exclaimed, "Of course it's a violation of international law, that's why it's a covert action. The guy is a terrorist. Go grab his ass."[29] The rendition process changed in the mid-1990s under Michael Scheuer, a CIA officer who transformed the rendition program to break up terrorist (namely, al Qaeda) cells.[30] The CIA and Albanian intelligence service cooperated to capture an Egyptian terrorist cell in Tirana in 1998—an operation that made the press when the Albanians revealed the CIA's involvement.[31] The men were sent to Egypt, where they were tortured and two were executed. In response, al Qaeda's second-in-command, Ayman al-Zawahiri, promised revenge. Two days later, al Qaeda struck the American embassies in Kenya and Tanzania. Rendition was part of an ongoing war on terror even before the Global War on Terror.[32]

After 9/11, the rendition program expanded beyond al Qaeda leaders, such as Abu Zubaydah and Khalid Sheikh Mohammed, to include dozens of less valuable targets, such as Abu Omar. While intelligence officials certainly wanted to take down senior terrorists, they also urgently sought information that might help prevent a terrorist attack, so they identified lower-level figures for rendition. The expansion of the program raised questions about its purposes. According to Scheuer, intelligence gathering was not the priority pre-9/11. The goal was to get the target "off the street."[33] This changed with the Global War on Terror. Baer described how the destination of the rendered individual signaled the desired outcome: "If you want a serious interrogation, you send a prisoner to Jordan. If you want them to be tortured, you send them to Syria. If you want someone to disappear—never to see them again—you send them to Egypt."[34] Egypt became the preferred destination for the CIA's extraordinary renditions.

In the case of Abu Omar, the CIA failed to obtain information from him or get him "off the streets." Contrary to Baer's assertion, Abu Omar did not "disappear" in Egypt but was released on two different occasions pursuant to Egyptian court rulings. Furthermore, Spataro, the prosecutor who built the case against the CIA, claimed that Abu Omar would have ended up in an Italian jail for terrorist activities and that the abduction actually "damaged counterterrorism efforts in Italy and Europe."[35] Indeed, an Italian court convicted Abu Omar on terrorism charges in absentia in December 2013.[36] There is no evidence that Abu

Omar yielded any significant information to his Egyptian torturers. Instead, snatching Abu Omar out from under DIGOS surveillance damaged collection efforts that might have yielded intelligence on terrorist networks and plots. If the CIA had any prevailing purpose in abducting Abu Omar, it remains a mystery, or, in the case of intelligence, classified.

On its face, the Imam Rapito affair was a startling failure that exposed a deeply guarded US covert action program. It also led to the convictions, and therefore outing, of around two dozen CIA officers. Despite the scandal, the US government preserved the policy of extraordinary rendition with promises of better oversight.[37] Because terrorists were not like traditional spies, criminals, or prisoners of war, they could not be tried publicly in US courts or incarcerated according to normal legal practices.[38] The USIC faced the additional problem of eliciting information from those it captured to prevent future terrorist attacks. Besides, American rules on interrogation were ostensibly more restrictive than practices common in other states, perhaps explaining—although not justifying—extraordinary rendition. Terrorists had to be held somewhere, so sending them to other countries must have seemed like a good option at the time.

Enhanced Interrogation and Enhanced Scrutiny

Apparently, extraordinary rendition was how the US government handled "lower-level captives." As one US official explained, "We don't kick the [expletive] out of them. We send them to other countries so they can kick the [expletive] out of them." So-called high-value targets received special treatment. The United States held certain terrorists in CIA-operated "black sites" where the CIA would "kick the [expletive] out of them."[39]

What became known as "enhanced interrogation techniques" were not new to the CIA. In 1963, the CIA produced a manual on counterintelligence interrogation called *KUBARK* that included "coercive" techniques.[40] The CIA also drafted a *Human Resource Exploitation Training Manual* in 1983 that CIA officers and Army Special Forces used to train allied military forces and proxies in Latin America.[41] Following 9/11, the CIA revisited the dark art of interrogation. In a memorandum of February 2002, Bush recorded that "none of the provisions of Geneva apply to our conflict with al Qaeda in Afghanistan or elsewhere throughout the world." While the memorandum claimed that "our values as a Nation... call for us to treat detainees humanely," it included a caveat that this treatment would be "to the extent appropriate and consistent with military necessity."[42]

Deputy Assistant Attorney General John Yoo drafted and Assistant Attorney General Jay Bybee signed several "torture memos" that addressed the constitutional and legal issues surrounding "enhanced interrogation techniques." These legal opinions went so far as to analyze and approve specific techniques, including waterboarding. The DOJ's OLC then provided them to the CIA and DOD as guidance for their programs. The DOD also had internal memoranda approved by Rumsfeld that authorized harsh interrogation methods for military detainees.[43] The consensus, at least within senior national security circles, was that enhanced interrogation techniques were not only lawful but also critical tools in the Global War on Terror. However, the consensus among national security officials ran up against the rapidly collapsing post-9/11 consensus.[44]

As early as December 2002, an article in the *Washington Post* by Dana Priest and Barton Gellman reported a "brass-knuckled quest for information...in which the traditional lines between right and wrong, legal and inhumane, are evolving and blurred." Several anonymous officials who spoke about enhanced interrogation "defended the use of violence against captives as just and necessary," expressing "confidence that the American public would back their view." One official who supervised renditions even cavalierly remarked, "If you don't violate someone's human rights some of the time, you probably aren't doing your job."[45] The CIA's detention facilities where enhanced interrogation took place were restricted sites, so there were no attorneys, Red Cross workers, or others who could provide external oversight. Medical, psychological, and legal oversight was left to the CIA.

But CIA headquarters did not maintain sufficiently vigorous oversight of the techniques and practices its officers and contractors used overseas. In 2005, another article by Priest revealed that a detainee named Gul Rahman froze to death after he was left shackled, half naked, in his cell at a CIA site referred to as the "Salt Pit" in Afghanistan in November 2002. No one notified the man's family. He was not on any US government registry of detainees—not even as a "ghost detainee," the CIA's term for its prisoners. An official said, shrugging, "He just disappeared from the face of the earth."[46] Rahman died after a delegation from the US Federal Bureau of Prisons visited the Salt Pit and was reportedly "WOW'ed" by the sensory deprivation techniques used at the facility. The visitors also collectively decided that "the detainees were not being treated inhumanely."[47]

The CIA IG, John Helgerson, ascertained that there were no guidelines for the CIA's enhanced interrogation techniques at the Salt Pit. Interrogators admitted that "literally, a detainee could go for days or weeks without anyone looking at him." One detainee spent seventeen days chained to a wall in a standing position.[48] Moreover, senior CIA officials expressed no real knowledge or understanding of what went on there.[49] In response to Rahman's death, Tenet issued guidelines for enhanced in January 2003 that set minimal standards for a detention facility. Even the Salt Pit, where "detainees were kept shackled in complete darkness and isolation, with a bucket for human waste, and without notable heat during the winter months, met the standard."[50] The CIA IG investigation expanded to the entire CIA detention and interrogation program.

So, too, did Priest's investigative journalism. In November 2005, Priest reported on the CIA's global network of black sites spanning eight countries, including Thailand and "several democracies in Eastern Europe."[51] A few days later, a small group of CIA officials decided to destroy the tape-recorded interrogations of several al Qaeda terrorists at CIA black sites.[52] By contrast, the DOD "produced volumes of public reports and testimony about its detention practices and rules after the abuse scandals at Iraq's Abu Ghraib prison and at Guantanamo Bay" drew national outcry.[53] The DOD's detention and interrogation program put additional pressure on the CIA program.

The US government faced a rising tide of legal challenges by DOD detainees. The Supreme Court's decision to review the case of *Rasul v. Bush* shook the CIA, which began to move detainees out of its facility at Guantanamo Bay.[54] One detainee, Mamdouh Habib, a dual Egyptian and Australian citizen, caught a break thanks to Dana Priest and the *Washington Post*. In January 2005, Priest reported that Habib was initially arrested in Pakistan, rendered by the CIA to Egypt, where he was tortured, and then sent to Guantanamo Bay.[55] The DOD suddenly released Habib without charges. Habib's attorney explained that the "CIA feared legal exposure if Habib's case was ever heard in an open court."[56] Following the Supreme Court decision in *Hamdan v. Rumsfeld*, the CIA further curtailed its detention and interrogation program.[57]

The legal issues with the CIA's detention and interrogation program distressed Jack Goldsmith, whose short tenure in the DOJ's OLC ended with his resignation. He reviewed Yoo's memoranda and determined that they were "legally flawed, tendentious in substance and tone, and overbroad and thus largely unnecessary."[58] But Goldsmith also recognized the challenges that civil-intelligence relations imposed on the intelligence community:

> The executive branch and Congress pressure the community to engage in controversial action at the edges of the law, and then fail to protect

> it from recriminations when things go awry. This leads the community to retrench and become risk averse, which invites complaints by politicians that the community is fecklessly timid.[59]

Tracing the cases from the 1960s to the Global War on Terror, Goldsmith determined these "cycles of timidity and aggression are the bane of the intelligence community, and are a terrible problem for our national security." He sympathized with the USIC but was less forgiving of the President and Congress. He criticized the Bush administration for a "go-it-alone approach to many terrorism-related legal policy issues." Congress "dropped the ball in exercising its national security responsibilities," which Goldsmith found "unsurprising" given that Congress's "natural posture is to inquire and complain but not make hard decisions…[which] minimizes congressional responsibility and allows Congress to decide whether to jump on the bandwagon or confer blame, depending on how things turn out."[60]

Congress predictably exculpated itself from blame for the CIA's detention and interrogation program. SSCI chair Dianne Feinstein admitted that "the Intelligence Committee…often pushes intelligence agencies to act quickly in response to threats and world events," but quickly defended SSCI by claiming that "such pressure, fear, and expectation of further terrorist plots do not justify, temper, or excuse improper actions taken by individuals or organizations in the name of national security." Repeating a well-worn sentiment in American civil society, Feinstein concluded that the "major lesson…is that regardless of the pressures and the need to act, the Intelligence Community's actions must always reflect who we are as a nation, and adherence to our laws and standards."[61]

Once again, a congressional investigation cast the CIA as a "rogue elephant." SSCI's report on the CIA's detention and interrogation program claimed that the CIA deliberately avoided or impeded oversight by both the executive and legislative branches. However, the report also admitted that the CIA did, in fact, brief SSCI in September 2002, albeit after the initial approval and employment of enhanced interrogation techniques.[62] Furthermore, the chairmen and vice chairmen of HPSCI and SSCI received briefings on the program, while Congress appropriated tens of millions of dollars for the CIA to establish its detention system, implying that Congress failed to exert any meaningful oversight of these activities and simply rubber-stamped them.[63] Then again, the mood in Congress mirrored the mood of the entire country following 9/11—equal parts vengeful and fearful. For example, following the capture of Khalid Sheikh Mohammed, SSCI member Jay Rockefeller implied that he would not object if the United States transferred Mohammed to a country that would use torture to obtain information to prevent another attack.[64]

Not only did congressional oversight fail to prevent intelligence abuses but SSCI became embroiled in its own intelligence scandal. Feinstein reached an accord with DCIA Leon Panetta to gain access to the CIA's records when SSCI started its review of the detention and interrogation program in 2009. During the investigation, SSCI staffers discovered an internal CIA report called the "Panetta Review," a document that the CIA never intended for SSCI to see. In perhaps the most remarkable back-and-forth in the history of congressional intelligence oversight, the CIA and SSCI sparred over who was spying on whom.

In January 2014, CIA officials intimated that SSCI staffers had gained unauthorized access to the agency's computer network to access the files.[65] That March, Feinstein took to the Senate floor to accuse the CIA of infiltrating congressional computers.[66] DCIA John Brennan, who at first denied that the CIA had spied on the Senate, later issued an apology. An internal CIA review revealed that some of its officers read congressional emails, sent a criminal referral to the Justice Department based on false information, and claimed that they acted at the request of Brennan himself.[67] Rather than coming clean, the CIA was compounding one scandal with another.

The CIA mistakenly believed that cover from the top would protect it in the event of exposure. Tenet later argued, "The attorney general of the United States told us that these techniques are legal under U.S. law and do not in any way compromise our adherence to international torture statutes," also maintaining that the CIA "briefed members of Congress fully on what we were doing at all times."[68] One particularly notorious OLC memorandum of May 2005 determined that "CIA interrogation techniques . . . do not 'shock the conscience.' "[69] But it was the American people, not executive branch attorneys, who would determine what shocked the conscience. By the time that OLC memorandum was written, an overwhelming majority of Americans had rejected several of the CIA's interrogation methods that were made public, including waterboarding.[70]

If the means were unacceptable, then perhaps the ends would at least justify them. CIA officials defended the detention and interrogation program by arguing that it played a critical role in counterterrorism. Tenet intimated that enhanced interrogation techniques produced intelligence that eliminated one-third of al Qaeda's leadership.[71] The OLC memorandum of May 2005 claimed that the interrogations of Abu Zubaydah and Khalid Sheikh

Mohammed provided information on al Qaeda's structure and operations, while intelligence from CIA detainees provided more than six thousand intelligence reports.[72]

However, the "Panetta Review" confided that the CIA "repeatedly overstated the value of intelligence gained during the brutal interrogations of some of its detainees." The CIA even deceptively attributed intelligence to the interrogation of Khalid Sheikh Mohammed when the information came from other sources. Moreover, Mohammed also fabricated plots to stop interrogations.[73] Troublingly, SSCI determined that the CIA "coordinated the release of classified information to the media, including inaccurate information concerning the effectiveness of the CIA's enhanced interrogation techniques," such as waterboarding.[74] Tenet dismissed the SSCI report as "dead wrong on every account, period, end of paragraph."

Former DCIs and DCIAs were divided on the value of the program. Some, like Porter Goss, Michael Hayden, and former acting director Michael Morell, argued that "the techniques were a necessary evil, justified by the context of the times," especially the fear of another impending attack following 9/11. Others disagreed. Stansfield Turner stated, "I just don't think a country like ours should be culpable of conducting torture. I just think it's beneath our dignity," while General David Petraeus argued, "You will pay a price for what you do, and it will be vastly greater than whatever it is you got out of taking this action."[75]

When Bush defended the program in a public speech on September 6, 2006, he tried to capture the uncertainty, fear, and resolve of the US government and the USIC in the immediate aftermath of 9/11. He claimed the United States "had to wage an unprecedented war against an enemy unlike any [the country] had fought before." Bush called the program "one of the most vital tools in our war against the terrorists," adding, "Were it not for this program, our intelligence community believes that al Qaeda and its allies would have succeeded in launching another attack against the American homeland." He also insisted that "the procedures were tough and they were safe and lawful and necessary," and argued that the program survived scrutiny by DOJ and CIA lawyers, the CIA IG, and congressional leadership. However, Bush's speech ended up being more a justification of the program than an argument for its continuation. By the time he gave the speech, the CIA was already closing the curtain on another sordid chapter of American covert action history.[76]

Rapidly improvised to meet the exigencies of the Global War on Terror, the CIA's detention and interrogation program exacerbated long-standing tensions in the CIA's organizational culture. One CTC official believed the program undermined the CIA's HUMINT-oriented mission, asserting, "It was against the culture and they [i.e., CIA officers] believed information was best gleaned by other means." Other CIA officers argued "that the system was unsustainable and diverted the agency from its unique espionage mission."[77] Faced with an assault from all sides, the CIA effectively ended its detention and interrogation program by 2006. It last used enhanced interrogation techniques in November 2007 and did not hold any detainees after April 2008.[78] The CIA also assured the OLC that the interrogation program was "not conducted in the United States... and that it [was] not authorized for use against United States persons."[79] But the USIC had another intelligence program initiated after 9/11 that was.

The Rise of the American Surveillance State

In December 2005, the *New York Times* published details of the President's Surveillance Program, initiated by the Bush administration after 9/11.[80] James Risen broke the story, calling it "the biggest secret in the U.S. government." He also revealed that many government officials "believed... [the program] was illegal, and possibly unconstitutional." In fact, the Bush administration had pressured the *Times* to kill the story in 2004, arguing that it "would severely damage national security." NSA Director Michael Hayden protested that the NSA program "was the 'crown jewel' in America's war on terror."[81]

NSA surveillance became an entrenched feature of the new American intelligence state. Bush reauthorized the PSP every forty-five days. The Attorney General also certified the program as legal and constitutional. John Yoo, who emerged as the legal force behind so many controversial intelligence activities during the Global War on Terror, had drafted the OLC opinion defending the PSP in November 2001. After Yoo's departure in 2004, new OLC lawyers, including Jack Goldsmith, wavered on the earlier legal analysis justifying the program. A schism developed between the White House and DOJ over the PSP. White House staff even went to the hospital bedside of Attorney General John Ashcroft for PSP reauthorization in March 2004. When they failed to obtain his signature, Bush simply reauthorized the program anyway. Eventually, the Bush administration agreed to modify the PSP in response to the DOJ's concerns. A new OLC memorandum coauthored by Goldsmith claimed that the AUMF gave the President the "authority to use both domestically and abroad 'all necessary and appropriate force,' including signals intelligence capabilities, to prevent future acts of international terrorism against the United States."[82]

Bush decided not to reauthorize the program in February 2007, in part due to the negative publicity surrounding it.[83] But rather than eliminate this cornerstone of the surveillance state, the three branches of the US government worked together to preserve it. The FISA Court and Congress retained key features of the PSP in new judicial and legislative structures. For example, the FISC began issuing orders authorizing intelligence activities that were originally part of the PSP.[84] Congress went even further. The Protect America Act of 2007 enhanced the executive branch's authority to conduct warrantless wiretapping. A subsequent ruling by the Foreign Intelligence Surveillance Court of Review (FISCR) upheld the legislation, which included provisions that compelled private companies to provide communications records to the federal government.[85] The FISA Amendments Act of 2008, which superseded the Protect America Act of 2007, essentially codified the transfer of the PSP to FISA authorities.[86] Thus, the President no longer needed the PSP because the basic elements of the program continued with both congressional and judicial approval.

Like other intelligence programs during the Global War on Terror, congressional oversight had once again failed to prevent abuse. In the face of public outcry, the congressional intelligence committees offered the familiar protest that they were not fully informed of the program. To be fair, a few members of Congress, such as Representative Nancy Pelosi, expressed their concerns about surveillance activities after DNSA Michael Hayden briefed members of HPSCI and SSCI on October 1, 2001, about the NSA's response to 9/11.[87] Under Hayden's authority, the NSA began targeting terrorist-associated foreign phone numbers communicating between the United States and foreign countries on September 14, 2001. The NSA Office of General Counsel determined that Hayden's decision was legal, although it represented "more aggressive use of E.O. 12333 authority than that exercised by former Directors." The NSA IG's report on the PSP noted that "General Hayden was operating in a unique environment in which it was a widely held belief that additional terrorist attacks on U.S. soil were imminent."[88] Still, the NSA's initiative left the impression that the organization had "acted on its own authority, without a formal directive from President Bush, to expand its domestic surveillance operations in the weeks after the Sept. 11 attacks."[89] At least initially, the PSP looked like another case of American intelligence once again going rogue.

By the time Pelosi voiced her apprehensions to Hayden, Bush had already signed off on the order creating the PSP. Subsequently, other members of HPSCI and SSCI briefed on the PSP and NSA activities continued to equivocate. Some later claimed that these briefings lacked "specific details."[90] Nevertheless, the PSP continued. An executive branch official who had complained to a member of Congress about the constitutional and legal issues associated with the PSP explained, "People just looked the other way because they didn't want to know what was going on."[91] Furthermore, when the Bush administration briefed the Gang of Eight in 2004, although "individual Congressional leaders expressed thoughts and concerns related to the program . . . the consensus was that the program should continue."[92] Between 2001 and 2007, two different NSA directors and other officials involved in the program briefed Congress forty-nine times, with Hayden reporting that "no one ever suggested that the NSA should stop the program."[93] That some members of Congress "declined to comment about the matter, while others did not return phone calls," suggests they knew enough about the PSP to understand just how secretive, likely valuable, and undoubtedly controversial it was.[94]

Secret, valuable, and controversial were the perfect ingredients for another intelligence scandal. Furious at the exposure of the highly classified PSP, the Bush administration ordered the FBI to investigate the leaks and initiated a "legal campaign" against journalist James Risen.[95] The Obama administration likewise aggressively targeted journalists, including Risen, over intelligence leaks.[96] The Global War on Terror therefore generated a "war on leaks" in which the FBI used "intrusive measures against reporters more often than any time in recent memory."[97]

It was not journalists but intelligence insiders, privy to the program, who proved to be the real problem. Edward Snowden briefly served with the CIA before resigning and becoming a contractor for the NSA. He began downloading classified information from the NSA's Hawaii Cryptologic Center, where he was a general systems administrator, ultimately taking more than 1.5 million classified files.[98] He subsequently contacted journalist Glenn Greenwald, who published the first of several blockbuster revelations regarding the scale of NSA surveillance in *The Guardian* in June 2013.[99] Copies of classified documents provided by Snowden accompanied Greenwald's reports. Echoing Herbert Yardley and *The American Black Chamber*, Snowden published a tell-all book, *Permanent Record*, in which he revealed his disillusionment with the USIC and offered a glimpse into the NSA's sources and methods.[100] Also like Yardley, there was a public debate over whether Snowden was a traitor or a whistleblower.

Both men claimed they exposed secret intelligence for the good of the American people. Snowden explained that he had reached his "breaking point" when DNI James Clapper stated that the NSA did not collect information on Americans in response to a question from Senator Ron Wyden during a congressional hearing.[101] Clapper amended his answer to "not wittingly," adding that the NSA "could inadvertently perhaps collect" data from American citizens.[102] Wyden, who sat on SSCI, probably already knew the answer. So, too, did other members of Congress, according to Snowden, who presumed that "more than a few of the congresspeople to whom Clapper was testifying knew very well that what he was saying was untrue, yet they refused, or felt legally powerless, to call him out on it."[103] Snowden's revelations proved that both Clapper and Congress were not being fully transparent with the American people. But Snowden was equally disingenuous: He had started downloading classified files in July 2012, eight months before Clapper's testimony.[104] HPSCI insisted that "Snowden was not a whistleblower" and pointed out that the majority of files he stole had "nothing to do with programs impacting individual privacy interests—they instead pertain to military, defense, and intelligence programs of great interest to America's adversaries."[105] It did not help Snowden's case that he eventually made his way to Russia. Traitor or whistleblower, Snowden is another reminder of the dangers of a spy once scorned.

Snowden's book included the names and descriptions of several secret surveillance programs conducted by the NSA. STELLARWIND was the heart of the PSP and the "NSA's deepest secret."[106] It was so secret that Cheney ordered the program concealed from both FISC and the congressional intelligence committees.[107] In fact, the NSA apparently exceeded Bush's original mandate in its collection efforts, leading Bush to "retroactively authorize" the NSA's overreach under STELLARWIND.[108] Although the NSA closed STELLARWIND in 2008, aspects of the program were reproduced in other programs such as PRISM.[109]

The NSA collected information with the help of private companies under the PRISM program, which began in 2007 following scrutiny of the PSP. Former NSA Director General Keith Alexander explained that "the U.S. SIGINT system would be irrevocably damaged" if the NSA could not maintain the cooperation or at least compliance of private companies "because the NSA would have sacrificed America's home field advantage as the primary hub for worldwide telecommunications."[110] The NSA's reach via PRISM was staggering, as it incorporated data from Microsoft, Yahoo, Google, Facebook, Skype, YouTube, and Apple. Perhaps invoking their own plausible deniability, these companies have variously denied their role in NSA surveillance.[111] However, public exposure led one unnamed company to ask

FISC to issue a court order for its records so the company could claim it was "compelled" to provide the information.[112] These corporations and the unwitting American citizens who believed their information and privacy were safe with them had very little choice in the matter.

Snowden believed that the NSA's vast surveillance empire was the result of a collapse of oversight and control by the three branches of government.[113] In reality, it was a product of the cooperation of all three branches. The executive branch initiated and maintained invasive surveillance practices after 9/11. The USA PATRIOT Act's "business records" provision empowered the government to obtain orders from FISC forcing private companies to hand over information that included private communications by American citizens.[114] Congress reauthorized, extended, modified, or restored the USA PATRIOT Act over the years and preserved key features of it in subsequent legislation like the Protect America Act and the FISA Amendments Act of 2008, which provided authorities that the NSA used as part of its PRISM program.[115] At the same time, the FISC created precedents that expanded the scope of the federal government's surveillance powers without the scrutiny of legal scholars or the public. In this respect, Snowden also exposed the workings of FISC to the American people.[116] With the backing of the entire US government, the USIC was only too happy to accommodate.

In a refrain of the domestic intelligence campaign preceding the Church Committee era, the CIA, FBI, and NSA all cooperated in building the post-9/11 American intelligence state. The CIA "prepared the threat assessment memoranda that were used to support the PSP authorizations and reauthorizations."[117] The FBI originally used the PSP to provide leads to its field offices but eventually adopted an active role by providing information like telephone numbers and internet addresses to the NSA.[118] Both the FBI and CIA requested and received information from the NSA surveillance program.[119] For its part, the NSA had "the capacity to collect data about virtually every phone call made in America" and also "infiltrated video games, cell-phone apps, and every corner of the digital universe." Whenever the NSA encountered resistance through encryption, it simply broke the encryption or created "back doors" to gain access.[120] Snowden decided that the USIC "had come to understand the rules of our system better than the people who had created it, and they used their knowledge to their advantage," concluding, "They'd hacked the Constitution."[121]

Like the enhanced interrogation program, senior officials from across the USIC tried to salvage the surveillance program by arguing for its effectiveness. They claimed that the PSP and NSA activities "addressed a gap in intelligence collection." However, several USIC IGs found that it was "difficult to assess the overall impact of the PSP on IC counterterrorism efforts" because, with the exception of the FBI, there were no "systematic processes for tracking how PSP reporting was used."[122] Even with FBI records, the DOJ IG found it difficult to document the PSP's effects, and a report on the PSP determined that "the program generally played a limited role in the FBI's overall counterterrorism efforts."[123] As for the CIA, it did not "systematically assess the usefulness of the product of the PSP." Additionally, too few CIA officers were read into the PSP, and those who were had "too many competing priorities, and too many other information sources and analytic tools available to them, to fully utilize PSP."[124] Meanwhile, the National Counterterrorism Center reported that the PSP "was not of greater value than other sources of intelligence," and NCTC analysts interviewed "could not recall specific examples where PSP information provided what they considered actionable intelligence."[125] The net benefit of NSA mass domestic surveillance remains unclear or at least unproven.

Amnesia or Myopia?

Shortsightedness or a lack of long-term memory has afflicted all Americans—including politicians, government officials, intelligence officers, and members of the public—in terms of US intelligence history and the role they have played in it. For example, the legacy of CIA black sites and torture marred the Senate confirmation hearings for the appointment of Gina Haspel as the first female DCIA. Haspel presided over a CIA black site in Thailand. She was also one of the CIA officials involved in the decision to destroy the taped interrogations of al Qaeda terrorists. Haspel wrote, "With the benefit of hindsight and my experience as a senior Agency leader, the enhanced interrogation program is not one the CIA should have undertaken."[126]

Hindsight permitted innumerable condemnations of executive officials like John Yoo, author of so many controversial legal memoranda. Yoo reminded his critics of the impact that the security context and threat environment had on the actions of the Bush administration and USIC. In the aftermath of 9/11, they feared that more terrorist attacks by al Qaeda were imminent, and this fear imposed "an urgency to decide [on enhanced interrogation techniques] so that valuable intelligence could be acquired... before further attacks could occur." Yoo also stressed that he "didn't have [the] luxury in the spring of 2002" of time or patience, as policymakers and the USIC were scrambling to respond to terrorism.[127] But they were not the only actors involved in what was a collective national response to 9/11.

The American people had also rallied around the flag, which suggested that the US government and USIC had a public mandate to keep the country safe by any means necessary. Disturbingly, although public opposition to enhanced interrogation soared in 2005, polling even after SSCI released its damning report in 2014 indicated that Americans would support torturing terrorist suspects in order to prevent another attack.[128] And while a majority of Americans considered waterboarding to be torture, roughly half decided that it was still justified at times.[129] Americans also broadly backed intrusive domestic intelligence activities after 9/11, although that support tapered off over time.[130] Finally, a majority of Americans consistently agreed that the US government had not gone far enough in protecting the country versus had gone too far in restricting civil liberties, although they briefly reversed themselves in the wake of Snowden's leaks.[131] As they always have, the American people will vacillate between preferring liberty and transparency or security and secrecy depending on their perception of threats to national security. In one moment, they will support decisive action to protect themselves, only to moralize about the methods later and forget all the lessons when the next emergency arises.

Pop culture only compounds the problem. A study of media stories involving the CIA during the Church Committee period of the 1970s revealed that "the most persistent theme was that the CIA engages in immoral or illegal activities."[132] Despite the criticism of the CIA and USIC for intelligence excesses during the Global War on Terror, movies like *Zero Dark Thirty* and television shows like *24* glorified or at least endorsed aggressive or abusive intelligence practices. The USIC must therefore exercise its duties on behalf of an American public that at best has no idea how intelligence actually operates and at worst has bad ideas about how intelligence should operate.

The revelations of the Global War on Terror did not generate the same national debate and demand for reform as the Church Committee period. As a result, the American people may have to get used to their intelligence state. Due to the cooperation of the three branches of the US government and the ubiquity of information technology, pervasive surveillance is a fixture of the American intelligence system. One of the last acts of the Obama administration was to amend EO 12333 to expand the NSA's ability to share the fruits of its massive surveillance efforts across the entire USIC—ironically, a sign of greater intelligence coordination, yet regrettably a graver threat to civil liberties.[133]

24

In Intelligence We Trust?

THE AMERICAN INTELLIGENCE state survived a succession of scandals during the Global War on Terror that likely would have compelled reform and retrenchment at any other point in US history. The government and the USIC subsequently wielded secret intelligence against American citizens based on a "trust us" approach to national security. In the absence of judicial precedents, they set troubling intelligence precedents that conflicted with core constitutional principles. Intelligence targeted American citizens at home and abroad, with lethal results in the latter case. In turn, the two intelligence organizations representing the division between domestic and foreign intelligence, the FBI and CIA, exhibited some of the persistent tensions rooted in their organizational histories and cultures.

Rather than prevent intelligence scandals, congressional oversight exacerbated them. In a reprise of earlier episodes in American history, accusations of spying on the President or collusion with foreign powers flew back and forth across the political divide. Intelligence became entangled in partisan politics, and as the public became more politically polarized, so, too, did support for the USIC. These political conflicts came at a cost to civil-intelligence relations, as mutual suspicions spread among the government, the intelligence community, and the American people.

Intelligence has accompanied the highs and lows of US history, if often only in the shadows. At times, policymakers and intelligence officers might have preferred it to stay there because intelligence activities that once seemed legal, ethical, or wise did not always remain so. Intelligence has recently been at the center of controversies that erode the foundations of the American republic. Even if contemporaries judge what was done as necessary or acceptable, posterity may not be so kind.

Caught in the Crosshairs

The Global War on Terror signaled open season on accused terrorists, and the United States had an especially effective hunting tool in the form of drones.

With names that signified their purpose, Predator and Reaper drones would find, fix, and often finish off the targets of intelligence manhunts that could take days, weeks, or even years. In September 2011, armed American drones hovering over the desert of Yemen set their crosshairs on one such target. They launched their missiles, killing Anwar al Awlaki, a US citizen born in New Mexico who later became a radical Islamist cleric and alleged senior leader of al-Qaeda in the Arabian Peninsula (AQAP).[1]

President Barack Obama announced the death of al-Awlaki the same day, crediting the work of the intelligence community for the successful operation.[2] He later declared, "We are very pleased that Mr. Awlaki is no longer going to be in a position to directly threaten the United States homeland, as well as our allies around the world."[3] The Obama administration claimed Awlaki had "inspired" terrorist plots. But the administration's public case against Awlaki rested primarily on his rhetoric and allegations of his involvement in terrorist plots. For proof of Awlaki's guilt, the administration would have had to produce the intelligence it had on him. Following his death, AQAP argued that the US government "did not prove the accusations against [him], and did not present evidence against [him] in their unjust laws of their freedom."[4] In one of the most controversial actions in American intelligence history, the US government executed one of its own citizens in a secret intelligence operation.

The Obama administration's counterterrorism policies may be one reason it resorted to killing Awlaki. During his presidential campaign, Obama promised to restrict extraordinary rendition and enhanced interrogation, which placed him in the challenging position of having to figure out what to do with terrorists given that capturing, detaining, and interrogating them had proven so troublesome. Apparently, the administration concluded that it was easier to kill them, evidenced by the considerable increase in drone strikes between the Obama and Bush administrations.[5] Senator Saxby Chambliss described the shift: "Their [the Obama administration's] policy is to take out high-value targets, versus capturing high-value targets.... They are not going to advertise that, but that's what they are doing."[6] However, Awlaki's citizenship distinguished him from other terrorist targets.

The Awlaki killing raised enormous constitutional questions regarding the President's power to order the extrajudicial killing of an American citizen. The Obama administration leaned on the 2001 AUMF as justification for its decision.[7] In February 2010, the OLC drafted a meager seven-page memorandum arguing, based on information provided by the CIA and the USIC, that killing al-Awlaki would not violate EO 12333 or the US Constitution.[8] Furthermore, the Obama administration approved using lethal force against

Awlaki sometime between January and April, months before the OLC produced its more comprehensive July memorandum that presented the legal justification for Awlaki's killing.[9] Worse still, after the strike that killed Awlaki the DOJ drafted a white paper outlining the conditions under which the executive branch could target an American citizen.[10] Like the legal memoranda supporting NSA surveillance or CIA rendition and interrogation, the US government continued the Global War on Terror's tradition of putting "the policy cart before the constitutional horse."[11] The publicly available documents redacted the portions of these memoranda providing the intelligence qua evidence that proved Awlaki was an operational terrorist leader. In a nod to internal executive branch oversight, the July OLC memorandum confidently asserted that the "highest officers in the Intelligence Community have reviewed the factual basis" for targeting Awlaki.[12] The US government could apparently use secret intelligence to target an American citizen, with the executive branch acting as judge, jury, and executioner.

The Awlaki extrajudicial killing also illustrated how the judiciary deferred to presidential control and oversight of intelligence. In December 2010, the DC District Court dismissed a petition by Awlaki's father, Nasser al-Awlaki, seeking an injunction to prevent the targeted killing of his son nine months before the strike that ultimately killed him. The court began its opinion by noting an incongruity in intelligence policy: "How is it that judicial approval is required when the United States decides to target a U.S. citizen overseas for electronic surveillance, but that, according to defendants [the US government], judicial scrutiny is prohibited when the United States decides to target a U.S. citizen overseas for death?"[13] Additionally, government attorneys would neither confirm nor deny that Awlaki was on the "kill list" that was reviewed by Obama and his national security team at their so-called Terror Tuesday meetings.[14] The unsettling result of the government's logic is that American citizens presumably cannot know if they are being targeted for death until the actual strike takes place—although reports leaked out that Awlaki was on the kill list months before the strike that killed him.

The DC District Court avoided the weighty constitutional questions entirely and dismissed the case. On the one hand, the court recognized "that there are circumstances in which the Executive's unilateral decision to kill a U.S. citizen overseas is 'constitutionally committed to the political branches' and judicially unreviewable." On the other, it stated, "this Court does not hold that the Executive possesses 'unreviewable authority to order the assassination of any American whom he labels an enemy of the state.'"[15] Awlaki's father brought another case to the DC District Court following his son's death. The court briefly paid lip service to the constitutional quandary, noting, "The powers granted to the Executive and Congress to wage war and provide for national security does not give them *carte blanche* to deprive a U.S. citizen of his life without due process and without any judicial review."[16] Nonetheless, the court dismissed this case, too.

The controversy following Awlaki's death probably explains why the Obama administration ultimately decided not to extrajudicially kill another US citizen, Mohanad Mahmoud Al Farekh. Instead, the USIC provided intelligence to the Pakistani government, which captured Farekh and extradited him to the United States to stand trial. Both the Pentagon and CIA wanted to place Farekh on the kill list. This time, Attorney General Eric Holder, who had defended the killing of Awlaki, demurred due to his doubts about the intelligence.[17] Even if the US government decided not to kill Farekh, the decision was made within the executive branch and the question never reached the courts. The extrajudicial killing of US citizens based on secret intelligence remains an unsettled area of American constitutional law.

The CIA's role in the targeted killing of Awlaki and the wider CIA drone campaign also raised a matter of international humanitarian law with respect to civilians directly participating in hostilities. Various news articles reported that US officials claimed "the CIA was in control of all the aircraft, as well as the decisions to fire" or that "the operation was carried out by Joint Special Operations Command [JSOC], under the direction of the CIA."[18] In either case, the US government arguably violated the laws of armed conflict by authorizing the CIA, a civilian agency, to control or conduct drone strikes.[19]

The CIA was not the only US organization in the targeted killing business. JSOC, composed of some of the military's most elite special operations forces, had a wide range of intelligence capabilities and a drone fleet.[20] Drone strikes became a potential bureaucratic battleground between the CIA and the military. At first, policymakers avoided the problem by separating the two organizations' operations geographically: The CIA was responsible for drone strikes in Pakistan, while JSOC was responsible for drone strikes in Yemen. However, after JSOC missed Awlaki a few times and launched airstrikes that killed Yemeni civilians, the CIA opened a Yemen-Somalia Department and built a secret drone base in Saudi Arabia.[21] Reports suggest that it was the CIA that was able to finally gather the intelligence that revealed Awlaki's location.[22] Furthermore, according to US officials, the "first time the C.I.A. used the Saudi base was to kill Mr. Awlaki in September 2011."[23] When the CIA and JSOC later cooperated to target the Islamic State in Syria, the *Washington*

Post pointed out that this contrasted with "the friction and turf battles that have surfaced between the CIA and JSOC in other conflict zones, particularly Yemen, where each operates a fleet of armed drones, relying on separate streams of intelligence and lethal authorities."[24]

Perhaps due to the scrutiny from the Awlaki killing and public reports of errant strikes that killed civilians, the Obama administration attempted to transfer responsibility for drone strikes from the CIA to the military in 2014. But Congress showed a preference for keeping the CIA in the targeted killing game.[25] The Obama administration renewed its effort, and CIA drone strikes fell off in Pakistan, Yemen, and Syria by 2016. Even though the CIA was "not ordered to disarm its fleet of drones," shifting drone strikes to the military "enable[d] greater transparency and end[ed] an often awkward charade in which the U.S. government refuse[d] to acknowledge its role in strikes that [were] abundantly covered by news organizations and tallied by watchdog groups."[26]

If questions of constitutional law, international humanitarian law, and bureaucratic competition were not enough, organizational culture provided another good reason to minimize the CIA's role in drone strikes. The drone mission hurt the CIA as an intelligence organization. Senior officials, including from the CIA, observed with some alarm that it "morphed into a paramilitary force," also worrying that the "agency's emphasis on lethal operations deviates from its traditional mission and could impair its ability to focus on gathering intelligence."[27] Obama himself insisted, "I don't want our intelligence agencies being a paramilitary organization. That's not their function."[28]

The CIA paramilitarized at the expense of the intelligence profession. Meanwhile, the DOD continued to compete with the CIA in the realm of HUMINT, eventually creating the Defense Clandestine Service (DCS) in 2012. The DCS would purportedly work with the CIA and sharpen military intelligence collection while alleviating stress on the CIA's HUMINT officers.[29] However, it also represented yet another potential area of bureaucratic competition as part of a "decades-long knife fight between the Pentagon and Langley . . . for control of America's spies."[30] The congressional armed services and intelligence committees entered the fray. HPSCI wanted the DOD to demonstrate that DCS would actually "provide unique capabilities to the intelligence community."[31] SASC protested that the CIA was going to foist some of its responsibilities onto DCS at the DOD's expense.[32] Thus, cooperation between the CIA and DOD during the Global War on Terror did not guarantee comity in DC's rough-and-tumble of bureaucratic politics.

The tactical nature of counterterrorism also undermined the CIA's role in all-source, strategic intelligence analysis, one of its original core missions rooted in its legislative design. Analysts became "targeteers," charged with tracking wanted terrorists for eventual drone strikes or special operations raids. Former DCIA Michael Hayden admitted, "A lot of things that pass for analysis right now is really targeting."[33] The drive for "current intelligence" in the Global War on Terror distracted the CIA from its global strategic intelligence requirements at a time when the United States desperately needed them.[34] Changing the analytical culture of the CIA could prove challenging for an organization in which over half of its employees joined after 2001 and "have done nothing but tactical work," making it "very difficult to go from a tactical approach to seeing things more strategically."[35]

The wars in Iraq and Afghanistan affected the clandestine culture of the CIA as well. Alex Finley, the pen name of a former CIA officer of the post-9/11 class, recounted a perceptible shift during the Global War on Terror: "As more and more CIA officers spent time with their military counterparts... a more military-style mentality seep[ed] into the agency," as did a military-style appearance. While Finley concedes that the "transformation was a necessary one, given the nature of the threat," she cautioned that "our Cold War adversaries hadn't actually gone away." For example, "while American attention was turned elsewhere, Russia had quietly continued applying its formidable knowledge of traditional spy tradecraft," obliging the CIA to "pivot back toward traditional espionage."[36]

That pivot has not been an easy one. When Russia detained an alleged CIA officer in 2013, the man supposedly carried with him two wigs, a compass, and a street map of Moscow.[37] Between rolling around the Middle East in armored SUVs under the watchful eye of heavily armed contractors or walking around the streets of Moscow poorly disguised and under the equally watchful eye of an adversary's intelligence service, it is hard to say the transformation to fight the Global War on Terror served the CIA well. The CIA must reacquire some of its Cold War–era tradecraft, made even more difficult by new surveillance technology.

The CIA is reorienting back to threats and challenges that look less like those of the Global War on Terror and more like those of the Cold War. In fact, for both the CIA and the United States, the Cold War was perhaps better preparation for the twenty-first century than the Global War on Terror was. Facing challenges more akin to those of the Cold War, the CIA will have to rediscover what Allen Dulles called the "Craft of Intelligence."[38]

Caught in the Crossfire

During the Global War on Terror, the already blurry blue line between domestic intelligence and law enforcement got even blurrier. Already endowed with these two functions, the FBI grew stronger after 9/11. Several commissions and congressional investigations expressed their desire for greater FBI intelligence capabilities and closer cooperation between law enforcement and intelligence efforts within the FBI itself. Congress therefore enhanced the FBI's domestic intelligence powers through legislation like the USA PATRIOT Act and IRTPA.

The FBI did not waste the opportunity. For example, it expanded its use of National Security Letters (NSLs), which are administrative, rather than judicial, subpoenas that allow the FBI to collect information from individuals. The number of NSLs exploded to tens of thousands per year, despite many of those targeted not being suspected of any misconduct. The only pretext the FBI needs for NSLs is that the information is "relevant to" an investigation into terrorism or intelligence matters, which extended to practically anything or anybody in the post-9/11 era.[39] NSLs also contain nondisclosure provisions that prevent the target from revealing to anyone that the FBI is seeking information from them, thereby giving the FBI the power both "to investigate and to silence."[40]

The Attorney General's guidelines to the FBI in 2008 further blended the FBI's dual domestic intelligence and law enforcement roles. The document cited presidential directives, legislative intent, and commission reports, including the WMD Commission's mandate that "the FBI and other agencies do a better job of gathering intelligence inside the United States" and "that [the FBI] eliminate the remnants of the old 'wall' between foreign intelligence and domestic law enforcement." Furthermore, the guidelines no longer required the FBI to distinguish between its "information gathering activities" by labeling them as "'criminal investigations,' 'national security investigations,' or 'foreign intelligence collections,'" or to separate the personnel who carried them out. These new guidelines, signed by Attorney General Michael Mukasey, therefore demonstrated no appreciation for the distinctions between the intelligence and law enforcement professions or the problems associated with blurring the two.[41]

If that was not enough, the FBI had access to the NSA's massive domestic surveillance campaign. One NSA official agreed that the proper "way to do it, was to put this under FBI control, using FBI authorities, and just let the FBI use [the NSA's] tools."[42] While placing such powerful surveillance tools in the hands of a law enforcement agency like the FBI may seem preferable to keeping them in a military component, the Bureau's troubling history of political opportunism and intelligence abuse made it no better a candidate to conduct domestic surveillance than the NSA. Furthermore, the Global War on Terror's dual effects of weakening the FISA process and empowering the FBI made it even easier for the Bureau to spy on American citizens.

During the 2016 US presidential election the FBI proved yet again why mixing intelligence and law enforcement is problematic for civil-intelligence relations and invariably leads to political controversies. In July, the FBI opened an investigation, code-named Crossfire Hurricane, into the campaign of Republican nominee Donald Trump as part of a larger USIC effort to monitor Russian interference in the upcoming presidential election.[43] One source for the FBI's investigation was a former British MI6 officer named Christopher Steele. A DC firm named Fusion GPS had hired Steele to investigate ties between Trump and Russia. It was paid to conduct "opposition research" by the Democratic National Committee and a law firm working for Hillary Clinton's presidential campaign. Steele personally maintained contact with a DOJ attorney named Bruce Ohr, whose wife worked as an independent contractor for Fusion GPS. Ohr became an intermediary for information between the FBI and Steele, who "was 'desperate' that Trump not be elected."[44] Steele not only provided his reports to the FBI but also supplied information to the media without informing the FBI. These reports, which collectively became known as the "Steele dossier," contained bombastic allegations pertaining to Trump's ties to Russia as well as his personal life. However, the Steele dossier relied on Russian sources, a dubious foundation given Russian intelligence's history spreading of disinformation.[45]

Aside from the conflicts of interest in the Steele-DOJ-FBI-media nexus, there were also disturbing signs of politicization in the FBI. Two FBI officials, Peter Strzok and Lisa Page, who were also having an affair, exchanged text messages that included statements like "Trump should go f himself" and "maybe you're meant to stay where you are because you're meant to protect the country from that menace [i.e., a Trump presidency]." Perhaps the most notorious and unsettling message was a response by Strzok to Page's anxious inquiry whether Trump was "ever going to become president": "No. No he's not. We'll stop it."[46] These expressions of outright partisanship—including an ominous threat to intervene in the US political process—suggested the FBI had not overcome its history of politicization and tainted the Bureau's image in subsequent coverage of the investigation.

Worse yet, it later emerged that the FBI manipulated information to obtain four FISA warrants to spy on Carter Page, an American citizen and foreign policy advisor to the Trump campaign. For over eleven months, the FBI surveilled Page under FISA authorities in an effort to uncover the nature of his contacts with Russians. Since the FBI considered Steele a "reliable source," it incorporated pieces of his dossier into its FISA request despite the Bureau having no corroborating evidence for these claims and knowing about Steele's conflict of interest in being paid to provide information to the Clinton campaign and DNC.[47] The FBI also knew that Page had been an operational contact to the CIA for several years and had shared information he obtained from his interactions with Russian intelligence officials. Incredibly, one FBI agent opposed including this exculpatory evidence in the FISA application, and an FBI attorney altered an email from the CIA confirming Page's work for the Agency.[48] The Justice Department belatedly conceded to the FISC in December 2019 that it had "insufficient predication to establish probable cause to believe that Page was acting as an agent of a foreign power."[49] Nonetheless, the FBI had abused its domestic intelligence powers, violating American civil liberties in the process.

American intelligence was its own worst enemy in this case. The ODNI concluded that Russia's paramount goal in interfering in the 2016 US presidential election was to undermine the American people's faith in their political system.[50] As it turned out, the United States did not need Russia's help. While the USIC—and the rest of the country along with it—fretted over foreign interference, elements of the USIC itself were actively intervening in the American political process.

While perhaps claiming or even believing themselves to be above politics, intelligence organizations can entangle themselves in the messy arena of American domestic politics. In the case of Crossfire Hurricane, either the FBI was spying on American citizens, including a presidential candidate, on its own initiative or it was conducting a politicized intelligence operation on behalf of the incumbent administration. The two are equally problematic for civil-intelligence relations. Josh Campbell, a former FBI special agent who was involved in the Crossfire Hurricane investigation, insisted the FBI was independent and "not an arm of the executive branch."[51] The dangerous result of this logic would be that the FBI is an extraconstitutional security service in the United States, existing outside the executive, legislative, and judicial branches. Meanwhile, the extent to which the FBI was following the orders of senior Obama administration officials remains a matter of controversy. However, evidence from Peter Strzok's notes suggests that President Barack

Obama, Vice President Joe Biden, and FBI Director James Comey were actively involved in and aware of the FBI's activities. Comey or Biden allegedly considered using the Logan Act, which makes it illegal for private American citizens to conduct unauthorized diplomacy with a foreign government and was originally passed by the Federalist administration to target the Democratic-Republicans back in 1799, as leverage against members of the Trump campaign and its transition team.[52]

Intelligence sharpened political divisions in the country, which in turn made the USIC subject to political attacks. Many of the most visible and visceral attacks came from Trump himself. Throughout his candidacy and presidency, Trump consistently voiced strong opinions about the USIC, ranging from skepticism to hostility.[53] For example, he sided with Russian President Vladimir Putin over his own intelligence community on the question of whether Russia interfered in the 2016 presidential election. Former DCIA John Brennan, an especially virulent critic of Trump, called the comments "nothing short of treasonous" and insisted that the President was "wholly in the pocket of Putin."[54] Trump and Brennan took their grievances with each other to the American people through social media.[55] Their mutual animosity escalated to the point where Trump threatened to revoke Brennan's security clearance. Former members of the USIC rushed to defend one of their own against the President. A dozen former senior intelligence officials signed a letter denouncing the President's decision. The list expanded to sixty former CIA officials and eventually reached 175 former national security officials across the USIC, DOD, NSC, and State Department.[56] The consistent, passionate, and often partisan outspokenness of former intelligence officers during the Trump administration exacerbated the strains in civil-intelligence relations.

Even before the 2016 presidential election, former acting DCIA Michael Morrell published an op-ed in the *New York Times* provocatively titled "I Ran the C.I.A. Now I'm Endorsing Hillary Clinton."[57] The op-ed presented several problems for civil-intelligence relations. By leaning on his CIA experience as a qualification to arbitrate American domestic politics, Morrell was linking intelligence and politics. The article also risked rekindling old fears about CIA or USIC involvement in domestic politics, especially in an extraordinarily polarized and bitter political climate. Although Morrell and other former intelligence officers certainly have the right to air their opinions about domestic politics as private citizens, the public may not decouple their prior status as intelligence professionals and affiliation with the USIC from their personal political beliefs and endorsements.[58] Finally, Morrell's op-ed ignored a fundamental lesson of American intelligence history: Anytime intelligence and partisan politics have mixed—regardless of the motivations or intentions of the actors involved—the outcome was bad for both the USIC and the country.

In their own defense, some of these individuals claimed they had a professional responsibility to "speak truth to power," which has become a common refrain in recent years and is enshrined in ODNI's Principles of Professional Ethics for the Intelligence Community.[59] But the intelligence profession is not tasked with knowing "the truth," and instead is meant to exercise good analytical judgment and provide the best possible analysis to policymakers. In fact, it is problematic if intelligence professionals claim to know the truth since intelligence fundamentally involves uncertainty and requires expressing uncertainty to policymakers who can accept or reject what the USIC tells them.[60] Moreover, American intelligence history is replete with examples of intelligence officers being wrong in their analysis or politicizing intelligence.[61] Above all, due to secrecy, intelligence professionals cannot reveal how or why they would know "the truth"—an especially fraught proposition in an area as delicate as American domestic politics.

Instead of claiming to know "the truth," the USIC should be more concerned with trust, and Trump certainly did not trust the USIC. He claimed there was a "deep state" of intelligence officers determined to subvert his presidency. The words and actions of former and current members of the USIC did not help dispel the accusation. In one unquestionably unhelpful episode, former acting DCI John McLaughlin declared, "Thank God for the deep state" during a panel on election security that included former senior CIA and FBI officials.[62] McLaughlin was addressing yet another political intelligence scandal that quickly overshadowed the Crossfire Hurricane investigation and resulted in the third House impeachment of a President in American history.

In the fall of 2019, a CIA whistleblower accused Trump of pressuring Ukrainian President Volodymyr Zelensky to launch an investigation designed to damage former Vice President Joe Biden, who was campaigning on the Democratic ticket for the 2020 presidential election. During a July phone call, Trump asked for this "favor" in response to Zelensky's expression of gratitude for US military support to Ukraine, which had been fighting Russian-backed separatists in the country's Donbas region since 2014. In the weeks preceding the phone call, Trump had ordered his administration to withhold $400 million in military aid to Ukraine, which he subsequently released only after he became aware of the whistleblower complaint. Notably, the whistleblower did not have firsthand knowledge of the phone call but heard details about it from NSC and Situation Room staffers assigned to listen to presidential calls and document them in a Memorandum of Conversation.[63]

The whistleblower complaint quickly spread to the politically polarized venue of Congress, which erupted in partisan conflict. The congressional intelligence committees, especially HPSCI, were internally divided between the two political parties. Intelligence politicization proliferated as each side weaponized leaks against the other.[64] Rather than focus on the USIC and American intelligence policy, HPSCI devoted its attention to producing a nearly four-hundred-page report on what primarily was a domestic political question—and an extremely divisive one at that—concerning whether the President was inappropriately using his position to pressure a foreign government to help his reelection campaign.[65]

Echoing some of the controversies and debates of the early American republic, the US government continued to prove itself incapable of separating intelligence and politics. The conflicts between the Trump administration and the USIC jeopardized intelligence professionalism and civilian control over intelligence, a core tenet of civil-intelligence relations. Beyond that, intelligence controversies sowed mistrust across the US government and between the two political parties who share responsibility for it.

A Crisis of Confidence in the Constitutional System

The USIC's visible forays into politics made public support for intelligence a matter of political affiliation. A significantly higher percentage of Democrats than Republicans expressed trust in the FBI.[66] Favorable opinions about the CIA reflected the same political divide.[67] Nonetheless, public support for intelligence as a whole remained high, although Americans were split when asked whether they believed the USIC adequately safeguarded their constitutional rights.[68] A poll reported that nearly two-thirds of Americans believed the FBI broke the law when it spied on US citizens, with a nearly bipartisan consensus between Democrats and Republicans.[69] Meanwhile, roughly half of Americans believed the CIA and other members of the USIC were trying to steer the outcome of US elections.[70] Despite all the controversies, the FBI and CIA still maintained higher public approval ratings than both the President and Congress.[71] The American people remain consistently inconsistent.

Trust between policymakers and intelligence professionals is essential for national security, but trust between the American people and their government is foundational to the constitutional system. Trust in the US government has tumbled in recent years.[72] Intelligence has been one of the reasons for the decline. Troublingly, the American people currently vest more trust in the unelected intelligence community than in the representatives they elect to control and oversee it. Thus, they trust intelligence more than they trust themselves in the sense of the diminished faith they have in their own constitutional system and institutions. Of the many challenges facing American civil-intelligence relations, there is no greater one than that.

Conclusion

AMERICA AND THE INTELLIGENCE REVOLUTION

THERE ARE TWO overarching themes that emerge from the history of American intelligence. First, intelligence has been a feature of US history since the beginning, but throughout it, the American people have often been uncomfortable with the idea of their country engaging in sneaky intelligence activities, particularly when those activities involved their own government spying on them. Second, and partly in response to the first, the United States has continuously faced problems with how it has organized, incorporated, and controlled the American intelligence system. Today, intelligence is changing the world in ways that will force the United States to confront the conflicts and tensions inherent in this history.

Since the outset of the twenty-first century, intelligence studies have claimed that there has been a "revolution in intelligence affairs."[1] But what has happened over the course of American intelligence history suggests that there is an even greater revolution occurring—an Intelligence Revolution.[2] Briefly, a revolution in intelligence affairs refers to transformations in intelligence brought about by changes in technology, tradecraft, or functions. The Intelligence Revolution refers to changes in intelligence that have taken place over roughly the past century and are transforming states and societies.[3]

The twentieth century witnessed several marked advances in intelligence.[4] It was during this time that the Intelligence Revolution took shape. The "world's second-oldest profession" became an independent profession of national security. Technological innovations like the airplane and radio transformed the battlefield during the First World War and fostered an early revolution in intelligence affairs.[5] During the Second World War, intelligence was a central feature of the war effort for all the great powers involved. It was equally clear that intelligence was going to be an integral instrument of statecraft after the end of the war.

Intelligence exploded in the second half of the twentieth century with the onset of the Cold War. The Cold War drove developments in technology and tradecraft as the United States and the Soviet Union looked to intelligence to gain a competitive advantage against each other. This intelligence competition birthed, employed, and advanced the technological developments that formed the foundation of the Information Age, including computers, satellites, and the internet. In this respect, the Cold War was not just a competition involving the US government. It extended to American civil society as private companies, civic groups, academic institutions, and even individuals participated, whether as sources of intelligence, proxies for intelligence operations, or innovators in intelligence technology.[6] A key transition also took place over the course of the Cold War and into the post–Cold War period as technology originally intended for intelligence applications shifted to dual use—that is, for both civil and intelligence purposes—and then eventually commercial use.

The intelligence monopoly that states have traditionally held is eroding as private companies rival governments and intelligence services in their ability to collect and analyze information. Not only have they acquired hardware and software previously used for intelligence operations, but they have also innovated new technology and new approaches to using it. Large corporations now employ surveillance to monetize information and compete in both national and global marketplaces. For example, Amazon uses its website, its Kindle device, and its personal assistant program, Alexa, to collect private information from its users.[7] Google, Apple, Samsung, and Microsoft also vacuum up personal data.[8] Furthermore, private corporations hire former intelligence officers and analysts to bring the training and tradecraft of national security intelligence into the field of business intelligence. The titans of information technology and social media have combined technology and intelligence to target citizens as consumers at the individual level while amassing information on billions of people. These corporations also provide pathways for the US government and other states like China to collect more intelligence for their own purposes either through complicity or compulsion. Across the world, governments and their intelligence communities both cooperate and compete with large corporations over information, using the methods and tools of intelligence to acquire, analyze, and exploit it. Intelligence, the age-old practice of collecting and using information to shape events, set the conditions for these changes in human history and stands to benefit from them. The cost will be to everyday people hoping to preserve some shred of personal privacy.

The twenty-first century is on course to be the most surveilled century in human history. Personal computers and smartphones have turned individuals into sources of intelligence and targets for the massive surveillance apparatuses of state intelligence organizations and private corporations. Everywhere on earth, people are participants in their own surveillance, but it remains to be seen how their behavior will change as the result of living in a global panopticon. And while the United States helped ignite the Intelligence Revolution, it also appears unprepared for its challenges.

Blowback: The Revenge of History

In the same span of time that witnessed the steady march of the United States from small republic to global superpower, American intelligence has also experienced incredible transformations. The United States created intelligence services in the nineteenth and early twentieth centuries and subordinated them to other professions and institutions of national security, namely, military, law enforcement, and diplomacy. They all fought with each other to control key intelligence functions and to prevent coordination through an independent intelligence organization. After the Second World War, the looming threat of the Soviet Union and communism provided the basis for a Cold War consensus that largely unified the American people and their government behind the creation of a national security state with a formidable peacetime intelligence system. The structure of this intelligence system reflected rather than resolved long-term conflicts in American intelligence history.

When the United States finally established an independent intelligence organization in 1947, the CIA had a congressional mandate to coordinate intelligence but quickly faced bureaucratic competition from the State, Defense, and Justice Departments. At the same time, Congress constructed an illusory wall between foreign and domestic intelligence, reinforced by the organizational and professional divisions between the CIA and FBI.[9] Over the course of the Cold War, the United States also created more intelligence organizations like the NSA and NRO that developed based on bureaucratic competition over core intelligence functions and reflected a long-standing tradition of subordinating intelligence to war planning and warfighting. It was during the Cold War that the United States cemented the technophilic or perhaps technocentric posture of the USIC and the foundation for its "techno-spy empire."[10] The USIC today, including its structure, functions, and legal authorities, therefore reflects the Industrial Age context of the Cold War.

But it is not the path intelligence took in the United States that signals the principal challenge, indeed threat, that the Intelligence Revolution poses. Instead, it was the example set by its ideological rival and Cold War adversary that should concern the American people and shape future US intelligence reform efforts. The Stalinist Soviet Union used intelligence to try to surveil the entire body politic and force people to conform to the state's vision of model civic behavior.

One of the sorely misplaced assumptions at the dawn of the twenty-first century was that the Information Age would witness the global spread of liberty and democracy. It would purportedly free people's minds, which in turn would free people. Cellphones, computers, and the internet would allow individuals to access information that would create states full of informed citizens who would choose democracy over authoritarianism. In fact, the exact opposite is occurring.

The combination of intelligence, technology, and state surveillance signals the looming threat that authoritarianism poses in the twenty-first century. Governments and their intelligence services have surveillance powers the likes of which past authoritarian leaders, like Stalin or Mao, could have only dreamed of. Russia is becoming a "cyber gulag" that exploits wiretapping, facial recognition, and censorship to root out and crush dissent.[11] China is experimenting with a "social credit system," in which the state constantly monitors people going about their everyday lives with the goal of shaping people's actions, behavior, relationships, and even minds.[12] Rather than turning out to be the tools of democracy and freedom, computers, phones, and the internet are being used as tools of authoritarianism and repression.

The United States is not immune from the authoritarian effects of the Intelligence Revolution. Over the same period of time that intelligence changed so dramatically, the US government amassed more power than the Founders intended, despite a persistent strand of American thought that opposes "big government."[13] Intelligence has only reinforced a strong central government. The enduring tension between liberty and security is intensifying with the Intelligence Revolution, tipping the scales away from liberty. During the Global War on Terror, the US government unleashed its powerful intelligence apparatus, undermining civil liberties and eroding constitutional rights in the process. Individually and collectively, Americans were living under a massive intelligence microscope. As the Global War on Terror fades into recent history, new challenges have surfaced that struck fault lines in US civil-intelligence relations and left the country fumbling for responses to the Intelligence Revolution.

The COVID-19 pandemic reinforced the consequences of the Intelligence Revolution. Countries around the world, from China and South Korea to Israel and Singapore, leveraged intelligence organizations and capabilities to respond to COVID. Some observers in the United States praised South Korea's invasive surveillance measures, which included data collection from smartphones and credit cards, to identify and isolate potential human COVID hosts.[14] COVID exposed the world to sterilized terms like "contact tracing" to justify state surveillance. But governments were not merely tracing a virus; they were tracing people. Many Americans were suspicious of contact tracing apps and other surveillance measures that were imposed in the name of public health, safety, and welfare.[15] The result was dissension in American civil society and schisms between the American people and their government, which exposed flaws in how the United States collectively deals with crises that adversaries could exploit in future conflicts.

The United States must also adjust to intelligence threats that undermine its traditional assumptions about competition, conflict, and warfare. The military is the most powerful institution in the United States, and the DOD continues to play a dominant role in the American intelligence system through its control of many of the USIC's organizations and the majority of its personnel and resources. The technology used by DOD agencies like the NSA, NRO, and NGA gives the military more bureaucratic power in terms of budget and sensitive collection capabilities, which means more influence in national intelligence policy. The military also wields immense surveillance powers that can pose profound threats to American liberty when its technical intelligence services are combined with the effects of the Intelligence Revolution. For example, the NSA, created to carry out intelligence operations "conducted against foreign governments," has engaged in massive domestic and global surveillance that eclipses strictly military matters, yet it is still a DOD component.[16] The military has the potential to exercise wider domestic intelligence power than the FBI. Ceding so much domestic surveillance capability not only to the government but especially to the military presents a fundamental challenge to both civil-intelligence and civil-military relations.

Paradoxically, the US military is more powerful, and therefore potentially more dangerous to American liberty, today than in generations past, but also less effective in responding to the core threats the country must confront. As intelligence increasingly impacts American civil society at home, and as the United States embarks on a new era of geopolitical competition with rivals like China and Russia, the wisdom of allowing the DOD to dominate the

American intelligence system requires reexamination. The United States organized its intelligence community in response to warfare in the Industrial Age, but subordinating intelligence to the military in the Information Age will not satisfy the demands of the coming century.[17]

Nikita Khrushchev supposedly once declared the Soviet Union would defeat the United States without firing a shot. Today, not only are America's adversaries using cyberoperations to steal US military secrets or plan cyberattacks that would blind the US military in a fight, but they are also harnessing intelligence in other ways to damage American national security without resorting to outright war.[18] Russia's use of disinformation has eroded the American public's faith in its constitutional institutions. While the United States itself has used intelligence to shape elections in foreign countries, including Russia, the American people have utterly failed to unify against this intelligence threat and instead have rewarded Russia's efforts by dividing themselves further politically.

Intelligence is at the forefront of competition with China as well. China boasts the largest national intelligence apparatus in the world. Chinese economic and industrial espionage is prolific, and the FBI opens a new China-related counterintelligence investigation roughly every ten hours.[19] But China's intelligence activities go far beyond traditional espionage. China is targeting the American people themselves by collecting their most private information, including their DNA. The US government estimates that China has collected personal information on 80 percent of American adults.[20] Mao Zedong worried that the United States was trying "to change countries like ours, and to carry out sabotage activities so as to change the nature of society into what they like."[21] But now China is honing its ability to influence American citizens both individually and collectively. How and (perhaps even more perplexingly) why China is leveraging its massive and growing intelligence and surveillance system to target the American people is one of the great puzzles and potential threats facing the USIC and the United States.[22]

Khrushchev and Mao were perceptive and perhaps prescient. They recognized the intersection of intelligence and ideas, and they understood how the nature of national security and international competition involved both. Other states are currently using intelligence to undermine America's political, military, economic, and even social strength. And while the United States still regards military might as the ultimate measure of national power, intelligence can have disruptive effects that cause tumult and civil unrest, weakening a state from within. Democracies like the United States appear especially vulnerable to the effects of intelligence, while authoritarian regimes are harnessing intelligence to secure their domestic control and expand their foreign influence. There is no boundary between foreign and domestic intelligence in these states, and the Intelligence Revolution will demolish what little is left of the wall the United States constructed between the two. Surveillance through technology has even united the two old organizational rivals that represent the wall. The CIA, which operates programs outside the authority of FISA, has accessed intelligence on American citizens through its databases.[23] Meanwhile, the FBI has abused Section 702 of FISA, which was created by statute as a legacy of the PSP, to avoid the warrant process and gather intelligence on American citizens, including members of Congress and political donors.[24] The ongoing global intelligence competition also eviscerates the equally artificial American distinction between war and peace, and so the USIC must remain vigilant and proactive, which is to say aggressive and intrusive in its activities.

Conflict and competition make democracies more imperial abroad and less liberal at home.[25] As in other eras, for the United States to become more secure, it will have to become less free in terms of using intelligence to root out threats at home while also projecting power abroad. But the country should proceed with caution: The Intelligence Revolution will permanently change states and societies in ways that contemporary observers cannot yet fully understand or appreciate.

Even Intelligence Isn't Safe

If the United States faces challenges and uncertainties in adapting to the Intelligence Revolution, the USIC is encountering its fair share as well. New technology holds as much peril as promise. It is not just the technology itself but also how states and even members of the public are using it that is disrupting traditional approaches to intelligence. In response, the USIC will have to adjust not only how it operates but also how it engages with the world around it.

Intelligence officers have always had to find ways to work undetected in foreign states. The risks are especially acute in "hard target" countries with robust counterintelligence systems, such as Russia or China. If intelligence can use new technology to monitor people, then the same principle applies to intelligence officers. The USIC is confronting the difficulties associated with what it calls "ubiquitous technical surveillance," as cameras, phone tracking software, and biometrics make it much harder for intelligence officers to travel, meet and recruit assets, and conduct the full range of human espionage operations, all without discovery.[26] A combination of hacking, Big Data, and social network analysis has allowed adversaries like Iran and China to find and identify American intelligence officers.[27] A new generation of intelligence officers could enter the field already compromised by their "digital dust"—traces of their online existence like consumer activity and social media accounts.

Espionage still offers insights that other sources of intelligence cannot. Some targets shun the conveniences and dangers of modern communication. For example, al Qaeda's leadership shifted to using human couriers rather than phones and the internet. The notoriously paranoid Vladimir Putin does not have a smartphone, which encumbered the USIC's effort to gather information about his plans and intentions; instead, the CIA relied on a high-placed spy in the Kremlin who had to be extracted suddenly in 2017.[28] Essentially, the difficulty of HUMINT puts a premium on it. Spy games will continue to offer states the paradoxical possibility of either mitigating conflict or escalating it from the shadows.[29]

While new technology makes espionage more difficult, it also makes the process of collecting information easier. Open-source intelligence, the collection and analysis of publicly available information, is ostensibly revolutionizing intelligence—or at least that is the common perception among policymakers, the public, and the USIC itself. Although OSINT elements exist within several members of the USIC, there has recently been debate over the need to establish a new agency dedicated specifically to it. Beyond yet another bureaucratic battle over a key intelligence function, OSINT puts the intelligence profession in jeopardy.

On the surface, OSINT suggests that anyone can "do" intelligence. With just a computer and internet access, a private citizen can mine satellite imagery, social media, news reports, and any number of sources of information. Analysis is then a matter of using one's best judgment, perhaps with the help of the same structured analytic techniques used by intelligence organizations and readily available online. Certainly, some conduct OSINT better than others. For example, Bellingcat, an independent collective of researchers, investigators, and journalists, has provided OSINT on a range of security topics of global interest, including a demonstrable record of success in exposing Russian intelligence activities.[30] Many US intelligence officers and officials have praised OSINT and the work of organizations like Bellingcat as a workaround to having to risk revealing classified sources and methods.[31] But in trying to exploit OSINT to protect secrecy, the USIC undermines itself.

It was a long and hard-won fight to professionalize intelligence in the United States. Allowing OSINT to take credit for what was obtained through secret activities diminishes the value of the USIC and its expensive, secretive organizations in the eyes of the public and those policymakers not privy to special collection programs. Alternatively, if OSINT amateurs can collect or analyze information as well as, if not better than, intelligence officers and organizations, it calls into question the need for professional intelligence. As the youngest, most precarious profession of national security, intelligence must carefully guard its professional prerogatives and continue to prove itself. To this end, former intelligence officers have recently started a foundation to professionalize OSINT within the USIC.[32] Perhaps the USIC will be able to distinguish its own sphere of OSINT from private sector OSINT. Even then, OSINT risks blurring intelligence analysis with what some might consider mere research and investigation. Moreover, the windfall of OSINT risks overwhelming analysts with a deluge of publicly available data that also contains misinformation and disinformation. Finally, OSINT could distract intelligence professionals from their heretofore core competency in gathering and analyzing information that is protected and not publicly available.[33] Like HUMINT, secret intelligence will remain indispensable and even more valuable as it becomes more difficult to collect or as states feel more secure in their secrets.[34]

Perhaps the greatest unknown for the USIC is how artificial intelligence (AI), machine learning, and quantum computing will change intelligence. The USIC is trying to keep pace with the dramatic speed of technological change. For example, the CIA recently created a Directorate of Digital Innovation to ensure it continues to develop and incorporate technological breakthroughs into its operations and analysis. It is the hope of intelligence professionals that AI will help sort through the ever-growing mass of data, freeing up human analysts to apply their skills to providing policymakers with finished intelligence products and reasoned judgments.[35] But AI holds even more prospects for intelligence. Not only could machines autonomously collect information, but they could also become consumers, analysts, and counterintelligence "agents."[36] Eerily echoing the CIA's early Cold War mind control experiments, researchers are also using a combination of AI and fMRI scanners to learn to read human thoughts.[37] It is not hard to imagine intelligence services adopting this breakthrough to collect from the hardest target of all: the human mind.

Even if the USIC were able to successfully integrate all the new advances in technology, there are still old questions of US civil-intelligence relations that it will never overcome. The USIC will always face trial in the court of public opinion. The swift American withdrawal from Afghanistan in

August 2021 and the equally sudden conquest of the country by the Taliban once again ignited a debate over intelligence failure. There was a consensus among the members of the USIC that the Afghan government would not be able to successfully resist the Taliban without US support, though intelligence assessments failed to predict the precise timeline for the rapid fall of Kabul and the Taliban takeover of the country. There was also disagreement among intelligence agencies regarding the Afghans' will to resist and the Afghan Army, which quickly collapsed. In the event, intelligence was unlikely to affect the outcome, as the Biden administration had already announced the withdrawal in April 2021.[38] Reflecting their mercurial temperament, while a majority of Americans favored the withdrawal, they also disapproved of the Biden administration's handling of it.[39] As in other instances of intelligence failure, policy failures both preceded and followed intelligence failure.

In contrast to Afghanistan, the USIC predicted the Russian invasion of Ukraine in February 2022 with remarkable accuracy in terms of both the timeline and Russia's plan of attack. Yet, it also anticipated the Russians would capture the Ukrainian capital in just a few days, underestimating the Ukrainians' remarkable resilience and fierce resistance. Apparently, even when the USIC is successful, it still manages to fail. However, intelligence allowed the United States to prepare allies and signal Russia ahead of the invasion. The US government also did something unexpected by declassifying intelligence to shore up domestic and global public support for Ukraine, which publicly foiled Russian intelligence attempts to use disinformation or a "false flag" operation as a pretext for war.[40] As always, it is only a matter of time until policymakers and the public will again blame intelligence for larger, collective failures, and they will again question the value of intelligence in US national security.

The Spy, the State, and the American People

Perhaps American intelligence's failures, scandals, and abuses do overshadow its successes. Intelligence organizations and officers are sometimes scapegoats and other times heroes. In some conspiracy theories, they form a cabal that manipulates the United States and global order from the shadows. In other accounts, they are a bumbling lot whose secret operations are half-cocked and whose analytical skills are no better than those of average citizens. It can be difficult to separate fact from fiction and perception from reality in the shadowy world of intelligence.

It is true that American intelligence activities have done injury to the US constitutional system, regardless of the intentions or exigencies that motivated them. Too often, the American people discovered these trespasses in spite of secrecy rather than on account of transparency. While congressional hearings or leaks to the press have been two common pathways for public access to information, and FOIA and mandatory declassification review continue to provide records for research and study, the relationship between intelligence and the American people should not be one based on force or manipulation.

Similarly, intelligence officials occasionally call for a national debate on intelligence that purportedly includes the American people, but the debate never actually materializes.[41] Even then, secrecy would still very much inform the parameters of this debate. Intelligence officers cannot, on the one hand, profess to welcome fair and frank public debate and, on the other, insist that if average Americans had access to the same secrets—ones they cannot know and therefore cannot assess for themselves—then they might change their minds about national security issues. Trite phrases and jokes like "It's classified," "That's need-to-know," or, worst of all, "I can tell you, but then I'd have to kill you" serve only to stifle rather than encourage debate. To be fair, such phrases more often are used to caricature intelligence officers than are used by them, but secrecy creates much of the misunderstanding and mistrust that burdens US civil-intelligence relations. If the intelligence community wants the trust of the American people, then it must trust them in return.

The USIC has taken some steps toward more transparency or at least a more public face. Many organizations in the USIC now have social media accounts, although the CIA's first tweet, "We can neither confirm nor deny that this is our first tweet," and another about not knowing the whereabouts of the dead rapper Tupac Shakur led to recriminations about the CIA reproducing conspiracy theories or trying to cover its controversial history through humor.[42] One former CIA officer even suggested it should step away from social media and get back to the business of intelligence, commenting, "The CIA does not need to be on Twitter, because it can't be transparent."[43]

But transparency is essential for trust. In introducing the 2019 National Intelligence Strategy, DNI Dan Coats emphasized, "We need to reassure the policymakers and the American people that we can be trusted." The 2023 National Intelligence Strategy has made information exchange with civil society, including private corporations and civic groups, one of its central goals.[44] Transparency, an American principle, runs at cross-purposes to secrecy, an intelligence principle, and in this, the USIC must find balance.

In a reversal of the intelligence tradition, some representatives of the USIC are suggesting that transparency not only can help harmonize US civil-intelligence relations but also can help make the country safer. One test of transparency will be if the USIC declassifies and publicizes its own abuses or failures before they become public. In previous eras, the USIC only declassified documents relating to its wrongdoings following leaks, press reports, or congressional investigations. Whether the USIC truly achieves more transparency, only time will tell.

Aside from this purported attempt to change its organizational culture and operating principle, the USIC is also trying to change its composition to be more representative of the country it serves. The USIC remains one of the least representative institutions of the US government, despite prioritizing workforce diversity in recent years.[45] Even if the USIC manages to "look like America," the intelligence profession still involves inherently un-American practices and lacks democratizing features like the military draft, which means it constantly faces the problem of elitism even when trying to give itself a more democratic face. Tempering elitism requires intelligence professionals to understand not only the relationship between the spy and the state but also the fragile relationship between the spy and the citizen.

Samuel Huntington ended his classic, *The Soldier and the State*, with a poetic comparison of the United States Military Academy at West Point and the nearby village of Highland Falls, New York. Writing in 1957, he wondered, "Is it possible to deny that the military values... are the ones America most needs today?" then declared, "America can learn more from West Point than West Point from America."[46] But the same cannot be said for intelligence.

This history cannot end with a description of the CIA headquarters as a foil to some idyllic town in northern Virginia or even the hustle and bustle of nearby Washington, DC. Secrecy prevents outsiders from visiting the CIA compound and witnessing its daily life, or interacting transparently with many CIA officers, who often conceal their identities and their profession. The CIA has an organizational culture based on secrecy; it is an insular world of insiders who keep secrets from outsiders—their fellow citizens, their friends, and even their own families. Few would conclude that the country needs more secrecy, an intelligence principle, though it could probably use more privacy, an American principle.[47]

The Spy and the State has aimed to provide a history of intelligence and the American people, including how their perceptions, prejudices, and principles have shaped it. It has offered an overview of the ideas and influences that have informed the creation and evolution of American intelligence in order to explain a subject that too often has been shrouded in secrecy and mythology. Intelligence has served the dual, if conflicting, causes of American liberty and security since the Revolutionary War, even if imperfectly. While it has its faults, it has also often taken the blame for the flaws of the country and culture at large. The American people have been complicit in terms of overreacting to threats and aiding—or at least supporting—aggressive intelligence activities. The public cannot offer sweeping mandates to the USIC out of collective fear, only to recoil at the methods it uses to address the problem. The American people have also harbored unrealistic expectations of intelligence as a silver bullet for many of the challenges and threats they face, while exhibiting zero tolerance for intelligence scandals, abuses, or failures. They continue to prefer the sexy Hollywood image of James Bond or Jason Bourne to the more rote and relevant role of the analyst working on a National Intelligence Estimate. It is easier and perhaps more exciting to associate intelligence with clandestine and covert activities instead of its analytical role. Ironically, the CIA has suffered the same identity problem since its inception. The American people and the CIA—indeed, the entire USIC—still have much to learn from each other and from their intertwined history.

Securing the Blessings of Liberty

Liberty and security exist at opposite poles. Movement toward one pole implies a shift away from the other. Critics may claim that this is a false choice and that there is an alternative: The United States must defend freedom, or, as Gouverneur Morris wrote in the Preamble to the Constitution, "secure the Blessings of Liberty." But the idea of securing liberty has been problematic in its application when it involves intelligence.

Throughout US history, defending freedom has involved intelligence activities that infringe upon constitutional rights and offend American principles, even if temporarily, in the name of protecting the nation and its people. Intelligence requires continuity and support, but there has been a tug-of-war in the country's search for liberty and security that has dragged intelligence back and forth along with it. While the United States has often managed to roll back controversial and egregious intelligence measures after a war or threat has passed, advances in intelligence and the advent of the Intelligence Revolution now portend changes not only to US civil-intelligence relations but also to the American way of life, with the result that the country will be both less safe and less free. The American people must therefore assert their role in the US intelligence system more directly in the future than they have in the past—their liberty and security depend on it.

How should the United States balance intelligence with American principles? How the country has answered this question in the past has charted the course for American intelligence to the present. How the American people answer this question in the present will determine the future of their republic as intelligence transforms the twenty-first century.

Notes

INTRODUCTION

1. The field of intelligence studies has expanded to nonstate actors and private sector or corporate intelligence, but this book is a history of intelligence as it is traditionally understood in terms of national security.
2. The term "civil-intelligence relations" has appeared in only a few places. See, for example, Douglas Porch, *The French Secret Services: From the Dreyfus Affair to the Gulf War* (New York: Farrar, Straus and Giroux, 1995); Thomas C. Bruneau and Steven C. Boraz, eds. *Reforming Intelligence: Obstacles to Democratic Control and Effectiveness* (Austin: University of Texas Press, 2007). I initially proposed a field of American civil-intelligence relations to frame what eventually became this book and received recognition for this earlier work: "2019 'Bobby R. Inman Award' Winners Announced," Intelligence Studies Project, University of Texas at Austin, August 5, 2019, https://intelligencestudies.utexas.edu/news/2019-bobby-r-inman-award-winners-announced/. This book is hopefully a starting point for further studies of civil-intelligence relations not only in the United States but elsewhere as well.
3. Samuel Huntington, *The Soldier and the State: The Theory and Politics of Civil-Military Relations* (Cambridge, MA: Belknap Press of Harvard University Press, 1957).
4. Huntington preferred the term "American liberalism" rather than "the American people" to explain how a set of beliefs and principles acted as an "ideological constant" in US civil-military relations. See Huntington, *The Soldier and the State*, chap. 6.
5. Document 550, Gouverneur Morris to James LaCaze, February 21, 1788, *The Documentary History of the Ratification of the Constitution Digital Edition*, ed. John Kaminski, Gaspare J. Saladino, Richard Leffler, Charles H. Schoenleber, and Margaret A. Hogan (Charlottesville: University of Virginia Press, 2009). Other sources attribute the quotation to Robert Morris.

6. George Washington to Noah Webster, July 31, 1788, *The Writings of George Washington from the Original Manuscript Sources, 1745–1799*, ed. John C. Fitzpatrick, vol. 30 (Washington, DC: GPO, 1939), 27–28.
7. George Washington to Gouverneur Morris, October 13, 1789, Founders Online, National Archives.
8. Henry Merritt Wriston, *Executive Agents in American Foreign Relations* (Gloucester, MA: Peter Smith, 1967), 210.
9. Stephen F. Knott, *Secret and Sanctioned: Covert Operations and the American Presidency* (New York: Oxford University Press, 1996), 145–48.
10. "The City upon a Hill Speech" (1961), JFKL.
11. "Election Eve Address 'A Vision for America'" (1980), RRL.
12. "The President and the Press: Address Before the American Newspaper Publishers Association," April 27, 1961, Digitized Content, JFKL.
13. Allen W. Dulles, *The Craft of Intelligence* (Guilford, CT: Lyons Press, 2006), 177.
14. Rhodri Jeffreys-Jones, *Cloak and Dollar: A History of American Secret Intelligence* (New Haven, CT: Yale University Press, 2002), 63.
15. Samuel Huntington explains that American civil society has attempted to force the military to reflect its social values in a process he calls "transmutation." To Huntington, this is a trade-off of military professionalism for American principles. The same applies to intelligence. Huntington, *The Soldier and the State*, 155–57.
16. There is a spirited debate over whether secrecy is an essential ingredient of intelligence. There is open-source intelligence, or OSINT, that is available from public sources of information like social media, commercial satellites, or news articles. A state can also choose to reveal the intelligence it has collected and analyzed, so an intelligence product may not be secret, like the Annual Threat Assessment produced by the US Intelligence Community. Even the most secretive and sensitive covert action operations sometimes become public, like the famous CIA-sponsored coup in Iran or plans to assassinate Fidel Castro, covered later in this book. Crucially, at some point in any of the above examples, intelligence always involves secrecy.
17. See, for example, Robert Stinnett, *Day of Deceit: The Truth About FDR and Pearl Harbor* (New York: Free Press, 2001); Max Holland, "The Lie That Linked CIA to the Kennedy Assassination: The Power of Disinformation," *Studies in Intelligence* 45, no. 5 (2001); Garrett M. Graff, *UFO: The Inside Story of the US Government's Search for Alien Life Here—and Out There* (New York: Avid Reader Press/Simon & Schuster, 2023).
18. "Remarks upon Presenting the National Security Medal to Allen W. Dulles, 28 November 1961," Digitized Content, JFKL.
19. "C.I.A.: Maker of Policy, or Tool," *New York Times*, April 25, 1966.
20. Rhodri Jeffreys-Jones, *The CIA and American Democracy*, 3rd ed. (New Haven, CT: Yale University Press, 2003), 54.

21. Archibald MacLeish, *The Hamlet of A. MacLeish* (Cambridge: Riverside Press, 1928), 38.

CHAPTER 1

1. George Dudley Seymour, *Documentary Life of Nathan Hale* (New Haven, CT: privately printed, 1941), 318, 339.
2. Seymour, *Documentary Life of Nathan Hale*, 308–9.
3. Kenneth A. Daigler, *Spies, Patriots, and Traitors: American Intelligence in the Revolutionary War* (Washington, DC: Georgetown University Press, 2014), 96–97, 100.
4. James Hutson, "Nathan Hale Revisited," *Information Bulletin*, July/August 2003, LOC.
5. Daigler, *Spies, Patriots, and Traitors*, 101–2.
6. Benjamin Tallmadge, *Memoir of Colonel Benjamin Tallmadge*, ed. Henry Phelps Johnston (New York: Gillis Press, 1904), 134.
7. Tallmadge, *Memoir of Colonel Benjamin Tallmadge*, 56.
8. GEN MSS 817, Box 17, Folder: Church, R Benjamin, WLPP.
9. G. J. A. O'Toole, *Honorable Treachery: A History of U.S. Intelligence, Espionage, and Covert Action from the American Revolution to the CIA* (New York: Grove Press, 2014), 17.
10. November 7, 1775, *Journals of the Continental Congress 1774–1789*, ed. Worthington Chauncey Ford, vol. 3 (Washington, DC: GPO, 1905), 331, 334.
11. Don Higginbotham, *The War of American Independence: Military Attitudes, Policies, and Practice, 1763–1789* (New York: Macmillan, 1971), 58.
12. O'Toole, *Honorable Treachery*, 13.
13. Bernard Bailyn, *The Ideological Origins of the American Revolution* (Cambridge, MA: Belknap Press of Harvard University Press, 2017), 144; Forrest McDonald, *Novus Ordo Seclorum: The Intellectual Origins of the Constitution* (Lawrence: University Press of Kansas, 1985), 78.
14. *The Revolutionary Diplomatic Correspondence of the United States*, ed. Francis Wharton, vol. 3 (Washington, DC: GPO, 1889), 12n.
15. Philip Davidson, *Propaganda and the American Revolution, 1763–1783* (Chapel Hill: University of North Carolina Press, 1941).
16. Samuel Adams, *The Writings of Samuel Adams*, ed. Harry Alonzo Cushing, vol. 2 (New York: G. P. Putnam's Sons, 1906), 356.
17. Secret Journals of Congress, November 29, 1775, *Revolutionary Diplomatic Correspondence*, vol. 2, 61.
18. Franklin et al., Committee of Secret Correspondence, to Arthur Lee, December 12, 1775, *Revolutionary Diplomatic Correspondence*, vol. 2, 63.
19. A. Lee to Lieutenant-Governor Colden, February 13, 1776, *Revolutionary Diplomatic Correspondence*, vol. 2, 72. The letters were addressed on the outside to

Benjamin Franklin but in the contents to Lieutenant-Governor Colden (the former British-appointed governor of New York), causing Francis Wharton to propose that the actual recipient was neither man. *Revolutionary Diplomatic Correspondence*, vol. 2, 71, 72, 76.

20. A. Lee to Lieutenant-Governor Colden, February 14, 1776, *Revolutionary Diplomatic Correspondence*, vol. 2, 76–77.
21. Secret Journals of Congress, May 10, 1776, *Revolutionary Diplomatic Correspondence*, vol. 2, 90.
22. Franklin, Morris et al., Memorandum of October 1, 1776, *Revolutionary Diplomatic Correspondence*, vol. 2, 151–52.
23. John Jay to Robert Morris, October 6, 1776, *Revolutionary Diplomatic Correspondence*, vol. 2, 165.
24. *Revolutionary Diplomatic Correspondence*, vol. 1, 369.
25. Committee of Secret Correspondence to Silas Deane, March 3, 1776, *Revolutionary Diplomatic Correspondence*, vol. 2, 78–80.
26. Milton C. Van Vlack, *Silas Deane: Revolutionary War Diplomat and Politician* (Jefferson, NC: McFarland, 2013), 99–100.
27. *Revolutionary Diplomatic Correspondence*, vol. 1, 562–64.
28. Deane to Committee of Secret Correspondence, October 1, 1776, *Revolutionary Diplomatic Correspondence*, vol. 2, 153–57.
29. Deane to Committee of Secret Correspondence, November 6, 1776, *Revolutionary Diplomatic Correspondence*, vol. 2, 190–92.
30. Deane to Jay, December 3, 1776, *Revolutionary Diplomatic Correspondence*, vol. 2, 214.
31. Deane to Jay, December 3, 1776, *Revolutionary Diplomatic Correspondence*, vol. 2, 214–15.
32. Franklin to Deane, December 4, 1776, *Revolutionary Diplomatic Correspondence*, vol. 2, 217.
33. Van Vlack, *Silas Deane*, 121.
34. Van Vlack, *Silas Deane*, 122–23.
35. Van Vlack, *Silas Deane*, 133–37; Jonathan R. Dull, “Franklin the Diplomat: The French Mission,” *Transactions of the American Philosophical Society* 72, no. 1 (1982): 24–25.
36. September 26, 1776, *Journals of the Continental Congress*, vol. 5, 827.
37. October 22, 1776, *Journals of the Continental Congress*, vol. 6, 897.
38. *Revolutionary Diplomatic Correspondence*, vol. 1, 561, 564–68.
39. The Committee for Foreign Affairs became the Department of Foreign Affairs and it, in turn, became the State Department. Thus, the State Department’s revolutionary roots lie in both intelligence and diplomacy.
40. April 17, 1777, *Journals of the Continental Congress*, vol. 7, 274.
41. Knott, *Secret and Sanctioned*, 33.
42. *Revolutionary Diplomatic Correspondence*, vol. 3, 12.

43. Gerard to the President of Congress, January 5, 1779, *Revolutionary Diplomatic Correspondence*, vol. 3, 11–12.
44. *Revolutionary Diplomatic Correspondence*, vol. 3, 17.
45. Knott, *Secret and Sanctioned*, 34.
46. Anonymous, "Edward Bancroft (@ Edwd. Edwards), Estimable Spy," *Studies in Intelligence* 5, no. 1 (1961).
47. Juliana Ritchie to Benjamin Franklin, January 12, 1777, Founders Online, NARA.
48. Benjamin Franklin to [Juliana Ritchie], January 19, 1777, Founders Online, NARA.
49. P. K. Rose, "A Counterintelligence Debacle: British Penetration of America's First Diplomatic Mission," *Studies in Intelligence* 41, no. 4 (1997): 61.
50. Rose, "A Counterintelligence Debacle," 62–63.
51. *Revolutionary Diplomatic Correspondence*, vol. 1, 462.
52. Daigler, *Spies, Patriots, and Traitors*, 85.
53. Dull, "Franklin the Diplomat," 27.
54. George Washington to Elias Dayton, July 26, 1777, GEN MSS 817, Box 46, WLPP.
55. See, for example, *Writings of George Washington*, vol. 10, 413, 464, 468.
56. Washington to Major John Clark, Junior, November 4, 1777, *Writings of George Washington*, vol. 10, 8.
57. Washington to Benjamin Tallmadge, November 20, 1778, GEN MSS 817, Box 17, Folder: Washington, George ALS to Major Tallmadge 1778 Nov 20, WLPP.
58. Knott, *Secret and Sanctioned*, 16–17.
59. Washington to Governor William Livingston, January 20, 1778, *Writings of George Washington*, vol. 10, 329.
60. Knott, *Secret and Sanctioned*, 20.
61. Washington to Major General Thomas Mifflin, April 10, 1777, *Writings of George Washington*, vol. 7, 385.
62. Washington to Reverend Alexander McWhorter, October 12, 1778, *Writings of George Washington*, vol. 13, 71–72.
63. Washington to Philip Schuyler, May 14, 1781, *Writings of George Washington*, vol. 22, 81.
64. Daigler, *Spies, Patriots, and Traitors*, 243.
65. Washington to Nathaniel Sackett, April 8, 1777, *Writings of George Washington*, vol. 7, 371–72.
66. O'Toole, *Honorable Treachery*, 43–44.
67. Knott, *Secret and Sanctioned*, 23.
68. April 27, 1779, *Secret Journals of the Acts and Proceedings of Congress*, vol. 1 (Boston: Thomas B. Wait, 1821), 112.
69. Daigler, *Spies, Patriots, and Traitors*, 243.

70. Samuel Purviance Jr., Letter of May 4, 1777, GEN MSS Box 17, Folder Purviance, Samuel, Jr., WLPP.
71. Washington to Josiah Quincy, March 24, 1776, *Writings of George Washington*, vol. 4, 422.
72. *Writings of George Washington*, vol. 5, 266, fn. 23.
73. Washington to the Secret Committee of the New York Legislature, July 13, 1776, *Writings of George Washington*, vol. 5, 267.
74. *Journals of the Provincial Congress, Provincial Convention, Committee of Safety and Council of Safety of the State of New York, 1775–1777*, vol. 1 (Albany, NY: Thurlow Weed, 1842), 638.
75. *Minutes of the Committee and of the First Commission for Detecting and Defeating Conspiracies in the State of New York*, vol. 1 (New York: Printed for the Society, 1924).
76. Fishkill, NY, November 8, 1776, *Minutes of the Committee and of the First Commission for Detecting and Defeating Conspiracies in the State of New York*, vol. 1, 13.
77. Daigler, *Spies, Patriots, and Traitors*, 113.
78. Rhodri Jeffreys-Jones, *American Espionage: From Secret Service to CIA* (London: Endeavour Press, 2017), 23.
79. Washington to Webster, July 31, 1788, *Writings of George Washington*, vol. 30, 28.

CHAPTER 2

1. Charles Mathias, Proposed Standing Committee on Intelligence Activities, S. Res. 400, 122 Cong. Rec. 13695 (1976).
2. O'Toole, *Honorable Treachery*, 83.
3. James Madison, *Notes of Debates in the Federal Convention of 1787* (New York: W. W. Norton, 1987), 364.
4. Madison, *Notes of Debates in the Federal Convention of 1787*, 28.
5. Richard Kohn, *Eagle and Sword: The Beginnings of the Military Establishment in America* (New York: Free Press, 1975).
6. Nathan Miller, *Spying for America: The Hidden History of U.S. Intelligence* (New York: Marlowe, 1997), 56; Adam Mill, "How Yanking John Brennan's Security Clearance Keeps Intelligence Accountable," *The Federalist*, August 22, 2018; Philip A. Lacovara, "Presidential Power to Gather Intelligence: The Tension Between Article II and Amendment IV," *Law and Contemporary Problems* 40, no. 3 (1976): 107.
7. Elizabeth B. Bazan and Jennifer K. Elsea, "Memorandum: Presidential Authority to Conduct Warrantless Electronic Surveillance to Gather Foreign Intelligence Information," Congressional Research Service, January 5, 2006, 3–4.
8. John Jay, *Federalist Papers*, No. 64.
9. Alexander Hamilton, *Federalist Papers*, No. 70.

10. Hamilton, *Federalist Papers*, No. 75.
11. For Hamilton's role in intelligence operations during the Revolutionary War, see Knott, *Secret and Sanctioned*, 37–42; O'Toole, *Honorable Treachery*, 45; Daigler, *Spies, Patriots, and Traitors*, 187, 244.
12. "No Money shall be drawn from the Treasury, but in Consequence of Appropriations made by Law; and a regular Statement and Account of Receipts and Expenditures of all public Money be published from time to time." For more on the debate, see John S. Warner, "Where Secrecy Is Essential," *Studies in Intelligence* 3, no. 2 (1987).
13. Warner, "Where Secrecy Is Essential," 48. The original debate of September 14, 1787, may be found in Madison, *Notes of Debates in the Federal Convention*, 641.
14. David Robertson, *Debates and Other Proceedings of the Convention of Virginia* (Richmond, VA: Ritchie & Worlsey and Augustine Davis, 1805), 47, 50, 46, and 51, respectively.
15. Robertson, *Debates and Other Proceedings of the Convention of Virginia*, 53.
16. Robertson, *Debates and Other Proceedings of the Convention of Virginia*, 128.
17. Robertson, *Debates and Other Proceedings of the Convention of Virginia*, 326.
18. Robertson, *Debates and Other Proceedings of the Convention of Virginia*, 328.
19. Alexander Hamilton, *The Federalist Papers*, No. 64.
20. For example, *Hamdi v. Rumsfeld*, 542 US 507 (2004); *Al-Aulaqi v. Obama*, 717 F. Supp. 2d 1 (DDC 2010); *Al-Aulaqi v. Panetta*, 35 F. Supp. 3d 56 (DDC 2014).
21. Huw Dylan and Michael S. Goodman, "Guide to Study of Intelligence: British Intelligence," *The Intelligencer: Journal of U.S. Intelligence Studies* 21, no. 2 (2015): 35; Steven E. Maffeo, *Most Secret and Confidential: Intelligence in the Age of Nelson* (Annapolis, MD: Naval Institute Press, 2000), 4, 8.
22. George Washington, "First Annual Message to Congress," January 8, 1790, Founders Online, NARA.
23. *Annals of Congress*, 1st Cong., 2nd sess., 1129. NB: There is another existing volume of the *Annals of Congress* from the same publisher and edition and for the same Congress and session in which the page of this speech of January 27, 1790, is 1091. The author has no explanation for the variance except perhaps a printing error at the time of publication in 1834.
24. Act of July 1, 1790, An Act Providing the Means of Intercourse Between the United States and Foreign Nations, ch. 22, 1 Stat. 128–29.
25. Wriston, *Executive Agents*, 211n13.
26. List of Special Agents, 1785–1912, RG 59, Entry 38, Box 1, NACP.
27. Wriston, *Executive Agents*, 212.
28. Act of February 9, 1793, An Act to Continue in Force for a Limited Time, and to Amend the Act Intituled "An Act Providing the Means of Intercourse Between the United States and Foreign Nations," ch. 4, 1 Stat. 300.
29. *Aurora General Advertiser*, October 23, 1795, M2478, Jan 1, 1795–Dec 31, 1795, LOC. Secretary of the Treasury Oliver Wolcott Jr. repudiated these charges in a

letter to Bache published in the *Aurora* on October 24, 1795. Also, see Alexander Hamilton to George Washington, October 26, 1795, Founders Online, NARA.

30. Thomas Paine, "Letter to George Washington," July 30, 1796, Thomas Paine National Historical Association.
31. James Monroe to Timothy Pickering, July 30, 1797, *Annals of Congress*, 5th Cong., Appendix, 3169.
32. George Washington, Farewell Address, September 19, 1796, Founders Online, NARA.

CHAPTER 3

1. Christopher Andrew, *For the President's Eyes Only: Secret Intelligence and the American Presidency from Washington to Bush* (New York: HarperPerennial, 1996), 29.
2. John Gardner, *Brief Consideration of the Important Services, and Distinguished Virtues and Talents, Which Recommend Mr. Adams for the Presidency of the United States* (Boston: Manning & Loring, 1796), No. 5, 23–24.
3. There was also a W. (Nicholas Hubbard).
4. Act of June 25, 1798, An Act Concerning Aliens, ch. 58, 1 Stat. 570–72; Act of July 6, 1798, An Act Respecting Alien Enemies, ch. 66, 1 Stat. 577–78.
5. *Annals of Congress*, 5th Cong., 2nd sess., 1575.
6. *Annals of Congress*, 5th Cong., 2nd sess., 1576–77.
7. *Annals of Congress*, 5th Cong., 2nd sess., 2005–15.
8. *Annals of Congress*, 5th Cong., 3rd sess., 2895.
9. *Annals of Congress*, 5th Cong., 2nd sess., 2900–2901.
10. *Annals of Congress*, 5th Cong., 2nd sess., 3000–3001.
11. Act of July 14, 1798, An Act in Addition to the Act, Entitled "An Act for the Punishment of Certain Crimes Against the United States," ch. 74, 1 Stat. 596.
12. Jasper M. Trautsch, *The Genesis of America: US Foreign Policy and the Formation of National Identity, 1793–1815* (Cambridge: Cambridge University Press, 2018), 162.
13. John C. Miller, *Crisis in Freedom: The Alien and Sedition Acts* (Boston: Little, Brown, 1951), 146–50.
14. James Morton Smith, "The 'Aurora' and the Alien and Sedition Laws: Part II: The Editorship of William Duane," *Pennsylvania Magazine of History and Biography* 77, no. 2 (1953): 129.
15. Timothy Pickering to John Adams, July 24, 1799, Founders Online, National Archives.
16. Charles J. Ingersoll, *Recollections, Historical, Political, Biographical, and Social*, vol. 1 (Philadelphia: J. B. Lippincott, 1861), 192. George Logan is the namesake of the Logan Act.
17. "Secret Service Money," *Columbian Centinel*, GEN MSS 817, Box 46, WLPP.

18. Knott, *Secret and Sanctioned*, 66–79.
19. Knott, *Secret and Sanctioned*, 88–104, 107–15.
20. This history derives from E. A. Cruikshank, *The Political Adventures of John Henry: The Record of An International Imbroglio* (Toronto: Macmillan, 1936).
21. Cruikshank, *The Political Adventures of John Henry*, 23–24.
22. JHP, Microfilm Shelf 16, 731, pp. 9–10.
23. JHP. The cipher may be found at 5–6.
24. JHP, 11–13.
25. JHP, 4, No. 4.
26. JHP, 4, No. 7.
27. JHP, 4, No. 13.
28. Henry to Craig, January 31, 1809, JHP, 4, No. 1.
29. Cruikshank, *The Political Adventures of John Henry*, 64.
30. Henry Memorial to Lord Liverpool, JHP, 17–18.
31. Cruikshank, *The Political Adventures of John Henry*, 73; Francis F. Beirne, *The War of 1812* (New York: E. P. Dutton, 1949), 78.
32. JHP, 29; Elbridge Gerry to James Madison, January 2, 1812, Founders Online, National Archives.
33. Cruikshank, *The Political Adventures of John Henry*, 74; JHP, 81.
34. Cruikshank, *The Political Adventures of John Henry*, 75; JHP, 36, 92.
35. Cruikshank, *The Political Adventures of John Henry*, 93; JHP, 81.
36. *Annals of Congress*, 12th Cong., 1st sess., 1162.
37. "Documents of John Henry, Communicated to Mr. Monroe," University of Alberta Canadian Institute for Historical Microreproductions, CIHM/ICMH microfilm no. 51217, 3.
38. *Annals of Congress*, 12th Cong., 1st sess., 1181–84.
39. *Annals of Congress*, 12th Cong., 1st sess., 1184–88.
40. Statement of Count Edward de Crillon, March 14, 1812, *Annals of Congress*, 12th Cong., 1st sess., 1220–24.
41. Samuel Eliot Morison, "The Henry-Crillon Affair of 1812," *Proceedings of the Massachusetts Historical Society* 3, no. 69 (1947–51): 221.
42. Edmund Quincy, *Life of Josiah Quincy of Massachusetts* (Boston: Ticknor and Fields, 1868), 252.
43. Quincy, *Life of Josiah Quincy*, 251; Cruikshank, *The Political Adventures of John Henry*, 85, 133.
44. Quincy, *Life of Josiah Quincy*, 252.
45. Payments 4322 for $1,000 and 4321 for $49,000, respectively. General Treasury Ledger, No. 22 (1812), RG 217, Entry 2, vol. 15, NAB.
46. Morison, "The Henry-Crillon Affair of 1812," 213.
47. *Annals of Congress*, 12th Cong., 1st sess., 2198.
48. Cruikshank, *The Political Adventures of John Henry*, 131, 134.
49. Morison, "The Henry-Crillon Affair of 1812," 223.

50. Henry Adams, "Count Edward de Crillon," *American Historical Review* 1, no. 1 (1895): 54.
51. JHP, 74, 76.
52. Morison, "The Henry-Crillon Affair of 1812," 228.
53. *Annals of Congress*, 12th Cong., 2nd sess., 762.
54. March 5, 1814, *Niles Weekly Register* 6, no. 1 (Baltimore: Franklin Press, 1814), 4.
55. James Fenimore Cooper, *The Spy: A Tale of the Neutral Ground* (1821; reprint, New York: Penguin Books, 1997).
56. Cooper, *The Spy*, 1.
57. Cooper, *The Spy*, 398.
58. Cooper, *The Spy*, 310.
59. Cooper, *The Spy*, 233.
60. Cooper, *The Spy*, 331.
61. Maria Edgeworth, *The Port Folio* 16 (1823): 86.
62. *North American Review* 32, no. 71 (1831): 519.
63. William Gilmore Simms, "The Writings of Cooper," in *Fenimore Cooper: The Critical Heritage*, ed. George Dekker and John P. McWilliams (London: Routledge and Kegan Paul, 1973), 218–19.
64. F.A.S., "The United States: American Literature, Novels of Mr. Cooper," in Dekker and McWilliams, *Fenimore Cooper: The Critical Heritage*, 129.
65. Sarah Hale, *The Port Folio* 13 (1822): 96.
66. W. H. Gardiner, *North American Review* 15, no. 36 (1822): 259.
67. Gardiner, *North American Review*, 261.
68. Cooper, *The Spy*, 3–6.
69. Harry Edward Miller, "The Spy of the Neutral Ground," *New England Magazine* (n.s.) 18: 308; Dave McTiernan, "The Novel as 'Neutral Ground': Genre and Ideology in Cooper's *The Spy*," *Studies in American Fiction* 25, no. 1 (1997): 8; Alison Marie Weir, "The Spy in Early America: The Emergence of a Genre" (Ph.D. diss., University of Illinois at Urbana-Champaign, 1998), 98.
70. H. L. Barnum, *The Spy Unmasked; or, Memoirs of Enoch Crosby, Alias Harvey Birch, the Hero of Mr. Cooper's Tale of the Neutral Ground; Being an Authentic Account of the Secret Services Which He Rendered His Country During the Revolutionary War* (New York: J. & J. Harper, 1828).
71. Cooper, *The Spy*, 398.
72. Cooper, *The Spy*, 400.

CHAPTER 4

1. *Annals of Congress*, 5th Cong., 2nd sess., 894.
2. *Annals of Congress*, 5th Cong., 2nd sess., 916–17.
3. *Annals of Congress*, 5th Cong., 2nd sess., 935.
4. *Annals of Congress*, 5th Cong., 2nd sess., 1112.

5. *Annals of Congress*, 7th Cong., 2nd sess., 1264–66.
6. *Annals of Congress*, 12th Cong., 2nd sess., 920–22.
7. List of Special Agents, 1785–1912, RG 59, Entry 38, Box 1, NAB.
8. Knott, *Secret and Sanctioned*, 107–15; Charles Lyon Chandler, "The Life of Joel Roberts Poinsett," *Pennsylvania Magazine of History and Biography* 59, no. 1 (1935): 1–31.
9. Chandler, "The Life of Joel Roberts Poinsett," 26.
10. Wriston, *Executive Agents*, 219.
11. Wriston, *Executive Agents*, 220.
12. *Annals of Congress*, 15th Cong., 1st sess., 1465–66.
13. *Annals of Congress*, 15th Cong., 1st sess., 1467.
14. *Annals of Congress*, 15th Cong., 1st sess., 1466.
15. *Annals of Congress*, 15th Cong., 1st sess., 1468.
16. Wriston, *Executive Agents*, 224.
17. *Register of Debates in Congress*, 19th Cong., 1st sess., 235.
18. Wriston, *Executive Agents*, 227.
19. *Register of Debates in Congress*, 19th Cong., 1st sess., 339.
20. *Register of Debates in Congress*, 19th Cong., 1st sess., 602–4.
21. *Register of Debates in Congress*, 19th Cong., 1st sess., 608–11. Archival records list John Paul Jones as a "special agent." List of Special Agents, 1785–1912, RG 59, Entry 38, Box 1, NAB.
22. List of Special Agents, 1785–1912, RG 59, Entry 38, Box 1, NAB.
23. Act of May 1, 1810, *An Act Fixing the Compensation of Public Ministers, and of Consuls Residing on the Coast of Barbary, and for Other Purposes*, Ch. 44, 2 Stat. 608–10.
24. Wriston, *Executive Agents*, 236–37.
25. *Register of Debates in Congress*, 19th Cong., 1st sess., 610.
26. *Register of Debates in Congress*, 21st Cong., 2nd sess., 232.
27. *Register of Debates in Congress*, 21st Cong., 2nd sess., 233.
28. *Register of Debates in Congress*, 21st Cong., 2nd sess., 252.
29. *Register of Debates in Congress*, 21st Cong., 2nd sess., 294.
30. *Register of Debates in Congress*, 21st Cong., 2nd sess., 295.
31. *Register of Debates in Congress*, 21st Cong., 2nd sess., 293.
32. *Register of Debates in Congress*, 22nd Cong., 1st sess., 783.
33. *Register of Debates in Congress*, 22nd Cong., 1st sess., 776.
34. *Congressional Globe*, 27th Cong., 2nd sess., 469.
35. *Congressional Globe*, 27th Cong., 2nd sess., 473.
36. *Congressional Globe*, 27th Cong., 2nd sess., 473.
37. *Journal of the Executive Proceedings of the Senate of the United States of America*, vol. 6 (Washington, DC: GPO, 1887), 319.
38. *Journal of the Executive Proceedings of the Senate*, vol. 6, 352; James D. Richardson, *A Compilation of the Messages and Papers of the Presidents*, vol. 6 (New York: Bureau of National Literature, 1897), 2181.

39. Richardson, *Compilation*, vol. 6, 2281.
40. Richardson, *Compilation*, vol. 6, 2284.
41. Richardson, *Compilation*, vol. 6, 2285.
42. Richardson, *Compilation*, vol. 6, 2285.
43. Matthew Karp, *This Vast Southern Empire: Slaveholders at the Helm of American Foreign Policy* (Cambridge, MA: Harvard University Press, 2016), 116.
44. Wriston, *Executive Agents*, 719–21.
45. Thomas Hart Benton, *Thirty Years' View; or, A History of the Working of the American Government for Thirty Years, from 1820–1850*, vol. 2 (New York: D. Appleton, 1858), 680–82.
46. "Affairs of Hungary, 1849–1850," Senate, 61st Cong., 2nd sess., Document No. 279.
47. Ambrose Dudley Mann to John M. Clayton, October 8, 1849, "Affairs of Hungary," 27–28.
48. Chevalier J. G. Hülsemann to Daniel Webster, September 30, 1850, *Congressional Globe*, 31st Cong., 2nd sess., Appendix, 45.
49. Webster to Hülsemann, December 21, 1850, *Congressional Globe*, 31st Cong., 2nd sess., Appendix, 47.
50. Mann to Clayton, January 10, 1850, "Affairs of Hungary," 37.

CHAPTER 5

1. Henry Shelton Sanford to William Seward, September 24, 1861, Despatches from U.S. Ministers to Belgium, M193, Roll 6, NACP.
2. For more on Lincoln's style of managing the war, see Eliot A. Cohen, *Supreme Command: Soldiers, Statesmen, and Leadership in Wartime* (New York: Free Press, 2002), chap. 2.
3. The details of this plot and Pinkerton's role in uncovering it are the subject of some debate. Allan Pinkerton, *The Spy of the Rebellion: Being a True History of the Spy System of the United States Army During the Late Rebellion* (1883; reprint, Lincoln: University of Nebraska Press, 1989), chap. 2. For an alternative account, see Edwin C. Fishel, *The Secret War for the Union: The Untold Story of Military Intelligence in the Civil War* (New York: Houghton Mifflin, 1996), 14.
4. Pinkerton, *Spy of the Rebellion*, chap. 8.
5. Pinkerton, *Spy of the Rebellion*, 24.
6. Secret Service Accounts File, Records of the Provost Generals Office, RG 110, Entry 95, Box 1, NAB.
7. Pinkerton to Watson, October 7, 1862, Accounts of Allan Pinkerton, RG 110, Entry 106, NAB.
8. Pinkerton to Watson, October 7, 1862.
9. Pinkerton, *Spy of the Rebellion*, 247.
10. Pinkerton, *Spy of the Rebellion*, 247–48.

11. Secret Service Accounts File, Records of the Provost Generals Office, Accounts of Secret Service Agents, Record Group 110, Entry 95, Box 7, NAB.
12. Joseph A. Fry, *Henry Sanford: Diplomacy and Business in Nineteenth-Century America* (Reno: University of Nevada Press, 1982).
13. Seward to Sanford, March 26, 1861, Diplomatic Instructions of the Department of State, 1801–1906, M77, Roll, 19 (Belgium, April 14, 1832–December 23, 1870), NACP.
14. Draft, Sanford to Seward, May 10, 1861, Box 140, HSSP.
15. M95, Box 140, HSSP.
16. Draft, Sanford to Seward, May 10, 1861, Box 140, HSSP.
17. Sanford to Seward, September 24, 1861, Despatches from U.S. Ministers to Belgium, M193, Roll 6, NACP .
18. For further accounts of individual spies, see Fishel, *The Secret War for the Union*; Donald E. Markle, *Spies and Spymasters of the Civil War* (New York: Hippocrene Books, 2000); and Harnett T. Kane, *Spies for the Blue and Gray* (Garden City, NY: Hanover House, 1954).
19. Lafayette C. Baker, *History of the United States Secret Service* (Philadelphia: L. C. Baker, 1867), 34–35, Kindle ed.
20. Sanford to Seward, May 7, 1861, Despatches from U.S. Ministers to Belgium, M193, Roll 6, NACP.
21. Draft, Sanford to Seward, August 15, 1861, Box 140, HSSP.
22. Sanford to Seward, September 24, 1861, Despatches from U.S. Ministers to Belgium, M193, Roll 6, NACP.
23. Sanford to Seward, October 8, 1861, Despatches from U.S. Ministers to Belgium, M193, Roll 6, NACP.
24. Fry, *Henry Sanford*, 46.
25. Don H. Doyle, *The Cause of All Nations: An International History of the American Civil War* (New York: Basic Books, 2015), 75.
26. Secret Service Accounts File, Records of the Provost Generals Office, RG 110, Entry 95, Box 1, NAB.
27. Sanford to Seward, September 24, 1861, Despatches from U.S. Ministers to Belgium, M193, Roll 6, NACP.
28. Sanford to Seward, March 28, 1862, Despatches from U.S. Ministers to Belgium, M193, Roll 6, NACP.
29. RG 59, Entry A1 13, Volume 103, NACP.
30. Despatches from U.S. Ministers to Great Britain, M30, Roll 73, NACP.
31. Sanford to Seward, October 10, 1861, Despatches from U.S. Ministers to Belgium, M193, Roll 6, NACP.
32. Adams to Seward, October 18, 1861.
33. Adams to Seward, October 18, 1861, Despatches from U.S. Ministers to Great Britain, M30, Roll 73, NACP.
34. Seward to Sanford, November 4, 1861, Diplomatic Instructions of the Department of State, M77, Roll 19, NACP.

35. Seward to Sanford, January 30, 1862, Diplomatic Instructions of the Department of State, M77, Roll 19, NACP.
36. The Pinkerton Detective Agency's logo was an eye with the motto "We never sleep"—thus the origin of the term "private eye."
37. George B. McClellan to Abraham Lincoln, September 13, 1862, Series 1, General Correspondence, 1833–1916, ALP; John Gibbon, *Personal Recollections of the Civil War* (New York: G. P. Putnam's Sons, 1928), 73.
38. James McPherson, *Battle Cry of Freedom: The Civil War Era* (New York: Oxford University Press, 1988), 537–39.
39. Stephen W. Sears, *Landscape Turned Red: The Battle of Antietam* (New York: Ticknor & Fields, 1983), 296.
40. McPherson, *Battle Cry of Freedom*, 544.
41. Edwin Fishel, "Pinkerton and McClellan: Who Deceived Whom?," *Civil War History* 34, no. 2 (1988): 141.
42. James D. Horan and Howard Swiggett, *The Pinkerton Story* (New York: G. P. Putnam's Sons, 1951), 108–9, 110–14, 115–22.
43. O'Toole, *Honorable Treachery*, 148.
44. Fishel, *The Secret War for the Union*, 278–79.
45. Peter G. Tsouras, *Major General George H. Sharpe and the Creation of American Military Intelligence in the Civil War* (Philadelphia: Casemate, 2018), 40.
46. Tsouras, *Major General George H. Sharpe*, 12.
47. Tsouras, *Major General George H. Sharpe*, 1.
48. Fishel, *The Secret War for the Union*, 294.
49. Tsouras, *Major General George H. Sharpe*, 52.
50. O'Toole, *Honorable Treachery*, 202; Fishel, *The Secret War for the Union*, 3.
51. Tsouras, *Major General George H. Sharpe*, 158.
52. Tsouras, *Major General George H. Sharpe*, chap. 6.
53. Bruce W. Bidwell, *History of the Military Intelligence Division, Department of the Army General Staff: 1775–1941* (Frederick, MD: University Publications of America, 1986), 32.
54. Article 88, General Orders No. 100, Instructions for the Government of Armies of the United States in the Field, April 24, 1863 (Lieber Code).
55. Article 101, Lieber Code.
56. Article 87, Lieber Code.
57. Article 98, Lieber Code.
58. Seward to Adams, September 10, 1861, Diplomatic Instructions of the Department of State, M77, Roll 77, NACP.
59. Muir is also spelled "Mure" in some accounts.
60. Seward to Adams, August 17, 1861, Diplomatic Instructions of the Department of State, M77, Roll 77, NACP.
61. Seward to Adams, October 22, 1861, Diplomatic Instructions of the Department of State, M77, Roll 77, NACP.

62. Christopher Dickey, *Our Man in Charleston: Britain's Secret Agent in the Civil War South* (New York: Crown, 2015), 282–83.
63. Seward to Adams, October 23, 1861, Diplomatic Instructions of the Department of State, M77, Roll 77, NACP.
64. Dickey, *Our Man in Charleston*, 40–43, 75, 157, and passim.
65. Dickey, *Our Man in Charleston*, 220–21.
66. Dickey, *Our Man in Charleston*, 285.
67. Dickey, *Our Man in Charleston*, 283.
68. "Important Political Arrest," *New York Herald*, August 15, 1861.
69. "Important Developments from the Carpet Bag of a Spy—Russell, of the London Times, Aiding the Rebels," *New York Herald*, August 25, 1861.
70. "Alleged Complicity of the British Minister with the Rebels," *New York Herald*, August 30, 1861.
71. *New York Times*, September 25, 1861; *Chicago Daily Tribune*, August 17, 1861; *Cincinnati Daily Press*, December 30, 1861; *Richmond Dispatch*, August 29, 1861.
72. Henry Sanford to William Seward, September 24, 1861, Despatches from U.S. Ministers to Belgium, M193, Roll 6, NACP.
73. Margaret Clapp, *Forgotten First Citizen: John Bigelow* (Boston: Little, Brown, 1947), 149–56.
74. Sanford to Seward, November 25, 1864, Despatches from U.S. Ministers to Belgium, M193, Roll 6, NACP.
75. Sanford to Seward, December 21, 1864, Diplomatic Instructions of the Department of State, M77, Roll 19, NACP.
76. Seward to Sanford, February 14, 1865, Diplomatic Instructions of the Department of State, M77, Roll 19, NACP.
77. Fishel, *The Secret War for the Union*, 286.
78. James Barron, "Sherman Letters Show Civil War General Regarded Reporters as 'Spies,'" *New York Times*, June 21, 1987.
79. Randy D. Ferryman, "The Unresolved Tension Between Warriors and Journalists During the Civil War," *Studies in Intelligence* 58, no. 3 (2014): 6.
80. Ferryman, "The Unresolved Tension Between Warriors and Journalists During the Civil War," 4.
81. Knott, *Secret and Sanctioned*, 145.
82. Ferryman, "The Unresolved Tension Between Warriors and Journalists During the Civil War," 9.
83. Records of Correspondence of Scouts, Guides, Spies, RG 110, Entry 36, Box 1, NAB.
84. Frank L. Klement, *Dark Lanterns: Secret Political Societies, Conspiracies, and Treason Trials in the Civil War* (Baton Rouge: Louisiana State University Press, 1984), 153.
85. *Ex parte Milligan*, 71 U.S. 2 (1866).
86. Klement, *Dark Lanterns*, 179.

87. Klement, *Dark Lanterns*, 159.
88. Klement, *Dark Lanterns*, 179.
89. Records of the Provost Marshal General's Bureau (Civil War) Correspondence, Reports Accounts, and Related Records of Two or More Scouts, Guides, Spies, and Detectives 1861–1864, RG 110, Entry 31, Box 1, NAB.
90. Gavin Mortimer, *Double Death: The True Story of Pryce Lewis, the Civil War's Most Daring Spy* (New York: Walker, 2010), 229–32.
91. S. Paul O'Hara, *Inventing the Pinkertons or, Spies, Sleuths, Mercenaries, and Thugs: Being a Story of the Nation's Most Famous (and Infamous) Detective Agency* (Baltimore: Johns Hopkins University Press, 2016), 14.
92. O'Toole, *Honorable Treachery*, 151; Fishel, *The Secret War for the Union*, 598–99.
93. Andrew, *For the President's Eyes Only*, 18.
94. Tsouras, *Major General George H. Sharpe*, vii.
95. Tsouras, *Major General George H. Sharpe*, vii.
96. Tsouras, *Major General George H. Sharpe*, 47.
97. O'Toole, *Honorable Treachery*, 202, 206; Tsouras, *Major General George H. Sharpe*, v, 1, 2, 9, 10, and passim.
98. Baker, *History of the United States Secret Service*, 35.
99. Baker, *History of the United States Secret Service*, 36.
100. Baker, *History of the United States Secret Service*, 604, 608.
101. Anonymous, "The Spy System in Europe," *Beadle's Monthly: A Magazine of To-Day* 1 (1866): 80–84.

CHAPTER 6

1. Knott, *Secret and Sanctioned*, 150–51.
2. John Stevens to W. Q. Gresham, March 7, 1893, *Appendix II, Foreign Relations of the United States 1894, Affairs in Hawaii* (Washington, DC: GPO, 1895), 414.
3. *Papers Relating to the Annexation of the Hawaiian Islands to the United States*, 52nd Cong., 2nd sess. (Washington, DC: GPO, 1893), 1–6.
4. Stephen Kinzer, *The Brothers: John Foster Dulles, Allen Dulles, and Their Secret World War* (New York: Times Books, 2013), 11.
5. "For Hawaiian Annexation," *New York Times*, December 17, 1897.
6. *Appendix II, FRUS 1894, Affairs in Hawaii*, 493; for more evidence of the preexisting agreement between the coup plotters and Stevens, see esp. 583, 1029, 1030, 1063.
7. *Appendix II, FRUS 1894, Affairs in Hawaii*, 218.
8. *Appendix II, FRUS 1894, Affairs in Hawaii*, 462, 484.
9. *Appendix II, FRUS 1894, Affairs in Hawaii*, 594.
10. Allan Nevins, *Grover Cleveland: A Study in Courage* (New York: Dodd, Mead, 1964), 555–59.
11. *Appendix II, FRUS 1894, Affairs in Hawaii*, 445–58.
12. Cong. Rec., 53rd Cong., 2nd sess., 430.

13. Cong. Rec., 53rd Cong., 2nd sess., 430–31.
14. Nevins, *Grover Cleveland*, 554.
15. Cong. Rec., 53rd Cong., 2nd sess., 432.
16. American military theorists and historians Samuel Huntington, Morris Janowitz, and Allan Millett all identify the Civil War as the hinge point heralding the professionalization of the US military. See Huntington, *The Soldier and the State*, esp. 194, 199, 237; Allan R. Millett, *Military Professionalism and Officership in America* (Columbus, OH: Mershon Center, 1977), 16, 17; Morris Janowitz, *The Professional Soldier: A Social and Political Portrait* (New York: Free Press, 2017), 57, 151.
17. For more on this history, see Jeff Rogg, "Military-Intelligence Relations: Explaining the Oxymoron," *International Journal of Intelligence and CounterIntelligence* 36, no. 4 (2023): 1067–84.
18. Mark Shulman attributes the foundation of ONI in 1882 to the rise of naval theorists in the American national security establishment, while Bruce Bidwell identifies American military observers in Europe and intelligence activities against Native Americans as the proximate causes for the foundation of MID in 1885. See Mark Russell Shulman, "The Rise and Fall of American Naval Intelligence, 1882–1917," *Intelligence and National Security* 8, no. 2 (1993): 214–15; and Bidwell, *History of the Military Intelligence Division*, 39, 43–52.
19. *Army and Navy Journal*, April 20, 1889, Correspondence of War College Division and Related Gen. Staff Offices, 1903–19, RG 165, M1024, Roll 1, NACP.
20. O'Hara, *Inventing the Pinkertons*, 144.
21. Shulman, "Rise and Fall of American Naval Intelligence," 215.
22. Jeffery M. Dorwart, *The Office of Naval Intelligence: The Birth of America's First Intelligence Agency 1865–1918* (Annapolis, MD: Naval Institute Press, 1979), 44–45, 47–49.
23. Dorwart, *The Office of Naval Intelligence*, 54.
24. Dorwart, *The Office of Naval Intelligence*, 54, 56.
25. Chapter 1266, An Act to Increase the Efficiency and Reduce the Expenses of the Signal Corps of the Army, and to Transfer the Weather Service to the Department of Agriculture, sec. 2, October 1, 1890, 51st Cong., 1st sess., 26 Stat. 653.
26. A. W. Greely, January 12, 1892, Correspondence of War College Division and Related Gen. Staff Offices, 1903–19, RG 165 M1024, Roll 1, NACP.
27. Memorandum of the Secretary of War, January 1892, Correspondence of War College Division and Related Gen. Staff Offices, 1903–19, RG 165 M1024, Roll 1, NACP.
28. Memorandum outlining the functions of the Adjutant General's Department and tracing the origin and development of an Intelligence Division as part of the office of the Adjutant General, John C. Kelton, 1892, Correspondence of War College Division and Related Gen. Staff Offices, 1903–19, RG 165 M1024, Roll 1, NACP.
29. Memorandum of General John Schofield, January 20, 1892, Correspondence of War College Division and Related Gen. Staff Offices, 1903–19, RG 165 M1024, Roll 1, NACP.

30. General Orders No. 23, March 18, 1892, *General Orders and Circulars, Adjutant General's Office. 1892* (Washington, DC: GPO, 1893).
31. Bidwell, *History of the Military Intelligence Division*, 60.
32. Dorwart, *The Office of Naval Intelligence*, 56.
33. Dorwart, *The Office of Naval Intelligence*, 64–65.
34. Brief Outline of the Origin, Growth and Work of the Military Information Division, Adjutant General's Office, February 21, 1902, Correspondence of War College Division and Related Gen. Staff Offices, 1903–19, RG 165 M1024, Roll 1, NACP.
35. Bidwell, *History of the Military Intelligence Division*, 62.
36. Dorwart, *The Office of Naval Intelligence*, 65.
37. Alfred McCoy, *Policing America's Empire: The United States, the Philippines, and the Rise of the Surveillance State* (Madison: University of Wisconsin Press, 2009), 28.
38. McCoy, *Policing America's Empire*, 39.
39. Ralph H. Van Deman, *The Final Memoranda*, ed. Ralph E. Weber (Wilmington, DE: SR Books, 1988), 7.
40. Van Deman, *The Final Memoranda*, 8.
41. Van Deman, *The Final Memoranda*.
42. McCoy, *Policing America's Empire*, 46, 50, chaps. 3–5.
43. Affairs in the Philippines Islands, Hearings Before the Committee on the Philippines, 57th Cong., 1st sess., S. Doc. 331, Part 2, 1527–49.
44. Trials or Courts-Martial in the Philippine Islands in Consequence of Certain Instructions, Letter from the Secretary of War, 57th Cong., 2nd sess., S. Doc. 213, 42.
45. T. R. Brereton, "First Lessons in Modern War: Arthur Wagner, the 1898 Santiago Campaign, and U.S. Army Lesson-Learning," *Journal of Military History* 64, no. 1 (2000): 79.
46. Arthur L. Wagner, *The Service of Security and Information* (Kansas City, MO: Hudson-Kimberly, 1903), 16.
47. Wagner, *The Service of Security and Information*, 180.
48. Wagner, *The Service of Security and Information*, 181.
49. Wagner, *The Service of Security and Information*, 182.
50. Wagner, *The Service of Security and Information*, 190.
51. Wagner, *The Service of Security and Information*, 3.
52. Memorandum of John B. Babcock, September 28, 1893, Correspondence of War College Division and Related Gen. Staff Offices, 1903–19, RG 165, M1024, Roll 1, NACP.
53. Dorwart, *The Office of Naval Intelligence*, 69.
54. Richardson Clover to Chief of the Bureau of Navigation, June 30, 1899. Records of the Chief of Naval Operations, Letters Sent, 1899–1911, RG 38, Entry 69, Vol. 1, 195, NAB.

55. Richardson Clover to Chief of the Bureau of Navigation, June 30, 1899, 196–98.
56. Dorwart, *The Office of Naval Intelligence*, 78.
57. Charles D. Sigsbee to Chief of the Bureau of Navigation, March 6, 1900, Records of the Chief of Naval Operations, Letters Sent, 1899–1911, RG 38, Entry 69, Vol. 2, 433–36, NAB.
58. Dorwart, *The Office of Naval Intelligence*, 89.
59. Dorwart, *The Office of Naval Intelligence*, 96.
60. Memorandum of Secretary of War Elihu Root, August 8, 1903, Correspondence of War College Division and Related Gen. Staff Offices, 1903–19, RG 165 M1024, Roll 1, NACP.
61. Bidwell, *History of the Military Intelligence Division*, 77.
62. Bidwell, *History of the Military Intelligence Division*, 79.
63. Bidwell, *History of the Military Intelligence Division*, 81.
64. Memorandum. Office Chief of Second Section, General Staff, June 27, 1908. National Archives. Correspondence of War College Division and Related Gen. Staff Offices, 1903–19, RG 165 M1024, Roll 1, NACP.
65. Bidwell, *History of the Military Intelligence Division*, 87.
66. April 10, 1890, Records of the Office of the Chief of Naval Operations, Office of Naval Intelligence, General Correspondence, 1886–1899, RG 38, Entry 68, Vol. 7, NAB.
67. "Report of the Secretary of War and Reports of Bureau Chiefs," *Annual Reports of the War Department for the Fiscal Year Ended June 30, 1902*, vol. 1 (Washington, DC: GPO, 1903), 322.
68. William Crozier, Chief of War College Division, January 27, 1913, Correspondence of War College Division and Related Gen. Staff Offices, 1903–19, RG 165 M1024, Roll 1, File 639–79, NACP.
69. John W. Foster, *The Practice of Diplomacy as Illustrated in the Foreign Relations of the United States* (Boston: Houghton, Mifflin, 1906), 381.

CHAPTER 7

1. Larry B. Sheafe, "The United States Secret Service: An Administrative History" (unpublished manuscript, 1983), 1.
2. David R. Johnson, *Illegal Tender: Counterfeiting and the Secret Service in Nineteenth-Century America* (Washington, DC: Smithsonian Institution Press, 1995), 71.
3. H. McCulloch to Edwin Stanton, July 5, 1865, Solicitor of the Treasury, Letters Received from the Secret Service, RG 206, Entry 35, Box 80, NACP.
4. Johnson, *Illegal Tender*, 73–77.
5. Sheafe, *The United States Secret Service*, 9; Johnson, *Illegal Tender*, 81.
6. H. C. Whitley, *Circular of Instructions to Operatives, Secret Service Division, Treasury Department* (Washington, DC: GPO, 1873), 3, 4, 5, 9, 12; Solicitor of the

Treasury, Letters Received from the Secret Service, RG 206, Entry 35, Box 80, NACP.

7. Charles Lane, *Freedom's Detective: The Secret Service, the Ku Klux Klan and the Man Who Masterminded America's First War on Terror* (New York: Hanover Square Press, 2019).
8. "The Safe-Burglary Conspiracy," *Michigan Argus*, April 21, 1876. For more on the Safe-Burglary Plot, see Johnson, *Illegal Tender*, 83–85.
9. Bluford Wilson to Benjamin Bristow, July 27, 1874, Solicitor of the Treasury, Letters Received from the Secret Service, RG 206, Entry 35, Box 80, NACP.
10. Wilson to Bristow, September 5, 1874, Solicitor of the Treasury, Letters Received from the Secret Service, RG 206, Entry 35, Box 80, NACP.
11. H. F. French to Robinson, January 24, 1879, Solicitor of the Treasury, Letters Received from the Secret Service, RG 206, Entry 35, Box 80, NACP.
12. Frederick M. Kaiser, "Origins of Secret Service Protection of the President: Personal, Interagency, and Institutional Conflict," *Presidential Studies Quarterly* 18, no. 1 (1988): 103.
13. Kaiser, "Origins of Secret Service Protection of the President," 103–4.
14. John E. Wilkie, "The Secret Service in the War," in *The American-Spanish War: A History by the War Leaders* (Norwich, CT: Chas. C. Haskell & Son, 1899), 423.
15. Wilkie, "The Secret Service in the War," 424–25.
16. Wilkie, "The Secret Service in the War," 426–28.
17. Jeffreys-Jones, *Cloak and Dollar*, 49–53. For the contents of the Carranza Letter, see Wilkie, "The Secret Service in the War," 433–36.
18. Jeffreys-Jones, *Cloak and Dollar*, 55; Jeffreys-Jones, *American Espionage*, 52.
19. Jeffreys-Jones, *American Espionage*, 52–55.
20. Wilkie, "The Secret Service in the War," 429.
21. Records Relating to Spy Suspects During the Spanish-American War, Feb.–Aug. 1898, RG 87, Entry 16, Box 1, NACP.
22. "Hunting Spanish Spies," *Indianapolis News*, June 25, 1898, Hoosier State Chronicles.
23. Kaiser, "Origins of Secret Service Protection of the President," 110.
24. Kaiser, "Origins of Secret Service Protection of the President," 113.
25. Cong. Rec., 57th Cong., 1st sess., 2276.
26. Cong. Rec., 57th Cong., 1st sess., 3049.
27. Stephen Skowronek, *Building a New American State: The Expansion of National Administrative Capacities, 1877–1920* (New York: Cambridge University Press, 1982). In chap. 4, Skowronek argues that military professionalization was an integral part of building the modern state.
28. Skowronek, *Building a New American State*, chap. 6.
29. Kaiser, "Origins of Secret Service Protection of the President," 117.
30. Skowronek, *Building a New American State*, 185–86.
31. "Wilkie Would Be the Fouché of the United States," *Chicago Inter Ocean*, January 3, 1904, The Inter Ocean, Chicago, Ill., Dec. 28, 1903–Feb. 2, 1904, M1065, LOC.

32. Theodore Roosevelt, January 4, 1909, Richardson, *Compilation of the Messages and Papers of the Presidents,* vol. 15 (1917), 7247.
33. Wilkie intimated as much in a letter to William Loeb Jr., secretary to the President, on December 12, 1908, U.S. Secret Service Correspondence, Letters Sent, RG 87, Entry 20, Box 41, NACP.
34. *Evening Star*, April 21, 1908, LOC.
35. *Evening Star*, April 22, 1908, LOC.
36. *Evening Star*, April 22, 1908. LOC.
37. Cong. Rec., 60th Cong., 1st sess., 5555.
38. Cong. Rec., 60th Cong., 1st sess., 5558.
39. Cong. Rec., 60th Cong., 1st sess., 5559.
40. John Wilkie to William B. Allison, May 5, 1908. U.S. Secret Service Correspondence, Letters Sent, RG 87, Entry 20, Box 39, NACP.
41. 35 Stat. 328 (1908).
42. Cong. Rec., 60th Cong., 2nd sess., 25. To be fair, one Secret Service investigation resulted in the conviction of a senator and a congressman for land fraud in Oregon.
43. Kaiser, "Origins of Secret Service Protection of the President," 118.
44. *New York Times*, December 13, 1908.
45. Theodore Roosevelt, January 4, 1909, Richardson, *Compilation of the Messages and Papers of the Presidents*, Vol. 15, 7252.
46. Cong. Rec., 60th Cong., 2nd sess., 671.
47. Cong. Rec., 60th Cong., 2nd sess., 678.
48. Cong. Rec., 60th Cong., 2nd sess., 2183.
49. Cong. Rec., 60th Cong., 2nd sess., 672.
50. January 27, 1909, *Hearings before Subcommittee of House Committee on Appropriations in Charge of Sundry Civil Appropriations Bill for 1910* (Washington, DC: GPO, 1909), 247–48.
51. *Hearings Before Subcommittee of House Committee on Appropriations in Charge of Sundry Civil Appropriations Bill for 1910*, 250.
52. *Annual Report of the Attorney-General of the United States for the Year 1907* (Washington, DC: GPO, 1907), 9–10; *Annual Report of the Attorney-General of the United States for the Year 1908* (Washington, DC: GPO, 1908), 7.
53. *Evening Star*, April 22, 1908, LOC.
54. *Annual Report of the Attorney-General of the United States for the Year 1909* (Washington, DC: GPO, 1909), 9–10.
55. Stanley Finch to J. D. Harris, July 3, 1908, Records of the Federal Bureau of Investigation, Letters Sent by the Chief Examiner, 1907–1911, RG 65, Entry A1 17, Box 1, NACP.
56. January 27, 1909, *Hearings Before Subcommittee of House Committee on Appropriations in Charge of Sundry Civil Appropriations Bill for 1910* (Washington, DC: GPO, 1909), 214–15.
57. Cong. Rec., 60th Cong., 2nd sess., 662.

58. John Wilkie to James M. Wright, April 5, 1909, U.S. Secret Service Correspondence, Letters Sent, RG 87, Entry 20, Box 42, NACP.
59. There are several letters to operatives dismissing them from service on April 9, 1909, contained in U.S. Secret Service Correspondence, Letters Sent, RG 87, Entry 20, Box 42, NACP.
60. Kaiser, "Origins of Secret Service Protection of the President," 118, citing 65 Stat. 122 (1951).
61. *Hearings Before Subcommittee of House Committee on Appropriations in Charge of Sundry Civil Appropriations Bill for 1910*, 1006.
62. *Hearings Before Subcommittee of House Committee on Appropriations in Charge of Sundry Civil Appropriations Bill for 1910*, 1007.
63. *Hearings Before Subcommittee of House Committee on Appropriations in Charge of Sundry Civil Appropriations Bill for 1910*, 1039.
64. *Hearings Before Subcommittee of House Committee on Appropriations in Charge of Sundry Civil Appropriations Bill for 1910*, 1041–42.
65. *Hearings Before Subcommittee of House Committee on Appropriations in Charge of Sundry Civil Appropriations Bill for 1910*, 1040.
66. *Hearings Before Subcommittee of House Committee on Appropriations in Charge of Sundry Civil Appropriations Bill for 1910*, 1041.
67. *Annual Report of the Attorney-General of the United States for the Year Ended June 30, 1910* (Washington, DC: GPO, 1910), 25–26; Max Lowenthal, *The Federal Bureau of Investigation* (Westport, CT: Greenwood Press, 1950), 13–21.
68. Richard A. Posner, *Uncertain Shield: The U.S. Intelligence System in the Throes of Reform* (Lanham, MD: Rowman & Littlefield, 2006), 93–97.

CHAPTER 8

1. This sequence of events is derived from Frank J. Rafalko, ed., *A Counterintelligence Reader*, vol. 1 (Washington, DC: National Counterintelligence Center, 2001), chap. 3.
2. *The World* (New York), August 15, 1915.
3. *Report of the Commission on Protecting and Reducing Government Secrecy* (Washington, DC: GPO, 1997), A-9.
4. "FBI Nabs More Subversive Agents," *Circleville Herald*, July 25, 1942; "Central Figure in 1917 Blast Is Seized by FBI," New York *Daily News*, July 25, 1942.
5. Lansing to Wilson, November 20, 1915, Series 2: Family and General Correspondence, MSS46029, Reel 74, WWP.
6. Lansing to Wilson, November 20, 1915.
7. Lansing to Wilson, November 20, 1915.
8. Robert Lansing, *War Memoirs of Robert Lansing* (Indianapolis, IN: Bobbs-Merrill, 1935), 318.
9. April 4, 1916, Desk Diaries and Notes, MSS29454, Box 66, Reel 2, RLP.

10. Lansing, *War Memoirs*, 318–29.
11. Jeffreys-Jones, *American Espionage*, 66.
12. *History of the Bureau of Diplomatic Security of the United States Department of State* (Global Publishing Solutions, 2011), 7, nn. 24, 26.
13. Rafalko, *A Counterintelligence Reader*, 109.
14. Lansing to Wilson, April 8, 1917, Series 2: Family and General Correspondence, MSS46029, Reel 87, WWP.
15. McAdoo to Wilson, April 16, 1917, Woodrow Wilson Correspondence, Feb. 10–July 10, 1917, Box 522, WGMP.
16. Burleson to Wilson, April 17, 1917, Series 2: Family and General Correspondence, MSS46029, Reel 87, WWP.
17. It is unclear if Gregory knew that Wilson himself had authorized the Secret Service to aid the State Department in domestic intelligence investigations back in May 1915.
18. Gregory to Wilson, April 17, 1917, Series 2: Family and General Correspondence, MSS46029, Reel 87, WWP.
19. McAdoo to Wilson, May 16, 1917, Woodrow Wilson Correspondence, Feb. 10–July 10, 1917, Box 522, WGMP.
20. McAdoo to Gregory, June 2, 1917, Woodrow Wilson Correspondence, Feb. 10–July 10, 1917, Box 522, WGMP.
21. McAdoo to Wilson, July 5, 1917, Woodrow Wilson Correspondence, Feb. 10–July 10, 1917, Box 522, WGMP.
22. McAdoo to Wilson, July 9, 1917, Woodrow Wilson Correspondence, Feb. 10–July 10, 1917, Box 522, WGMP.
23. Wilson to Gregory, July 12, 1917, Series 3: Letterbooks, 1913–1921, Vol. 42, 1917, MSS46029, Reel 151, WWP.
24. Wilson to McAdoo, November 19, 1917, Series 3: Letterbooks, 1913–1921, Vol. 42, 1917, MSS46029, Reel 152, WWP.
25. 40 Stat. 217 (1917).
26. 40 Stat. 553 (1918).
27. 40 Stat. 120 (1917).
28. 40 Stat. 643 (1918).
29. Joan M. Jensen, *Army Surveillance in America, 1775–1980* (New Haven, CT: Yale University Press, 1991), 167.
30. *Hearings Before the Committee on Military Affairs, United States Senate, 65 Congr., 2nd Sess., S. 4364* (Washington, DC: Government Printing Office, 1918), 38–39.
31. Joan M. Jensen, *The Price of Vigilance* (Chicago: Rand McNally, 1968), 103.
32. O'Brian to Gregory, March 12, 1918, Department of Justice Straight Numerical File 190470, RG 60, Entry 112, Box 2823, NACP.
33. O'Brian to Gregory, March 1, 1918, Department of Justice Straight Numerical File 190470, RG 60, Entry 112, Box 2823, NACP.

34. O'Brian to Gregory, March 7, 1918, Department of Justice Straight Numerical File 190470, RG 60, Entry 112, Box 2823, NACP.
35. Jensen, *Price of Vigilance*, 102–3; Roy Talbert Jr., *Negative Intelligence: The Army and the American Left, 1917–1941* (Jackson: University Press of Mississippi, 1991), 43.
36. Jensen, *Army Surveillance in America*, 167.
37. Michael Warner, *The Rise and Fall of Intelligence: An International Security History* (Washington, DC: Georgetown University Press, 2014), 45–62.
38. William Henry Smyth, *Technocracy: First, Second and Third Series* (Berkeley, CA: n.p., 1921), 7.
39. Mark Stout traces the "technophilic" origins of the US Intelligence Community to the First World War and views the war as an inflection point during which those involved in intelligence began to recognize the distinctiveness of their work. Mark Stout, *World War I and the Foundations of American Intelligence* (Lawrence: University Press of Kansas, 2023). See also Mark Stout, "World War I and the Birth of American Intelligence Culture," *Intelligence and National Security* 32, no. 3 (2017): 378–94.
40. Bidwell, *History of the Military Intelligence Division*, 96, 110–25.
41. John Patrick Finnegan and Romana Danysh, *Military Intelligence* (Washington, DC: Center of Military History, 1998), 25–26.
42. McCoy, *Policing America's Empire*, 299.
43. Finnegan and Danysh, *Military Intelligence*, 24.
44. Talbert, *Negative Intelligence*, 43.
45. Talbert, *Negative Intelligence*, 45.
46. Jensen, *Army Surveillance in America, 1775–1980*, 171.
47. Talbert, *Negative Intelligence*, 27.
48. General Orders No. 80, August 26, 1918. War Department. *General Orders and Bulletins, War Department 1918* (Washington, DC: GPO, 1919).
49. Bidwell, *History of the Military Intelligence Division*, 237.
50. Bidwell, *History of the Military Intelligence Division*, 252.
51. Dorwart, *The Office of Naval Intelligence*, 107, 117–25.
52. Dorwart, *The Office of Naval Intelligence*, 117.
53. Dorwart, *The Office of Naval Intelligence*, 139–40.
54. Eric Setzekorn, "The Office of Naval Intelligence in World War I: Diverse Threats, Divergent Responses," *Studies in Intelligence* 61, no. 2 (2017): 52.
55. Cameron Givens, "The Color of Loyalty: Rumors and Race-Making in First World War America," *Journal of American Ethnic History* 42, no. 2 (2023): 42–76.
56. McCoy, *Policing America's Empire*, 299.
57. Dorwart, *The Office of Naval Intelligence*, 119.
58. Jensen, *The Price of Vigilance*, 17–25; David Joseph Williams, "'Without Understanding': The FBI and Political Surveillance, 1908–1941" (PhD dissertation, 1314, University of New Hampshire, 1981), 83–85.

59. Records of the Federal Bureau of Investigation, Sample of Record Cards of Badge-Holding Members, RG 65, Entry 14, Box 1, NACP.
60. McCoy, *Policing America's Empire*, 301.
61. Records of the Federal Bureau of Investigation, APL Newsletters (Spyglass), RG 65, Entry 16, Box 1, NACP.
62. Jensen, *The Price of Vigilance*, 43.
63. McAdoo to Gregory, June 2, 1917, Woodrow Wilson Correspondence, Feb. 10–July 10, 1917, Box 522, WGMP.
64. Wilson to Gregory, June 4, 1917, Series 3: Letterbooks, 1913–1921, Vol. 42, 1917, MSS46029, Reel 151, WWP.
65. Gregory to Wilson, June 14, 1917, Series 2: Family and General Correspondence, MSS46029, Reel 88, WWP.
66. Jensen, *The Price of Vigilance*, 44–51.
67. Dorwart, *The Office of Naval Intelligence*, 113, 117.
68. Van Deman, *The Final Memoranda*, 30.
69. Bidwell, *History of the Military Intelligence Division*, 189–90.
70. Finnegan and Danysh, *Military Intelligence*, 29.
71. Jensen, *Army Surveillance in America*, 173.
72. Jensen, *Army Surveillance in America*, 171; Miller, *Spying for America*, 201.
73. O'Toole, *Honorable Treachery*, 333.
74. Miller, *Spying for America*, 200.
75. "An Analysis of FBI Domestic Security Intelligence Investigations: Authority, Official Attitudes, and Activities in Historic Perspective," October 28, 1975, *Hearings Before the Select Committee to Study Governmental Operations with Respect to Intelligence Activities of the United States Senate*, vol. 6, *Federal Bureau of Investigation* (Washington, DC: GPO, 1976), 549.
76. "The Slacker Raids," *New York Times*, September 13, 1918.
77. Jensen, *Army Surveillance in America*, 191.
78. *Annual Report of the Attorney General of the United States for the Year 1918* (Washington, DC: GPO, 1918), 21.
79. Lansing, *War Memoirs*, 83–84.
80. Lansing, *War Memoirs*, 84.

CHAPTER 9

1. For a comprehensive account of this century-long war, see Calder Walton, *Spies: The Epic Intelligence War Between East and West* (New York: Simon & Schuster, 2023).
2. "36 Were Marked as Victims by Bomb Conspirers," *New York Times*, May 1, 1919.
3. "Radicals Watched in Bomb Plot," *New York Times*, May 4, 1919.
4. "Russian Reds Are Busy Here," *New York Times*, June 8, 1919.
5. "Palmer Warns Reds They Can Not Succeed," *New York Times*, June 18, 1919.

6. Beverly Gage, *G-Man: J. Edgar Hoover and the Making of the American Century* (New York: Viking, 2022), 61.
7. Tim Weiner, *Enemies: A History of the FBI* (New York: Random House, 2012), 23.
8. Weiner, *Enemies*, 40–41.
9. Cont. 1, Reel 1, Shelf No. 18,958, JDP.
10. Josephus Daniels, *The Wilson Era: Years of War and After, 1917–1923* (Chapel Hill: University of North Carolina Press, 1946), 546.
11. Weiner, *Enemies*, 41.
12. "City Under Guard Against Red Plot Threatened Today," *New York Times*, May 1, 1920.
13. "Says Palmer Upsets Nerves of the People," *New York Times*, May 11, 1920.
14. "Lawyers Denounce Raids on Radicals," *New York Times*, May 28, 1920.
15. Robert Lansing, *The Peace Negotiations: A Personal Narrative* (Boston: Houghton Mifflin, 1921), 221.
16. Bidwell, *History of the Military Intelligence Division*, 247–49.
17. Jeffreys-Jones, *Cloak and Dollar*, 78–80.
18. Albert P. Niblack, *The History and Aims of the Office of Naval Intelligence* (Washington, DC: GPO, 1920), 6.
19. Niblack, *The History and Aims of the Office of Naval Intelligence*, 24.
20. Setzekorn, "The Office of Naval Intelligence in World War I," 52.
21. Jensen, *Army Surveillance*, 197.
22. Army and Navy Register, February 10, 1923, GEN MSS 817, Box 13, WLPP.
23. Army and Navy Register, February 10, 1923, WLPP.
24. Walter C. Sweeney, *Military Intelligence: A New Weapon in War* (New York: Frederick A. Stokes, 1924), 1–4.
25. Sweeney, *Military Intelligence*, 209–12.
26. Sweeney, *Military Intelligence*, 217–23.
27. Williams, *Without Understanding*, 222.
28. Gage, *G-Man*, 98–99.
29. Gara LaMarche, "The ACLU's Fifth Column?," December 20, 2019, ACLU.
30. Weiner, *Enemies*, 61; Rob Warden and Bob Tamarkin, "FBI Dossiers Bare ACLU Infiltration," *Washington Post*, June 19, 1977.
31. Roger Baldwin Letter, August 13, 1924, ACLU.
32. *Hearings Before the Select Committee to Study Governmental Operations with Respect to Intelligence Activities*, vol. 6 (Washington, DC: GPO, 1976), 314. NB: These hearings and final reports will be referred to as the "Church Committee" from here on out.
33. "An Analysis of FBI Domestic Security Intelligence Investigations," Church Committee, vol. 6, 553.
34. Weiner, *Enemies*, 62–63.
35. Williams, *Without Understanding*, 259, 277; for more on these activities, see 259–80.

36. John F. Fox Jr, "Bureaucratic Wrangling over Counterintelligence, 1917–18," *Studies in Intelligence* 49, no. 1 (2005): 9–17.
37. Weiner, *Enemies*, 69–70.
38. William Pinkerton, "How to Deal with the Bolsheviki," *American Industries* 19, no. 12 (July 1919): 30–31.
39. Woodrow Wilson, "Address at Coliseum, St. Louis, Mo.," September 5, 1919, *Addresses of President Wilson: Addresses Delivered by President Wilson On His Western Tour, September 4 to September 25, 1919 on The League of Nations, Treaty of Peace with Germany, Industrial Conditions, High Cost of Living, Race Riots, Etc.* (Washington, DC: GPO, 1919), 42–43.
40. Wilson, "Address at Coliseum, St. Louis, Mo."
41. John F. Dooley, *Codes, Ciphers and Spies: Tales of Military Intelligence in World War I* (New York: Copernicus Books, 2016), 5.
42. David Kahn, *The Codebreakers: The Story of Secret Writing* (New York: Macmillan, 1967), 353.
43. Kahn, *The Codebreakers*, 353–54; Bidwell, *History of the Military Intelligence Division*, 169.
44. David Kahn, *The Reader of Gentlemen's Mail: Herbert O. Yardley and the Birth of American Codebreaking* (New Haven, CT: Yale University Press, 2004), 50.
45. Herbert O. Yardley, *The American Black Chamber* (Annapolis, MD: Bluejacket Books, 1931), 203–4.
46. Friedman, "A Brief History of the Signal Intelligence Service," *Cryptologia* 15, no. 3 (1991): 264.
47. Liza Mundy, *Code Girls: The Untold Story of the American Women Code Breakers of World War II* (New York: Hachette Books, 2017).
48. Bidwell, *History of the Military Intelligence Division*, 253.
49. February 3, 1919, RG 59 Decimal File 110.7/95–110.75.75/33 Box 0990, NACP.
50. Friedman provides a detailed accounting of the estimate in "A Brief History of the Signal Intelligence Service," 265.
51. Yardley, *The American Black Chamber*, 240.
52. Yardley, *The American Black Chamber*, 241; Friedman, "A Brief History of the Signal Intelligence Service," 268.
53. Yardley, *The American Black Chamber*, 366.
54. Yardley, *The American Black Chamber*, 277.
55. Yardley, *The American Black Chamber*, 322–23.
56. Letter from Acting Secretary of War F. H. Payne to the Secretary of State, September 1, 1931, Code Breaking Collection, Call No. Xerox 2440, WFFC.
57. Yardley, *The American Black Chamber*, 348–49.
58. February 3, 1919, RG 59 Decimal File 110.7/95–110.75.75/33, Box 0990, NACP.
59. Friedman, "A Brief History of the Signal Intelligence Service," 267.
60. Friedman, "A Brief History of the Signal Intelligence Service," 266.

61. The Navy had a Code and Signal Section and a "Research Desk" responsible for cryptology, but they were apparently unable to meet the Navy's COMINT needs.
62. Draft of "History of the Military Intelligence Division, Department of the Army General Staff," Codes and Ciphers section, 136, Folder ID 493, Document ID A72903, WFFP.
63. Friedman, "A Brief History of the Signal Intelligence Service," 265.
64. Anonymous, "The Many Lives of Herbert O. Yardley," unclassified NSA document, n.d., 9, FOIA; Draft of "History of the Military Intelligence Division, Department of the Army General Staff," Codes and Ciphers section, 139.
65. Bidwell, *History of the Military Intelligence Division*, 328.
66. Yardley, *The American Black Chamber*, 368; Anonymous, "The Many Lives of Yardley," 9.
67. Friedman, "A Brief History of the Signal Intelligence Service," 267–68; Anonymous, "The Many Lives of Yardley," 10.
68. Louis Kruh, "Stimson, The Black Chamber, and the 'Gentlemen's Quote,'" *Cryptologia* 12, no. 2 (1988): 65, 75.
69. Henry L. Stimson and McGeorge Bundy, *On Active Service in Peace and War* (New York: Harper & Brothers, 1947), 188. It is also on this page in his autobiography where Stimson recollects stating "Gentlemen do not read each other's mail!" in reaction to learning about the Cipher Bureau.
70. McGeorge Bundy to William Bundy, November 15, 1950, National Security Agency Folder ID ACC8833, Document ID A99807, WFFP.
71. David Kahn, "Why Weren't We Warned?" in *The American Experience in World War II: Volume 4 Pearl Harbor in History and Memory*, ed. Walter L. Hixson (New York: Routledge, 2003), 85.
72. Bidwell, *History of the Military Intelligence Division*, 330.
73. Edward Barnett, Memorandum, January 30, 1939, 12. Folder 001, Document ID A61782, WFFP.
74. Kahn, *The Reader of Gentlemen's Mail*, 122; Letter from Lester Condit to Capt. Hotson, Subject: Herbert Yardley, Folder ID 057, Document ID A40274, WFFP.
75. Kahn, *The Reader of Gentlemen's Mail*, 125.
76. Kahn, *The Reader of Gentlemen's Mail*, 129.
77. Herbert O. Yardley, "Are We Giving Away Our State Secrets: A Cipher Expert's View of the Methods Used by the Government in Its Diplomatic Correspondence," *Liberty Magazine*, December 19, 1931, Folder ID 142, Document ID A44766, WFFP.
78. Anonymous, "The Many Lives of Yardley," 12.
79. Yardley, *The American Black Chamber*, 289–90.
80. Yardley, *The American Black Chamber*, 312–13.
81. Kahn, *The Reader of Gentlemen's Mail*, 162.
82. An Act for the Protection of Government Records, Pub. L. 73-37, Stat. 48-122, June 10, 1933.

83. Thomas F. Troy, *Donovan and the CIA: A History of the Establishment of the Central Intelligence Agency* (Frederick, MD: University Publications of America, 1984), 3–6.
84. Jeffery M. Dorwart, "The Roosevelt-Astor Espionage Ring," *New York History* 62, no. 3 (1981): 309–10.
85. O'Toole, *Honorable Treachery*, 346; Jeffreys-Jones, *Cloak and Dollar*, 63.
86. Stout, *World War I and the Foundations of American Intelligence*, 195.
87. O'Toole, *Honorable Treachery*, 347.
88. Stout, *World War I and the Foundations of American Intelligence*, 195.
89. Jeffreys-Jones, *Cloak and Dollar*, 63–64; Hugh Wilford, *The CIA: An Imperial History* (New York: Basic Books, 2024).
90. "An Analysis of FBI Domestic Security Intelligence Investigations," Church Committee, vol. 6, 550.

CHAPTER 10

1. Arthur Schlesinger Jr., *The Imperial Presidency* (New York: Houghton Mifflin, 2004), chap. 5.
2. Church Committee, vol. 6, 556.
3. Church Committee, book III, 391.
4. Church Committee, vol. 6, 557.
5. Church Committee, vol. 6, 558–59.
6. Church Committee, vol. 6, 560.
7. Weiner, *Enemies*, 67.
8. Douglas M. Charles, "Informing FDR: FBI Political Surveillance and the Isolationist-Interventionist Foreign Policy Debate, 1939–1945," *Diplomatic History* 24, no. 2 (2000): 213.
9. Confidential Memorandum, August 24, 1936, Records of the Federal Bureau of Investigation, Office of the Director, J. Edgar Hoover, Official and Confidential Subject Files, 1924–1972, RG 65, Entry UD05D14, Box 22, Folder 136, NACP.
10. Confidential Memorandum, August 24, 1936, NACP.
11. Church Committee, book III, 396.
12. Confidential Memorandum, August 25, 1936, Records of the Federal Bureau of Investigation, Office of the Director, J. Edgar Hoover, Official and Confidential Subject Files, 1924–1972, RG 65, Entry UD05D14, Box 22, NACP.
13. Church Committee, book III, 393.
14. Church Committee, vol. 6, 559.
15. Church Committee, book III, 395.
16. Athan G. Theoharis, "The FBI's Stretching of Presidential Directives, 1936–1953," *Political Science Quarterly* 91, no. 4 (1976–77): 652.
17. Memorandum for Mr. Tamm, September 10, 1936, Records of the Federal Bureau of Investigation, Office of the Director, J. Edgar Hoover, Official and

Confidential Subject Files, 1924–1972, RG 65, Entry UD05D14, Box 22, Folder 136, NACP.

18. Confidential Memorandum, August 24, 1936, NACP.
19. Confidential Memorandum, August 25, 1936, NACP.
20. Theoharis, "The FBI's Stretching of Presidential Directives," 655.
21. Kenneth O'Reilly, "A New Deal for the FBI: The Roosevelt Administration, Crime Control, and National Security," *Journal of American History* 69, no. 3 (1982): 646–48.
22. Charles, "Informing FDR," 212.
23. Charles, "Informing FDR," 220–24.
24. Memorandum for the Attorney General, May 21, 1940, Records of the Federal Bureau of Investigation, Office of the Director, J. Edgar Hoover, Official and Confidential Subject Files, 1924–1972, RG 65, Entry UD05D14, Box 24, Folder 163, NACP; *Nardone v. US*, 308 US 338 (1939).
25. Athan Theoharis, "FBI Wiretapping: A Case Study of Bureaucratic Autonomy," *Political Science Quarterly* 107, no. 1 (1992): 101, 103.
26. Charles, "Informing FDR," 223.
27. Tamm to Hoover, December 3, 1940, Records of the Federal Bureau of Investigation, Office of the Director, J. Edgar Hoover, Official and Confidential Subject Files, 1924–1972, RG 65, Entry UD05D14, Box 16, Folder 73, NACP.
28. Charles, "Informing FDR," 232.
29. Executive Order 6166, June 10, 1933.
30. 74th Congr., sess. 1, Act of March 22, 1935, ch. 39, title II, 49 Stat. 77. Later enabling legislation would eventually claim intelligence as the first of the four principal missions of the FBI, followed by counterterrorism and counterintelligence, with criminal enterprises/federal crimes ranking third. See 118 Stat. 3701–2 (2004).
31. Church Committee, vol. 6, 562.
32. For a detailed account of the Rumrich case and FBI debacle, see Raymond J. Batvinis, *The Origins of FBI Counterintelligence* (Lawrence: University Press of Kansas, 2007), chap. 1.
33. Batvinis, *The Origins of FBI Counterintelligence*, 10.
34. Batvinis, *The Origins of FBI Counterintelligence*, 24–25.
35. Batvinis, *The Origins of FBI Counterintelligence*, 51.
36. Batvinis, *The Origins of FBI Counterintelligence*, 54.
37. Batvinis, *The Origins of FBI Counterintelligence*, 53; Church Committee, book III, 397–98.
38. Cummings to Roosevelt, October 20, 1938, 1850–1956, Accession #9973, Special Collections Dept., Box 100, HSC.
39. Cummings to Roosevelt, October 20, 1938, HSC.
40. Cummings to Roosevelt, October 20, 1938, HSC.
41. J. Edgar Hoover, Memorandum, November 7, 1938, Records of the Federal Bureau of Investigation, Office of the Director, J. Edgar Hoover, Official and

Confidential Subject Files, 1924–1972, RG 65, Entry UD05D14, Box 22, Folder 136, NACP.
42. "Spies," *New York Times*, December 1, 1938.
43. Don Whitehead, *The FBI Story: A Report to the People* (New York: Random House, 1956), 165.
44. Weiner, *Enemies*, 81.
45. Troy, *Donovan and the CIA*, 12–13.
46. Whitehead, *The FBI Story*, 165.
47. Church Committee, book III, 400–402.
48. Presidential Directive, June 26, 1939, to All Federal Departments and Agencies, Records of the Federal Bureau of Investigation, Office of the Director, J. Edgar Hoover, Official and Confidential Subject Files, 1924–1972, RG 65, Entry UD05D14, Box 15, Folder 66, NACP.
49. Church Committee, book II, 26.
50. Reissued in a memorandum by J. Edgar Hoover to the FBI on September 6, 1939, Records of the Federal Bureau of Investigation, Office of the Director, J. Edgar Hoover, Official and Confidential Subject Files, 1924–1972, RG 65, Entry UD05D14, Box 15, Folder 66, NACP.
51. Church Committee, book III, 405.
52. OF1661a, Boxes 1, 2, Fifth Column, 1940, FDRL.
53. OF 1661, Boxes 1, 2, Espionage, 1933–45, FDRL.
54. OF10b, Box 11, FBI, 1943–1945, FDRL.
55. "Declare U.S. Ready to Run Down Spies," *New York Times*, October 1, 1939.
56. Church Committee, book II, 29.
57. O'Reilly, "A New Deal for the FBI," 651–53.
58. Jerry Voorhis to Robert Jackson, December 10, 1940, Records of the Federal Bureau of Investigation, Office of the Director, J. Edgar Hoover, Official and Confidential Subject Files, 1924–1972, RG 65, Entry UD05D14, Box 15, Folder 59, NACP.
59. Albert Alexander, "The President and the Investigator: Roosevelt and Dies," *Antioch Review* 15, no. 1 (1955): 106–17.
60. O'Reilly, "A New Deal for the FBI," 650–53.
61. For example, "Dies Predicts Plane Sabotage in 3 Months; FBI Negligent in Ignoring Proof, Says Congressman," *Chicago Times-Herald*, November 5, 1940; Hoover to AG, November 16, 1940, Records of the Federal Bureau of Investigation, Office of the Director, J. Edgar Hoover, Official and Confidential Subject Files, 1924–1972, RG 65, Entry UD05D14, Box 15, Folder 59, NACP.
62. Bidwell, *History of the Military Intelligence Division*, 396.
63. Troy, *Donovan and the CIA*, 13.
64. McCoy, *Policing America's Empire*, 327–28; Talbert, *Negative Intelligence*, 256–58.
65. February 9, 1942, Subject: Delimitation of Investigative Duties of the Federal Bureau of Investigation, the Office of Naval Intelligence and the Military Intelligence Division, Records of the Federal Bureau of Investigation, Office of the

Director, J. Edgar Hoover, Official and Confidential Subject Files, 1924–1972, RG 65, Entry UD05D14, Box 15, Folder 64, NACP.

66. This is not to say that the military did not continue to conduct domestic intelligence operations after the Second World War. Furthermore, domestic intelligence operations by military components have continued even to the present through agencies like the NSA.
67. Bidwell, *History of the Military Intelligence Division*, 397–98; Troy, *Donovan and the CIA*, 17.
68. February 25, 1942, Subject: Agreement Between MID, ONI, and FBI for Coordinating Special Intelligence Operations in the Western Hemisphere, Records of the Federal Bureau of Investigation, Office of the Director, J. Edgar Hoover, Official and Confidential Subject Files, 1924–1972, RG 65, Entry UD05D14, Box 15, Folder 64, NACP.
69. Secret Memorandum, date unknown, Army Intelligence Decimal File, 1941–1948, RG 319, Entry NM347B, Box 423, NACP.
70. Troy, *Donovan and the CIA*, 20.
71. Talbert, *Negative Intelligence*, 256.
72. Dorwart, *Conflict of Duty*, 118.
73. Dorwart, *Conflict of Duty*, 118; Batvinis, *The Origins of FBI Counterintelligence*, 74.
74. Whitehead, *The FBI Story*, 169–70.
75. Troy, *Donovan and the CIA*, 20–21.

CHAPTER 11

1. Douglas Waller, *Wild Bill Donovan: The Spymaster Who Created the OSS and Modern American Espionage* (New York: Free Press, 2011), 13–14.
2. The 69th was redesignated the 165th during the war.
3. Waller, *Wild Bill Donovan*, 35.
4. Brian R. Sullivan, "'A Highly Commendable Action': William J. Donovan's Intelligence Mission for Mussolini and Roosevelt, December 1935–February 1936," *Intelligence and National Security* 6, no. 2 (1991): 338.
5. Sullivan, "'A Highly Commendable Action,'" 342.
6. Sullivan, "'A Highly Commendable Action,'" 356.
7. Troy, *Donovan and the CIA*, 30.
8. Troy, *Donovan and the CIA*, 31–32.
9. Nicholas Reynolds, *Need to Know: World War II and the Rise of American Intelligence* (New York: Mariner Books, 2022), 23.
10. Troy, *Donovan and the CIA*, 53–54.
11. Reynolds, *Need to Know*, 40, 50, 57.
12. McKenzie Porter, "The Biggest Private Eye of All," *MacLean's Magazine*, December 1, 1952, 68. The article mentions that J. Edgar Hoover also wrote a personal letter of thanks to Stephenson for his intelligence efforts during the war.

13. Reynolds, *Need to Know*, 45.
14. Troy, *Donovan and the CIA*, 39.
15. William Stevenson, *A Man Called Intrepid* (Guilford, CT: Lyons Press, 2000), 264.
16. Michael S. Goodman, *The Official History of the Joint Intelligence Committee, Volume I: From the Approach of the Second World War to the Suez Crisis* (London: Routledge, 2014), chaps. 1–4; Christopher Andrew, *Her Majesty's Secret Service: The Making of the British Intelligence Community* (New York: Elizabeth Sifton Books, 1986), chap. 14.
17. Goodman, *History of the Joint Intelligence Committee*, 100.
18. Reynolds, *Need to Know*, 51–57.
19. David F. Rudgers, *Creating the Secret State: The Origins of the Central Intelligence Agency, 1943–1947* (Lawrence: University Press of Kansas, 2000), 10.
20. Copy of Henry Stimson Notes After Cabinet Meeting, April 4, 1941, Army Intelligence Decimal File, 1941–1948, RG 319, Entry NM347B, Box 423, NACP.
21. John Ranelagh, *The Agency: The Rise and Decline of the CIA* (New York: Simon and Schuster, 1986), 58.
22. Joseph E. Perisco, *Roosevelt's Secret War: FDR and World War II Espionage* (New York: Random House, 2002), 7–9.
23. Dorwart, *Conflict of Duty*, 59.
24. PSF, Boxes 97–100, FDRL; Bradley Smith, *The Shadow Warriors: O.S.S. and the Origins of the C.I.A* (New York: Basic Books, 1983), 63–64.
25. Waldo Heinrichs, "The United States Prepares for War," in *The Secrets War: The Office of Strategic Services in World War II*, ed. George C. Chalou (Washington, DC: NARA, 2002), 10–11, 13.
26. *History of the S.I.S. Division*, vol. 1 (Washington, DC: FBI, 1947), 36, 62, FBI, The Vault.
27. *History of the S.I.S. Division*, vol. 1, 71–72.
28. Dorwart, *Conflict of Duty*, 153.
29. Biddle to Hoover, May 29, 1942, Records of the Federal Bureau of Investigation, Office of the Director, J. Edgar Hoover, Official and Confidential Subject Files, 1924–1972, RG 65, Entry UD05D14, Box 22, Folder 136, NACP.
30. Dorwart, *Conflict of Duty*, 164–66; Dorwart, "The Roosevelt-Astor Espionage Ring," 312–18.
31. Dorwart, "The Roosevelt-Astor Espionage Ring," 318.
32. Enclosure in letter from Adolf Berle to Sherman Miles, Army Intelligence Decimal File, 1941–1948, RG 319, Entry NM347B, Box 423, NACP.
33. Dorwart, "The Roosevelt-Astor Espionage Ring," 320.
34. John Franklin Carter, "Report on Talk with Vincent Astor," December 5, 1941, PSF, Box 97, Folder Carter, John F.: Nov.–Dec. 1941, FDRL.
35. Grace Tully, "Memorandum for the President," December 11, 1941, PSF, Box 97, Folder Carter, John F.: Nov.–Dec. 1941, FDRL.

36. Dorwart, *Conflict of Duty*, 167–69.
37. Dorwart, "The Roosevelt-Astor Espionage Ring," 322.
38. Sherman Miles. Memorandum for the Chief of Staff, Subject: Coordinator for the Three Intelligence Agencies of the Government. April 8, 1941, Army Intelligence Decimal File, 1941–1948, RG 319, Entry NM347B, Box 423, NACP.
39. Troy, *Donovan and the CIA*, 43–44.
40. Troy, *Donovan and the CIA*, 45.
41. Sherman Miles, Memorandum for the Chief of Staff, Subject: Coordinator for the Three Intelligence Agencies of the Government. April 8, 1941, Army Intelligence Decimal File, 1941–1948, RG 319, Entry NM347B, Box 423, NACP.
42. J. Edgar Hoover to Edwin Watson, Secretary to the President, May 22, 1941, Army Intelligence Decimal File, 1941–1948, RG 319, Entry NM347B, Box 423, NACP.
43. Report on Coordination of the Three Intelligence Services, the Federal Bureau of Investigation, the Military Intelligence Division, and the Office of Naval Intelligence, May 29, 1941, Army Intelligence Decimal File, 1941–1948, RG 319, Entry NM347B, Box 423, NACP.
44. Report of Sub-Committee of Intelligence Conference on Trends and Coverage in Intelligence and Intelligence Investigational Operations, March 26, 1941, Army Intelligence Decimal File, 1941–1948, RG 319, Entry NM347B, Box 423, NACP; Report of Conference held in San Juan, P. R., on subject of cooperation between ONI, MID and FBI, May 21, 1941, Army Intelligence Decimal File, 1941–1948, RG 319, Entry NM347B, Box 423, NACP.
45. Troy, *Donovan and the CIA*, appendix A, 417–18.
46. Hoover Memorandum, August 1, 1940, Records of the Federal Bureau of Investigation, Office of the Director, J. Edgar Hoover, Official and Confidential Subject Files, 1924–1972, RG 65, Entry UD05D14, Box 14, Folder 45, NACP.
47. Douglas M. Charles, "'Before the Colonel Arrived': Hoover, Donovan, Roosevelt, and the Origins of American Central Intelligence, 1940–41," *Intelligence and National Security* 20, no.2 (2005): 235.
48. Charles, "'Before the Colonel Arrived,'" 232.
49. Charles, "'Before the Colonel Arrived,'" 234.
50. Troy, *Donovan and the CIA*, 57, 59.
51. Memorandum, June 10, 1941, Office of Strategic Services, RG 226, Entry 190, Container 471, NACP.
52. Troy, *Donovan and the CIA*, 66–69.
53. Folder on the organization and functions of the COI, Budgetary Administration Records for Emergency and War Agencies and Defense Activities, 1939–1949, RG 51, Entry A1 107-A, Box 37, NACP.
54. "Col. Donovan, Who Studied Nazi Espionage, Is Slated for Big Post, Capital Reports," *New York Times*, July 6, 1941.
55. "Donovan Will Take Information Post," *New York Times*, July 10, 1941.

56. "Historical Intelligence Documents: From COI to CIG," *Studies in Intelligence* 37, no. 5 (1994): 111–23.
57. Statement on the Appointment of William J. Donovan as Coordinator of Information, July 11, 1941, American Presidency Project, UCSB.
58. "Donovan Is Named Information Head," *The New York Times*, July 12, 1941.
59. William Hall to Fred Lawton, August 6, 1941, Budgetary Administration Records for Emergency and War Agencies and Defense Activities, 1939–1949, RG 51, Entry A1 107-A, Box 37, NACP.
60. Series of letters between Bernard Gladieux and William Hall, July-September 1941, RG 51, Entry A1 107-A, Box 37, NACP.
61. Hall to Lawton, August 6, 1941, NACP.
62. "Historical Intelligence Documents."
63. Ranelagh, *The Agency*, 49.
64. Troy, *Donovan and the CIA*, 104–105.
65. Smith, *The Shadow Warriors*, 93.
66. For more on R&A, see Barry M. Katz, *Foreign Intelligence: Research and Analysis in the Office of Strategic Services, 1942–1945* (Cambridge, MA: Harvard University Press, 1989); Robin W. Winks, *Cloak and Gown: Scholars in the Secret War, 1939–1961*, 2nd ed. (New Haven, CT: Yale University Press, 1996).
67. Bradley Smith, *The Shadow Warriors*, 76–77.
68. *History of the Office of the Coordinator of Inter-American Affairs: Historical Reports on War Administration* (Washington, DC: GPO, 1947), 197.
69. Office of the Coordinator of Information document circa January 1942, Budgetary Administration Records for Emergency and War Agencies and Defense Activities, 1939–1949, RG 51, Entry A1 107-A, Box 37, NACP.
70. William O. Hall to Bernard L. Gladieux, October 29, 1942, Budgetary Administration Records for Emergency and War Agencies and Defense Activities, 1939–1949, RG 51, Entry A1 107-A, Box 23, NACP.
71. Miles to Chief of Staff, September 5, 1941, Army Intelligence Decimal File, 1941–1948, RG 319, Entry NM347B, Box 423, NACP.
72. "These Are U.S. Army's Six Foremost Generals," *Life*, December 2, 1940.
73. Records of the Federal Bureau of Investigation, Office of the Director, J. Edgar Hoover, Official and Confidential Subject Files, 1924–1972, RG 65, Entry UD05D14, Box 15, Folder 64, NACP.
74. Memo for the Attorney General, December 31, 1941, William J. Donovan File #77-58706, Part 3, 58, FBI, The Vault.
75. Memorandum for the President. July 30, 1941, Budgetary Administration Records for Emergency and War Agencies and Defense Activities, 1939–1949, RG 51, Entry A1 107-A, Box 37, NACP.
76. Stone to Gladieux, September 16, 1941, RG 51, Entry A1 107-A, Box 37, NACP.
77. Conference with Colonel Donovan, November 2, 1941, RG 51, Entry A1 107-A, Box 37, NACP.

78. For a copy of the document, see Troy, *Donovan and the CIA*, 112.
79. Tamm to Hoover, November 18, 1941, Records of the Federal Bureau of Investigation, Office of the Director, J. Edgar Hoover, Official and Confidential Subject Files, 1924–1972, RG 65, Entry UD05D14, Box 15, Folder 62, NACP.
80. Breckinridge Long, *The War Diary of Breckinridge Long: Selections from the Years 1939–1944*, ed. Fred L. Israel (Lincoln: University of Nebraska Press, 1966), fc234.

CHAPTER 12

1. See, for example, "Historian Offers New Report on Pearl Harbor," *New York Times*, March 13, 1982.
2. Troy, *Donovan and the CIA*, 117; Smith, *The Shadow Warriors*, 106–7.
3. Document 399, The Ambassador in Japan (Grew) to the Secretary of State, November 17, 1941, *FRUS, Japan, 1931–1941, Volume II.*
4. Document 80, The Ambassador in Japan (Grew) to the Secretary of State, January 27, 1941, *FRUS, Japan, 1931–1941, Volume II.*
5. Roberta Wohlstetter concludes that Pearl Harbor represented a failure of analysis, especially the failure to distinguish "signals," or key pieces of intelligence, from "noise," the morass of information that can bury signals. David Kahn argues that collection, rather than analysis, was the source of the failure, particularly because Japan had made it difficult for foreign states to collect information about it. See Roberta Wohlstetter, *Pearl Harbor: Warning and Decision* (Stanford, CA: Stanford University Press, 1962) and David Kahn, "Why Weren't We Warned?" December 30, 2017, HistoryNet, https://www.historynet.com/why-werent-we-warned.htm.
6. Bidwell, *History of the Military Intelligence Division*, 456.
7. Bidwell, *History of the Military Intelligence Division*, 457.
8. Dorwart, *Conflict of Duty*, 179–80.
9. Bidwell, *History of the Military Intelligence Division*, 475.
10. Office of Naval Intelligence Memorandum, Subject: Japanese Intelligence and Propaganda in the United States During 1941, December 4, 1941, http://www.mansell.com/e09066/1941/41-12/IA021.html.
11. *Report of the Joint Committee on the Investigation of the Pearl Harbor Attack*, 79th Cong., 2nd sess., Document No. 244 (Washington, DC: GPO, 1946), 132.
12. For a picture of the message, see Kahn, *The Codebreakers*, 43.
13. Yardley, *The American Black Chamber*, 312–13.
14. Anonymous, "Many Lives of Yardley," 11–12.
15. Kahn, *The Reader of Gentlemen's Mail*, 136.
16. United States Senate Committee on Armed Services, *Enhancing Further the Security of the United States by Preventing Disclosures of Information Concerning the Cryptographic Systems and the Communication Intelligence Activities of the United States*, 80th Cong, 2nd sess., S. Rept. 1433 (Washington, DC: GPO, 1948).
17. 48 Stat. 1104.

18. Stephen Budiansky, *Battle of Wits: The Complete Story of Codebreaking in World War II* (New York: Touchstone, 2000), 35.
19. Reynolds, *Need to Know*, 113.
20. Budiansky, *Battle of Wits*, 168–69.
21. Thomas L. Burns, *The Origins of the National Security Agency, 1940–1952* (Fort Meade, MD: Center for Cryptologic History, 1990), 8–9.
22. Frederick D. Parker, *Pearl Harbor Revisited: U.S. Navy Communications Intelligence 1924–1941*, Series IV: World War II, vol. 6, 3rd ed. (Fort Meade, MD: Center for Cryptologic History, 2013), 48. For SIS's deficiencies in personnel ahead of Pearl Harbor, see Friedman, "A Brief History of the Signal Intelligence Service," 271.
23. Parker, *Pearl Harbor Revisited*, 31.
24. Parker, *Pearl Harbor Revisited*, 40–41.
25. Dorwart, *Conflict of Duty*, 172–81; Entry December 7, 1941, Berle Papers, Adolf A. Berle Diary, Box 213, Folder Diary December 1–11, 1941, FDRL.
26. *Report of the Joint Committee on the Investigation of the Pearl Harbor Attack*, 184; *Hearings Before the Joint Committee on the Investigation of the Pearl Harbor Attack*, Part 36, Proceedings of Hewitt Inquiry (Washington, DC: GPO, 1946), 233.
27. Reynolds, *Need to Know*, 82.
28. Reynolds, *Need to Know*, 83.
29. Smith, *The Shadow Warriors*, 100–103; Waller, *Wild Bill Donovan*, 104.
30. "Wild Bill Donovan—Washington's Mystery Man," *Look*, December 16, 1941, Office of Strategic Services, RG 226, Entry 190, Container 471, NACP.
31. Office of the Coordinator of Information Circa January 1942, Budgetary Administration Records for Emergency and War Agencies and Defense Activities, 1939–1949, RG 51, Entry A1 107-A, Box 37, NACP.
32. Troy, *Donovan and the CIA*, 117–18.
33. Ranelagh, *The Agency*, 59.
34. Smith, *The Shadow Warriors*, 107.
35. Smith, *The Shadow Warriors*, 109.
36. Troy, *Donovan and the CIA*, 129–31; Smith, *The Shadow Warriors*, 113–14.
37. Troy, *Donovan and the CIA*, 106; Smith, *The Shadow Warriors*, 91–92. For more on Solborg, see Richard Harris Smith, *OSS: The Secret History of America's First Central Intelligence Agency* (Guilford, CT: Lyons Press, 2005), 37–38.
38. Solborg to Donovan, January 13, 1942, MPGP.
39. Joseph F. Jakub III, *Spies and Saboteurs: Anglo-American Collaboration and Rivalry in Human Intelligence Collection and Special Operations, 1940–45* (New York: St. Martin's Press, 1999), 44.
40. Troy, *Donovan and the CIA*, 134.
41. William Hall to Bernard Gladieux, March 21, 1942, Budgetary Administration Records for Emergency and War Agencies and Defense Activities, 1939–1949, RG 51, Entry A1 107-A, Box 37, NACP.
42. Harris Smith, *OSS*, 38; Smith, *The Shadow Warriors*, 115.

43. Troy, *Donovan and the CIA*, 126.
44. Ranelagh, *The Agency*, 61.
45. Beatrice Bishop Berle and Travis Beal Jacobs, eds., *Navigating the Rapids 1918–1971: From the Papers of Adolf A. Berle* (New York: Harcourt Brace Jovanovich, 1973), 397.
46. Entry January 6, 1942, Berle Papers, Adolf A. Berle Diary, Box 213, Folder Diary January 1942, FDRL.
47. Long, *War Diary*, 257.
48. Gladieux Notes, February 20, 1942, Budgetary Administration Records for Emergency and War Agencies and Defense Activities, 1939–1949, RG 51, Entry A1 107-A, Box 37, NACP.
49. FY 1942 Coordinator of Information Budget, Budgetary Administration Records for Emergency and War Agencies and Defense Activities, 1939–1949, RG 51, Entry A1 107-A, Box 37, NACP.
50. Captain F. C. Denebrink to Joint U.S. Chiefs of Staff, Proposed Utilization of the Facilities of the Office of the Coordinator of Information to Best Advantage by the U.S. Military Services, March 8, 1942, Records of the U.S. Joint Chiefs of Staff, Central Decimal File 1942–45, RG 218, Entry UD1, Box 371, NACP.
51. Troy, *Donovan and the CIA*, 136–37.
52. Troy, *Donovan and the CIA*, 137; Smith, *The Shadow Warriors*, xv, 118–19.
53. Smith to Hopkins, March 26, 1942, Budgetary Administration Records for Emergency and War Agencies and Defense Activities, 1939–1949, RG 51, Entry A1 107-A, Box 37, NACP.
54. Troy, *Donovan and the CIA*, 146, 149.
55. Donovan to Roosevelt, April 14, 1942, Records of the OSS Washington Director's Office, RG 226, M1642 Roll 23, Frames 70–73, NACP.
56. Berle and Jacobs, *Navigating the Rapids*, 412.
57. Troy, *Donovan and the CIA*, 138.
58. Hirshberg to Gladieux, October 7, 1942, Budgetary Administration Records for Emergency and War Agencies and Defense Activities, 1939–1949, RG 51, Entry A1 107-A, Box 23, NACP.
59. Hall to Gladieux, October 27, 1942, Budgetary Administration Records for Emergency and War Agencies and Defense Activities, 1939–1949, RG 51, Entry A1 107-A, Box 67, NACP.
60. Records of the OSS, Washington Director's Office, RG 226, M1642, Roll 110, Frames 31–35, NACP.
61. William O. Hall to Bernard L. Gladiuex, October 29, 1942, Budgetary Administration Records for Emergency and War Agencies and Defense Activities, 1939–1949, RG 51, Entry A1 107-A, Box 23, NACP.
62. Mark Stout, "The Alternate Central Intelligence Agency: John Grombach and the Pond," in *Spy Chiefs: Intelligence Leaders in the United States and United Kingdom*, ed. Christopher Moran, Mark Stout, Ionna Iordanou, and Paul Maddrell

(Washington, DC: Georgetown University Press, 2018). See also Mark Stout, "The Pond: Running Agents for State, War, and the CIA," *Studies in Intelligence* 48, no. 3 (2004).

63. Reynolds, *Need to Know*, 133–34.
64. Waller, *Wild Bill Donovan*, 118–19.
65. Donovan to Strong, March 29, 1943, Records of the U.S. Joint Chiefs of Staff, Central Decimal File 1942–45, RG 218 Entry UD1, Box 368, NACP.
66. Waller, *Wild Bill Donovan*, 147.
67. Gladieux to Director, 9/42, Budgetary Administration Records for Emergency and War Agencies and Defense Activities, 1939–1949, RG 51, Entry A1 107-A, Box 23, NACP.
68. J.P.W.C. 45/D, October 24, 1942, Records of the U.S. Joint Chiefs of Staff, Central Decimal File 1942–45, RG 218, Entry UD1, Box 371, NACP.
69. Troy, *Donovan and the CIA*, 179–209.
70. Reynolds, *Need to Know*, 200–206.
71. Waller, *Wild Bill Donovan*, 164–66; Reynolds, *Need to Know*, 261–62.
72. A history skillfully addressed in Reynolds, *Need to Know*.
73. See, for example, Colin Beavan, *Operation Jedburgh: D-Day and America's First Shadow War* (New York: Penguin Books, 2007).
74. Dixee Bartholomew-Feis, *The OSS and Ho Chi Minh: Unexpected Allies in the War Against Japan* (Lawrence: University Press of Kansas, 2006); Maochun Yu, *OSS in China: Prelude to Cold War* (New Haven, CT: Yale University Press, 1996).
75. Reynolds, *Need to Know*, 295–310.
76. *The Office of Strategic Services: America's First Intelligence Agency* (Washington, DC: CIA, 2000).
77. Jennifer Davis Heaps, "Tracking Intelligence Information: The Office of Strategic Services," *American Archivist* 61 (1998): 287–308, 301.
78. William Colby and Peter Forbath, *Honorable Men: My Life in the CIA* (New York: Simon and Schuster, 1978), 55.
79. Harris Smith, *OSS*, 9.
80. Harvey Klehr, John Earl Haynes, and Fridrikh Igorevich Firsov, *The Secret World of American Communism* (New Haven, CT: Yale University Press, 1995), 278.
81. Mark A. Bradley, *A Very Principled Boy: The Life of Duncan Lee, Red Spy and Cold Warrior* (New York: Basic Books, 2014).

CHAPTER 13

1. Troy, *Donovan and the CIA*, 209, 218.
2. Eliot to Donovan, October 13, 1942, Records of the OSS Washington Director's Office, RG 226, M1642, Roll 75, NACP.
3. J.P.W.C. 45/D, October 24, 1942, Records of the U.S. Joint Chiefs of Staff, Central Decimal File 1942–45, RG 218, Entry UD1, Box 371, NACP.

4. Director of Strategic Services to Joint Psychological Warfare Committee, Response to J.P.W.C. 45/D, October 31, 1942, Records of the U.S. Joint Chiefs of Staff, Central Decimal File 1942–45, RG 218, Entry UD1, Box 371, NACP.
5. Donovan to Smith, September 17, 1943, Office of Strategic Services, OSS, Washington Director's Office Administrative Files, 1941–1945, RG 226, M1642, Roll 2, NACP.
6. Troy, *Donovan and the CIA*, 219.
7. "Organization of an Intelligence System," August 11, 1944, Records of the OSS Washington Director's Office, RG 226, M1642, Roll 134, NACP.
8. "A Projected Post War Intelligence Service," September 1, 1944, Office of Strategic Services, OSS, Washington Director's Office Administrative Files, 1941–1945, RG 226, M1642, Roll 3, NACP.
9. Troy, *Donovan and the CIA*, 219–20.
10. Office of Strategic Services, OSS, Washington Director's Office Administrative Files, 1941–1945, RG 226, M1642, Roll 3, NACP.
11. Hughes to Donovan, October 21, 1944, OSS, Washington Director's Office Administrative Files, 1941–1945, RG 226, M1642, Roll 3, NACP.
12. Stacy B. Lloyd to Donovan, October 1944?, OSS, Washington Director's Office Administrative Files, 1941–1945, RG 226, M1642, Roll 3, NACP.
13. Roosevelt to Donovan, October 31, 1944, OSS, Washington Director's Office Administrative Files, 1941–1945, RG 226, M1642, Roll 3, NACP.
14. Troy, *Donovan and the CIA*, 226.
15. Unknown to Roosevelt, October 26, 1944, Office of Strategic Services, OSS, Washington Director's Office Administrative Files, 1941–1945, RG 226, M1642, Roll 3, NACP.
16. Donovan to Roosevelt, November 7, 1944, OSS, Washington Director's Office Administrative Files, 1941–1945, RG 226, M1642, Roll 3, NACP.
17. Drafts, November 1944, OSS, Washington Director's Office Administrative Files, 1941–1945, RG 226, M1642, Roll 3, NACP.
18. Donovan to Roosevelt, November 18, 1944, OSS, Washington Director's Office Administrative Files, 1941–1945, RG 226, M1642, Roll 3, NACP.
19. Donovan to Roosevelt, November 18, 1944, NACP.
20. James Donovan to Magruder, November 23, 1944, Office of Strategic Services, OSS, Washington Director's Office Administrative Files, 1941–1945, RG 226, M1642, Roll 7, NACP.
21. See Troy, *Donovan and the CIA*, 225, for a graph of the FBI proposal.
22. See, generally, *History of the S.I.S. Division*.
23. Weiner, *Enemies*, 126–28.
24. Smith, *The Shadow Warriors*, 350–59.
25. Troy, *Donovan and the CIA*, 222, fn. 51.
26. See, *History of the S.I.S. Division*.
27. Troy, *Donovan and the CIA*, 222.

28. JIC 89/1, October 24, 1944, Office of Strategic Services, OSS, Washington Director's Office Administrative Files, 1941–1945, RG 226, M1642, Roll 7, NACP. NB: The many iterations of these proposals include JCS, JIC, and JIS qualifiers. For simplicity, the book will refer to these plans under the umbrella of the JCS.
29. Troy, *Donovan and the CIA*, 211.
30. Report by the Joint Intelligence Committee, "Post-War Intelligence Policy of the United States," October 7, 1944, Office of Strategic Services, OSS, Washington Director's Office Administrative Files, 1941–1945, RG 226, M1642, Roll 13, NACP.
31. JIS 89/2 Report by the Joint Intelligence Committee, "Post-War Intelligence Policy of the United States," November 15, 1944, Office of Strategic Services, OSS, Washington Director's Office Administrative Files, 1941–1945, RG 226, M1642, Roll 7, NACP.
32. JIS 89/2 Report by the Joint Intelligence Committee, "Post-War Intelligence Policy of the United States," November 15, 1944, NACP.
33. Troy, *Donovan and the CIA*, 228.
34. Troy, *Donovan and the CIA*, 231–34.
35. Joint Intelligence Staff, "Proposed Establishment of a Central Intelligence Service," December 9, 1944, Office of Strategic Services, OSS, Washington Director's Office Administrative Files, 1941–1945, RG 226, M1642, Roll 7, NACP.
36. JIC 121st Meeting, December 22, 1944, OSS, Washington Director's Office Administrative Files, 1941–1945, RG 226, M1642, Roll 7, NACP.
37. JIC 121st Meeting, December 22, 1944.
38. JIC 121st Meeting, December 22, 1944.
39. Donovan to Roosevelt, December 26, 1944, CIA/ERR.
40. Report by the Joint Strategic Survey Committee, "Proposed Establishment of a Central Intelligence Service," January 18, 1945, Office of Strategic Services, OSS, Washington Director's Office Administrative Files, 1941–1945, RG 226, M1642, Roll 7, NACP.
41. Report by the Joint Strategic Survey Committee, "Proposed Establishment of a Central Intelligence Service," Office of Strategic Services, OSS, Washington Director's Office Administrative Files, 1941–1945, RG 226, M1642, Roll 134, NACP.
42. Stanley P. Lovell to Ned Buxton, December 1944, Office of Strategic Services, OSS, Washington Director's Office Administrative Files, 1941–1945, RG 226, M1642, Roll 3, NACP.
43. Rudgers, *Creating the Secret State*, 25–27.
44. See, for example, Rudgers, *Creating the Secret State*, 30–31; Waller, *Wild Bill Donovan*, 311–12; Troy, *Donovan and the CIA*, vi, 281–82.
45. The unknown interlocutor was possibly CIA official Walter Pforzheimer.
46. GEN MSS 817, Box 21, Folder CIA Memorandum, WLPP.
47. Troy, *Donovan and the CIA*, vi; Rudgers, *Creating the Secret State*, 31; Waller, *Wild Bill Donovan*, 311.
48. Troy, *Donovan and the CIA*, 282.

49. Stout, "The Alternate Central Intelligence Agency," 82.
50. Rudgers, *Creating the Secret State*, 29.
51. Donovan to Roosevelt, February 23, 1945, Office of Strategic Services, Washington Director's Office Administrative Files, 1941–1945, RG 226, M1642, Roll 3, NACP.
52. Troy, *Donovan and the CIA*, 260–61.
53. Roosevelt to Donovan, April 5, 1945, Records of the OSS Washington Director's Office, RG 226, M1642, Roll 134, NACP.
54. For the letters, see GEN MSS 817, Box 13, Folder Donovan Papers and Pictures, WLPP.
55. C. Thomas Thorne Jr. and David S. Patterson, "Introduction," *FRUS, 1945–1950, Emergence of the Intelligence Establishment* (Washington, DC: GPO, 1996).
56. Troy, *Donovan and the CIA*, 265–67.
57. FBI memorandum, May 2, 1945, FBI, The Vault, William J. Donovan, Part 3, 130.
58. Drew Pearson's "Washington Merry-Go-Round," April 24, 1945, American University Library Special Collections.
59. Troy, *Donovan and the CIA*, 277, 280–83.
60. Kilgore to Donovan, August 13, 1945, Records of the OSS Washington Director's Office, RG 226, M1642, Roll 3, NACP.
61. Waller, *Wild Bill Donovan*, 434.
62. Troy, *Donovan and the CIA*, 292.
63. Magruder to Donovan, August 25, 1945, Records of the OSS Washington Director's Office, RG 226, M1642, Roll 3, NACP.
64. Donovan to Smith, August 25, 1945, Records of the OSS Washington Director's Office, RG 226, M1642, Roll 1, NACP.
65. Document 14, Executive Order 9621, *FRUS, 1945–1950, Emergence of the Intelligence Establishment*.
66. Michael Warner, ed., *The CIA Under Harry Truman*, (Washington, DC: Center for the Study of Intelligence, CIA, 1994), 15.
67. Troy, *Donovan and the CIA*, 308.
68. Document 5, Memorandum from the Director of the Federal Bureau of Investigation (Hoover) to Attorney General Clark, August 29, 1945, *FRUS, 1945–1950, Emergence of the Intelligence Establishment*.
69. Document 17, Memorandum from Attorney General Clark to President Truman, Washington, undated, *FRUS, 1945–1950, Emergence of the Intelligence Establishment*.
70. Document 17, Memorandum from Attorney General Clark to President Truman, Washington, undated, *FRUS, 1945–1950, Emergence of the Intelligence Establishment*.
71. Document 11, Memorandum from Arnold Miles of the Bureau of the Budget Staff to the Assistant Director for Administration Management of the Bureau of Budget (Stone), September 19, 1945, *FRUS, 1945–1950, Emergence of the Intelligence Establishment*, 116–22.

72. Zachary Selden, "Special Intelligence Service of the Federal Bureau of Investigation: Forgotten Forerunner of the Central Intelligence Agency," *International Journal of Intelligence and CounterIntelligence* 36, no. 4 (2023): 1210–27.
73. Weiner, *Enemies*, 134–35.
74. Document 15, Letter from President Truman to Secretary of State Byrnes, *FRUS, 1945–1950, Emergence of the Intelligence Establishment*.
75. Troy, *Donovan and the CIA*, 313, 325–26.
76. Troy, *Donovan and the CIA*, 326. See p. 327 for a chart of the State Department plan.
77. For the first State Department plan, see Troy, *Donovan and the CIA*, 327.
78. For the revised State Department plan, see Troy, *Donovan and the CIA*, 332.
79. Troy, *Donovan and the CIA*, 314–16, 326.
80. John Magruder to Robert Lovett, October 26, 1945, OSS Washington Director's Office, RG 226, M1642, Roll 134, NACP.
81. John Magruder to Robert Lovett, October 26, 1945, NACP.

CHAPTER 14

1. Jeff Rogg, "Coordinating Intelligence: An American Drama in Three Acts…of Congress," *International Journal of Intelligence and CounterIntelligence* 36, no. 2 (2023): 423–43.
2. A considerable body of scrutiny, debate, and folklore surrounds the creation of the CIA. For different interpretations, see Ranelagh, *The Agency*, 37; Thomas F. Troy, "The Quaintness of the U.S. Intelligence Community: Its Origin, Theory, and Problems." *International Journal of Intelligence and CounterIntelligence* 2, no. 2 (1988): 246–51; Rudgers, *Creating the Secret State*, 3; Amy Zegart, *Flawed by Design: The Evolution of the CIA, JCS, and NSC* (Stanford, CA: Stanford University Press, 1999), 7.
3. Smith, *The Shadow Warriors*, xvi; Rudgers, *Creating the Secret State*, 3; Ranelagh, *The Agency*, 21–36; Zegart, *Flawed by Design*, 185; Richard Immerman, *The Hidden Hand: A Brief History of the CIA* (West Sussex, UK: Wiley Blackwell, 2014), 20.
4. See, for example, "Centralized Intelligence," *Washington Star*, January 24, 1946; "The Gallup Poll: Public Favors Maintenance of Secret Agents Abroad," *Washington Post*, March 22, 1946.
5. O'Toole, *Honorable Treachery*, 511.
6. Warner, ed., *The CIA Under Truman*, 29–32.
7. Troy, *Donovan and the CIA*, 346.
8. For a history of the President's Daily Brief, see David Priess, *The President's Book of Secrets: The Untold Story of Intelligence Briefings to America's Presidents* (New York: PublicAffairs, 2016).
9. Troy, *Donovan and the CIA*, 359.
10. N.I.A. Directive No. 5, July 8, 1946, CIA/ERR.
11. Weiner, *Enemies*, 145.

12. Troy, *Donovan and the CIA*, 365.
13. "Organization and Functions of the Central Intelligence Group," first speech by member of CIG contingent at the second Frankfort Conference, May 1947, CIA/ERR.
14. Troy, *Donovan and the CIA*, 369–75.
15. Troy, *Donovan and the CIA*, 376; Zegart, *Flawed by Design*, 165.
16. Cong. Rec., 80th Cong., 1st sess., 2069.
17. Hearings Before the Committee on Expenditures in the Executive Department on H.R. 2319, 80th Cong., 1st sess., 125–28.
18. Hearings on H.R. 2319, 171.
19. Hearings on H.R. 2319, 438.
20. Hearings on H.R. 2319, 454.
21. Hearings on H.R. 2319, 479–81.
22. Hearings Before the United States Senate Committee on Armed Services on S. 758, 80th Cong., 1st sess., 492–99.
23. Hearings on S. 758, 649–51.
24. Hearings on H.R. 2319, 438–39.
25. Hearings on H.R. 2319, 454–56.
26. Hearings on S. 758, 497–99.
27. Hearings on S. 758, 525–28.
28. Correspondence from William J. Donovan to Senator Chan Gurney Regarding National Security, May 7, 1947, Manuscripts, Box 11A, Folder 12, RDP.
29. Troy, *Donovan and the CIA*, 382–84; Rudgers, *Creating the Secret State*, 140–41.
30. Document 215, Memorandum for the Record, May 26, 1947, *FRUS, Emergence of the Intelligence Establishment*.
31. C. P. Trussell, "Unification Voted by House; Senate to Act on Changes," *New York Times*, July 20, 1947.
32. National Security Act of 1947, Pub. L. 253, 80th Cong., 1st sess., July 26, 1947.
33. National Security Act of 1947.
34. National Security Act of 1947.
35. National Security Act of 1947.
36. In later years, Clark Clifford insisted the act's drafters intended for the CIA to conduct covert action through a "'catch-all' clause." Statement of Clark Clifford, Church Committee, vol. 7, 51; Clark Clifford with Richard Holbrooke, *Counsel to the President: A Memoir* (New York: Random House, 1991), 169–70. Thomas Troy reached the same conclusion based on his own study of the history. See Troy, *Donovan and the CIA*, 415.
37. Samuel A. Tower, "Intelligence Net to Be World-Wide," *New York Times*, August 3, 1947.
38. Address of the President to Congress, Recommending Assistance to Greece and Turkey, March 12, 1947, The Truman Doctrine, Harry S. Truman Administration, HSTL.

39. Document 250, Memorandum of Discussion at the 2d Meeting of the National Security Council, November 14, 1947, *FRUS, Emergence of the Intelligence Establishment.*
40. Church Committee, book IV, 28–29.
41. Document 257, Memorandum From the Executive Secretary of the National Security Council (Souers) to Director of Central Intelligence Hillenkoetter, *FRUS, Emergence of the Intelligence Establishment.*
42. Document 269, Policy Planning Staff Memorandum, May 4, 1948, *FRUS, Emergence of the Intelligence Establishment.*
43. Document 292, National Security Directive on Office of Special Projects NSC 10/2, June 18, 1948, *FRUS, Emergence of the Intelligence Establishment.*
44. John Prados, *Safe for Democracy: The Secret Wars of the CIA* (Chicago: Ivan R. Dee, 2006), 40.
45. Document 298, Memorandum of Conversation and Understanding, August 6, 1948, *FRUS, Emergence of the Intelligence Establishment.*
46. Document 292, *FRUS, Emergence of the Intelligence Establishment.*
47. The Commission on Organization of the Executive Branch of the Government, Task Force Report on National Security Organization, January 1949, 37–38, 51–52. Hereafter "Eberstadt Report."
48. Eberstadt Report, 37.
49. Eberstadt Report, 44.
50. Eberstadt Report, 45.
51. Eberstadt Report, 57–58.
52. Eberstadt Report, 40.
53. The Central Intelligence Agency and National Organization for Intelligence, A Report to the National Security Council, January 1, 1949, 11. Hereafter "Dulles Report."
54. Dulles Report, 41–42.
55. Dulles Report, 4.
56. Dulles Report, 10.
57. Dulles Report, 36.
58. Document 241, Memorandum from the General Counsel of the Central Intelligence Agency (Houston) to Director of Central Intelligence Hillenkoetter, *FRUS, Emergence of the Intelligence Establishment.*
59. Rudgers, *Creating the Secret State*, 165–66.
60. "Martin Questions Spy Bill Secrecy," *New York Times*, March 7, 1949.
61. Rudgers, *Creating the Secret State*, 166.
62. Central Intelligence Agency Act of 1949, Pub. L. 81-110, 63 Stat. 208, June 20, 1949.
63. Clifford, *Counsel to the President*, 170.
64. CIA Act of 1949. The Contingent Fund reauthorization of 1793 reads: "Every such certificate shall be deemed a sufficient voucher for the sum or sums therein expressed to have been expended."

65. Ranelagh, *The Agency*, 194, quoting Houston memorandum to the director of Central Intelligence, May 25, 1949.
66. L. Britt Snider, *The Agency and the Hill: CIA's Relationship with Congress, 1946–2004* (Washington, DC: Center for the Study of Intelligence, 2008), 6–9.
67. Church Committee, book IV, 40.
68. Church Committee, book IV, 39.
69. Ranelagh, *The Agency*, 283; Snider, *The Agency and the Hill*, 10, 40.
70. Snider, *The Agency and the Hill*, 40.
71. For three principal features of the Cold War consensus, see Bruce W. Jentleson, *American Foreign Policy: The Dynamics of Choice in the 21st Century*, 2nd ed. (New York: W. W. Norton, 2004), 129.
72. Ranelagh, *The Agency*, 281; Jeffreys-Jones, *The CIA and American Democracy*, 74.
73. Snider, *The Agency and the Hill*, 10.
74. Ranelagh, *The Agency*, 285.
75. Marvin C. Ott, "Partisanship and the Decline of Intelligence Oversight," *International Journal of Intelligence and CounterIntelligence* 16, no. 1 (2003): 74.
76. Snider, *The Agency and the Hill*, 40–42.
77. Ranelagh, *The Agency*, 283n.
78. Snider, *The Agency and the Hill*, 40.
79. Jeffreys-Jones, *The CIA and American Democracy*, 27; Troy, *Donovan and the CIA*, 376.

CHAPTER 15

1. Document 34, Acting Secretary of State to the Secretary of State, *FRUS, 1948 Volume IX, The Western Hemisphere* (Washington, DC: GPO, 2018); Bertram D. Hulen, "Marshall Blames Reds in Colombia; Parley to Continue," *New York Times*, April 13, 1948.
2. "Dewey Holds U.S. Lax in Colombia," *New York Times*, April 13, 1948.
3. Jack Davis, "The Bogotazo," *Studies in Intelligence* 13, no. 4 (1969): 82.
4. "The X at Bogota," *Washington Post*, April 13, 1948; "Crisis in Defense," *Washington Post*, April 17, 1948.
5. Jeffreys-Jones, *The CIA and American Democracy*, 54.
6. Ranelagh, *The Agency*, 188–89.
7. U.S. Department of Energy, "The Manhattan Project," n.d., https://www.osti.gov/opennet/manhattan-project-history/Events/1942-1945/espionage.htm.
8. As late as 2019, evidence surfaced of yet another Soviet spy who was integral to providing the Soviet Union with instructions on how to detonate a nuclear weapon. See Harvey Klehr and John Early Haynes, "On the Trail of a Fourth Soviet Spy at Los Alamos," *Studies in Intelligence* 63, no. 3 (2019); William J. Broad, "Fourth Spy at Los Alamos Knew A-Bomb's Inner Secrets," *New York Times*, January 27, 2020.
9. Director of Central Intelligence R. H. Hillenkoetter, Memorandum to the President, "Estimate of the Status of the Russian Atomic Energy Project," July 25, 1948, DNSA.

10. Vince Houghton, *The Nuclear Spies: America's Atomic Intelligence Operation Against Hitler and Stalin* (Ithaca, NY: Cornell University Press, 2019), 147–48.
11. Memorandum from Director of Central Intelligence Rear Admiral R. H Hillenkoetter, "Report of Surveillance," Central Intelligence Agency, September 9, 1949, DNSA.
12. Document 399, Memorandum from the Assistant Director for Scientific Intelligence (Machle) to Director of Central Intelligence Hillenkoetter, *FRUS, 1945–1950, Emergence of the Intelligence Establishment.*
13. Donald P. Steury, "How the CIA Missed Stalin's Bomb," *Studies in Intelligence* 9, no. 1 (2005).
14. "The Korean War Controversy: An Intelligence Success or Failure?" June 25, 2015, CIA.
15. Clayton Laurie, "The Korean War and the Central Intelligence Agency," Center for the Study of Intelligence, 6–7, CIA/ERR.
16. "Current Capabilities of the Northern Korean Regime," June 19, 1950, CIA/ERR.
17. Jeffreys-Jones, *The CIA and American Democracy*, 63, 65.
18. Jeffreys-Jones, *CIA and American Democracy*, 66–67; Ranelagh, *The Agency*, 190.
19. Donald P. Steury, ed., *Sherman Kent and the Board of National Estimates: Collected Essays* (Washington, DC: Center for the Study of Intelligence, 1994).
20. Document 29, Minutes of a Meeting of the Intelligence Advisory Committee, *FRUS, 1950–1955, The Intelligence Community* (Washington, DC: GPO, 2007).
21. Ludwell Lee Montague, *General Walter Bedell Smith as Director of Central Intelligence: October 1950–February 1953* (University Park: Pennsylvania State University Press, 1992), 128.
22. Introduction in "Sherman Kent and the Board of National Estimates: Collected Essays."
23. Montague, *General Walter Bedell Smith*, 135.
24. Sherman Kent, *Strategic Intelligence for American World Policy* (Princeton, NJ: Princeton University Press, 1966), 180, 200, 218.
25. Willmoore Kendall, "The Function of Intelligence," *World Politics* 1, no. 4 (1949): 548–50. Italics appear in the original source.
26. Jeffreys-Jones, *The CIA and American Democracy*, 68.
27. Document 298, Memorandum of Conversation and Understanding, August 6, 1948, *FRUS, 1945–1950, Emergence of the Intelligence Establishment.*
28. Document 298, *FRUS, 1945–1950, Emergence of the Intelligence Establishment.*
29. Colby and Forbath, *Honorable Men*, 73.
30. Immerman, *The Hidden Hand*, 28.
31. Colby and Forbath, *Honorable Men*, 73.
32. NSC 68: United States Objectives and Programs for National Security, April 14, 1950, Section IX, D.
33. Church Committee, book IV, 32.
34. Church Committee, book IV, 32–34.
35. Church Committee, book IV, 36–37.

36. Church Committee, book IV, 37; Ranelagh, *The Agency*, 199.
37. Ranelagh, *The Agency*, 199; Immerman, *The Hidden Hand*, 41.
38. Dulles Report, 116.
39. Document 90, Note from the Executive Secretary of the National Security Council (Lay) to the National Security Council, *FRUS, 1950–1955, The Intelligence Community*.
40. Church Committee, book IV, 38.
41. Immerman, *The Hidden Hand*, 42–43.
42. Document 107, Memorandum from Director of Central Intelligence Smith to the National Security Council, *FRUS, 1950–1955, The Intelligence Community*. In this memorandum, Smith also explained that the Office of National Estimates "utilizes the resources of the total United States intelligence community." This memorandum by Smith therefore represents one of the earliest—if not the earliest—use of the term. Michael Warner adopts Ludwell Lee Montague's reading that the earliest use of the term "intelligence community" was in the minutes of a 1952 meeting of the Intelligence Advisory Committee. See Michael Warner, ed., *Central Intelligence: Origin and Evolution* (Washington, DC: Center for the Study of Intelligence, 2001), 6n13. Meanwhile, Troy credits the Second Hoover Commission and Clark Report of 1955 with cementing the use of the term. See Troy, "Quaintness of the U.S. Intelligence Community," 253.
43. Quoted in Rudgers, *Creating the Secret State*, 183.
44. Kent, *Strategic Intelligence*, 182.
45. Kent, *Strategic Intelligence*, 166–68.
46. Kendall, "The Function of Intelligence," 545–46.
47. D. H. Berger, The Use of Covert Paramilitary Activity as a Policy Tool: An Analysis of Operations Conducted by the United States Central Intelligence Agency, 1949–1951 (written in fulfillment of a requirement for the Marine Corps Command and Staff College, May 22, 1995); Roger B. Jeans, *The CIA and Third Force Movements in China During the Early Cold War: The Great American Dream* (Lanham, MD: Lexington Books, 2018).
48. Berger, *The Use of Covert Paramilitary Activity as a Policy Tool*. Italics appear in original source.
49. Jeffreys-Jones, *The CIA and American Democracy*, 72.
50. Immerman, *The Hidden Hand*, 43–44.
51. Immerman, *The Hidden Hand*, 47.
52. To be fair, Árbenz had helped initiate a military coup in 1944, although he did succeed to office in a democratic election in 1950.
53. John Lewis Gaddis, *George F. Kennan: An American Life* (New York: Penguin Books, 2012), 318–19.
54. Colby and Forbath, *Honorable Men*, 73.
55. Harry Rositzke, *The CIA's Secret Operations* (New York: Reader's Digest Press, 1977), 252, 258, 270–71.

56. Rositzke, *The CIA's Secret Operations*, 50.
57. Document 338, Letter from Secretary of Defense's Special Assistant (McNeil) to Mathias F. Correa, *FRUS, 1945–1950, Emergence of the Intelligence Establishment.*
58. Kendall, "The Function of Intelligence," 548–49. Italics appear in original source.
59. "The Concept of the Junior Officer Training Program," Memorandum for Deputy Director of Central Intelligence, March 19, 1956, CIA/ERR.
60. Milt Bearden and James Risen, *The Main Enemy: The Inside Story of the CIA's Final Showdown with the KGB* (New York: Random House, 2003), 19–20.
61. Colby and Forbath, *Honorable Men*, 86–87.
62. Victor Marchetti and John D. Marks, *The CIA and the Cult of Intelligence* (New York: Dell, 1974), 5. I incorporate this resource with a degree of caution over the controversy surrounding the book and, especially, the author. That said, his explanation of a "cult of intelligence" merits further discussion for what it reveals about the differences between professional intelligence and American principles.
63. Marchetti and Marks, *The CIA and the Cult of Intelligence*, 6–10.
64. Colby and Forbath, *Honorable Men*, 20.
65. Rositzke, *The CIA's Secret Operations*, 258–62.
66. Kendall, "The Function of Intelligence," 549–50.
67. Clifford, *Counsel to the President*, 170.
68. Rositzke, *The CIA's Secret Operations*, 272.

CHAPTER 16

1. Allen W. Dulles to Donald B. Lourie, Under Secretary of State, August 5, 1953, GEN MSS 817, Box 79, Folder McCarthy, WLPP.
2. Memorandum for the Record, July 9, 1953, GEN MSS 817, Box 79, Folder McCarthy, WLPP.
3. William S. White, "McCarthy Strikes at Allen Dulles," *New York Times*, July 10, 1953.
4. Ranelagh, *The Agency*, 240; Jeffreys-Jones, *The CIA and American Democracy*, 75.
5. Church Committee, book IV, 44.
6. Commission on Organization of the Executive Branch of the Government, Commission Report on Intelligence Activities, June 29, 1955, CIA/ERR.
7. Document 220, Report by the Task Force on Intelligence Activities of the Commission on Organization of the Executive Branch of the Government, May 1955, *FRUS, 1950–1955, The Intelligence Community*. Hereafter "Clark Report to President."
8. Clark Report to President.
9. Memorandum for the Director of Central Intelligence on DCI Responsibility for the Coordination and Effective Guidance to the U.S. Intelligence Effort, May 25, 1965, CIA/ERR.
10. Clark Report to President.

11. Document 221, Report by the Commission on Organization of the Executive Branch of the Government to the Congress, June 1955, *FRUS, 1950–1955, The Intelligence Community*. Hereafter "Clark Report to Congress."
12. Clark Report to Congress.
13. Document 185, Letter from President Eisenhower to General James H. Doolittle, *FRUS, 1950–1955, The Intelligence Community*.
14. Michael Warner and J. Kenneth McDonald, *US Intelligence Community Reform Studies Since 1947* (Washington, DC: Center for the Study of Intelligence, 2005), 15.
15. Document 192, Report by the Special Study Group, *FRUS, 1950–1955, The Intelligence Community*.
16. The Chargé in the Soviet Union (Kennan) to the Secretary of State, February 22, 1946, DNSA.
17. Eminent military theorist and West Point professor Dennis Hart Mahan understood that the American people were "warlike but unmilitary," while his son Alfred Thayer Mahan, an equally renowned naval theorist and Naval War College president, echoed his father and called them "aggressive, combative, and even warlike." Huntington, *The Soldier and the State*, 266.
18. "Congress Is Asked to Supervise C.I.A.," *New York Times*, January 15, 1955.
19. Cong. Rec., 84th Cong., 2nd sess., 5924.
20. Cong. Rec., 84th Cong., 2nd sess., 5931.
21. Cong. Rec., 84th Cong., 2nd sess., 5937.
22. Cong. Rec., 84th Cong., 2nd sess., 5939.
23. Cong. Rec., 84th Cong., 2nd sess., 5931–35.
24. Cong. Rec., 84th Cong., 2nd sess., 5924.
25. Cong. Rec., 84th Cong., 2nd sess., 5933.
26. Snider, *The Agency and the Hill*, 17.
27. Jeffreys-Jones, *The CIA and American Democracy*, 78.
28. Kenneth Michal Absher, Michael C. Desch, and Roman Popadiuk, *Privileged and Confidential: The Secret History of the President's Intelligence Advisory Board* (Lexington: University Press of Kentucky, 2012), 18.
29. EO 10656, CIA/ERR.
30. *The President's Foreign Intelligence Advisory Board* (Washington, DC: Hale Foundation, 1981), 11, 15–19.
31. Document 212, National Security Council Directive; Document 250, National Security Council Directive, *FRUS, 1950–1955, The Intelligence Community*.
32. Immerman, *The Hidden Hand*, 45; Jeffreys-Jones, *The CIA and American Democracy*, 93. It was known as the 303 Committee under the Johnson administration and later the 40 Committee in the Nixon and Ford administrations. David Wise, "The Secret Committee Called '40,'" *New York Times*, January 19, 1975.
33. Prados, *Safe for Democracy*, 150.
34. Rositzke, *The CIA's Secret Operations*, 239.

35. Burns, *Origins of the NSA*, 20–21.
36. Document 435, National Security Council Intelligence Directive No. 9, *FRUS, 1945–1950, Emergence of the Intelligence Establishment.*
37. Burns, *Origins of the NSA*, 54–56.
38. James Bamford, *The Puzzle Palace: Inside the National Security Agency, America's Most Secret Intelligence Organization* (New York: Penguin Books, 1983), 72.
39. Burns, *Origins of the NSA*, 59.
40. Burns, *Origins of the NSA*, 59; Memorandum for the Director: Establishment of the Armed Forces Security Agency, September 1, 1949, WFFP.
41. Document 97, Memorandum from Director of Central Intelligence Smith to the Executive Secretary of the National Security Council (Lay), *FRUS, 1950–1955, The Intelligence Community.*
42. Burns, *Origins of the NSA*, 103–5.
43. Memorandum on Communications Intelligence Activities, October 24, 1952, https://media.defense.gov/2021/Jul/15/2002763653/-1/-1/0/TRUMAN-MEMO.PDF.
44. Memorandum on Communications Intelligence Activities, October 24, 1952.
45. Raphaël Ramos, "The National Security Act, SIGINT, and the Origins of an Intelligence Diarchy," *International Journal of Intelligence and CounterIntelligence* 36, no. 2 (2023): 444–65.
46. Frederic Oder, James Fitzpatrick, and Paul Worthman, *The Corona Story* (Chantilly, VA: Center for the Study of National Reconnaissance, 2013), 1.
47. Karl Weber, *The Office of Scientific Intelligence, 1949–68*, The Directorate of Science and Technology Historical Series, No. OSI-1 (Washington, DC: Central Intelligence Agency, 1972), annex III, tab A, 1, 6.
48. Amy Ryan and Gary Keeley, "Sputnik and US Intelligence: The Warning Record," *Studies in Intelligence* 61, no. 3 (2017): 3.
49. Oder et al., *The Corona Story*, 3.
50. President Dwight D. Eisenhower's Farewell Address (1961), NARA.
51. Weber, *The Office of Scientific Intelligence, 1949–68*, annex III, tab A, 3.
52. Oder et al., *The Corona Story*, 7.
53. Bruce Berkowitz, *The National Reconnaissance Office at 50 Years: A Brief History* (Chantilly, VA: Center for the Study of National Reconnaissance, 2011), 11.
54. Weber, *The Office of Scientific Intelligence, 1949–68*, annex III, tab A, 8–9.
55. Oder et al., *The Corona Story*, 20, 28.
56. Aaron Bateman, "Technological Wonder and Strategic Vulnerability: Satellite Reconnaissance and American National Security During the Cold War," *International Journal of Intelligence and CounterIntelligence* 33, no. 2 (2020): 335.
57. Aaron Bateman, "Trust but Verify: Satellite Reconnaissance, Secrecy and Arms Control During the Cold War," *Journal of Strategic Studies* 46, no. 5 (2023): 1039.
58. Re: Management of the National Reconnaissance Program, September 6, 1961, DNSA.

59. Oder et al., *The Corona Story*, 67–71.
60. *The Directorate for Science and Technology 1962–1970*, vol. 2, chaps. V–VI (Washington, DC: CIA Historical Staff, 1972), 192, CIA.
61. Oder et al., *The Corona Story*, 73–75, 90–91.
62. *The Directorate for Science and Technology 1962–1970*, 203–6.
63. Agreement Between the Secretary of Defense and the Director of Central Intelligence on Management of the National Reconnaissance Program, March 13, 1963, DNSA.
64. Proposed D/NRO-JCS/JRC Agreement, July 8, 1963, CIA/ERR.
65. Agreement for Reorganization of the National Reconnaissance Program, signed August 13, 1965, DNSA.
66. Bateman, "Trust but Verify," 1054.
67. Rogg, "Military-Intelligence Relations."
68. Joint Study Group Report on Foreign Intelligence Activities of the United States Government, December 15, 1960, 89–93, CIA/ERR.
69. Joint Study Group Report on Foreign Intelligence Activities of the United States Government, 8–32. The tension between the Secretary of Defense and JCS is a subject of considerable study in civil-military relations but is beyond the scope of this discussion.
70. Document 80, Memorandum of Discussion at the 473rd Meeting of the National Security Council, *FRUS, 1961–1963, Volume XXV: Organization of Foreign Policy; Information Policy; United Nations; Scientific Matters* (Washington, DC: GPO, 2001).
71. Memorandum for the Chairman, Joint Chiefs of Staff, February 8, 1961, in *Defense Intelligence Agency: At the Creation, 1961–1965*, ed. Deane J. Allen and Brian G. Shellum (Washington, DC: DIA History Office, 2002), 22–25.
72. Memorandum for the President, July 6, 1951, DNSA.
73. DOD Directive 5105.21, Papers of President Kennedy, NSF, Departments and Agencies, Box 280, Folder Department of Defense, Defense Intelligence Agency, 1961, JFKL.
74. DOD Announcement of August 2, 1961, DNSA.
75. Rogg, "Military-Intelligence Relations," 1076.

CHAPTER 17

1. Rositzke, *The CIA's Secret Operations*, 239.
2. Memorandum for the President, June 30, 1961, Papers of President Kennedy, NSF Departments and Agencies, Box 271, Folder Central Intelligence Agency General 5/61–8/61, JFKL.
3. "Volunteers" means that the individuals were willing participants in these "medical" experiments even if they were unaware that the CIA was sponsoring the experiments.

4. Madeleine G. Kalb, "The C.I.A. and Lumumba," *New York Times*, August 2, 1981. For more on Gottlieb, see Stephen Kinzer, *Poisoner in Chief: Sidney Gottlieb and the CIA Search for Mind Control* (New York: Henry Holt, 2019).
5. Ranelagh, *The Agency*, 208.
6. Mark Riebling, *Wedge: The Secret War Between the FBI and CIA* (New York: Alfred A. Knopf, 1994), 84.
7. Dulles, *The Craft of Intelligence*, 39.
8. Dulles, *The Craft of Intelligence*, 177.
9. Harry S. Truman, "Limit CIA Role to Intelligence," *Washington Post*, December 22, 1963.
10. David Wise and Thomas B. Ross, *The Invisible Government* (New York: Random House, 1964), 3.
11. Wise and Ross, *The Invisible Government*, 222.
12. Wise and Ross, *The Invisible Government*, 223.
13. Wise and Ross, *The Invisible Government*, 225.
14. "C.I.A.: Maker of Policy, or Tool," *New York Times*, April 25, 1966.
15. Ramparts advertisement, *New York Times*, February 14, 1967.
16. Neil Sheehan, "A Student Group Concedes It Took Funds from C.I.A.," *New York Times*, February 14, 1967.
17. Sol Stern, "NSA and the CIA," *Ramparts*, March 1967, 29–39, 35.
18. Marcus Raskin "... and a Judgment," *Ramparts*, March 1967, 39.
19. Frances Stonor Saunders, *The Cultural Cold War: The CIA and the World of Arts and Letters* (New York: New Press, 2013), 427.
20. Hugh Wilford, *The Mighty Wurlitzer: How the CIA Played America* (Cambridge, MA: Harvard University Press, 2008), 7–8, 240, 251, 254.
21. Thomas W. Braden, "I'm Glad the CIA Is 'Immoral,'" *Saturday Evening Post*, May 20, 1967, 10–14.
22. Peter Grose, *Gentleman Spy: The Life of Allen Dulles* (New York: Houghton Mifflin, 1994), 563.
23. Tity de Vries, "The 1967 Central Intelligence Agency Scandal: Catalyst in a Transforming Relationship Between State and People," *Journal of American History* 98, no. 4 (2012): 1076.
24. The law was originally enacted in July 1966 with an effective date of one year later, but then was repealed and reenacted in substantially the same form in July 1967.
25. Church Committee, book III, 11.
26. Memorandum of W. C. Sullivan to C. D. DeLoach, Subject: "Black Bag Jobs," July 19, 1966, Records of the Federal Bureau of Investigation, Office of the Director, J. Edgar Hoover, Official and Confidential Subject Files, 1924–1972, RG 65, Entry UD05D14, NACP. For more on Sullivan's role in the FBI letters to King, see Michael E. Ruane, "'You Are Done': A Secret Letter to Martin Luther King Jr. Sheds Light on FBI's Malice," *Washington Post*, December 13, 2017.
27. Church Committee, book II, 14.

28. Memorandum for the Files, J. Edgar Hoover, April 12, 1971, Records of the Federal Bureau of Investigation, Office of the Director, J. Edgar Hoover, Official and Confidential Subject Files, 1924–1972, RG 65, Entry UD05D14, NACP.
29. Church Committee, book III, 3.
30. Memorandum of March 25, 1971, Records of the Federal Bureau of Investigation, Office of the Director, J. Edgar Hoover, Official and Confidential Subject Files, 1924–1972, RG 65, Entry UD05D14, NACP.
31. Church Committee, book III, 765.
32. Church Committee, book II, 108, 189.
33. Church Committee, book III, 739.
34. Church Committee, book II, 97–98.
35. Church Committee, book II, 100–107, 180.
36. Robert M. Smith, "F.B.I. Is Said to Have Cut Direct Liaison with C.I.A.," *New York Times*, October 10, 1971.
37. Warner and McDonald, *US Intelligence Community Reform Studies Since 1947*, 21.
38. "A Review of the Intelligence Community," March 10, 1971, DNSA, 4–5, 13–16, 25–26.
39. Warner and McDonald, *US Intelligence Community Reform Studies Since 1947*, 22.
40. Seymour Hersh, "Hunt Tells of Early Work for a C.I.A. Domestic Unit," *New York Times*, December 31, 1974.
41. Ranelagh, *The Agency*, 547–48.
42. Memorandum for All CIA Employees, May 9, 1973, DNSA.
43. Douglas F. Garthoff, *Directors of Central Intelligence as Leaders of the U.S. Intelligence Community 1946–2005* (Washington, DC: Center for the Study of Intelligence, 2005), 83n8; The CIA's "Family Jewels," 107, DNSA.
44. The CIA's "Family Jewels," 326.
45. Seymour M. Hersh, "Huge C.I.A. Operation Reported in U.S. Against Antiwar Forces, Other Dissidents in Nixon Years," *New York Times*, December 22, 1974.
46. Hersh, "Huge C.I.A. Operation Reported in U.S."
47. Lucien N. Nedzi, "Oversight or Overlook: Congress and the U.S. Intelligence Agencies," remarks to the CIA Senior Seminar, November 14, 1973, *Studies in Intelligence* 18, no. 2 (1974).
48. Church Committee, book II, 111–14.
49. Hersh, "Huge C.I.A. Operation Reported in U.S."
50. Church Committee, book II, 115.
51. Church Committee, vol. 2, Huston Plan, 72–73.
52. Hersh, "Huge C.I.A. Operation Reported in U.S."
53. Church Committee, vol. 2, Huston Plan, 108.
54. Kathryn Olmsted, "Lapdog or Rogue Elephant? CIA Controversies from 1947 to 2004," in *The Central Intelligence Agency: Security Under Scrutiny*, ed. Athan Theoharis, Richard Immerman, Loch Johnson, Kathryn Olmsted, and John Prados (Westport, CT: Greenwood Press, 2006), 203.

55. *Report to the President by the Commission on CIA Activities Within the United States* (Washington, DC: GPO, 1975), 1–15.
56. John Prados and Arturo Jimenez-Bacardi, "Gerald Ford White House Altered Rockefeller Commission Report in 1975; Removed Section on CIA Assassination Plots," National Security Archive, February 29, 2016, DNSA.
57. Jeffreys-Jones, *The CIA and American Democracy*, 202–3.
58. 88 Stat. 1804.
59. Knott, *Secret and Sanctioned*, 166.
60. Ranelagh, *The Agency*, 678.
61. Knott, *Secret and Sanctioned*, 166.
62. Memorandum of Conversation, January 4, 1975, National Security Adviser, Memoranda of Conversations, 1973–1977, Box 8, GRFL.
63. Schlesinger, *The Imperial Presidency*, 163.
64. Robert David Johnson, "The Unintended Consequences of Congressional Reform: The Clark and Tunney Amendments and U.S. Policy Toward Angola," *Diplomatic History* 27, no. 2 (2003): 234.
65. Transcript, *CBS Reports*, "The Hot and Cold Wars of Allen Dulles," Papers of President Kennedy, NSF Departments & Agencies, Folder Central Intelligence Agency General 3/62–4/62, JFKL.
66. John M. Maury, "CIA and the Congress," *Studies in Intelligence* 18, no. 2 (1974).
67. George Lardner Jr., "House Supports Nedzi," *Washington Post*, June 11, 1975.
68. Ranelagh, *The Agency*, 595.
69. Gerald K. Haines, "The Pike Committee Investigations and the CIA," *Studies in Intelligence* 42, no. 5 (1999): 81–92.
70. Harold P. Ford, *William E. Colby as Director of Central Intelligence 1973–1976* (Washington, DC: Center for the Study of Intelligence, 1993), 164, 166.
71. Haines, "The Pike Committee Investigations and the CIA."
72. Aaron Latham, "The Report on the CIA that President Ford Doesn't Want You to Read," *Village Voice*, February 16, 1976.
73. Haines, "The Pike Committee Investigations and the CIA."
74. Ranelagh, *The Agency*, 592.
75. Jeffreys-Jones, *The CIA and American Democracy*, 208.
76. "'Disreputable if Not Outright Illegal,' The National Security Agency Versus Martin Luther King, Muhammad Ali, Art Buchwald, Frank Church, *et al.*," ed. Matthew M. Aid and William Burr, September 25, 2013, DNSA.
77. John M. Crewdson, "Church Doubts Plot Links to Presidents," *New York Times*, July 19, 1975.
78. Loch K. Johnson, *A Season of Inquiry: The Senate Intelligence Investigation* (Lexington: University Press of Kentucky, 1985), 54.
79. Church Committee, book IV, 31.
80. Church Committee, vol. 7, 51.
81. Ranelagh, *The Agency*, 597.
82. Colby and Forbath, *Honorable Men*, 403–404.

83. Ranelagh, *The Agency*, 589.
84. Church Committee, vol. 1, 17.
85. Church Committee, vol. 1, 41.
86. Church Committee, vol. 1, 21.
87. Ranelagh, *The Agency*, 554–55.
88. Memorandum of Conversation, January 4, 1975, GRFL.
89. National Security Adviser, Memoranda of Conversations, Box 10, March 28, 1975, GRFL.
90. CIA Employee Bulletin, February 28, 1975, GEN MSS 817 Box 21, WLPP.
91. Tim Weiner, "William E. Colby, 76, Head of C.I.A. in a Time of Upheaval," *New York Times*, May 7, 1996.
92. Church Committee, vol. 7, Covert Action, 45.
93. Richard Helms and William Hood, *A Look over My Shoulder: A Life in the Central Intelligence Agency* (New York: Random House, 2003), 442.
94. *Covert Action in Chile 1963–1973,* Church Committee Staff Report (Washington, DC: GPO, 1975), 2.
95. Lee Lescaze, "Probing Helms & Co.," *Washington Post*, October 31, 1979.
96. Helms and Hood, *A Look over My Shoulder*, 445.
97. Walter Pincus, "Colby-Helms Feud Goes Public at Hill Hearing," *Washington Post*, October 23, 1979.
98. Rositzke, *The CIA's Secret Operations*, 238. There is even some debate over just which parts of the "Family Jewels," if any, were actually illegal under existing US law. See, for example, Daniel L. Pines, "The Central Intelligence Agency's 'Family Jewels': Legal Then? Legal Now?" *Indiana Law Journal* 84, no. 2 (2009): 637–88.
99. Ford, *William E. Colby as Director of Central Intelligence*, 166.
100. Memorandum for the President, June 30, 1961, JFKL.

CHAPTER 18

1. Document 83, Minutes of a National Security Council Meeting, *FRUS, 1969–1976*, vol. XXXVIII, part 2, *Organization and Management of Foreign Policy; Public Diplomacy, 1973–1976* (Washington, DC: GPO, 2014).
2. For many years, defenders of the Rosenbergs claimed they were wrongfully convicted until evidence from the highly classified SIGINT project known as VENONA proved the guilt of at least Julius.
3. Document 83, Minutes of a National Security Council Meeting, *FRUS, 1969–1976*.
4. Gerald Ford, Letter to the Chairman and Members of the Senate Select Committee to Study Governmental Operations with Respect to Intelligence Activities, October 31, 1975.
5. Johnson, *A Season of Inquiry*, 108.

6. Johnson, *A Season of Inquiry*, 195.
7. Remarks by W. E. Colby before Pacem in Terris IV, December 4, 1975, 8, GRFL.
8. Executive Order 11905, February 18, 1976, GRFL.
9. Johnson, *A Season of Inquiry*, 195.
10. J. Kenneth McDonald, "Secrecy, Accountability, and the CIA: The Dilemma of Intelligence in a Democracy," in *The United States Military Under the Constitution of the United States, 1789–1989*, ed. Richard H. Kohn (New York: New York University Press, 1991), 396.
11. Proposed Standing Committee on Intelligence Activities, S. Res. 400, 94th Cong., 2nd sess., 13695.
12. S. Res. 400, 94th Cong., 2nd sess., 13978.
13. S. Res. 400, 94th Cong., 2nd sess., 13981.
14. Cong. Rec., 94th Cong., 2nd sess., 13974.
15. Cong. Rec., 94th Cong., 2nd sess., 13975.
16. Cong. Rec., 94th Cong., 2nd sess., 13995–96.
17. Cong. Rec., 94th Cong., 2nd sess., 13978–79.
18. Frederick M. Kaiser, *Legislative History of the Senate Select Committee on Intelligence* (Washington, DC: CRS, 1978), 54.
19. Cong. Rec., 94th Cong., 2nd sess., 13983.
20. Cong. Rec., 94th Cong., 2nd sess., 13693.
21. *The Public Papers of the Presidents of the United States*, Jimmy Carter, 1978, book I (Washington, DC: GPO, 1979), 190–93.
22. Executive Order 12036, January 24, 1978.
23. Jimmy Carter, *White House Diary* (New York: Picador, 2010), 165.
24. Ranelagh, *The Agency*, 632.
25. Ranelagh, *The Agency*, 633.
26. Stansfield Turner, *Secrecy and Democracy: The CIA In Transition* (New York: Perennial Library, 1986), 17–18.
27. Edward Jay Epstein, "Who Killed the CIA," *Commentary*, October 1985, CIA/ERR.
28. Bearden and Risen, *The Main Enemy*, 63.
29. Bearden and Risen, *The Main Enemy*, 63.
30. To be fair, Colby planned to cut an even higher percentage of the Operations branch, but both he and his successor, George H. W. Bush, never followed through with the dismissals.
31. Bill Richards, "CIA Shaken by Job Cutbacks," *Washington Post*, December 4, 1977.
32. Ranelagh, *The Agency*, 636.
33. Epstein, "Who Killed the CIA?"
34. "Washington Whispers," *U.S. News & World Report*, April 3, 1978.
35. Benjamin F. Schemmer, "The Intelligence Community Against Turner," *The Washington Post*, April 8, 1979.

36. *Hearings Before the Select Committee on Intelligence . . . on Nomination of Admiral Stansfield Turner to be Director of Central Intelligence*, February 22 and 23, 1977, 95th Cong., 1st sess. (Washington, DC: GPO, 1977), 11.
37. *Hearings Before the Select Committee on Intelligence . . . on Nomination of Admiral Stansfield Turner to be Director of Central Intelligence*, 14.
38. Turner, *Secrecy and Democracy*, 28.
39. Stansfield Turner and George Thibault, "Intelligence: The Right Rules," *Foreign Policy* 48 (1982): 129–30. Turner's deference to the executive did not extend to the Reagan administration, which he openly and unabashedly criticized as part of the article and his book *Secrecy and Democracy*, both written during Reagan's presidency.
40. Loch K. Johnson, *America's Secret Power: The CIA in a Democratic Society* (New York: Oxford University Press, 1989), 208.
41. Ranelagh, *The Agency*, 635. The CIA held Nosenko for three years and interrogated him before finally declaring him a genuine defector in 1969. The subject of Nosenko's bona fides remains a matter of debate with Agency officers.
42. Epstein, "Who Killed the CIA?"
43. Address by Admiral Stansfield Turner to the National Press Club, October 25, 1978.
44. Turner, *Secrecy and Democracy*, 178–79.
45. George Lardner Jr., "Moynihan Unleashes the C.I.A.," *The Nation*, February 12, 1980, CIA/ERR.
46. Bearden and Risen, *The Main Enemy*, 63.
47. Turner, *Secrecy and Democracy*, 87.
48. Document 102, n. 9, Minutes of a Presidential Review Committee Meeting, *FRUS, 1977–1980*, vol. XII, *Afghanistan* (Washington, DC: GPO, 2018).
49. Elaine Kamarck, "The Iranian Hostage Crisis and Its Effect on American Politics," Brookings Institution, November 4, 2019.
50. McDonald, "Secrecy, Accountability, and the CIA," 397.
51. National Intelligence Reorganization and Reform Act, S. 2525, 95th Cong. (1978).
52. McDonald, "Secrecy, Accountability, and the CIA," 398.
53. *Hearings Before the Select Committee on Intelligence on S. 2525, National Intelligence Reorganization and Reform Act of 1978*, 95th Cong., 2nd sess. (Washington, DC: GPO, 1978), 11.
54. *Hearings on S. 2525*, 37, 45–46.
55. *Hearings on S. 2525*, 47, 49.
56. *Hearings on S. 2525*, 194–95.
57. Michael M. Uhlmann, "Approaches to Reform of the Intelligence Community," in *Intelligence Requirements for the 1980's: Elements of Intelligence*, ed. Roy Godson (Washington, DC: National Strategy Information Center, 1979), 14.
58. Hugh Tovar, "Covert Action," in *Intelligence Requirements for the 1980's: Elements of Intelligence* ed. Roy Godson (Washington, DC: National Strategy Information Center, 1979), 78.

59. Uhlmann, "Approaches to Reform of the Intelligence Community," 13–16.
60. Uhlmann, "Approaches to Reform of the Intelligence Community," 18.
61. *Hearings on S. 2525*, 48.
62. Like Presidents Tyler's and Polk's messages to Congress to protect their intelligence prerogatives vis-à-vis the Contingent Fund, in *Totten v. United States*, 92 U.S. 105 (1875), the executive successfully asserted its prerogative against intelligence oversight by the judicial branch. The precedent had lasting effects on judicial oversight of intelligence with respect to the state secrets privilege.
63. For example, *Katz v. United States*, 389 U.S. 347 (1967).
64. *US v. US District Court*, 407 U.S. 297 (1972).
65. See, for example, Senator Bayh's statement in *Hearings Before the Subcommittee on Intelligence and the Rights of Americans on S. 1566, Foreign Intelligence Surveillance Act of 1978*, 95th Congr., 2nd sess. (Washington, DC: GPO, 1978), 3, and Attorney General Bell's statement at 12.
66. Foreign Intelligence Surveillance Act. Pub. L. 95-511, 92 Stat. 1783. Originally proposed as S. 3197 in 1976, the act failed to reach the floor, but returned to the Senate as S. 1566 in 1977 before finally passing Congress in October 1978.
67. *Hearings on S. 1566*, 9.
68. There are exceptions outlined in the law that allow for warrantless collection.
69. William E. Conner, *Intelligence Oversight: The Controversy Behind the FY 1991 Intelligence Authorization Act* (McLean, VA: Association of Former Intelligence Officers, 1993), 13.
70. *Hearings on S. 2284, National Intelligence Act of 1980*, 96th Congr., 2nd sess. (Washington, DC: GPO, 1980), 11.
71. *Hearings on S. 2284*, 9.
72. Lardner, "Moynihan Unleashes the C.I.A."
73. "Moynihan Agonistes," *The Nation*, July 12, 1980, CIA/ERR.
74. Hearings on S. 2284, 100.
75. "Moynihan Agonistes"; *Hearings on S. 2284*, 17.
76. *Hearings on S. 2284*, 2–3.
77. *Hearings on S. 2284*, 45–46.
78. Presidential Finding of December 28, 1979, DNSA.
79. McDonald, "Secrecy, Accountability, and the CIA," 397. They were the House and Senate Armed Services Committees, the House and Senate Appropriations Committees, the House Foreign Affairs and Senate Foreign Relations Committees, and finally, HPSCI and SSCI.
80. *Hearings on S. 2284*, 47.
81. Philip Agee, *Inside the Company: CIA Diary* (New York: Farrar, Straus and Giroux, 1975).
82. *Hearings on S. 2284*, 165.
83. Memorandum of January 16, 1978, DNSA. The memorandum cites six examples, including MKULTRA and the Kennedy assassination.

84. "Archive Calls on CIA and Congress to Address Loophole Shielding CIA Records from the Freedom of Information Act," October 15, 2004, DNSA.

CHAPTER 19

1. Nicholas Dujmovic, "Reagan, Intelligence, Casey, and the CIA: A Reappraisal," *International Journal of Intelligence and CounterIntelligence* 26, no. 1 (2013): 5–9.
2. Dujmovic, "Reagan, Intelligence, Casey, and the CIA," 10–11.
3. Republican Party Platform of 1980, July 15, 1980, American Presidency Project, UCSB, https://www.presidency.ucsb.edu/documents/republican-party-platform-1980.
4. Turner and Thibault, "Intelligence: The Right Rules," 124.
5. Leslie H. Gelb, "Reagan Aides Describe Operations to Gather Inside Data on Carter," *New York Times*, July 7, 1983.
6. Quoted in article, "Did CIA Boss Spy for Reaganites?" UPI, July 21, 1983, FG006-02 Central Intelligence Agency, Box 191 (Folder 150000-164999), RRL.
7. Donald Freed, "A Question of Treason," *The Rebel*, November 22, 1983, CIA/ERR.
8. Freed, "A Question of Treason."
9. Joint Report of the Task Force to Investigate Certain Allegations Concerning the Holding of American Hostages by Iran in 1980, 102nd Cong., 2nd sess., H. Rept. No. 102-1102 (1993); David D. Kirkpatrick, "How a Chase Bank Chairman Helped the Deposed Shah of Iran Enter the U.S.," *New York Times*, December 29, 2019; Peter Baker, "A Four-Decade Secret: One Man's Story of Sabotaging Carter's Re-election," *New York Times*, March 18, 2023.
10. Rhoda Koenig, "Basket Casey," October 15, 1990, *New York Magazine*, 87.
11. Koenig, "Basket Casey," 88.
12. For example, Casey sent the President a clipping from the UK's *Sunday Express* in August 1983 with a cover letter advising him, "This is the greatest piece of political advocacy I have ever seen. If it can be translated into US terms, there'[ll] be another landslide." Casey to Reagan, August 13, 1983, Executive Secretariat, NSC: Agency File: Records, RAC Box 2 (Box 91373), CIA (4/21/82–8/7/82), RRL.
13. Bob Woodward, *Veil: The Secret Wars of the CIA, 1981–1987* (New York: Simon & Schuster, 2005), 21, 43.
14. See, for example, George Lardner Jr., "As Congress' Resolve Faded, so Did Proposed CIA Charter Commentary," *Washington Post*, May 5, 1980. Also see Jeffreys-Jones, *The CIA and American Democracy*, 227, although it is unclear if Reagan himself used these words.
15. *Hearing on Nomination of William J. Casey to be Director of Central Intelligence*, 97th Cong., 1st sess. (Washington, DC: GPO, 1981), 16, 25.
16. Executive Order 12333, December 4, 1981.
17. See EO 12036 sec. 3–4 vs. EO 12333 sec. 3.1.
18. Turner and Thibault, "Intelligence: The Right Rules," 128, 132.

19. Conner, *Intelligence Oversight*, 16.
20. John Brecher et al., "A Secret War for Nicaragua," *Newsweek*, November 8, 1982, CIA/ERR.
21. Milt Freudenheim and Barbara Slavin, "The World in Summary; Guerrillas Regroup as Carter Switches on Salvador Arms," *New York Times*, January 25, 1981.
22. "Radio Address to the Nation on the Situation in Central America," March 30, 1985, RRL.
23. "Finding Pursuant to Section 662 of the Foreign Assistance Act of 1961, As Amended, Concerning Operations Undertaken by the Central Intelligence Agency in Foreign Countries, Other than Those Intended Solely for the Purpose of Intelligence Collection," March 9, 1981, https://www.brown.edu/Research/Understanding_the_Iran_Contra_Affair/documents/d-nic-5.pdf.
24. "Finding Pursuant to Section 662 of the Foreign Assistance Act of 1961."
25. Steve Coll, *Ghost Wars: The Secret History of the CIA, Afghanistan, Bin Laden, from the Soviet Invasion to September 10, 2001* (New York: Penguin, 2004), 58.
26. Patrick Tyler et al., "Casey Enforces 'Reagan Doctrine' with Reinvigorated Covert Action," *Washington Post*, March 9, 1986.
27. "Summary of Boland Amendment Provisions," Arthur B. Culvahouse, Folder Title: Iran/Arms Transaction: Legal Memoranda—Nicaraguan Contra Aid [Boland Amendment], Box CFOA 1131, RRL.
28. 96 Stat. 1865.
29. *Report of the Congressional Committees Investigating the Iran-Contra Affair*, S. Rep. No. 216, H. Rep. No. 100-433, 100th Cong., 1st sess. (Washington, DC: GPO, 1987), 33. Hereafter "Iran-Contra Report."
30. H. Res. 159, 98th Cong. (1983).
31. Memorandum for Stanley Sporkin, General Counsel, from David S. Addington, Legislation Division, April 29, 1983, FG006-02 Central Intelligence Agency, Box 191 (Folder 330000-331999), RRL.
32. Finding of September 19, 1983, DNSA.
33. Iran-Contra Report, 35.
34. Iran-Contra Report, 36.
35. Philip Taubman, "How Congress Was Informed of Mining of Nicaragua Ports," *New York Times*, April 16, 1984; Employee Bulletin, April 12, 1984, GEN MSS 817, Box 21, WLPP.
36. Knott, *Secret and Sanctioned*, 179.
37. Iran-Contra Report, 37.
38. The accord and its addendum appeared in Robert Gates's confirmation hearing for DCI in 1987. See *Hearings Before SSCI on the Nomination of Robert M. Gates to be Director of Central Intelligence* (Washington, DC: GPO, 1987), 16–18.
39. Philip Taubman, "Aggressive C.I.A. Chief," *New York Times*, April 19, 1984.
40. Koenig, "Basket Casey," 88.
41. NSDD 159, January 18, 1985, RRL.

42. 98 Stat. 1935.
43. Iran-Contra Report, 43, 403–404.
44. Don Wallace Jr. and Allan Gerson, "The Dubious Boland Amendments," *Washington Post*, June 5, 1987.
45. Finding of January 17, 1986, DNSA.
46. *Report of the President's Special Review Board* (Washington, DC: GPO, 1987), I-1, IV 1-9. Hereafter "Tower Commission."
47. Tower Commission, IV-11, 14.
48. J. Y. Smith, "Former CIA Director William J. Casey Dies," *Washington Post*, May 7, 1987.
49. Tower Commission, V-4.
50. Address to the Nation on the Iran Arms and Contra Aid Controversy, March 4, 1987, RRL.
51. Tower Commission, V-6.
52. Iran-Contra Report, 11.
53. Iran-Contra Report, 16.
54. Iran-Contra Report, 17.
55. Testimony of William Casey to Senate Select Committee on Intelligence, December 16, 1986, White House Legal Task Force: Records Casey's Knowledge of Diversion Box 332 (Formally 92835), RRL.
56. Iran-Contra Report, 21.
57. *Final Report of the Independent Counsel for Iran/Contra Matters* (Washington, DC: U.S. Court of Appeals for the District of Columbia Circuit, 1993), 561.
58. "Excerpts from the Iran-Contra Report: A Secret Foreign Policy," *New York Times*, January 19, 1994.
59. Minority Report of Iran-Contra Report, 437–38.
60. Jeffreys-Jones, *The CIA and American Democracy*, 219.
61. Lee H. Hamilton, "The Trouble with 'Covert' Action," *Washington Post*, August 17, 1986.
62. Knott, *Secret and Sanctioned*, 177–78.
63. Stephen F. Knott, *Rush to Judgment: George W. Bush, The War on Terror, and His Critics* (Lawrence: University Press of Kansas, 2012), 59.
64. Knott, *Secret and Sanctioned*, 176.
65. Knott, *Rush to Judgment*, 61; Knott, *Secret and Sanctioned*, 179.
66. Hamilton, "The Trouble with 'Covert' Action."
67. Russell Watson with David C. Martin, "Is Covert Action Necessary?," *Newsweek*, November 8, 1982.
68. John P. Wallach, "CIA Plan Revealed: Mine 3 Nicaragua Harbors to Halt the Flow of Arms," *San Francisco Examiner & Chronicle*, July 17, 1983, CIA/ERR.
69. *Newsweek*, October 10, 1983, CIA/ERR.
70. Tyler et al., "Casey Enforces 'Reagan Doctrine' with Reinvigorated Covert Action."

71. Diana I. Bolsinger, "Overt Action: Congressional Oversight, Private Activism and Afghan Covert Action policy in the Reagan Administration," *Intelligence and National Security* 39, no. 5 (2024): 824–40.
72. See, for example, Stephen Kinzer, "Soviet Help to Sandinistas: No Blank Check," *New York Times*, March 28, 1984.
73. Tyler et al., "Casey Enforces 'Reagan Doctrine' with Reinvigorated Covert Action."
74. NSDD 159, January 18, 1985, RRL.
75. "What We Face," Fulton, Missouri, October 29, 1983, FG, Box 191, WHORM Subject File FG006-02 (Central Intelligence Agency) (190000-201999), RRL.
76. Dennis Volman, "Salvador Death Squads, a CIA Connection?" *Christian Science Monitor*, May 8, 1984.
77. "Address to the Nation on United States Policy in Central America," May 9, 1984, RRL.
78. Francis X. Clines, "The Reagan Speech," *New York Times*, May 10, 1984.
79. Memorandum for Robert C. McFarlane, May 10, 1984, FG, Box 191, WHORM Subject File FG006-02 (Central Intelligence Agency) (220000-249999), RRL.
80. "Radio Address to the Nation on the Situation in Central America," March 30, 1985, RRL.
81. "Radio Address to the Nation on the Central American Peace Proposal," April 20, 1985, RRL.
82. "Address to the Nation on the Iran Arms and Contra Aid Controversy," March 4, 1987, DNSA.
83. "Reagan Says U.S. Favors Covert Aid to Angola Rebels," *New York Times*, November 23, 1985.
84. William W. Pascoe III, "Angola Tests the Reagan Doctrine," Heritage Foundation, November 14, 1985.
85. Jim Hoagl, "The Year of the Spy," *Washington Post*, September 5, 1986.
86. For more on the National Security Archive's history, see https://nsarchive.gwu.edu/about.
87. WHORM Alpha File, Casey, William J., Folder 2 of 2, RRL.
88. Schlesinger, *The Imperial Presidency*, 453; Philip Geyelin, "Clark Clifford and the Iran-Contra 'Debacle,'" *Washington Post*, August 10, 1987.
89. Chester Pach, "The Reagan Doctrine: Principle, Pragmatism, and Policy," *Presidential Studies Quarterly* 36, no. 1 (2006): 88.
90. Watson and Martin, "Is Covert Action Necessary?"
91. Loch K. Johnson, "Covert Action and Accountability: Decision-Making for America's Secret Foreign Policy," *International Studies Quarterly* 33, no. 1 (1989): 105–7.
92. "Covert Action in the 80s," Memorandum from Robert M. Gates to DCI, September 16, 1981, CIA/ERR.
93. George Crile, *Charlie Wilson's War: The Extraordinary Story of the Largest Covert Operation in History* (New York: Atlantic Monthly Press, 2003), 514, 521.

CHAPTER 20

1. Schlesinger, *The Imperial Presidency*, 454–56.
2. NSDD 286, October 15, 1987.
3. Conner, *Intelligence Oversight*, 26.
4. Conner, *Intelligence Oversight*, 29.
5. Hearings Before the Select Committee on Intelligence on S. 1818, 100th Cong., 2nd sess., March 1, 1988.
6. Iran-Contra Report, 425.
7. Frederick M. Kaiser, "Inspector General in the CIA Compared to Other Statutory Inspectors General," CRS Report, December 21, 1989.
8. L. Britt Snider, "Creating a Statutory Inspector General at the CIA," *Studies in Intelligence* 44, no. 5 (2001): 15–21, 17–20.
9. Snider, *The Agency and the Hill*, 149.
10. Conner, *Intelligence Oversight*, 27.
11. Conner, *Intelligence Oversight*, 35–36.
12. Pub. L. 102-88, 105 Stat. 429 (1991).
13. Conner, *Intelligence Oversight*, 39.
14. Samuel Huntington framed American civil society's posture toward the military as one of "conform or die." Besides the policy of "transmutation," which forces the military to act in concordance with American principles, he also explained there was a policy of "extirpation," which meant the elimination of the military to "do away with the problem of civil-military relations entirely." The CIA teetered precariously between transmutation and extirpation in the early 1990s. Huntington, *The Soldier and the State*, 155.
15. Turner and Thibault, "Intelligence: The Right Rules," 138.
16. David L. Boren, "New World, New C.I.A.," *New York Times*, June 17, 1990.
17. Bearden and Risen, *The Main Enemy*, 518.
18. S. 236, End of the Cold War Act of 1991, January 17, 1991.
19. Eric Kocher, "Usually Unnecessary, Often Undesirable, That's the C.I.A.," *New York Times*, June 16, 1991.
20. "About Us—Bureau of Intelligence and Research," US Department of State, https://www.state.gov/about-us-bureau-of-intelligence-and-research/.
21. Stansfield Turner, "Intelligence for a New World Order," *Foreign Affairs* 70, no. 4 (1991): 161–62.
22. Turner, "Intelligence for a New World Order," 158–65.
23. Bruce D. Berkowitz, "US Intelligence Estimates of the Soviet Collapse: Reality and Perception," *International Journal of Intelligence and CounterIntelligence* 21, no. 2 (2008): 245.
24. Daniel P. Moynihan, "The State Dept. Can Do the Job," *New York Times*, May 19, 1991.
25. Indeed, the CIA faced the continued problem of subordination not only to the State Department but also the DOD following the end of the Cold War, just as it

had at the beginning. See David P. Oakley, *Subordinating Intelligence: The DoD/CIA Post-Cold War Relationship* (Lexington: University Press of Kentucky, 2019).

26. Bud Shuster, "Independence Means Integrity," *New York Times*, May 19, 1991.
27. David Boren, "The Intelligence Community: How Crucial?" *Foreign Affairs* 71, no. 3 (1992): 54.
28. Walter Pincus, "Specter Urges Splitting Top CIA Post, Tougher Penalty for Lying," *Washington Post*, October 28, 1987.
29. Pub. L. 99-433, 100 Stat. 992, October 1, 1986. For more on the history of Goldwater-Nichols, see James R. Locher III, *Victory on the Potomac: The Goldwater-Nichols Act Unifies the Pentagon* (College Station: Texas A&M University Press, 2002).
30. H.R. 4165, National Security Act of 1992, 102nd Cong.; S. 2198, Intelligence Reorganization Act of 1992, 102nd Cong.
31. The House bill specified that the DNI would not be an active-duty officer of the armed forces while the Deputy DNI would be. The Senate bill said that one or the other, but not both, would be either an active-duty or retired military officer.
32. Elaine Sciolino, "Lawmakers Unveil Spy Agency Plan," *New York Times*, February 6, 1992.
33. George Lardner Jr., "Intelligence Overhaul Urged," *Washington Post*, February 6, 1992.
34. Lardner, "Intelligence Overhaul Urged."
35. Cong. Rec., 102nd Cong., 2nd sess., 1543.
36. Lardner, "Intelligence Overhaul Urged."
37. *Joint Hearing Before SSCI and HPSCI on S. 2198 and S. 421 to Reorganize the United States Intelligence Community* (Washington, DC: GPO, 1993), 3.
38. Sciolino, "Lawmakers Unveil Spy Agency Plan"; Lardner, "Intelligence Overhaul Urged."
39. Sciolino, "Lawmakers Unveil Spy Agency Plan."
40. *Joint Hearing Before SSCI and HPSCI on S. 2198 and S. 421*, 17–19.
41. Letter from Dick Cheney to Les Aspin, March 17, 1992, https://fas.org/irp/congress/1992_cr/cheney1992.pdf.
42. ACLU Memorandum of February 20, 1992, *Joint Hearing Before SSCI and HPSCI on S. 2198 and S. 421*, 92–99; Letter to David Boren and Frank Murkowski from Morton Halperin, April 24, 1992, *Joint Hearing Before SSCI and HPSCI on S. 2198 and S. 421*, 119–21.
43. Cong. Rec., 102nd Cong., 2nd sess., 30523.
44. Pub. L. 102-496, 106 Stat. 3180 (1993).
45. Frank J. Smist Jr., *Congress Oversees the United States Intelligence Community, 1947–1994*, 2nd ed. (Knoxville: University of Tennessee Press, 1994), 293.
46. Sciolino, "Lawmakers Unveil Spy Agency Plan."
47. Lardner, "Intelligence Overhaul Urged."
48. Cong. Rec., 102nd Cong., 2nd sess., 1543.

49. Cong. Rec., 102nd Cong., 2nd sess., 1674.
50. Cong. Rec., 102nd Cong., 2nd sess., 1543.
51. Cong. Rec., 102nd Cong., 2nd sess., 30522.
52. Cong. Rec., 102nd Cong., 2nd sess., 16237–38.
53. Cong. Rec., 102nd Cong., 2nd sess., 30523.
54. Cong. Rec., 102nd Cong., 2nd sess., 16237.
55. Turner, "Intelligence for a New World Order," 151–59.
56. See, for example, *Hearings Before the Committee on Foreign Affairs House of Representatives, 102nd Cong., 2nd Sess.* (Washington, DC: GPO, 1992); *Special Report Committee Activities of SSCI, 103rd Cong., 1st sess., January 3, 1991, to October 8, 1992* (Washington, DC: GPO, 1993).
57. *Hearings Before the Committee on Foreign Affairs, 102nd Congr., 2nd Sess.*, 211.
58. *Joint Hearing Before SSCI and HPSCI on S. 2198 and S. 421*, 11.
59. Elaine Sciolino, "C.I.A. Casting About for New Missions," *New York Times*, February 4, 1992.
60. Sciolino, "C.I.A. Casting About for New Missions."
61. R. Jeffrey Smith, "As Woolsey Struggles, CIA Suffers," *Washington Post*, May 10, 1994.
62. Jeffreys-Jones, *Cloak and Dollar*, 261.
63. Stephen Engelberg, "Spy Agency Under Siege," *New York Times*, December 29, 1994.
64. R. Jeffrey Smith, "As Woolsey Struggles, CIA Suffers."; Tim Weiner, "Director of C.I.A. to Leave, Ending Troubled Tenure," *New York Times*, December 29, 1994.
65. Weiner, "Director of C.I.A. to Leave, Ending Troubled Tenure."
66. Riebling, *Wedge*, 432–33, 445–46.
67. Tim Weiner, "Director of C.I.A. to Leave, Ending Troubled Tenure."
68. Tim Weiner, "Agency Chief Pledges to Overhaul 'Fraternity' Atmosphere at C.I.A.," *New York Times*, July 19, 1994.
69. Engelberg, "Spy Agency Under Siege"; Weiner, "Director of C.I.A. to Leave, Ending Troubled Tenure."
70. S. 126, introduced January 4, 1995.
71. For the six, see Warner, *Central Intelligence: Origin and Evolution*, 13.
72. Loch K. Johnson, "The Aspin-Brown Intelligence Inquiry: Behind the Closed Doors of a Blue Ribbon Commission," *Studies in Intelligence* 48, no. 3 (2004): 1–20.
73. L. Britt Snider, "A Different Angle on the Aspin-Brown Commission," *Studies in Intelligence* 49, no. 1 (2005).
74. Smist, *Congress Oversees the United States Intelligence Community*, 316–17.
75. Commission on the Roles and Capabilities of the US Intelligence Community, 149. Hereafter "Aspin-Brown Commission Report."
76. Snider, "A Different Angle on the Aspin-Brown Commission."
77. Johnson, "The Aspin-Brown Intelligence Inquiry."

78. Warner, "Central Intelligence: Origin and Evolution," 14–15.
79. Aspin-Brown Commission Report, xvi.
80. Johnson, "The Aspin-Brown Intelligence Inquiry."
81. Aspin-Brown Commission Report, 61.
82. "Making Intelligence Smarter," Council on Foreign Relations, 1996.
83. Daniel Schorr, "Get Smart: Spies Posing as Reporters Is a Stupid Idea," *Washington Post*, February 4, 1996.
84. Richard N. Haass, "Don't Hobble Intelligence Gathering," *Washington Post*, February 15, 1996.
85. Mark D. Gearan, "Don't Spook the Peace Corps," *Washington Post*, March 02, 1996.
86. *Commission on Protecting and Reducing Government Secrecy* (Washington, DC: GPO, 1997), XXXI.
87. *Commission on Protecting and Reducing Government Secrecy*, XXXVI–XXXVII, A-3.
88. Daniel Patrick Moynihan, *Secrecy* (New Haven, CT: Yale University Press, 1998).
89. Jeffreys-Jones, *Cloak and Dollar*, 272.
90. Jeffreys-Jones, *Cloak and Dollar*, 263, 270.
91. Seymour M. Hersh, "The Intelligence Gap: How the Digital Age Left Our Spies Out in the Cold," *New Yorker*, December 6, 1999: 58–76.
92. Aspin-Brown Commission Report, 24.
93. Haass, "Don't Hobble Intelligence Gathering."

CHAPTER 21

1. Gary C. Schroen, *First In: An Insider's Account of How the CIA Spearheaded the War on Terror in Afghanistan* (New York: Presidio Press, 2006), 46–47.
2. National Commission on Terrorist Attacks upon the United States, *The 9/11 Commission Report* (Washington, DC: GPO, 2004), 357, http://govinfo.library.unt.edu/911/report/911Report.pdf.
3. For more on the CIA and its relationship with Massoud before 9/11, see Coll, *Ghost Wars*, 346–47, 458–59, 488–89.
4. Schroen, *First In*, 63.
5. *The 9/11 Commission Report*, 114.
6. Coll, *Ghost Wars*, 487–89. The 9/11 Commission Report claims the operation took place in December 1999. See *The 9/11 Commission Report*, 187–88.
7. Gary Berntsen and Ralph Pezzullo, *Jawbreaker: The Attack on bin Laden and Al-Qaeda: A Personal Account by the CIA's Key Field Commander* (New York: Three Rivers Press, 2005), 62.
8. Coll, *Ghost Wars*, 490.
9. James Risen, "The Nation: The Clinton Administration's See-No-Evil C.I.A.," *New York Times*, September 10, 2000.

10. For the Phoenix Memo, see *The 9/11 Commission Report*, 272; for the PDB, see *The 9/11 Commission Report*, 261–62.
11. See, for example, Memorandum, "The Phoenix and Provincial Reconnaissance Unit Programs," December 16, 1969, CIA/ERR.
12. Barton Gellman, "CIA Weighs 'Targeted Killing' Missions," *Washington Post*, October 28, 2001; James Risen and David Johnston, "Threats and Responses: Hunt for Al Qaeda; Bush Has Widened Authority of C.I.A. to Kill Terrorists," *New York Times*, December 15, 2002; David Johnston, "At a Secret Interrogation, Dispute Flared over Tactics," *New York Times*, September 10, 2006.
13. Bob Woodward, *Bush at War* (New York: Simon & Schuster, 2002), 100.
14. Schroen, *First In*, 38.
15. Woodward, *Bush at War*, 97.
16. Bearden and Risen, *The Main Enemy*, 530–33.
17. Berntsen, *Jawbreaker*, 87.
18. Convergence of civilian intelligence and military special operations posed problems ranging from the laws of armed conflict and just-war theory to issues in control and oversight as the CIA and military special operations can attempt to shift activities between Title 10 and Title 50 authorities to evade congressional oversight or budget restrictions. In recent years, the military has conducted more intelligence-style operations under the Title 10 banner of "traditional military activities," obstructing congressional oversight. See, for example, Robert Chesney, "Military-Intelligence Convergence and the Law of the Title 10/Title 50 Debate," *Journal of National Security Law and Policy* 5, no. 2 (2012): 539–629; Andru Wall, "Demystifying the Title 10–Title 50 Debate: Distinguishing Military Operations, Intelligence Activities and Covert Action," *Harvard National Security Journal* 3, no. 1 (2011): 85–142.
19. Barton Gellman, "Secret Unit Expands Rumsfeld's Domain," *Washington Post*, January 23, 2005.
20. Gellman, "Secret Unit Expands Rumsfeld's Domain."
21. Douglas Jehl and Eric Schmitt, "Reports on Pentagon's New Spy Units Set Off Questions in Congress," *New York Times*, January 25, 2005.
22. Gellman, "Secret Unit Expands Rumsfeld's Domain"; Jehl and Schmitt, "Reports on Pentagon's New Spy Units Set Off Questions in Congress."
23. 50 USC § 3093(e).
24. Jehl and Schmitt, "Reports on Pentagon's New Spy Units Set Off Questions in Congress."
25. John Walcott and Andy Pasztor, "Reagan Ruling to Let CIA Kidnap Terrorists Overseas Is Disclosed," *Wall Street Journal*, February 20, 1987.
26. Gellman, "CIA Weighs 'Targeted Killing' Missions."
27. Knott, *Rush to Judgment*, 60.
28. Joint Resolution to Authorize the Use of United States Armed Force Against Those Responsible for the Recent Attacks Launched Against the United States, Pub. L. 107-40, 115 Stat. 224 (2001).

29. Richard F. Grimmett, "Authorization for Use of Military Force in Response to the 9/11 Attacks (P.L. 107-40): Legislative History," CRS Report, January 16, 2007.
30. Most recently with U.S. troops fighting ISIS in Syria. See "Trump Approves Wider Syria Oil-Protection Mission, Raising Questions on Whether U.S. troops Can Launch Strikes in Region," Associated Press, November 5, 2019.
31. See, for example, "Reforming the Authorizations for Use of Military Force," Session 13 of the Congressional Study Group, Brookings Institution, May 11, 2022, https://www.brookings.edu/articles/reforming-the-authorizations-for-use-of-military-force/; Brian Finucane, "The House Tackles Zombie War Authorizations: Possibilities and Perils," Just Security, August 14, 2023, https://www.justsecurity.org/87560/the-house-tackles-zombie-war-authorizations-possibilities-and-perils/; David Cole, "Killing Citizens in Secret," *New York Times Review of Books*, October 9, 2011.
32. USA PATRIOT Act of 2001, Pub. L. 107-56.
33. 115 Stat. 389.
34. 115 Stat. 281.
35. 115 Stat. 284–85.
36. Working Draft, Office of the Inspector General, National Security Agency, March 24, 2009, ACLU (henceforth "Working Draft, NSA OIG Report"); Report on the President's Surveillance Program, OIG Report by DOD, DOJ, CIA, NSA, ODNI, July 10, 2009, DOJ/OIG.
37. John Yoo, Memorandum for the Attorney General, November 2, 2001, ACLU.
38. Report on the President's Surveillance Program, 9–14.
39. Working Draft, NSA OIG Report, 5.
40. Report on the President's Surveillance Program, 6.
41. Report on the President's Surveillance Program.
42. Genevieve Lester and Jeffrey Rogg, "Intelligence and Oversight: A View of the US System," in *Intelligence Oversight in the Twenty-First Century*, ed. Ian Leigh and Njord Wegge (London: Routledge, 2019), 146.
43. Report on the President's Surveillance Program, 26.
44. Working Draft, NSA OIG Report, 36.
45. Working Draft, NSA OIG Report, 43–46.
46. Working Draft, NSA OIG Report, 29.
47. "Two Decades Later, the Enduring Legacy of 9/11," Pew Research Center, September 2, 2021. Italics appear in the original source.

CHAPTER 22

1. David Kohn, "Bush on 9/11: Moment to Moment," CBS News, September 3, 2002.
2. Bootie Cosgrove-Mather, "9-11 Relatives Grill Bush Administration," CBS News, September 20, 2002.

3. Report of the National Commission on Terrorism, "Countering the Changing Threat of International Terrorism," Pursuant to Public Law 277, 105th Cong., iv, 7–31, DNSA.
4. United States Commission on National Security/21st Century, "Road Map for National Security: Imperative for Change," January 2001, 82–85.
5. Henry Kissinger, "Destroy the Network," *Washington Post*, September 12, 2001.
6. Joint Inquiry into Intelligence Community Activities Before and After the Terrorist Attacks of September 11, 2001, 107th Cong., 2nd sess., S. Rept. No. 107–351, H. Rept. No. 107-792, December 2002, xi. Hereafter "9/11 Joint Inquiry Report."
7. 9/11 Joint Inquiry Report, 39.
8. 9/11 Joint Inquiry Report, 2–13.
9. Cosgrove-Mather, "9-11 Relatives Grill Bush Administration."
10. Jim Dwyer, "Investigating 9/11: An Unimaginable Calamity, Still Largely Unexamined," *New York Times*, September 11, 2002.
11. Pete Brush, "Bush Opposes 9/11 Query Panel," CBS News, May 15, 2002.
12. "Bush Asks Daschle to Limit Sept. 11 Probes," *CNN*, January 29, 2002.
13. Intelligence Authorization Act for FY 2003, Pub. L. 107-306, 116 Stat. 2408, Title VI, Section 602(3).
14. Final Report of the National Commission on Terrorist Attacks upon the United States, *The 9/11 Commission Report*, xviii.
15. *The 9/11 Commission Report*, 377.
16. *The 9/11 Commission Report*, 411, 415.
17. *The 9/11 Commission Report*, 426.
18. *The 9/11 Commission Report*, 419–21.
19. "Senate and House Intelligence Committees Announce Joint Inquiry into the September 11th Terrorist Attacks," SSCI press release, February 14, 2002.
20. Richard Posner explains that policymakers have displayed a "preference for bipartisan over nonpartisan composition, which tends to politicize the commissions." Furthermore, they suffer from the "pressure for unanimity—in part to dispel the impression of politicization, but with the effect of making the commission's recommendations a product of political compromise." Posner, *Uncertain Shield*, 7.
21. "Congress Sets Inquiry on U.S. Flaws in Attack," *New York Times*, February 12, 2002.
22. "Senate and House Intelligence Committees Announce Joint Inquiry into the September 11th Terrorist Attacks," SSCI press release.
23. Thomas H. Kean and Lee H. Hamilton, *Without Precedent: The Inside Story of the 9/11 Commission* (New York: Alfred A. Knopf, 2006), 17, 290, 308.
24. See, for example, Glenn Kessler, "Bill Clinton and the Missed Opportunities to Kill Osama bin Laden," *Washington Post*, February 16, 2016.; Warren Bass, "The Bin Laden Attack That Two Presidents Failed to Answer," *Wall Street Journal*, January 10, 2019; Chris Whipple, "CIA Director Documentary: 'The Attacks Will Be Spectacular,'" Politico, November 12, 2015.

25. "Transcript: Interview with Bob Graham," *New York Times*, September 6, 2002.
26. *The 9/11 Commission Report*, 107.
27. *The 9/11 Commission Report*, 105. Amy Zegart agrees: "While Congress has been instrumental in many post-9/11 executive branch reforms, Congress has largely been unable to reform itself." In fact, "by the fall of 2007, the Senate Select Committee on Intelligence grew so deeply concerned that it held a hearing on itself." Amy Zegart, *Eyes on Spies: Congress and the United States Intelligence Community* (Stanford, CA: Hoover Institution Press, 2011), 3–4.
28. Transcript of 9/11 Commission News Conference, CNN, July 22, 2004.
29. Thomas H. Kean and Lee H. Hamilton, "Stonewalled by the C.I.A.," *Washington Post*, January 2, 2008.
30. Statement of Cofer Black, Hearings Before the Joint Inquiry, September 26, 2002.
31. Testimony of Attorney General John Ashcroft, April 13, 2004, National Commission on Terrorist Attacks upon the United States.
32. Neil A. Lewis, "Rule Created Legal 'Wall' to Sharing Information," *New York Times*, April 14, 2004.
33. David Stout, "Ashcroft Faults Clinton Era at 9/11 Panel," *New York Times*, April 13, 2004; "Jamie Gorelick's Wall," *Washington Times*, April 15, 2004.
34. Jamie S. Gorelick, "The Truth About 'the Wall,'" *Washington Post*, April 18, 2004.
35. Slade Gorton, "Defending the September 11 Commission," *Washington Times*, August 17, 2005.
36. *The 9/11 Commission Report*, 79.
37. See, for example, James Gordon Meek, "Exclusive: CIA's Tenet Blames FBI for 9/11 in Memoir," New York *Daily News*, February 21, 2013; Jeff Stein, "FBI Agent: The CIA Could Have Stopped 9/11," *Newsweek*, June 19, 2015.
38. Michael Allen, *Blinking Red: Crisis and Compromise in American Intelligence After 9/11* (Washington, DC: Potomac Books, 2013), 42.
39. Allen, *Blinking Red*, 43.
40. Allen, *Blinking Red*, 43.
41. Richard Gid Powers, *Broken: The Troubled Past and Uncertain Future of the FBI* (New York: Free Press, 2004), 404, 424.
42. *The 9/11 Commission Report*, 423.
43. Posner, *Uncertain Shield*, 101. For more of Posner's work on the subject, see Richard A. Posner, "Our Domestic Intelligence Crisis," *Washington Post*, December 21, 2005; Richard A. Posner, "Time to Rethink the FBI," *Wall Street Journal*, March 19, 2007.
44. Statement of Pat Roberts, *Hearings on Reform of the United States Intelligence Community*, 108th Cong., 2nd sess., S. Hrg. 108-835, September 7, 2004 (Washington, DC: GPO, 2005), 82–83.
45. Intelligence Reform and Terrorism Prevention Act of 2004, Pub. L. 108-458.
46. 118 Stat. 3656.
47. 118 Stat. 3650.

48. President's Remarks on Intelligence Reform, August 2, 2004, https://georgewbush-whitehouse.archives.gov/news/releases/2004/08/20040802-2.html.
49. For a few examples, see Allen, *Blinking Red*, 13–14. Rumsfeld was Secretary of Defense from 1975 to 1977, and Cheney held the post from 1989 to 1993.
50. Allen, *Blinking Red*, 53–54.
51. Allen, *Blinking Red*, 60–63, 86–88, 106.
52. *The 9/11 Commission Report*, 410.
53. 118 Stat. 3645; Allen, *Blinking Red*, 171.
54. John D. Bansemer, *Intelligence Reform: A Question of Balance* (Maxwell AFB, AL: Air University Press, 2006), 96.
55. Allen, *Blinking Red*, 160–62.
56. Gellman, "Secret Unit Expands Rumsfeld's Domain."
57. John Hamre, "A Better Way to Improve Intelligence," *Washington Post*, August 9, 2004.
58. Allen, *Blinking Red*, 68.
59. *The 9/11 Commission Report*, 412.
60. Allen, *Blinking Red*, 172–73.
61. EO 12333, United States Intelligence Activities, as amended 2008.
62. Pam Benson, "In Today's Intelligence Hierarchy, Who *Really* Runs the Show?" CNN, February 12, 2009.
63. Allen, *Blinking Red*, 34–36, 86–89; *The 9/11 Commission Report*, 413.
64. Robert M. Gates, "Racing to Ruin the C.I.A.," *New York Times*, June 8, 2004.
65. Douglas Jehl, "Will More Power for Intelligence Chief Mean Better Results?" *New York Times*, December 8, 2004.
66. Allen, *Blinking Red*, 169; Gates, "Racing to Ruin the C.I.A."
67. SSCI Hearings on Reform of the United States Intelligence Community, S. Hrg. 108-835, 75, 77, 86, 105, 106.
68. S. Hrg. 108-835, 106.
69. 118 Stat. 3655.
70. Benson, "In Today's Intelligence Hierarchy, Who *Really* Runs the Show?"
71. 118 Stat. 3660.
72. Benson, "In Today's Intelligence Hierarchy, Who *Really* Runs the Show?"
73. 118 Stat. 3661.
74. Allen, *Blinking Red*, 176.
75. Mark Mazzetti, "Turf Battles on Intelligence Pose Test for Spy Chiefs," *New York Times*, June 8, 2009.
76. 118 Stat. 3649.
77. 118 Stat. 3662; William Y. Chin, "Diversity in the Age of Terror: How Racial and Ethnic Diversity in the U.S. Intelligence Community Enhances National Security," *Florida A&M University Law Review* 6, no. 1 (2010): 49–88.
78. 118 Stat. 3700-02.
79. Troy, *Donovan and the CIA*, 346.

80. Michael Turner, "A Distinctive U.S. Intelligence Identity," *International Journal of Intelligence and CounterIntelligence* 17, no. 1 (2004), 51.

CHAPTER 23

1. R. Jeffrey Smith, "Hussein's Prewar Ties to Al-Qaeda Discounted," *Washington Post*, April 6, 2007.
2. Michelle Nichols, "Ex-CIA Chief Says 'Slam Dunk' Iraq Quote Misused," Reuters, April 26, 2007.
3. "Report on Postwar Findings About Iraq's WMD Programs and Links to Terrorism and How They Compare with Prewar Assessments," 109th Cong., 2nd sess., S. Report 109-331.
4. Executive Order 13328, February 6, 2004.
5. Dana Milbank, "After 14-Month Inquiry, Many Questions Remain," *Washington Post*, April 1, 2005.
6. "Authorization for Use of Military Force Against Iraq Resolution of 2002," Pub. L. 107-243, 116 Stat. 1498.
7. Milbank, "After 14-Month Inquiry, Many Questions Remain."
8. Letter to the President delivered with the report. "The Commission on the Intelligence Capabilities of the United States Regarding Weapons of Mass Destruction: Report to the President of the United States," March 31, 2005. Hereafter "Robb-Silberman Report."
9. Mark M. Lowenthal, "The Real Intelligence Failure? Spineless Spies," *Washington Post*, May 25, 2008.
10. Seymour M. Hersh, "Selective Intelligence," *New Yorker*, May 5, 2003.
11. Hersh, "Selective Intelligence."
12. Robert D. Novak, "Mission to Niger," *Washington Post*, July 14, 2003.
13. Joseph C. Wilson IV, "What I Didn't Find in Africa," *New York Times*, July 6, 2003.
14. Novak, "Mission to Niger."
15. The FBI investigated the case as a violation of the Intelligence Identities Protection Act of 1982. Ultimately, only Libby was charged and convicted for perjury and obstruction of justice. Bush commuted his sentence, and President Donald Trump pardoned him in 2018.
16. *Hearing Before the Committee on Oversight and Government Reform, White House Procedures for Safeguarding Classified Information*, Serial No. 110-28, 110th Cong., 1st sess. (Washington, DC: GPO, 2008), 18, 32.
17. *Report on Prewar Intelligence Assessments About Postwar Iraq*, SSCI, S. Report 110-76, 110th Cong., 1st sess. (Washington, DC: GPO, 2007), 207–11.
18. For a detailed account, see Steven Hendricks, *A Kidnapping in Milan: The CIA on Trial* (New York: W. W. Norton, 2010).
19. John Crewdson, "Italy Says CIA May Have Had Distorted View of Cleric," *Chicago Tribune*, January 8, 2007.

20. Craig Whitlock, "CIA Ruse Is Said to Have Damaged Probe in Milan," *Washington Post*, December 6, 2005.
21. Dana Priest, "Italy Knew About Plan to Grab Suspect," *Washington Post*, June 30, 2005.
22. Richard Norton-Taylor, "High-Flying Lifestyle of the CIA's Rendition Men," *The Guardian*, October 25, 2006.
23. Peter Bergen, "Exclusive: I Was Kidnapped by the CIA," *Mother Jones*, March/April 2008; H. D. S. Greenway, "The CIA's Italian Job," *New York Times*, July 20, 2005.
24. Priest, "Italy Knew About Plan to Grab Suspect."
25. Hendricks, *A Kidnapping in Milan*, 270; John Crewdson, "CIA Chiefs Reportedly Split over Cleric Plot," *Chicago Tribune*, January 8, 2007.
26. Crewdson, "CIA Chiefs Reportedly Split over Cleric Plot."
27. Alan Clarke, *Rendition to Torture* (New Brunswick, NJ: Rutgers University Press: 2012), 78.
28. Stephen Grey, "America's Gulag," *New Statesman*, May 17, 2004.
29. Richard A. Clarke, *Against All Enemies: Inside America's War on Terror* (New York: Free Press, 2004), 144.
30. Dick Marty (Switzerland, ALDE), "Alleged Secret Detentions and Unlawful Inter-State Transfers Involving Council of Europe Member States," Draft Report—Part II (Explanatory Memorandum), Parliamentary Assembly of the Council of Europe, Committee on Legal Affairs and Human Rights, June 7, 2006, 10.
31. R. Jeffrey Smith, "U.S. Probes Blasts' Possible Mideast Ties," *Washington Post*, August 12, 1998; Andrew Higgins and Christopher Cooper, "CIA-Backed Team Used Brutal Means to Break Up Terrorist Cell in Albania," *Wall Street Journal*, November 20, 2001.
32. Jane Mayer, *Dark Side: The Inside Story of How the War on Terror Turned into a War on American Ideals* (New York: Doubleday, 2008), 114.
33. Marty, "Alleged Secret Detentions and Unlawful Inter-State Transfers Involving Council of Europe Member States."
34. Grey, "America's Gulag."
35. Whitlock, "CIA Ruse Is Said to Have Damaged Probe in Milan."
36. "Italy: Egyptian Cleric Convicted," *New York Times*, December 7, 2013.
37. David Johnston, "U.S. Says Rendition to Continue, but With More Oversight," *New York Times*, August 24, 2009.
38. Jane Mayer, "Outsourcing Torture: The Secret History of America's 'Extraordinary Rendition' Program," *New Yorker*, February 7, 2005.
39. Dana Priest and Barton Gellman, "U.S. Decries Abuse but Defends Interrogations," *Washington Post*, December 26, 2002.
40. *KUBARK Counterintelligence Interrogation*, July 1963, DNSA.
41. *Human Resource Exploitation Training Manual*, 1983, DNSA.
42. Presidential Memorandum of February 7, 2002, DNSA.

43. Memorandum for William J. Haynes, II, General Counsel, Department of Defense, from Office of Legal Counsel, US Department of Justice, March 14, 2003, DNSA; Memorandum for John Rizzo, Acting General Counsel of the Central Intelligence Agency from Office of Legal Counsel, US Department of Justice, August 1, 2002; Scott Shane, "Waterboarding Used 266 Times on 2 Suspects," *New York Times*, April 19, 2009; Tim Golden and Don van Natta Jr., "U.S. Said to Overstate Value of Guantánamo Detainees," *New York Times*, June 21, 2004.
44. The following events are drawn heavily from SSCI's "Committee Study of the Central Intelligence Agency's Detention and Interrogation Program," 113th Cong., 2nd sess., S. Report 113-288. Hereafter "SSCI Report on CIA's Detention and Interrogation Program."
45. Priest and Gellman, "U.S. Decries Abuse but Defends Interrogations."
46. Dana Priest, "CIA Avoids Scrutiny of Detainee Treatment," *Washington Post*, March 3, 2005.
47. Memorandum for Deputy Director for Operations, Subject: Death Investigation—Gul Rahman, January 28, 2003, CIA/ERR; SSCI Report on CIA's Detention and Interrogation Program, 60.
48. SSCI Report on CIA's Detention and Interrogation Program, 50n240.
49. SSCI Report on CIA's Detention and Interrogation Program, 57.
50. SSCI Report on CIA's Detention and Interrogation Program, 62.
51. Dana Priest, "CIA Holds Terror Suspects in Secret Prisons," *Washington Post*, November 2, 2005.
52. Mark Mazzetti and Scott Shane, "Bush Lawyers Discussed Fate of C.I.A. Tapes," *New York Times*, December 19, 2007.
53. Dana Priest, "CIA Holds Terror Suspects in Secret Prisons."
54. *Rasul v. Bush*, 542 U.S. 466 (2004); SSCI Report on CIA's Detention and Interrogation Program, xxv.
55. Dana Priest and Dan Eggen, "Terror Suspect Alleges Torture," *Washington Post*, January 6, 2005.
56. Mayer, *Dark Side*, 127.
57. *Hamdan v. Rumsfeld*, 548 U.S. 557 (2006); SSCI Report on CIA's Detention and Interrogation Program, xxv.
58. Jack L. Goldsmith, *The Terror Presidency* (New York: W. W. Norton), 151.
59. Goldsmith, *The Terror Presidency*, 163.
60. Goldsmith, *The Terror Presidency*, 163–64, 205–7.
61. SSCI Report on CIA's Detention and Interrogation Program, v.
62. SSCI Report on CIA's Detention and Interrogation Program, xiv–xv.
63. Priest, "CIA Avoids Scrutiny of Detainee Treatment."
64. Jose A. Rodriguez, "Today's CIA Critics Once Urged the Agency to Do Anything to Fight al-Qaeda," *Washington Post*, December 5, 2014.
65. Mark Mazzetti, "Behind Clash Between C.I.A. and Congress, a Secret Report on Interrogations," *New York Times*, March 7, 2014.

66. Mark Mazzetti and Jonathan Weisman, "Conflict Erupts in Public Rebuke on C.I.A. Inquiry," *New York Times*, March 11, 2014.
67. Conor Friedersdorf, "A Brief History of the CIA's Unpunished Spying on the Senate," *The Atlantic*, December 23, 2014.
68. Chris Whipple, "CIA Director Documentary: 'The Attacks Will Be Spectacular,' " *Politico Magazine*, November 12, 2015.
69. OLC Memorandum of May 30, 2005, 38, OLC.
70. "Terrorism," Gallup, https://news.gallup.com/poll/4909/terrorism-united-states.aspx.
71. Priest and Gellman, "U.S. Decries Abuse but Defends Interrogations."
72. OLC Memorandum of May 30, 2005, 10–11.
73. Mark Mazzetti, "C.I.A. Report Found Value of Brutal Interrogation Was Inflated," *New York Times*, January 20, 2015; SSCI Report on CIA's Detention and Interrogation Program, 85–87.
74. SSCI Report on CIA's Detention and Interrogation Program, xvii.
75. Whipple, "CIA Director Documentary: 'The Attacks Will Be Spectacular.' "
76. "Transcript: President Bush's Speech on Terrorism," *New York Times*, September 6, 2006.
77. Priest, "CIA Holds Terror Suspects in Secret Prisons."
78. SSCI Report on CIA's Detention and Interrogation Program, xxiv–xxv.
79. OLC Memorandum of May 30, 2005, 39.
80. James Risen and Eric Lichtblau, "Bush Lets U.S. Spy on Callers Without Courts," *New York Times*, December 16, 2005.
81. James Risen, *Pay Any Price: Greed, Power, and Endless War* (Boston: Mariner Books, 2015), 270–71.
82. Report on the President's Surveillance Program, 44–45, 49.
83. Report on the President's Surveillance Program, 54.
84. Report on the President's Surveillance Program, 50–53, 250–51; Working Draft, NSA OIG Report, 37–42.
85. James Risen and Eric Lichtblau, "Court Affirms Wiretapping Without Warrants," *New York Times*, January 15, 2009; Del Quentin Wilber and R. Jeffrey Smith, "Intelligence Court Releases Ruling in Favor of Warrantless Wiretapping," *Washington Post*, January 16, 2009.
86. Report on the President's Surveillance Program, 259–66.
87. Eric Lichtblau and Scott Shane, "Files Say Agency Initiated Growth of Spying Effort," *New York Times*, January 4, 2006.
88. Working Draft, NSA OIG Report, 3.
89. Lichtblau and Shane, "Files Say Agency Initiated Growth of Spying Effort."
90. Risen and Lichtblau, "Bush Lets U.S. Spy on Callers Without Courts"; Frederick A. O. Schwarz Jr. and Aziz Z. Huq, *Unchecked and Unbalanced: Presidential Power in a Time of Terror* (New York: New Press, 2007), 140.
91. Risen and Lichtblau, "Bush Lets U.S. Spy on Callers Without Courts."

92. Report on the President's Surveillance Program, 42.
93. Report on the President's Surveillance Program, 26–27.
94. Risen and Lichtblau, "Bush Lets U.S. Spy on Callers Without Courts."
95. Risen, *Pay Any Price*, 272.
96. Erik Wemple, "Seizing Journalists' Records: An Outrage That Obama 'Normalized' for Trump," *Washington Post*, June 8, 2018.
97. James Risen, "If Donald Trump Targets Journalists, Thank Obama," *New York Times*, December 30, 2016.
98. *Review of the Unauthorized Disclosures of Former National Security Agency Contractor Edward Snowden*, HPSCI, 114th Cong., 2nd sess., H. Report No. 114-891 (Washington, DC: GPO, 2016), 3–4, 10, 14. Hereafter "HPSCI Report on Snowden."
99. Glenn Greenwald, "NSA Collecting Phone Records of Millions of Verizon Customers Daily," *The Guardian*, June 6, 2013.
100. Edward Snowden, *Permanent Record* (New York: Henry Holt, 2019).
101. "Transcript: ARD Interview with Edward Snowden," Courage Foundation, January 27, 2014.
102. Glenn Kessler, "James Clapper's 'Least Truthful' Statement to the Senate," *Washington Post*, June 12, 2013.
103. Snowden, *Permanent Record*, 231.
104. HPSCI Report on Snowden, 10.
105. HPSCI Report on Snowden, i–ii.
106. Snowden, *Permanent Record*, 177.
107. Barton Gellman, "Inside the NSA's Secret Tool for Mapping Your Social Network," *Wired*, May 24, 2020.
108. Charlie Savage, "George W. Bush Made Retroactive N.S.A. 'Fix' After Hospital Room Showdown," *New York Times*, September 20, 2015.
109. Barton Gellman, "U.S. Surveillance Architecture Includes Collection of Revealing Internet, Phone Metadata," *Washington Post*, June 15, 2013. For the end of STELLARWIND, see Report on the President's Surveillance Program, 276.
110. Working Draft, NSA OIG Report, 29.
111. Barton Gellman and Laura Poitras, "U.S., British Intelligence Mining Data from Nine U.S. Internet Companies in Broad Secret Program," *Washington Post*, June 7, 2013.
112. Working Draft, NSA OIG Report, 40.
113. Snowden, *Permanent Record*, 230.
114. Snowden, *Permanent Record*, 223.
115. Timothy B. Lee, "How Congress Unknowingly Legalized PRISM in 2007," *Washington Post*, June 6, 2013.
116. Peter Wallsten, Carol D. Leonnig, and Alice Crites, "For Secretive Surveillance Court, Rare Scrutiny in the Wake of NSA Leaks," *Washington Post*, June 22, 2013.
117. Report on the President's Surveillance Program, 10.

118. Report on the President's Surveillance Program, 271–75.
119. Working Draft, NSA OIG Report, 18.
120. Burrough, Ellison, and Andrews, "The Snowden Saga: A Shadowland of Secrets and Light," *Vanity Fair*.
121. Snowden, *Permanent Record*, 232.
122. Report on the President's Surveillance Program, 60–61.
123. Report on the President's Surveillance Program, 61.
124. Report on the President's Surveillance Program, 63–64.
125. Report on the President's Surveillance Program, 65.
126. Cong. Rec., 115th Cong., 2nd sess., S2748.
127. Jeffrey Rosen, "Conscience of a Conservative," *New York Times Magazine*, September 9, 2007.
128. "Terrorism," Gallup; Bruce Drake, "Americans' Views on Use of Torture in Fighting Terrorism Have Been Mixed," Pew Research Center, December 9, 2014.
129. Adam Goldman and Peyton Craighill, "New Poll Finds Majority of Americans Think Torture Was Justified After 9/11 Attacks," *Washington Post*, December 16, 2014.
130. "Opinion Data on U.S. Attitudes Toward Government Counterterrorism Efforts," appendix M in National Research Council, *Protecting Individual Privacy in the Struggle Against Terrorism: A Framework for Program Assessment* (Washington, DC: National Academies Press, 2008); "Poll Finds U.S. Split over Eavesdropping," CNN, January 11, 2006; George Gao, "What Americans Think About NSA Surveillance, National Security and Privacy," Pew Research Center, May 29, 2015.
131. Shiva Maniam, "Americans Feel the Tensions Between Privacy and Security Concerns," Pew Research Center, February 19, 2019; A. W. Geiger, "How Americans Have Viewed Government Surveillance and Privacy Since Snowden Leaks," Pew Research Center, June 4, 2018.
132. Ernest W. Lefever and Roy Godson, *The CIA and the American Ethic: An Unfinished Debate* (Washington, DC: Ethics and Public Policy Center of Georgetown University, 1979), 112.
133. Alex Emmons, "Obama Opens NSA's Vast Trove of Warrantless Data to Entire Intelligence Community, Just in Time for Trump," *The Intercept*, January 13, 2017.

CHAPTER 24

1. Another American citizen, Samir Khan, was killed in the strike, although he was not intentionally targeted.
2. Remarks by the President at the "Change of Office" Chairman of the Joint Chiefs of Staff Ceremony, White House, September 30, 2011.
3. Lloyd C. Gardner, *Killing Machine: The American Presidency in the Age of Drone Warfare* (New York: New Press, 2013), 174.

4. Lesley Wexler, "Litigating the Long War on Terror: The Role of al-Aulaqi v. Obama," *Loyal University Chicago International Law Review* 9 (2011): 170.
5. See, for example, Micah Zenko, "Obama's Final Drone Strike Data," Council on Foreign Relations, January 20, 2017.
6. Jo Becker and Scott Shane, "Secret 'Kill List' Proves a Test of Obama's Principles and Will," *New York Times*, May 29, 2012.
7. Memorandum for the Attorney General, Re: Applicability of Federal Criminal Laws and the Constitution to Contemplated Lethal Operations Against Shaykh Anwar al-Aulaqi, July 16, 2010, OLC.
8. Memorandum for the Attorney General, Re: Lethal Operation Against Shayk Anwar Aulaqi, February 19, 2010, DNSA.
9. Scott Shane, "U.S. Approves Targeted Killing of American Cleric," *New York Times*, April 6, 2010; Memorandum for the Attorney General, Re: Applicability of Federal Criminal Laws and the Constitution to Contemplated Lethal Operations Against Shaykh Anwar al-Aulaqi, July 16, 2010, OLC.
10. "Department of Justice White Paper on Lawfulness of a Lethal Operation Directed Against a U.S. Citizen Who Is a Senior Operational Leader of Al-Qa'ida or an Associated Force," November 8, 2011, OIP. See also Jeffrey P. Rogg, "'That the Republic Should Suffer No Harm': The Constitutional Conundrum of the Executive, Secret Intelligence, and the Rule of Law," *International Journal of Intelligence and CounterIntelligence* 32, no. 3 (2019): 600–628.
11. Rogg, "'That the Republic Should Suffer No Harm,'" 613.
12. Memorandum for the Attorney General, Re: Applicability of Federal Criminal Laws and the Constitution to Contemplated Lethal Operations Against Shaykh Anwar al-Aulaqi, July 16, 2010, 40.
13. *Al-Aulaqi v. Obama*, 717 F. Supp. 2d 1, 2 (D.D.C. 2010).
14. Becker and Shane, "Secret 'Kill List' Proves a Test of Obama's Principles and Will."
15. *Al-Aulaqi v. Obama*, 717 F. Supp. 2d 1, 78, 80.
16. *Al-Aulaqi v. Panetta*, 35 F. Supp. 3d 56, 69 (D.D.C. 2014).
17. Mark Mazzetti and Eric Schmitt, "Terrorism Case Renews Debate over Drone Hits," *New York Times*, April 12, 2015.
18. Greg Miller, "Strike on Aulaqi Demonstrates Collaboration Between CIA and Military," *Washington Post*, September 30, 2011; Jennifer Griffin and Justin Fishel, "Two U.S.-Born Terrorists Killed in CIA-Led Drone Strike," Fox News, September 30, 2011.
19. See, for example, Geoffrey Corn, "Unarmed but How Dangers? Civilian Augmentees, the Law of Armed Conflict, and the Search for a More Effective Test for Permissible Civilian Battlefield Functions," *Journal of National Security Law and Policy* 2 (2008): 273; Joseph B. Berger III, "Covert Action: Title 10, Title 50, and the Chain of Command," *Joint Force Quarterly* 67, no. 4 (2012): 32–39.
20. Dana Priest and William M. Arkin, "'Top Secret America': A Look at the Military's Joint Special Operations Command," *Washington Post*, September 2, 2011.

21. Miller, "Strike on Aulaqi Demonstrates Collaboration Between CIA and Military"; Robert F. Worth, Mark Mazzetti, and Scott Shane, "Drone Strikes' Risks to Get Rare Moment in the Public Eye," *New York Times*, February 5, 2013; Greg Miller, "Obama's New Drone Policy Leaves Room for CIA Role," *Washington Post*, May 25, 2013.
22. Mark Mazzetti, Eric Schmitt, and Robert F. Worth. "Two-Year Manhunt Led to Killing of Awlaki in Yemen," *New York Times*, September 30, 2011.
23. Worth, Mazzetti, and Shane, "Drone Strikes' Risks to Get Rare Moment in the Public Eye."
24. Greg Miller, "U.S. Launches Secret Drone Campaign to Hunt Islamic State Leaders in Syria," *Washington Post*, September 1, 2015.
25. Miller, "Obama's New Drone Policy Leaves Room for CIA Role"; Greg Miller, "Lawmakers Seek to Stymie Plan to Shift Control of Drone Campaign from CIA to Pentagon," *Washington Post*, January 15, 2014.
26. Greg Miller, "Why CIA Drone Strikes Have Plummeted," *Washington Post*, June 16, 2016.
27. Miller, "Lawmakers Seek to Stymie Plan to Shift Control of Drone Campaign from CIA to Pentagon."
28. Miller, "Why CIA Drone Strikes Have Plummeted."
29. Robert Chesney, "DOD-CIA Convergence: The DIA Defense Clandestine Service Initiative Runs into Trouble," *Lawfare*, December 11, 2012.
30. Noah Shachtman, "Congress Smashes Pentagon's New Den of Spies," *Wired*, May 21, 2013.
31. Shachtman, "Congress Smashes Pentagon's New Den of Spies."
32. Greg Miller, "Pentagon's Plans for a Spy Service to Rival CIA Have Been Pared Back," *Washington Post*, November 1, 2014.
33. Mark Mazzetti, "C.I.A. to Focus More on Spying, a Difficult Shift," *New York Times*, May 23, 2013.
34. See, for example, John A. Gentry and Joseph S. Gordon, *Strategic Warning Intelligence: History, Challenges, and Prospects* (Washington, DC: Georgetown University Press, 2019).
35. Mazzetti, "C.I.A. to Focus More on Spying, a Difficult Shift."
36. Alex Finley, "How the CIA Forgot the Art of Spying," *Politico Magazine*, March/April 2017.
37. Mazzetti, "C.I.A. to Focus More on Spying, a Difficult Shift."
38. See also Douglas London, *The Recruiter: Spying and the Lost Art of American Intelligence* (New York: Hachette Books, 2021).
39. Barton Gellman, "The FBI's Secret Scrutiny," *Washington Post*, November 6, 2005.
40. "National Security Letters," Electronic Frontier Foundation, https://www.eff.org/issues/national-security-letters.
41. "The Attorney General's Guidelines for Domestic FBI Operations," September 29, 2008, 5, 7, OPA.

42. Robert O'Harrow Jr. and Ellen Nakashima, "President's Surveillance Program Worked with Private Sector to Collect Data After September 11, 2001," *Washington Post*, June 27, 2013.
43. This background derives from the Office of the Inspector General of the US Department of Justice, "Review of Four FISA Applications and Other Aspects of the FBI's Crossfire Hurricane Investigation," December 9, 2019, DOJ/OIG. Hereafter "DOJ OIG Report on FBI and FISA."
44. DOJ OIG Report on FBI and FISA, 259.
45. Howard Blum, "How Ex-Spy Christopher Steele Compiled His Explosive Trump-Russia Dossier," *Vanity Fair*, March 30, 2017.
46. DOJ OIG Report on FBI and FISA, 67.
47. DOJ OIG Report on FBI and FISA, 127–30, 139, 160.
48. DOJ OIG Report on FBI and FISA, 79, 157–60.
49. United States Foreign Intelligence Surveillance Court, In Re Carter W. Page, Order Regarding Handling and Disposition of Information, January 7, 2020, FISC.
50. ODNI Report, "Assessing Russian Activities and Intentions in Recent US Elections," January 6, 2017, 1, ODNI.
51. Josh Campbell, *Crossfire Hurricane: Inside Donald Trump's War on the FBI* (Chapel Hill, NC: Algonquin Books of Chapel Hill, 2019), 230; also 22, 28, 91, 102, 229.
52. Glenn Kessler, "Michael Flynn, Barack Obama and Trumps's Claims of 'Treason,'" *Washington Post*, June 26, 2020.
53. Mary Louise Kelly, "A History of Trump's Broken Ties to the U.S. Intelligence Community," NPR, October 28, 2019; Robert Draper, "Unwanted Truths: Inside Trump's Battles with U.S. Intelligence Agencies," *New York Times*, August 8, 2020.
54. Matthew Nussbaum, "Trump Publicly Sides with Putin on Election Interference," Politico, July 16, 2018.
55. See, for example, https://twitter.com/realDonaldTrump/status/819164172781060096; https://twitter.com/JohnBrennan/status/974978856997224448.
56. Maegan Vazquez, "175 Former US Officials Added to List Denouncing Trump for Revoking Brennan's Security Clearance," CNN, August 20, 2018.
57. Michael J. Morrell, "I Ran the C.I.A. Now I'm Endorsing Hillary Clinton," *New York Times*, August 5, 2016.
58. Peter S. Usowski, "Former CIA Officers Writing About Intelligence, Policy, and Politics, 2016–2017," *Studies in Intelligence* 62, no. 3 (2018): 11–12.
59. Principles of Professional Ethics for the Intelligence Community, ODNI.
60. Mark M. Lowenthal, "Intelligence Is NOT About 'Telling Truth to Power,'" *International Journal of Intelligence and CounterIntelligence* 34, no. 4 (2021): 795–98.
61. John A. Gentry, "'Truth' as a Tool of the Politicization of Intelligence," *International Journal of Intelligence and CounterIntelligence* 32, no. 3 (2019): 217–47.
62. Ian Schwartz, "Former Acting CIA Director John McLaughlin on Impeachment: 'Thank God for the Deep State,'" Real Clear Politics, November 1, 2019.

63. "Document: Read the Whistle-Blower Complaint," *New York Times*, September 26, 2019.
64. Matthew Rosenberg, Maggie Haberman, and Adam Goldman, "2 White House Officials Helped Give Nunes Intelligence Reports," *New York Times*, March 30, 2017; Nicholas Fando, "Senate Intelligence Leaders Say House G.O.P. Leaked a Senator's Text," *New York Times*, March 1, 2018; Julia Mueller, "Pompeo Accuses Schiff of Leaking Classified Information," The Hill, January 25, 2023.
65. House Report 116-335, 116th Cong., 1st sess. (2019).
66. Michael Berkman and Eric Plutzer, "Poll Report: Republicans No Longer Trust the FBI," McCourtney Institute for Democracy, February 20, 2018; "Growing Partisan Differences in Views of the FBI; Stark Divide over ICE," Pew Research Center, July 24, 2018.
67. Sonam Sheth, "Public Opinion of the CIA Shows How Even Bureaucratic Organizations Have Become Politicized," *Business Insider*, January 5, 2017.
68. Joshua Busby, Archit Oswal, and Steve Slick, "Public Attitudes on U.S. Intelligence in 2020," *Lawfare*, June 7, 2021.
69. Carrie Sheffield, "FISA Fallout: Nearly Two-Thirds of Americans Believe FBI Breaks Law When Spying," *Just the News*, April 8, 2020.
70. "Election 2024: Many Voters Suspicious Toward Intelligence Agencies," Rasmussen Reports, March 7, 2024.
71. "Majorities Express Favorable Opinions of Several Federal Agencies, Including the FBI," Pew Research Center, February 14, 2018; Kathy Frankovic, "Americans Like the CIA—Not Congress," YouGov, March 26, 2014.
72. Dan Balz and Clara Ence Morse, "American Democracy Is Cracking. These Forces Help Explain Why," *Washington Post*, August 18, 2023.

CONCLUSION

1. See, for example, Deborah G. Barger, *Toward a Revolution in Intelligence Affairs* (Santa Monica, CA: RAND Corporation, 2005).
2. A 1989 article by John Lewis Gaddis and a 1991 Air Force publication both use the term "intelligence revolution." The former attempts to contextualize the role of intelligence in terms of helping shape national security policy during the Cold War, while the latter discusses what I would argue is a revolution in intelligence affairs. A 1993 article by Wesley K. Wark, republished by the CIA's Center for the Study of Intelligence, uses the term "intelligence revolution" in a manner closer to how it is used here but still more reflective of a revolution in intelligence affairs. See John Lewis Gaddis, "Intelligence, Espionage, and Cold War Origins," *Diplomatic History* 13, no. 2 (1989): 191–212; *The Intelligence Revolution: A Historical Perspective*, Proceedings of the Thirteenth Military History Symposium, ed. Walter T. Hitchcock (Washington, DC: Office of Air Force History, 1991); Wesley K. Wark, "One of Time's Arrows: The Intelligence Revolution and the Future," *Studies in Intelligence* 37, no. 4 (1994): 9–16.

3. Military historians have distinguished between a "revolution in military affairs" and the "Military Revolution." Revolutions in military affairs are changes in warfare brought about by innovations in areas like technology, training, or tactics. By contrast, the Military Revolution refers to changes in warfare that brought about fundamental transformations to the states and societies of Europe over the course of centuries and led them to dominate the world. This book therefore proposes an analogous concept for intelligence history. See, for example, Michael Roberts, *The Military Revolution, 1560–1600: An Inaugural Lecture Delivered Before the Queen's University of Belfast* (Belfast: M. Boyd, 1956); Geoffrey Parker, *The Military Revolution: Military Innovation and the rise of the West, 1500–1800* (Cambridge: Cambridge University Press, 1988).
4. See, for example, Warner, *The Rise and Fall of Intelligence*.
5. See generally Stout, *World War I and the Foundations of American Intelligence*.
6. Aaron Bateman, "Secret Partners: The National Reconnaissance Office and the Intelligence-Industrial-Academic Complex," *Intelligence and National Security* 38, no. 6 (2023): 885–901.
7. Grant Clauser, "Amazon's Alexa Never Stops Listening to You. Should You Worry?" *New York Times*, August 8, 2019.
8. Jason Cohen, "Amazon's Alexa Collects More of Your Data than Any Other Smart Assistant," *PCMag*, March 30, 2022.
9. For more on the organizational divisions between the CIA and FBI, see Riebling, *Wedge*.
10. Kristie Macrakis, *Nothing Is Beyond Our Reach: America's Techno-Spy Empire* (Washington, DC: Georgetown University Press, 2023).
11. Dasha Litvinova, "The Cyber Gulag: How Russia Tracks, Censors and Controls Its Citizens," Associated Press, May 23, 2023; Paul Mozur, Adam Satariano, Aaron Krolik, and Aliza Aufrichtig, "'They Are Watching': Inside Russia's Vast Surveillance State," *New York Times*, September 22, 2022.
12. Stanley Lubman, "China's 'Social Credit' System: Turning Big Data into Mass Surveillance," *Wall Street Journal*, December 21, 2016; Nicole Kobie, "The Complicated Truth About China's Social Credit System," *Wired*, July 6, 2019; Charlie Campbell, "'The Entire System Is Designed to Suppress Us': What the Chinese Surveillance State Means for the Rest of the World," *Time*, November 21, 2019; Charlie Campbell, "How China Is Using 'Social Credit Scores' to Reward and Punish Its Citizens," *Time*, January 16, 2019.
13. See, for example, Gary Gerstle, *Liberty and Coercion: The Paradox of American Government From the Founding to the Present* (Princeton, NJ: Princeton University Press, 2015).
14. Derek Thompson, "What's Behind South Korea's COVID-19 Exceptionalism?" *The Atlantic*, May 6, 2020; Mark Zastrow, "How South Korea Prevented a Coronavirus Disaster—and Why the Battle Isn't Over," *National Geographic*, May 12, 2020.

15. Kate Blackwood, “Study: Americans Skeptical of COVID-19 Contact Tracing Apps,” Cornell Chronicle, January 12, 2021.
16. Memorandum on Communications Intelligence Activities, October 24, 1952, NSA.
17. I am indebted to James Kurth for many enriching discussions on American civil-military relations, national security policy, and related topics that helped me form the ideas for this section.
18. David E. Sanger and Julian E. Barnes, “U.S. Hunts Chinese Malware That Could Disrupt American Military Operations,” *New York Times*, July 29, 2023.
19. Christopher Wray, “The Threat Posed by the Chinese Government and the Chinese Communist Party to the Economic and National Security of the United States,” Hudson Institute, July 7, 2020, FBI.
20. Jon Wertheim, “China’s Push to Control Americans’ Health Care Future,” CBS News, January 31, 2021.
21. He Di, “The Most Respected Enemy: Mao Zedong’s Perception of the United States,” *China Quarterly* 137 (March 1994): 153.
22. Intelligence and Security Committee of Parliament, HC 1605, July 23, 2023, 25, https://isc.independent.gov.uk/wp-content/uploads/2023/07/ISC-China.pdf.
23. Katie Bo Lillis, “Senators Allege CIA Collected Data on Americans in Warrantless Searches,” CNN, February 11, 2022.
24. United States Foreign Intelligence Surveillance Court, Section 702 Memorandum Opinion and Order, April 11, 2023, INTEL.gov.
25. Jeff Rogg, “An American-Made Greek Tragedy: Coronavirus and the Thucydides Trap,” *National Interest*, September 27, 2020.
26. Warren P. Strobel, “Biometrics, Smartphones, Surveillance Cameras Pose New Obstacles for U.S. Spies,” *Wall Street Journal*, November 27, 2021.
27. Jenna McLaughlin and Zach Dorfman, “‘Shattered’: Inside the Secret Battle to Save America’s Undercover Spies in the Digital Age,” Yahoo News, December 30, 2019.
28. Simon Shuster, “Putin’s Fear of Texting Kept U.S. Spymasters in the Dark,” *Time*, March 24, 2014; Julian E. Barnes, Adam Goldman, and David E. Sanger, “C.I.A. Informant Extracted from Russia Had Sent Secrets to U.S. for Decades,” *New York Times*, September 9, 2019.
29. William M. Arkin, “Exclusive: The CIA’s Blind Spot About the Ukraine War,” *Newsweek*, July 5, 2023.
30. Bellingcat, https://www.bellingcat.com/about/who-we-are/.
31. Amy Mackinnon, “Bellingcat Can Say What U.S. Intelligence Can’t,” *Foreign Policy*, December 17, 2020.
32. Justin Doubleday, “New OSINT Foundation Aims to ‘Professionalize’ Open Source Discipline Across Spy Agencies,” Federal News Network, July 27, 2022. Also see https://www.osintfoundation.com/osint/default.asp.
33. Gavin Wilde, “The IC’s Biggest Open-Source Intelligence Challenge: Mission Creep,” Just Security, February 3, 2023.

34. Dan Lomas, "The Death of Secret Intelligence? Think Again," RUSI, July 5, 2023.
35. William Burns, "A World Transformed and the Role of Intelligence," Ditchley Annual Lecture, July 1, 2023, CIA.
36. Anthony Vinci, "The Coming Revolution in Intelligence Affairs," *Foreign Affairs*, August 31, 2020.
37. Oliver Whang, "A.I. Is Getting Better at Mind-Reading," *New York Times*, May 1, 2023.
38. Vivian Salama, "Four U.S. Intelligence Agencies Produced Extensive Reports on Afghanistan, but All Failed to Predict Kabul's Rapid Collapse," *Wall Street Journal*, October 28, 2021; Mark Mazzetti, Julian E. Barnes, and Adam Goldman, "Intelligence Warned of Afghan Military Collapse, Despite Biden's Assurances," *New York Times*, August 17, 2021.
39. Ariel Edwards-Levy, "Most Americans Favor Afghanistan Withdrawal but Say It Was Poorly Handled," CNN, August 23, 2021.
40. Shane Harris, Karen DeYoung, Isabelle Khurshudyan, Ashley Parker, and Liz Sly, "Road to War: U.S. Struggled to Convince Allies, and Zelensky, of Risk of Invasion," *Washington Post*, August 16, 2022; Julian E. Barnes and Adam Entous, "How the U.S. Adopted a New Intelligence Playbook to Expose Russia's War Plans," *New York Times*, February 23, 2023.
41. See, for example, Statement for the Record by Lt Gen Michael V. Hayden, USAF, Director Before the House Permanent Select Committee on Intelligence, April 12, 2000, NSA; Remarks as Delivered by James R. Clapper, Director of National Intelligence, October 29, 2013, INTEL.gov.
42. Elias Groll, "Sorry to Be a Killjoy, but the CIA's First Tweet Isn't Funny," *Foreign Policy*, June 6, 2014; Matthew Gault, "The CIA's Tweets About Tupac Are 'Vital to the Legitimation of the Agency,'" Vice, April 13, 2021.
43. Emily Brandwin, "The CIA Doesn't Need to Be on Twitter, It Needs a Serious Public Makeover," *The Guardian*, July 10, 2014.
44. Jeff Seldin, "New US Intelligence Strategy Calls for More Partners, More Sharing," VOA, August 10, 2023.
45. Devin Dwyer and Cindy Smith, "US Spy Agencies Face 'Shocking' Lack of Diversity," ABC News, October 6, 2020; Warren P. Strobel, "Diversity in U.S. Spy Agencies Ticks Up, Report Finds," *Wall Street Journal*, July 8, 2021.
46. Huntington, *The Soldier and the State*, 465–66.
47. Mary Madden and Lee Rainie, "Americans' Attitudes About Privacy, Security and Surveillance," Pew Research Center, May 20, 2015; Brooke Auxier, Lee Rainie, Monica Anderson, Andrew Perrin, Madhu Kumar, and Erica Turner, "Americans and Privacy: Concerned, Confused and Feeling Lack of Control over Their Personal Information," Pew Research Center, November 15, 2019.

Select Bibliography

ARCHIVES, LIBRARIES, AND COLLECTIONS

American Presidency Project, University of California Santa Barbara, Santa Barbara, CA (UCSB)

Central Intelligence Agency (CIA)

Freedom of Information Act Electronic Reading Room (CIA/ERR)

Department of Justice (DOJ)

Office of Public Affairs (OPA)

Office of Information Policy (OIP)

OLC FOIA Electronic Reading Room (OLC)

OIG Reports (DOJ/OIG)

Digital National Security Archive, National Security Archive, The George Washington University, Washington, DC (D NSA)

Federal Bureau of Investigation (FBI)

The Vault

Foreign Relations of the United States (FRUS)

Appendix II, FRUS 1894, Affairs in Hawaii

FRUS, Japan, 1931–1941, Volume II

FRUS, 1945–1950: Emergence of the Intelligence Establishment

FRUS, 1948 Volume IX: The Western Hemisphere

FRUS, 1950–1955, The Intelligence Community

FRUS, 1961–1963 Volume XXV: Organization of Foreign Policy; Information Policy; United Nations; Scientific Matters

FRUS, 1969–1976, Volume XXXV', Organization and Management of Foreign Policy; Public Diplomacy, 1973–1976

FRUS, 1977–1980 Volume XII, Afghanistan

Franklin D. Roosevelt Presidential Library (FDRL), Hyde Park, NY

Gerald R. Ford Presidential Library, Ann Arbor, MI (GRFL)

Harry S. Truman Library, Independence, MO (HSTL)
Henry Shelton Sanford Papers, Sanford Historical Society, Sanford, FL (HSSP)
John F. Kennedy Presidential Library, Boston, MA (JFKL)
Library of Congress, Washington DC (LOC)
CHRONICLING AMERICA HISTORIC AMERICAN NEWSPAPERS
Argus Leader
Aurora General Advertiser
Boston Evening Transcript
Chicago Inter Ocean
The Chicago Daily Tribune
Chicago Times-Herald
The Cincinnati Daily Press
The Circleville Herald
New York Daily News
The Evening Star
The Inter Ocean
The Michigan Argus
The New York Herald
The New York Times
The Richmond Dispatch
The World
PERSONAL PAPERS
Abraham Lincoln Papers (ALP)
John Henry Papers (JHP)
Josephus Daniels Papers (JDP)
Robert Lansing Papers (RLP)
W. G. McAdoo Papers (WGMP)
Woodrow Wilson Papers (WWP)
Millard Preston Goodfellow Papers, Hoover Archives, Stanford, CA (MPGP)
National Archives Founders Online (Founders Online, NARA)
National Archives at College Park, College Park, MD (NACP)
RECORD GROUPS
RG 51 Office of Management and Budget
RG 59 Department of State
RG 60 Department of Justice
RG 65 Federal Bureau of Investigation
RG 87 U.S. Secret Service
RG 165 War Department General and Special Staffs
RG 206 Solicitor of the Treasury
RG 226 Office of Strategic Services
RG 319 Army Staff
MICROFILM
Despatches from U.S. Ministers to Belgium, 1832–1906.

Despatches from U.S. Ministers to Great Britain, 1791–1906.
Diplomatic Instructions of the Department of State, 1801–1906.
National Archives Building, Washington DC (NAB)
RECORD GROUPS
RG 38 Office of the Chief of Naval Operations
RG 107 Office of the Secretary of War
RG 110 Provost Marshal General's Bureau (Civil War)
RG 217 Records of the Accounting Officers of the Department of the Treasury
MICROFILM
Correspondence and Issuances, Headquarters of the Army of the Potomac, 1861–1865.
National Security Agency (NSA)
Herbert O. Yardley Collection (HOYC)
William F. Friedman Collection of Official Papers (WFFP)
Office of the Director of National Intelligence (ODNI)
Papers of Homer Stillé Cummings (HSC), University of Virginia Library, Charlottesville, VA (HSC)
Richard Dunlop Papers (RDP), US Army Heritage & Education Center, Carlisle Barracks, PA (RDP)
Ronald Reagan Presidential Library, Simi Valley, CA (RRL)
Walter L. Pforzheimer Papers, Beinecke Rare Book and Manuscript Library, Yale University, New Haven, CT (WLPP)
William F. Friedman Collection (WFFC), The George C. Marshall Foundation, Charlottesville, VA (WFFC)

CASE LAW

Al-Aulaqi v. Obama, 717 F. Supp. 2d 1 (D.D.C. 2010).
Al-Aulaqi v. Panetta, 35 F. Supp. 3d 56 (D.D.C. 2014).
Ex parte Milligan, 71 U.S. 2 (1866).
Hamdan v. Rumsfeld, 548 U.S. 557 (2006).
Hamdi v. Rumsfeld, 542 U.S. 507 (2004).
Katz v. United States, 389 U.S. 347 (1967).
Nardone v. U.S., 308 U.S. 338 (1939).
Rasul v. Bush, 542 U.S. 466 (2004).
Totten v. United States, 92 U.S. 105 (1875).
United States v. United States District Court, 407 U.S. 297 (1972).
United States Foreign Intelligence Surveillance Court, In Re Carter W. Page, Order Regarding Handling and Disposition of Information, January 7, 2020.

CONGRESSIONAL RECORDS

Annals of Congress
The Congressional Globe

Congressional Record (Cong. Rec.)
Congressional Research Service (CRS)
Federal Register
Journal of the Executive Proceedings of the Senate of the United States of America
Register of Debates in Congress
U.S. Statutes at Large
Reports and Hearings of Congress

NEWSPAPERS, PERIODICALS, WEBSITES

ABC News
American Civil Liberties Union
Associated Press
The Atlantic
Brookings Institution
Business Insider
CBS News
Chicago Tribune
Christian Science Monitor
CNN
The Federalist
Federal News Network
Foreign Affairs
Foreign Policy
Fox News
GQ
The Guardian
The Hill
Hudson Institute
The Indianapolis News
The Intercept
Just Security
Lawfare
Look
Mother Jones
National Geographic
The National Interest
Newsweek
New Statesman
The New Yorker
New York Magazine
New York Post

The New York Review of Books
The New York Times
The New York Times Magazine
PCMag
Politico
Politico Magazine
Ramparts
Real Clear Politics
Reuters
RUSI
The Saturday Evening Post
Scientific American
Time
Twitter
U.S. News & World Report
Vanity Fair
The Village Voice
VOA
The Wall Street Journal
The Washington Post
The Washington Times
Wired
The World
Yahoo News

POLLS

Cornell Chronicle
CNN
Gallup
McCourtney Institute, Pennsylvania State University
NBC News/*Wall Street Journal*
Pew Research Center
Rasmussen
YouGov

PUBLISHED PRIMARY SOURCES

Adams, Samuel. *The Writings of Samuel Adams*. Edited by Harry Alonzo Cushing. Vol. 2. New York: G. P. Putnam's Sons, 1906.
Annual Report of the Attorney-General of the United States, 1907–10, 1918.

Annual Reports of the War Department for the Fiscal Year Ended June 30, 1902. Vol. 1. Washington, DC: GPO, 1903.

Anonymous, "The Spy System in Europe." *Beadle's Monthly: A Magazine of To-Day*, I (1866): 80–84.

Baker, Lafayette C. *History of the United States Secret Service*. Philadelphia: L. C. Baker, 1867. Kindle edition.

Barnum, H. L. *The Spy Unmasked; or, Memoirs of Enoch Crosby, Alias Harvey Birch, the Hero of Mr. Cooper's Tale of the Neutral Ground; Being an Authentic Account of the Secret Services Which He Rendered his Country During the Revolutionary War*. New York: J. & J. Harper, 1828.

Benton, Thomas Hart. *Thirty Years' View; or, A History of the Working of the American Government for Thirty Years, From 1820–1850*. 2 vols. New York: D. Appleton, 1858.

Berle, Beatice Bishop, and Travis Beal Jacobs, eds. *Navigating the Rapids 1918–1971: From the Papers of Adolf A. Berle*. New York: Harcourt Brace Jovanovich, Inc, 1973.

Brownell Report: Report to the Secretary of State and the Secretary of Defense by a Special Committee Appointed Pursuant to Letter of 28 December 1951 to Survey Communications Intelligence Activities of the Government, June 13, 1952.

Carter, Jimmy. *White House Diary*. New York: Picador, 2010.

The Central Intelligence Agency and National Organization for Intelligence, A Report to the National Security Council, January 1, 1949. "The Dulles-Jackson-Correa Report" or "Dulles Report."

The Commission on Organization of the Executive Branch of the Government, Task Force Report on National Security Organization, January 1949. "The Eberstadt Report."

The Commission on the Intelligence Capabilities of the United States Regarding Weapons of Mass Destruction. "Robb-Silberman Report."

Commission on the Roles and Capabilities of the US Intelligence Community. "Aspin-Brown Commission Report." 1996.

Cooper, James Fenimore. *The Spy: A Tale of the Neutral Ground*. 1821; reprint, New York: Penguin Books, 1997.

Daniels, Josephus. *The Wilson Era: Years of War and After, 1917–1923*. Chapel Hill: University of North Carolina Press, 1946.

Defense Intelligence Agency: At The Creation, 1961–1965. Edited by Deane J. Allen and Brian G. Shellum. Washington, DC: DIA History Office, 2002.

Drew Pearson's Washington Merry-Go-Round, April 24, 1945. American University Library Special Collections.

Edgeworth, Maria. *The Port Folio* 16 (1823).

Final Report of the Independent Counsel for Iran/Contra Matters. Washington, DC: US Court of Appeals for the District of Columbia Circuit, 1993.

Final Report of the National Commission on Terrorist Attacks Upon the United States. https://9-11commission.gov/report/.

"Finding Pursuant to Section 662 of the Foreign Assistance Act of 1961, As Amended, Concerning Operations Undertaken by the Central Intelligence Agency in Foreign Countries, Other than Those Intended Solely for the Purpose of Intelligence

Collection," March 9, 1981, https://www.brown.edu/Research/Understanding_the_Iran_Contra_Affair/documents/d-nic-5.pdf.

"Finding Pursuant to Section 662 of the Foreign Assistance Act of 1961, As Amended, Concerning Operations Undertaken by the Central Intelligence Agency in Foreign Countries, Other than Those Intended Solely for the Purpose of Intelligence Collection," December 1, 1981, https://www.brown.edu/Research/Understanding_the_Iran_Contra_Affair/documents/d-all-45.pdf.

Ford, Worthington Chauncey, ed. *Journals of the Continental Congress 1774–1789*. Vols. 1–15. Washington, DC: GPO, 1904–9.

Foster, John W. *The Practice of Diplomacy as Illustrated in the Foreign Relations of the United States*. Boston: Houghton, Mifflin, 1906.

Gardiner, W. H. *North American Review* 15, no. 36 (1822): 250–82.

Gardner, John. *Brief Consideration of the Important Services, and Distinguished Virtues and Talents, Which Recommend Mr. Adams for the Presidency of the United States*. Boston: Manning & Loring, 1796.

General Orders No. 23, March 18, 1892. *General Orders and Circulars, Adjutant General's Office. 1892*. Washington, DC: GPO, 1893.

General Orders No. 80, August 26, 1918. War Department. *General Orders and Bulletins, War Department 1918*. Washington, DC: GPO, 1919.

General Orders No. 100: The Lieber Code. "Instructions for the Government of Armies of the United States in the Field." April 24, 1863.

Gibbon, John. *Personal Recollections of the Civil War*. New York: G. P. Putnam's Sons, 1928.

Hale, Sarah. *The Port Folio* 13 (1822): 90–101.

Hamilton, Alexander, John Jay, and James Madison. *The Federalist Papers*. LOC Online.

"Historical Intelligence Documents: From COI to CIG." *Studies in Intelligence* 37, no. 5 (1994): 111–23.

History of the Office of the Coordinator of Inter-American Affairs: Historical Reports on War Administration. Washington, DC: GPO, 1947.

Hunt, Gaillard, ed. *Journals of the Continental Congress, 1774–1789*. Vols. 16–27. Washington, DC: GPO, 1910–1928.

Ingersoll, Charles J. *Recollections, Historical, Political, Biographical, and Social*. 2 vols. Philadelphia: J. B. Lippincott, 1861.

Journals of the Provincial Congress, Provincial Convention, Committee of Safety and Council of Safety of the state of New York, 1775–1777. 2 vols. Albany, NY: Thurlow Weed, 1842.

Kaminski, John, Gaspare J. Saladino, Richard Leffler, Charles H. Schoenleber, and Margaret A. Hogan, eds. *The Documentary History of the Ratification of the Constitution Digital Edition*. Charlottesville: University of Virginia Press, 2009.

Kendall, Willmoore. "The Function of Intelligence." *World Politics* 1, no. 4 (1949): 542–52.

Lansing, Robert. *The Peace Negotiations: A Personal Narrative*. Boston: Houghton Mifflin, 1921.

Lansing, Robert. *War Memoirs of Robert Lansing*. Indianapolis, IN: Bobbs-Merrill, 1935.

Letter from Dick Cheney to Les Aspin, March 17, 1992. https://fas.org/irp/congress/1992_cr/cheney1992.pdf.

Long, Breckinridge. *The War Diary of Breckinridge Long: Selections from the Years 1939–1944*. Edited by Fred L. Israel. Lincoln: University of Nebraska Press, 1966.

Madison, James. *Notes of Debates in the Federal Convention of 1787*. New York: W. W. Norton, 1987.

"Making Intelligence Smarter." Council on Foreign Relations, 1996.

Marty, Dick (Switzerland, ALDE). "Alleged Secret Detentions and Unlawful Inter-State Transfers Involving Council of Europe Member States," Draft Report—Part II (Explanatory Memorandum), Parliamentary Assembly of the Council of Europe, Committee on Legal Affairs and Human Rights, June 7, 2006.

Memorandum for the Chairman, Joint Chiefs of Staff, February 8, 1961. In *Defense Intelligence Agency: At The Creation, 1961–1965*, edited by Deane J. Allen and Brian G. Shellum. Washington, DC: DIA History Office, 2002.

Memorandum on Communications Intelligence Activities, October 24, 1952. https://media.defense.gov/2021/Jul/15/2002763653/-1/-1/0/TRUMAN-MEMO.PDF.

Minutes of the Committee and of the First Commission for Detecting and Defeating Conspiracies in the State of New York. Vol. 1. New York: Printed for the Society, 1924.

Niblack, Albert P. *The Office of Naval Intelligence: Its History and Aims*. Washington, DC: GPO, 1920.

Niles Weekly Register 6, no. 1. Baltimore: Franklin Press, 1814.

Office of Naval Intelligence Memorandum. Subject: Japanese Intelligence and Propaganda in the United States During 1941, December 4, 1941. http://www.mansell.com/e09066/1941/41-12/IA021.html.

Paine, Thomas. "Letter to George Washington." July 30, 1796. https://thomaspaine.org/major-works/letter-to-george-washington.html.

"Papers Relating to the Annexation of the Hawaiian Islands to the United States." Washington, DC: GPO, 1893.

Pinkerton, William. "How to Deal with the Bolsheviki." *American Industries* 19, no. 12 (July 1919): 30–31.

Pinkerton, Allan J. *The Spy of the Rebellion: Being a True History of the Spy System of the United States Army During the Late Rebellion*. 1883; reprint, Lincoln: University of Nebraska Press, 1989.

Porter, McKenzie. "The Biggest Private Eye of All." *MacLean's Magazine*, December 1, 1952.

President's Special Review Board. "Tower Commission Report."

The Public Papers of the Presidents of the United States, Jimmy Carter, 1978, Book I. Washington, DC: GPO, 1979.

Quincy, Edmund. *Life of Josiah Quincy of Massachusetts*. Boston: Ticknor and Fields, 1868.

Report by the Task Force on Intelligence Activities of the Commission on Organization of the Executive branch of the Government, May 1955.

Report by the Commission on Organization of the Executive Branch of the Government to the Congress, June 1955.

Report by the Special Study Group, Report on the Covert Activities of the Central Intelligence Agency, 1954.

Report to the President by the Commission on CIA Activities Within the United States. Washington, DC: GPO, 1975.

Richardson, James D. *A Compilation of the Messages and Papers of the Presidents*. 20 vols. New York: Bureau of National Literature, 1897–1922.

Robertson, David. *Debates and Other Proceedings of the Convention of Virginia*. Richmond: Ritchie & Worlsey and Augustine Davis, 1805.

Stimson, Henry L., and McGeorge Bundy. *On Active Service in Peace and War*. New York: Harper & Brothers, 1947.

Sweeney, Walter C. *Military Intelligence: A New Weapon in War*. New York: Frederick A. Stokes, 1924.

Tallmadge, Benjamin. *Memoir of Colonel Benjamin Tallmadge*. Edited by Henry Phelps Johnston. New York: Gillis Press, 1904.

Turrou, Leon G. *Where My Shadow Falls: Two Decades of Crime Detection*. New York: Doubleday, 1949.

The United States Commission on National Security/21st Century, *Road Map for National Security: Imperative for Change*.

Van Deman, Ralph H. *The Final Memoranda*. Edited by Ralph E. Weber. Wilmington, DE: SR Books, 1988.

Wagner, Arthur L. *The Service of Security and Information*. Kansas City, MO: Hudson-Kimberly, 1903.

Wait, Thomas B. *Secret Journals of the Acts and Proceedings of Congress*. 4 vols. Boston: Thomas B. Wait, 1820–21.

Washington, George. "First Annual Message to Congress." January 8, 1790. https://millercenter.org/the-presidency/presidential-speeches/january-8-1790-first-annual-message-congress.

Washington, George. *The Writings of George Washington from the Original Manuscript Sources, 1745–1799*. Edited by John C. Fitzpatrick. 39 vols. Washington, DC: GPO, 1931–1944.

Wharton, Francis, ed. *The Revolutionary Diplomatic Correspondence of the United States*. 6 vols. Washington, DC: GPO, 1889.

Wilkie, John E. "The Secret Service in the War." In *The American-Spanish War: A History by the War Leaders*. Norwich, CT: Chas. C. Haskell & Son, 1899.

Wilson, Woodrow. "Address at Coliseum, St. Louis, Mo." September 5, 1919, in *Addresses of President Wilson: Addresses Delivered by President Wilson on His Western Tour, September 4 to September 25, 1919 on the League of Nations, Treaty of Peace with*

Germany, Industrial Conditions, High Cost of Living, Race Riots, Etc. Washington, DC: GPO, 1919.

Yardley, Herbert O. *The American Black Chamber*. Annapolis: Bluejacket Books, 1931.

SECONDARY SOURCES

Absher, Kenneth Michael, Michael C. Desch, and Roman Popadiuk. *Privileged and Confidential: The Secret History of the President's Intelligence Advisory Board*. Lexington: University Press of Kentucky, 2012.

Adams, Henry. "Count Edward de Crillon." *American Historical Review* 1, no. 1 (1895): 51–69.

Agee, Philip. *Inside the Company: CIA Diary*. New York: Farrar, Straus and Giroux, 1975.

Aldrich, Richard. *The Hidden Hand: Britain, America and Cold War Secret Intelligence*. Woodstock, NY: Overlook Press, 2002.

Alexander, Albert. "The President and the Investigator: Roosevelt and Dies." *Antioch Review* 15, no. 1 (1955): 106–17.

Allen, Michael. *Blinking Red: Crisis and Compromise in American Intelligence After 9/11*. Washington, DC: Potomac Books, 2013.

Andrew, Christopher. *For the President's Eyes Only: Secret Intelligence and the American Presidency from Washington to Bush*. New York: HarperPerennial, 1996.

Andrew, Christopher. *Her Majesty's Secret Service: The Making of the British Intelligence Community*. New York: Elizabeth Sifton Books, 1986.

Anonymous. "Edward Bancroft (@ Edwd. Edwards), Estimable Spy." *Studies in Intelligence* 5, no. 1 (1961).

Bailyn, Bernard. *The Ideological Origins of the American Revolution*. Cambridge, MA: Belknap Press of Harvard University Press, 2017.

Bamford, James. *The Puzzle Palace: Inside the National Security Agency, America's Most Secret Intelligence Organization*. New York: Penguin Books, 1983.

Bansemer, John D. *Intelligence Reform: A Question of Balance*. Maxwell AFB, AL: Air University Press, 2006.

Barger, Deborah G. *Toward a Revolution in Intelligence Affairs*. Santa Monica, CA: RAND Corporation, 2005.

Bartholomew-Feis, Dixee. *The OSS and Ho Chi Minh: Unexpected Allies in the War Against Japan*. Lawrence: University Press of Kansas, 2006.

Bateman, Aaron. "Secret Partners: The National Reconnaissance Office and the Intelligence-Industrial-Academic Complex." *Intelligence and National Security* 38, no. 6 (2023): 885–901.

Bateman, Aaron. "Technological Wonder and Strategic Vulnerability: Satellite Reconnaissance and American National Security During the Cold War." *International Journal of Intelligence and CounterIntelligence* 33, no. 2 (2020): 328–53.

Bateman, Aaron. "Trust but Verify: Satellite Reconnaissance, Secrecy and Arms Control During the Cold War." *Journal of Strategic Studies* 46, no. 5 (2023): 1037–61.

Batvinis, Raymond J. *The Origins of FBI Counterintelligence*. Lawrence: University Press of Kansas, 2007.

Bearden, Milt, and James Risen. *The Main Enemy: The Inside Story of the CIA's Final Showdown with the KGB*. New York: Ballantine Books, 2003.

Beavan, Colin. *Operation Jedburgh: D-Day and America's First Shadow War*. New York: Penguin Books, 2007.

Beeman, Richard. *Plain, Honest Men: The Making of the American Constitution*. New York: Random House, 2010.

Beirne, Francis F. *The War of 1812*. New York: E. P. Dutton, 1949.

Berger, D. H. "The Use of Covert Paramilitary Activity as a Policy Tool: An Analysis of Operations Conducted by the United States Central Intelligence Agency, 1949–1951." Written in fulfillment of a requirement for the Marine Corps Command and Staff College, May 22, 1995.

Berger, Joseph B., III. "Covert Action: Title 10, Title 50, and the Chain of Command." *JFQ* 67, no. 4 (2012): 32–39.

Berkowitz, Bruce. *The National Reconnaissance Office at 50 Years: A Brief History*. Chantilly, VA: Center for the Study of National Reconnaissance, 2011.

Berkowitz, Bruce D. "US Intelligence Estimates of the Soviet Collapse: Reality and Perception." *International Journal of Intelligence and CounterIntelligence* 21, no. 2 (2008): 237–250.

Berntsen, Gary, and Ralph Pezzullo. *Jawbreaker: The Attack on Bin Laden and Al-Qaeda: A Personal Account by the CIA's Key Field Commander*. New York: Three Rivers Press, 2005.

Bidwell, Bruce. *History of the Military Intelligence Division, Department of the Army General Staff: 1775–1941*. Frederick, MD: University Publications of America, 1986.

Bolsinger, Diana I. "Overt Action: Congressional Oversight, Private Activism and Afghan Covert Action policy in the Reagan Administration." *Intelligence and National Security* 39, no. 5 (2024): 824–40.

Bradley, Mark A. *A Very Principled Boy: The Life of Duncan Lee, Red Spy and Cold Warrior*. New York: Basic Books, 2014.

Brereton, T. R. "First Lessons in Modern War: Arthur Wagner, the 1898 Santiago Campaign, and U.S. Army Lesson-Learning." *Journal of Military History* 64, no. 1 (2000): 79–96.

Bruneau, Thomas C., and Steven C. Boraz, eds. *Reforming Intelligence: Obstacles to Democratic Control and Effectiveness*. Austin: University of Texas Press, 2007.

Budiansky, Stephen. *Battle of Wits: The Complete Story of Codebreaking in World War II*. New York: Touchstone, 2000.

Burns, Thomas L. *The Origins of the National Security Agency, 1940–1952*. Center for Cryptologic History, 1990.

Callanan, James. *Covert Action in the Cold War: US Policy, Intelligence and CIA Operations*. New York: I. B. Tauris, 2009.

Campbell, Josh. *Crossfire Hurricane: Inside Donald Trump's War on the FBI*. Chapel Hill: Algonquin Books of Chapel Hill, 2019.

Chambers, John Whiteclay, II. *OSS Training in the National Parks and Service Abroad in World War II*. Washington, DC: US National Parks Service, 2008.

Chandler, Charles Lyon. "The Life of Joel Roberts Poinsett." *Pennsylvania Magazine of History and Biography* 59, no. 1 (1935): 1–31.

Charles, Douglas M. " 'Before the Colonel Arrived': Hoover, Donovan, Roosevelt, and the Origins of American Central Intelligence, 1940–41." *Intelligence and National Security* 20, no. 2 (2005): 225–37.

Charles, Douglas M. "Informing FDR: FBI Political Surveillance and the Isolationist-Interventionist Foreign Policy Debate, 1939–1945." *Diplomatic History* 24, no. 2 (2000): 211–32.

Chesney, Robert. "Military-Intelligence Convergence and the Law of the Title 10/Title 50 Debate." *Journal of National Security Law and Policy* 5, no. 2 (2012): 539–629.

Chin, William Y. "Diversity in the Age of Terror: How Racial and Ethnic Diversity in the U.S. Intelligence Community Enhances National Security." *Florida A&M University Law Review* 6, no. 1 (2010): 49–88.

Clapp, Margaret. *Forgotten First Citizen: John Bigelow*. Boston: Little, Brown, 1947.

Clarke, Alan. *Rendition to Torture*. New Brunswick, NJ: Rutgers University Press: 2012.

Clarke, Richard A. *Against All Enemies: Inside America's War on Terror*. New York: Free Press, 2004.

Clifford, Clark, with Richard Holbrooke. *Counsel to the President: A Memoir*. New York: Random House, 1991.

Cohen, Eliot A. *Supreme Command: Soldiers, Statesmen, and Leadership in Wartime*. New York: Free Press, 2002.

Colby, William, and Peter Forbath. *Honorable Men: My Life in the CIA*. New York: Simon and Schuster, 1978.

Coll, Steve. *Ghost Wars: The Secret History of the CIA, Afghanistan, Bin Laden, from the Soviet Invasion to September 10, 2001*. New York: Penguin, 2004.

Conner, William E. *Intelligence Oversight: The Controversy Behind the FY 1991 Intelligence Authorization Act*. McLean, VA: Association of Former Intelligence Officers, 1993.

Corn, Geoffrey. "Unarmed but How Dangerous? Civilian Augmentees, the Law of Armed Conflict, and the Search for a More Effective Test for Permissible Civilian Battlefield Functions." *Journal of National Security Law and Policy* 2 (2008): 257–95.

Crile, George. *Charlie Wilson's War: The Extraordinary Story of the Largest Covert Operation in History*. New York: Atlantic Monthly Press, 2003.

Cruikshank, E. A. *The Political Adventures of John Henry: The Record of An International Imbroglio*. Toronto: Macmillan, 1936.

Crumpton, Frank. *The Art of Intelligence: Lessons from a Life in the CIA's Clandestine Service*. New York: Penguin, 2012.

Daigler, Kenneth A. *Spies, Patriots, and Traitors: American Intelligence in the Revolutionary War*. Washington, DC: Georgetown University Press, 2014.

Davidson, Philip. *Propaganda and the American Revolution, 1763–1783*. Chapel Hill: University of North Carolina Press, 1941.

Davies, Philip H. J., and Kristian C. Gustafson. *Intelligence Elsewhere: Spies and Espionage Outside the Anglosphere*. Washington, DC: Georgetown University Press, 2013.

Davis, Jack. "The Bogotazo." *Studies in Intelligence* 13, no. 4 (1969): 75–87.

De Vries, Tity. "The 1967 Central Intelligence Agency Scandal: Catalyst in a Transforming Relationship Between State and People." *Journal of American History* 98, no. 4 (2012): 1075–92.

Di, He. "The Most Respected Enemy: Mao Zedong's Perception of the United States." *China Quarterly*, No. 137 (March 1994): 144–58.

Dickey, Christopher. *Our Man in Charleston: Britain's Secret Agent in the Civil War South*. New York: Crown, 2015.

Dooley, John F. *Codes, Ciphers and Spies: Tales of Military Intelligence in World War I*. New York: Copernicus Books, 2016.

Dorwart, Jeffery M. *Conflict of Duty: The U.S. Navy's Intelligence Dilemma, 1919–1945*. Annapolis, MD: Naval Institute Press, 1983.

Dorwart, Jeffery M. *The Office of Naval Intelligence: The Birth of America's First Intelligence Agency 1865–1918*. Annapolis, MD: Naval Institute Press, 1979.

Dorwart, Jeffery M. "The Roosevelt-Astor Espionage Ring." *New York History* 62, no. 3 (1981): 307–22.

Doyle, Don H. *The Cause of All Nations: An International History of the American Civil War*. New York: Basic Books, 2015.

Draper, Theodore. *A Very Thin Line: The Iran-Contra Affairs*. New York: Hill & Wang, 1991.

Dujmovic, Nicholas. "Reagan, Intelligence, Casey, and the CIA: A Reappraisal." *International Journal of Intelligence and CounterIntelligence* 26, no. 1 (2013): 1–30.

Dull, Jonathan R. "Franklin the Diplomat: The French Mission." *Transactions of the American Philosophical Society* 72, no. 1 (1982): 1–76.

Dulles, Allen W. *The Craft of Intelligence*. Guilford, CT: Lyons Press, 2006.

Dunlop, Richard. *Donovan: America's Master Spy*. New York: Skyhorse, 2014.

Dylan, Huw, and Michael S. Goodman. "Guide to Study of Intelligence: British Intelligence." *The Intelligencer: Journal of U.S. Intelligence Studies* 21, no. 2 (2015): 35–40.

Ekirch, Arthur A., Jr. *The Civilian and the Military*. New York: Oxford University Press, 1956.

Ferryman, Randy D. "The Unresolved Tension Between Warriors and Journalists During the Civil War." *Studies in Intelligence* 58, no. 3 (2014): 1–12.

Finnegan, John Patrick, and Romana Danysh. *Military Intelligence*. Washington, DC: Center of Military History, 1998.

Fishel, Edwin C. "Pinkerton and McClellan: Who Deceived Whom?" *Civil War History* 34, no. 2 (1998): 115–42.

Fishel, Edwin C. *The Secret War for the Union: The Untold Story of Military Intelligence in the Civil War*. New York: Houghton Mifflin, 1996.

Ford, Harold P. *William E. Colby as Director of Central Intelligence 1973–1976*. Washington, DC: Center for the Study of Intelligence, 1993.

Fox, John F., Jr. "Bureaucratic Wrangling over Counterintelligence, 1917–18." *Studies in Intelligence* 49, no. 1 (2005): 9–17.

Friedman, William F. "A Brief History of the Signal Intelligence Service." *Cryptologia* 15, no. 3 (1991): 263–72.

Fry, Joseph A. *Henry Sanford: Diplomacy and Business in Nineteenth-Century America*. Reno: University of Nevada Press, 1982.

Gaddis, John Lewis. *George F. Kennan: An American Life*. New York: Penguin, 2012.

Gaddis, John Lewis. "Intelligence, Espionage, and Cold War Origins." *Diplomatic History* 13, no. 2 (1989): 191–212.

Gage, Beverly. *G-Man: J. Edgar Hoover and the Making of the American Century*. New York: Viking, 2022.

Gardner, Lloyd C. *Killing Machine: The American Presidency in the Age of Drone Warfare*. New York: New Press, 2013.

Garthoff, Douglas F. *Directors of Central Intelligence as Leaders of the U.S. Intelligence Community 1946–2005*. Washington, DC: Center for the Study of Intelligence, 2005.

Gentry, John A., and Joseph S. Gordon. *Strategic Warning Intelligence: History, Challenges, and Prospects*. Washington, DC: Georgetown University Press, 2019.

Gentry, John A. " 'Truth' as a Tool of the Politicization of Intelligence." *International Journal of Intelligence and Counterintelligence* 32, no. 2 (2019): 217–47.

Gerstle, Gary. *Liberty and Coercion: The Paradox of American Government From the Founding to the Present*. Princeton, NJ: Princeton University Press, 2015.

Givens, Cameron. "The Color of Loyalty: Rumors and Race-Making in First World War America." *Journal of American Ethnic History* 42, no. 2 (2023): 42–76.

Goldsmith, Jack L. *The Terror Presidency*. New York: W. W. Norton, 2007.

Goodman, Michael S. *The Official History of the Joint Intelligence Committee Volume I: From the Approach of the Second World War to the Suez Crisis*. London: Routledge, 2014.

Graff, Garrett M. *UFO: The Inside Story of the US Government's Search for Alien Life Here—and Out There*. New York: Avid Reader Press/Simon & Schuster, 2023.

Grose, Peter. *Gentleman Spy: The Life of Allen Dulles*. New York: Houghton Mifflin, 1994.

Haines, Gerald K. "The Pike Committee Investigations and the CIA." *Studies in Intelligence* 42, no. 5 (1999): 81–92.

Hanson, Victor Davis. *Carnage and Culture: Landmark Battles in the Rise of Western Power*. New York: Anchor Books, 2002.

Hartz, Louis. *The Liberal Tradition in America*. San Diego: Harcourt Brace, 1980.

Heaps, Jennifer Davis. "Tracking Intelligence Information: The Office of Strategic Services." *American Archivist* 61 (1998): 287–308.

Heinrichs, Waldo. "The United States Prepares for War." In *The Secrets War: The Office of Strategic Services in World War II*, edited by George C. Chalou. Washington, DC: NARA 2002.

Helms, Richard, and William Hood. *A Look Over My Shoulder: A Life in the Central Intelligence Agency*. New York: Random House, 2003.

Hendricks, Steven. *A Kidnapping in Milan: The CIA on Trial*. New York: W. W. Norton, 2010.

Hendrickson, David C. *Union, Nation, or Empire: The American Debate over International Relations, 1789–1941*. Lawrence: University Press of Kansas, 2009.

Herspring, Dale R. *The Pentagon and the Presidency: Civil-Military Relations from FDR to George W. Bush*. Lawrence: University Press of Kansas, 2005.

Higginbotham, Don. *The War of American Independence: Military Attitudes, Policies, and Practice, 1763–1789*. New York: Macmillan, 1971.

History of the Bureau of Diplomatic Security of the United States Department of State. n.p.: Global Publishing Solutions, 2011.

Holland, Max. "The Lie That Linked CIA to the Kennedy Assassination: The Power of Disinformation." *Studies in Intelligence* 45, no. 5 (2001).

Horan, James D., and Howard Swiggett. *The Pinkerton Story*. New York: G. P. Putnam's Sons, 1951.

Houghton, Vince. *The Nuclear Spies: America's Atomic Intelligence Operation Against Hitler and Stalin*. Ithaca, NY: Cornell University Press, 2019.

Huntington, Samuel P. *The Soldier and the State: The Theory and Politics of Civil-Military Relations*. Cambridge, MA: Belknap Press of Harvard University Press, 1957.

Immerman, Richard H. *The Hidden Hand: A Brief History of the CIA*. Chichester, UK: John Wiley & Sons, 2014.

Immerwahr, Daniel. *How to Hide an Empire: A History of the Greater United States*. New York: Picador, 2019.

The Intelligence Revolution: A Historical Perspective. Proceedings of the Thirteenth Military History Symposium, edited by Walter T. Hitchcock. Washington, DC: Office of Air Force History, 1991.

Jakub, Joseph F., III. *Spies and Saboteurs: Anglo-American Collaboration and Rivalry in Human Intelligence Collection and Special Operations, 1940–45*. New York: St. Martin's Press, 1999.

Janowitz, Morris. *The Professional Soldier: A Social and Political Portrait*. New York: Free Press, 2017.

Jeans, Roger B. *The CIA and Third Force Movements in China During the Early Cold War: The Great American Dream*. Lanham, MD: Lexington Books, 2018.

Jeffreys-Jones, Rhodri. *American Espionage: From Secret Service to CIA*. London: Endeavour Press, 2017.

Jeffreys-Jones, Rhodri. *Cloak and Dollar: A History of American Secret Intelligence*. New Haven, CT: Yale University Press, 2002.

Jeffreys-Jones, Rhodri. *The CIA and American Democracy*. 3rd edition. New Haven, CT: Yale University Press, 2003.

Jensen, Joan M. *Army Surveillance in America, 1775–1980*. New Haven, CT: Yale University Press, 1991.

Jensen, Joan M. *The Price of Vigilance*. Chicago: Rand McNally, 1968.

Jentleson, Bruce W. *American Foreign Policy: The Dynamics of Choice in the 21st Century*. 2nd edition. New York: W. W. Norton, 2004.

Johnson, David R. *Illegal Tender: Counterfeiting and the Secret Service in Nineteenth-Century America*. Washington, DC: Smithsonian Institution Press, 1995.

Johnson, Loch K. *America's Secret Power: The CIA in a Democratic Society*. New York: Oxford University Press, 1989.

Johnson, Loch. *A Season of Inquiry: The Senate Intelligence Investigation*. Lexington: University Press of Kentucky, 1985.

Johnson, Loch K. "Covert Action and Accountability: Decision-Making for America's Secret Foreign Policy," *International Studies Quarterly* 33, no. 1 (1989): 81–109.

Johnson, Loch K. "The Aspin-Brown Intelligence Inquiry: Behind the Closed Doors of a Blue Ribbon Commission." *Studies in Intelligence* 48, no. 3 (2004).

Johnson, Robert David. "The Unintended Consequences of Congressional Reform: The Clark and Tunney Amendments and U.S. Policy Toward Angola." *Diplomatic History* 27, no. 2 (2003): 215–43.

Kahn, David. *The Codebreakers: The Story of Secret Writing*. New York: Macmillan, 1967.

Kahn, David. *The Reader of Gentlemen's Mail: Herbert O. Yardley and the Birth of American Codebreaking*. New Haven, CT: Yale University Press, 2004.

Kahn, David. "Why Weren't We Warned?" In *The American Experience in World War II*, volume 4, *Pearl Harbor in History and Memory*, edited by Walter L. Hixson. New York: Routledge, 2003.

Kaiser, Frederick M. "Origins of Secret Service Protection of the President: Personal, Interagency, and Institutional Conflict." *Presidential Studies Quarterly* 18, no. 1 (1988): 101–27.

Kane, Harnett T. *Spies for the Blue and Gray*. Garden City, NY: Hanover House, 1954.

Karp, Matthew. *This Vast Southern Empire: Slaveholders at the Helm of American Foreign Policy*. Cambridge, MA: Harvard University Press, 2016.

Katz, Barry M. *Foreign Intelligence: Research and Analysis in the Office of Strategic Services, 1942–1945*. Cambridge, MA: Harvard University Press, 1989.

Kean, Thomas H., and Lee H. Hamilton. *Without Precedent: The Inside Story of the 9/11 Commission*. New York: Alfred A. Knopf, 2006.

Keegan, John. *Intelligence in War: The Value—and Limitations—of What the Military Can Learn About the Enemy*. New York: Vintage Books, 2004.

Keithly, David M. "Intelligence Sesquicentennial: Testament of Bleeding War." *Journal of Strategic Security* 8, no. 5 (2015): 53–66.

Kent, Sherman, *Strategic Intelligence for American World Policy*. Princeton, NJ: Princeton University Press, 1966.

Kinzer, Stephen. *The Brothers: John Foster Dulles, Allen Dulles, and Their Secret World War*. New York: Times Books, 2013.

Kinzer, Stephen. *Poisoner in Chief: Sidney Gotlieb and the CIA Search for Mind Control*. New York: Henry Holt, 2019.

Klaidman, Daniel. *Kill or Capture: The War on Terror and the Soul of the Obama Presidency*. New York: First Mariner Books, 2013.

Klehr, Harvey, and John Early Haynes. "On the Trail of a Fourth Soviet Spy at Los Alamos." *Studies in Intelligence* 63, no. 3 (2019).

Klehr, Harvey, John Earl Haynes, and Fridrikh Igorevich Firsov. *The Secret World of American Communism*. New Haven, CT: Yale University Press, 1995.

Klement, Frank L. *Dark Lanterns: Secret Political Societies, Conspiracies, and Treason Trials in the Civil War*. Baton Rouge: Louisiana State University Press, 1984.

Koestler, Arthur, et al. *The God that Failed: A Confession*. New York: Harper & Brothers, 1949.

Kohn, Richard. *Eagle and Sword: The Beginnings of the Military Establishment in America*. New York: Free Press, 1975.

Knott, Stephen F. *Rush to Judgment: George W. Bush, The War on Terror, and His Critics*. Lawrence: University Press of Kansas, 2012.

Knott, Stephen F. *Secret and Sanctioned: Covert Operations and the American Presidency*. New York: Oxford University Press, 1996.

Kruh, Louis. "Stimson, The Black Chamber, and the "'Gentlemen's Quote.'" *Cryptologia* 12, no. 2 (1988): 65–89.

Lacovara, Philip A. "Presidential Power to Gather Intelligence: The Tension Between Article II and Amendment IV." *Law and Contemporary Problems* 40, no. 3 (1976): 106–31.

Lane, Charles. *Freedom's Detective: The Secret Service, the Ku Klux Klan and the Man Who Masterminded America's First War on Terror*. New York: Hanover Square Press, 2019.

Lefever, Ernest W., and Roy Godson. *The CIA and the American Ethic: An Unfinished Debate*. Washington, DC: Ethics and Public Policy Center of Georgetown University, 1979.

Lester, Genevieve, and Jeffrey Rogg. "Intelligence and Oversight: A View of the US System." In *Intelligence Oversight in the Twenty-First Century: Accountability in a Changing World*, edited by Ian Leigh and Njord Wegge. London: Routledge, 2019.

Locher, James R., III. *Victory on the Potomac: The Goldwater-Nichols Act Unifies the Pentagon*. College Station: Texas A&M University Press, 2002.

London, Douglas. *The Recruiter: Spying and the Lost Art of American Intelligence*. New York: Hachette Books, 2021.

Lowenthal, Mark M. "Intelligence Is NOT About 'Telling Truth to Power.'" *International Journal of Intelligence and CounterIntelligence* 34, no. 4 (2021): 795–98.

Lowenthal, Max. *The Federal Bureau of Investigation*. Westport, CT: Greenwood Press, 1950.

Lynn, John A. *Battle: A History of Combat and Culture*. Cambridge, MA: Westview Press, 2003.

MacLeish, Archibald. *The Hamlet of A. MacLeish*. Cambridge: Riverside Press, 1928.

Macrakis, Kristie. *Nothing Is Beyond Our Reach: America's Techno-Spy Empire*. Washington, DC: Georgetown University Press, 2023.

Maffeo, Steven E. *Most Secret and Confidential: Intelligence in the Age of Nelson*. Annapolis, MD: Naval Institute Press, 2000.

Marchetti, Victor, and John D. Marks. *The CIA and the Cult of Intelligence*. New York: Dell, 1980.

Markle, Donald E. *Spies and Spymasters of the Civil War*. New York: Hippocrene Books, 2000.

Maury, John M. "CIA and the Congress." *Studies in Intelligence* 18, no. 2 (1974).

May, Ernest. *American Imperialism: A Speculative Essay*. New York: Atheneum, 1968.

Mayer, Jane. *Dark Side: The Inside Story of How the War on Terror Turned into a War on American Ideals*. New York: Doubleday, 2008.

McCoy, Alfred. *Policing America's Empire: The United States, the Philippines, and the Rise of the Surveillance State*. Madison: University of Wisconsin Press, 2009.

McDonald, Forrest. *Novus Ordo Seclorum: The Intellectual Origins of the Constitution*. Lawrence: University Press of Kansas, 1985.

McDonald, J. Kenneth. "Secrecy, Accountability, and the CIA: The Dilemma of Intelligence in a Democracy." In *The United States Military Under the Constitution of the United States, 1789–1989*, edited by Richard H. Kohn. New York: New York University Press, 1991.

McPherson, James. *Battle Cry of Freedom: The Civil War Era*. New York: Oxford University Press, 1988.

McTiernan, Dave. "The Novel as 'Neutral Ground': Genre and Ideology in Cooper's *The Spy*." *Studies in American Fiction* 25, no. 1 (1997): 3–20.

Mendez, Antonio J. *The Master of Disguise: My Secret Life in the CIA*. New York: William Morrow, 1999.

Miller, Henry Edward. "The Spy of the Neutral Ground." *New England Magazine* (new series) 18 (1898).

Miller, John C. *Crisis in Freedom: The Alien and Sedition Acts*. Boston: Little, Brown, 1951.

Miller, Nathan. *Spying for America: The Hidden History of U.S. Intelligence*. New York: Marlowe, 1997.

Millett, Allan R. *Military Professionalism and Officership in America*. Columbus, OH: Mershon Center, 1977.

Montague, Ludwell Lee. *General Walter Bedell Smith as Director of Central Intelligence: October 1950–February 1953*. University Park: Pennsylvania State University Press, 1992.

Morison, Samuel Eliot, Commager, Henry Steele, and William E. Leuchtenburg. *The Growth of the American Republic*. Vol. 2. New York: Oxford University Press, 1969.

Morison, Samuel Eliot. "The Henry-Crillon Affair of 1812." *Proceedings of the Massachusetts Historical Society* 3, no. 69 (1947–51): 207–31.

Mortimer, Gavin. *Double Death: The True Story of Pryce Lewis, the Civil War's Most Daring Spy*. New York: Walker, 2010.

Moynihan, Daniel Patrick. *Secrecy*. New Haven, CT: Yale University Press, 1998.

Mundy, Liza. *Code Girls: The Untold Story of the American Women Code Breakers of World War II*. New York: Hachette Books, 2017.

Nagy, John A. *George Washington's Secret Spy War: The Making of America's First Spymaster*. New York: St. Martin's Press, 2016.

Nedzi, Lucien. "Oversight or Overlook: Congress and the U.S. Intelligence Agencies." *Studies in Intelligence* 18, no. 2 (1973).

Nevins, Allan. *Grover Cleveland: A Study in Courage*. New York: Dodd, Mead, 1964.

O'Hara, S. Paul. *Inventing the Pinkerton's or, Spies, Sleuths, Mercenaries, and Thugs: being a Story of the Nation's Most Famous (and Infamous) Detective Agency*. Baltimore: Johns Hopkins University Press, 2016.

O'Reilly, Kenneth. "A New Deal for the FBI: The Roosevelt Administration, Crime Control, and National Security." *Journal of American History* 69, no. 3 (1982): 638–58.

O'Toole, G. J. A. *Honorable Treachery: A History of U.S. Intelligence, Espionage, and Covert Action from the American Revolution to the CIA*. New York: Grove Press, 2014.

Oakley, David P. *Subordinating Intelligence: The DoD/CIA Post–Cold War Relationship*. Lexington: University Press of Kentucky, 2019.

Oder, Frederic, James Fitzpatrick, and Paul Worthman. *The Corona Story*. Chantilly, VA: Center for the Study of National Reconnaissance, 2013.

Olmsted, Kathryn. "Lapdog or Rogue Elephant? CIA Controversies from 1947 to 2004." In *The Central Intelligence Agency: Security Under Scrutiny*, edited by Athan Theoharis, Richard Immerman, Loch Johnson, Kathryn Olmsted, and John Prados. Westport, CT: Greenwood Press, 2006.

Olson, James. *Fair Play: The Moral Dilemmas of Spying*. Lincoln: University of Nebraska Press, 2011.

Ott, Marvin C. "Partisanship and the Decline of Intelligence Oversight." *International Journal of Intelligence and CounterIntelligence* 16, no. 1 (2003): 69–94.

Owsley, Harriet Chappell. "Henry Shelton Sanford and Federal Surveillance Abroad, 1861–1865." *Mississippi Valley Historical Review* 48, no. 2 (1961): 211–28.

Pach, Chester. "The Reagan Doctrine: Principle, Pragmatism, and Policy." *Presidential Studies Quarterly* 36, no. 1 (2006): 75–88.

Parker, Frederick D. "Pearl Harbor Revisited: Navy Communications Intelligence 1924–1941." Series IV, World War II, Volume 6. Fort George G. Meade, MD: Center for Cryptologic History, National Security Agency, 2013.

Parker, Geoffrey. *The Military Revolution: Military Innovation and the Rise of the West, 1500–1800*. Cambridge: Cambridge University Press, 1988.

Pascoe, William W., III. "Angola Tests the Reagan Doctrine." Heritage Foundation, November 14, 1985.

Perisco, Joseph E. *Roosevelt's Secret War: FDR and World War II Espionage*. New York: Random House, 2002.

Pines, Daniel L. "The Central Intelligence Agency's 'Family Jewels': Legal Then? Legal Now?" *Indiana Law Journal* 84, no. 2 (2009): 637–88.

Pinheiro, John C. *Manifest Ambition: James K. Polk and Civil-Military Relations During the Mexican War*. Westport, CT: Praeger Security International, 2007.

Porch, Douglas. *The French Secret Services: From the Dreyfus Affair to the Gulf War*. New York: Farrar, Straus and Giroux, 1995.

Posner, Richard A. *Uncertain Shield: The U.S. Intelligence System in the Throes of Reform*. Lanham, MD: Rowman & Littlefield, 2006.

Powers, Richard Gid. *Broken: The Troubled Past and Uncertain Future of the FBI*. New York: Free Press, 2004.

Prados, John. *Safe for Democracy: The Secret Wars of the CIA*. Chicago: Ivan R. Dee, 2006.

The President's Foreign Intelligence Advisory Board. Washington, DC: The Hale Foundation, 1981.

Priess, David. *The President's Book of Secrets: The Untold Story of Intelligence Briefings to America's Presidents*. New York: PublicAffairs, 2016.

Protecting Individual Privacy in the Struggle Against Terrorism: A Framework for Program Assessment. Washington, DC: National Academies Press, 2008.

Rafalko, Frank J., ed. *A Counterintelligence Reader*. Washington, DC: National Counterintelligence Center, 2001.

Ramos, Raphaël "The National Security Act, SIGINT, and the Origins of an Intelligence Diarchy," *International Journal of Intelligence and CounterIntelligence* 36, no. 2 (2023): 444–65.

Ranelagh, John. *The Agency: The Rise and Decline of the CIA*. New York: Simon and Schuster, 1986.

Ransom, Harry Howe. *Central Intelligence and National Security*. Cambridge, MA: Harvard University Press, 1958.

Reynolds, Nicholas. *Need to Know: World War II and the Rise of American Intelligence*. New York: Mariner Books, 2022.

Richelson, Jeffrey T. *The US Intelligence Community*. 6th edition. Boulder, CO: Westview Press, 2012.

Riebling, Mark. *Wedge: The Secret War Between the FBI and CIA*. New York: Alfred A. Knopf, 1994.

Risen, James. *Pay Any Price: Greed, Power, and Endless War*. Boston: Mariner Books, 2015.

Roberts, Michael. *The Military Revolution, 1560–1660: An Inaugural Lecture Delivered Before the Queen's University of Belfast*. Belfast: M. Boyd, 1956.

Rogg, Jeff. "Coordinating Intelligence: An American Drama in Three Acts... of Congress." *International Journal of Intelligence and CounterIntelligence* 36, no. 2 (2023): 423–43.

Rogg, Jeff. "Military-Intelligence Relations: Explaining the Oxymoron." *International Journal of Intelligence and CounterIntelligence* 36, no. 4 (2023): 1067–84.

Rogg, Jeff. "The U.S. Intelligence Community's 'MacArthur Moment.'" *International Journal of Intelligence and CounterIntelligence* 33, no. 4 (2020): 666–81.

Rogg, Jeffrey P. "'That the Republic Should Suffer No Harm': The Constitutional Conundrum of the Executive, Secret Intelligence, and the Rule of Law." *International Journal of Intelligence and CounterIntelligence* 32, no. 3 (2019): 600–628.

Rose, P. K. "A Counterintelligence Debacle: British Penetration of America's First Diplomatic Mission." *Studies in Intelligence* 41, no. 4 (1997): 57–64.

Rositzke, Harry. *The CIA's Secret Operations*. New York: Reader's Digest Press, 1977.

Rudgers, David. *Creating the Secret State: The Origins of the Central Intelligence Agency, 1943–1947*. Lawrence: University of Kansas Press, 2000.

Ryan, Amy and Keeley, Gary. "Sputnik and US Intelligence: The Warning Record," *Studies in Intelligence* 61, no. 3 (2017).

Saunders, Frances Stonor. *The Cultural Cold War: The CIA and the World of Arts and Letters*. New York: New Press, 2013.

Sayle, Edward F. "The Historical Underpinnings of the U.S. Intelligence Community." *International Journal of Intelligence and Counterintelligence* 1, no. 1 (1986): 1–27.

Schlesinger, Arthur, Jr. *The Imperial Presidency*. New York: Houghton Mifflin, 2004.

Schroen, Gary C. *First In: An Insider's Account of How the CIA Spearheaded the War on Terror in Afghanistan*. New York: Presidio Press, 2006.

Schwarz, Frederick A. O., Jr., and Aziz Z. Huq. *Unchecked and Unbalanced: Presidential Power in a Time of Terror*. New York: New Press, 2007.

Sears, Stephen W. *Landscape Turned Red: The Battle of Antietam*. New York: Ticknor & Fields, 1983.

Selden, Zachary. "Special Intelligence Service of the Federal Bureau of Investigation: Forgotten Forerunner of the Central Intelligence Agency." *International Journal of Intelligence and CounterIntelligence* 36, no. 4 (2023): 1210–27.

Setzekorn, Eric. "The Office of Naval Intelligence in World War I: Diverse Threats, Divergent Responses." *Studies in Intelligence* 61, no. 2 (2017): 43–54.

Seymour, George Dudley. *Documentary Life of Nathan Hale*. New Haven, CT: Private Print for Author, 1941.

Sheafe, Larry B. "The United States Secret Service: An Administrative History." Unpublished manuscript, 1983.

Shulman, Mark Russell. "The Rise and Fall of American Naval Intelligence, 1882–1917." *Intelligence and National Security* 8, no. 2 (1993): 214–26.

Simms, William Gilmore. "The Writings of Cooper." In *Fenimore Cooper: The Critical Heritage*, edited by George Dekker and John P. McWilliams. London: Routledge and Kegan Paul, 1973.

Skowronek, Stephen. *Building a New American State: The Expansion of National Administrative Capacities, 1877–1920*. New York: Cambridge University Press, 1982.

Smist, Frank J., Jr. *Congress Oversees the United States Intelligence Community, 1947–1994*. 2nd edition. Knoxville: University of Tennessee Press, 1994.

Smith, Bradley. *The Shadow Warriors: O.S.S. and the Origins of the C.I.A.* New York: Basic Books, 1983.

Smith, James Morton. "The 'Aurora' and the Alien and Sedition Laws: Part II: The Editorship of William Duane." *Pennsylvania Magazine of History and Biography* 77, no. 2 (1953): 123–55.

Smith, Richard Harris. *OSS: The Secret History of America's First Central Intelligence Agency*. Guilford, CT: Lyons Press, 2005.

Smyth, William Henry. *Technocracy: First, Second and Third Series*. Berkeley, CA: n.p., 1921.

Snider, L. Britt. "A Different Angle on the Aspin-Brown Commission." *Studies in Intelligence* 49, no. 1 (2005).

Snider, L. Britt. "Creating a Statutory Inspector General at the CIA." *Studies in Intelligence* 44, no. 5 (2001): 15–21.

Snider, L. Britt. *The Agency and the Hill: CIA's Relationship with Congress, 1946–2004*. Washington, DC: Center for the Study of Intelligence, 2008.

Snowden, Edward. *Permanent Record*. New York: Henry Holt, 2019.

Stephanson, Anders. *Manifest Destiny: American Expansion and the Empire of Right*. New York: Hill and Wang, 1995.

Steury, Donald P. "How the CIA Missed Stalin's Bomb." *Studies in Intelligence* 49, no. 1 (2005).

Stevenson, William. *A Man Called Intrepid*. Guilford, CT: Lyons Press, 2000.

Stinnett, Robert. *Day of Deceit: The Truth About FDR and Pearl Harbor*. New York: Free Press, 2001.

Stout, Mark. "The Alternate Central Intelligence Agency: John Grombach and the Pond." In *Spy Chiefs: Intelligence Leaders in the United States and United Kingdom*, edited by Christopher Moran, Mark Stout, Ionna Iordanou, and Paul Maddrell. Washington, DC: Georgetown University Press, 2018.

Stout, Mark. "The Pond: Running Agents for State, War, and the CIA." *Studies in Intelligence* 48, no. 3 (2004).

Stout, Mark. "World War I and the Birth of American Intelligence Culture." *Intelligence and National Security* 32, no. 3 (2017): 378–94.

Stout, Mark. *World War I and the Foundations of American Intelligence*. Lawrence: University Press of Kansas, 2023.

Stuart, Reginald C. *Civil-Military Relations During the War of 1812*. Westport, CT: Praeger, 2009.

Sulick, Michael. *Spying in America: Espionage from the Revolutionary War to the Dawn of the Cold War*. Washington, DC: Georgetown University Press, 2012.

Sullivan, Brian R. "'A Highly Commendable Action': William J. Donovan's Intelligence Mission for Mussolini and Roosevelt, December 1935–February 1936." *Intelligence and National Security* 6, no. 2 (1991): 334–66.

Talbert, Roy, Jr. *Negative Intelligence: The Army and the American Left, 1917–1941*. Jackson: University Press of Mississippi, 1991.

Theoharis, Athan G. "The FBI's Stretching of Presidential Directives, 1936–1953." *Political Science Quarterly* 91, no .4 (1976–1977): 649–72.

Theoharis, Athan. "FBI Wiretapping: A Case Study of Bureaucratic Autonomy." *Political Science Quarterly* 107, no. 1 (1992): 101–22.

Tovar, Hugh. "Covert Action." In *Intelligence Requirements for the 1980's: Elements of Intelligence*, edited by Roy Godson. Washington, DC: National Strategy Information Center, 1979.

Trautsch, Jasper M. *The Genesis of America: US Foreign Policy and the Formation of National Identity, 1793–1815*. Cambridge: Cambridge University Press, 2018.

Troy, Thomas F. *Donovan and the CIA: A History of the Establishment of the Central Intelligence Agency*. Frederick, MD: University Publications of America, 1984.

Troy, Thomas F. "The Quaintness of U.S. Intelligence Community: Its Origin, Theory, and Problems." *International Journal of Intelligence and CounterIntelligence* 2, no. 2 (1988): 245–66.

Tsouras, Peter G. *Major General George H. Sharpe and the Creation of American Military Intelligence in the Civil War*. Philadelphia: Casemate, 2018.

Turner, Michael. "A Distinctive U.S. Intelligence Identity." *International Journal of Intelligence and Counterintelligence* 17, no. 1 (2004): 42–61.

Turner, Stansfield. *Secrecy and Democracy: The CIA in Transition*. New York: Perennial Library, 1986.

Uhlmann, Michael M. "Approaches to Reform of the Intelligence Community." In *Intelligence Requirements for the 1980's: Elements of Intelligence*, edited by Roy Godson. Washington, DC: National Strategy Information Center, 1979.

Usowski, Peter S. "Former CIA Officers Writing About Intelligence, Policy, and Politics, 2016–2017." *Studies in Intelligence* 62, no. 3 (2018): 1–14.

Van Doren, Carl. *Secret History of the American Revolution*. Clifton, NJ: Augustus M. Kelley, 1973.

Van Vlack, Milton C. *Silas Deane: Revolutionary War Diplomat and Politician*. Jefferson, NC: McFarland, 2013.

Wall, Andru. "Demystifying the Title 10–Title 50 Debate: Distinguishing Military Operations, Intelligence Activities and Covert Action." *Harvard National Security Journal* 3, no. 1 (2011): 85–142.

Waller, Douglas. *Wild Bill Donovan: The Spymaster Who Created the OSS and Modern American Espionage*. New York: Free Press, 2011.

Walton, Calder. *Spies: The Epic Intelligence War Between East and West*. New York: Simon & Schuster, 2023.

Wark, Wesley K. "One of Time's Arrows: The Intelligence Revolution and the Future." *Studies in Intelligence* 37, no. 4 (1994): 9–16.

Warner, John S. "Where Secrecy Is Essential." *Studies in Intelligence* 3, no. 2 (1987): 45–64.

Warner, Michael, ed. *Central Intelligence: Origin and Evolution*. Washington, DC: Center for the Study of Intelligence, 2001.

Warner, Michael, ed. *The CIA Under Harry Truman*. Washington, DC: Center for the Study of Intelligence, 1994.

Warner, Michael. *The Rise and Fall of Intelligence: An International Security History*. Washington, DC: Georgetown University Press, 2014.

Warner, Michael, and J. Kenneth McDonald. *US Intelligence Community Reform Studies Since 1947*. Washington, DC: Center for the Study of Intelligence, 2005.

Weiner, Tim. *Enemies: A History of the FBI*. New York: Random House, 2013.

Weiner, Tim. *Legacy of Ashes: The History of the CIA*. New York: Anchor Books, 2007.

Weir, Alison Marie. "The Spy in Early America: The Emergence of a Genre." PhD diss., University of Illinois at Urbana-Champaign, 1998. https://apps.dtic.mil/sti/tr/pdf/ADA348213.pdf.

Wettemann, Robert P., Jr. *Privilege vs. Equality: Civil-Military Relations in the Jacksonian Era, 1815–1845*. Westport, CT: Praeger, 2009.

Wexler, Lesley. "Litigating the Long War on Terror: The Role of al-Aulaqi v. Obama." 9 Loyal University Chicago International Law Review 159 (2011): 159–76.

Whitehead, Don. *The FBI Story: A Report to the People*. New York: Random House, 1956.

Wilford, Hugh. *The CIA: An Imperial History*. New York: Basic Books, 2024.

Wilford, Hugh. *The Mighty Wurlitzer: How the CIA Played America*. Cambridge, MA: Harvard University Press, 2008.

Williams, David Joseph. *"Without Understanding": The FBI and Political Surveillance, 1908–1941*. Doctoral Dissertations. 1314. University of New Hampshire, 1981.

Winks, Robin W. *Cloak and Gown: Scholars in the Secret War, 1939–1961*. 2nd edition. New Haven, CT: Yale University Press, 1996.

Wise, David. *The Politics of Lying: Government Deception, Secrecy, and Power*. New York: Random House, 1973.

Wise, David and Thomas B. Ross. *The Invisible Government*. New York: Random House, 1964.

Wohlstetter, Roberta. *Pearl Harbor: Warning and Decision*. Stanford, CA: Stanford University Press, 1962.

Wood, Gordon S. *The Creation of the American Republic, 1776–1787*. Chapel Hill: University of North Carolina Press, 1998.

Woods, Brett F. *Neutral Ground: A Political History of Espionage Fiction*. New York: Algora, 2008.

Woodward, Bob. *Bush at War*. New York: Simon & Schuster, 2002.

Woodward, Bob. *Veil: The Secret Wars of the CIA, 1981–1987*. New York: Simon & Schuster Paperbacks, 2005.

Wriston, Henry Merritt. *Executive Agents in American Foreign Relations*. Gloucester, MA: Peter Smith, 1967.

Yu, Maochun. *OSS in China: Prelude to Cold War*. New Haven, CT: Yale University Press, 1996.

Zegart, Amy. *Eyes on Spies: Congress and the United States Intelligence Community*. Stanford, CA: Hoover Institution Press, 2011.

Zegart, Amy *Flawed by Design: The Evolution of the CIA, JCS, NSC*. Stanford, CA: Stanford University Press, 1999.

Zenko, Micah. "Obama's Final Drone Strike Data." *Council on Foreign Relations*, January 20, 2017.

MISCELLANEOUS SOURCES

Bellingcat. https://www.bellingcat.com/about/who-we-are/.

Bureau of Intelligence and Research, US State Department. https://www.state.gov/about-us-bureau-of-intelligence-and-research/.

Frontline Interview with Gary Schroen. https://www.pbs.org/wgbh/pages/frontline/darkside/interviews/schroen.html.

Intelligence and Security Committee of Parliament HC 1605, July 23, 2023. https://isc.independent.gov.uk/wp-content/uploads/2023/07/ISC-China.pdf.

Kahn, David. "Why Weren't We Warned?" December 30, 2017. HistoryNet. https://www.historynet.com/why-werent-we-warned.htm.

"National Security Letters." Electronic Frontier Foundation. https://www.eff.org/issues/national-security-letters.

The OSINT Foundation. https://www.osintfoundation.com/osint/default.asp.

President's Remarks on Intelligence Reform, August 2, 2004. https://georgewbush-whitehouse.archives.gov/news/releases/2004/08/20040802-2.html.

US Department of Energy. "The Manhattan Project." https://www.osti.gov/opennet/manhattan-project-history/Events/1942-1945/espionage.htm.

Index

For the benefit of digital users, indexed terms that span two pages (e.g., 52–53) may, on occasion, appear on only one of those pages.